Cambridge Studies in Early Modern British History

AN UNCOUNSELLED KING

In a struggle of protest over the government of Scotland, the concept of kingship as Charles I understood it was challenged by the Covenanters. Although many aspects of this episode have received recent attention, Charles's own role has not hitherto been investigated in detail. Using a large body of newly available evidence Dr Donald here attempts to redress the balance, and in doing so offers a substantially new perspective on the Scottish troubles in the crisis years of 1637–41.

The collapse of the king's government in Scotland was by no means due to Charles alone. The problems of ruling over multiple kingdoms in a time of social upheaval were immense. The controversial liturgy of 1637 was certain to meet resistance; but what was less predictable was the extensive organisation of protest on national, religious and·legal grounds. Charles's response was nevertheless important in shaping the events of this major crisis in which presbyterianism became established and the king's prerogative powers circumscribed.

Critics of royal policy were most ready to denounce the king's counsel rather than the king himself. But the criticism rebounded on a monarch who readily assumed a role of sole responsibility. Charles was especially intolerant of protest against his rule and – despite a poverty of means – was more eager to suppress than to listen to complaint. Principles tended to come before politics. This study sheds light on the processes whereby Charles, with counsel and yet often in spite of it, tried to uphold his case.

Cambridge Studies in Early Modern British History

Series editors

ANTHONY FLETCHER
Professor of Modern History, University of Durham

JOHN GUY
Reader in British History, University of Bristol

and JOHN MORRILL
*Lecturer in History, University of Cambridge, and
Fellow and Tutor of Selwyn College*

This is a series of monographs and studies covering many aspects of the history of the British Isles between the late fifteenth century and the early eighteenth century. It includes the work of established scholars and pioneering work by a new generation of scholars. It includes both reviews and revisions of major topics and books which open up new historical terrain or which reveal startling new perspectives on familiar subjects. All the volumes set detailed research into broader perspectives and the books are intended for the use of students as well as of their teachers.

For a list of titles in the series, see end of book.

AN UNCOUNSELLED KING

Charles I and the Scottish troubles, 1637–1641

PETER DONALD

New College, University of Edinburgh

The right of the
University of Cambridge
to print and sell
all manner of books
was granted by
Henry VIII in 1534.
The University has printed
and published continuously
since 1584.

CAMBRIDGE UNIVERSITY PRESS

Cambridge
New York   Port Chester
Melbourne   Sydney

Published by the Press Syndicate of the University of Cambridge
The Pitt Building, Trumpington Street, Cambridge CB2 1RP
40 West 20th Street, New York, NY 10011, USA
10 Stamford Road, Oakleigh, Melbourne 3166, Australia

First published 1990

Printed in Great Britain at the University Press, Cambridge

British Library cataloguing in publication data
Donald, Peter
An uncounselled king: Charles I and the Scottish
troubles, 1637–1641. – (Cambridge studies in early modern
British history)
1. Scotland. Political events, 1625–1649
I. Title
941.106′2

Library of Congress cataloguing in publication data
Donald, Peter
An uncounselled king: Charles I and the Scottish troubles,
1637–1641 / Peter Donald.
p.   cm. – (Cambridge studies in early modern British history)
ISBN 0-521-37235-6
1. Scotland – History – Charles I, 1625–1649. 2. Charles I, King of
Great Britain, 1600–1649. I. Title. II.Series.
DA803.3.D66 1990
941.106′2 – dc20   89–77392 CIP

ISBN 0 521 37235 6 hardback

WD

For Brigid

CONTENTS

PREFACE

Recent scholarship on the Scottish troubles, or 'Scottish Revolution' as it is often called, has tended to concentrate on those who became Covenanters, with only sidelong glances at the king whose ways of government they challenged. This book differs in making its sidelong glances from the opposite perspective and attempting to explore Charles I's response to the troubles. Given the sequence of troubles met by Charles in three kingdoms, it is clearly desirable to be alert to a British story, which at the same time is a daunting prospect. Although the great narrative historian S. R. Gardiner attempted as much and was followed by C. V. Wedgwood, time and space in my first researches necessarily limited what was to be said concerning England and Ireland.[1] In expectation now of the Earl Russell's major study of the 1637–42 period, it has seemed prudent to confine remarks on English and Irish history still to a minimum. Nevertheless the importance of Charles's handling of the Scottish troubles extended far beyond Scotland, and any assessment of the high politics of the reign must seriously engage with this fact.

In itself the narrative here provides a particularly well-documented account of Charles and his counsel, a subject which partly on account of Charles's liking for privacy historians have little dealt with beyond passing remarks. Professor Hibbard's account of the reality of the popish plot which animated so many contemporaries has informed us of the extent to which Catholics and Catholic sympathisers surrounded the king and sought to influence him. Dr Cust's recent study of the history of the forced loan in England has tried courageously and with good success to delineate lines of counsel around the king in the 1620s.[2] Many questions remain with regard to the Scottish troubles, but the copious survival of hitherto unexploited manuscript evidence permits, relatively speaking, a very good insight into the workings of the king and his counsel.

---

[1] S. R. Gardiner, *A History of England . . . 1603–1642* (10 vols., 1883–4); C. V. Wedgwood, *The King's Peace 1637–1641* (1955).

[2] C. Hibbard, *Charles I and the Popish Plot* (Chapel Hill, NC, 1983); R. Cust, *The Forced Loan and English Politics 1626–1628* (Oxford, 1987).

The king ruled, but criticisms and attacks on his government were directed against his counsel. People expected the king to be counselled, and Charles for his part was often prepared to talk and listen, but problems arose when he was thought to be inadequately or badly counselled. The form of complaint avoided casting direct aspersions since it was proper to accept the king's determined pleasure without question, but people would be aiming, whether indirectly or diplomatically, to steer his tracks. Charles's government was rarely standing still but care was needed if questions were to be asked; he was a king especially prone to take offence, all too ready to denounce sincere objections. A determination to have the rights of majesty vindicated brought him near the position of being beyond counsel. Principle threatened to overwhelm the necessary considerations of practice.

Narrative has seemed the only way possible to trace the ambiguities, double intentions and intrigue that were as much part of the Scottish troubles as major episodes of conflict. I am indebted to the work of Drs Stevenson and Makey for providing such stimulating, different approaches to the history of the period.[3] To some extent the narrative follows familiar ground yet at almost all points the use of unexploited primary sources has brought new things to light. I have sought to provide a readable account which does not presuppose knowledge of this other work; much is made here of chronology but I have mostly desisted from signalling differences, particularly with Dr Stevenson's narrative account, *The Scottish Revolution 1637–1644*.

Though I have attempted to draw attention to the vitally important internal dynamic of the protest movement in Scotland, relatively little is said on the better-studied detail of Covenanting history. This with the pre-1637 period, moreover, has recently been the subject of more work, including a valuable effort at a local study. Our relative ignorance of local history generally in the field is a serious gap, certainly for analysis of motivation and organisation within Scotland, and for understanding of the interplay of local politics, issues and interests within the national scene.[4]

Given the British significance of the Scottish troubles, current English historiography raises many important questions which could be better followed up with regard to Scotland and it will be clear that I have attempted to address some of these at least in a preliminary way. I remain unhappy

[3] D. Stevenson, *The Scottish Revolution 1637–1644* (Newton Abbot, 1974); W. Makey, *The Church of the Covenant 1637–1651* (Edinburgh, 1979). Dr Stevenson has also published numerous articles and other relevant books. M. Lee, Jr, *The Road to Revolution: Scotland under Charles I, 1625–1637* (Urbana and Chicago, 1985) is the only narrative account in print of the early part of Charles's reign in Scotland.

[4] A. I. Macinnes, 'The origin and organization of the Covenanting movement during the reign of Charles I, 1625–1641; with a particular reference to the west of Scotland' (unpublished University of Glasgow Ph.D. dissertation, 1988). See too K. M. Brown, 'Aristocratic finances and the origins of the Scottish Revolution', *EHR*, 104 (1989), 46–87.

about usage of the term 'Scottish Revolution' because of the problems in tying down when and what revolution occurred. There are questions about religion and politics which make it not at all straightforward to look always for a separation of the two, or for the sharp dichotomy between ministers and all laymen which has usually been suggested. Some distinctions may be made, but a root concern must be with the very heated politics of the church – which Charles certainly regarded as his main struggle; though the field of tensions became large, there was a very particular starting-point. Anti-popery, on which such excellent work has appeared in England, was a phenomenon which obviously was not merely or even mainly directed to studies of comparative religion. There was a concern in Scotland for 'religion and liberties', which included a patriotic element while not being exclusively Scottish. Propaganda for an internal as well as in time external readership offers helpful insight here, although a limited central perspective.[5] In this period of crisis – or opportunity – religious people could be skilful politicians with more than religious aims, and Johnston of Wariston is the prime example.

On the main theme, the account here presented extends and modifies our knowledge concerning the role of king and counsel in the handling of the troubles. The option of going with the king or at least not with the Covenant has too often been neglected in modern study of the period, though not all Scots eagerly came forward to be Covenanters. Again there is a need for further study of the local dimension, and some more direct work on various prominent individuals – although the evidence is not always available. But a focus on the swings of the king's actions and the efforts of his leading counsellors enlarges our understanding of how the troubles grew to their considerable height in the crucial years of 1637–41. Indeed Charles had major problems with which to deal, and across a multiple-kingdom situation which for no European ruler in the seventeenth century was easy, but singlemindedness and a religious attachment to monarchical ideals multiplied difficulties; it is with this that we must try to grapple.

In large part this book is a revision of my doctoral dissertation completed in the University of Cambridge. Many debts were incurred there, in the friendly and stimulating research seminars, in my home college of Gonville and Caius, but above all through the enthusiasm and patient guidance of my supervisor Dr John Morrill. From before the beginnings of my research he has been a much appreciated friend and ally. North of the border I have had great encouragement and friendship from fellow Scottish historians; in London I

---

[5] See especially P. Lake, 'Anti-popery: the structure of a prejudice', in R. Cust and A. Hughes (eds.), *Conflict in Early Stuart England* (1989), pp. 72–106. I use the word 'propaganda' for its original meaning – without derogatory overtones.

was no less fortunate, but especially around my year as Scouloudi research fellow in the Institute of Historical Research. Acknowledgement of the benefits conferred by the seminars, facilities and people of that Institute seem now almost to be commonplace: I can only add my own heartfelt thanks. Professor Conrad Russell, now the Earl Russell, arrived back in this country after I had begun my work, but even before that, and in great measure afterwards, he has been a constant inspiration and guide. It seems hard beyond this to single out names, because it has been to me a joy of historical research that for the most part we do all share and help each other, whether in small ways or large, known and unknown. May that long continue. I am especially grateful to those who have opened up to me their unpublished work, short papers and doctoral dissertations. Responsibility for this text is of course entirely my own.

In the course of my research I have been excellently served by the staff of record offices and libraries in Scotland and England, but especially in the Scottish Record Office, the National Library of Scotland, Cambridge University Library and New College, Edinburgh. I am grateful to the Director of Libraries and Information Services, Sheffield City Libraries and Olive, Countess Fitzwilliam's Wentworth Settlement Trustees for access to the Strafford papers, and to the Duke of Northumberland, the Earl of Crawford and Balcarres, the Earl of Dalhousie, the Viscount De L'Isle and Major-General Sir Humphry Tollemache, 6th Bt, for permission to cite from their family collections. The late Peter Maxwell Stuart was especially generous in enabling me to consult the Traquair manuscripts; my thanks go also to His Grace the Duke of Argyll for the use of his archives and The Argyll Historical Project. The costs of research and publication were aided by a grant from the Twenty-Seven Foundation.

Latterly a move to Edinburgh has changed my life in many ways, and I am grateful for the forbearance of many in and around New College who have tolerated an academic concern continuing outside my present training. Professor Anthony Fletcher has given generously of his time to help me through the processes of publication; Raymond Brown and Violet Sim have assisted most ably in reading through the typescript. I owe much to my family, some of whom are no longer with us, but my greatest debt is to my wife who has been alongside me, supporting me in all kinds of ways in these last three years; the dedication can be but a token acknowledgement of this.

ABBREVIATIONS

Aldis	Aldis, H. G., *A List of Books Printed in Scotland before 1700* (rev. edn, Edinburgh, 1970)
AO	Archives Office
APS	*The Acts of the Parliaments of Scotland*
AUL	Aberdeen University Library
BC	Bannatyne Club
BIHR	*Bulletin of the Institute of Historical Research*
BL	British Library, London
Bod.	Bodleian Library, University of Oxford
CC	Christ Church College, Oxford
CJ	*Journals of the House of Commons*
CSPD	*Calendar of State Papers, Domestic Series* (note: references are to printed volume by year, then to manuscript volume and item)
CSPI	*Calendar of State Papers . . . Ireland*
CSPV	*Calendar of State Papers . . . Venice*
CUL	Cambridge University Library
D'Ewes (C)	Coates, W. H. (ed.), *The Journal of Sir Simonds D'Ewes* (Yale, 1942)
D'Ewes (N)	Notestein, W. (ed.(, *The Journal of Sir Simonds D'Ewes* (Yale, 1923)
DNB	*Dictionary of National Biography*
EHR	*English Historical Review*
EUL	Edinburgh University Library
GD	Gifts and Deposits, Scottish Record Office, Edinburgh
HJ	*Historical Journal*
HLRO	House of Lords Record Office, London
JBS	*Journal of British Studies*
LJ	*Journals of the House of Lords*
MC	Maitland Club
NLS	National Library of Scotland, Edinburgh

NRA (S)	National Register of Archives (Scotland), Survey
P and P	*Past and Present*
PCR	*Privy Council Registers in Facsimile* (1967–8)
PRO	Public Record Office, London
RO	Record Office
RPCS	*The Register of the Privy Council of Scotland*
RSCHS	*Records of the Scottish Church History Society*
SHR	*Scottish Historical Review*
SHS	Scottish History Society
SRA	Strathclyde Regional Archives, Glasgow
SRO	Scottish Record Office, Edinburgh
STC	Pollard, A. W., and G. R. Redgrave, *A Short-Title Catalogue of Books Printed in England, Scotland and Ireland and of English Books Printed Abroad, 1475–1640*, 2 vols. (2nd edn, eds. W. A. Jackson, F. S. Ferguson and K. A. Pantzer, 1976–86)
STS	Scottish Text Society
TRHS	*Transactions of the Royal Historical Society*
Wing	Wing, D., *Short-Title Catalogue 1641–1700*, 3 vols. (2nd edn, New York, 1951–88)
WS	Wodrow Society
WWM	Wentworth Woodhouse Muniments, Sheffield Central Library

NOTE ON THE TEXT

All dates are Old Style, with calendar year beginning on 1 January, as was the style in Scotland.
Spelling and capitalisation, and sometimes punctuation have been modernised in all quotations.
The place of publication for all printed works cited is London unless otherwise stated.

1

The king and his counsel

In a struggle deriving from alienation felt in church and in state the Scots offered a major challenge to kingship as Charles I understood it. At first they argued merely that the king was badly counselled – in general terms a line of criticism quite common in the Europe of the day, but a charge that could threaten far-reaching remedies. It was one that Charles I was singularly disposed to reject. A remedy pushed from below was to his mind more aggravation than cure. An assault on his authority deserved only the name of treason.

The challenge, which developed considerably through the period of his troubles, has attracted good attention in recent years from historians, although many questions undoubtedly remain. Charles's response has been less thoroughly dealt with, crucial though it was for the history of the period. How he managed in these crisis years is the principal concern of this study. Stability was no easy matter: built into the situation were problems of multiple-kingdom government undoubtedly relevant to the complex of troubles which Charles became obliged to face. His line towards the Scots illustrates clearly a style of operation which was ill-suited across all of his kingdoms at the time. The limited brief here of investigating the handling of the Scottish troubles has implications which range more widely.

The King of England, Scotland and Ireland enjoyed considerable authority in the early seventeenth century. If practically there were strangleholds on the effectiveness and range of policy, in name and presence the king was highly impressive. Because according to scripture the king was the Lord's anointed, changes in the course of government had to have royal assent. But was the king's will not to be questioned? The alienated Scots found it both politic and necessary to denounce evil counsellors, and bishops in particular, for their part in influencing the king's direction. Over a church policy seen as both unpopular and wrong they dared to suggest that Charles ought to consult a general assembly and parliament. The troubles burgeoned when the king despite everything denied that there was a problem.

The tensions of high politics in the early modern state lay often in the

1

attempts by governments to enforce centralised rule and, not least, a single
variety of religion. The consensus of their peoples, and the very means to
effect their aims of government, were rarely assured. Programmes varied on
the ideals appropriate to the national churches, as indeed on the desirability
of interventionism in the localities.[1] In the three-kingdom situation after 1603
faced first by James VI and then by Charles I after 1625, the problems were
multiplied and intensified. Matters of and around the church came to be of
considerable significance – although this must be said without prejudice to
the very real concerns in all three kingdoms over taxation, trade and other
matters of social or economic policy. Nevertheless, the conversion of
common dissent into major crisis requires explanation.

After the regnal Union of 1603 the Scots had been placed in the novel situation of having an absentee king, and this in the midst of a period already
marked by radical social change engendered not least by the Reformation.
Within the Protestant ecclesiastical settlement were further questions of a disruptive nature as committed standpoints on presbyterian church government
lasted throughout and beyond the revival of episcopacy by James around the
period of union; determined nonconformity was often the response to other
ecclesiastical initiatives. The prominent opposition to the prayer book of
1637 arose out of this and it became entrenched to an extent well beyond
expectations. The reaction of Charles I was uncompromising. From royal
fury, the situation even came to war, and then back to an uneasy peace in
1641.

The kingdoms of England, Ireland and Scotland were united under one king
in 1603 on the death of the childless Queen Elizabeth. James VI of Scotland,
long since prepared, enthusiastically took up the wealth and power of the late
queen's dominions. By this dynastic accident, problems of centuries past
between Scotland and her strong southern neighbour seemed capable of
being solved. The best possible means was now at hand to conclude good
relations. Royal authority might equally be enhanced. There was a chance to
curb effectively the history of border raids where the two countries joined;
James wanted the area to be renamed the 'Middle Shires'. In a different part
of the periphery, Ireland, only newly free from rebellion, could now be controlled with the best cooperation of both England and Scotland; the prospect
for the Irish, as for all marginal sectors, was an ever fuller subjection to the
king's writ.[2]

The Union of 1603, as has recently been argued, was a 'starting-point, a

[1] H. G. Koenigsberger, *Politicians and Virtuosi* (1986), pp. 1–25.
[2] T. W. Moody, F. X. Martin and F. J. Byrne (eds.), *A New History of Ireland*, vol. III (Oxford, 1978), pp. 140–1, 187.

basis, a *sine qua non*.[3] What actually was united by a single crowned head was a subsequent political process. Residual hostilities between the kingdoms were considerable, although there had been links – religious, economic and cultural – long before 1603. A single king drew prestige and power. Scots were proud that their king had gone south; James's pursuit of the title 'Great Britain' indicated something of what he thought should accrue from a joining of the kingdoms. Abroad he was happy to remain *rex pacificus*; the Union offered extra security. At home his consuming vision was to promote the idea and reality of union and amity between his peoples. But the potential tensions of the situation were as great as its promise, and they became quickly manifest.

The problems emerged through the opening years as the king cautiously but insistently forwarded his project of union. At the earliest stage, provision was made in the Scottish parliament to exclude laws and religion from the brief of the Union Commission, for English takeover was feared. The Scots' sensitivity to being trampled under the feet of the more wealthy and numerous English was justifiable. James treasured the project of union, but it foundered on both sides. English people for their part harboured distrust of Scots from the past, and were all too prone to jealousies and arrogance in the present. Lasting agreement on trade was elusive; even settlement on the administration of the renamed 'Middle Shires' was not straightforward. On a number of matters the king proceeded outside the parliaments, with mixed measure of success. The flag called the Union Jack was never popular; Calvin's case, to establish rights of the *post nati*, those born after 1603, achieved the desired target of rights of naturalisation though raising important legal and constitutional points too, for allegiance due to the king and for the sovereign status of Scotland in English law. James also reformed the coinage and did what he could to ease the disagreements on commerce between the nations. Laws and the church were left for further action.[4]

A formal settlement of a union that would satisfy both Scots and English was not achieved. The Scots wanted a more federal arrangement than the English would allow. A well-developed sense of patriotic identity continued to sustain Scottish independence feeling long after the first union schemes. James himself had no wish to eliminate all Scottish distinctiveness, however much he wanted it to be assimilable, in a unity of hearts and minds, to that of

---

[3] B. Galloway, *The Union of England and Scotland, 1603–1608* (Edinburgh, 1986), p. 1.

[4] The best account is in Galloway, *The Union of England and Scotland.* See also M. Lee, Jr, *Government by Pen: Scotland under James VI and I* (1980), pp. 34–8, 83–6; B. R. Galloway and B. P. Levack (eds.), *The Jacobean Union*, SHS (Edinburgh, 1985); B. P. Levack, *The Formation of the British State: England, Scotland and the Union, 1603–1707* (Oxford, 1987). For the 'Middle Shires', see C. M. F. Ferguson, 'Law and order on the Anglo-Scottish border, 1603–1707' (unpublished University of St. Andrews Ph.D. dissertation, 1981).

the English. At least one dimension of it though was to be erased. The
presbyterians of Scotland were forming their own sense of Scottish national
identity. The British church vision that had fired some of the first-generation
reformers was somewhat left behind, as alongside less influential English
counterparts the Scots made criticism of the church as it was established in
England. As an element which thus challenged the royal authority which
upheld the establishment, they were eminently worthy of suppression.[5]

Without closer union, administrative separation – an expedient in 1603
eyes – lasted. England provided a seat for the monarchy and so became the
centre of government. In all three kingdoms privy councils helped by handling administration – the putting out of orders, the hearing of petitions, the
resolving of local disputes – with variable degrees of efficiency.[6] How much
they advised is an important point. Only for English affairs could the king
easily sit in person in his privy council and so hear their consultations. Advice
written from a distance was less sure of success; the Scots sent delegations or
representatives south over major issues. In practice James and Charles were
also open to counsel from anyone who gained the necessary access to their
persons, a personal dimension of government which was highly important.
The chain of patronage stretched downwards from the king, who preferred
and rewarded servants at his discretion. Court was the centre stage of
national politics. The institutional machinery of government, because it was
the king's, had limited room for sustained opposition to him. As positions
and policy ultimately depended on the king, all politicking, statesmanlike or
otherwise, hung absolutely on gaining his approval.[7]

The handling of 'British' policy was not straightforward, given the lack of
any British machinery of government. With the diverse needs of the kingdoms, decisions over trade or foreign policy easily risked causing offence,
particularly in the outlying kingdoms, Scotland and Ireland. Communication
by letter achieved a measure of contact, but neither this nor the visits of individuals, officially or otherwise, to the king at Court could fully compensate
for the problems raised by monarchy over a number of separate kingdoms.
Predictably England became the measure for at least most things, but not
without tensions. In Ireland, where anglicisation was equated with Protestantism and civilisation, advances were made despite a largely Catholic and

[5] G. Donaldson, *The Making of the Scottish Prayer Book of 1637* (Edinburgh, 1954),
   pp. 4–23; A. H. Williamson, *Scottish National Consciousness in the Age of James VI*
   (Edinburgh, 1979).
[6] K. Sharpe, 'Crown, parliament and locality: government and communication in early Stuart
   England', *EHR*, 101 (1986), 321–50; P. G. B. McNeill, 'The jurisdiction of the Scottish privy
   council 1532–1708' (unpublished University of Glasgow Ph.D. dissertation, 1960);
   H. F. Kearney, *Strafford in Ireland, 1633–41* (Manchester, 1959).
[7] C. S. R. Russell, *Parliaments and English Politics 1621–1629* (Oxford, 1982), pp. 5–18;
   D. Starkey *et al.*, *The English Court from the Wars of the Roses to the Civil War* (1987).

culturally variant people. Institutionally the subordination remained England-bound, despite the potential contribution Scotland could now make to the management of the situation there.[8] For Protestant Scots at home the anglicising tendency over the church and other policies tendered to them was a considerable source of aggravation.

The track towards integration by the awards of titles or office to non-nationals, for instance, was as muddied as any other. Protests over privilege were raised in the parliaments. Nevertheless honour was served in 1617 when, during the one visit he achieved after the Union, James had the Scottish privy council admit some English members nominally into its ranks. Charles repeated the gesture in 1626 and during his coronation visit of 1633.[9] Various Scots had been appointed to the English council, where they played a more active role than their English counterparts in Scottish affairs; since most were courtiers, they had the English council meetings readily at hand. On a more official note, Viscount Alexander was apparently admitted into the English ranks in 1629 in respect of his being the Scottish Secretary of State. He was mostly resident in London, and there had been a request from Edinburgh for early knowledge through him of the various matters that affected Scotland.[10]

The Court itself preserved a constant Scottish interest around both James and Charles. Many Scots could be numbered close to the royal person, in the Bedchamber or Privy Chamber. Such individuals kept up links with 'home' in Scotland despite their protracted residence in the south. The English resented the exclusion of themselves that resulted from the arrangement; however, with Court contacts so vital in the climate of the day, the Scots expected as much as they got.[11] Whatever the alienation by royal policies, the monarchy remained a unique force of patronage and mystique. Charles, acclaimed as the 108th king, touched for the 'king's evil' in Edinburgh during the coronation visit. The Earl of Rothes, surely contrary to his taste and yet surely understandably, held the sceptre while Charles took communion kneeling during that 1633 coronation. The equally puritan Earl of Eglinton was utterly committed to winning a place for his son in the Prince of Wales's Household which was to be settled in the 1630s.[12]

---

[8] Moody, Martin and Byrne, *New History of Ireland, passim.*

[9] *RPCS*, 1st Series, vol. XI, pp. 136–7, 163–6, 169; 2nd Series, vol. I, pp. 248–50, vol. V, pp. 116–17.

[10] GD 22/3/785 – undated, but early 1629; *Acts of the Privy Council of England*, May 1629–May 1630 (1960), p. 26.

[11] N. Cuddy, 'The revival of the entourage: the Bedchamber of James I, 1603–1625' and K. Sharpe, 'The image of virtue: the court and household of Charles I, 1625–1642', in D. Starkey *et al.*, *The English Court*, pp. 173–260; P. Heylyn, *Cyprianus Anglicus* (1668), pp. 377–9; GD 40/2/XV.4.

[12] Bod. Rawlinson Ms. D49, fols. 4–5; NLS Ms. 21183, fol. 73; Sir W. Fraser, *Memorials of the Montgomeries Earls of Eglinton* (2 vols., Edinburgh, 1859), vol. I, pp. 236–7. In the event, Scots were denied places around the prince – W. Knowler (ed.), *The Earl of*

However, with the removal of the Court to England, a mighty vacuum had been created in Scotland. At a stroke the king had been released from the distinctively Scottish risks of personal attack, but his subjects were deprived of an outlet for the expression of frustrations and debate. Informal and proud of his own quality of debate, James had regularly met with his leading subjects. Scots now had to journey far if they were to see their king. James hoped that his privy council in Edinburgh would represent his person. How effectively it achieved this was another variable in the balance, for there could be contrary demands made on it. Even if Scots reckoned the privy council good enough, it was not automatic that the king would be content with its conduct.[13]

King James VI of Scotland as James VI and I managed as best he could to promote his sovereignty over kingdoms still in many respects divided. That his Scottish background shaped his reign after 1603 is a most persuasive argument concerning a king of England who has often been cricitised over-severely.[14] The Union was not bound to succeed. It is a measure of James's success that tensions were contained within reason, although it certainly was not solely his achievement. The link between administration in Scotland and a king who boasted in 'government by pen' was helped by responsible and efficient leading councillors who travelled regularly between Scotland and England. There was no shortage of difficulties, including notably on matters of the church. James's ineptitude with finance was a constant blot on a record generally of caution and moderation.[15]

More positively on the financial side, James for his part would at least have kept out of war. The outbreak of the Thirty Years' War near the end of the reign led to troubles he would dearly have avoided. The 'hotter sort of Protestants' would willingly have seen the British flag enter the fray against the armies perceived to be of the Roman antichrist. James's resistance had, among others, the support of the ecclesiastical faction which called such people 'puritans'. He died as the crisis was developing, but the church antagonisms only became more acute under the rise of the so-called Arminians. The war years exposed a number of serious areas of conflict between the king and various subjects in his three kingdoms. The costs of war

Strafforde's Letters and Dispatches (2 vols., 1739), vol. II, p. 167. On the importance of patronage, see K. M. Brown, 'Aristocratic finances and the origins of the Scottish Revolution', *EHR*, 104 (1989), 46–87.

[13] J. Wormald, *Court, Kirk and Community: Scotland 1470–1625* (1981), pp. 156–7, 192; R. Mitchison, *Lordship to Patronage: Scotland 1603–1745* (1983), p. 12; GD 124/10/97; *RPCS*, 1st Series, vol. IX, pp. 745–6.

[14] J. Wormald, 'James VI and I: two kings or one?', *History*, 68 (1983), 187–209.

[15] Lee, *Government by Pen*; Mitchison, *Lordship to Patronage*, pp. 1–21; Cuddy, 'The revival of the entourage'.

alone would have been disruptive, but there were ideological elements to the troubles. In Ireland, Charles antagonised the Protestant hierarchy, not to mention puritans everywhere, by contemplating major concessions to the Catholics in return for supply. In England, sensitivities about the role of parliaments were heightened as various non-parliamentary expedients were tried. Scottish loyalties were vulnerable when arguments could be made about foreign policy being decided upon without due reference to their national (and vested) interests. Across the kingdoms high-sounding political statements were made while locally hardship and non-cooperation marred the militarisation effort. Some of Charles's difficulties with armies in 1639–40 arose in similar fashion.[16]

Although the king would seek to restrict trouble for the sake of good order in government, conflict did not necessarily mean civil war. In normal circumstances, and in days without paid bureaucracies, central rule would be as reactive as initiating. In Scotland this was particularly true, though a long tradition of *laissez-faire* monarchy had begun to change in the sixteenth century as central demands for money, and a widening judicial system, penetrated into the localities. The other main sphere of active royal policy, church reformation, in origins had proceeded against the will of the Crown in Scotland, but it was James's battle from the earliest opportunity to assume the more common role of leadership.[17]

Scottish society in some ways underwent a rapid transition in the period before and after the Union. The coincidence of the Reformation and the increased rule of law was significant. The local authority of the magnates was still employed by the king, but the developments in civil law and the judicial experiments in the localities were incursions tending to undermine that. More significant still were the effects of the Reformation which, joined with the king's best efforts, helped to counteract blood feud and the organisation of followings by bonds of manrent. Protestantism awakened an active religious consciousness through all ranks of the population. The presbyterian organisation which evolved, alongside the changes in civil order, promoted the roles of the lairds and lesser men in society; the feuing of kirklands benefited especially the same group. Regular taxation from 1581 caused the standardisation of lairds' or barons' representatives from the shires being summoned

---

[16] I summarise here very major points which are under controversy. K. Fincham and P. Lake, 'The ecclesiastical policy of King James I', *Journal of British Studies*, 24 (1985), 169–207; Russell, *Parliaments and English Politics*; C. Russell, 'Monarchies, wars and estates in England, France and Spain, c. 1580–1640', *Legislative Studies Quarterly*, 7 (1982), 205–20; M. Lee, Jr, *The Road to Revolution: Scotland under Charles I, 1625–1637* (Urbana and Chicago, 1985), pp. 79–83; R. Cust, *The Forced Loan and English Politics 1626–1628* (Oxford, 1987); R. Cust and A. Hughes (eds.), *Conflict in Early Stuart England* (1989); J. P. Sommerville, *Politics and Ideology in England, 1603–1640* (1986).

[17] Wormald, *Court, Kirk and Community*, pp. 20–6, 148–76; Wormald, 'James VI and I'.

to parliaments. Union with England made Scots even more want to disown a violent medieval past. The highlands, assumed to be areas of barbarism and lawlessness, were shunted roughly into isolation by lowland and government attitudes.[18]

Changes met problems, whether the newness originated from below or above. The social effects of the breakdown of familiar landmarks have not yet been fully assessed; but trouble came notably with the more energetic regime of Charles I. The victories of the lawyers and administrators, the 'new men' who wanted to govern society, faced conservative indifference if not opposition in the localities, and some tension where their ambitions were restrained by vested interests, usually of the king or the nobility. The leaders in the church were vociferous in denouncing the old order. Loudly they preached change, for the individual as for the established church. They too had their frustrations. Aside from lingering error and 'popery', as they would call it, the notion of the godly prince held by James and Charles embraced a wish for a control and obedience that was certainly challengeable.[19]

Royal supremacy in matters ecclesiastical was a topic of relevance all over Europe. Reformation in religion involved hopes for reformation in the state as a whole, in which case the role of the prince or the magistrate could be vital. He could be protector and benefactor of the reforming church; or his opposition might be a principal obstacle. The question of whether or not a prince might be resisted was raised in this context; and it sometimes had to be answered in practical action. Reformation was but rarely a purely spiritual issue.[20]

Given the origins of the Reformation in England, the royal supremacy had never seriously been challenged, but there had been large disagreements about the course of reform. Puritan critics who wanted more godly (purer) reform beyond matters of order and moderation made only limited headway. Some of these people stood on a presbyterian platform, for which they found scriptural justification; they first made headway in a time of anti-episcopal

[18] Wormald, *Court, Kirk and Community*, pp. 148–94; J. Wormald, *Lords and Men in Scotland: Bonds of Manrent 1442–1603* (Edinburgh, 1985), esp. pp. 1–6; K. M. Brown, *Bloodfeud in Scotland 1573–1625* (Edinburgh, 1986); M. Sanderson, *Scottish Rural Society in the Sixteenth Century* (Edinburgh, 1982); M. Lynch, 'The Crown and the burghs, 1500–1625', in M. Lynch (ed.), *The Early Modern Town in Scotland* (1987), pp. 55–80.

[19] Wormald, *Court, Kirk and Community*, pp. 148–9, 165–6; Lee, *Government by Pen*, pp. 8–10, 42–4. See too A. I. Macinnes, 'The origin and organization of the Covenanting movement during the reign of Charles I, 1625–1641; with a particular reference to the west of Scotland' (unpublished University of Glasgow Ph.D. dissertation, 1988).

[20] R. A. Mason, 'Covenant and commonweal: the language of politics in Reformation Scotland', in N. Macdougall (ed.), *Church, Politics and Society: Scotland 1408–1929* (Edinburgh, 1983), pp. 97–126; G. Donaldson, *Scotland: James V–James VII* (Edinburgh, 1965), pp. 107–31, 157–70; P. Collinson, 'The monarchical republic of Queen Elizabeth I', *Bulletin of the John Rylands University Library of Manchester*, 69 (1987), 394–424.

feeling in the 1560s but never managed to break through. By the 1590s they were in decline, and their opponents in controversy increasingly confident on *iure divino* arguments for episcopacy and positive arguments in favour of the ceremonies and liturgy the others hoped to reject.[21]

The terms by which royal and episcopal authority were justified tended towards being absolutist in response to the challenge that came from both puritans and Roman Catholics. The king had his power conferred directly from God and so strictly speaking was limited only by natural and divine law, and punishable only by God. Charles I distanced himself particularly from any suggestion that his church supremacy was subject to popular consent. He stood for a great deal belonging to him as God's viceregent on earth. The ideas of James VI and I were probably little different; but significantly they were tempered by moderation in practice.[22]

James's upbringing in Scotland lay in the shadow of his mother's enforced abdication in 1567, but he successfully left behind the threats of resistance theory. The prestige of the monarchy survived the upheaval of the 1560s and 1570s. James's greatest battle, it has been argued, came to be over the church and with the presbyterians who would limit his authority over it.[23] The local and national organisation of a presbyterian church battled for establishment by the godly prince, rightly critical of the ill-reformed episcopal bench, but was royally resisted because it radically claimed its full independence from the state.

James's own religious politics began to win the advantage in the closing years of the sixteenth century. In 1584 presbyterians had been persecuted by the so-called 'Black Acts', but in 1592 the king, again in parliament, passed the contrasting 'Golden Act' which upheld the presbyterian system. This political compromise marked a temporary resting-point. Episcopacy was never formally abolished, but it ceased for some time to have an ecclesiastical function. James's success in restoring it was gradual, the first move being to appoint individuals to the parliament for filling the first estate. Royal appointees were likely to be compliant. The presbyterians held out as best they could in the national or general assemblies. The general assembly held at Montrose in 1600 enacted that clerical representatives in parliaments were to be strictly accountable to general assemblies. However, by the time of the Glasgow Assembly of 1610 and the *selective* ratification of its conclusions in the parliament of 1612, diocesan episcopacy was fully restored. James had worked for his ends by attempting close control of the various representative

---

[21] P. Lake, *Anglicans and Puritans? Presbyterianism and English Conformist Thought from Whitgift to Hooker* (1988); P. Collinson, *The Birthpangs of Protestant England* (1988).
[22] W. R. Foster, *The Church before the Covenants* (Edinburgh, 1975), pp. 125–6; Sommerville, *Politics and Ideology*, pp. 203–8.
[23] Wormald, *Court, Kirk and Community*, pp. 143–9.

meetings. After Glasgow, it was not clear that any future assembly would be called to meet.[24]

Arguments for presbyterianism by divine right derived from the reading of scripture, but were something of a second stage to deeply felt prejudice against ungodly bishops. There was more of a priority in the hoped-for creation of a new godly commonwealth – an all-encompassing vision, imbued with a sense of rightness that wished to hear no contrary voices. Sympathies to the godly prince, as the king might easily be seen to be, could be very conditional – and the royal imperatives that expected obedience as a matter of necessity less compelling.[25] Hard-line insistence on an unlimited royal supremacy could not simply rule the field.

The kings stood by bishops for political as much as religious reasons, although it is unwise to play too much on distinctions here. Possibly Charles was more committed to *iure divino* episcopacy than his father – but political rather than theological arguments justified the case for unity on the subject. The political advantage of bishops was emphasised in the opening procla- mation on the church of Scotland issued by Charles.[26] Episcopacy com- plemented monarchy in a way that parity of ministers did not. No authority in the kingdoms was in theory to be outwith the control of the monarch – and certainly none potentially against him – yet some presbyterians dared to defend the convening of an assembly at Aberdeen in 1605 that James had prorogued. James insisted on having them pursued for treason for declining his authority. By isolating those he viewed to be extreme, he hoped to quieten the moderate majority. The problem was that the presbyterians did not accept his authority so to act. Regardless, the king had a statute passed in the parliament of 1606 which acknowledged him as supreme governor over all persons, estates and causes, both spiritual and temporal, within his realm of Scotland. It was to be a buttressing legal foundation for the royal claims.[27]

James's achievement over episcopacy owed its success to a number of factors. The politic management of the nobility, most notably by rewards in land, worked against a united alliance against him. It was probably a small number who were rigidly opposed to having bishops; scriptural evidence was not unambiguous on the subject. The caution with which the policy was

---

[24] G. Donaldson, *The Scottish Reformation* (Cambridge, 1960); J. Kirk (ed.), *The Second Book of Discipline* (Edinburgh, 1980); D. G. Mullan, *Episcopacy in Scotland: The History of an Idea, 1560–1638* (Edinburgh, 1986).

[25] Cf. Donaldson, *The Scottish Reformation*, pp. 144–5.

[26] *RPCS*, 2nd Series, vol. I, pp. 91–2. Cf. [Charles I], *A Large Declaration*, STC 21906 (1639), pp. 424–5.

[27] Donaldson, *Scotland: James V–James VII*, pp. 197–207; Wormald, *Court, Kirk and Community*, pp. 143–9; Mullan, *Episcopacy*, pp. 87–113; Lee, *Government by Pen*, pp. 48–56; Fincham and Lake, 'The ecclesiastical policy'. See also M. J. Mendle, *Dangerous Positions* (Alabama, 1985).

advanced was exemplary, and typically Jacobean. However wide the discrepancy between legislation and what might have been preferred, an unintended but lasting compromise with presbyterian organisation minimised causes for grievance. At the local level, kirk sessions and presbyteries continued; bishops were more of an addition than an alteration to the church's constitution. The more secular dimension of episcopacy was tempered as ambitious individuals infiltrated only slowly into civil positions extra to their role in parliaments, where they were fully employed to royal advantage. Sensitive individuals like the Earl of Rothes were irked, but politics was at least half, if not more, of the battle. The contrast is to be drawn with Charles's reign.[28]

A battle won by James in practice did not put an end to argument by words, albeit by a particularly vocal minority. Episcopacy had its critics, at first even men who later accepted preferments, but subsequently amongst a small resolute hard-core. David Calderwood was one of the most prominent here; by several publications the debate was kept alive, and in measure answered by the other side.[29] What exactly might be bracketed under the royal supremacy was among the subjects disputed, despite the 1606 legislation, but it is noteworthy that even Calderwood in subsequent years dropped his challenge of the king's right to summon assemblies, as if to recognise the weakness of his ground on this point.[30] The issue resurfaced as it were with a vengeance in the Covenanting period – perhaps a predictable development of a new phase of confidence in presbyterianism, but one that powerfully indicates the shaping force of politics alongside ideas, and not one or the other in isolation.

Antipathies to anglicisation rumbled in the background of the troubles over James's policy for church government, but provocation was sought to be avoided. When in 1610 three Scottish bishops went to England for their consecration, the Archbishop of Canterbury was deliberately not involved, so as to avert suspicions of the English claiming superiority. In the same decade, when the Catholic Marquis of Huntly chose to conform whilst he was in

---

[28] Foster, *Church*, pp. 11–36; D. Laing (ed.), *Correspondence of Sir Robert Kerr, First Earl of Ancrum, and his Son, William, Third Earl of Lothian* (2 vols., Edinburgh, 1875), vol. I, pp. 35–8; Lee, *The Road to Revolution*, pp. 6–7.

[29] For example, [D. Calderwood], *The Altar of Damascus . . .* , STC 4352 ([Amsterdam], 1621); [D. Calderwood], *Quaeres Concerning the State of the Church of Scotland*, STC 4361.5 ([Amsterdam], 1621); D. Lyndesay, *A True Narration of all the Passages of the Proceedings in the General Assembly of the Church of Scotland . . .* , STC 15657 (1621); [D. Calderwood], *The Pastor and the Prelate . . .* , STC 4359 (n.p., 1628); E. G. Selwyn (ed.), *The First Book of the Irenicum [1629] of John Forbes of Corse* (Cambridge, 1923); [D. Calderwood], *A Re-examination of the Five Articles Enacted at Perth, Anno 1618*, STC 4363.5 (n.p., 1636).

[30] I owe this point to P. H. R. Mackay, 'The Five Articles of Perth' (unpublished University of Edinburgh Ph.D. dissertation, 1975), p. 36. I am grateful to Dr Mackay for permission to cite from his work.

England, the opportunity was not lost, but Archbishop Abbot took care to cover himself with the Scottish bishops.[31] James certainly valued the support of English bishops. In 1606 against the presbyterians and in subsequent years, Englishmen preached on behalf of the royal cause. English echoes of the new worship directives for the Scottish church in 1616 were indicative of the British dimension behind what technically were to be Scottish changes. James felt the need to persuade his Scottish subjects that some things English were good and to be recommended.[32]

These last-mentioned changes in worship, which were embodied in the so-called Five Articles of Perth, were undoubtedly more troublesome than the reintroduction of episcopacy. On the king's side, however, it seemed altogether undesirable to tolerate disparities across the kingdoms under his headship. Aside from theology the argument that he and his clergy should be respected in the ordering of the church worked for the sake of civil order; but the Scottish changes were expected to edify, or give spiritual benefit to the people. The element of anglicisation was to be incidental.[33]

There was a British problem in so far as discontent smouldered still in England over aspects of liturgical worship, including what was to be most contentious in Scotland, kneeling at the celebration of the Lord's Supper.[34] James would insist that scruples on matters which historically could be regarded at least as 'indifferent' had to be abandoned in favour of obedience to authority.[35] The difficulty was that, as like-minded efforts towards the Channel Islands had found, such changes met with strong opposition.[36] A principal argument in Scotland was that anything not explicitly warranted in scripture was to be avoided in worship, and especially lest it lead the ignorant populace back into the ways of superstition and popery. This had been a cardinal imperative of the Scottish Reformation. More specifically, some-

[31] Foster, *Church*, p. 29; B. Botfield (ed.), *Original Letters Relating to the Ecclesiastical Affairs of Scotland* (2 vols., Edinburgh, 1851), vol. II, pp. 474–8; Lee, *Government by Pen*, pp. 158–9.

[32] Mullan, *Episcopacy*, pp. 98–103; Lee, *Government by Pen*, pp. 158–9; T. Morton, *A Defence of the Innocencie of the Three Ceremonies of the Church of England* . . . , STC 18179 (1618); J. Buckeridge, *A Sermon Preached before His Maiestie at Whitehall March 22 1617* . . . , STC 4005 (1618); L. Andrewes, *A Sermon Preached before His Maiestie at Whitehall, on Easter Day Last, 1618*, STC 623 (1618); W. Laud, *The Works of the Most Reverend Father in God, William Laud, D.D.*, eds. W. Scott and J. Bliss (7 vols., Oxford, 1847–60), vol. III, p. 160; Botfield, *Original Letters*, vol. II, pp. 535–40. For James's speech in 1617, see CUL Ms. Ee.5.23, fols. 442–5.

[33] Foster, *Church*, pp. 192, 199–205; cf. P. Heylyn, *A Full Relation of Two Journeys* . . . (1656), pp. 363–423.

[34] For example, cf. Botfield, *Original Letters*, vol. II, p. 559.

[35] J. Craigie (ed.), *The Basilicon Doron of King James VI*, STS, 3rd Series (2 vols., Edinburgh, 1944, 1950) esp. vol. I, pp. 16–17. This was a minimal stance.

[36] A. J. Eagleston, *The Channel Islands under Tudor Government, 1485–1642* (Cambridge, 1949), pp. 128–45.

thing like kneeling at the time of communion was taken to be idolatry. Words for respecting the continuity of the church from earliest times were alien to Scottish evangelical thinking. The proposals did not seem at all 'indifferent'.

Although a few in Scotland would have felt little hostility to the proposals, the predominant line was to oppose. The English background helped little but James did not even enjoy the support of all the Scottish bishops. He pressed hard, though, the line of obedience, and the policy got carried through general assemblies, not without reluctance. The use of the assemblies the king regarded merely as a necessary means to an end. He maintained consistently that he had the authority in any case to enforce his will. A statute was drafted in 1617 that affirmed that the king with consent of his clergy might make what changes he pleased in the Scottish church. It was tactically dropped, but signposted clearly enough James's thinking.[37]

Despite all the various efforts to coerce membership, the passing of the Five Articles at the general assembly of Perth in 1618 was messy, with quite a number of those present dissenting. James subsequently demanded on his own authority the enforcement of all the Articles – kneeling at communion, private administration of the two sacraments, the observance of major Feast Days and episcopal confirmation. The assembly Act was not explicit that these were rigorously to be observed, but the king passionately ordered just that. A very loud protest was made in return. That James took his reading of the Perth Articles to a statute in the parliament which met in 1621 tacitly acknowledged this, although he maintained that this was merely strengthening an injunction he had already been fully competent to make.[38] The king's wish for uniformity of practice was now quite explicit. Opponents tried but in vain to block the manœuvre.[39]

This account of James's ecclesiastical policy is important background to the troubles of Charles's reign since the issues at stake did not die. The son's passions also echoed those of his royal father.[40] Yet there were differences. James took advice to proceed through representative assemblies, albeit packed ones; his pragmatism in this respect, despite his passion, was not to be copied. Moreover, James's designs for a new confession of faith, liturgy and canons, having begun with the Five Articles, were quietly left aside in the midst of the troubles. The king to some extent at least recognised his limitations. He could suffer compromise, although on church affairs he did

[37] Lee, *Government by Pen*, pp. 167–8; J. Spottiswood, *The History of the Church of Scotland*, BC (3 vols., Edinburgh, 1850), vol. III, p. 246.
[38] *APS*, vol. IV, pp. 596–7; Foster, *Church*, pp. 181–92; Lee, *Government by Pen*, pp. 157–94, 204–7; Mullan, *Episcopacy*, pp. 151–9.
[39] NLS Wod, Fo. 31, fol. 5; [Calderwood], *Quaeres Concerning the State of the Church of Scotland*.
[40] Cf. Laud, *Works*, vol. V, pp. 338, 355, 366.

not like it. It seemed politic, however, not to press too far.[41] Still, the bishops were commanded to enforce the Articles. The observance of changes in worship depended on local consent and cooperation, however, and success was at best patchy.[42]

Division over the Five Articles, however, need not have been lastingly significant. Local enforcement was sporadic and, if anything, eased off slightly. At the same time, it might be supposed that patterns of conformity were slowly made. At James's death in 1625 there were serious divisions in the church, but they were not in themselves critical. Other troubles were inherited besides by Charles, the debt, the uncertainties engendered by social change, the unresolved tensions of union. James had failed in his promise to visit his native kingdom often, and on his one visit had brought disliked taxation in addition to the church policies. Scotland was not an easy kingdom to succeed to, but it was not on any certain path to rebellion.

As has been suggested, Charles in his basic ideas about the monarchy probably differed very little from his father, though publicly he was less eloquent on the subject. His sense, however, was to brook no compromise. He would believe that his word was final, and disobedience he would take as an insult to his person. Order and authority were the life-blood of the state. How he regulated his Court offers one insight into his world, one of decorum and propriety. More authoritarian and more energetic than James, whether for his self-protection or out of a consuming vision, he struck from his accession an altogether new note.[43]

A change of monarch naturally had wide ramifications, despite what continuity there was within the Court and institutional machineries of government. From a high political perspective, Charles's inflexibility and concern to make his mark raised problems very quickly, and not simply on account of the burdens of war. How the king saw things did not necessarily command agreement. Fears for property were felt, in the Forced Loan in England but also through the Revocation for Scotland. Certainly conflicts in church and state were not simply of Charles's making, but there were troubles and disputes which he liked very little; and when he was committed, he was slow indeed to be turned.

Historians debate the extent to which Charles was personally involved in

---

[41] Botfield, *Original Letters*, vol. II, p. 524; G. Donaldson, 'Reformation to Covenant', in D. Forrester and D. Murray (eds.), *Studies in the History of Worship in Scotland* (Edinburgh, 1984), pp. 33–51.

[42] P. H. R. Mackay, 'The reception given to the Five Articles of Perth', *RSCHS*, 19 (1977), 185–201. There is an interesting attempt at a statistical approach in A. B. Birchler, 'The influence of the Scottish clergy on politics: 1616–1638' (unpublished Lincoln, Nebraska, Ph.D. dissertation, 1966).

[43] Sharpe, 'The image of virtue'; C. Carlton, *Charles I* (1983).

government. As a keen sportsman and aesthete, did he give much time over to its routine business? How much was selectively read to him for approval? It can be said that Charles could be very concerned, even to the point of fine detail, and in all kinds of spheres. This pertained whether or not he had actively originated the lines of policy.[44] Business was always coming to him. Suitors who lacked close access themselves to the king would try many and various ways to seek his favour. For all Archbishop Laud's importance in the 'British' church, he was not considered the only person to enjoy weight of influence on this. The hopeful candidate for a Scottish see, for instance, might find Patrick Maule of Panmure, a Bedchamber servant, a useful potential figure of support.[45]

Everything revolved around the king, and it is also important that Charles rose to assume responsibility, as was generally expected of him. Even if to do otherwise would have been unfitting, we might see his assertion of the kingly role as the practical manifestation of the high political thought to which he adhered. His counsellors, whether as individuals in private or in a full institutional setting, had to acknowledge the finality of his arbitration; he was not always prepared to come to a decision in public.[46] Utterly determined to answer expectations, his personal commitment to his role was asserted most forcefully in crisis, as will later appear. The king regularly turned to counsel. How open he was to persuasion is another matter – indeed it is our key theme.

In the fragile context of Union, Charles's style with the policies he actively espoused created trouble. The Court, distant as ever, became more and more the seat of decisions about what was 'good' for Scotland. Discontent grew through the general hostility to anglicisation and burdensome rule. However, it would be dangerous to assume that all was tending towards the explosion that came in 1637 and beyond. On the one hand it is important to consider what in retrospect seems to have been of general preparatory significance. Yet it may be argued that the direction of changes in the church in the mid-1630s was the critical determinant for what we know as the 'Scottish troubles'; and

---

[44] K. Sharpe, 'The personal rule of Charles I', in H. Tomlinson (ed.), *Before the English Civil War* (1983), esp. pp. 58–9; Carlton, *Charles I*, pp. 154–60. For primary examples, see HMC *R. R. Hastings* (78), vol. IV, pp. 71–2; NLS Ms. 81, no. 46; GD 406/1/153.
[45] See, for example, *A Diary of the Public Correspondence of Sir Thomas Hope of Craighall, Bart., 1633–1645*, ed. T. Thomson, BC (Edinburgh, 1843), p. 22; GD 45/14/14 (ii); NLS Ms. 81, no. 60; *The Memoirs of Henry Guthry, Late Bishop of Dunkeld* (Glasgow, 1747), pp. 16–17; W. H. Hutton, 'Two letters of Archbishop Laud', *EHR*, 45 (1930), 107–8.
[46] Cf. HMC *Denbigh* (68), pp. 256–7; K. Sharpe, *Criticism and Compliment: The Politics of Literature in the England of Charles I* (Cambridge, 1987), pp. 189, 212; Cust, *The Forced Loan*, pp. 41–3.

that the short-term movements within those troubles contributed vitally to the shape that they took.[47]

The use of separate Scottish institutions continued under the new king, although not without some attempts at reform. Charles could easily overlook Scottish distinctiveness, despite Wentworth's later criticism that he governed Scotland too much by the hands of Scotsmen.[48] Lip-service was paid by the use of the term 'native kingdom', but it is far from clear that Charles regularly sought information from the north, despite the advice for instance from Lord Napier to do so.[49] Like James, he could find English perspectives as serviceable. Ideas for local and criminal justice had English echoes; economic regulation often happened to advantage English interests, sometimes to Scottish detriment. What was the best policy was open to discovery. Instability in Scotland through the Union was exacerbated.[50]

More specifically, the reforming policies of 1625 betrayed a quite loose approach to matters of Scottish import. In consequence meetings were held in January 1626 at Whitehall between Charles and a specially summoned group of the Scottish privy council. At issue were the notorious Revocation and the restructuring of various component parts of the Scottish administration – policies which to a greater or lesser extent gave grounds for trouble. Fortunately it is possible to describe in some detail Charles's conduct.[51] The encounter was held at the request of councillors who felt distinctly unconsulted, not to mention aggrieved. Charles apparently met them willingly enough. At such an early stage, and conscious of some ignorance on his part concerning Scotland (albeit loath to admit it), the idea seemed both politic and wise. His personal presence served to affirm the authority behind the policies of the previous months; the presence of advisers of those policies gave him the necessary back-up support.

The sessions were held in the Withdrawing Chamber on various afternoons. The king sat while everyone else stood, the Duke of Buckingham at the king's left and the Lord Chancellor of Scotland, Sir George Hay, at his right; whenever anyone contributed to the discussion, he knelt. In effect the king

---

[47] Cf. interpretations in Lee, *The Road to Revolution*; W. Makey, *The Church of the Covenant 1637–1651* (Edinburgh, 1979), pp. 1–15; Macinnes, 'The origin and organization of the Covenanting movement'; Stevenson, *The Scottish Revolution*, pp. 15–55.

[48] Knowler, *Strafforde Letters*, vol. II, p. 190. Cf. Stevenson, *The Scottish Revolution*, p. 32.

[49] M. Napier (ed.), *Memorials of Montrose and his Times*, MC (2 vols., Edinburgh, 1848–51), vol. I, pp. 25–7, 70–8.

[50] Cf. *RPCS*, 2nd Series, vol. VI, p. 457; GD 406/M1/328/2; Lee, *The Road to Revolution*, pp. 90–4.

[51] My account is very substantially drawn from NLS Adv. Ms. 33.1.4 (vol. XVIII of the Denmilne papers), fols. 1–20. This was written retrospectively by an eye-witness. See too the better-known evidence in *HMC Mar and Kellie* (60), pp. 133–46 (GD 124/10/309–11, 313–14). In what follows, I shall reference only specific points of detail.

was holding an audience rather than a council meeting. When the council met on their own with Buckingham to view the text of the Revocation, they assembled in the Council Chamber and sat round a table. Buckingham, incidentally, on this occasion was insistent on the ordinary precedence of the Scots council being observed; he refused the seniority which was offered to him. Charles, when he was present, always initiated, calling for explanations of various objections that had been raised to royal policy. To avoid giving offence, the councillors frequently justified their words as their official duty, which was to speak honestly and plainly for the king's honour and the service of the common good.

This was not the only occasion of talk concerning the propriety of counsel in the first year of Charles's reign. The Earl of Mar at another time explained to Charles his view of James's Scottish government, which, although it often involved the sending of orders, also permitted the reformulation or even rejection of policy within Scotland. If he thus overlooked the Five Articles of Perth, he also had a measure of truth in his words.[52] Another remarkably early comment of 1625, presumably elicited on account of the contrast with Charles's father, came from James Douglas, who as Secretary-depute for Scotland attended Charles at Court. He noted that the king, once his mind was decided, was not easily swayed from a matter of policy.[53] On both occasions the subject was the highly contentious Revocation policy. At Whitehall Charles himself took occasion to give some instruction to his councillors relevant to their recent behaviour. When he sent to ask their advice, he said, there was good reason for them to give it to him; but when he sent down his pleasure and commanded them, there was reason to obey. He recalled having 'checked' the Earl of Melrose once before, who had asked leave for the council to delay any course they feared prejudicial to his service until they sent him their opinion. Melrose acknowledged that the king had said as much – but once again begged leave for the same, should there be risk of prejudice to the king's service or his laws: they were, he said, sworn to do it. Charles's reply, if any, is not recorded but a cleric, Patrick Lindsay, Bishop of Ross, subsequently spoke out for him, challenging the councillors for impertinence in their responses.

The giving of counsel to this king, therefore, even in reasonable circumstances, was no straightforward matter. Nevertheless, it is important to note that, despite the willingness of councillors to express their duty to give advice, they equally admitted their obligation to adhere to the king's resolution – even if contrary to their counsel. All together accepted the right of Charles to

---

[52] HMC *Mar and Kellie*, p. 145; cf. Lee, *Government by Pen.*
[53] HMC *Mar and Kellie*, p. 123.

make all final determinations. There was an implied limitation though, which Charles accepted in theory. The king was not to act contrary to the laws.

Before this meeting, Charles had relied seemingly on a combination of people available and his own ideas. The reporter of the debates took note that the king had something to learn on a number of points of law; practice did not always match theory. Charles appealed to the precedent of his father's actions or wishes, including on the restructuring of the court of session, but the detailed labour of matching current policy with precedents was not well known to him.[54] Courtiers Sir William Alexander and Sir John Scot of Scotstarvet made the case for the Session reforms; the king asked the assembled councillors for information about Acts of parliament which might frustrate his declared purpose. The experts on the highly contentious king's Revocation were Lord Ochiltree and a Mr Robert Johnston. They had been asked, *since* the receipt of news of complaints, to make detailed comparison between Charles's action and the parallel actions of Scottish rulers before him.

Even now, we are still unsure how Charles originally settled on the details of the troublesome Revocation. The extract from the Register of the Privy Seal which has come to light names four Scots as present with the king in Salisbury on 12 October 1625 when the text was settled – the Earl of Nithsdale, unpopular initiator of other parts of policy as we shall see, and a privy councillor; Sir James Fullarton, Gentleman of the Bedchamber; Sir George Elphinstone, Justice-clerk and privy councillor; and Sir Robert MacLellan of Bombie.[55] This may be helpful or not; Buckingham too was almost certainly involved. Informed by Ochiltree and Johnston, Charles took a determined line in these later Court discussions that his Revocation had no substantial differences from that of his father or progenitors.[56] This was simply not true, and the king's case was mounted somewhat disingenuously from precedents. As it stood, Charles revoked not only grants made in his minority but all grants of royal patrimony ever made to his or the Crown's prejudice. In debate he acknowledged some minor novelties, but also noted that his father had made some erections to his 'lessioun'; smiling, he pointed a finger at the Earl of Mar as one amongst many who had benefited.

The Revocation scheme embraced a threefold purpose, to provide maintenance for ministers and colleges, schools and hospitals; to end the feudal superiorities of the lords of erection, which were alleged to limit the freedom of the gentry who held land from them; and to enlarge and fix the patrimony

[54] Cf. Laing (ed.), *Ancrum Correspondence*, vol. I, pp. 36–7.
[55] I have discovered three copies – NLS Wod. Fo. 61, fol. 113; NLS Ch. 16396 (Fleming of Wigtown papers), GD 406/M9/326 (Hamilton papers).
[56] For Ochiltree, see *HMC Mar and Kellie Supp.*, p. 234. Reasons for the Revocation, citing Jacobean statutes and principles of state, are marshalled in GD 124/10/365.

of the Crown, latterly dilapidated, so it claimed, by ill-advised grants of land, and thus to increase Crown revenues. The explanation, we might note, was given in response to fears, not in anticipation of them.[57] A Revocation of grants made during royal minorities was an accustomed means of redress open to Scottish monarchs when they came of age. Charles's sweeping measure, a full-blown policy more than a simple remedial action, understandably raised Scottish fears of a wholesale attack on property rights.[58]

Charles complained that none of his principal councillors had advised him to make the entitled Revocation before his twenty-fifth birthday, even though they had not lacked opportunity.[59] It was a clear example of tunnel vision. The fact was that advice received had not suited him. The Earl of Melrose spoke to correct him. He had raised the subject before Charles when he was last at Court and, having received directions, had solicited the King's Advocate's help in composing terms that would stand with law. Charles did not deny it. It seems likely that the document presented to the privy council in July 1625 had resulted, for Charles complained that only grants from the Principality of Scotland had been covered.[60] Melrose replied that the Advocate had been prepared to allow no more. The final text, far broader in scope, was offered without apology. As will be noted again, no written text had actually been made available to the Scots before this time. Lord Ochiltree made observations concerning a (superseded) precedent of James V, and Charles was distinctly cool on the plea that there was widespread anxiety in Scotland. He said that he would respect 'sufficient' historical rights of possession – but could not answer for what his successors might do. The councillors understandably were not reassured.[61]

On one point, however, an advance was made against the standing text. It was observed that the king revoked all deeds done to the hurt of the Crown, the royal conscience 'or against the laws of our realm', and moreover that was only mentioned once, in the introduction of the text. The Scots insisted that the normal form was '*and*' contrary to the laws. Ochiltree had the face to argue that there was no great difference; Buckingham was more concessionary, saying that this might be redressed – which was subsequently done, partly at first by royal declaration and then by comprehensive modification

---

[57] *RPCS*, 2nd Series, vol. I, pp. 227–32, 351–3.

[58] Cf. Lee, *The Road to Revolution*, pp. 9–42; Mitchison, *Lordship to Patronage*, pp. 29–34. Macinnes, 'The origin and organization of the Covenanting movement', gives a very full account of the outworkings of the Revocation.

[59] See also *HMC Mar and Kellie*, pp. 238–9.

[60] See *RPCS*, 2nd Series, vol. I, pp. 81–2. I take as confirmation of this more harmless document Gilbert Primrose's matter of factness in reporting its composition – *ibid.*, p. 651.

[61] In July 1626 the determination to establish an inalienable patrimony seems to have been a measure to answer fears – *RPCS*, 2nd Series, vol. I, pp. 351–2.

of the text.[62] Again the original thinking should command our attention. Buckingham argued that having the crucial phrase about the laws only once in the introductory section was in line with English form![63] Clearly attention to Scottish precedent had not been rigorous. At the same time what had been repeated frequently in the text, namely the idea of prejudice to the Crown without mention of laws, seemed to reflect the priorities which had been at hand.

Royal provocation in the substance of the policy was not helped by ill-advised politics. The subsequent outworkings of the Revocation scheme would be complex and only partially successful as far as the king's aims were concerned. Dictation was hardly a satisfactory way to avoid complications, and yet that seemed the order of the day. In November 1625 the fully enlarged Revocation was read in the privy council and proclaimed at the Mercat Cross in Edinburgh. Incredibly, no one was then given a copy to study and, as a result, natural worries increased by rumour. It was not accidental. We know that the Earl of Nithsdale, Charles's messenger, got reprimanded by the king for letting a copy fall accidentally into the Chancellor's hands.[64] Only in January 1626 at Whitehall did Charles allow his privy council to scrutinise the text and compare it with the texts of his predecessors.

What might have been seen as disregard for even minimal channels of consent evidently did not appear a problem to the absentee king. When present with his councillors, he accepted their written objections, but typically remitted decisions to a later date. The result was a proclamation in which the king gave some explanation of the measure but no changes and, to boot, a boast that he had carefully taken the advice of his chief officers and councillors; he warned that the spreading of rumours of hostile criticism would be accounted as sedition.[65] Charles declared the Revocation as of himself, anticipating the standard parliamentary ratification but insistent that failure to observe 'solemnities' (i.e. formalities) because of his present absence from Scotland should be no hindrance to the effecting of the action. While he talked with councillors, he happily ignored suggestions that he should go forthwith to a parliament – 'our kingly power and authority royal' being sufficient.[66]

---

[62] *RPCS*, 2nd Series, vol. I, pp. 227–8. I have compared the 1625 text with that in *APS*, vol. V, pp. 23–7.

[63] The Earls of Nithsdale and Annandale had tried to use an English means of parliamentary management, the committee, for getting the taxation of 1625 through the convention of estates – NLS Adv. Ms. 33.1.4, fols. 1–2.

[64] The Chancellor tried to keep Charles's favour by saying that he had kept secrecy as then requested – but for talking with some noblemen about it on the last day of the convention of estates (he claimed, before Nithsdale had enjoined secrecy!).

[65] *RPCS*, 2nd Series, vol. I, pp. 227–32.

[66] Parliamentary ratification was anticipated on the Privy Seal text of the Revocation. By mid-

Poor politics is well documented also for the king's proposal to restructure the council and court of session.[67] This had met with rejection in Edinburgh, partly on the grounds that Charles lacked the authority to do as he had ordered, namely to dismiss some Lords of Session so as to empty the court of the nobility.[68] The scheme can probably be traced to a memorandum from the Earl of Nithsdale.[69] Charles's commitment to it was linked with a belief that nobles served more appropriately for their rank as privy councillors – strange, since it was a mistaken idea that criminal judgements were passed in the court of session, which in fact was the supreme court for civil disputes. He scorned the suggestion that nobles found honour in serving there, until he was corrected on the point by the Lord Chancellor.[70] However, the main controversy of the Whitehall discussions was on the king's powers of dismissal. Charles's councillors advised him that he simply could not dismiss existing members of the court without due cause. Since two members, the Earl of Lauderdale and Lord Carnegie, were most unwilling to quit their places, this was a problem. The king's recourse to the arguments of Scot of Scotstarvet, who rather passionately believed himself able to mount a case in the king's favour, was offered to the assembled councillors. They accepted it in writing and promptly formulated a hasty, but in their minds decisive, refutation of the arguments.[71]

The division over this issue was felt very strongly by Charles. He himself offered the additional argument that, since he appointed Lords of Session, he must by logical inference be able to dismiss them. He was instructed that even the first part did not hold, since customarily the existing Lords vetted and tried any royal nominations. Charles was obviously not well informed, but on principle wished to achieve his desire; indeed he regarded it as a prime issue, affecting directly the prerogative.

Once more, the propriety of counsel denying the king's will was raised. Charles's big question was who should judge the point at dispute. The first time he asked this, Hay, the Chancellor, declined to offer a ruling in such a delicate matter, although he ventured to suggest that the king might take the advice of 'the Estates'. Answering a second time the same question, although as cautiously, Hay expanded what he had meant by suggesting the advice of

1627 Archbishop Spottiswood felt confident enough that this could successfully be achieved – NLS Adv. Ms. 33.1.3, no. 87.

[67] The principal sources are still NLS Adv. Ms. 33.1.4, fols. 1–20; *HMC Mar and Kellie*, pp. 133–46. See also Sir J. Scot of Scotstarvet, 'A trew relation of the principall affaires concerning the state', *SHR*, 11 (1914), 164–91.

[68] *APS*, vol. V, p. 183. The objection had been moved by the 'small barons'.

[69] Macinnes, 'The origin and organization of the Covenanting movement', p. 118; *HMC Mar and Kellie*, p. 234. The idea was not apparently wholly novel – cf. BL Harl. Ms. 4707, fol. 47.

[70] Cf. Lee, *The Road to Revolution*, p. 18. Charles's ignorance was manifest – *ibid.*, p. 14.

[71] Preserved in NLS Adv. Ms. 33.1.4, fol. 23.

a parliament. The first time, Charles seemingly did not want to engage with this – as over the Revocation – and advanced his argument of logic already described. On the second occasion, after Nithsdale had first exploded at the presumption of the Lord Chancellor's suggestions, the king took the whole council to task that they had forwarded advice from the 1625 convention of estates to call a parliament. Hay offered the interesting response that they had indeed hesitated to send this advice, which so nearly called the king's authority into question, but that on his initiative the advice had been rephrased. Before, it was that the king 'would not alter anything in the Session without advice of his parliament'; after, that he 'would be pleased not to alter any of these things in the Session, without advice of his parliament, which had been established in parliament'. The argument of this was that by the original parliamentary constitution of the court in 1532, nobles had been entitled to sit.[72]

All of this did not close the issue, but Charles obviously hesitated to impose his will categorically where there was such doubt surrounding his right. Presumably as a compromise, Hay suggested submitting to the judgement of the Lords of Session who were to be retained in their office; Sir Alexander Strachan of Thornton, as already earlier in the debate, spoke up to justify the king's absolute authority. Archbishop Spottiswood's following suggestion was evidently preferred by Charles as a compromise, namely that the two lords who resisted dismissal should be offered extraordinary places on the Session. This much had been the tenor of Scotstarvet's paper. It respected the original institution of the court, which allowed for noble members, but without cutting too far against the king's wishes to have nobles out of ordinary membership.

Agreement seemed possible here although the king's basic aim had been moderated. As extraordinary lords, the nobles concerned, and those who later in the reign received similar appointments (including Lord Lorne, later Earl of Argyll), could play a near-indistinguishable role in the business of the court.[73] But, as if to make a kingly stand, Charles in closing declared his intention to have no officers of state on the Session, contrary to his own earlier statement. This was challenged both by the Earl of Mar and the Chancellor, who maintained that the King's Advocate, and usually the Clerk-register sat as members. Charles would concede the point in time; for the immediate future, he kept his position.[74]

The king's prerogative power arose frequently as an issue in these Session

---

[72] *APS*, vol. V, p. 183.
[73] Cf. G. Brunton and D. Haig, *An Historical Account of the Senators of the College of Justice* (Edinburgh, 1832), pp. xlvii–xlviii.
[74] See Lee, *The Road to Revolution*, p. 24. The Earl of Traquair tried in 1637 to be the first noble since Charles's reconstitution to become an ordinary lord – GD 406/1/778.

discussions. Charles's allies defended it with more or less skill; the others were not setting out to oppose it, but by reference to laws and what they thought most reasonable found themselves giving offence. Charles had offered the presidency of the privy council to the Earl of Melrose as compensation for his loss of a place on the court of session. Melrose, though piqued, had declined what he thought was an unprecedented and unnecessary honour that might be unpopular in Scotland; but it was the Earl of Morton's words, that the king would need to consult the Estates if the president was *ex officio* to have a parliamentary place, which caused the most trouble. Although Charles protested this had not been his intention, he found it 'sedition' even to suggest that it was not within his power so to act. He believed that he had a right to give anyone he wanted a place. Similar passion was vented by Charles during discussion over privileges he had proposed to award privy councillors, which the Scots had argued were against law. He told them that they were challenging his prerogative. There were the same words over opposition to the scheme to give good-ranking baronetcies to those who would offer to colonise Nova Scotia.

The Bishop of Ross discredited himself on more than one occasion by what were taken to be foolish and uninformed words on the question in hand. He readily took refuge in the capacious concept of the royal prerogative, and John Spottiswood, Archbishop of St Andrews, followed him when a proposal was made from below to reform the powers of the court of high commission. This court, erected by James in 1609 for oversight of ecclesiastical matters in Scotland, caused particular problems for nonconformists in the church there. The councillors' suggestion was that the court of session might have power to block the other court's letters of horning (a way of denouncing people as rebels) if there was reasonable cause, on the grounds that High Commission had no official power to suspend ministers from their charges, and letters of horning were presumably being used as an alternative. Spottiswood found this a 'puritanical argument', but more than that a challenge to the royal prerogative which had first set up the court. Melrose doubted that the proposals for reform were at all that. The bishops' words, however, made the authority of the king the issue of contention. Whether or not the councillors were being sympathetic to nonconformists – people who would have challenged the king's right to order the church by proclamation – the incident illustrates the possible tensions which could bring in dispute over royal sovereignty.

The king's authority came into the reckoning when problems arose over policy, but it was no easy subject. Recourse taken by the king's advisers in high-sounding doctrine could be an effective silencer of argument, but not without the cost of heightening tensions. It was difficult, then as now, to determine where the drive for policy was coming from, but always it was more seemly to attack those who counselled the king – seemly, if not totally accurate. The bishops and not James himself, despite many pleas, had suffered criticism for the policy of the Five Articles of Perth.[75] However, the king's part was not overlooked; the Earl of Rothes, who played the role of an attacker, looked keenly for the 'first fruits' of the new king's reign in 1625, amongst other things on religion. He must have been disappointed.[76]

As far as Charles was concerned, if the issue of the royal prerogative was raised, it had to be vindicated.[77] If the royal counsellors needed defence, the same story generally held, for as they gave support to Charles, and so opened themselves to criticism in the case of unpopular policies, the king was no cipher. At least where policy was at stake, Charles rarely abandoned those who were close to him. It was in this that someone like the unpopular Catholic Earl of Nithsdale found his security against attacks.[78] This could be a block that did not necessarily serve the best ends. As this detailed account of the early council debates has shown, there could be personal risk in making even justifiable criticism, especially if it was sustained. Whether or not the king's counsellors were mentioned, Charles was quick to suspect disloyalty and 'sedition'.

Was this the real 'crisis of counsel'? In England the parliaments of the 1620s ended on sour notes, being followed by proclamations about the evil plotting which had spoiled their wished-for harmony; the king moved to rule without parliaments. But there were attendant dramas in the English privy council, disagreements amongst those who had the king's ear. Charles expected much to follow his determined wishes – and to some extent himself steamrollered over the varying lines of counsel in evidence. A number followed him; some plainly wished to dissent.[79]

As far as Scotland was concerned, Charles tended to exacerbate the difficulties of the absentee situation by his approach to government. Dangerously he reserved to himself, and so to those to whom he showed personal favour, the direction of policy. The risks can be seen from the 1626 scenario. Determinations taking little heed of the written objections were dispatched north before the displeased councillors' own return.[80] The nobility's

---

[75] Cf. Spottiswood's defence in Lyndesay, *A True Narration*, pp. 21–46; Spottiswood, *History*, vol. III, pp. 235–71.
[76] Laing, *Ancrum Correspondence*, vol. I, pp. 35–8; Lee, *The Road to Revolution*, pp. 44, 46. NLS Adv. Ms. 33.1.4, fol. 5 reports Charles speaking with the Earl of Rothes in private on 13 January 1626; I have not yet found any corroborative evidence of this, however.
[77] For precisely this in a case in the court of session in 1634, see Traqr. Ms. 8/3–5, 37/5.
[78] NLS Ms. 21174, fol. 72; NLS Adv. Ms. 33.1.4, fol. 21.
[79] Cf. K. Sharpe (ed.), *Faction and Parliament* (Oxford, 1978), pp. 37–42; Cust, *The Forced Loan*, pp. 16–90; L. J. Reeve, 'Sir Robert Heath's advice for Charles I in 1629',*BIHR*, 65 (1986), pp. 220–1.
[80] NLS Adv. Ms. 33.1.4, fol. 19v; *RPCS*, 2nd Series, vol. I, pp. 220–1, 230–2.

'liberties' were damaged by their exclusion from the Session, but Charles would still have all kinds of expectations of them; the ill-motivated exclusion of officers of state could only be a temporary gesture. What might have deepened wounds was the boost given to the bishops. The Bishop of Ross gained a seat as an Extraordinary Lord of Session; Archbishop Spottiswood was made president both of the Exchequer Commission and the highly unpopular Commission of Grievances, and was named first on the roll of the council. No change was made in the court of high commission.[81] Anti-clericalism would build up through the reign.

The counsel of Charles I may have been contentious, but it cannot be said that he was uninformed. He did not live in isolation. It was apparently more a problem of his being set on fairly fixed courses of actions which aroused antagonisms. The cooperative counsellor would have to be careful not to diverge too far from the king's mind. How far counsel could dare to engage with the king's ends (as opposed to his means) should be asked. Personal interest constantly mixed with state policy for those who had office or Court favour to guard. The counsel of the king might not always be what he wanted, but his taking offence was certainly to be avoided.[82] There was criticism, as we have seen; Scottish councillors even seriously discussed offering Charles taxations as an alternative to the Revocation in 1626 – Charles would hear nothing of it.[83] Most often points of administration would be debated. In 1629 the privy council as a body begged leave, through Menteith, to be free from danger should a majority amongst them decide on a course of action contrary to the king's direction.[84]

Energy in centrally directed policy was also a comparative novelty for Scotland. In the months and years following the Whitehall debates, the Revocation was forwarded in its various aspects. The administration of the policy called for considerable efforts, which were given in mixed measure. Panic fears subsided, but the scheme never worked easily or very successfully. It remains debatable how far the shock impact of it had long-term consequences; Sir James Balfour of Denmilne's suggestion of this should probably not be rejected too hastily – though the Revocation was not an issue on which a united front could readily be formed.[85]

---

[81] Lee, *The Road to Revolution*, pp. 29, 32; GD 124/10/315. For a hostile reaction, see Laing, *Ancrum Correspondence*, vol. I, p. 42.

[82] Cf. in Scottish politics the falls of Lord Napier and the Earl of Strathearn, or in the English situation of Sir Robert Heath – Lee, *The Road to Revolution*, pp. 85–7, 119–27; Reeve, 'Sir Robert Heath's advice', pp. 220–2.

[83] NLS Ms. 21174, fol. 72.

[84] GD 22/3/785.

[85] Sir J. Balfour, *Historical Works* (4 vols., Edinburgh, 1824–5), vol. II, p. 128; *The Diary of Sir Archibald Johnston, Lord Wariston, 1639*, ed. G. M. Paul, SHS (Edinburgh, 1896), p. 76; Lee, *The Road to Revolution*, pp. 16, 24–9, 43–62, 66–71.

Charles had declared his commitment. It was a common note. Another problem of the opening convention of estates in Scotland had been the refusal of supply for two thousand men in addition to the taxation granted. The king carefully questioned the proceedings; and went forward by affirming that he would use some of the taxation for the required purpose, and supply the remainder himself! Further heavy taxations were requested and granted in 1630 and 1633, with widely burdensome effects.[86]

The scheme for the Common Fishing, originated at Court in 1630 for the consideration of the convention of estates, met a cool response. It was drafted in the context of Dutch fishing competition, a subject on Charles's mind even in 1625, but English interests backed it; indeed it was referred to the English privy council for discussions with the Scots. That Englishmen should get equal rights of fishing in inshore Scottish waters offended vested interests in the north, particularly of the burghs. A national interest was claimed to be at stake. Characteristically, Charles appealed for cooperation on the matter by declaring his deep personal concern. The Scots retorted by asking for the name 'Great Britain' to be dropped, so that by separate mention of the kingdoms their separate interests could be better remembered. In effect the absentee king was asked to take seriously his triple status.[87]

Disparities between Scotland and England also got overlooked in Charles's agreement to customs and controls in the salt and coal industries. Duties in Scotland were relatively low by English standards. Increase benefited the Crown financially – and English merchants incidentally. Charles was not seeking to give deliberate offence surely; but he provoked urgent efforts by the offended interests to marshal protests. The coinage was another subject of grievance, where the personal advancement of entrepreneurs with the king stirred up trouble. In James's reign after 1603, economic 'policy', such as it was, had been more directed from the Scottish privy council.[88]

Was there a crisis of Scottish counsel? There was a national problem since, after Charles's accession, serious blows had been dealt to the independent traditions of the Scottish administration. Professor Lee has rightly praised the atypical contribution of the Earl of Menteith in managing a temporary restoration of sorts here, a moderation of royal anglicised direction in the northern kingdom. Others less successfully filled the gaps, most notably the Earl of

[86] APS, vol. V, pp. 166–75, 209–17, 13–20; NLS Adv. Ms. 33.1.4, fol. 2. For the war effort, see Lee, The Road to Revolution, pp. 29–30, 79–85.
[87] NLS Adv. Ms. 33.1.4, fol. 7v; APS, vol. V, pp. 229–30; Lee, The Road to Revolution, pp. 100–8.
[88] Lee, The Road to Revolution, pp. 14, 87, 101, 105–7, 151, 168, 186–7; Government by Pen, pp. 86–90. Dr Macinnes's unpublished dissertation deals at length with all of these important subjects.

Traquair, who like Menteith travelled when he could to the king in person.[89] Yet it is almost certain that Scots regularly had the king's ear on Scottish affairs, those resident about Court as well as those who travelled there more sporadically. Again, how Charles listened is the question; and he did not turn to them alone. Buckingham was clearly well informed at those 1626 talks; his involvement had begun under James.[90] Sir Dudley Carleton was pleased to note the successes of the 1630 convention of estates, an indication perhaps of an increasing British interest around this British king.[91] Mercantile or monopolist interests obviously clambered in on economic questions. The separation of the kingdoms was hard fact despite all of this, however – and Archbishop Laud, most notoriously and fully involved with the affairs of Scotland, acknowledged his limitations of knowledge and perspective. The king would be pressed to remember the same point.

It has long been asked what would have happened in England had Charles not gone to war with the Scots. The hypothetical question for Scotland is what would have happened had he not espoused the liturgical policy which brought about the troubles of 1637. It is not to the purpose to answer such questions, but we should be concerned for instance to consider how far the strong national element in these troubles brought in support from people not much bothered about the substance of Charles's prayer book. It seems a likelihood though it is not easily demonstrable; there are many difficulties, not least evidential, in pinning down motivation.[92] As has always been the case, religion and the church were never far from being of political significance; in Scotland in the 1630s this became particularly true.

In one respect the controversial religious politics of James and Charles in Scotland were anglicising; as importantly they were innovatory and overriding in respect to ways of counsel. They were resisted by an opposition which therefore made itself strong both ideologically and politically. Innovation was a dirty word in this period, especially when set against a panegyric in defence of the acts and laws of the sixteenth-century Reformation, or a defence by scripture alongside principles of reason and nature. Charles, with a rather different interpretation of the same principles, insisted like his father on his authority to rule the church, and by his bishops. Innovation might be acceptable if it introduced practices warranted by the Early Church; this was

---

[89] Lee, *The Road to Revolution*, pp. 43–126.
[90] Cf. Warwickshire RO CR 2017/C1/55.
[91] PRO SP 63/251, fol. 133v, cited in L. J. Reeve, 'The Secretaryship of State of Viscount Dorchester 1628–1632' (unpublished University of Cambridge Ph.D. dissertation, 1983), pp. 202–3.
[92] Cf. Macinnes, 'The origin and organization of the Covenanting movement'; Brown, 'Aristocratic finances'; Makey, *Church of the Covenant*.

a statement about the catholicity of the faith.[93] The vision glossed over the problems. There were major divergences of opinion in England and Scotland on what was legitimate for the church, and therefore there would be conflict in following the principle of *cuius regio, eius religio*. The single and allegedly popish line backed by Charles was bound to stir up opposition; that he proceeded by authoritarian tactics helped to push things to a major crisis.

The first royal statement in Charles's reign on the Five Articles of Perth was in tiny measure conciliatory, in so far as it accepted non-enforcement of the policy on ministers admitted before 1618. Such men might have taught different principles before this date, and so, it might be argued, could not be expected to offend against conscience; but it was laid down that none should presume now to speak out against the Articles or discourage ordinary folk from observing them. New ministers were to accept the Articles, subscribing at their admission a 'band of conformity' now to be common to all dioceses. The king was giving no *carte blanche* to nonconformity, more being persuaded to accept limitations on the 'ideal' of instant change.[94] The town of Edinburgh in 1628 discovered that no leeway was to be allowed, when it petitioned in vain for relief from what it claimed to be a major source of divisions, the article concerning kneeling at communion.[95]

The disturbances of 1637 were not simply doctrinal. The reformed thinkers in Scotland feared and disliked the 'new' doctrines in England, and more rarely at home, of Arminian or anti-Calvinist theologians, but this cannot be said to have been the sole irritant. In the more detailed critiques of the Scottish prayer book and the Laudian establishment, certainly such issues were taken up;[96] but at the first view the troubles in Scotland were raised by changes felt both to be badly conceived and introduced by irregular means.

A very vital strand of nonconformity was continuous through the reign, which may here be followed in its high political manifestations. In 1630 a convention of estates met in Edinburgh. The king wanted a taxation and also some consultation on the Revocation scheme; the taxation was granted with little difficulty. Commissioners for the shires submitted a fairly lengthy list of

---

[93] Lyndesay, *A True Narration*, esp. pp. 38–45; NLS Wod. 4to. 106, fols. 31, 39; *HMC Hastings*, vol. IV, pp. 71–2; Laud, *Works*, vol. III, pp. 321–2; vol. VI, pp. 88, 443; vol. VII, p. 292. Cf. R. Baillie, *The Letters and Journals*, ed. D. Laing, BC (3 vols., Edinburgh, 1841–2), vol. I, p. 27.

[94] C. Rogers (ed.), *The Earl of Stirling's Register of Royal Letters Relative to the Affairs of Scotland* (2 vols., Edinburgh, 1885), vol. I, pp. 62–4. For another measure of the continuity with James, cf. NLS Wod. Fo. 43, fol. 206.

[95] Lee, *The Road to Revolution*, pp. 63–4.

[96] Notably in the work of Robert Baillie – EUL New College Ms. X15b 3/1, vol. II, fols. 44–67, 114–16. Copies of his work were circulated – NLS Wod. Fo. 42, fols. 270–86. For other like products, cf. NLS Wod. Fo. 43, fol. 254; Wod. Fo. 64, fol. 193.

articles and grievances for action.[97] However, silenced on the official record was a supplication to organise the Estates into petitioning for relief from the enforcement of the Five Articles of Perth. Its origins are unclear, but some noblemen, including Lord Balmerino, were involved. The privy council met to discuss what should be done. On the conclusion that the Estates would assent to it, it was decided to prevent it being read at all. This raised the question of whether the councillors could actually block a matter intended for the convention of estates. A fuss arose when they attempted to do so; but, by arguing that they corporately represented the king's person, the action was carried.

The same subject in effect was subsequently raised in the convention in a more subtle way through a petition as from the lay patrons. Lord Balmerino was to the fore; the content was to object to bishops frustrating the patrons' choices for ministers because of the oath they urged on new entrants, an oath, they observed, which had no sanction of parliament. The point of offence was obvious enough; and blame for enjoining the practice of the Five Articles was laid squarely on the bishops. The petitioners may have had direct help from ministers; certainly in 1633 patrons were kept well informed of the ministers' own corporate moves of protest.[98] But privy councillors, well aware of the king's mind, silenced the protest now; amongst those who carried the motion were the Earls of Menteith and Morton, assisted by Sir William Alexander, Charles's London-based Secretary. The royal cause was upheld by such loyalty.[99]

In 1633 Charles made his long-promised journey to Scotland for his coronation. A parliament was at last held, under the closest possible control of the king. Charles had hitherto avoided the institution though James had striven hard to find ways of making his parliaments compliant. The Lords of the Articles were a committee which looked over all proposed business in advance of the full sessions, when very little debate was customary. Since the restoration of episcopacy, bishops' choices had shaped the composition of that committee, and they did so again in 1633. Less predictably, a single conformist official, Sir John Hay, the Clerk-register, was appointed to receive any petitions; and meetings of the nobility and others in organised groups in advance of the parliament were proscribed.[100]

---

[97] *APS*, vol. V, pp. 219–20.

[98] NLS Wod. Fo. 43, fols. 225, 227–8.

[99] NLS Wod. Fo. 42, fols. 233–4. The original account was probably written by Sir William Alexander for the king. Cf. W. Scot, *An Apologeticall Narration of the State and Government of the Kirk of Scotland Since the Reformation*, WS (Edinburgh, 1846), pp. 327–9; J. Row, *The Historie of the Estate of the Kirk of Scotland*, MC (2 vols., Edinburgh, 1842), vol. I, pp. 142–3; GD 22/1/518. See also Lee, *The Road to Revolution*, pp. 99–100.

[100] Lee, *The Road to Revolution*, pp. 128, 131–3. For James and parliaments, see Wormald, *Court, Kirk and Community*, pp. 20–2, 156–8.

The occasion for pressing the king to reform was not missed however. A petition was composed and signed by a number of ministers for submission to the Lords of the Articles. The programme began on a presbyterian note by taking up issues concerning episcopacy which had been overruled in James's time. It expressed a wish for church representatives to be fully accountable and bishops to be censurable in general assemblies, which it asked to be held annually. Non-enforcement of the Perth Articles was requested. Further objections concerned the ministers' admission oath and the suspensions of nonconformist ministers. Sir John Hay refused to accept the petition. The king was then directly approached, but to no avail.[101]

The next move was during the meetings of the Lords of the Articles. The Revocation was now to be ratified, containing all the alterations of detail made since its first publication. Another taxation was being requested. Various private suits were born of the former matter, and controversy arose over the planned taxation, but dispute over proposed legislation bearing on the church drew much of the limelight. One of these repeated the Act of 1606 on the royal supremacy together with re-enacting another Jacobean statute, or rather part of one, that placed the regulation of kirk apparel in the hands of the king; the second more generally ratified and approved all acts and statutes in force regarding the established church.[102] Another petition was organised, to be signed by two members from the three lay groups represented, the nobility, the shire and the burgh commissioners. It was hostile to the intention to ratify the 1621 statute on the Perth Articles, and further levelled criticism at the heavy taxation proposals. However, it was not in the end presented. The Earl of Rothes and Lord Loudoun argued its case before Charles, but evidently got poor countenance; the outcome was that it was decided not to present the petition.[103]

A block on the mere expression of opposition cannot be supposed to have quietened the trouble. The king's insistence that the parliament should have only one day to vote all the legislation, private and public, was the final aspect of this. Debate was supposed to be avoided. On both taxation and ecclesiastical policy, this was not the case. In the voting the Crown achieved success, but not without imputations that the count had been wrong.[104] A minority of the nobility, but a majority of the gentry and burgh commissioners, voted against – despite Charles's attempt to intimidate opposition by keeping a

---

[101] Row, *Historie*, vol. I, pp. 146–50; Scot, *Apologeticall Narration*, pp. 329–35; NLS Wod. Fo. 43, fol. 256. For a variant version which made reference to the then current rumours of canons and a service-book, see NLS Wod. Fo. 43, fol. 225.

[102] *APS*, vol. V, pp. 20–1.

[103] Row, *Historie*, vol. I, pp. 151–5; Scot, *Apologeticall Narration*, pp. 337–8; NLS Wod. Fo. 43, fols. 234–5.

[104] *APS*, vol. V, pp. 7–165; Lee, *The Road to Revolution*, pp. 131–7.

personal record of who did what. Rothes was the primary spokesman on the church legislation. He would have allowed the Act on the royal supremacy, he said, but not the Act on apparel linked with it; he would have agreed to the ratification of existing ecclesiastical legislation, but only if the 1621 Act concerning the Perth Articles had been excepted.

They were calculated words, expressing surely a wish for a bargain – for the consensus that was ordinarily the ideal. The nonconformist source which lists the names of those who supported Rothes admitted the second stand was less fully upheld. It may suggest a reluctance for commitment over what was implied, namely that parliamentary legislation concerning the church should stretch no further than general assembly enactments permitted, a strongly presbyterian stance. It is probably risky to make too much of this, but it is known that the hard-core nonconformists were politically tentative about raising such an issue.[105] The superiority of general assemblies in church affairs was not sanctioned by James or Charles, and the king's direction continued as ever to hold considerable influence. Our recorder of the votes also had to note that some who had voted against ratification of the Perth Articles in the parliament in 1621 now in 1633 bowed under pressure to vote the other way.[106]

Rothes's words for allowing the royal supremacy may have been little more than tactical, but politics was the art of the possible. It would have been difficult, to say the least, to argue otherwise before Charles. As it was, the king withheld two promotions of rank for Lords Loudoun and Lindsay because they opposed him.[107] Charles was demanding rather than soliciting consent. On the one hand, his controlling tactics over the parliament rested on recent precedent, with a few additions; but on the other it seems undeniable that many were overtly unhappy about this. The central public forum of debate in Scotland had less of a history than in England, but in these days of Union it was witnessing comparable troubles.

Tactical phrasing was not absent from the cause of complaint within the notorious supplication drawn up for the nonconformist group after the parliament was ended. Statements critical of the king's handling of his parliament suggested that a 'good' king would not want to be misled into bad conduct. Charles was informed that James had desisted from conjoining any

---

[105] NLS Wod. Fo. 43, fol. 228.

[106] NLS Wod. Fo. 43, fols. 235–8; see also a variant copy, *ibid.*, fols. 239–44. For supporting accounts, see Sir W. Fraser, *Memoirs of the Maxwells of Pollok* (2 vols., Edinburgh, 1863), vol. II, pp. 232–41; BL Add. Ms. 63057A, fols. 60–1; *HMC Salisbury* (9), vol. XXII, p. 303 (there misdated).

[107] Fraser, *Maxwells of Pollok*, vol. II, p. 244; GD 406/1/252. For Loudoun's stance, see too Baillie, *Letters*, vol. I, pp. 477–8. The Earl of Lothian was also challenged – GD 40/2/XIII.86.

statute on the prerogative with innovations in 1617 – a reference to the then dropped legislation concerning the king's right with his clergy to rule in the church. The fears and reasons for the troubles were explained. But, however it was phrased, the message was very clear in appealing for reform, and above all that there should be no change in the doctrine or discipline of the Scottish church 'not compatible with the honour thereof and your good people's conscience or that has been rejected by public acts and laws of our reformed church'.[108]

The supplication was notorious because it led to the prosecution of Lord Balmerino. Basically an apology, said to be from the nobles and other members in retrospect of the parliament, it was not actually presented, but rather fell into Archbishop Spottiswood's hands about October 1633. The authorship was fixed on William Haig, who conveniently fled the country to escape persecution. Haig's zeal had not affected his desire for royal service prior to this; he had been an unsuccessful suitor for the clerkship of the new taxation under the Marquis of Hamilton.[109] The supplication text went further than anything before in the relative starkness of its criticisms, which was probably the reason for people hesitating to avow it. There was a recognition that some individuals would push hard to denounce what had been written; Balmerino presumably did not offer himself for attack. Once the persecution was begun, however, the intention to plead innocence of the charges was not to entail denying the value of the supplication. While Balmerino was under trial, his cause was upheld by prayer meetings and fastings.[110]

Balmerino of course had played a regular part in church protest. It seems likely that bishops and king together readily took offence, but for anything more there was delay. Depositions relating to the case were taken in June 1634, some three months after the case came to the king's notice; only in October that year was the decision taken to pursue him, after a visit by the Bishop of Ross to Court. The hesitations involved here were apparently linked with uncertainties on how best to proceed for the desirable outcome.[111] Balmerino was charged under the specially revived law against leasing-making, the purposeful spreading of slander against the Crown; but it seems that the king was advised to look for his free submission. The Earl of Traquair did what he could on this, but Balmerino held out presumably for unacceptable terms, for a trial followed.[112] In the end Balmerino was found

---

[108] The supplication is printed in Row, *Historie*, vol. I, pp. 162–7. A better copy, correctly arranged under three main heads, is in NLS Wod. Fo. 43, fol. 249.

[109] GD 406/1/255, 256, 258.

[110] *HMC 9 (II)*, pp. 262–3; NLS Wod. Fo. 43, fols. 239–44, 251, 254–3 (*sic* – the folios are bound in the wrong order); Row, *Historie*, vol. I, pp. 167–74.

[111] Traqr. Ms. 8/5, 13/23.

[112] GD 406/1/998; *HMC 9 (II)*, p. 263; GD 45/14/7.

guilty of very little, indeed only of hearing, concealing and not revealing the supplication or 'libel', as the prosecution described it. The verdict was reached only by the casting vote of Traquair over the jury. Nevertheless Balmerino was subsequently relieved of pressure, in stages, with no sentence being carried out. The king's cause was evidently considered to be on somewhat weak ground. As much loss of face was suffered by the prosecutors, and amongst them the bishops.[113]

The more respectable ministers' grievances of 1633 were published with a number of related documents in 1635; if nothing else the battle might be by words.[114] For some, however, prayer and tears or even exile marked the times. Robert Baillie, later important against the prayer book, tended to shy from public protest; the presbyterian Lord Kenmure had hesitated to express his discontent alongside the others.[115] The natural advantage lay with the monarch, but Charles would have been well advised to play cautiously. The apparel controversy indicated that this was far from likely. The travesty of the Balmerino case moreover was no help to stability. It showed a measure of vindictiveness against what after all was presented as a petition. Some might easily argue this to be rule badly counselled; it was certainly often cited after 1637 if not before. The king was strong – but his government was not unimpeachable.

Bishops and others stuck with the king. At the coronation and in public worship during the royal visit to Scotland, English vestments were worn.[116] Orders subsequent to the contentious Act of parliament enforced new regularity of apparel in the Chapel Royal and then elsewhere. There was opposition.[117] The king's proceedings were being regarded as unacceptable. But Charles and his clergy went on with plans for a new liturgy and canons. They would have expected again minor troubles; they got far more.

Liturgy in the church of Scotland was less regularly used than in England. James's ideas for reform on this count had met with some sympathy in 1616 and after, but at the same time with fears of wholesale anglicisation. Some again were disturbed when rumours picked up news of the reforms being

---

[113] *Cobbett's Complete Collection of State Trials* (34 vols., 1809–28), vol. III, pp. 591–713; GD 406/1/998, 8310; SRO SP 13/154; Row, *Historie*, vol. I, pp. 167–74; Lee, *The Road to Revolution*, pp. 157–62.

[114] *The Grievances Given in by the Ministers before the Parliament Holden in June 1633*, Aldis 856.5 (n.p., 1635). Cf. NLS Wod. Fo. 43, fol. 224.

[115] Baillie, *Letters*, vol. I, p. 1; D. Mathew, *Scotland under Charles I* (1955), pp. 35–42; Sir W. Brereton, *Travels in Holland, the United Provinces, England, Scotland and Ireland M.DC.XXXIV–M.DC.XXXV*, Chetham Society (1844), p. 101.

[116] J. Spalding, *The History of the Troubles and Memorable Transactions in Scotland and England from M.DC.XXIV to M.DC.XLV*, BC (2 vols., Edinburgh, 1828), vol. I, pp. 17–21; Balfour, *Works*, vol. IV, pp. 383–404; NLS Adv. Ms. 15.2.17; NLS Ms. 21183, fols. 72–3.

[117] Laud, *Works*, vol. VI, pp. 340–1, 383–4, 395–6, 409, 419–20.

revived late in 1629, but secrecy on the part of Charles and those with whom he worked kept much from being publicly expressed for some time.[118] However, the use of the English Book of Common Prayer at services during the royal visit of 1633, with subsequent orders for its use elsewhere, indicated ominously in Scotland the king's preferred direction.[119]

In 1616 King James had asked, successfully, some members of the general assembly to revise the Book of Common Order and 'to set down a common form of ordinary service to be used in all time hereafter'. Although this took up on earlier calls for reform of the forms of set prayer already existing and used in the church of Scotland, James's readiness to wait on consultative channels should not be exaggerated. Publication of this liturgy was supposed to proceed if a general assembly committee, heavily staffed with bishops, approved it. The early work – seemingly done without the knowledge of one of the presbyterian members of that very committee – was further revised, twice, in following years by a different committee, including prominently the Bishop of Galloway, William Cowper. There was some clear borrowing from the English order. The Scottish stage thus completed, Dr Peter Young, the Scottish Dean of Winchester, was amongst those in England who scrutinised the product. In 1619 the liturgy was ready for printing.[120] Years later, Bishop John Maxwell of Ross was one who strongly remembered the Jacobean precedent. He ascribed the non-appearance of the liturgy then to the lamented death of King James.[121] More accurately, as has already been noted, it was held back on political grounds, on account of the intense and sustained opposition to the separate policy of the Five Articles of Perth.

The same John Maxwell, while still only an ambitious minister, was the carrier of the Jacobean production to Charles and Laud, then Bishop of London, in 1629. Probably hopeful of the healing force of time, Maxwell's own churchmanship willingly embraced the common argument for reforming liturgy in Scotland, namely the desire for well-ordered uniformity of practice across the kingdoms, free from division and consonant with the best practices of the church. Laud apparently was not well enough to meet his Scottish visitor, but conveniently so since the purpose of Maxwell's mission got dented. On his own account, Laud managed to persuade the king that the

---

[118] William Struthers to the Earl of Menteith – Balfour, *Works*, vol. II, pp. 181–4; also see NLS Wod. Fo. 43, fol. 225.

[119] Struthers's letter (note above) was published with the ministers' grievances in 1635 – *The Grievances Given in by the Ministers* . . .

[120] G. W. Sprott, *Scottish Liturgies of the Reign of James VI* (Edinburgh, 1871); Donaldson, *Making of the Scottish Prayer Book of 1637*; G. Donaldson (ed.), 'A Scottish liturgy of the reign of James VI', in *Miscellany of the Scottish History Society* (Edinburgh, 1965), vol. X, pp. 87–117.

[121] NLS Wod. Fo. 66, fol. 77. Holograph of John Maxwell, Bishop of Ross (wrongly ascribed in Baillie, *Letters*, vol. I, p. 444).

imposition of the English Book of Common Prayer on Scotland was rather more preferable.[122]

Predictable nonconformity was not a major factor in shaping royal aims, but neither king nor archbishop, as Laud became, could overstep completely the local bishops who were the agents of church government in Scotland. A period of Anglo-Scottish debates concerning the liturgical policy therefore ensued – debates at least concerning the finer points of detail. Archbishop Spottiswood recognised that the aim was to form documents as close to accepted English forms as possible. In 1633, the first Scottish editions of the English Book of Common Prayer came off the presses, the text which was to be used in the interim period of talks. In October 1634 Charles asked the Scottish bishops to scrutinise an annotated copy of this book, as a likely progress stage.[123]

It is striking that John Maxwell later omitted to remember these interim orders, though he probably helped with the annotations. His account written for the purposes of royal propaganda in the height of the troubles emphasised rather the efforts by the episcopate to draw up a *Scottish* liturgy.[124] There was truth in his words, since as late as August 1634 the 1619 book seems still to have been in the Scottish bishops' minds. Once the king's revised English version was received and deliberated, they had to apologise to Court that 'full conformity' would be a 'work of time'. Nevertheless it was a slightly changed English prayer book that, after revisions in both kingdoms, was authorised for the press, in Maxwell's care, in 1635.[125] Canons were also prepared, much in line with the English model, which in 1634 had also been extended to Ireland; Ireland already had the English liturgy. The long-perceived need for an ordinal was explored. The canons placed a predictably high emphasis on form and obedience to matters of royal direction.[126]

There can be no doubt that Charles was intimately involved with this whole project, however creative the professional churchmen were.[127] Whatever details came from below him, the policy and the style of its introduction clearly suited Charles's wishes. Another stage of revision took place after copies of the service-book had begun to be printed. It was strongly connected

---

[122] Laud, *Works*, vol. III, p. 427, vol. VII, pp. 489–90.
[123] Laud, *Works*, vol. VI, pp. 554–5; Baillie, *Letters*, vol. I, p. 442; Donaldson, *Scottish Prayer Book*, pp. 40, 43–7.
[124] Baillie, *Letters*, vol. I, pp. 443–5 (cf. n. 121 above).
[125] Donaldson, *Scottish Prayer Book*, pp. 49–50.
[126] The canons are printed in Laud, *Works*, vol. V, pp. 583–606. For Ireland, see *ibid.*, vol. VI, p. 354, vol. VII, p. 66; A. Ford, *The Protestant Reformation in Ireland, 1590–1641* (Frankfurt on Main, 1985), p. 269. For the ordinal, see Foster, *Church*, pp. 133–51.
[127] See, for example, Donaldson, *Scottish Prayer Book*, pp. 104–5. Charles's general role in church matters is the subject of some debate, as explained but not wholly resolved in A. Foster, 'Church policies of the 1630s', in Cust and Hughes, *Conflict*, pp. 197–223.

with the new Dean of the Chapel Royal in Scotland, James Wedderburn, who owed his early clerical career in England to the patronage of Laud. Laud presented the new ideas to Charles; in return the king was pleased to command him to write out the approved alterations, as before in a copy of the English prayer book. Laud felt persuaded that these changes would be to Scotland's benefit. In later days, they would be held unfairly against him personally.[128]

A substantial list can be made of the concessions to Scottish variation made in the liturgy. Admittedly some of these, like the rubric for celebration of communion facing eastwards, Laud could have seen as positive gains; Charles won a small battle to have Apocrypha readings included. Elsewhere, however, the newness could be striking, as in the preface which replaced the English version Charles would have been happy to retain. This quoted with approval John Knox's sanction of liturgy as well as almost apologising for the inclusion of 'festivals and some other rites not as yet received nor observed in our church'. It has been argued that by 1584 presbyterian standards, the finished product of 1637, had it been judged on its merits, had a serious claim to acceptability.[129]

However, the circle consulted had been small. It seems unlikely that even all of the Scottish bishops, the 'representative body of the church' as Charles called them, were actively involved.[130] Nine of the thirteen attended the public introduction in July 1637, but the absentees seem to have been the most reluctant of backers. On the other hand, one or two not on the episcopal bench were forward in their support. At the English end, Bishops Wren, and to a lesser extent Juxon, met with Archbishop Laud.[131] Above all, where James had worked, albeit reluctantly, with general assemblies, the 1636 canons were simply published from Aberdeen and the service-book reform authorised by royal proclamation issued by the privy council on 20 December at the end of that year. The proclamation was printed in the final text of the book; English prayer books carried a (Jacobean) proclamation but alongside the Elizabethan Act of Uniformity. The Scots were commanded everywhere to adopt the form which 'we [Charles] (having taken the counsel of our clergy) think fit to be used in God's public worship'.[132]

Nothing so narrowly directed was tried in Ireland or England. Amongst many in Scotland, there was little likelihood of the book being judged on its

---

[128] Donaldson, *Scottish Prayer Book*, pp. 49–59; Laud, *Works*, vol. VI, pp. 495–6.
[129] Donaldson, *Scottish Prayer Book*, pp. 60–80, 101–5.
[130] The term was defended later by reference to the bishops' special role in parliaments – as opposed to general assemblies – NLS Wod. Fo. 66, fol. 74v.
[131] Donaldson, *Scottish Prayer Book*, pp. 43–7; Laud, *Works*, vol. VI, pp. 504, 554–5. Three absentees were not privy councillors, and they were later prepared to disown and even abjure episcopacy – George Graeme, John Abernethy and Alexander Lindsay. The fourth and last, Neil Campbell, had close connections with Lord Lorne, later Earl of Argyll – GD 112/39/17.
[132] Donaldson, *Scottish Prayer Book*, p. 100.

merits. The Perth Articles had caused great trouble; however much the Scottish bishops had achieved with the king, a crisis ensued over church government with such controversial lines of direction. Religion in this context could not but be political. Opposition had time to get planned. Some of the clearest evidence on this points to a committee meeting of nonconformist ministers at the beginning of July 1637, when they prepared to make their stand on the historic Scottish reformed cause. Against what threatened to encourage a reading and not a preaching ministry they upheld the form of worship accepted in Scotland and not yet abolished through the proper channels of general assembly and parliament. English practice, established or otherwise, was apprehended on a number of points to be popish and thus boded no satisfaction; they knew that the English themselves were not everywhere conforming. It was in advance of consideration of the textual niceties that lines were drawn.[133]

In its most basic form this critique struck hard against the government of Charles I and his bishops, although the confidence to write as much explicitly was lacking. In an early petition format, the advice of bishops and archbishops was a target of attack drafted but then deleted.[134] The king's government nevertheless had seriously alienated itself and, though the extent of the trouble at the outset should not be exaggerated, it became in time very substantial. A fairly widespread reaction of dissent could be roused if it did not spontaneously rise of itself. People of all estates were involved as damage, actual and impending, was feared to the laws of church and state. Cries of popish innovation moved large numbers of Scots, the majority in south-west Scotland and Fife, quickly to petition for redress. To overcome the consequences of bad counsel there were appeals for the use of general assembly and parliament, the institutions of government where the whole nation might be represented.[135]

This was no opening statement of revolution, far more a means to an end or ends – although the possibility of reading it otherwise, as Charles did, existed. It seems more accurate, however, to read the appeals in terms of expediency. The Supplicants, as they became known, soon moved also to claiming the support of the legislation of 1633, which ratified the existing church establishment, as a bulwark against the service-book. They, or at least

---

[133] J. M. Henderson (ed.), 'An "Advertisement" about the service book, 1637', *SHR*, 23 (1925–6), 199–204; Baillie, *Letters*, vol. I, pp. 1–2, 4–5.

[134] NLS Wod. Fo. 43, fols. 260–1. Undated. The terms correspond closely to the 'Advertisement' cited above, n. 133 (for the original, see NLS Wod. Fo. 43, fol. 262).

[135] See petitions in *RPCS*, 2nd Series, vol. VI, pp. 699–716. Again the statistical approach in Birchler, 'The influence of the Scottish clergy' is worthwhile. Lee, *The Road to Revolution*, pp. 223–4, gives a misleading impression of universal opposition amongst the nobility.

many of them, were not wishing thereby to rest their cause at that; the point is that they felt that the circumstances gave such a claim purpose.[136]

The defence was to be of 'religion and liberties'. The general terms left plenty of room for definition, and were not completely distinct from one another. While 'religion' addressed the relation between the believer and God, it had a social as well as an individual aspect. 'Liberties' were perhaps more earth-bound, a concept about social roles bestowed under the king and his government and ultimately through the grace of God. Out from the service-book policy the liberties at stake were those of the Scottish people – their laws, their civil peace, their freedom, their nationhood. Serious ecclesiastical opposition to royal policy would develop into a wide-ranging protest; prominent Scots would subsequently labour hard in contemplating what measure of religion and liberties they were bound to defend.

Even at the outset the shot fired by Charles and his bishops probably had various splinter effects. It intensified antipathy to the church hierarchy notably amongst nobility and laymen ambitious for office, for example. If clerical ambitions had been moderated under James, this was not so under Charles, when jealousies had multiplied as the leading bishops successfully took royal favour. The precedency granted early to Archbishop Spottiswood and challenged by the Earl of Kinnoul in 1633 had been confirmed in 1637 as *ex officio*, the latest of a chain of advancements. In 1635 Spottiswood had been created the first clerical Lord Chancellor since the Reformation.[137] Bishops Maxwell of Ross and Whitford of Brechin competed keenly for other high offices of state, in fact unsuccessfully, but bishops were increasingly present on the many privy council and government commissions of the 1630s.[138] A new constitution for the court of high commission in 1634 named all kinds of people to sit on it, but the bishops were correctly perceived to dominate, by critics who questioned the very legality of the court.[139] Probably also distinctly unpopular was the bishops' role over the Revocation where, despite early scruples about the Crown's designs on the church, they generally assisted the king's aims. Archbishop Laud from afar was involved in promoting this; bishoprics, like many benefices, stood to gain. Strategies for the enrichment of the church were pursued across all the kingdoms.[140]

---

[136] Cf. D. H. Fleming, *Scotland's Supplication and Complaint against the Book of Common Prayer . . . the Book of Canons, and the Prelates* (Edinburgh, 1927).

[137] Rogers, *Stirling's Letters*, vol. I, p. 62; Fraser, *Maxwells of Pollok*, vol. II, p. 255; *RPCS*, 2nd Series, vol. VI, p. 471; Foster, *Church*, pp. 35–6.

[138] Baillie, *Letters*, vol. I, p. 6; Traqr. Ms. 12/14; GD 45/14/17; Foster, *Church before the Covenants*, pp. 32–9. See also G. I. R. McMahon, 'The Scottish episcopate, 1600–1638' (unpublished University of Birmingham Ph.D. dissertation, 1973).

[139] G. I. R. McMahon, 'The Scottish courts of high commission, 1610–1638', *RSCHS*, 15 (1965), 193–209.

[140] Macinnes, 'The origin and organization of the Covenanting movement', gives the fullest

The Scottish nobility, who held themselves to be the natural royal councillors, disliked the signs of the bishops amassing wealth and influence. The keen administrator figures who attended the privy council likewise rose to the competition. One notorious venture had raised all kinds of hackles. In 1635 a proposal to make one Andrew Learmouth Abbot of Lindores created fears of churchmen making permanent gain from the king's Revocation; and the related possibility of a new dynasty of clerical abbots advancing into parliament and the court of session was seen as appalling. Anti-clerical feeling was expressed both within and outside the privy council. Even the tenants and heritors who might have been materially affected were aroused.[141] More ill-feeling over church land issues, especially within the council, lay in the immediate background to the troubles that arose around the introduction of the service-book.

Charles was consciously employing the bishops as his agents for the handling of this last, unpopular policy. He had called no general assemblies since his accession and it seems improbable that any bishop tried to persuade him to seek any such national consent for the liturgy; if they had, he presumably would have refused.[142] While the liturgy came in through the half-accepted machinery of episcopacy, the privy council, which probably approved the December 1636 proclamation without even seeing a final text, had a distinct supporting role only. The bishops, or some of them, went to their synods in the spring of 1637. It was they who announced a week in advance the first reading in Edinburgh, and of course they who in strength attended that service which met with a popular riot. The Earls of Traquair and Roxburgh, leading lay councillors (and rivals of episcopal ambition), were not required to be present.[143] Thus the churchmen stood almost alone alongside the force of the king's proclamation. It was not a promising combination.

Royal government was generally weak on the enforcement of policy but the notable lack of a commanding royal presence in Scotland contributed significantly to the development of the troubles. In the recent major controversies

---

treatment. For the Jacobean background, see Foster, *Church*, pp. 156–72. For England and Ireland, see Laud, *Works*, vol. III, pp. 187–8; Kearney, *Strafford in Ireland*, pp. 120–5; Ford, *Protestant Reformation in Ireland*, pp. 67–8, 269–70. Scots were not oblivious to the British dimension of the land policy – GD 406/1/315.

[141] GD 406/1/315, 8217, 964, 354; Traqr. Ms. 8/13; SRO SP 13/153, E 5/2, fols. 21–2, E 17/3/36–7; Buckminster Park, Tollemache Ms. 5264; Laud, *Works*, vol. VI, pp. 438–9; Brereton, *Travels*, pp. 100–1; Scot, *Apologeticall Narration*, pp. 336–7; Lee, *The Road to Revolution*, pp. 167 f 8. For the earlier dispute over the Laird of Craigievar's surrender of Lindores, see GD 250/7/407.

[142] Cf. Laud, *Works*, vol. VII, p. 373; also vol. III, p. 278.

[143] Baillie, *Letters*, vol. I, pp. 440–5; Laud, *Works*, vol. VI, pp. 494–5; BL Sloane Ms. 650, fol. 16; BL Add. Ms. 23112, fol. 44v; GD 406/1/382.

of the church, the king personally, or his agents, had pressed with a firmness that had only a shaky parallel in 1637. As we shall see, Charles found himself with problems within as well as outside his administration. Uncertainties amongst those on whom the king relied worked against there being a powerful force of resistance to the protesters.

The crisis was more than the riot on 23 July 1637, but the subsequent course of events was assured to no one. The violence of that first Sunday may well have been spontaneous; we shall never know for certain.[144] Opposition, as we have noted, could be self-defeating under a monarchy with a strong claim to rule. Two cases in point, William Haig and Lord Balmerino, must have got very frustrated at the consequences of their expressions of discontent. Such people sought ways of persuading the king to take better counsel, but always the problem was that Charles resisted giving ground.

However, the ministers who made advance plans to oppose the introduction of the liturgy took the advice of a young, committed lawyer who subsequently figured at the centre of the movement that formed, Archibald Johnston of Wariston. Their purpose was to establish the risks of making opposition. Every minister was required to have two copies of the new liturgy for use; the relevant proclamation counted as rebels any who refused.[145] As implied within the appeals to representative assemblies, there was at the beginning a legal point. Could the king order as he had done? The point struck directly at the claimed royal prerogative. It would be important that a historical case in law could be made, but it was one which needed support of theological argument. God was to be obeyed before man; kings were but His servants – even if Charles was the 'Lord's deputy over his people'.[146] To develop the case took time, in prayer and in careful writing. It was equally important that the protest went ahead, and with gathering strength. Charles's hold on the guiding reins became very soon devoid of power.

In 1637 there was an obvious single and important matter for protest, and however much other areas of resentment at royal government were drawn in, a committed number of individuals in the background of the riot picked up with exemplary efficiency on that cause. Mass appeal, relatively speaking, was as assured as it could be; from early on therefore, there was a new daring in what was to be done. Hostility against anglicisation and other burdens, not

---

[144] Cf. Makey, *Church of the Covenant*, p. 18.
[145] *Diary of Sir Archibald Johnston of Wariston, 1632–1639*, ed. G. M. Paul, SHS (Edinburgh, 1911), p. 262; Baillie, *Letters*, vol. I, pp. 440–1, 447. For Johnston, see D. Mathew, *Scotland under Charles I* (1955), pp. 59–69.
[146] Johnston, *Diary*, pp. 258–9, 265–8, 270; Baillie, *Letters*, vol. I, pp. 449–50; J. Leslie, Earl of Rothes, *A Relation of Proceedings Concerning the Affairs of the Kirk of Scotland*, ed. D. Laing, BC (Edinburgh, 1830), p. 55.

least episcopal leadership, was readily channelled against a political course of action held to be unfair and even plain wrong.

As time advanced, it was to become more than a matter as it were of the last straw. The king's denial of what was powerfully demanded from within Scotland and his threats against his subjects obliged as much as excused increasing determinations of commitment. Charles staked his claims by affirming a discretionary right to rule; he reckoned he had consulted the 'representative body' of the church in Scotland by using her bishops. But words were not enough without power, and his threats met with determined response. His people appealed for representative assemblies. As his intransigence began to appear in its true sustained colours, they were organised on the other side to stand up and be counted.

Multiple-kingdom states were generally unstable; the Scots, with their strong tradition of nationhood, naturally rose to the defence of a 'patriotic' line.[147] Charles had to cope with a national movement – although in reality many were uncommitted or unwilling to lend support, which should not be forgotten. From a general aspect the movement drew its shape from the society in which it was formed. The various estates, with the lairds notably as an independent grouping, had conscious identities; appeals to national assemblies, whether of the church or the state, reflected the values of a people who respected religious commitment and written law. Popular lines were to be shaped by the politics of the church cause; in general, recent and longer-term experiences would be brought in together. What was possible for government began to assume a different shape.

A Scottish monarch in days past might have responded to crisis by direct personal and bloody intervention.[148] But as times had changed the society to be ruled, so the absence of the king in England complicated the royal response. Moreover, while Charles had not hesitated to direct in better times, he found himself in a crisis where his appointed servants fell far short of his expectations. It was not an easy situation to assess;[149] but nor was Charles a king easily counselled when faced with opposition to his purposes. As ever, he tried to dictate. He paid attention with great reluctance to what was most possible and his personal absence served only to magnify the shortcomings of that approach. Even when he made the effort to be present, he could be no better satisfied.

Charles's inability to respond was momentous. Remedial advice could make but small inroads. In what follows it will be seen that he was counselled to give way a little but refused. He preferred to resort to force, even to civil

---

[147] Cf. J. Wormald, *Mary, Queen of Scots: A Study in Failure* (1988), pp. 20–39.
[148] Wormald, *Mary, Queen of Scots*, pp. 37–8.
[149] Cf. Laud, *Works*, vol. VI, pp. 402, 489–90; vol. VII, p. 374.

war. So he brought on a challenge that ran far beyond a reaction to these latest policies or their antecedents in church and state. Distant from the stubborn king, the party of resistance exploited the situation. The analysis provided here makes a particular concentration on the centre, where sustained church ideology remained always important and for Charles touched most painfully on his religious concern for sovereignty. Though the king's direction fell as much under attack in the localities, the complexities of behaviour there are largely beyond our scope.

What were the ways forward for the king and his counsel? Perhaps because the Covenanters came to achieve so much in controlling the country, it has not always been remembered how much the approval of Charles as king remained the focus of their aspirations. There were many of significance who hesitated even to join with the 'patriotic' cause of the Covenant because they feared the king's disapproval. From all angles men were trying to find harmony and cooperation between the king and his subjects, despite the many differences being expressed. In retrospect we see, with some of them, that a perfect balance was beyond hope, that indeed something like a Jacobean compromise was more to be recommended. However, while few contemporaries were conscious revolutionaries, they could be radicals and with powerful effect. These were the king's troubles.

2

The king's troubles
July 1637–May 1638

Charles I was singularly indisposed to make response to popular protest against his rule. That which had beginnings in a riot in and around St Giles's Cathedral in Edinburgh on 23 July 1637 was referred peremptorily to those who represented him in that city; what grew out of that riot the king would have preferred not to know. There were several dimensions to all of this. Least visible to Charles was a groundswell of discontent over the impact of three-kingdom government in a decade of poor harvests and trade problems. Individuals more or less aggrieved according to circumstance might have seen the prospect of an 'English' or 'popish' liturgy as a further, painful subject of aggravation. Almost as obscure to Charles were the immense efforts which prominent and vociferous individuals applied to organising a positive campaign of protest. Serious issues were felt to be at stake, more than talk of preferences for styles of worship might suggest. More visible were the efforts of the king's privy councillors and other supposed supporters against the protesters, yet here too there were obscurities. Given a general assumption that popular disturbance was inimical to orderly government, Charles would happily have heard no more than that the troubles were quelled; but, even when his concern was more aroused, distance and the politics of keeping his favour inevitably meant that he was but partially informed. Moreover, his capacity for listening to complaint was limited. It is on these latter dimensions that the following narrative is concentrated.

The movement which was to develop under the banner of the National Covenant drew in a wide range of issues for remedy, but anything like a programme was slow to appear. At the outset, and in a controlling prominence, was protest at the rule which had brought service-book and canons, new psalm books, Perth Articles and the court of high commission, and disputes over clerical oaths and appointments and dismissals of ministers. It was over the politics of the church that Scots first articulated grounds of profound alienation.

The Scottish bishops were bound to be quickly under attack, with their recent history of civil promotions and administration giving little to support

43

them; privately, however, the king himself was not beyond criticism. He it was who typically entrusted churchmen alone with the task of introducing the service-book, which furthermore left the Scottish administration as a whole ill prepared to face the protest that was expressed. Bishops varied in their commitment to this latest policy – just as some had advised James against the policy of the Five Articles. Lay councillors, in these years especially, could be as anti-clericalist as any, and in the initial outburst against the service-book they clearly found it advantageous that they had been largely excluded from the preparations. The proper unity of the king's privy council was elusive.

The scale of the troubles could not initially be foreseen. The frightening impact of the organisation which capitalised on the violence of July subsequently forced the Earl of Traquair, the Lord Treasurer, into an uneasy alliance with his episcopal rivals in the administration. Ambitious and prospering, Traquair had to reckon that his own position might be at stake. Other privy councillors, lacking positive commitment to the liturgy, if not actually resenting its Englishness, were probably close to some in the ranks of those who petitioned or 'supplicated' the king. However, something like sympathy with the Supplicants was bound to secure royal anger. Charles took protest badly: his purpose was to secure obedience to rightful authority.

From the time of the Duke of Lennox's return in September 1637, the king was kept informed; he heard something of the noise, but resisted it. Not wanting to make any direct response to the supplications, his first statement in December was too brief for the Supplicants, and his verbal directions to the council virtually impracticable. While Traquair, Roxburgh and Spottiswood tried to conceive how king and subjects might best be accommodated, Charles was more concerned to assert his authority. He was correct in seeing that his understanding of this was under attack but sought to vindicate it by proclaiming in February 1638 his own responsibility for the liturgy. In his view the protest had become treasonable disloyalty.

Traquair's efforts to advise the king were anguished as at Court he found his words barely heeded, although his ideas, like those of the Earl of Nithsdale or Archbishop Spottiswood, were subsumed into policy as it suited the king. Hamilton, the target of approaches by councillors and Supplicants alike, in turn attempted to steer Charles along such lines. The king was counselled by Scots, albeit not Scots who were completely attuned to the thinking of the Covenant. Even in March 1638, Traquair's suggestions fell short of what was demanded from below; he did not suggest any concession over the Five Articles of Perth or ecclesiastical discipline. His first hope was to persuade Charles of the need to proceed by consultation on the other contentious matters.

The middle ground may have had the greatest room for compromise, but the problem was that it repelled Charles to recognise such an area. The distance between the king and the seat of the troubles served to exacerbate the antipathies latent in the situation, though even in face-to-face dialogue Charles was rarely accommodating. At four hundred miles, his pronouncements had the effect of obliging the opponents of his government to draw together on a platform which was one of increasing requests and demands. At the same time, measured long-distance reporting to the king allowed attempts at rapprochements to flourish. Although in the event they rarely rose beyond the attempts stage, they have been drastically neglected in the historiography of the Scottish troubles. Like Charles, historians have preferred in the main to see events in terms of the polar opposites which were made manifest. Both Charles and the hard-line nonconformists came to envisage settlement by conquest in pursuit of their rival visions, naming their enemies to be seditious practisants or agents of the antichrist; ideas of anything smacking of compromise were shunned. Toleration came much more easily to those without a hot religious bent; but there was a spectrum of attitudes in this Scottish crisis. People live together in states for the sake of peace: it is important to try to understand the various facets of the, at times, circuitous quest for the recovery of that in Scotland.

Shouting, stool-throwing and stonings were firm signals by the women and lads of Edinburgh and others less visible that the reading from the liturgy on 23 July 1637 met with considerable disapproval.[1] The riot was but the tip of the troubles for the king; although at first it seemed a small thing, it was very quickly followed up. As early petitioning followed the advance planning of protest against the liturgy, it was to be argued that, although the Scottish church already had a set form of worship, a new book would in any case require the approval of both general assembly and parliament, which had presided over past changes. Representative ministers appeared in Edinburgh in mid-August to appeal against judgement for not supplying themselves with copies of the new liturgy. Privy councillors were directly approached and more general petitions began to flow in in support from various regions. In October the mobs came out again, by then publicly alongside a group of committed nobles and representatives of shires and burghs from many parts of Scotland; ministers had played their part in the organisation, and the petition then presented added terms against the canons and the bishops. More than a single policy decision was at stake; any king would have had serious reckoning with such a movement of protest.

Those of the council present in Edinburgh tried to restore order in the

---

[1] D. Stevenson, *The Scottish Revolution 1637–1644* (Newton Abbot, 1974), pp. 61–3; W. Makey, *The Church of the Covenant 1637–1651* (Edinburgh, 1979), p. 18.

immediate aftermath of 23 July, organising the apprehension of rioters and asking the city magistrates to consider how to secure further use of the service-book.[2] On the 26th, when the council attendance was fuller, a report was sent to the king, one of Traquair's servants acting as the carrier, and the council sat on every day of that week – despite 'scandalous and reproachful' speeches – fulfilling its commission, namely to assist the clergy in the settling of the liturgy. Lay–clerical tensions were serious. Traquair and Roxburgh felt moved to send strong complaints concerning the management of the business, and specifically to complain of the unwillingness of some of the bishops to communicate with their lay colleagues in the council.[3]

Vulnerable in the circumstances of a possible tactical failure, 'the clergy', after the dispatch of the first council letter, wrote separately to Court, by a bishop's messenger, expressing concern at the violent reception given to the book. There was a distinct atmosphere of crisis in the air. The ageing Archbishop Spottiswood initially placed an interdict on all church services after the riot. On 29 July he with Bishop Maxwell of Ross recommended to the council that the new liturgy should be kept from use until the king's pleasure on the punishment of the troublemakers was known; meanwhile worship should be with sermon and neither old nor new order of service. The council formally deferred to the bishops 'to do therein according to the power incumbent unto them in the duty of their offices'.[4]

The king's earliest response naturally reflected on the separation of responsibilities. He told the council to punish the authors and actors of the tumult and to concur with the clergy 'as they from time to time shall require your help'. The clergy were encouraged to assist in the punishment of malefactors, particularly of any ministers involved, but more importantly to continue as they had begun with the service-book. A third letter recommended to the Edinburgh authorities their continued concurrence on both fronts.[5] Less formally, Archbishop Laud writing from Court scorned what he saw as weakness on the part of the clergy. The archbishop's informant was Traquair, who had not spared him a favourable gloss on his own efforts, but the bishops' ready reference to Court seemed timorous in the light of their

[2] *RPCS*, 2nd Series, vol. VI, pp. 483–4, 486.
[3] *RPCS*, 2nd Series, vol. VI, pp. 486–7, 489; *A Diary of the Public Correspondence of Sir Thomas Hope of Craighall, Bart., 1633–1645*, ed. T. Thomson, BC (Edinburgh, 1843), p. 64; Traqr. Ms. 12/18, 8/2; GD 406/1/382.
[4] NLS Adv. Ms. 33.7.26, fols. 10–11; *RPCS*, 2nd Series, vol. VI, p. 490; W. Laud, *The Works of the Most Reverend Father in God, William Laud, D.D.*, eds. W. Scott and J. Bliss (7 vols., Oxford, 1847–60), vol. VI, pp. 495, 503–4; (J. Leslie, Earl of) Rothes, *A Relation of Proceedings Concerning the Affairs of Scotland*, ed. D. Laing, BC (Edinburgh, 1830), pp. 3–4.
[5] *RPCS*, 2nd Series, vol. VI, p. 509; BL Add. Ms. 23112, fol. 73v.

responsibilities. Laud justly bemoaned the lack of 'thorough' (diligence), picking up on how the bishops disappointed expectations.[6]

Although the daily meetings of the privy council in the second week had seen attendance dropping off, the arrival of these letters from Court on 4 August prompted immediate action. It was ordained that the persons held responsible in the tumult should now be put on trial, and on the next day a committee of the council was named to carry out hearings. Spottiswood shouldered the leading role in this. The bishops further moved for the burgh council of Edinburgh to confer with the Bishop of Edinburgh to arrange for reading the service – but the majority of the clergy present advised that this could not be done in time for the next day, alleging there were too few readers available, and other difficulties besides.[7]

Assured of the king's backing, the clergy involved were to do what they could. There were to be further attempts to use the liturgy – in the event without success in the main Edinburgh churches.[8] The problems ahead, however, were more than tactical, and the question was how far the trouble might go. In a letter to Charles, Traquair alluded to 'groundless fears' fomented by 'some who profess openly, and others who in a more circumspect, the more dangerous way, oppose the good of your Majesty's service; the best part of both which are puritanically affected people'.[9] Rumour and conscious propaganda would fuel the Scottish fire – Traquair can have had little idea of how much – but such words spoke eloquently to Charles's most ingrained presuppositions about enemies to the royal 'service'.

Rivalries within the Scottish administration worked against any hope of Laudian 'thorough' in the introduction of the service-book. Another Laud-backed project, the re-endowment of the church with formerly annexed land happened to occupy Traquair and Archbishop Spottiswood as much as the new liturgy in July 1637. At least partly because of their competition, the parties requested to be allowed to come south to argue their cases, on both matters; it was the usual way of scoring points of advantage.[10] This time Charles refused direct access: in a single letter returned by the bishop's messenger, he affirmed his former directions on the liturgy to council and clergy together.[11]

---

[6] Laud, *Works*, vol. VI, pp. 495–6.
[7] *RPCS*, 2nd Series, vol. VI, pp. 509–11; NLS Wod. Fo. 66, fol. 51r.
[8] Rothes, *Relation*, pp. 4–5; NLS Wod. Fo. 62, fols. 3–8.
[9] Traqr. Ms. 12/18 (partly summarised in *HMC 9 (II)*, p. 258).
[10] The transfer of the St Andrews priory lands from the Duke of Lennox to the archbishopric was the main issue. Some bishops had backed Traquair's approach against Spottiswood earlier in the year; Sir John Hay had supported the archbishop, as he would again over this period – M. Lee, Jr, *The Road to Revolution: Scotland under Charles I, 1625–1637* (Urbana and Chicago, 1985), pp. 189–91; Traqr. Ms. 12/17, 12/18; GD 406/M9/93/15.
[11] *RPCS*, 2nd Series, vol. VI, p. 521; BL Add. Ms. 23112, fol. 72r (6 August).

This dispatch did not reach Edinburgh before the council rose for a break on 10 August. In the meantime, the truth of the bishops' worries as to who would dare to read from the service-book was confirmed; intimidation of likely helpers probably played its part.[12] Forwardness was not lacking on the other side. When the council heard the king's letter read on 24 August, a well-briefed trio of ministers came to protest at being charged for not having provided themselves with service-books as required by proclamation. Archibald Johnston of Wariston, the lawyer who had advised them, had spent a troubled month. However, councillors appeared sympathetic, telling the ministers that the proclamation enjoined only the buying of the book, not its use. A draft version of this statement would have gone even further, to say 'they had nor has [sic] no purpose nor intention to extend the same to the practice thereof'.[13] Having thus avoided confrontation, the council sent to the king, telling of their surprise at the general clamours and fears being expressed. In the request for a royal statement, it was suggested that he should summon some councillors or clergy to confer with him.[14]

The council was in no position to launch into public criticism of policy, for the sake of the king's honour, but there was clearly a gentle approach here. The Supplicants were already impressive; some councillors no doubt disliked the policy in substance or means, and there were letters composed for them on the subject. The Earl of Morton was addressed by the Earl of Rothes and Lord Burghley around 21 August; their promised 'further information' appeared at the time of the council meeting those few days afterwards.[15] Morton, the retired Lord Treasurer, was one who urged the council to take care in their response to the ministers. It may be that the response was in return for the control of the crowds on this day.[16] If civil order was the priority, Traquair meanwhile continued in his criticism of bishops; it was regrettably short-sighted but Laud took the same tack, offended at the bishops' cowardice. He forecast a similar reaction from the king, 'who to my knowledge hath carefully looked over, and approved every word in this liturgy'.[17]

---

[12] *RPCS*, 2nd Series, vol. VI, pp. 513–16. Cf. R. Baillie, *The Letters and Journals*, ed. D. Laing, BC (3 vols., Edinburgh, 1841–2), vol. I, pp. 20–1, 23.

[13] *RPCS*, 2nd Series, vol. VI, pp. 521, 694; Baillie, *Letters*, vol. I, pp. 449–50; *Diary of Sir Archibald Johnston of Wariston*, ed. G. M. Paul, SHS (Edinburgh, 1911), pp. 262, 267–8; Stevenson, *Scottish Revolution*, pp. 64–5.

[14] Baillie, *Letters*, vol. I, p. 451.

[15] NLS Ms. 79, fol. 54; Ms. 81, no. 14; Baillie, *Letters*, vol. I, pp. 450–1.

[16] Rothes, *Relation*, pp. 6–7; Baillie, *Letters*, vol. I, p. 20; NLS Wod. 4to. 9, fol. 416.

[17] Traquair's letter does not survive, but Laud's reply makes clear some of the points. The earl allowed particular criticism of the Bishops of Brechin and Ross, who both staunchly upheld the book but were disliked rivals – Laud, *Works*, vol. VI, pp. 504–6; Lee, *The Road to Revolution*, pp. 156–7, 176, 185.

Charles reprimanded the weakness he perceived, refusing, as he put it, to believe that he had a slack council or bad subjects. Noting that delinquents were still not punished from July, and that the service-book had not been read in Edinburgh a second time, he urged that there should be no turning back; he picked up on private information from Bishop Wedderburn to express optimism for that course. He expected obedience, not discussions or delays. Shortly afterwards Traquair and Spottiswood were specifically commanded not to leave Edinburgh until the book was settled.[18] In so far as the emphasis of reports to date had dwelt heavily on the imperfect carriage of the bishops, it was not incapable direction. Traquair had miscalculated the seriousness of what was happening; Charles would be more fully disabused of his optimism in September.

There were at least two levels to the problem. It is likely that the criticisms expressed, by among others Traquair and Roxburgh, that some of the bishops had conducted the affair with poor judgement and rash public expressions were relevant. An absentee royal policy had even less chance if divisions within the administration went unhealed. Doubtless the blame was not all on one side, however, though Charles's directions in any case encouraged a lay–clerical divide. At the same time, beyond this, fears both of what the new liturgy meant in itself and for the general well-being of religion had stimulated a massive response. The information delivered to the privy councillors was only a part of it; more emotive tracts and other similar items of propaganda against the service-book were already in production. Robert Baillie, the minister of Kilwinning in Ayrshire, first asked to show his stance verbally, was pressed to enter into writing.[19] Another month saw the production of numerous petitions in time for the council meeting in September.[20]

Charles would not take kindly complaints that he had proceeded by 'a way unacquainted'; as yet, he was barely informed. In Edinburgh, gathered nobles and ministers and others hoped that the courtier Duke of Lennox, who had come north for his mother's funeral, would carry a large supplication to the king. Baillie recounted hearing the duke say in Glasgow that the king was misinformed – but about what? It was possibly a recognition of the force of the objections being raised, although Traquair, who stood by Lennox, gave assistance to the Supplicants in redrafting the supplication to the king which apparently sought to pave ways of reform through the bishops.[21] Traquair's

[18] Baillie, *Letters*, vol. I, pp. 452–3, 22; Traqr. Ms. 4/87, 12/19.
[19] 'Reasons why the service-book cannot be received' (by George Gillespie) – Baillie, *Letters*, vol. I, p. 90; 'Jeshurun' was almost certainly an earlier production – EUL Laing Ms. I, 293. For Robert Baillie, see Baillie, *Letters*, vol. I, pp. 35–7; 'Meditation on the Canterburian faction' – EUL New College Ms. X15b 3/1, vol. I, fols. 32–4.
[20] Stevenson, *Scottish Revolution*, pp. 66–9; Makey, *Church of the Covenant*, pp. 19–22.
[21] Baillie, *Letters*, vol. I, p. 22; *RPCS*, 2nd Series, vol. VI, p. 523; Rothes, *Relation*, p. 9.

reckoning was that nothing more could be hoped for from Charles; but criticism of the improper means of introduction nevertheless remained. Lennox was to take two of the sixty-eight petitions available from various areas of the country, including one from the ministry of the Dunblane diocese, who plainly did not like the book – contrary to the information had by the king from their Bishop Wedderburn.[22]

The council hoped to persuade the king that their efforts to have the service-book brought into use were sincere. Denying the Supplicants' efforts to procure assurances to their advantage, a committee was appointed to remain constantly in Edinburgh, to work alongside the burgh magistrates.[23] Little, however, seems to have been achieved. A rumour went out that the book had been suspended until November, when the petitions would be answered. The baillies and officers of Edinburgh objected to being asked to do anything in the meantime; the resort of nobles and others with petitions had 'so alienated their minds that no such assurances can be expected now as formerly'.[24] By October their positive support for the Supplicants was being voiced. It should be asked whether this was a comment on the power of coercion as well as of arguments against the book. Sir John Hay, Charles's nominee provost of Edinburgh, maintained the former against the Earl of Rothes's belief in the effectiveness of the latter.[25]

Rothes, well experienced in the oppositions to various regal policies, was prominently committed to the present cause. Archbishop Spottiswood in debate with him drew comparisons with England and Ireland, and offered the argument of *cuius regio eius religio*; Rothes replied that religion was changed easily enough in sixteenth-century England: 'the two professions were near equally divided; but there were few here to concur to such a change, all being reformed . . . the reformation of England was not so full as that of Scotland, and had not so much law for it'. Attachment to the strengths of the national reformation of Scotland, which Rothes saw to be all but realised, gave an image of English impurity still too much akin to Rome that was quite widely felt. Spottiswood's theology could accommodate change, but Rothes's difference on that was further illustrated in his comparison of the law, where he seemed to imply that besides legislation divine law, the evidence of scripture

---

[22] Rothes, *Relation*, pp. 47–8; Baillie, *Letters*, vol. I, p. 22; NLS Wod. 4to. 24, fol. 75.
[23] *RPCS*, 2nd Series, vol. VI, pp. 528–9; Baillie, *Letters*, vol. I, pp. 453–4.
[24] *RPCS*, 2nd Series, vol. VI, p. 533; GD 112/39/694; SRA T-PM 113/275, Stirling-Maxwell of Pollok muniments; M. Wood (ed.), *Extracts from the Records of the Burgh of Edinburgh 1626 to 1641* (Edinburgh, 1936), pp. 194–5; Rothes, *Relation*, p. 11; NLS Wod. 4to. 9, fols. 418–19.
[25] Rothes, *Relation*, pp. 16, 21–2. See too Makey, *Church of the Covenant*, pp. 153–60.

alone, had to be taken into account. To detract from that was more than unnecessary; it was seen as wrong.[26]

The historic confessions of the church in Scotland gave the grounding for the scriptural argument; Sir Thomas Hope of Craighall, the King's Advocate, would, like Rothes, firmly endorse it.[27] In their eyes, arguments citing church history in support of liturgy and ceremonies fell flat as did talk merely of obedience to the king. The purity of the church was an ideal which beckoned beyond thoughts of tradition and order. Laymen stood out beside dissenting ministers, while clergy seem mostly to have spoken on the other side. Dr Robert Barron, one of the famous Aberdeen doctors, advanced his thoughts on the king's behalf in writing around this time. Not surprisingly, one of the Supplicants tried to refute the arguments.[28]

Traquair was always more the politician than the theologian. This fact, with the like-mindedness of some other crucial figures, probably helped to avert an early civil war in Scotland, such as Robert Baillie feared from early October 1637.[29] There was little determined backing for the king which could match the advancing confidence of the Supplicants. Charles in any case was to make no immediate response to the information now reaching him. According to his Secretary, the Earl of Stirling, he was most offended that petitions had been sent up with a public expectation of an answer. Policy once defined was not lightly to be reconsidered, let alone redefined. Charles insisted that he should hear and make resolutions concerning opposition; but his Scottish council should simply have received those petitions and allowed a private resolution from Court. Traquair, reprimanded, promised to have the service-book read in Edinburgh or else 'to perish by the way'. Even so, he still vituperated the 'folly and presumption' of some bishops who would not take advice. His naming of the Bishops of Galloway and Dunblane as his supporters would hardly have pleased the Supplicants; for him, they were amongst the less politically ambitious.[30]

The king had heard, but had not wanted to understand, the sense of the September petitions. George Con, the Papal nuncio who attended upon

---

[26] Rothes, *Relation*, pp. 10–11. Cf. A. H. Williamson, *Scottish National Consciousness in the Age of James VI* (Edinburgh, 1979). For Spottiswood's lasting commitment to the service-book, see his will – J. Spottiswood, *The History of the Church of Scotland*, BC (3 vols., Edinburgh, 1850), vol. I, p. cxxxi.

[27] See GD 45/1/54.

[28] 'A declaration of some regrets and grievances by some brethren well-affected to the church against these who supplicate his Majesty against the service-book'; 'Ane tryal of Dr Barron's apology' – NLS Wod. Fo. 29, fols. 30–7; another copy of Barron's work is NLS Adv. Ms. 29.2.8, fols. 181–4. Cf. J. Row, *The Historie of the Estate of the Kirk of Scotland*, MC (2 vols., Edinburgh, 1842), vol. I, p. 271. For Barron, see J. D. Ogilvie, 'The Aberdeen doctors and the National Covenant', *Papers of the Edinburgh Bibliographical Society*, 11 (1912–20), 73–86, where this controversial exchange is not, however, mentioned.

[29] Baillie, *Letters*, vol. I, p. 25.   [30] Traqr. Ms. 9/2, 12/19.

Charles, related the petitions' contents to Rome; the Earl of Stirling pressed him to persuade the king of their seriousness. Charles was determined to be obeyed; as yet he would do or say little more. Laud, like Stirling, would come to bemoan the inadequacy of this, but any alternative would have had doubtful effectiveness.[31] On 9 October Charles wrote to the council to discharge their intended meeting for the delivery of a response, and ordered their removal with the court of session firstly to Linlithgow, and in time to Dundee. He strictly forbade the gatherings of Supplicants under pain of horning; he confided that he was not prepared to give answer to their petitions at this time. The removal command was given in order to punish Edinburgh for not opposing the movement of supplications in September. In the classic fashion of Charles's absentee rule, it merely created another problem, since even Sir John Hay joined in petitioning against it, for the sake of Edinburgh's economic prosperity.[32]

The response of the Supplicants, however, advanced the trouble more. Mobs were once again violent in the streets of the capital on 18 October. More significantly, another major petition to present to the council was hastily composed, which demanded the trial of service-book and canons. Widely circulated for signatures, it was the first public document to make a charge of blame for the innovations directly against the bishops.[33]

The council, obedient to the king's charge, refused to accept anything; but Traquair, trying to preserve the face of authority in which he had such a great interest, spoke with the Earl of Rothes. Highly critical of the popular disorders, Traquair remained open in his criticism of the rashness of the bishops' proceedings but attempted to defuse any block attack. He explained that he was now in better affection with the Chancellor because Bishop Maxwell of Ross was no longer around, implying that Spottiswood alone might be more pliable. It was optimistic thinking.[34]

The king's distance was telling in the crisis now emerging. Traquair had honestly related to Rothes the form of the recent royal correspondence, which had been written by Lennox rather than by the Secretary; he confessed himself unsure of what might happen.[35] That Traquair now sent again for permission to go to Court was indication of his sense that Charles needed to be

---

[31] BL Add. Ms. 15390, fols. 436, 457; Laud, *Works*, vol. VII, p. 402.

[32] *RPCS*, 2nd Series, vol. VI, pp. 536–40; GD 406/1/389; [Charles I], *A Large Declaration*, STC 21906 (1639), pp. 41–2; Stevenson, *Scottish Revolution*, p. 71. Linlithgow could provide nowhere for the Session to meet – GD 112/39/700.

[33] D. H. Fleming, *Scotland's Supplication and Complaint . . . 18th October 1637* (Edinburgh, 1927); Stevenson, *Scottish Revolution*, pp. 72–4, 338–9; Makey, *Church of the Covenant*, pp. 21–2; Rothes, *Relation*, pp. 16–17, 19–21.

[34] Rothes, *Relation*, pp. 21–2.

[35] The letters, Lennox holograph, survive in SRO PC 11/6b/284–5; they were misplaced, and one left undated, when entered in Stirling's register – BL Add. Ms. 23112, fol. 76v.

persuaded to heed more keenly the turn of events. Given the king's former orders, however, Traquair trod carefully in proceeding to request permission to come south. First he approached indirectly the Marquis of Hamilton; a direct request was saved for the hands of Patrick Maule of Panmure, who was returning to Court.[36] He reiterated shortly afterwards to Panmure that he wanted to speak with the king, to offer in terms amenable to Charles, 'remedy . . . that might both pacify and quiet all their mutinies, or rather rebellions, secure us from the like hereafter, and get His Majesty's content of these who shall be found to have had a hand in that which is passed'.[37]

Traquair had no intentions of backing off from his own objections to episcopal conduct in this political contest, but the idea he offered failed to satisfy more serious opponents. He apparently upheld as a compromise the English Book of Common Prayer: this might be acceptable to those of good faith, among whom he counted himself, as a convert from Roman Catholicism. In theory the idea met the principal objections that there were popish innovations in the modifications of the Scottish text, but of course reflected poorly on the latest authors. Traquair's asseverations of personal commitment were obviously meant to impress Rothes, but he missed the target; and Charles would not permit his journey intended for the purpose of suggesting the same to him.[38]

Bishops were now public targets for the Supplicants, which in itself was a breakthrough of daring not attempted around the July time; encouragement through the achievement of widespread petitioning was surely important. But, whatever the bishops themselves had done, the king's own role had the attention of more than Traquair. Johnston of Wariston noted in his diary that the recent proclamation came in terms 'peremptory and absolute'. What about the good of the church of Scotland? What about the faith of the historic confessions of the sixteenth century? Charles was threatening, and Wariston, perhaps with others, doubted his right to do so. There had emerged a definite risk of persecution for the movement of protest by popular gatherings and petitions. As for the ministers in July, Wariston would be asked to prepare a legal defence. It was a very natural step to contemplate directly the scope of the royal prerogative.[39]

The king's councillors combined mediation with firmness. Traquair was in Edinburgh trying to deter crowds from gathering yet again on the day before the next meeting of the council in Linlithgow on 14 November. In explaining

---

[36] P. Yorke, *Miscellaneous State Papers, from 1501 to 1726* (2 vols., 1778), vol. I, pp. 95–7; GD 406/1/1000; Hope, *Diary*, p. 66.
[37] GD 45/14/14 (v).
[38] Rothes, *Relation*, p. 22 – cf. Baillie, *Letters*, vol. I, pp. 39–40; Traqr. Ms. 4/92 (15 November, from Court).
[39] Johnston, *Diary*, pp. 269–70, 273, 275, 278, 292, 298, 304–5, 308–14.

to Rothes how he had been maligned for correspondence with the Supplicants – not fairly, in his opinion – he affirmed his purpose to serve the king. By now it was a recurring matter to have the crowds kept under control. As an encouragement Traquair showed to Rothes the king's most recent letter, in which Charles had acknowledged the account of the Supplicant nobles' help in this regard during the October riot. Traquair wished to show that he had done his best to endear the Supplicants to the king. The question of whether ordered protest might reap rewards was still open. Traquair continued to turn over possible remedies in his mind. With Rothes he clarified whether concessions over High Commission and the canons would be required; he asked again concerning the English prayer book. The reply, phrased so that it would apply to all the Supplicants, was that they would only accept an order of service authorised first through a general assembly. There had been organised briefing for the Supplicants' negotiations with the councillors; the Five Articles of Perth were now included as a definite target for remedy.[40]

These discussions had the support of the council when it convened; but still no petition was to be received, although the one of October was offered again. The Supplicants tried to have bishops excluded from judging on the cause.[41] The councillors won time, but meanwhile Sir Thomas Hope gave near-official warrant to the idea of the Supplicants electing representatives to attend in Edinburgh. This could serve the practical interests of public order, but it also laid the way for the formation of the so-called Tables. Representative members of the estates, including the lairds and burghs taken separately, would comprise the powerful ruling centre of the Covenanting movement in days to come. Here in November 1637, the Supplicants remained unsure of the council, concerned particularly that there might be proceedings against the magistrates of Edinburgh and the nobles for the rioting of October. Johnston of Wariston received his calling. The confidence which would mark the movement in the future was still in the forming, but it was mounting.[42]

The seriousness of the October events had only a limited impact in the Court, because the failings of the divided Scottish administration were believed to be a major part of the problem. Charles still would not answer petitions, but he did try to offer reassurances about the fears of popery which were reported to him – amongst others by the Earl of Roxburgh, the Lord Privy Seal, who

---

[40] Rothes, *Relation*, pp. 30–2; HMC 9 *(II)*, p. 248 (Traqr. Ms. 4/88, 28 October); 'Memorandum for those who did confer with the councillors' – EUL New College Ms. X15b 3/1, vol. I, fol. 27v.
[41] RPCS, 2nd Series, vol. VI, pp. 544–5; Rothes, *Relation*, pp. 23–33; EUL New College Ms. X15b 3/1, vol. I, fols. 28–9; NLS Wod. Fo. 61, fols. 238–9.
[42] Johnston, *Diary*, p. 273; Stevenson, *Scottish Revolution*, pp. 75–8; Makey, *Church of the Covenant*, pp. 22–5.

attended Court in late October and November. A proclamation text therefore promised that he would alter nothing except to the advancement of the 'true religion as it is presently professed' in Scotland, as had always been the intention. Traquair, although not allowed to come to Court, was sent a personal note of assurance.[43]

As from the beginning of the reign, there was competition for the king's ear. Robert, the Catholic Earl of Nithsdale, had flourished precariously in the early years, and although latterly less to the fore in Scottish politics he kept favour at Court, where he journeyed at the end of October 1637 to forward some Irish land business.[44] He did not, however, keep silent about the troubles in Scotland, and the fortunate survival of his advice-papers enables a clearer understanding of Charles's attitude towards Traquair and his fellows.

In November 1637 Nithsdale was heavily critical of the councillors in Scotland and strongly advised that neither bishop nor officer of state be allowed to come to Court until the troubles were settled; it was far better that the king send commands by a minor servant, not necessarily explaining everything, and especially where men's fidelity was unproven. The mutual accusations of bishops and laymen in the council were best retained as a threatening means to induce obedience. 'Secrecy which none living hath in a fuller measure is the only means to effectuate what is intended' – a counsel to the king which was to make no exceptions, neither the nearest in the Bed-chamber, nor the councillor, and in this case the Earl of Roxburgh, who attended upon Charles for his commands and against whom Nithsdale spared little.[45]

Nithsdale maintained that neither the service-book nor High Commission should ever be discharged, for to do otherwise would stain the king's honour, but he thought that a period of not extending the business of the court or of not pressing the use of the liturgy might be possible. Some should suffer for making trouble – should come with copies tied round their necks – though the king's public statements should be of 'fair generals'.

At the same time, prominent figures should use their influence to gain the country. From Court, Hamilton should deal with the Earl of Cassilis, Lord Lindsay and others of his friends; the Duke of Lennox, the Earls of Morton

---

[43] *RPCS*, 2nd Series, vol. VI, pp. 546–7; Traqr. Ms. 4/92; *HMC 9 (II)*, p. 243.

[44] Laud, *Works*, vol. VI, pp. 386–7. Nithsdale was in Edinburgh still on 28 October – SRA T-PM 113/951, Stirling-Maxwell of Pollok muniments.

[45] On Roxburgh, Nithsdale wrote, 'to employ a puritan and acquaint him with what is intended were, as a man would think, to make the bad reform the Borders'. Roxburgh was prominent in the commission for the Middle Shires, to which Nithsdale himself had pretensions – *RPCS*, 2nd Series, vol. VI, pp. 161–5.

and Ancrum[46] and the men of government in Scotland should do likewise. Castles should be secured at Edinburgh, Stirling and Blackness, to which end James Livingstone and Patrick Maule, both Grooms of the Bedchamber, should send to those responsible, the Earls of Mar and Linlithgow; and money should be conveyed secretly to them before the turn of affairs worsened. On the siting of the council and Session, Nithsdale strongly advised against any leniency towards Edinburgh, and suggested the castle at Stirling as the most secure place.[47]

The warnings sounded grave, but Charles was not yet unduly disturbed. He may further have been given the impression that poverty rather than religion underlay the troubles.[48] In the first instance he seemed to be willing to wait on events. His note to Traquair on 20 November told somewhat deviously that Roxburgh would show him the 'very secrets of my thoughts';[49] the instruction written concerning the council and Session stated only that they should not meet in Edinburgh or Leith – but in the event both went to Stirling.[50] The gentler approach preferred aimed – rather as Nithsdale has suggested – to defuse tensions by giving a general reassurance of Charles's good intentions; to his privy council he perhaps even implied that he would attend the outcome of conciliation on the ground, before pressing further with the service-book. However, he did ask that Edinburgh sue for pardon in the wake of the riots.[51]

The differences of approach within the Scottish council still fostered tensions. Traquair, when he parted with the Supplicants in November, had promised to persuade the bishops that they should not enforce the 'innovations' until the king's answer arrived. Archbishop Spottiswood duly agreed, but the Bishop of Brechin, Walter Whitford, a few days later performed his infamous attempt to have the liturgy used in his own cathedral, wearing pistols and dirks at his side. He barely escaped to his house with his life. In December Traquair, following the statement in the proclamation to have Edinburgh submit peaceably for pardon on the earlier contempt shown against royal authority, was somewhat rivalled by Sir John Hay's more aggressive efforts to pursue for punishment.[52]

---

[46] Ancrum was to be threatened into cooperation by warning that the Earl of Lothian his son's part amongst the Supplicants would be used against him. Con described Ancrum as a 'puritan' – BL Add. Ms. 15391, fol. 51v.
[47] NLS Ms. 9303, fols. 14–15 (holograph, unsigned – rough copy?). Another note by Nithsdale referred to words 'spoken at my hithercoming'; Dumbarton Castle was also mentioned as needing defence – NLS Ms. 9303, fol. 16. It was seemingly Charles's practice to have advice tendered in writing for his reflection.
[48] BL Add. Ms. 15390, fol. 503; cf. [Charles I], *Large Declaration*, esp. pp. 6–12; K. M. Brown, 'Aristocratic finances and the origins of the Scottish Revolution', *EHR*, 104 (1989), 46–87.
[49] *HMC 9 (II)*, p. 243.
[50] *RPCS*, 2nd Series, vol. VI, p. 546; vol. VII, p. 3.
[51] *RPCS*, 2nd Series, vol. VI, pp. 546–7.
[52] BL Sloane Ms. 650, fol. 29; GD 112/39/703; GD 45/1/56; Baillie, *Letters*, vol. I, pp. 46–7.

Talks on the ground conducted by lay councillors kept the bishops out as a group, which effect was also managed ironically by the vague statement in the king's proclamation published on 7 December. Charles, assuming that the 'true religion' should be declared from above, gave in effect his delayed answer to the September petitions. He announced that he abhorred all popish superstition, and had no intentions of allowing it. The Supplicants read this as further grounds for attacking the bishops, who had apparently introduced precisely that. It was hardly Charles's intention, and in the days after the proclamation was published, the lay councillors tried to persuade Supplicants to moderate their carriage. They were asked to petition by shire as in September, to confine complaints to the service-book – and to avoid casting the bishops as irredeemable opponents. Traquair, to keep his grip, told Rothes now that he positively disliked the service-book and would be telling this to the king – a shift from his earlier conversations; his persistent pressing in matters 'esteemed the loss of their cause', however, could be taken by those more removed from him as unpleasantly provocative.[53]

Archibald Johnston of Wariston reflected in his diary on the hesitations within the close coterie of Supplicants' leaders, particularly concerning the matter of complaining against the bishops. Wariston did not hold back, determining clear views on the limited scope of the royal prerogative in the church; and he was closely involved, with the leading nobles of whom he named Rothes, Loudoun and Balmerino, on the composition of a declinator against the bishops, as well as of a new supplication and a protestation which expressed the frustration at not having petitions received, the last a consequence of the councillors' declining to receive petitions on 13 December.[54] The case was set down in writing against bishops and later against the court of high commission: the temptation to compromise was to be resisted.[55] The protestation was not in the end presented. Instead, on 21 December, Lord Loudoun and two ministere delivered speeches before the council which cast back on the history of the problem as revealed in recent months. The activities of the bishops underwent biting attack. The declinator was to state that the bishops were not acceptable to sit on these matters as judges, and it was presented with the supplication; Wariston at least thought of appealing even against their consulting with the king.[56]

[53] *RPCS*, 2nd Series, vol. VI, pp. 546–7; BL Sloane Ms. 1467, fol. 41; Sloane Ms. 650, fol. 33; Rothes, *Relation*, pp. 33–44; Baillie, *Letters*, vol. I, pp. 43–5.

[54] Johnston, *Diary*, pp. 287, 275, 278, 283–4; Baillie, *Letters*, vol. I, pp. 44–5.

[55] NLS Wod. 4to. 24, fols. 78–9; EUL Laing Ms. I, 291 and Johnston, *Diary*, pp. 293, 297, 302–4, 308 (wrongly dated in *HMC Laing*). The paper urging the attack on bishops not to be left aside attracted notice at Court – see below, p. 64.

[56] *RPCS*, 2nd Series, vol. VI, p. 554; BL Sloane Ms. 1467, fol. 44; GD 406/M1/38; NLS Wod. Fo. 61, fols. 242–5 (includes Wariston interlineations); Baillie, *Letters*, vol. I, pp. 45–6, 455–8; Rothes, *Relation*, pp. 45–51.

No promise was given that the declinator would be handed on to Charles, but the lay councillors, on their own, at last accepted supplications, those of September and October as well as the present new one; all the bishops chose to be absent that day. For Roxburgh and Traquair the move seemed necessary, principally to avoid the Supplicants themselves sending someone up to Court. This, and the protestation had it been made, would have compromised more than ever their authority besides surely displeasing Charles. They understood now that the king would have to take the protests seriously, but preferably under their own advice. To this end they worked on a new line of counsel.[57] This was to offer hope of some further trial of the liturgical policy as a means to restoring the peace, and thus to stem the tide of growing demands, a task of some urgency. Cooperation with the bishops was required, and care in phrasing for the king's approval. Given the firmness of the royal policy, this was the most realistic course. Equally, because of its sensitive nature, the counsel was formulated in close secrecy.

Spottiswood was sympathetic to the pragmatism of the strategy, but the fragility of the cultivated alliance within the council was all too apparent. The archbishop wished to send to Court his son, Sir Robert Spottiswood, Lord President of the court of session. Traquair and Roxburgh, trusting that his going would await the results of their mutual consultations, were left in consternation when the son took leave on 23 December. Not knowing what he would be saying, they wrote post-haste to Charles to ask him to wait for the coming of joint advice, which in the event was not agreed until the second week of January 1638. Copies of an interim account were also sent to Hamilton and Patrick Maule, to help the force of the appeal. Despite the panic, however, Roxburgh expressed his hope that unanimous agreement would shortly be found and mutual discords wholly forgotten.[58]

Meanwhile, in spite of the successful delivery of the petitions, the Supplicants' fear of the consequences of Spottiswood's journey prompted Lord Loudoun to write to the Marquis of Hamilton. He backed the arguments of the petitions which he trusted would be presented from the council and hoped that these 'truths' would not be deflected by the Lord President's information.[59] The Earl of Haddington, also at Court, was another hoped-for supporter.[60] Lord Lorne, from within the council in Edinburgh, suggested to Johnston of Wariston that he might like to accompany Traquair in his public venture of carrying the supplications to Court, a sign that Lorne entered more

---

[57] Rothes, *Relation*, p. 38; Traqr. Ms. 12/31.
[58] Traqr. Ms. 12/31; Spottiswood, *History*, vol. I, p. cxxvii; Hope, *Diary*, p. 69. The interim account survives in Traqr. Mss. Bundle 28[i] – 'Copy hereof sent to his Majesty by St Andrews, Traquair and Roxburgh, Decemb. 1637'; see also GD 406/1/8348.
[59] GD 406/1/394 (25 December).
[60] Baillie, *Letters*, vol. I, p. 47; Rothes, *Relation*, p. 53.

than a little into the arguments for the 'cause'.[61] The tide would not easily be stopped.

The earliest in the line of projected settlements, the joint work principally of Traquair, Roxburgh and Spottiswood, envisaged merely the possibility of revision of the 1637 liturgy. The documentation of these efforts shows that differences of approach were not easily reconciled; the will of the authors to find a solution is all the more impressive. 'A memorial to be humbly represented to his Majesty' urged Charles to proclaim that he had no intention of giving offence by his service-book and that he would not press it until it was revised by 'the most learned, godly, wise and moderate persons of the clergy'. Secondly, another proclamation should forbid unlawful conventions on pain of treason and provide for punishment according to the severity of the offence for the actors of tumults in Edinburgh, Glasgow and Brechin. All three signed the 'Memorial', and it was said that other councillors had been consulted. It seems to have uneasily included the two strains of thinking, being critical of the liturgy although playing still to the royal preference for clerical direction, and finally stern against the stirrers of public trouble.[62]

Two further papers, the one a preparatory draft in Traquair's hand of the other, gave an alternative design at some greater length which confirms the impression that Spottiswood's mark lay more heavily on the 'Memorial'. The introductory section of the draft, 'An advice for quieting the present troubles', dealt with the Edinburgh problem, suggesting that the burgh should beg pardon from the king for the tumults and the convocations; further on, it was argued that all convocations should be stopped, and all representatives sent away. Turning to the liturgy, Traquair suggested that the king should hold a conference with perhaps eight on each side, for and against, and if differences still remained should refer the matter to a general assembly. If the assembly decision were binding on everyone, tensions would be defused on both the substance of the book and the manner of its introduction with relation to the laws of the church. The king might determine when and where the assembly should meet, but April in St Andrews was offered as a suggestion. Less room for debate was permitted on other points, however, because the questioning of the episcopal estate or the Five Articles of Perth was not to be allowed. The court of high commission, resting on royal prerogative, was to command obedience but Traquair, noting that bishops might abuse its use, recommended that the king join nobles, officers of state and privy councillors always to convene with the clergy for the hearing of purely ecclesiastical cases in the normal meeting-place for the privy council.[63]

---

[61] Johnston, *Diary*, pp. 289–90.
[62] Traqr. Mss. – in bundle 'Traquair papers nos. 47 to 54, of Mr Fraser's list'.
[63] Traqr. Ms. 41/7.

This was probably intended to serve as a working paper for discussion, but was in large measure a comment on Traquair's vision for settlement. He stated a case for taking consultation over the service-book, despite what he knew of the king's view, and revealed his anti-clericalism in the comment on High Commission; his resistance to breaches of order was to be expected from a man in authority, but it was not vindictive. It surely reflected on his awareness of the fragile control which rested with the privy council. He fell short on both sides of the dispute. While the liturgy was of specific importance to the Supplicants, and the paper showed something of an understanding of the value of a general assembly, as was explicit in their demands, it is unlikely that what he offered was going to be enough. But it was in any case firstly a matter of persuading the bishops and the king.

The finished text, 'Ane humble advice for quieting the present troubles and controversies of the church', focused above all on the service-book. Thus there was no room for suggestions of a new superior body for ecclesiastical discipline, and indeed no mention of Edinburgh. Agreement on what should be done about the town had perhaps been difficult, and it certainly seems likely that Spottiswood had resisted over High Commission. But on the service-book, outlines had changed very little, with a proposal for a conference between approvers and disapprovers, not above seven or eight on each side, and an assembly to decide on any points still controversial. The canons were to be debated too: the onus was to be on the opponents to prove their case, who were therefore to admit their mistake if error was not proved – as seemed by implication to be expected. Points of procedure were more fully detailed than in the original version – means to ensure peaceful proceedings and order in speaking, notaries to keep precise notes of what was said.[64]

This paper was signed by Traquair and Roxburgh and four bishops – St Andrews, Argyll, Galloway and Dunblane. It should probably be taken that the small number of signatories was a sign of the close circulation of this paper, the limited and delayed achievement of the Traquair vision. The episcopal backing was important for taking it to the king.[65] 'Our judgements may be wrong, but we have been sincere and diligent': thus the Earl of Roxburgh respectfully commended to Charles the 'best course' for his honour and for peace in Scotland.[66]

Archbishop Spottiswood, however, had abandoned only with extreme

----

[64] Traqr. Ms. 13/33 (partly printed in *HMC 9 (II)*, p. 253).

[65] The advice was still under discussion on 6 January – Traqr. Ms. 12/20. Bishop Fairley of Argyll had enjoyed Traquair's backing; Sydserf of Galloway had expressed his confidence in him around this time – GD 45/14/14 (ii); Traqr. Ms. 8/1; Spottiswood, *History*, vol. I, pp. cxxvi–cxxvii. Of those around, the Bishops of Brechin and Edinburgh conspicuously did not sign.

[66] Traqr. Ms. 12/27.

reluctance the shorter 'Memorial', and five days after Traquair had left for Court on 17 January, he was writing to his son in London to tell how Traquair had urged that that other paper be put aside. Traquair's further argument had been that if the course projected made no quietness in the country, the king would direct instructions to the council, 'which I [Spottiswood] expounded to be done for excluding the Marquis of Huntly's employment, who is only [i.e. alone] feared and is only able to do service'.[67] The archbishop, unhappy about free debate over the objections to the policy, preferred evidently to hope for the support of Huntly on the council to back an approach both repressive and authoritarian – which Traquair as clearly wished to avoid. Sir John Hay, excluded from the secret talks which had taken place, urged Sir Robert Spottiswood separately that Traquair was double-dealing, that he had offered too many concessions to the Supplicants in the past and that he had ignored the bishops.[68] Traquair had propounded a line of accommodation, but he struggled even to get it put to the test. The administration was little more united than before, and this was a fact of which Charles would be well aware.

Furthermore, there was an element within the council that positively sided with the Supplicants. The King's Advocate, Sir Thomas Hope of Craighall, sent a packet with Traquair to be delivered to Patrick Maule at Court. Maule was a man concerned about the present troubles in the Scottish church; he wanted a good outcome to the efforts òf the Supplicants. Hope wished to argue a case that the imposition of the service-book had contravened various Acts of the parliament of Scotland. He sent another copy with a letter directly to the king.[69] Hope had met earlier in January with Archibald Johnston – with whom he had differences, and yet his thinking resembled closely the general line of the Supplicants.[70] By reciting articles of the 1560 Confession of Faith, his paper upheld the vital principle that to do without the warrant of God's Word was to do against that Word, and he noted the confirming legislation of general assemblies and parliaments. The recent 'innovations', introduced only by bishops and no general assembly, and moreover contrary to the confession of faith, 'cannot be received', he wrote. Hope was not so much suggesting debate; far from thinking in the same political terms as Traquair, he was asserting one particular argument.[71]

The Traquair counsels were secret and Charles was even less prepared to

---

[67] Spottiswood, *History*, vol. I, pp. cxxiii–cxxiv; Hope, *Diary*, pp. 69–70; cf. Bod. Bankes Ms. 65/28d.
[68] Spottiswood, *History*, vol. I, pp. cxxvi–cxxvii.
[69] Hope, *Diary*, pp. 69–70. For Patrick Maule, see *HMC 5*, p. 637.
[70] Johnston, *Diary*, pp. 292, 295.
[71] GD 45/1/30 (dated 13 January). See too another important paper, 'Anent the estate of the kirk of Scotland' – GD 45/1/54.

allow publicly the journey of the Lord Treasurer for the purposes of presenting more petitions; Traquair's official warrant to travel south was for
Exchequer business.[72] The earl had struggled in Edinburgh, and he would
struggle even more around Whitehall. His sense of affinity with the Supplicants, particularly his peers among them, although it had taken him so far in
one direction, had left probably an ideological gap, and certainly a political
one. At Court he was no more comfortable. His need to keep the king's trust
constrained his manœuvrings and obliged a course which was as difficult to
alter at source as it was to effect in Scotland.

   The serious tensions within the Scottish council had their part to play. In his
own later account at his trial, Traquair conveniently telescoped the story of
his conflicts with the bishops by omitting nearly all discussion of their joint
enterprise of conciliating the Supplicants.[73] As Sir Robert Spottiswood on
behalf of the bishops did his best to discredit him – if Nithsdale had not done
the job already – in a sense this truly represented the outcome of affairs. In
Court, English observers questioned Traquair's loyalty.[74] Traquair had far
better support from the Earl of Roxburgh, who wrote from Edinburgh to the
Marquis of Hamilton of his overriding concern to avert dangers he saw
threatening;[75] but Charles, above all detesting the challenge he saw to his
authority, was unsympathetic to the projected settlement. He gave Traquair
instead a warrant for a new proclamation.

   A further paper of advice written by the earl at this time tried to make
Charles fully aware of the dangers in his preferred course. If the king would
not answer the petitions nor state an intention to try the allegations in them
against the service-book and canons, 'which has been the cause and beginning of all that is passed', old pretexts for opposition would remain valid.
And if, secondly, Charles was resolved to proceed to try his opponents, it
would be taken that opposition to the service-book was a punishable offence,
and therefore all means possible would be employed to prevent its being used
again. The conclusion was obvious, that troubles would not cease. Traquair
raised thirdly a possibility that the Advocate and other advocates with him
might not enforce Charles's commands, and that it might not be legally
possible to override their judgements.[76]

   The new proclamation took little stock of such words, nor much

[72] Traqr. Ms. 4/104; GD 406/1/1311; BL Add. Ms. 23112, fol. 78v (Traqr. Ms. 4/94 –
Windebank holograph, unusually); GD 406/1/8309.
[73] Traqr. Mss. Bundle 26[iii] (defence around the second article).
[74] BL Add. Ms. 27962H, fol. 108v; Add. Ms. 15391, fols. 73–4; *CSPV 1636–9*, pp. 379, 387.
[75] GD 406/1/1311.
[76] Traqr. Mss. Bundle 27 (endorsed 'Inst. Feb. 1638'; Traquair holograph, signed) – printed in
Sir W. Fraser, *History of the Carnegies Earls of Southesk and their Kindred* (2 vols.,
Edinburgh, 1867), vol. I, pp. 97–8.

apparently of the 'Memorial'; Patrick Maule's opinion that it was substantially composed before even the Lord President arrived in Court may have been correct.[77] Charles reaffirmed for the public his personal, royal approval of the Scottish liturgy, which was 'a ready means to maintain the true religion already professed, and beat out all superstitions'. There was no positive provision for pressing the use of the book, but neither was there an indication that revision would be considered. The proclamation sternly berated those who had kept meetings in the past to organise petitions, and warned that any future petitions should not run in prejudice of royal authority; future convocations were now forbidden upon pain of treason. The king took on board only a small part of the advice from Scotland.[78]

Charles also sent a letter to the council to reprimand them for receiving petitions in his view more derogatory to authority than conducive to peace; kings deserved loyalty and obedience. The preservation of the king's authority, he continued, was the only means to peace.[79] In Edinburgh Sir John Hay would have reason to be pleased, and so apparently would Nithsdale. Once again 'fair generals' masked unspoken intentions in the royal proclamation text; and the Earl of Mar was to be approached quietly to assess the strength of Stirling and Edinburgh Castles.[80]

Traquair later recollected a frank interchange with Charles in criticism of the proclamation that possibly had a basis in historical fact; but however daring Traquair was in counsel, the king was not to be easily blocked.[81] As had happened in the 1626 debates, the prerogative was urgently to be defended – and clarification of the legal position was sought in support of the line already determined. Traquair was asked to write out questions for the three leading advocates in Edinburgh, possibly deriving from his own challenges. The offence in law of the popular convocations was one subject; and, with the Edinburgh problem in mind, it was asked how the violent troublemakers could be punished. The two other queries opened up broader issues – the standing of any persons, especially breakers of the peace, corresponding with foreigners or 'subjects of his Majesty's other kingdoms' without leave; and the question whether any statute in force obliged the king *not* to set down a 'decent way for the service of God'. The king of England and Ireland was alert to the Scottish example being infectious; and he addressed the statutory definition of his royal supremacy in Scotland so as to find the best means of

---

[77] *HMC 5*, p. 637.
[78] Printed in [Charles I], *Large Declaration*, pp. 46–8; Stevenson, *Scottish Revolution*, pp. 80–1.
[79] *RPCS*, 2nd Series, vol. VII, pp. 15–16.
[80] Complete secrecy was not however achieved! GD 406/1/982; *HMC Mar and Kellie* (60), p. 195; GD 406/M9/41.
[81] Traqr. Mss. Trial VIII, and Bundle 26[iii]. Cf. GD 406/1/981; *CSVP 1636–9*, p. 379.

overriding the appeal being made to national assemblies. The paper closed by enabling the Chancellor, Treasurer and Privy Seal to compose any further questions thought fitting. Despite rejecting the projected settlement, Charles still had certain uses for his men on the spot.[82]

Charles heard and knew a great deal about the trouble, but it was for him to lead. Traquair's advice was put aside, and he, the royal servant, was called upon to obey. For a king concerned about three-kingdom uniformity, it was worrying that there were the first indications of Scottish propaganda, even anti-episcopal material, circulating in England.[83] The trouble was to be dealt with at root. Charles looked for law by which he might enforce the rights of his case as he understood them; but law was not necessarily on his side. The Supplicants were already committed to searching for a case.[84]

The advocates Charles questioned ruled against convocations without legal warrant, but one, Sir Thomas Nicholson, observed a possible loophole for the Supplicants – gatherings *super re licita et ob bonum finem*. Might any of those gatherings since July be justified, given that all three advocates referred the determination of church policy in some measure to the general assemblies and parliaments? The advocates were cautious. Sir Thomas Hope in his prime position kept his answers brief; Sir Lewis Stewart allowed just a little more ground on the king's side. None dared to limit explicitly the sovereign's powers, but Sir Thomas Nicholson again observed that good kings lived by the laws, as they swore to do at their coronations.[85]

One of a supplementary triad of questions, also signed by Charles in January 1638, deserves final notice. It was asked 'whether the combination of subjects by oath to take part one with another, even if quarrelled [i.e. argued] by law, is warrantable'.[86] The new royal proclamation would set off the chain of events that led to the signing of the National Covenant. There the greatest legal care would be used to underpin the very course against which Charles was opposed. Law could be employed either way.[87] Mutual banding around a common confession of faith would have the effect of imposing conditions on Charles's government of the Scottish church. Talk of the Negative Confession of 1581 was in the air, and so perhaps also talk of a common subscription.

---

[82] Traqr. Ms. 4/95 (*HMC 9 (II)*, p. 248).
[83] The piece, 'No alteration', was referred to in the third question: for the text of this, see, for example, NLS Ms. 20775, fol. 173. I discuss the British dimension at some length in chapter 5 below.
[84] Rothes, *Relation*, p. 43; Johnston, *Diary*, pp. 309, 312.
[85] Traqr. Ms. 14/3.
[86] Traqr. Ms. 4/95.
[87] Williamson, *Scottish National Consciousness*, pp. 140–3; S. A. Burrell, 'The Covenant idea as a revolutionary symbol: Scotland, 1596–1637', *Church History*, 27 (1958), 338–50. Charles subsequently used the Act anent Bands on his side – [Charles I], *Large Declaration*, pp. 71–2.

There was almost an anticipation of the event in the king's question – and an indication that Charles would have little patience with it.

Traquair returned to Scotland beset with the difficulties of the situation. It was not easy to reconcile the contradictions between his advice for the troubles and the proclamation he carried with him, but he made a solid effort to serve the king. Speaking at length with Rothes on 17 February 1638, he did not reveal the contents of the proclamation, and tried to extract information on how far the Supplicants had organised themselves with legal help; the questions to the three advocates from the king were given over that same day.[88] The attempt to make the proclamation at Stirling free from disturbance was an elaborate operation. Traquair and Roxburgh actually managed to persuade Rothes and the Earl of Wemyss to undertake that there would be no protest, but when these changed their minds, they left in the middle of the night to avoid disturbance.[89] When this was then discovered, the proclamation was hurriedly issued on 20 February, even though the council was not quorate. On the next day the council was more fully attended, and the proclamation was ratified, but with great difficulty; the Advocate, Sir Thomas Hope, abstained. He argued that his signature was not necessary, but it was a gesture of solidarity with the Supplicants.[90]

The Supplicants argued that this new explicit avowal of the service-book by the king had been advised by the bishops. Again they tried to present a declinator, but, meeting with predictable refusal, offered instead a protestation – in other words a public statement of their position which blatantly bypassed the obstructiveness of the privy council. The hold of Charles's government was breaking. The officers of state, Traquair and Roxburgh, were now in disgrace. After the proclamation was published, there were further readings of the protestation, including in Linlithgow and Stirling.[91]

Archibald Johnston denied that he had seen the proclamation in advance by Traquair's means, and it does not seem necessary to doubt him. The Supplicants could make an informed guess at its contents since the Earl of Haddington's news from Court, received in Scotland by 8 February, bore bad tidings.[92] 'God's Providence' had been twice kind, however, in providing the main points of the proclamation and then the queries for the advocates for Johnston; and, in the early hours of 19 February, Lord Lindsay's care to keep tabs on Traquair had paid off. Sir Thomas Hope might be suspected of being

88 Rothes, *Relation*, pp. 54–5, 62–3; GD 112/40/2/1/119–20; *HMC 9 (II)*, p. 254.
89 *HMC 9 (II)*, p. 259; Johnston, *Diary*, p. 316; Rothes, *Relation*, p. 63; GD 45/1/32; Yorke, *State Papers*, vol. II, pp. 97–9.
90 GD 45/1/35; Rothes, *Relation*, pp. 64–6.
91 Rothes, *Relation*, pp. 57–67, 88–9; GD 26/10/14–15.
92 Baillie, *Letters*, vol. I, p. 50; Johnston, *Diary*, p. 312. Cf. Stevenson, *Scottish Revolution*, p. 80.

the not unwilling instrument of Providence; he saw the proclamation before Johnston knew it, and of course was a recipient of the queries.[93] Traquair and Roxburgh, notably assisted by Sir Lewis Stewart and not Hope, spoke to Johnston on the 23rd, to recommend a submissive course. Johnston rejected the idea – and received as his next visitors nobles who asked him to be the author of a band to be joined to the historic 1581 Negative Confession. Feelings of insecurity were heightened in the aftermath of the proclamation. It was apt that a lawyer together with a minister were given the charge of preparing a statement of both defence and vision.[94]

The National Covenant emerged on 28 February 1638, fundamentally assaulting the thinking that had led finally to the service-book. At its heart was the Negative Confession, so called because of its violent denunciation of the various popish 'errors' rejected in the reformation. Another section cited at length the statutes which had established that reformation in Scotland. Most importantly there was a band by which people might pledge commitment to the place of free assemblies and parliaments in determining the shape of the Scottish church, where truth would be upheld; with argument that the liturgy and other perceived 'innovations' recently complained of were unacceptable, it talked of defence of 'the true religion' alongside the king's authority. This was to be a covenant with God.[95]

Theology evidently was only a part of the process. The evangelical faith of a reformed church was affirmed in the face of popery but there was an equally prominent appeal to the legislation confirming that reformation in Scotland. This directed a political point, but the comprehensiveness of the legal case was not without problems. Robert Baillie went to some length to clarify that subscription did not entail the final rejection of episcopacy. He believed that he secured as much, and in written argument to persuade subscription argued the same; but the quoted parliamentary legislation of the Covenant remained ambiguous – recent Scottish history had fluctuated on the issue. Loud criticism of bishops prevailed and, though a clear-cut presbyterian case from the Covenant needed more, Baillie's efforts suggested that talk was in the air. The Five Articles of Perth, enacted in the parliament of 1621, remained semisecure on account of their statutory form – but were open to challenge as recent innovation.[96] Crucially at this point, propaganda directed to woo

93 Johnston, *Diary*, pp. 316–17; Rothes, *Relation*, p. 63; Hope, *Diary*, p. 70 (the date should probably be 15 February); GD 45/1/35; GD 112/40/2/1/28.
94 Johnston, *Diary*, pp. 318–19; Rothes, *Relation*, pp. 69–70; Baillie, *Letters*, vol. I, p. 50.
95 The text of the Covenant is accessible in W. C. Dickinson, G. Donaldson and I. A. Milne (eds.), *A Source Book of Scottish History* (3 vols., Edinburgh, 1958–61), vol. III, pp. 95–104.
96 Baillie, *Letters*, vol. I, pp. 52–4; NLS Wod. 4to. 24, fols. 108–15 or NLS Adv. Ms. 29.2.8, fols. 263–4; Rothes, *Relation*, pp. 69–80, 90–2; Johnston, *Diary*, pp. 318–23, 332–3; NLS Wod. Fo. 64, fols. 207–10.

support clearly discriminated between those already committed to protest and others it was now hoped to bring in. Nonconformity tended towards power politics. There was a great concern for unity; all together were called upon to desist from practice according to the Five Articles.[97] Determination of the ambiguities was left appropriately to the hoped-for national assemblies; for the ways of reformation leaders would hope to secure agreement.

Banding was a historic practice which James VI and I might have hoped finally to have outlawed. The Covenant text insisted that even fighting in mutual defence of 'the true religion, liberties and laws of the kingdom' was within the context of loyalty to the king: but in effect it made this conditional on Charles concurring in the cause. For some it was almost too much to take, and the text was closely debated. Charles was right in taking this section above all as the most dangerous to his authority. He was being asked to submit himself to the Covenant's imperatives. Direction from below was something Charles could not in any manner accept.[98]

The clash of interests between a king of three kingdoms and his Scottish subjects was of crisis proportions. More alert and active than most on the Covenant side, the young, enthusiastic Johnston of Wariston worked hard. His inspiration in political thought was probably widely derived in European as well as Scottish history; above all his zeal for what he thought to be the truth privately upheld him. It was important also to those who led against the present counsels of the king that so many concurred in seeing them as wrong. Considerable feeling against recent policies for the church had appeared and, though the Covenant was lengthy and technical, it laid a claim to national support by answering an evident need. The movement which took off from this powerful statement explicitly opposed the subversion of true religion through popery – popery which in affecting 'liberties, laws and estates' demanded concrete resistance. The protest was potentially open to all kinds of interests but the considerable effort in its organisation, already well begun, continued to employ many of the foremost Supplicants. Although many hesitated to join, Charles had moved the privy council away from Edinburgh and the Covenanters, dominating there, set about raising a voluntary contribution for funding. It tended towards a general upset of the king's government.[99]

Hindsight, however, should not hide the complexities of the times. Charles's Scottish counsel could still hope that some accommodation might

---

[97] Rothes, *Relation*, pp. 67–8, 73–5 (cf. p. 91!); Johnston, *Diary*, p. 323.
[98] Baillie, *Letters*, vol. I, pp. 53–4; see also the draft of the third section in NLS Wod. Fo. 64, fol. 210. For discussions, see Makey, *Church of the Covenant*, pp. 26–30; Williamson, *Scottish National Consciousness*, esp. pp. 140–3; Stevenson, *Scottish Revolution*, pp. 82–6.
[99] Johnston, *Diary*, pp. 319–24; Rothes, *Relation*, pp. 72–3, 79–81.

be found to redress the collapse of order. Despite serious problems within the privy council on account of Charles's proclamation, there were no overt defections. Traquair and Roxburgh's sense of aggravation, although the Covenanters did not acknowledge it, led them to send to the Marquis of Hamilton, hoping that he might persuade Charles to reconsider. Traquair told of how he was attacked now like a bishop. He argued that the service-book could only be imposed with blood; that it would be easier to 'establish the Missal'.[100] The counsel was not unreasonable. Only a little later Traquair reported that the Covenanters were buying up muskets and powder, possibly even from Holland.[101] Roxburgh was no less insistent, fearful that the king had been led to misunderstand the seriousness of the situation.[102]

While the Covenant was being signed in Edinburgh, the privy council in Stirling voted that the cause of the troubles was the fear of innovations in religion by the service-book and canons and High Commission. Therefore the king was to be advised to take trial of these, suspending them meanwhile from use. Sir John Hamilton of Orbiston, the Justice-clerk, was given the embassy, with other councillors to follow if further persuasion was required. Traquair and Roxburgh wrote personally to Charles, which the council supported by asking at least Hamilton and Morton at Court to lend their assistance.[103] Traquair's former settlement lay at the origins of this, but in his own letters to both Charles and Hamilton he advised the simple removal of the three 'innovations'.[104] The difference was explained by the need for a little political manœuvring. Spottiswood had supported laying aside the service-book for the sake of public order, so that he joined his signature to the instructions to Orbiston, but he still esteemed the fears of innovating religion to be 'false'; Bishop Whitford made a vain effort to evade signing altogether. Traquair took pains to get the episcopal backing, while at the same time fending off for a second time the Marquis of Huntly, their hoped-for ally. Nothing was said on bishops or the Perth Articles.[105]

Sir Thomas Hope included his support for a review of church policy, like the other councillors warning of 'fearful consequences' without it. In another note to Patrick Maule – 'to present to his sacred Majesty', if thought fit – Hope explained what the council had done, and entrusted the business to the king's justice, affirming Charles's sovereign place 'as God's lieutenant'. Hope

[100] Baillie, *Letters*, vol. I, p. 50; GD 406/1/982, 983.
[101] GD 406/1/971, 981. Cf. Baillie, *Letters*, vol. I, p. 71; *RPCS*, 2nd Series, vol. VII, p. 9; GD 406/1/521.
[102] GD 406/1/8308.
[103] *RPCS*, 2nd Series, vol. VII, pp. 7–11, 456–7; G. Burnet, *The Memoires of the Lives and Actions of James and William, Dukes of Hamilton and Castleherald . . .* (1677), pp. 36–7.
[104] Burnet, *Memoires*, pp. 36–7; Yorke, *State Papers*, vol. II, p. 101.
[105] *RPCS*, 2nd Series, vol. VII, pp. 7, 9; Traqr. Ms. 37/9; GD 406/1/971; GD 112/39/717. On Huntly, see Traqr. Ms. 41/8; Rothes, *Relation*, pp. 62–3.

was sending his answer to the king's queries on legal points, but he wanted to emphasise further that the king's mercy and compassion should be shown to his subjects, who had admittedly proceeded with some irregularity in the way of their supplications; private offence should be set aside and attention given rather to God's glory and the truth of religion. Hope therefore advised a public declaration to clear the fears of the king's subjects of being tried for their 'convocations, mutinies, tumults'.[106]

Charles returned Orbiston with permission for Roxburgh and Traquair to come south. He announced his 'surprise' that the council seemed to be advising a change in the church government established by King James; he had his own case but offered to listen to the perceptions of those on the spot.[107] The privy council confirmed their former instructions that wished the legal trial of the service-book, and referred also to James's use of assemblies and parliaments. The 'heavy and fearful estate' of the country was to be shown.[108]

Independently the signatories of the Covenant had resolved to make their own approaches to the king. A letter was written to the three leading nobles at Court, Lennox, Hamilton and Morton, who were asked, in respect of the past failure of the privy council, to prosecute the just cause of grievances by presenting a petition to the king.[109] The courtiers were chosen for their leading rank more than for any certain knowledge of their sympathy. The Covenanters, however, learning of the privy council's work, altered course, choosing then to send up the petition with the statesmen. The responsibility thus regained by Traquair and Roxburgh came to them though as something of a burden, since the paper of demands received from the Covenanters clearly went further than they might have wished: they supposed rightly that the king would not be easily persuaded.[110]

Though counsel to the king was becoming more forthright, it fell short of the Covenanters' demands. They, wary of the ways of compromise, formulated desires in a paper given to Lord Lorne to carry south. The substance of the articles, like the Covenant drafted by Wariston and Alexander Henderson, took just a little further proposals for remedy of grievances short and long term. With the council agenda described as insufficient they asked for settlement of the church through a general assembly and parliament; for a complete discharge of the court of high commission, not merely its limitation; for relief from urging of the Five Articles of Perth; for trial of bishops and

---

[106] GD 406/1/971, 973; GD 45/1/44. [107] *RPCS*, 2nd Series, vol. VII, p. 17.

[108] *HMC 9 (II)*, p. 254.

[109] M. Napier (ed.), *Memorials of Montrose and his Times*, MC (2 vols., Edinburgh, 1848–51), vol. I, pp. 245–7 (NLS Ms. 80, no. 80, 3(?) March); D. Dalrymple, *Memorials and Letters Relating to the History of Britain in the Reign of Charles the First* (Glasgow, 1766), p. 24. Lord Lindsay added a personal note for the Marquis of Hamilton – GD 406/1/521.

[110] Johnston, *Diary*, p. 324; Rothes, *Relation*, p. 96.

other ministers through the discipline of a general assembly; for the future
annual meeting of general assemblies according to the act of the 1610
Glasgow Assembly; for limiting the votes of ministers in parliaments according to the caveats of the 1600 Montrose Assembly; and for the free admission
of ministers – without 'unlawful' oaths and by presbyteries as freely as by
bishops. These were the words; countable as progress in terms of action were
admissions of excluded ministers by presbytery and the 'proper' administration of communion.[111]

Traquair was rather less sure of his ground in going south than he had been
in January. It was he who had advised that Lord Lorne accompany him.[112]
Lorne's usefulness in talks with the Supplicants doubtless gave Traquair
hopes of his eloquence; if the risk was of royal disfavour, the Lord Treasurer
himself would perhaps live to fight on. Problems with the bishops threatened
the latter. Two days' talks with Archbishop Spottiswood before Traquair
departed did nothing to stop an episcopal delegation setting off likewise for
Court, including Sir John Hay and Sir Robert Spottiswood.[113]

Archibald Johnston had hopes and fears for Lorne's journey at the beginning of April 1638. The young lord's influence in the west of Scotland was
potentially very important, although the signing of the Covenant went on
fairly happily without him.[114] Lorne knew too well the risk of losing the
king's favour, for himself and the public good. His subsequent report to the
prominent Campbell Covenanter, Lord Loudoun, was that at Court he
advised a policy of concessions, while colleagues, Traquair and Roxburgh,
tendered advice negative towards the Supplicants – 'all that the king would
have done'. However accurate the distinction, Traquair was obliged to fend
off attacks from the bishops, which may have restricted him in his talks with
Charles, and Lorne later gave more favourable accounts of him; they
travelled back north together, in a coach with the Bishop of Galloway![115]

Lorne's words to Loudoun about the importance of the Supplicants listening to 'honest men's advice' suggested hopes for accommodation on some
middle ground.[116] Another like strategy, expressed possibly by Sir Thomas
Hope, was that the way of solution should be drawn from the Supplicants'
petitions, they being careful to petition within the laws of the kingdom: 'His

---

[111] Rothes, *Relation*, pp. 69–71, 96–8; Johnston, *Diary*, pp. 330, 334–5, 338–40. Cf. Makey,
       Church of the Covenant, pp. 29–31.
[112] Yorke, *State Papers*, vol. II, p. 106; GD 406/1/1311, 8169, 8222, 973. See too Baillie,
       Letters, vol. I, p. 70.
[113] GD 112/39/720; Baillie, *Letters*, vol. I, p. 70; Johnston, *Diary*, p. 332.
[114] GD 112/1/510; GD 112/39/720, 725, 490. For varying Campbell action, see GD
       112/40/2/1/4, 28, 123.
[115] Traqr. Ms. 12/41; GD 112/39/724; Baillie, *Letters*, vol. I, pp. 464–5, 73–4; GD
       406/M9/61/12. Cf. Stevenson, *Scottish Revolution*, pp. 88–9.
[116] Baillie, *Letters*, vol. I, p. 465.

Majesty as sovereign prince and God's lieutenant on earth is tied to proceed by way of justice and to lay their grievances and complaints unto the square and line of the acts and laws of the kingdom, which is a general that none can put in question.' The author went on to extract main particulars of the points demanded – that nothing might be introduced into the kirk without the consent of a lawful assembly and ratification by parliament, hence the present request for both and justification for the present requests for the service-book, canons and High Commission to be declared void, for ministers to be admitted without oaths and – Hope's common concern – for pardon of any punishable offence in their proceedings to date.[117]

This summary omitted detail of the positive Covenanter demands, but still it exceeded what Charles felt able to offer. Moreover, coercive enforcement was offered to him as an alternative to concession. In January 1638, the young Catholic Earl of Antrim, Randal MacDonnell, had wished to offer Charles service with arms.[118] The Earl of Nithsdale formulated a wider scheme, enjoying support apparently from the queen.[119] Nithsdale's proposal was for a three-prong offensive, with strikes at Leith, Aberdeen and Ayr. Detesting the policy of delay, he pointed to the Scots' own accumulation of armed strength in order to emphasise the manifest disloyalty, in his view, of the privy councillors. If Charles from England was to reign peacefully in Scotland, he had to send home all of his Scottish nobles to gather their friends in a show of royal strength; armies should be sent to follow them, if possible all to land on one day. Nithsdale was less interested in how these troops (presumably English and Irish) should get to the Scottish rendezvous, but he did detail which Scottish nobles should join together at each point. Forces from Ireland should land in Ayr and Nithsdale himself with the Duke of Lennox, the Marquis of Douglas, the Earls of Abercorn, Dumfries and Galloway and Lords Sempill and Herries should join there – an almost entirely Catholic front.[120] Lorne, whose estates would otherwise have included him, was moreover explicitly excepted; 'considering all the Campbells are the most ingrained Puritans in Scotland' he should rather join with the group at Leith, with, among others, the Marquis of Hamilton, also a western landowner. The Covenanters were to have no warning of the offensive. 'Puritan' commanders for the troops were to be avoided, and, for the defence of

---

[117] GD 45/1/53 (*c.* April 1638?).
[118] BL Add. Ms. 15391, fol. 31.
[119] BL Add. Ms. 15391, fol. 128. Cf. C. Hibbard, *Charles I and the Popish Plot* (Chapel Hill, NC, 1983), pp. 96–7.
[120] Of the exceptions, Lennox was not a Catholic although he had Catholic family connections; the Earl of Galloway joined the Covenanters at the Glasgow Assembly; the Earl of Dumfries's position is unknown to me, other than that he tried to procure subscriptions of the King's Covenant in October 1638.

England, the Lords Marshal and Admiral (Arundel and Northumberland) were 'in a careless way' to be prepared.[121]

The scheme had its attractions, but at the same time Charles turned to the idea of a Commissioner, or perhaps more accurately turned to his friend, the Marquis of Hamilton. This had the effect of further weakening the role of the privy council in Scotland.[122] The Commissioner would act instead as the king's representative. The delegated responsibility necessitated close instructions; but discretion allowed to the Commissioner would also enable decisive action. In crisis Charles assumed the reins of government in a more personal way than yet seen.

Hamilton was a natural choice. His birth and estates made his interest in Scotland. With fairly close friendship and trust from the king his cousin, he had been used most recently by Charles as collector of his Scottish taxation, an assignment still uncompleted; he had military experience. The times called for ever greater participation by the courtier Scots in Scottish events, but Hamilton seems to have resisted his special appointment.[123] Was it simply the difficulty of the situation? He was if anything less attuned to the Covenanting spirit than the Earl of Traquair. With a pragmatism more amenable to compromise than any highly pitched ideology, he nevertheless accepted a role for solving the troubles; his sense of the best course, for himself and for his country, gave the king a servant who played a major part in shaping royal policy over the next three years and beyond.[124]

The decision to send Hamilton as Commissioner seems to have been made in the first two weeks of April 1638, very shortly after the arrival of the delegation from Scotland, but not until 18 May was work finished on the king's new declarations and instructions.[125] Originally Hamilton was to publish a declaration that overtly advanced very little the king's previous position on concessions. The offer was not to enforce the canons or the service-book except fairly, in a way that would satisfy subjects that no innovation was intended, a condition too ambiguous to give immediate satisfaction; the High

---

[121] NLS Ms. 9303, fol. 17. The stratagem of adding English force to loyal Scots nobles and their followings was somehow reported to the Covenanters, and its inspiration fastened on the Scottish bishops – Baillie, *Letters*, vol. I, pp. 65, 70–1.

[122] Cf. Hamilton's Instructions I, IV – Burnet, *Memoires*, pp. 50–1. (SRO Hamilton Red Book i, 64. Here the numbering and spelling are different, but I have kept to Burnet's edition for convenience.)

[123] S. R. Gardiner (ed.), *The Hamilton Papers*, Camden Society (1880), pp. 15–16, although also see p. 2.

[124] There is a biography in H. L. Rubinstein, *Captain Luckless. James, First Duke of Hamilton, 1606–1649* (1975); much more work remains to be done, especially with reference to the huge manuscript archive.

[125] Eleazar Borthwick, who delivered news of the commission, was ready to leave London on 16 April – *CSPD 1637–8*, 387/85; cf. Rothes, *Relation*, p. 103. On the delay, see Stevenson, *Scottish Revolution*, p. 93.

Commission's activities were to be overseen by the privy council. A pardon was offered for what was past. The main point was that the king expected all signed Covenants or 'bands' to be given up without exception. Charles took these to strike against monarchy itself.[126]

Hamilton's instructions were defined through a long set of queries that he put to the king. The answers made clear that force was to be used where necessary to compel obedience. Charles was not prepared to be generous to all Covenanters, only to some whom he would receive back.[127] The king thus made exceptions, just as in the 1620s he had seen a troublesome core in his English parliaments at the root of his problems. His notion of the obedience due badly clouded his judgement of almost any protest, and almost inevitably exacerbated his troubles. Those alienated in England, particularly those fearful for the good of the church, would watch with interest the persistence of the excepted Covenanters; the king's advisers would urge him in the face of their opposition to be conciliatory.[128]

Archbishop Spottiswood gave his advice on how Hamilton should carry himself in Scotland. The commission might take as a model one given to the Earl of Montrose shortly after the Union – with an extension to allow Hamilton to assemble armed men in case of rebellion. Hamilton should take care to be well accompanied, presumably a safeguard against intimidation as well as appropriate to his honour. Spottiswood insisted that the king should offer no public capitulation – although he might hold out the resolution of giving satisfaction on the service-book if the Covenanters did their duty. The essential point was to have the Covenants surrendered, but Spottiswood advised a slight modification of the policy. People should be labouring to divide the opponents until the royal declaration was published, for it seemed dangerous to risk the latter part, about the Covenants, being known before there were certain divisions that might give a hope of enforcing it.[129]

Traquair likewise discussed the risk involved should the second part of the declaration be published prematurely, and he suggested that the first part, which would mitigate the fury of the people, should be issued first, and only when that fury had died down should the second part be made known. He was obliged to write his comments after returning to Scotland – apparently, on account of the bishops' attacks, less able to speak his mind whilst at Court.[130]

[126] Burnet, *Memoires*, pp. 43–4.
[127] Query no. 21 – Burnet, *Memoires*, p. 48.
[128] R. Cust, *The Forced Loan and English Politics 1626–1628* (Oxford, 1987), pp. 16–23, 87–90. I am very grateful to Dr Cust for also sharing unpublished work on Charles's thought with me.
[129] GD 406/M9/88/3.
[130] Yorke, *State Papers*, vol. II, pp. 107–9 – letter to Hamilton. Draft is Traqr. Ms. 12/24.

Practical advice was heeded. The Scots at Court were told to repair home to give support, hopefully by their bringing followings in strength, and the king sent letters to be distributed to possible noble supporters.[131] Hamilton wrote on 7 May to encourage many to meet him on his arrival; two of these letters which survive were written to already committed Covenanters – which pointed to the common problem of assessing accurately the Scottish situation from Court.[132] A second declaration was also composed, and approved by the king, that indeed did not directly ask for the surrender of the Covenants. In a way it was hardly a concession. Six weeks were allowed under the first declaration for the surrender.[133] Under the second, the bands were still to be delivered up, but the phrasing was less explicit. It was after the six weeks that Hamilton was to issue a warning for obedience on this, but then within eight days, and as before on pain of a charge of treason.[134]

The changes were aimed to break more effectively the unity amongst the Supplicants. The king's public statement remained vaguely couched, but behind it there were possibilities for progress. A short set of accompanying instructions, dated 17 May, laid the emphasis on conciliation. Hamilton was left free to negotiate in his own words. The scheme hinged on whether the others would cooperate in abandoning the Covenant. At worst, it was hoped only a remnant would need to be pursued under the force of the law.[135]

The king assumed that the lawyers could uphold his course of action. He seemed to go far in agreeing to a policy of moderate concessions; there was talk even of indicting a general assembly. Bishops had concurred in advising as much.[136] Although either declaration was available for Hamilton's use, Charles had taken some real steps towards settlement. Hamilton had to press for the surrender of the Covenants, but otherwise could offer progress on the subjects complained about. However, counsel had made ground rather late, and in strange partnership. Charles's promises left him that freedom of movement which was potentially destabilising. His decision that the Covenant was an act of rebellion could only be provocative. Furthermore, at the very same time that he allowed a policy of settlement by division, he instructed Hamilton that he would come north in person with English forces if need be

---

[131] Baillie, *Letters*, vol. I, p. 76; SRO Hamilton Red Book i, 65; GD 406/1/523, 727.
[132] To the Earl of Eglinton and Lord Balcarres – Sir W. Fraser, *Memorials of the Montgomeries Earls of Eglinton* (2 vols., Edinburgh, 1859), vol. I, p. 238; NLS Crawford Ms. 14/6/37. Campbell of Glenorchy was also clearly invited – GD 112/40/2/1/127.
[133] Instruction XXII – Burnet, *Memoires*, p. 51.
[134] SRO Hamilton Red Book i, 66, 90; Burnet, *Memoires*, pp. 44–5. (SRO Hamilton Red Book i, 62; Gardiner, *Hamilton Papers*, pp. 2–3, corrected Burnet on the number of days but misread the date, which was 18, not 28 May.)
[135] SRO Hamilton Red Book i, 65.
[136] Instruction IX – Burnet, *Memoires*, p. 50; cf. Gardiner, *Hamilton Papers*, p. 2.

– 'resolved to suffer my life rather than to suffer authority to be contemned'.[137] Accommodation and force were spoken of together.

The option of settlement by conquest required various preparations. In Scotland priority was given to securing castles and fortifications. Spottiswood had mentioned this, advising that the Earl of Mar be replaced in Edinburgh. Traquair on his arrival in Edinburgh reported stores and victuals ready for Edinburgh and Stirling Castles; ammunition followed him by sea.[138] In England military preparations began before Hamilton left Court, with something like the Nithsdale plan in sight. Hamilton discussed the potential usefulness of the Earl of Antrim; and he was also expected to advise Sir Henry Vane on the size of frigates to be built to transport English soldiers north.[139] Subsequent correspondence considered that the king would himself come north; six thousand men would be sent to Leith; forces would be put on the English borders; there would be an Irish dimension. The Earl of Arundel would be given responsibility for affairs in the north of England.[140]

There were, therefore, two facets to Hamilton's commission, since he was to work for recovering obedience to the king and yet also advise on the needs for the way of force.[141] How much would the latter be necessary? Threats would be made from the first.[142] It would be a hard commission to settle Scotland; he did not doubt that. In Scotland, in the light of snippets of news filtering through, conflicting assessments of Hamilton prefigured the ambiguities and doubts which would characterise his commission – politics, in Sir Philip Warwick's phrase, of 'serpentine winding'.[143] Hamilton's effort would be directed somehow to bringing together king and subjects. It was a task of greater difficulty than he ever imagined.

Charles's councillors appreciated that the liturgical policy had been a mistake, some more readily than others – some indeed as strongly moved as the Covenanters themselves. However, before the scope of the troubles became clear, the divisions within the administration hindered its coordination of a

---

[137] Instruction XXIII – Burnet, *Memoires*, p. 51.
[138] GD 406/M9/88/3; Yorke, *State Papers*, vol. II, p. 109.
[139] GD 406/1/1156, 7543; Gardiner, *Hamilton Papers*, pp. 12–13; Hibbard, *Charles I and the Popish Plot*, pp. 97–8. Cf. Laud, *Works*, vol. VII, pp. 455, 571.
[140] W. Knowler (ed.), *The Earl of Strafforde's Letters and Dispatches* (2 vols., 1739), vol. II, p. 181; Laud, *Works*, vol. VII, p. 444; BL Add. Ms. 15391, fols. 191, 205, 317.
[141] Cf. Makey, *Church of the Covenant*, p. 32, where Laud's role is, I suggest, exaggerated; see also Gardiner, *Hamilton Papers*, p. 1.
[142] Cf. BL Add. Ms. 15391, fol. 164v.
[143] NLS Wod. 4to. 25, fol. 14v; Baillie, *Letters*, vol. I, p. 71; Sir P. Warwick, *Memoires of the Reigne of King Charles I* (1701), p. 104; P. Heylyn, *Cyprianus Anglicus* (1668), p. 370; W. Sanderson, *A Compleat History of the Life and Raigne of King Charles . . .* (1658), pp. 226–7; *The Memoirs of Henry Guthry, Late Bishop of Dunkeld* (Glasgow, 1747), p. 38. For contemporaries in England, the attacks grew sharper particularly after December 1638.

cure. This made a difference initially more to the king than to the people because it gave at least part of an explanation for the problems. Traquair dominated the Scottish council as far as he was able, but, having revelled in the opportunity to cast slurs on disliked episcopal colleagues, his strenuous efforts to find a solution to the troubles were marred by continuing mutual distrust. Other differences within the privy council had Sir Thomas Hope's ideas vying with calls for punishment and persecution.[144] While it was pleaded that Charles be well informed, he for his part had a plurality of options at hand. In Scotland much happened without him. But he was slow and ambiguous in his response – except in his readiness to condemn.

The fateful policies had been conceived in narrow terms with the assumption that royal declaration would secure obedience. The lesson that this was not the case took time to penetrate. It is understandable that Charles wished merely to disperse the trouble – even that he readily resorted to persecution before pardon or concession. However, as this exacerbated the situation, at least half the problem was that he never truly changed course. The king had high honour and authority, but exercise of power depended on more than that. Meanwhile, parishes had joined in supplicating against the service-book; crowds in Edinburgh had witnessed impressive assemblies around a common cause. The Lord Chancellor, bearer of the highest royal honour, was greatly disturbed; from the beginning of 1638 he was pleading to be allowed to retire.[145] The Supplicants looked for legal as well as religious justification and Charles's wishes in the first instance could do little to stop them, as their actions most eloquently showed.

From the organisation of representative 'Tables' towards the end of 1637, if not before, opposition to royal policy entered upon a self-entrenching process which any king, let alone Charles I, would have found difficult to answer. A wide impassioned reaction to the service-book and canons was steered skilfully to an articulate defence of 'religion and liberties'. With the Covenant a considerable body of people within Scotland came to be committed around a highly centralised common course for new reformation. If the first question was how to reverse the 'mystery of iniquity' the hopes of leaders took on board matters civil as well as ecclesiastical. The eight articles sent to Court with Lord Lorne were revised by Alexander Henderson in a form which made a very much clearer emphasis on the need for the king to call a general assembly and parliament for redress of grievances. Not for the last time, the Covenanters formulated an eighth article as a catch-all: 'The more particular notes for things expedient for the weel of the kirk and kingdom, for his

---

[144] See Spottiswood still in April–May 1638 – GD 406/M9/88/3.
[145] Spottiswood, *History*, vol. I, pp. cxxiv–cxxv.

Majesty's honour and satisfaction, and for extinguishing the present com-
bustion, may be given in to be considered in the assembly and parliament.'[146]

The seeds of radical thought lay within the Covenanting movement, bound
up with talk of divine as well as human law. In some measure appeals to a
general assembly and parliament, enunciated by the Supplicants from the
first, were in direct succession to the historic line of nonconformity in Reformation Scotland; cries for full presbyterianism would not be far distant. The
practical politics of achieving that, however, were by no means assured, and
most criticism of the bishops, even with the programme for controls and
limitations, fell short of it. The general assembly could be as much a national
convention as a presbyterian instrument; the Covenant's terms of reference
were Acts of parliament on which all could agree. All of Charles's counsellors
– except those who keenly advised suppressive use of force – came round to
the idea that consultation through assemblies had to be forwarded. The
king's stiff reaction in the February 1638 proclamation, however, was
blamed on the bishops. The process of polarisation extended through the
Covenant to the whole Scottish nation. Was it 'only . . . religion' at stake?[147]
With the great emphasis on unity and a rhetoric against compromise to the
fore, there were the beginnings of almost a power struggle.

The liturgical policy was ill-suited to the Scotland of Charles I. Within the
wider context of government, its offensiveness appeared all the greater.
Appeals to general assembly and parliament indicated patriotic and political
hopes amongst the king's subjects. Zeal for the truth of the faith would have
had little impact aside from this. Nevertheless people prayed and fasted in
expectation of the king's response.[148] The politics of religion gave fuel to
passionate ideology the existence of which Charles would have liked to deny.
He rejected the raised fears of popery, the 'pretence of religion'; he was after
all personally committed to the church of the prayer book. It was his own will
that he declared in February 1638 – a will for a policy but ultimately a stand
on the issue of royal government. He was to find himself distinctly vulnerable.

---

[146] Rothes, *Relation*, pp. 55, 78, 100–2; Johnston, *Diary*, p. 345; Baillie, *Letters*, vol. I,
pp. 464–6. For taxation within the agenda, see Rothes, *Relation*, pp. 165–7, although also
p. 56. For another eighth article, see below chapter 7.
[147] Rothes, *Relation*, p. 76.
[148] NLS Wod. Fo. 61, fol. 240; Rothes, *Relation*, pp. 28, 68, 71; Baillie, *Letters*, vol. I, p. 26.

3

The King's Commissioner

May–December 1638

However much welled up in Scotland outwith the king's control, Charles had a part in provoking the course of actions up to the signing of the Covenant; his continuing failure thereafter to be responsive to the problems of his Scottish government reaped a crisis of ever greater proportions. Neither his policy nor his style of rule was suited to difficult times. The decision to go to arms was as ill-fated as the liturgy, although in a way as inevitable. The king of three kingdoms looked everywhere for his strength; but crises in three kingdoms would follow one after the other.

From his appointment in May 1638 through to the general assembly at Glasgow and its immediate aftermath at the end of the same year, the Marquis of Hamilton as the King's Commissioner tried to serve Charles's best interests. The task was tension-ridden from the outset. The king was to rule well over his subjects; but, for many Scottish subjects, their king's rule for the preservation of religion and liberties had come to mean something rather different from Charles's own vision.

Hamilton had first to satisfy Charles. That was no mean job, given the king's high expectations and the run of personal and factional intrigue wooing his sympathies. Hamilton had at least an advantage in his closeness of birth, matched by a companionship with Charles that few others apart from the queen enjoyed. Nevertheless he was vulnerable. His high descent had given fuel to rumours of kingly aspirations in the past; Charles was not a lover of intimacy in the manner of his father. The enjoyment of royal favour could not be taken for granted.

The seriousness of the Scottish situation in the king's eyes through its challenge to monarchy as he understood it gave Charles an unparalleled concern for what was happening. Hamilton was obliged to write frequently, a task that demanded great care, as the surviving drafts and copies bear ample witness. In return Charles often wrote himself: the collection of lengthy royal holograph letters surviving from this period is not typical. Charles also used Archbishop Laud and the Earl of Stirling, his Scottish Secretary, to carry the burden but Hamilton's load was heaviest of all. Twice he returned to Court for personal discussions with the king. Charles's ill-conceived 'best interests' were not at all straightforward to maintain.

Within Scotland, Hamilton, like Traquair and others before him, found the trouble of the Covenant demanded negotiation rather than dictation. The royal counsellor therefore tried to point the way. He tried hard to win the trust of his Covenanting counterparts, in particular the Earl of Rothes. To some extent he succeeded, but it was a balancing act which involved some duplicity. Charles's passion for preparing the ways of armed force seemed always the last resort during this first period of Hamilton's commission. But it is significant that Hamilton was caught by this; he could not abandon it in his counsel, although he had doubts of its value except against the most intractable opponents. Charles's practical problems of getting men and money ready were an encouragement to postpone action, but never totally to abandon the idea of their use.

Hamilton, as far as he was entrusted, had a considerable task, and an account of what he did offers important insight into the tensions of the situation. Understanding the likely course of the troubles was no easier then than now. Under the potent rallying symbol of the Covenant, optimism for reformation of the new Israel gave momentum to a presbyterian drive within the protest movement. The outcome was in part due to the king's attitude. Force undertaken might be a means of threat, but threat was met with a no less determined response on the other side. As the Scots laid up arms for themselves, Hamilton attempted to bring the king and Covenanters together on something like a middle path. It required a yielding on both sides, which in the event proved to be elusive. At the close of the Glasgow Assembly the rift was sharp and deep.

In Scotland after the signing of the Covenant the cry of religion and liberties flourished with political strength and purpose – yet the Covenanting movement was never completely homogeneous. Conservatism would resist farflung vision. The radical consciousness of those who led the movement is still a matter for debate amongst historians: often we can only make informed guesses about what went on in people's minds. The external evidence is limited and confined to a very few individuals. However, we may do well to work with a sense of some quite radical spirits at the core, with Johnston of Wariston eloquent *par excellence*. It is not always possible to disentangle the threads of internal differences. Outwardly the imperative was to show unity, a point so important that directions on the matter were composed by early May 1638. In theory, all workers of compromise settlements – which included bishops – were to be shunned, that a true and lawful resolution might be found.[1] In practice, there was more wavering, although again the evidence, much of it in the counsellors' reports to Court, must be used with care. However, the period was full of unknowns and indeed misunderstandings. From this stems part of the difficulty in the attempt to recount what was happening.

With his prominent position at Court, Hamilton had not been forgotten either by privy councillors or Supplicants in the months before his direct involvement in Scotland. As significantly, his past linked him with the minister, Eleazar Borthwick, who arrived in Edinburgh on 1 May to give news of the marquis's commission. Borthwick spoke there of good news – of concessions on matters consonant with the law, and meetings of general assembly and parliament. In other words, he revealed the peacemaking half of Hamilton's commission. Baillie interpreted it as an encouragement to further petitions.[2]

Borthwick tried to discourage the sending of Henderson's revised eight articles, the carrier of which he met on his way north. He had been acting as an agent for the Covenanters in London; but association there with Hamilton evidently gave him a different perspective. In Edinburgh worry and distrust still lay thick in the wake of the king's February proclamation. The articles were sent on their journey and Borthwick, as requested, wrote back separately to the marquis. The advice-paper that has survived was a frank statement of moderation; if it is the same one referred to in Rothes's account, it was possibly less aggressive than might have been wished, but for that reason gives a fascinating insight into the play of the day's politics.[3]

The interest is not simply that Borthwick offered to Hamilton an open confession of what might be the means to settlement, in effect cutting out any radicals' hopes of the Scottish troubles. It is also that the link with Hamilton was almost certainly underhand as far as the king was concerned. Independently, we presume, Secretary Windebank in London had been monitoring Borthwick's correspondence.[4] Even before he came to Scotland, Hamilton dealt with approaches Charles could not possibly have approved of. Hamilton could at least play the role of one sympathetic to the cause. After his arrival, Borthwick would try further to play the role of intermediary between him and the Covenanters.[5]

---

[1]   (J. Leslie, Earl of) Rothes, *A Relation of Proceedings Concerning the Affairs of Scotland*, ed. D. Laing, BC (Edinburgh, 1830), pp. 69–71, 110–12; *Diary of Sir Archibald Johnston of Wariston, 1632–1639*, ed. G. M. Paul, SHS (Edinburgh, 1911), p. 346.

[2]   Rothes, *Relation*, p. 103; R. Baillie, *The Letters and Journals*, ed. D. Laing, BC (3 vols., Edinburgh, 1841–2), vol. I, p. 99; cf. GD 112/39/727.

[3]   Rothes, *Relation*, pp. 102–3; Johnston, *Diary*, pp. 346–7.

[4]   *CSPD 1637–8*, 387/85; PRO SP 16/393/52, Borthwick to Lady Seton, holograph.

[5]   GD 406/1/409; Rothes, *Relation*, pp. 141, 162; Baillie, *Letters*, vol. I, p. 98.

Borthwick's advice naturally recommended a way forward by royal concessions. The ceremonies which caused discontent were to be removed; interestingly, he did not believe this to be a matter of the substance of true religion, but he evidently feared more danger if nothing was done. Secondly, the bishops were to be limited at least according to the conditions made in the general assemblies earlier in the century. So far, Borthwick endorsed the programme of the eight articles, and he included the need for guarantee against innovation by the king's acceptance of the place of free representative assemblies.

Borthwick's distinctiveness showed in his proposals for strategy. Reminiscent of Traquair in September 1637, he suggested that the bishops take up petitioning for the means of remedy. He appreciated the need to satisfy the king's honour, hence the argument against ceremonies, and while he did not doubt that a full solution of the troubles would take time, he nevertheless wished to hope for that, by God's grace, since the controversy was not over 'substantial points of religion'. Short-term politics therefore were to stop the process of deterioration in the Scottish situation. While some intended only religion, others had state or other affairs in mind. The crisis needed gentle and quick management before it enlarged further – to appease nobles and ministers 'not only religious but wise' who might help to move the rest back towards a state of peace. Trust, then, had to be rediscovered; private talks by the Commissioner would serve well. The king's administration had given offence which sparked off fears; it was now wholly inadvisable to promote any of unsound religious opinion, a reference probably to the Marquis of Huntly. The way of force too seemed quite inexpedient, for its outcome could not be guaranteed; if there was success, it could only be short-term.[6]

The scheme held out hope for settlement by consultation, and the king as usual escaped direct criticism. Perhaps Borthwick's ideas erred by over-optimism within the Scottish situation; but certainly they erred more in optimism that the king would find, or even be free to find, time properly to listen. News was equally available in Scotland of the intention 'to make division' that was enshrined in the queries Hamilton put elsewhere to Charles. The preparation of force would go ahead. Archibald Johnston decided that overthrow of the whole system of episcopacy, the 'root of papacy', had to be the practical goal.[7]

The king's readiness for struggle showed in his encouragement of the Marquis of Huntly, who was already attempting in the north-east of Scotland

[6] GD 406/M9/88/15. Borthwick holograph, unsigned, no date.
[7] Johnston, *Diary*, pp. 347–8. See then NLS Wod. Fo. 62, fols. 14–15; Baillie, *Letters*, vol. I, p. 86; GD 406/1/556. Cf. D. G. Mullan, *Episcopacy in Scotland: The History of an Idea, 1560–1638* (Edinburgh, 1986), pp. 179–80.

to contest the pressing of the Covenant; Charles also sent letters to the town and Bishop of Aberdeen in early April.[8] Huntly had mixed success, but drew in the support of other northern nobles, who appreciated his encouragement. The Earl of Caithness and Lord Berriedale did what they could against the efforts of the latter's son, the Master of Berriedale.[9] One of the Aberdeen doctors, John Forbes of Corse, had Huntly's patronage in his publication, at first in manuscript, of 'A peaceable warning' on 4 May 1638. Forbes wrote in an attempt to 'relieve' people of their fears and uncertainties in the face of the Covenanters' threat. It was reminiscent of his earlier role in the controversy over the Five Articles of Perth.[10] Huntly operated in an area with a tradition of conservatism; but old divisions also frequently marked lines of allegiance, a pattern no doubt repeated elsewhere.[11]

The possible promise in Hamilton's commission lay overshadowed by the provision for harsh punishment of any who dared to defend the Covenant. Concern for self-preservation continued to be relevant within Scotland, and alongside increasing determination with respect to demands worked against the marquis's quest for settlement. It goes too far to suggest that 'Hamilton was deeply in sympathy' with his Covenanting counterparts.[12] His basis of wealth and influence made at least part of the difference and his closeness to the king and to Laud earned him some unpopularity. A courtier peer who was able to affect a variety of commitments was further bound to experience distance from a group which found itself subscribing to a single ideology. Yet, unlike the king, he might explore the common ground. It was a long and painful process. Charles's programme was far from that of the Covenant.

Both sets of instructions for Hamilton contained the command to have the Covenants delivered up, but few, the lawyers included, had sympathy towards that.[13] In Scotland from the beginning of June 1638, Hamilton faced

---

8 BL Add. Ms. 23112, fol. 82; Rothes, *Relation*, pp. 98, 104–10; Baillie, *Letters*, vol. I, p. 465; NLS Ms. 2263, fol. 92; Bod. Bankes Ms. 65/28d, no. 6.
9 D. Stevenson, *The Scottish Revolution 1637–1644* (Newton Abbot, 1974), pp. 91–2; Rothes, *Relation*, pp. 104–10; NLS Wod. 4to. 24, fol. 69.
10 J. Forbes, *A Peaceable Warning*, Aldis 910 (Aberdeen, 1638); GD 406/1/416, 639; E. G. Selwyn (ed.), *The First Book of the Irenicum [1629] of John Forbes of Corse* (Cambridge, 1923); AUL Ms. 635, p. 162.
11 Baillie, *Letters*, vol. I, pp. 82–3; B. McLennan, 'Presbyterianism challenged: a study of Catholicism and episcopacy in the north-east of Scotland, 1560–1650' (unpublished University of Aberdeen Ph.D. dissertation, 1977); E. M. Furgol, 'The northern highland Covenanter clans 1639–1651', *Northern Scotland*, 7 (1987), 119–31; D. Stevenson, *Alasdair MacColla and the Highland Problem in the Seventeenth Century* (Edinburgh, 1980), pp. 64–73.
12 W. Makey, *The Church of the Covenant 1637–1651* (Edinburgh, 1979), p. 33.
13 S. R. Gardiner (ed.), *The Hamilton Papers*, Camden Society (1880), pp. 8–9; GD 406/1/554, 556. Gardiner's edition of letters principally from Hamilton to the king published originals nowadays bound in the SRO Hamilton Red Books; the transcriptions are mostly accurate, but the run of correspondence is not complete, since some letters escaped the binding

considerable pressure, both from the presence of assembled crowds and from the nobles and others he talked with. At first his fears were of general riot and of the Covenanters proceeding to summon representative assemblies as of their own authority; his sense of the weakness of Charles's position within Scotland was heightened as news came through of the Covenanters' own efforts to gather arms. With the mob problem he had some success but in other respects he could only attempt to win time and advantage.[14]

Hamilton's notion of gaining time was linked with the terms for accommodation he carried within his instructions. It was very quickly clear that the less aggressive of the two declarations would have to be used. Before he had even entered Edinburgh, Hamilton had begun to question whether Charles's demand for surrender of the Covenant had to be pursued. He phrased carefully his thoughts to Court, and was still happier to give them to Laud for his consideration than to the king. What, he came to ask, if the Covenant were so explained that its signatories acknowledged their 'strictest allegiance' to the king? He added assurances that he did not at all approve of it. When he dared to put the idea directly to Charles, the king's reply uncompromisingly rejected it: if the Covenant was retained, explained or not, 'I have no more power in Scotland than as a duke of Venice, which I will rather die than suffer.'[15]

The gentler declaration text allowed that issue to be hedged. As a means to combat the force of a protestation expected to follow its publication, the marquis successfully procured an additional clause to be inserted in it. This was to persuade hearers that the king fully intended to indict a general assembly and parliament. The idea was contained in Hamilton's instructions; by making it 'official', he hoped in some measure to win standing against the prevailing cause of the Covenant.[16]

Charles approved the winning of time, not least because of the various preparations for the use of force. Hamilton was as fully involved with this, but hesitations about the subdual of the Scots marked some of his letters. On the one hand there seemed to be little alternative but to advise on the organis-

process. Furthermore, drafts of the letters have also mostly survived, which are often of interest.

[14] Gardiner, *Hamilton Papers*, pp. 3–7; GD 406/1/553, 554.

[15] Gardiner, *Hamilton Papers*, pp. 8–9; GD 406/1/553, 554, 555, 327; Rothes, *Relation*, p. 165; SRO Hamilton Red Book i, 76 (incompletely printed in G. Burnet, *The Memoirs of the Lives and Actions of James and William, Dukes of Hamilton and Castleherald...* (1677), p. 60). The originals of the king's letters to Hamilton are again to be found in the SRO Hamilton Red Books. Burnet chose not always to transcribe perfectly; I hope to deal elsewhere with his writing of the *Memoires*. For the alternative explanations under discussion, see NLS Wod. Fo. 61, fols. 270, 275–6.

[16] P. H. Donald, 'The king and the Scottish troubles, 1637–1641' (unpublished University of Cambridge Ph.D. dissertation, 1988), p. 91; GD 406/1/555; Gardiner, *Hamilton Papers*, pp. 11–12, 20; Burnet, *Memoires*, p. 62.

ation of men and supplies in the three kingdoms; Hamilton would himself commend such as Huntly and Nithsdale. On the other hand, he sounded pessimistic of the prospects, both for the management of a three-prong campaign on account of various difficulties, and for the achievement of anything like the desired end. Would Charles thus be able to reclaim his people? Hamilton's decision was to return himself to Court. He persuaded the Covenanters that he would tell the king of their desires if in return they would await the king's authority for the holding of a general assembly. He hoped that the situation would if anything get better for Charles in the wake of the declaration. Charles had noted Hamilton's concern, but had proceeded with his preparations; his optimism for what might be available reached quite a height, and he reaffirmed that he would if necessary lead in person. However, he allowed Hamilton his journey, trusting that no weak surrender would be made in the process.[17]

Hamilton would not stray far from Charles's expectations, but the circumstances demanded some measure of double-talk if the process of accommodation was to advance. It remains difficult to be sure how far Hamilton's critical description of the Covenanters was sincere, but he certainly could be frustrated by them and their supporters.[18] Nevertheless his concern that the king should be satisfied made him seek confirmation from friends at Court.[19] He kept the good wishes of the bishops, whose physical safety in Scotland was becoming a matter for concern. Spottiswood drafted another possible declaration for Hamilton to consider, and encouraged him in his effort to move the king to call a general assembly.[20] John Maxwell, Bishop of Ross, unconsciously repeated words used by Eleazar Borthwick in hoping that God might yet bring light out of darkness![21]

The marquis successfully wrote letters to Court which were acceptable. Yet he also heard and probably believed that a settlement could be initiated if a mutual trust between king and Covenanters could be created. In dialogue, he offered both personal assurances and threats.[22] He went as far as he could in talks about the possible explanation of the Covenant. It no doubt made an impact that Johnston of Wariston was as difficult about it as the king; but, before he left Scotland, Hamilton at least appeared to yield ground, for which

---

[17] GD 406/1/552, 325, 327, 422; Gardiner, *Hamilton Papers*, pp. 3–6, 8–9, 11–13, 16–17; Burnet, *Memoires*, pp. 55–7, 59–62.
[18] See GD 406/1/552, 555; Gardiner, *Hamilton Papers*, p. 6.
[19] GD 406/1/420, 421, 424, 425.
[20] GD 406/1/679 (Burnet, *Memoires*, p. 45, misdated this); Baillie, *Letters*, vol. I, pp. 466–7 (early July? – cf. GD 406/1/2360).
[21] Burnet, *Memoires*, pp. 62–3; cf. GD 406/1/655, 656.
[22] Cf. Rothes, *Relation*, pp. 135–40, 144.

trouble later rebounded on him.[23] The modification he suggested for the proclamation tried to meet the request put to him so often in these days – although because of Charles, Hamilton was unable to offer certain dates for the wished-for meetings.[24] In letters to Charles and Laud, Hamilton cursed the impertinent and damnable demands; yet with crisis in the air an inevitable part of the way forward was to explore means of giving satisfaction. The Covenanters expected much of his journey south.[25]

The king's cause was weak on the ground. It was not just that lawyers would not uphold it, for reasons of conviction or fear. Threats that the Covenanters themselves might indict the assembly were symptomatic of the confidence they were gaining in Scotland.[26] Subscriptions to the Covenant were widely encouraged; in the court of session and the privy council, Hamilton could not be assured of support. While he expressed thoughts of pursuing some indebted individuals on the other side, the Covenanters went on to compose a declinator and ultimately charges against Sir John Hay and Sir Robert Spottiswood. The immediate concern was to prevent them from sitting as judges, but they further named them with the bishops as 'incendiaries', people who had incensed the king against his own subjects; the title of odium would be of some lasting significance.[27] The king's physical distance made more plausible arguments that the problem merely concerned bad counsel: it was an important background aspect of the challenge Charles was facing.[28]

Responses to threats of force were no less daring. Thoughts of justification preceded action as muster orders were sent out only towards the end of June and a warning system of beacons arranged. Military supplies were sought abroad. Hamilton did not like it, but chronologically the Covenanters were following after news of what the king was doing. Lest the king try to use

---

[23] GD 406/1/553, 718; Johnston, *Diary*, pp. 353–4; Rothes, *Relation*, pp. 121–3, 150–3, 159–64; Baillie, *Letters*, vol. I, pp. 86–7; SRO Red Book i, 75; Makey, *Church of the Covenant*, p. 34; GD 112/40/2/1/5; Johnston, *Diary*, pp. 354, 377; NLS Wod. Fo. 62, fol. 17; *General Demands Concerning the Late Covenant*, Aldis 912 (1639); GD 406/1/564; BL Add. Ms. 15391, fols. 244–6.

[24] Cf. GD 406/1/650/1; Rothes, *Relation*, pp. 118, 121, 149; GD 406/M9/88/14.

[25] Gardiner, *Hamilton Papers*, p. 6; Rothes, *Relation*, pp. 154–5, 165–8, 181–2; NLS Wod. Fo. 61, fol. 279.

[26] See NLS Wod. Fo. 61, fols. 262v (28 May 1638), 277–8, 281–2; *Reasons against the Rendering of our Confession*, Aldis 930 (n.p., 1638); *Reasons for a Generall Assemblie*, Aldis 931 (n.p., 1638); Baillie, *Letters*, vol. I, pp. 92–3, 95–6.

[27] GD 406/1/555, 558, 623; NLS Wod. Fo. 61, fol. 251; cf. Rothes, *Relation*, pp. 171–2, 176–8.

[28] Cf. GD 406/1/554; also the prefaces of the various drafts of the Covenanter protestation – NLS Wod. Fo. 61, fols. 262, 264, 268–9.

English force, printed propaganda was turned to an English readership, to discourage their participation in any such campaign.[29]

Threatening words were not necessarily productive. Charles himself began to learn that when he asked if any course in law, if not the charge of treason, might be brought against his opponents; his private question reflected poorly on his proclamations.[30] The lesson still had some way to penetrate. Hamilton seems to have understood better; in any case he took seriously the task of wooing support in Scotland. There was no other immediate option, but it should not be thought that his talks had to be in vain. Hamilton returned to Court with Covenanter statements he knew the king would dislike, but it kept the possibilities open. Although in correspondence he suggested that he would come only for a few days, more probably he hoped to restrain any hasty violent action and to gain new terms for progressing by peaceful talks.[31]

If force was to be effective, it had to be more than a matter of words. Although he continued to argue that point to Charles, Hamilton worked keenly on the building of an accommodation. In the event circumstances helped him, but the damage done in Scotland through the other course was serious. Amongst those alarmed by threats of force were Lord Lorne and the Campbells. Hamilton had been far from calming all fears during his sojourn in Edinburgh. It could be called a weakness, but obligation if not inclination dictated it; the royal counsellor had to be in measure alongside his king. Hamilton moreover shared nothing with the Covenanters of how he actually advised Charles on the military questions. He lived perilously close to the possibility of being called an incendiary.[32]

Hamilton finished his first period as Commissioner in Scotland by publishing the king's declaration on 4 July. He had kept the text secret up to that point. The expected protestation was made. Hamilton managed to have the declaration approved in privy council, but within hours a body of members returned to ask for the act to be cancelled before being registered.[33] There was also an explicatory act that abrogated and discharged the service-book and

[29] NLS Wod. Fo. 61, fol. 264 (4 June 1638); Rothes, *Relation*, pp. 136–7, 155–6; NLS Wod. Fo. 61, fol. 279; Gardiner, *Hamilton Papers*, pp. 14–17, and draft GD 406/1/10814; NLS Adv. Ms. 29.2.8, fols. 243–5; NLS Wod. Fo. 61, fols. 326–7; Stevenson, *Scottish Revolution*, p. 101; Johnston, *Diary*, pp. 361, 367; *A Short Relation of the State of the Kirk of Scotland . . .*, Aldis 934.5 (n.p., 1638).

[30] Burnet, *Memoires*, p. 55.

[31] GD 406/1/556; Gardiner, *Hamilton Papers*, pp. 14–19, and draft GD 406/1/10814; cf. Rothes, *Relation*, pp. 165, 182.

[32] Baillie, *Letters*, vol. I, pp. 72–3, 93–4; GD 406/1/967; GD 14/19, pp. 135–7; W. Knowler (ed.), *The Earl of Strafforde's Letters and Dispatches* (2 vols., 1739), vol. II, pp. 184, 187; GD 112/39/738; GD 406/1/516; Stevenson, *Scottish Revolution*, pp. 98–102; Rothes, *Relation*, esp. pp. 155–7, 170–1.

[33] Stevenson, *Scottish Revolution*, pp. 97–8; GD 16/46/40; NLS Wod. Fo. 61, fol. 324; Rothes, *Relation*, pp. 174–6, 178–81.

canons – inhibiting all further use of them – and also discharged the court of high commission. This had a full backing, whilst a less far-reaching version bore the signatures of only Hamilton, Traquair, Roxburgh and one of the new privy councillors, the Earl Marischal: it discharged without abrogating, and made no mention of any inhibition. If this was Hamilton's preferred text, it was further reflection on his lack of control even in the privy council that it was the other version which was passed.[34] The Covenanters had clearly come to exercise considerable influence. A settlement on Charles's terms looked more remote than ever.

Hamilton's correspondence with friends in Scotland during his three weeks at Court hinted at his own inclination. Not long after his arrival he reported optimistically to Roxburgh that Charles would wait on negotiations; there would be no immediate resort to 'use of power'. The matter was not yet finally concluded, however, nor on 23 July, when Hamilton's tone reflected grave worries. There were active preparations for war, with the king very displeased at the whole business of the council not ratifying the declaration, and above all at the Covenant being upheld – 'he having drunk in this opinion that monarchy and it cannot stand together'. Still Hamilton found the remaining option of force horrible for the confusion and ruin it would bring.[35] Roxburgh's opinion of force being self-defeating, of the pointlessness in destroying 'this poor kingdom', hearkened back to the marquis's earlier letters to the king. A good king reclaimed and did not destroy his people, Roxburgh wrote further: 'we must all serve him when he commands, but who sincerely loves him will ever beg for peace with his own'.[36]

Counsel given directly to the king who had to be obeyed was effective only if Charles would accept it. Hamilton was at least partly successful in this regard, not least because Charles had little choice. Military force could not quickly be ready. One obvious problem was that the king's expectations concerning supply were not sufficiently matched by his administration; the threatening words lacked substantial backing. Nor did it help that Charles wished in these early stages to proceed with minimum publicity.

Since, strictly speaking, Scotland-related affairs were outwith the responsibility of the English privy council, official consideration there depended on the king. While troubles over the contentious levy of ship money, including the trial of John Hampden, stimulated speculation on how far the Covenanters might arouse general 'puritan' disturbance, the king apparently kept to

---

[34] *RPCS*, 2nd Series, vol. VII, p. 34; GD 406/M9/52, 53, 67/11; cf. Baillie, *Letters*, vol. I, pp. 91–2.
[35] GD 406/1/8306, 718.　　　　　　　[36] GD 406/1/8306, 687; GD 45/1/39.

a minimum direct discussion of the Scottish troubles.[37] He had raised the military questions in the foreign committee of the English council in June, where there was a favourable reaction. Sir Henry Vane's work on shipping for the transport of troops, however, was independently organised; the earliest consultations about money were apparently with Bishops Laud and Juxon; the full privy council was briefed only in general terms on 1 July. Thereafter a small junto was formed to meet as a committee for Scotland.[38] Even in this select group members divided on the advisability of having recourse to arms, some preferring to trust to a peaceful solution. Religious sentiment may have played a part in directing hostility against the Scots; Sir Henry Vane was on the other side, praying against the need for war, and with him was the Earl of Northumberland who, though he hated the Scots, was influenced by his concerns over the shortage of money, arms and commanders – not to mention discontents among the English, a point that very probably took its significance from an expectation that the king would need to call a parliament for the purposes of supply.[39]

Archbishop Laud feared the parliament prospect, but the king hardly appeared to consider it. In late June Charles had written optimistically of his forces, the budget being fixed at £200,000 sterling for an enterprise to involve potentially at least 14,000 foot and 2,000 horse.[40] By mid-July the money available by borrowing totalled just over half of the anticipated budget. Nothing was said about how to supply the difference, but the idea initially was to have men raised in the northern counties, 2,500 in all, and for these to be settled in the garrisons at Berwick and Carlisle, and also at Newcastle and Holy Island. Arms would be found locally to some extent, with further supplies coming from the Prince of Orange. These limited preparations were dictated at least in part by the desire to keep expenses low.[41] Charles's affirmation of coming north himself with an army seemed to be pushed into the background: in its place came a plan to give some defence to the borders.

It was still an important effort. There was to be a small blockade of the

[37] Cf. GD 406/1/423, 374, 327, 593, 9594; W. Laud, *The Works of the Most Reverend Father in God, William Laud, D.D.*, eds. W. Scott and J. Bliss (7 vols., Oxford, 1847–60), vol. VII, pp. 454, 468; Knowler, *Strafforde Letters*, vol. II, p. 186; WWM Str. P. LB 7, fols. 83–5, 106v. The Anglo-Scottish dimension is discussed further below in chapter 5.

[38] GD 406/1/422, 423; PRO SP 16/396, p. 3; WWM Str. P. LB 18, p. 55; Laud, *Works*, vol. VII, pp. 454, 468; Knowler, *Strafforde Letters*, vol. II, p. 181; PRO C 115/N.8/8820; *CSPV 1636–9*, pp. 435–6; BL Add. Ms. 15391, fol. 196.

[39] Knowler, *Strafforde Letters*, vol. II, p. 186; PRO SP 81/44, fol. 266. Cf. Laud, *Works*, vol. VII, p. 468; WWM Str. P. LB 10b, pp. 8–10.

[40] Burnet, *Memoires*, p. 59; GD 406/1/422.

[41] Bod. Clarendon Ms. 14, fols. 115–16; PRO SP 16/396. Professor Mark Fissel is preparing a full study on the king's war effort; see meanwhile M. C. Fissel, *'Bellum episcopale*: the bishops' wars and the end of the "Personal Rule" in England 1638–1640' (unpublished University of Berkeley Ph.D. dissertation, 1983).

Scottish coasts, to hinder Scottish trade and more specifically to stop their import of arms.[42] Charles had no intention of relinquishing the option of force, although he could do little presently. For what might come for him out of Scotland, he continued to rely on his Commissioner. Hamilton's counsel successfully steered him on the path of granting concessions – though he walked with ominous reluctance: 'you are by no means to permit a present rupture to happen, but to yield anything though unreasonable rather than now to break'.[43]

What Charles wished, were the means available, was shelved as a new strategy with some positive thinking took over. The February Covenant had to be rejected on the grounds that it lacked royal permission, but it was proposed that the council and the people sign an alternative, authorised Covenant. This was to centre around the relatively unpolemical statement of the early reformers in Scotland, the 1567 Confession, with a suitably phrased band of mutual combination. And, whatever the outcome, a general assembly was to be indicted; some details were prepared in this regard.[44] Finally the king allowed even the present indicting of a parliament – if absolutely necessary for avoiding a 'rupture'.[45]

The evidence suggests strongly that Charles and Hamilton talked this one out alone. Laud, despite his recent heavy involvement, did not see Hamilton's instructions, which were written on 27 July.[46] Nithsdale and Lennox may have spoken their turn, but, if so, more on the military dimension.[47] The marquis possibly tried to have Archbishop Spottiswood summoned to Court to give his opinions on the working of division, but in the event Spottiswood and the other bishops were commanded to stay in the north of England, where they now were; Bishop John Maxwell, who had begun a journey south already, reached London only on 29 July.[48] Spottiswood's comments on the instructions touching the general assembly imply that Hamilton had advised their substance, which is confirmed by a set of notes taken by Hamilton; a

[42] *CSPD 1637–8*, 397/39; HMC *Cowper* (23), vol. II, p. 191.
[43] Burnet, *Memoires*, p. 66 (GD 406/M9/65/4; draft in GD 406/M9/65/3).
[44] Burnet, *Memoires*, pp. 66–8 (GD 406/M9/72) – misprint reads '1557'. 1567 was the year that the 1560 Confession was established through parliament, and Charles referred to it only by the later date.
[45] GD 406/M9/65/2.
[46] Laud, *Works*, vol. VII, p. 468; GD 406/1/564. Cf. *CSPV 1636–9*, p. 447.
[47] Nithsdale was still in London, but no evidence has turned up for his counsel at this time. A speech fathered on Lennox strongly recommended avoiding war. Dated 15 July, it was forged, but circulated widely, in Scotland at the latest by August 1638 – *CSPD 1637–8*, 395/56; HMC R. R. *Hastings* (78), vol. IV, p. 79; Baillie, *Letters*, vol. I, p. 105; GD 112/39/738; PCR, vol. IV, pp. 586, 602. Lennox seems to have questioned the wisdom of war with the Scots in November 1638 and again in May 1639 – BL Add. Ms. 15391, fol. 313v; HMC *Rutland* (24), vol. I, p. 511.
[48] GD 406/M9/67/5; BL Add. Ms. 23112, fol. 85; GD 112/43/1/8/1.

stage in the making of the instructions, the paper probably reflects the outcome of some dialogue, and on it Charles subsequently added further comments.[49]

It was firstly thought that no band should be signed without 'all the council at least' approving – most probably an indicator of the king's unease with the idea.[50] For the assembly, it was to be held in winter, and not in Edinburgh: to interpret, there would be no military onslaught this year, but any open discussion should be over in time for the next campaigning season. Charles afterwards inserted Glasgow as the desirable venue. Tactics meanwhile for the border garrisons and Edinburgh Castle were to anticipate, cautiously, any likely trouble.[51] The discussions also took in the suggestion that the Covenanters might stop collecting subscriptions if this assembly was granted. Although this contained no illusions about the first Covenant being surrendered, Charles in his afterthought commented that a protestation should be made if the collecting of signatures did continue; he too might use that Covenanter tactic of protestation.[52] The king suggested having two Commissioners for the assembly, a bishop as well as Hamilton lest a bishop as Moderator was refused, and named John Guthrie of Moray as generally the most acceptable. He was also hopeful that the bishops in exile would return home, especially Spottiswood, who had his own 'justification', in other words his Chancellorship – proposals which certainly would have encountered problems.[53] Hamilton was to protest against anything there was hope of the king recovering in the future 'for his honour and the settlement of the church'.[54] It was a final reflection on Charles's thoughts which boded ill for the establishment of trust, let alone long-term settlement. The king was well informed, but his generosity of response was minimal.

In the event little of this got off the ground. The bishops gave their close cooperation to Hamilton on the details of the forthcoming assembly. Archbishop Spottiswood took up the controversial question of the part of elders in elections; the Bishops of Galloway, Edinburgh and Argyll also gave specific advice on articles that Hamilton then proposed in public to the Covenanters. There was some engagement with recent Covenanter publications.[55] This

---

[49] GD 406/1/677; GD 406/M9/67/9.

[50] Cf. GD 406/M9/67/10; GD 406/1/10781.

[51] The language of the document is ambiguous. For Glasgow, cf. Stevenson, *Scottish Revolution*, pp. 108–9. For the Earl of Mar, who was to be replaced in Edinburgh Castle, see GD 406/1/10782; Gardiner, *Hamilton Papers*, pp. 18–19.

[52] Cf. Burnet, *Memoires*, pp. 61–2.

[53] Cf. GD 406/1/594, 677, 966, 8298.

[54] GD 406/M9/67/9 (n.d.). Burnet (*Memoires*, p. 75) dates the paper too late, in September.

[55] GD 406/1/677, 630; NLS Wod. Fo. 66, fols. 73–6. I am grateful to Professor Russell for the last reference – an answer to *Reasons for a Generall Assemblie*; cf. Baillie, *Letters*, vol. I, pp. 92–3, 95–6, 100–1, 103.

debate on the future assembly dominated proceedings in Scotland in August when Hamilton returned north. He had briefly opened the subject in June and now he wished to imply that the option of force had been laid aside in preference for ordinary proceedings, but no agreement was found.[56] The deceit made little difference. The Covenanters would not allow the limitations proposed, fearing the stifling of reform; once more they threatened to convene the assembly and parliament themselves. In the end two matters pressed on the episcopal side stood out. One was the condition that elders should have no part in choosing commissioners from the presbyteries, which notably amongst Covenanter ministers was a divisive issue since clergy had tended to dominate before; the other attempted to restrict issues settled by parliamentary acts to reform only in a parliament – which obviously included the Five Articles of Perth, but more fundamentally raised questions about the status of general assemblies and their legislation. With the Covenanters refusing to accept these, Hamilton asked to be allowed again to return to the king.[57]

The lack of correspondence between the marquis and Court in this second period in Scotland contrasts with the regular and lengthy communications maintained during the first. Hamilton was entrusted with a good measure of discretion, but it also reflected on the loss of urgency in the situation as seen by the king.[58] Nothing much, however, was heard of the new Covenant.[59] Instead another alternative was to emerge as part of a new and further-reaching package of concessions.

An agreement was settled at Broxmouth immediately after Hamilton's departure from Edinburgh, his co-signatories being Traquair, Roxburgh and the Earl of Southesk. Southesk's arrival as a leading conciliator postdated his being recommended by the Justice-clerk at the end of July as a future Lord Chancellor to fill the rumoured impending vacancy; he had abstained from approving Hamilton's 4 July declaration, being then alongside the Earl of Annandale, Lord Lorne and Sir Thomas Hope. However, he acted consistently his changed role hereafter, and Hamilton himself came to be persuaded that his candidacy for the Chancellorship might be suitable.[60]

The proposed settlement was that service-book, canons and High Com-

---

[56] Burnet, *Memoires*, pp. 69–70; GD 406/M9/67/7–8; cf. Rothes, *Relation*, pp. 165–7, 169.
[57] [Charles I], *A Large Declaration*, STC 21906 (1639), pp. 116–21, 123; Stevenson, *Scottish Revolution*, pp. 103–4; J. Kirk, *The Second Book of Discipline* (Edinburgh, 1980), pp. 116–21; W. R. Foster, *The Church before the Covenants* (Edinburgh, 1975), pp. 88–91, 119–21. For the special care to be taken over the elders, see below, pp. 94, 98.
[58] Cf. GD 406/1/563.
[59] Johnston, *Diary*, p. 376 (23 August). Cf. Stevenson, *Scottish Revolution*, p. 102.
[60] GD 406/1/617; *RPCS*, 2nd Series, vol. VII, p. 32; P. Yorke, *Miscellaneous State Papers, from 1501 to 1726* (2 vols., 1778), vol. II, p. 116.

mission should be 'absolutely' discharged – 'fully and without doubtful expressions': up to this point Hamilton had been instructed short of this.[61] Further clauses went part way towards satisfying demands. The bishops' 'unlimited authority' was remitted to the general assembly; this implied reference to the caveats of the assemblies of 1600 and 1610 which had figured in the Covenanters' eight articles and took seriously the option of moderate compromise – since now the institution of episcopacy was being popularly challenged in the street and pulpit.[62] Furthermore, it was offered that the observance of the Articles of Perth might be forborne until a final ruling by the 'estates'. As the talks in Edinburgh had just shown, this faced problems with those who would have a general assembly as the primary determining authority for all church matters, but to suggest that the king should sanction non-observance was a step in itself.[63] Most novel of the ideas was that the king should authorise subscription of the 1581 Negative Confession which had formed the core of the National Covenant – although with a different band. Thus it was hoped to answer the pleas that Charles might endorse the religious dimension of the Covenant. All together, with a generous pardon to relieve fears of recriminatory persecution, the scheme was to be the means of quietening at least the majority.[64]

Hamilton's course of action was decided without prior reference to Laud or to the king. He sounded a note of urgency, and taking the initiative upon himself, probably to strengthen his case, did not mention his Scottish co-workers.[65] That it was a collaborative effort was probably nearer the truth; whatever the case, Traquair wrote out the various documents, including two forms of warrant for publishing the 1581 Confession and band.[66] He, and probably also Roxburgh, wrote to the king to persuade consideration of what was proposed, and after Hamilton's departure they kept regular contact.[67]

In explaining to Laud why he had not indicted an assembly as instructed, Hamilton referred to the extreme risk to episcopacy without being better assured of a 'party' to support the king. Dr Walter Balcanquhal, who came south with Hamilton, put similar arguments, with more clerical bias.[68] The imperative put for the king's acceptance of the scheme was that far worse

---

[61] Cf. Burnet, *Memoires*, p. 66 (27 July instructions).
[62] GD 406/M9/61/15–16; see too GD 406/M9/88/5. Cf. Baillie, *Letters*, vol. I, pp. 467–8.
[63] In the July instructions, the Articles were to be kept but as 'indifferent'.
[64] Burnet, *Memoires*, pp. 70–1 (GD 406/M9/73); GD 406/M9/67/6.
[65] GD 406/1/559 (*c.* 25 August).
[66] GD 406/M9/73, M9/61/6, M9/83; GD 406/M9/61/7 (Balcanquhal holograph); *RPCS*, 2nd Series, vol. VII, pp. 73–4.
[67] GD 406/1/8211; Traqr. Ms. 12/23 (undated).
[68] GD 406/1/560; Baillie, *Letters*, vol. I, pp. 467–8. Balcanquhal was a Scot with ambitions in the English church – *DNB*.

was to be expected from the other side: prospects for an assembly and parliament on their terms looked highly uncompromising – extending even to the possible abjuration of episcopacy as contrary to the Word of God.[69]

The language of party was akin to royal expectations, but the emphasis of the scheme was less on forcing the subjection of anyone than on building foundations for a concessionary settlement. Final arbitration was still to come in the assembly and parliament. The councillors were ready to struggle, and their advice was not without promise. By contrast, the Scottish bishops now despaired of their appearing in an assembly because of the Covenanters' obstinacy; Hamilton courteously talked with Spottiswood at Newcastle on the way south.[70]

From Court at the beginning of September 1638 Hamilton reported his difficulties to Traquair: Charles found the remedy worse than the disease, since, while he would readily proclaim a disinclination to innovation of religion or laws, repeal or concession without assured results seemed distasteful. Few of course in Scotland could share Charles's understanding of innovation; but Hamilton's problem, as he expressed it to Traquair, was the risk of losing the king's favour if he undertook such a thing and failed, since the advice was contrary to that espoused by others and by the king's own intention. Charles still only wished the Covenant to be surrendered.[71]

The argument that worse impended nevertheless moved Charles to approve the Broxmouth advice – or at least to permit new instructions for Hamilton, which the marquis and Balcanquhal drafted.[72] However, the king, with Laud, held back still from any great shift of mind, as is clear from significant alterations on the text of the related proclamation. The concessions were worded as vaguely as possible – giving no public guarantee against future reintroduction of anything like the service-book; acknowledging no particular obligation to limit the bishops. In effect Charles insisted that change ultimately depended on himself; he allowed Hamilton to proceed with summoning assembly and parliament, but committed himself not at all to anything to be concluded there.[73]

Thus the distinctly moderate settlement suggested to Charles was taken barely half on board; only over the new authorised subscription to the Negative Confession had Hamilton made genuine progress. All privy councillors

---

[69] 'Inconveniences' (31 August) – GD 406/M9/82/1; see also M9/67/6.
[70] GD 406/1/676, 678.
[71] GD 406/1/716, 719.
[72] GD 406/M9/67/6 (Hamilton holograph); GD 406/M9/61/8–9 (Balcanquhal holograph); the final instructions, written by Hamilton and initialled by the king, are in Burnet, *Memoires*, pp. 72–4 (GD 406/M9/65/5).
[73] The draft, in Balcanquhal's hand, is GD 406/M9/61/15–16; for the final text, see *RPCS*, 2nd Series, vol. VII, pp. 64–6. For Laud's part, see GD 406/1/561, 546, 716.

were to approve of the new course of action, as in July/August, but the threat of dismissal was raised for any dissenters; Charles was to be told if any Lords of Session refused. On the original draft of the instructions, neither general assembly nor parliament were to be indicted if the majority of the council did not acquiesce, but Hamilton added the clause – 'or not a considerable part of other lords and gentlemen in case our council refuse'.[74] The purpose was somehow to create a solid core for the king's party.

Concerning the intended assembly, the membership provisions upheld by the Scottish bishops were now to be left aside. For though Hamilton had reckoned, probably correctly, that a majority of ministers preferred the old clerical system of elections, it was decided to make a priority out of fostering divisions over this amongst the Covenanters. The draft instructions had expressed the hope that elections would be held as in James's reign, a vague provision which could be argued either way; more explicitly in the final version laymen were to be encouraged to resist clericalism – and ministers likewise on the opposite tack! Thus a way of proceeding whereby Covenanter leaders had hoped to steer a powerful course to decisive conclusions in the general assembly was to be turned against them; despite their impressive planning made in advance, Hamilton was prepared to struggle.[75]

Charles's agreement was most reluctant, constrained by his having little political option; Hamilton was rather more positive. Although the marquis later claimed that it 'strained his conscience' to subscribe the Negative Confession, Sir Edward Stanhope, in a reply to a hostile judgement by Wentworth, the Lord Deputy of Ireland, seemed to quote the moderate reformist reasoning of this 'safe and honest policy': 'If they could by that means get their laws, privileges and immunities (which are very great, questioned and perhaps in danger of being disannulled) confirmed and established, I answer, they do their country good service, and offend not this kingdom [England] in defending it from wars.' At the same time Stanhope's hostility to the unreasonableness of some of the Covenanters reflected sympathies with the Hamilton-Traquair approach.[76]

George Con was one of the Catholics naturally hostile to the new strategy; the king would be advised by such people to press on with the military option.[77] The border garrisons remained as the leading point of the military

---

[74] GD 406/M9/65/5. This emendation was made in the very copy signed by Charles.
[75] GD 406/1/560, 962; GD 406/M9/61/8–9 (Burnet, *Memoires*, pp. 72–4). For the Covenanters' line, see Baillie, *Letters*, vol. I, pp. 469–73; GD 406/M9/61/4, M9/87/1.
[76] Yorke, *State Papers*, vol. II, p. 113; Knowler, *Strafforde Letters*, vol. II, pp. 239–41. Stanhope may be quoting Sir James Hamilton, the marquis's close servant.
[77] BL Add. Ms. 15391, fols. 244–6, 290, 260; Knowler, *Strafforde Letters*, vol. II, p. 238. See too the Catholic military scheme, possibly originating from this circle – *CSPD 1638–9*, 400/65.

strategy but Hamilton clearly expected to have a say on troop movements. He successfully countermanded a move ordered by Charles the day after he left Court, for supplies to proceed to Newcastle and Hull without his signal: the king in his impatience had argued that the Covenanters had no justification for complaint, given the supplies they had themselves collected.[78] Arms for the larger army continued to be sought, but Hamilton, while covering for security, aimed to minimise the need for force.[79]

Instructed to tell the bishops the details concluded, Hamilton met St Andrews, Ross and Brechin and urged them to consult on what was fit to be done at the assembly. Although they disliked the idea of an assembly being held at all, they agreed to attend when it met.[80] Spottiswood's demission of the Chancellorship was at last to be accepted, a gain for anti-clericalism. Hamilton himself was entrusted with the keeping of the Great Seal until a new Chancellor was appointed at his own recommendation, a sign of the king's continuing close trust.[81] Favour, moreover, was being shown to Traquair, who in recent months had battled with the bishops. A signature to his advantage which had been long held up by Spottiswood was referred to Hamilton's consideration.[82]

Archbishop Laud's support for the policy rested on his sense of expediency, which Hamilton could appreciate. Laud's former concern about the expense of military effort was still not allayed, and the approach of concessions for Scotland seemed to be the lesser evil ('*minus malum*') in an awkward situation, as he wrote in letters to Wentworth. Contemplating what had gone wrong, he returned frequently to the failure of government before as well as since the outbreak of the troubles.[83] Wentworth responded privately with a reflection that came close to direct criticism of the king and urged that minds be set on the supreme good, '*summum bonum*'. His heavy personal criticism of the Marquis of Hamilton was subsumed in a critique of the frame of mind that upheld 'indifferency'.[84] The rhetoric for decisive action Laud accepted to some extent, although Wentworth was the more outspoken. Laud agreed that too much was being yielded, but remained unable to see a present alternative, since neither money nor men in England were ready. Reflections on the

[78] GD 406/1/10793; Gardiner, *Hamilton Papers*, p. 25; GD 406/1/10796.
[79] PRO SP 16/398/46, 47, 48, 67, 70; SP 16/396, p. 5; HMC *Cowper*, vol. II, p. 193; *Calendar of Clarendon State Papers Preserved in the Bodleian Library*, eds. O. Ogle and W. H. Bliss, vol. I (Oxford, 1872), p. 158 (n. 1127); Fissel, '*Bellum episcopale*', pp. 11–21.
[80] Burnet, *Memoires*, pp. 74–5; GD 406/1/562; Gardiner, *Hamilton Papers*, p. 23. The Bishops of Galloway, Edinburgh and Moray still argued against it – GD 406/1/705, 659.
[81] Burnet, *Memoires*, pp. 74–5; GD 406/1/594, 604, 397, 709.
[82] GD 406/1/612, 746, 963. Sir Thomas Hope had also attacked him. For Traquair's defence against charges, see Traqr. Ms. 12/41; GD 406/1/748; BL Harl. Ms. 4612, fol. 60.
[83] Laud, *Works*, vol. VII, pp. 453–4, 468, 482, 489–90, 507.
[84] WWM Str. P. LB 7, fols. 144–7, 123, 131–2.

government of England came round to a similar analysis of the lack of 'thorough'.[85]

Wentworth, in Ireland, was removed from the inner circles of Scottish policy-making, and had little original to offer as practical counsel, despite his loud complaints. Writing for instance to the Earl of Northumberland after the latter's appointment to the Scottish committee, his ideas were for securing the border garrisons, an embargo on trade, and for the need to have a party in Scotland.[86] One theme, however, was his alone. Taking up from Northumberland's description of the Scots as a 'miserly nation', he expounded his thoughts concerning the ordinary government of Scotland. With the bad conduct of the Scots, he regretted the separate conduct of their affairs from those of England. Charles had been ill-advised to follow the practice of James before him; the long-term solution would be to lean more on the English in the control of the northern kingdom. Wentworth repeated the idea one month later: 'His Majesty must press to be absolute master, using an English deputy if not an English law, which may curb insolences by always foreseeing them, boost revenues, improve customs. So as then the king were king of Great Britain indeed.'[87] This would mean that the Book of Common Prayer used in England could be imposed, episcopal authority peaceably upheld and conformity established 'wholly to the government and laws of England . . . at least as we are here'.[88] The Deputy of Ireland projected his own approach to government directly on to the Scottish situation. In his dislike for the Scots, probably of some years' standing, he saw a likely ally in Northumberland. The thoughts were aired a little later to Laud.[89]

The Scottish advisers to the king, including the Marquis of Hamilton, would not think in similar terms, of Britain's salvation resting in the triumph of unadulterated anglicisation. Nor indeed would Charles go as far as to deny the Scottish identity; he kept Scottish councillors for his 'native kingdom'. Wentworth's scepticism on the use of ways of moderation with the Scots may not have reached the king. Laud passed on only parts of the correspondence to Charles, and not ordinarily the side papers in which these thoughts were contained. To his great frustration, Wentworth was instructed via Laud to hold off severe action against the Scots in Ireland until the results of Hamilton's mission were known; he was obliged to be accommodating on the

---

[85] Laud, *Works*, vol. VII, pp. 484, 490, 497, 505. Efforts to prove Hamilton's links with the Covenanters were inconclusive. WWM Str. P. LB 7, fols. 146–9; Laud, *Works*, vol. VII, pp. 485, 507; Knowler, *Strafforde Letters*, vol. II, pp. 125, 145–6; GD 406/1/569.

[86] Knowler, *Strafforde Letters*, vol. II, p. 191; WWM Str. P. LB 7, fols. 129–32.

[87] WWM Str. P. LB 10b, pp. 13–15. Cf. Knowler, *Strafforde Letters*, vol. II, p. 257.

[88] Knowler, *Strafforde Letters*, vol. II, pp. 190–1.

[89] WWM Str. P. LB 7, fol. 132; see too LB 3, p. 311; LB 11, pp. 190–1; T. Carte, *An History of the Life of James, Duke of Ormond* (3 vols., London, 1736), vol. III, pp. 19–20.

prospective use of the Earl of Antrim.[90] Limited to his own sphere, he investigated means of punitive action against the Covenanters in Ireland.[91]

Hamilton returned to Scotland in mid-September 1638. His hope for change was expressed in his earliest dispatches as, for example, he singled out the Earl of Haddington, whose willingness to serve seemed to bode well, given his recent history of sympathetic contacts particularly with the Earl of Rothes.[92] To the Marquis of Huntly, on the eve of issuing the new proclamation, Hamilton announced his hopes that the assembly and parliament might make a 'final conclusion' to the troubles. Huntly was to stay in the north to keep order, and further use his best efforts to have good men chosen in the elections now to be held.[93] The latter direction was not unique: a further part of the strategy was to compete with the Covenanters on their own ground to secure advantageous election results.[94]

But was Hamilton genuinely hopeful after the king's half-hearted espousal of moderate courses? At the outset his obvious support was patchy. Huntly had published the declaration of 4 July, despite its not being ratified by act of council, and looked to encourage others – indeed through his wider connections going beyond the north-east – but by no means with universal success.[95] The impact of the Aberdeen doctors' contribution is not easily assessed, but Forbes's *Peaceable Warning* had run to five hundred copies in the revised, printed version; the debate that began with the *Queries* and *Replyes*, approved through its stages in Court, had in addition allowed Hamilton a chance to make clear a critical stance on the Covenant – where his double-talk had confused matters. The Bishops of Aberdeen and Moray had lent their help.[96] Elsewhere the doctors of St Andrews, for example, who had also engaged in controversy, had had less staying power, since their area was generally behind the Covenant.[97] The Catholic nobles were loyal, but generally without large followings.[98] Various supporters received letters from Hamilton or Charles; but often they felt it necessary to request clear royal

---

[90] Laud, *Works*, vol. VII, pp. 464, 444, 455; WWM Str. P. LB 7, fols. 123–4, 132–3.
[91] M. Perceval-Maxwell, 'Strafford, the Ulster Scots and the Covenanters', *Irish Historical Studies*, 18 (1973), 524–51.
[92] GD 406/1/563; Gardiner, *Hamilton Papers*, p. 25; Baillie, *Letters*, vol. I, p. 47; Rothes, *Relation*, pp. 92–3; see also GD 406/1/689.
[93] GD 406/1/441, 439.
[94] GD 406/1/441, 961, 757, 692, 444; Gardiner, *Hamilton Papers*, p. 35; Johnston, *Diary*, pp. 377–8, 394; GD 406/1/567.
[95] GD 406/1/431, 639, 763, 428, 427, 1794.
[96] GD 406/1/433, 426, 564; GD 406/M9/88/16; J. D. Ogilvie, 'The Aberdeen doctors and the national covenant', *Papers of the Edinburgh Bibliographical Society*, 11 (1912–20), 73–86.
[97] See NLS Wod. Fo. 43, fol. 273 (copy in Wod. 4to. 25, fol. 32 has date 20 March); Wod. 4to. 26, fols. 128–34; also Wod. 4to. 76, fols. 56–7; Baillie, *Letters*, vol. I, p. 98; Johnston, *Diary*, pp. 348, 366.
[98] Cf. Rothes, *Relation*, p. 169; C. Hibbard, *Charles I and the Popish Plot* (Chapel Hill, NC, 1983), pp. 43, 93.

direction, which was a comment on one aspect of Charles's problem. The king, probably sensibly, referred much to Hamilton's discretion.[99]

Hamilton would look further for support amongst local officeholders but had little success in efforts at influencing appointments. Rigour in an anti-Covenanter line varied. When the Earl of Montrose complained at the interference in the impending burgh elections in Aberdeen, Roxburgh interestingly seems to have been sympathetic, fearing dangers if such a course were pressed through; personal sympathy probably had its part to play.[100] Traquair, however, positively gave advice for the last year's sheriffs to be retained, since it would be impossible in some places to find non-Covenanters.[101] Clergy dispossessed by the Covenanters would be keen supporters, but they clearly suffered economically and socially.[102] To win over some of their colleagues, the efforts of Hamilton and Dr Balcanquhal to foment hostility to Covenanter activity bore fruit: many ministers disliked the campaign for the participation of elders in the elections to the forthcoming assembly, especially when now particular gentry and nobles were specially infiltrated into the system.[103] The ministers' resistance was an encouraging point, since at a local level they played a not unimportant part in the Covenanter organisation.[104]

Charles had not given free rein. Hamilton once again was obliged to phrase his reports to Court with care – taking pains to enclose the documentation of what he was doing, and defending policy always in terms of its expediency. With Charles most happy on the negative thrust, Hamilton's optimism was cautiously restrained, as even at the beginning he held out only that the assembly might not be 'altogether damnable' – that at least if the assembly

---

[99] GD 112/43/1/6/36; Rothes, *Relation*, pp. 185–6; Stevenson, *Scottish Revolution*, p. 102. Not all of the king's letters came direct from Court; Hamilton carried blanks with him bearing the king's signature, and used apparently twenty-five – GD 406/1/747, 438; GD 406/M1/50.

[100] GD 406/1/531, 8170, 81, 8219; cf. Rothes, *Relation*, p. 149. Montrose sent his complaint via the Earl of Lauderdale; Hamilton pressed on, with only part success – GD 406/1/441, 669, 447, 757.

[101] GD 406/1/1003, 2360. For the Caithness story, see GD 406/1/439, 455, 471, 752; *RPCS*, 2nd Series, vol. VII, p. 102.

[102] GD 406/1/654. How many clergy were dispossessed at this time is not known, but names of those exiled to England in 1639 are extant – GD 406/M1/72/1–2; see too PRO E 351/1748 (I am grateful to Professor Mark Fissel for first drawing my attention to this); P. Heylyn, *Cyprianus Anglicus* (1668), p. 378; D. Stevenson, 'Deposition of ministers in the church of Scotland under the Covenanters, 1638–1651', *Church History*, 44 (1975), 321–35.

[103] On Covenanter management of elections, see Makey, *Church of the Covenant*, pp. 37–47, 123–38; Stevenson, *Scottish Revolution*, pp. 105–8.

[104] GD 406/1/563, 962, 766; Gardiner, *Hamilton Papers*, pp. 56, 57n.; GD 406/M9/88/9–10; GD 150/3444/1; Stevenson, *Scottish Revolution*, pp. 109–10; Makey, *Church of the Covenant*, pp. 17–25, 94–105. The showing of ministers' petitions at the assembly itself was less impressive – Baillie, *Letters*, vol. I, p. 138.

concluded on matters unacceptable to the king, there would be little support in the country at large for such conclusions.[105]

Having trusted only a small number of the privy councillors before September, Hamilton looked to see who would come over.[106] Probably at this time also, he compiled general lists, particularly of the nobility, which noted whether or not they were cooperative.[107] Nobility were prominent amongst the Covenanters on account of their rank but, as far as can be told, as an estate they tended to divide more than the others; besides Catholicism, personal allegiance to the king was doubtless a principal contributing factor in restraining their politics of alienation. Royal letters of course fostered such an effect. However, an important part of the Scottish problem was that the Covenant had moved all estates together in protest.[108]

Hamilton looked for grounds on which to hope, but he also quickly found difficulties. The noble Supplicants pleaded to be secured in religion on their terms before the royal proclamation was approved by the privy council. Hamilton resisted, but did make alterations in the text of the proclamation. Most strikingly the offer for episcopacy to be limited was omitted. It was justified to Court by the argument that it would be better for the king not to be necessarily committed to that, although Hamilton saw it as likely.[109] The fuller truth not contained in the dispatches is of interest. Archibald Johnston, considering what to say about the bishops at this stage, had decided to say nothing, presuming that Charles would not include any relevant statement in the proclamation. Surprised on learning the contrary, initially from Eleazar Borthwick, he was then favoured by Lord Lorne with more particular information. A presbyterian protestation seemed the only option; but then Lorne instead procured the omission of the proclamation statement.[110]

Hamilton had decided to risk postponing conflict on the issue of episcopacy so that the moderate settlement might stand a chance. Might Lorne work for a compromise settlement, though he had sympathy with the Covenant? In August he had served Hamilton crucially in persuading the Covenanters' agreement to the second journey south; Hamilton had wished security against any premature assembly elections taking place. At the same

---

[105] Gardiner, *Hamilton Papers*, p. 25; GD 406/1/563.

[106] GD 406/1/564, 569; cf. Gardiner, *Hamilton Papers*, pp. 27–8.

[107] GD 406/M9/88/6; the copy of a list in Bod. Dep. c. 172, fol. 11 has mistakes, but probably came from another original.

[108] Cf. D. Stevenson, 'The burghs and the Scottish Revolution', in M. Lynch (ed.), *The Early Modern Town in Scotland* (1987), pp. 167–91; GD 406/M1/35, M9/88/7; Makey, *Church of the Covenant, passim*.

[109] GD 406/1/564; cf. Gardiner, *Hamilton Papers*, p. 31. For the draft and the final text, see GD 406/M9/61/15–16; *RPCS*, 2nd Series, vol. VII, pp. 64–6. Even the statement of thanks by the privy council became muted – *ibid.*, pp. 66–7; cf. GD 406/M9/61/4.

[110] Johnston, *Diary*, pp. 390–2; also Yorke, *State Papers*, vol. II, p. 115; GD 406/1/986.

time their mutual understanding was strained – and in this present crisis through Hamilton's efforts in June for the employment of the Earl of Antrim and by his critical words in Court against Lorne in early September; more longstanding rivalries should not be discounted. The passing of time only heightened the tensions. The Covenanters were impatient for the elections; Lorne had reservations about the projected settlement brought back north by Hamilton.[111]

Hamilton's engagement of tactics did not belie his notions of limits on what the assembly might settle. The abolition of episcopacy lay outside these. Many Covenanters now may have had strong hopes for this, but it was left for the assembly to determine.[112] That did not of course preclude a concerted effort towards it, and Hamilton's intention to win nationwide support on the new but vague programme met a determined response. Trust was a rare commodity while there were still scares of the English arming.[113] This was important, but so were the demands of substance. Sir Thomas Hope, technically not a rebel, with Lorne and the Earl of Wigton inserted a qualifying clause for the 1581 Confession now to be signed by the privy council – 'as it was then professed'. This was a modification of Lorne's proposal, 'as it was then professed both in doctrine and discipline'; compromise with the reforming Covenanters may have been the intention, but the question arising was whether episcopacy was compatible with the Confession.[114] No elaboration was offered, for Hope and Lorne probably yet had to decide; Hamilton, happy enough with the king, would defend only the affirmative interpretation.

The interpretation of the King's Covenant, as it became known, was debated in council on 24 September, two days after the proclamation. It was asserted that the Negative Confession of 1581, in abjuring all things of popery, included matters of discipline and ceremonies. Hamilton doubted that the Covenanters all agreed on this, where 'matters indifferent' were concerned. This had certainly been true in the past, but Hamilton reckoned that some members of the council now inclined towards abolishing episcopacy.[115] At least Sir Thomas Hope and Lord Lorne would come to accept further that the Confession involved the abjuration of episcopacy. Hope was convinced that the Confession gave a true definition of the church in Scotland, as he argued

[111] Johnston, *Diary*, pp. 376, 393; GD 112/39/742; Baillie, *Letters*, vol. I, pp. 100–1; Burnet, *Memoires*, p. 109; GD 406/M9/61/12, M9/64/5.
[112] Cf. Johnston, *Diary*, p. 390.
[113] Makey, *Church of the Covenant*, pp. 35–6.
[114] Baillie, *Letters*, vol. I, pp. 107–8; GD 406/M9/64/5 – dated 22 September, although endorsed by Hamilton 'as *Argyll* would have had it' (my emphasis). Cf. Baillie, *Letters*, vol. I, pp. 144–7, 157–8; Makey, *Church of the Covenant*, p. 35.
[115] GD 406/1/565; Gardiner, *Hamilton Papers*, p. 33.

to Rothes on 2 October. His certainty probably extended little further at that time; but it seems possible that Sunday 28 October was a turning-point, after which he found it 'impossible' that the 1581 oath did not show that episcopacy was abjured within the church of Scotland as contrary to the Word of God. Lord Lorne first definitely wrote of the abjuration of episcopacy as the historical truth on 13 December, the day the resolution on it passed the Glasgow Assembly.[116] Hard courses by the king would produce a very hard reaction.

Hamilton would not agree, either now in September or later in the year, but this was a complicating element and the question of what was abjured by the Negative Confession arose frequently in the intervening period. With questions of ambiguity because of what the sixteenth-century reformers had wished, the Aberdeen doctors felt obliged to subscribe the King's Covenant conditionally in order to make clear their continuing faith in episcopacy, and the Marquis of Huntly confessed that he felt like doing the same. Covenanters in the north-east complained justifiably that by subscribing in the sense of 1581 they might be more obliged than before to the abjuring of episcopacy, the Articles of Perth and other recent 'innovations'.[117] Hamilton was frustrated in an attempt to remove the taint of ambiguity by a signed council declaration.[118]

The problems loomed large, yet as a move to convince the people of Scotland – including very much the 'vulgar sort' – of the king's 'good' intentions in religion, the policy of the King's Covenant had promise. The name of the king appended to this particular Confession compelled obedience, as Sir Thomas Hope himself insisted. Could Charles believe in it? Hamilton wished it so. To Laud he wrote of his hope to secure honest folk in religion 'in despite of the devil'.[119]

Perhaps he with his co-workers underestimated the strength of the opposition. The moderate Robert Baillie feared the implications of divisions and worried still at news of the king's military preparations, and this underpinned the extension of demands put for settlement beyond what the royal councillors offered.[120] Although Archibald Johnston confessed himself unsure of success at the outset – never expecting, on 21 September, so clear a means 'to

---

[116] *A Diary of the Public Correspondence of Sir Thomas Hope of Craighall, Bart, 1633–1645,* ed. T. Thomson, BC (Edinburgh, 1843), pp. vi–vii, 78; GD 406/1/10831. For Lorne, GD 45/1/42 but see GD 406/1/573. Cf. Makey, *Church of the Covenant,* pp. 51–2.

[117] Burnet, *Memoires,* pp. 86–7; GD 406/1/450, 448; [Charles I], *Large Declaration,* p. 177. Cf. Kirk, *Second Book of Discipline,* esp. pp. 130–45.

[118] GD 406/1/714; Hope, *Diary,* p. 79; GD 112/40/2/1/131; Johnston, *Diary,* p. 396; NLS Wod. Fo. 61, fol. 300; Baillie, *Letters,* vol. I, p. 112; GD 406/M9/91/3.

[119] Hope, *Diary,* pp. vi–vii; GD 406/1/566. Wariston saw the devil elsewhere – Johnston, *Diary,* pp. 392–3.

[120] Baillie, *Letters,* vol. I, p. 104.

divide and ruin us' – he would not let the movement be trapped. For himself he had long since argued the implications of the Confession against episco-pacy. In the large protestation made after Hamilton's proclamation, he argued that the band within the King's Covenant was insufficiently explicit against all 'innovations' since 1581; it courted danger, therefore, to subscribe it. He was harshly critical of Sir Thomas Hope for accepting it at all. The Covenanters subsequently did all they could to hinder subscriptions across the country.[121]

The collection of subscriptions against that was strained. A tactical gamble whereby existing Covenanters were amongst those commissioned on the task was not successful; but Lord Lorne, not technically a Covenanter, was no more diligent in his work, and Hamilton's explanation was accepted by the questioning Laud.[122] The efforts to gain ministers' support went as far as they could, but there was a setback with the Aberdeen doctors. Hamilton pushed them, against their own preference, to send representatives to the assembly in order to provide good disputes, but this failed to come off in the end, owing in some measure to accidental misunderstandings. Johnston was very relieved, attributing it to divine providence.[123] The Marquis of Huntly managed, reportedly, to get some twelve thousand signatures by his diligence and the receptivity of his area. On the way he furnished a large list of the prin-cipal barons and freeholders of Aberdeenshire who had subscribed: every one of these individuals was to be accountable. The people of Moray were beyond his responsibility and were mostly Covenanters, but he reported that some 'landed men' had offered their subscriptions to him.[124] Hamilton was encouraged in other quarters, where he reported sixteen thousand signatures – Bedchamber men Patrick Maule and James Maxwell were joined by the Earl of Nithsdale, sent by the king;[125] Lord Ogilvie worked valuably.[126]

---

[121] Johnston, *Diary*, pp. 391–3; NLS Wod. Fo. 62, fols. 14–16, 30, 32–3. For the protestation of 22 September, see [Charles I], *Large Declaration*, pp. 156–73. Cf. Stevenson, *Scottish Revolution*, p. 109.

[122] Stevenson, *Scottish Revolution*, pp. 112, 110; Gardiner, *Hamilton Papers*, pp. 43–4; GD 406/1/570, 454. The Earl of Dumfries also performed poorly – HMC *Hamilton Supplementary* (21), pp. 53–4.

[123] GD 406/1/665, 457, 666, 452, 463; HMC 6, p. 620 – Hamilton to [Huntly – not Argyll]; Johnston, *Diary*, p. 402. Cf. [Charles I], *Large Declaration*, pp. 244, 288.

[124] Burnet, *Memoires*, p. 86; GD 406/1/575, 473, 456/2, 460.

[125] Gardiner, *Hamilton Papers*, p. 56; BL Add. Ms. 15391, fols. 274–5. Patrick Maule of Panmure was otherwise outside the king's inner confidence. On 28 November he asserted confidently, and mistakenly, in a letter to Hamilton that Laud was not involved – GD 406/1/544.

[126] NLS Adv. Ms. 34.5.15. Lord Ogilvie was a Catholic – W. Forbes-Leith, *Memoirs of Scottish Catholics during the XVIIth and XVIIIth Centuries* (2 vols., 1909), vol. I, p. 9; GD 406/1/425, 726.

Hamilton was prepared to intimidate by threats of persecution. Lord Dalzell was accused by his opponents of using force to obtain subscriptions.[127]

By way of material inducements, Traquair and Stirling were instructed not to allow any grants to pass to Covenanters which were not 'absolutely' just in law; it was better to reward 'the deserving'.[128] At the end of October, Hamilton and Traquair were told to protect the estates of non-Covenanters, an order made on the day after the king recommended the Earl of Nithsdale for particular protection against creditors.[129] Nothing was to be done against the law, but favour was to be shown, and 'inconveniences' avoided as much as possible. The Earl of Stirling's register for subsequent months shows that this was not an empty directive.[130]

Hamilton was not limited to the politics of management. Dr Strang, the Principal of Glasgow University who previously had been pushed to sign the Covenant, wrote a tract to answer the protestation of 22 September and to encourage subscriptions for the King's Covenant, but he wanted it published anonymously. His wish being refused by Laud, the work was never published, but the surviving manuscript shows that Hamilton made some textual additions.[131]

Strang argued that the king's present concessions should satisfy all fears of innovation. The question of church government might still concern some people, but because practice varied around the reformed churches as did opinion within Scotland, it was best to strive for peace 'but not to think we can have earthly perfection'; the purity of doctrine was maintained in the kirk as it was. Then a number of reasons for subscribing the King's Covenant was avouched, the main purpose being to answer Johnston's protestation. When it was observed how the ministers had not backed the protestation as a group, Hamilton inserted in the manuscript some extensive points of factual detail, and almost immediately followed it with another section which attacked the defence offered for the National Covenant. Where it had been said that it was 'sealed from heaven by the fire of the Spirit', Hamilton objected that this made no sense and tended to blasphemy, since the Covenanters had compared the document's authority, its 'inspiration' and 'infallibility', with holy scripture.[132]

---

[127] GD 406/1/452; Johnston, *Diary*, p. 393; NLS Wod. Fo. 54, p. 174; Gardiner, *Hamilton Papers*, p. 41.

[128] BL Add. Ms. 23112, fol. 87v.

[129] BL Add. Ms. 23112, fols. 88–9; GD 406/1/736, 744; also Baillie, *Letters*, vol. I, pp. 75–6.

[130] BL Add. Ms. 23112, fols. 90–2. There may have been bribery on the eve of the assembly – NLS Wod. Fo. 65, fol. 192.

[131] Baillie, *Letters*, vol. I, pp. 476–7, 482–3; GD 406/1/573; NLS Wod. Fo. 66, fol. 65. For Strang, see Baillie, *Letters*, vol. I, pp. 66–9, 106, 134–5, 138; Johnston, *Diary*, pp. 367–9; [Charles I], *Large Declaration*, pp. 267–8.

[132] NLS Wod. Fo. 31, fol. 10 – Hamilton holograph; the attention to factual detail is characteristic of the marquis. Cf. here GD 406/1/564.

Strang proceeded to argue against the assertion that religion in 1581 in Scotland differed from the present. On the Articles of Perth and episcopacy, he wrote how many ministers were resolved with the king that neither of these were comprehended as being condemned or abjured – although this did not mean the opposite extreme, that they were upheld on oath. The band attached to the Confession was explained and, in conclusion, fears of royal insincerity answered: where there had been fear of arms, it was asserted that the king was making real efforts to solve the question peaceably.[133]

Hamilton's involvement in the issues deserves notice. The truth behind the misleading last point in the tract made his line of argument, stated both to Charles and Huntly, that religion could no longer be at stake not altogether well founded – though as he knew there was a real challenge to the king's understanding of sovereignty.[134] Strang's work, however, was an aid to Hamilton in defence against horrendous accusations now being levelled at him. In the pressure of the situation he began to restrain less the military dimension, at first more in response to Charles's pressure, but then to show more clearly to the waverers the king's controlled intentions. He put up money, amongst other things for arms to be brought into Edinburgh Castle. On 14 October he consented to supplies being put into Newcastle and Northumberland; the time schedule for manning garrisons in Berwick and Carlisle, instead of being between the assembly and parliament, was advanced so that they would be filled by the time the assembly convened. Not long afterwards he wrote to ask Huntly to consider what supplies of arms he would need.[135]

Hamilton had covered himself by undertaking his mission cautiously. He still wished leeway to do what he could to gain a party for the king, but was in agreement that a final punitive course should be taken with the most recalcitrant: this, as he frankly wrote to Charles, was the only way that it could be hoped to achieve a settlement 'acceptable' to him. Force from England would bolster the support looked for within Scotland.[136] It was no doubt a correct judgement that the present strength of the Covenanters rested on more than ideas and programmes, but whether coercive power from outside would achieve a conclusion in the king's favour remained to be tested. In Scotland Covenanter control was impressive, with the saints apparently as ready as the

---

[133] NLS Wod. Fo. 31, fols. 7–24; Wod. Fo. 66, fol. 65. For other similar tracts, see NLS Wod. Fo. 63, fols. 41–2; NLS Ms. 20774, fol. 67; *Whereas Some Have Given Out . . .*, Aldis 917 (Edinburgh, 1638).
[134] GD 406/1/443; Gardiner, *Hamilton Papers*, pp. 37, 60; also Yorke, *State Papers*, vol. II, p. 118.
[135] GD 406/1/10798; *PCR*, vol. IV, p. 438; GD 406/1/567, 575, 455; Gardiner, *Hamilton Papers*, pp. 42, 45–6, 49–55. Up to this point, Huntly had simply had to be prepared for any 'rupture' – GD 406/1/443.
[136] Gardiner, *Hamilton Papers*, p. 45; GD 406/1/570.

king to take the dispute to arms for the battle against the antichrist; but the management of the short-term politics was as crucial. The original Covenant was upheld despite Hamilton's efforts.[137] In England, meanwhile, the king was not even able to fulfil his limited plan of showing that his military threat was in earnest. Supplies from the Low Countries for the English north-east failed for some reason; and the five hundred Irish troops summoned to garrison Carlisle could not be ready.[138]

Preparations laid for the assembly allowed it to be dissolved if necessary at its opening, but Hamilton resisted the efforts of the Scottish bishops to have it prorogued altogether.[139] With lay advice, four statements to be used at the assembly were composed for approval at Court – a protestation in case a bishop was not accepted as Moderator, a speech for Hamilton to deliver, propositions to be offered in the king's name and a paper to show the nullities of the assembly – in other words something to excuse its dissolution. It was assumed that a future assembly would be more pliable. These were sent on 22 October to Laud, who was to explain everything to the king. As the king had wished, should this assembly have some days of meeting, protestations would prevent final resolutions on contentious issues; in particular Hamilton would not allow debate on the choosing of the Moderator, the validity of elections or the place of bishops, lest the way was opened for the overthrow of episcopacy. It would be essential for the king to keep verbatim to what was offered on his behalf, for, even if the assembly was dissolved at its opening, a declaration having been read to his 'best advantage' would maintain and increase the party won over already by concessions.[140]

The proposed declaration of propositions was written out by Traquair, together with a form which set out the demands of the Covenanters alongside suggested answers. Charles was advised here not simply to repeat the terms of his proclamation, but to uphold decisive roles for assembly and parliament on everything from the service-book through to the Perth Articles. In other words, Hamilton returned to the advice offered to Charles but rejected in September. Other answers met demands part way. Lawful oaths for ministers remained against a wider demand that asked both for presbyteries to be allowed to admit ministers and for the consent of parishioners to appointments, even in cases of episcopal presentation. For bishops, the demand that they be censured and their powers limited according to the caveats of Glasgow and Montrose, or further as the general assembly might determine, had the vague response that 'persons censurable' were subject to the assembly. This kept in line with Hamilton's decision around the publication

---

[137] Johnston, *Diary*, pp. 390–7.
[138] Burnet, *Memoires*, p. 90; Knowler, *Strafforde Letters*, vol. II, pp. 228, 233–5.
[139] See GD 406/1/957, 567, 706, 683, 682.   [140] GD 406/1/569.

of the September proclamation. As an institution episcopacy was not up for debate; Hamilton would make this as public as possible. The demand for general assemblies to be held once a year was answered by the formula that they might be kept 'so oft and as oft as the affairs of this kirk shall require', with the next assembly being indicted for a particular time and place, here left blank. Finally there was to be a statement of the king's disavowal of innovation and of his hope for everyone to subscribe the Confession of Faith.[141]

The obvious novelty was the notion touching the meeting of future assemblies. A second assembly was foreseen but with no clear commitment to a regular process thereafter; the formula was as far as the king would go.[142] When the statement was returned from Court, however, Charles blocked it more generally. Again he refused to commit all future decisions on liturgy and canons to the judgement of general assemblies, merely proposing the ambiguous statement that no other would be introduced 'but by a fair and legal way', and he deleted altogether the referral of High Commission and the Articles of Perth to the present assembly and parliament.[143] It was his typical entrenched response, far from meeting what had been proposed to him; whatever Laud or anyone else advised, his position was clear. Enraged at the insolence of the Covenanters' protestation in September, he did not see on principle why the Scots should not accept his accommodation.[144]

It remained uncertain whether the assembly should be allowed to meet beyond the opening day. Hamilton concentrated as much on trying to persuade Charles to uphold a full statement of concessions. Although he corresponded directly, Hamilton addressed his pleas to Laud as the useful ally in the circumstances: principle needed to take account of politics. In September the king had agreed that a future Act of parliament might repeal the 1621 Act that had ratified the Five Articles of Perth. While Hamilton was well aware of the sensitivity of the issues at stake, he argued plainly that there could be no satisfaction if it was said only that they would not be urged, as Charles now suggested; he wanted the possibility of an Act. As an interim sop, he did not deny that the king might use 'all fair persuasive means' to support practice according to the Articles, observing that this was the original state of affairs.[145] Charles was persuaded, but insisted that he should not be represented as 'pleased', only 'content'. All things being equal, he would have

---

141 GD 406/M1/67; GD 406/M9/91/1 is Hamilton's copy of the demands and answers; M9/65/7 is the copy sent to Court and returned, initialled by the king.
142 Cf. [Charles I], *Large Declaration*, p. 278; A. Peterkin, *Records of the Kirk of Scotland* (Edinburgh, 1838), p. 142; GD 406/1/163.
143 GD 406/M9/65/7; [Charles I], *Large Declaration*, pp. 277–8; Burnet, *Memoires*, p. 88.
144 Burnet, *Memoires*, pp. 82–3; Gardiner, *Hamilton Papers*, p. 39; Laud, *Works*, vol. VI, p. 543. Cf. also GD 406/1/10783.
145 GD 406/M9/71; Burnet, *Memoires*, p. 73; GD 406/1/565, 572; cf. Gardiner, *Hamilton Papers*, p. 55.

omitted the concession, 'that I should not be thought to desire the abolishing of that in Scotland which I approve and maintain in England'; the comment pointed back to part of the rationale behind the policy.[146]

For the 'nullities' to be exposed at the assembly for excusing dissolution the prime concentration was on the irregularities in elections, and the bishops apparently were forward in giving their advice here.[147] Hamilton would reveal dramatically at Glasgow his extensive knowledge of the secret directions sent out by the Tables, the Covenanter executive, for local elections.[148] In the background to the paper of nullities, there was some legal debate whether the assembly could be dissolved by the king alone. Hamilton and Charles assumed it could be done, although the marquis warned Laud that the event might override the theory. More doubtful theoretically was the king's negative voice in assemblies; that this was assured in a parliament added to the importance of the protestations planned to save the king being wrongly committed at Glasgow.[149]

The Court response to the nullities was constructive, observing the difficulty of the one argued for the non-subscription by electors and elected of the King's Covenant, which Hamilton, on reflection, marked to be omitted – probably because of the interpretation controversies. It was further suggested that if the marquis was to use the nullities, proclamation would be better than protestation; if the bishops on the other hand employed them, a protestation might be used. Hamilton as the king's representative should not be vulnerable to challenge on his judgement of nullities. A form of such a proclamation was appended, which was subsequently used with additions to cover what proceedings of the assembly did take place.[150]

Bishop John Maxwell had been to Court, and Hamilton was relieved to learn that he was seemingly moderate in his conduct. He was persuaded that the assembly should meet, despite his original mission almost certainly being

---

[146] Burnet, *Memoires*, p. 93 (12, not 20 November – SRO Hamilton Red Book i, 124). Cf. Baillie, *Letters*, vol. I, pp. 119–20.

[147] GD 406/M9/66/1; see too GD 406/M9/109/1. The former paper may have derived from another paper of nullities, certainly of episcopal composition, which tried firstly to suggest alternatives for a general assembly – a general council of all three kingdoms (prophetic?!), or a debate of differences by some clergy and laity before the king (retrospective). Neither was suitable in the present circumstances – GD 406/M9/66/2.

[148] Cf. GD 406/M9/61/4, M9/87/1; GD 406/1/962, 689.

[149] GD 406/M9/56/3 (Sir Thomas Hope); M9/56/2 (Sir Lewis Stewart?); Gardiner, *Hamilton Papers*, p. 33; GD 406/1/569; Baillie, *Letters*, vol. I, pp. 95–6, 467. Cf. J. P. Sommerville, *Politics and Ideology in England, 1603–1640* (1986), pp. 191–2; B. P. Levack, *The Formation of the British State: England, Scotland and the Union, 1603–1707* (Oxford, 1987), pp. 57–8.

[150] GD 406/M9/64/4; GD 406/1/400; Burnet, *Memoires*, pp. 99–100; [Charles I], *Large Declaration*, pp. 290–4.

to the contrary.[151] When Maxwell arrived in Edinburgh, he and Hamilton together settled the form of the bishops' general declinator of this assembly, which had been examined and commented on already by Charles. As a faith standard, the bishops referred to the 1567 Confession. The declinator was formed to incorporate the nullities.[152]

In theory, therefore, Charles's integrity in religion was to be made manifest in a short assembly; and, if the nullities were remedied, a new assembly might be indicted. The advent of military strength might be hoped to deal with the 'disturbers' of the country. Hamilton now held back little on this and Charles, on the eve of the meeting, announced his wish for 'wholesome resolutions', warning determinedly how he was set, by the advice of his council in England, on preparations for involving England in the business should these not be achieved. Mention of his council indicated how his attentions were shifting to the wooing of support outside Scotland; he would wish to appear innocently obliged to take up arms.[153] However, the 'advice' had hardly been crucial to his decision. To date Hamilton's own work had shaped the measure of the English preparations. Only on 15 November had Charles put the Scottish business for the second time before the assembled English privy council. As in July, the emphasis was more on getting support for the decided policy rather than opening up Scottish politics for debate – although there was apparently some discussion, with a mixture of opinions on possible ways forward. The greatest point of debate was on how much Scottish strength could be counted on, and how far therefore aggression needed to be pushed from England. It was reported that there were at least hesitations, but in any case detailed administrative work had proceeded through the small committee for Scotland four days earlier; this inner circle of advisers met frequently thereafter.[154]

Since even the limited scheme for the English border garrisons had not yet succeeded, Hamilton offered to protract the sitting of the assembly in the hope that this might help, but the Scottish bishops were uneasy.[155] Arguments over tactics nearly led to a confrontation, which was avoided only at the last minute. Archbishop Spottiswood was wanting to represent his claim to be Moderator, while Hamilton considered the more vital thing to be the declaration of the king's concessions. Their final agreement concluded at least that

[151] Burnet, *Memoires*, pp. 90–1, 88.
[152] Gardiner, *Hamilton Papers*, p. 58; GD 406/1/573, 704; Burnet, *Memoires*, p. 93; [Charles I], *Large Declaration*, p. 262.
[153] GD 406/1/400, 713, 10794, 10779; Yorke, *State Papers*, vol. II, p. 113; Burnet, *Memoires*, pp. 99–100.
[154] BL Add. Ms. 15391, fols. 313–14; GD 406/1/10794; cf. BL Add. Ms. 27962H, fols. 210–11; *CSPD 1638–9*, 402/61. That it was only the second time is an argument based on silence.
[155] Gardiner, *Hamilton Papers*, p. 58.

dissolution was still to be achieved by demonstrating the illegality of the elections.[156]

The general assembly convened at Glasgow on Wednesday 21 November.[157] There was no doubting that Hamilton from the outset was weak. He failed in his attempt to have six privy councillors as his assessors to attend alongside him with voting powers. Few of the elected commissioners had not been candidates of the Covenanters, and Archibald Johnston was well prepared with a programme. On bishops, Johnston had long since moved beyond the idea of merely limiting them; a paper in advance of the assembly contained few doubts that episcopal government would go – despite, or perhaps because of, the firmness of line on the other side. Johnston's worries focused more around the subject of clerical votes in parliament. In James's day this had been a prime motive for the royal nomination of bishops, who were subsequently used to steer Scottish parliaments; kings had made it a highly political matter. The proposal was to rule against all holding of civil office by churchmen.[158]

For one week the marquis covered Charles by protesting at every possible point of offence. He raised the point of disputable elections as soon as he arrived, but gave way easily on it; similarly the bishops' declinator was offered and withdrawn at the inevitable refusal – tactics to waste time and score for readiness to accommodate. At the elections of the Moderator and Clerk, the bishops' short protestation was delivered. Traquair spoke out frequently, though he lacked a commission; Lorne, now Earl of Argyll, spoke also, but not with Hamilton's backing.

When the commissions were read, Johnston, acting as Clerk, came to read aloud the names of those who backed the election of Sir Alexander Erskine of Dun against Lord Carnegie, the Earl of Southesk's son. It was a deliberate trial of strength, for the Erskine election had been made first, and by an adequate number of presbytery members; the rival was a king's man. Southesk had not backtracked on the help he had given Hamilton, and Carnegie was like-minded.[159] Apart from the personalities, however, Hamilton was obliged to meet the challenge, because it clearly showed a Covenanter fixing of an election; the problem was that it came too soon, before the king's 'good' intentions were proclaimed. Hamilton was not ready for a breaking-point.

---

[156] GD 406/1/671, 707, 673; Burnet, *Memoires*, pp. 96–8.

[157] I have drawn the following brief account from the three principal sources and shall not reference daily proceedings – Peterkin, *Records*, pp. 128–93; Robert Douglas's account in NLS Wod. 8vo. 10, fols. 68–120 (copy of Wod. 4to. 72, fols. 1–40); Baillie, *Letters*, vol. I, pp. 119–76. See too BL Sloane Ms. 650, fols. 78–83; GD 406/M9/88/11; Stevenson, *Scottish Revolution*, pp. 116–26; Makey, *Church of the Covenant*, pp. 48–52.

[158] Johnston, *Diary*, pp. 398, 403–4; NLS Wod. Fo. 63, fols. 103–4; GD 406/M9/82/1; Baillie, *Letters*, vol. I, pp. 174–5.

[159] Johnston, *Diary*, p. 350; GD 406/1/541, 650/1, 614; Yorke, *State Papers*, vol. II, p. 114.

The day was saved by other Covenanters speaking up to escape the issue. Business resuming, the commissions were all read, and Hamilton did not engage much in the other debates which took place. Instead he made protestation that he might raise future objections.[160]

He decided however on the next day, 27 November, to declare for the king. It did not seem possible, he wrote to Charles, to prolong the meeting any longer. With the assembly constituted, events so far had only confirmed his earlier fears of what was to come.[161] Therefore when the business turned again to controverted elections, he pushed the reading of the bishops' declinator, their appeal to the king that the assembly was illegal. Hamilton sounded apologetic that the assembly was thus doomed because of this division among its rightful 'members'; the aim was to win support for the king in the process. The day after, avouching the illegality of the assembly, he positively declined to acknowledge the authenticity of the old registers which were under scrutiny, and the assembly voted without him. A reply was read to the declinator, which at first he would not answer, but Balcanquhal spoke up. The example of the Synod of Dort had been raised, and Balcanquhal, who had attended there, wished to observe that Dort had dealt with fundamental points of religion; in contrast, he said, the present matters were indifferent, 'policy and order'.[162] The distinction was not so readily accepted by the other side; but Hamilton interrupted to read the king's statement of concessions.[163] In his speech he emphasised that the assembly met to consider not changes in religion but its preservation. This might include just criticism of bishops – such assemblies would be held for that purpose as often as necessary – but to do more was excessive. He proceeded to expose the Covenanters' organisation of the recent elections.

Hamilton intended to say nothing further. He fended off Lord Loudoun and Alexander Henderson as they tried to introduce full discussions concerning the bishops, and would not at first justify his objections to the elections. His words repeated the ideas he had often conveyed in writings to Court – 'If you persist [in this assembly against bishops] it is the king, not the bishops you have ado with.' As he began to criticise the ignorance of the lay elders, Rothes pushed him, with more success, to say more about the Covenanter influence on elections. He performed poorly, according to the account falling back 'on generals'. 'I know all my master's commands are justifiable, such as good Christians ought to obey': this was anger that the orders of the Tables

[160] See on this Makey, *Church of the Covenant*, pp. 42, 49.
[161] Gardiner, *Hamilton Papers*, pp. 60–1.
[162] Cf. N. R. N. Tyacke, *Anti-Calvinists* (Oxford, 1987), pp. 92, 95–8; Baillie, *Letters*, vol. I, pp. 139–41.
[163] A copy of this signed by Hamilton is NLS Ms. 7032, fol. 36. Cf. Peterkin, *Records*, p. 108; [Charles I], *Large Declaration*, pp. 277–8.

had been commanding greater obedience.[164] Argyll then spoke up to protest his belief that the assembly was lawful, and he explained his thoughts on the Negative Confession. Hamilton, refusing to allow debate of the interpretation of the Covenants, stood up and left. But the assembly sat on.

A protestation was made alleging that the Commissioner had lacked sufficient reason to end the meeting; therefore it had to go ahead. The minister, David Dickson, called attention in his subsequent speech to the clear lesson of fidelity Hamilton had given, the lesson of obedience, in Hamilton's case to his commission, but here to be rendered absolutely to God – which restricted obedience to the king. Hamilton's arguments had rung emptily for those who preferred the assembly's mind on the will of God. They sat on and passed resolutions; episcopacy and the Perth Articles were subsequently abjured, the civil places of kirkmen declared unlawful.

The considerable differences with Charles were now more sharply defined than ever. His politics pushed the Covenant movement to this state as much as did religious faith. Divided opinions were evident in the votes on the abjuration Acts.[165] Charles had answered the appeals for a general assembly only belatedly and under pressure, and had committed himself very little. The service-book and canons were to have been withdrawn upon a proclamation, not by a definitive assembly ruling; the assembly, had it been 'legally' constituted in his eyes, would merely have been a tool to be used, not a forum of free discussion.[166] He, like the Covenanter leaders, mixed law and the politics he wished to pursue. In the event, with authority in the church the fundamental issue, they gained the advantage. To defy the order to dissolve was a step of great significance. For the king, it was the most visible assertion of the power of the Covenant movement; it was actually the climax of the achievements of the internal organisation of the past year.

Those who remained in this assembly believed in a settlement to be made there, no doubt with varying degrees of commitment – the group included a whole spectrum of opinions, from the newest convert, Lord Erskine, to the convinced zealot Archibald Johnston.[167] It was, however, essential that the king who, it could be said, had been misled might in due course be persuaded of these determinations. Argyll told Traquair on 29 November that, although he would not sign the proclamation of dissolution, as he was now otherwise conscientiously committed, he would try to keep the assembly proceedings

---

[164] Cf. NLS Ms. 79, fol. 76 (5 October 1638). The whole day was also described in a long letter to the king – Yorke, *State Papers*, vol. II, pp. 113–21.

[165] See NLS Wod. Fo. 42, fols. 289–98; Baillie, *Letters*, vol. I, pp. 158–60, 175, 177–82; EUL New College Ms. X15b 3/1, vol. I, fol. 171v; vol. II, fols. 103–16. See too Stevenson, *Scottish Revolution*, pp. 123–5.

[166] Cf. GD 406/1/671; Baillie, *Letters*, vol. I, pp. 113–14, 141.

[167] Makey, *Church of the Covenant*, pp. 49–53.

'justifiable'. However, while his conscience conformed with assembly conclusions, the term 'justifiable' would have meant almost nothing to Charles. Nevertheless, one proposal he apparently made was somehow to reconcile the King's Covenant and that of the mainstream. It could conceivably have allowed freedom of conscience to everyone on the issue of episcopacy; politically it was a dead letter. That Hamilton had to maintain Charles's commitment effectively destroyed the idea.[168]

Others of the king's servants, Traquair and Southesk, obediently claimed that they could take no Covenant which excluded episcopacy.[169] Hamilton managed to get council backing for the proclamation of dissolution, but with extreme difficulty; two of the signatories, the Earls of Galloway and Kinghorn, soon after deserted to the assembly.[170] When a protestation was published from the general assembly, Hamilton responded with a further proclamation on 17 December, which recited at greater length the reasons for dissolution; it closed by insisting that subscription to the King's Covenant did not abjure episcopacy, an argument which was also published separately in a fuller form.[171]

There were clearly polarised standpoints on the issues but the whole was more complex. Rumours of English arming contributed to the general excitement. On the other hand Hamilton's achievement of council support owed much to his forceful appeal.[172] The assembly, however, was saying that the king had to change his position, and while the Scottish bishops, named for their bad counsel, were now punished, people hoped for more – and by Hamilton's means. Of course Hamilton was to be 'well' informed so as to counter further ill counsel, but Charles himself was not free from criticism. Argyll ultimately parted with the marquis on seemingly good terms. Having met personally with the king earlier in the year, he clearly reckoned that Charles himself needed to alter his resolutions and so allow others to do the same in the light of persuasive arguments of truth and reason. Hamilton's efforts to date under direct royal command had confirmed that, though his manœuvrings had successfully kept him Scottish trust. Johnston of Wariston meditated perhaps with a greater intensity in wishing Charles's personal

[168] GD 406/1/1010; GD 112/40/2/1/9; Yorke, *State Papers*, vol. II, p. 115; Johnston, *Diary*, p. 404; GD 45/1/42; Makey, *Church of the Covenant*, p. 52.
[169] GD 406/1/1010.
[170] Baillie, *Letters*, vol. I, pp. 146, 169. The proclamation is in [Charles I], *Large Declaration*, pp. 290–4; the manuscript draft in Traquair's hand shows the late alterations – GD 406/M9/45.
[171] J. D. Ogilvie, 'A bibliography of the Glasgow Assembly, 1638', *Records of the Glasgow Bibliographical Society*, 7 (1923), 1–12; Gardiner, *Hamilton Papers*, p. 66; GD 406/1/580, 611, 466.
[172] GD 406/1/10779. The document as in Gardiner, *Hamilton Papers*, pp. 66–8, was printed from the badly damaged original (SRO Hamilton Red Book i, 113).

reform; he placed his trust more in his God, and those called to be His instruments.[173]

General hopes of Hamilton's counsel did not necessarily mean that he would fully cooperate, nor indeed that Charles, any more than before, would heed new advice. However, the hopes were well placed, given that Hamilton preserved the king's favour. For himself, Hamilton was deeply troubled at the turn of events. His assessments for Charles of the loyalties of individuals were honest and judicious. Besides concentration mainly on the privy councillors and various nobles among the opponents, he included specific criticism of the Scottish bishops; the observation that they had not used the 'ordinary and legal way' for the church in Scotland struck pointedly at the course preferred by the king and Laud; Laud, and no doubt Charles, would not be willing hearers.[174] At the same time Hamilton had accepted for the king's sake that authority would have to be recovered by force. He concluded his paper with detailed ideas of strategy to reduce Scotland to obedience.

Hamilton committed himself to being involved until the country was quietened, but beyond that no longer – an interesting indication of his commitment to his already strained task. He projected an alternative for the future. Government by privy council having failed, he recommended a 'lieutenant or commissioner' for the whole kingdom, and at best the Duke of Lennox; Huntly, for all his good service, might lack general acceptability.[175] Thus, unconsciously, Hamilton repeated the similar long-term conclusion drawn by his enemy Viscount Wentworth.[176] There was a crucial difference, informed by their differing political experiences. The Scot put his faith in a Scottish permanent Commissioner; the Englishman in Ireland had wished the extension of English hegemony.

With English military preparedness forecast for February or March of the new year, Charles would not cancel the promised parliament in Scotland. Sir Henry Vane, himself drawing back from the prospect of bloodshed, reported the king's hopes for support beyond the assembly; Charles, he wrote, was concerned for the care of his loyal party in Scotland. Hamilton was therefore invited to come to Court to give counsel, or, if not himself, the Earl of Traquair, a suggestion by Lennox left to Hamilton's discretion.[177] Charles was certainly angry; Vane, who clearly had thought that Charles was think-

---

173 GD 112/40/2/1/8, 131, 9, 126; Baillie, *Letters*, vol. I, pp. 143–4; GD 406/M9/61/12; Johnston, *Diary*, pp. 402–5.
174 Cf. Laud, *Works*, vol. VI, pp. 554–5.
175 Yorke, *State Papers*, vol. II, pp. 113–21. The king's brief approving reply is in Burnet, *Memoires*, p. 99.
176 Above, p. 96. In August 1639, Hamilton's opinion was different – in changed circumstances – GD 406/1/948.
177 SRO Hamilton Red Book i, 111 – Burnet, *Memoires*, pp. 107–8, deliberately omitted the postscript about Traquair; HMC 9 (II), p. 249.

ing in terms of defence before the news came of the attempted dissolution of the assembly, was afterwards less sure.[178] However, the Scottish committee which had been entrusted with practical arrangements anticipated a smaller force than might have been, probably on account of cost; and the king did not rush to dramatise the situation in England.[179] Letters were sent out on 8 December for the mustering of trained bands, for which the king's final version gave away even less than the draft, which had hinted only that it was 'now of more importance than usual for us and our kingdom'.[180]

In Scotland the situation looked poor. Hamilton reflected somewhat despondently on how, lacking supportive force, he and the anti-Covenanters were vulnerable.[181] Nevertheless he sent out letters to loyal supporters, and provided funds for the clergy in difficulties.[182] He asked the Lords of Session to pass nothing upon the acts of the general assembly, but under pressure withdrew the order to have the letter registered, trying to avoid provoking a tumult; a few days later he applied his own influence on the same matter on the four Lords who had refused the King's Covenant, if only to create grounds for later punishment.[183] He planned the Marquis of Huntly's appointment as a lieutenant of forces in the north, assuming that the English forces would be coming soon. Charles agreed, but updated English news caused Hamilton to postpone the plan, which included other projected lieutenancies.[184] Huntly probably gave the greatest support in looking to the king's party. Besides talk about supplies there was mention that Dr Barron of Aberdeen was prepared to argue a strong case for the king's *iure divino* right to call and dissolve assemblies. Hamilton was grateful, for the question of the right to dissolve was very important.[185] Here had been the greatest affront of recent days to royal authority. The struggle was to continue.

The months between the signing of the National Covenant and the Glasgow Assembly undoubtedly made the ground that it has been tempting since to characterise as the 'Scottish Revolution'. Whether in campaigns to gather

---

[178]   Gardiner, *Hamilton Papers*, pp. 62–4; GD 406/1/578, 319, 549; Burnet, *Memoires*, pp. 99 (3 December), 107; GD 406/1/10799, 10797.

[179]   BL Add. Ms. 15391, fol. 317v; Bod. Clarendon Ms. 15, fols. 36, 44, 45v, 48; *CSPD 1638–9*, 404/22, 33; S. R. Gardiner, *A History of England . . . 1603–1642* (10 vols., 1883–4), vol. VIII, pp. 385–6.

[180]   PRO SP 16/404/38. The earlier action had been to encourage Lords Lieutenant to see to musters in the counties – *PCR*, vol. IV, pp. 542–4; GD 406/1/10794.

[181]   Gardiner, *Hamilton Papers*, p. 66; GD 406/1/579, 465.

[182]   GD 406/1/466, 468, 470, 472; *HMC Hamilton Supp.*, p. 55; GD 406/1/401; PRO E 351/1748.

[183]   Hope, *Diary*, p. 83; Traqr. Mss. Bundle 28; GD 112/39/751; GD 406/1/625.

[184]   GD 406/1/10779.

[185]   GD 406/1/469, 471. I have not located Barron's work, but see NLS Wod. Fo. 66, fol. 17v; GD 406/1/758, 412.

subscriptions to the Covenant or to assess potential military strength, the Covenanters undermined royal sovereignty as Charles had wished to shape it. Through elections to the general assembly and in its proceedings, the pattern was repeated. Central organisation, internal propaganda and sheer commitment in strength were the means of this achievement; social patterns and skilful politics underlay the course fashioned but not wholly limited by the name of religion.

Royal notions of policy and authority were naturally bound up together. Authority could not be surrendered, but its maintenance in accordance with the dictates of law and realism was highly problematic, given the Covenanter challenge over the importance of assemblies. Parliamentary law could not help Charles on the central issues when the contrary arguments were maintained with such force. The situation clearly required negotiation towards settlement, but Charles chose still to be very limited in his responsiveness. He was advised otherwise, but he held firm. Because of obsession with authority, policy was little altered. On the one hand he determined to have punishment of the most outright opposers of his rule; on the other he offered inadequate means for the building of support.

The two together were an unpromising mixture, not least because they militated against a relaxation of the general sense of crisis that counted against the king in Scotland. Yet there was no simple alternative. Force in itself provided no guaranteed solution – Charles was told this often enough – but in the circumstances was the only means of punishing those who were seen to be in rebellion. The Earl of Roxburgh questioned whether the times suited the desire for punishment. Charles was apparently vindictive in this regard; but his councillors shared the policy at least to some extent. Hamilton, with the likes of Roxburgh and Traquair, might apply considerable efforts to advancing peaceable approaches, but when the other side attacked royal authority, threat of persecution had to be applied. When presbyterianism loomed, Hamilton went into defence for the sake of the royal prerogative. Archbishop Laud was not so different – although he may have been less happy about conciliation on account of his positive beliefs; his realism pushed him to cooperate, except when insubordination seemed too hard to tolerate, and the marquis easily communicated with him.[186] Charles, then, exemplified the extreme pole of an approach that his counsellors felt themselves bound in part to share.

That the development of ways of force was not immediately feasible compelled Charles to attend to ways of conciliation, but these equally had their problems. The king would dabble in the suggestions put to him for concessions in the interests of winning support away from the Covenant he so

[186] Cf. GD 406/1/569, 570.

utterly detested. He would not, however, yield a reasonable programme. At all times his concessions not only lagged timewise behind demands – thus continuing the general sense of insecurity – but failed to come near even to what was advised. The ideas that Hamilton brought to Court at the beginning of September 1638 were the best. The king's name commanded wide respect; his endorsement of the Negative Confession, distasteful though he found it, could have won wide support. But Charles's chosen vagueness in expressing the concessions advised worked against the restoration of trust. Admittedly the Covenanter leadership did what they could to sabotage the operation, but, in the light of Charles's outright refusal to give way to general assembly and parliament decisions, the royal scheme was genuinely flawed. Whatever causes drove those who stood up against him, the appeals to representative Scottish assemblies were probably of fundamental importance.

Royal government was under attack, but this was not necessarily revolution. The whole imperative for the moderate schemes upheld by Hamilton and the others was that division at least might be created within the Covenant movement. Division of any sort might have been productive, given the attentions on the other side to concert the unity which was, among other things, a sign of God's Providence. The Scottish troubles were serious: the people cried down bishops in the streets, and a determined group of ministers and others wished and prayed for their removal, but the united advances of the Covenant movement depended on more than that; indeed, only gradually did a full reformation programme become integrated within it. The judgement that satisfaction of the majority was possible despite what had arisen never died amongst the king's counsellors; and it would be unwise to dismiss that. Was this not an important part of Lord Lorne's behaviour too, the hope that normality would soon return? Potentially conservatism would have tended to help the resolution of crisis; the undoubted daring of the core who kept the unrest going flourished only in the abnormal circumstances. They worked hard, but Charles's continuing obstinacy did little to stop them.

The king dragged his feet. His basic position seems to have been to abstain temporarily from the troublesome policies if and only if in return the movement of protest would quietly disperse. He was persuaded to hope for division but never committed himself generously to that. Principle was at odds with pragmatism; he had his own ways, regardless of what was said to him, and they were neither consistent nor realistic. In effect he grabbed at straws as they came to him. His physical distance from the troubles only reinforced the tendency, though for England and Ireland the pattern was probably little different. Some at Court, like the Earl of Arundel or Secretary Windebank, may have encouraged Charles's desire for revenge, but he lacked realism with regard to his military strength. Much of the work he referred beneath him, where it was acted upon slowly and with difficulty; occasionally he burst into action on points of offensive organisation, sometimes to Hamilton's dismay for the harm done to peacemaking talks in Scotland. Charles observed the customary separation between Scottish and English affairs, but his relative secrecy as to what was coming boded ill for a concerted effort within his other kingdoms. These were not the only problems, for practical, efficient administration depended on far more than the king's personal activity, but, given his power to make decisions, they were serious ones.

That Charles had other kingdoms on which to draw was evidently significant. Whatever the questions over Scottish support, the king could place his confidence elsewhere. It was another reason as to why the crisis became so inflated, that the king felt always urgently the need to maintain authority and policy which had implications in other kingdoms. He could not easily respect the independent line of the Scots; and they, for their part, would become increasingly concerned about the high politics both of those under Charles's rule and of the powers in Europe who might supply arms or other aid.

Hamilton, as the Commissioner, was most obviously responsible for the king's counsel, but he did not work alone. This is important for an assessment of his contribution where some questions remain. His chief ability may have been simply to talk well – whether to Scottish bishops, Covenanters or the king himself. Keeping all together in balance was no easy matter. In June he risked royal disfavour for almost giving approval to the Covenant as it stood; in August he supported a 'King's Covenant' which may have appealed enough to the Scottish bishops but rather missed the mark with their countrymen opponents. Especially with Traquair and Roxburgh he felt his way forward with Charles on a more far-reaching scheme of concessions, but despite all efforts was frustrated, first at Court and then in Scotland. Since at least he had a 'King's Covenant', Hamilton kept up optimism for Charles's cause, even with the other shortcomings; but he could also eloquently echo the words of command that prepared for bloodshed. He should not be too quickly condemned for indecision: often he or his colleagues anticipated well, but he could never know in advance the outcome. As importantly, two-sided approaches were at the origin of his commission. It proved impossible to break out of them.

As Charles's adviser, Hamilton knew better than most the king's limitations, his contrary counsels or dispositions, and he had to work with them. If the decisive stroke of force dreamed of by Wentworth could have destroyed the present movement of protest, it was neither practicable nor likely to be of long-term value. The long as well as the short term was bound to be in Hamilton's mind, for this was the standing of his native country and part source of wealth within the regnal union. He committed himself even after the awful 'rupture' of the Glasgow Assembly to continue working. By his reckoning Charles was an obstacle, but not the unique one, to a peaceful accommodation of the Scottish troubles. A real show of force might indeed be needed to persuade a yielding from the other side on some kind of middle ground.

In 1638 the duration of the troubles had worked mostly to the advantage of the Covenant cause. The machinations of leaders in response to the opportunities and threats received found their climax at Glasgow, when religion and liberties fully embraced presbyterianism. It was a political gain under very special circumstances. The minority who led for far-reaching reformation were undoubtedly pleased. It remains to be said that the unity sought so assiduously, even obsessively, was fragile and would be increasingly so as time went on. Few desired a prolonged situation of crisis, and the ambitions and visions of individuals ranged over a wide spectrum. Charles, however, chose to go to war. It was a powerful reflection on the Scottish troubles that the Covenanters undaunted marshalled their forces.

4

The king and war

January–July 1639

In the summer of 1638 Charles had found that his high words for using force against the Covenanters could not be matched by the means at his disposal. Within England and, more peripherally, Wales and Ireland, the administrative effort of organising armies and shipping was both expensive and slow. From within the particular troublespot of Scotland Charles's advisers urged upon him patience and caution, but as he remained fixed in his purpose his attention to counsel was selective. After the Glasgow Assembly the chosen path of the new year was a military drive of grand proportions. For all three kingdoms it was to be a powerful assertion of royal authority; whether or not the Covenanters dared to answer by use of arms, Charles was committed to overwhelming their challenge. Their rebellion could not be tolerated.

Because of the seriousness of the Scottish troubles, Charles himself was to go north. A commitment to the rights of royal majesty was to be vindicated in person; he would proceed at least to York, the northern capital of England. The Marquis of Hamilton continued as the King's Commissioner, but with a less inclusive brief of rallying the loyal forces in Scotland and commanding a naval assault up the east coast. His direct contact with Charles became more a matter of strategic communications. However, because the element of winning Scottish support remained, he kept contact both with Covenanter leaders and anti-Covenanters in the hope of forging a middle way. From Scotland, some hopes were still held of his achieving a major shift on the part of the king. Hamilton received the approaches, but for some time was unable to see a way forward.

The gritty resolution on the Covenanter side to mount a defence against threat of invasion only took the king's troubles into deeper waters. The control of the Covenanter leaders within Scotland was tightened; the royal institutions of government in consequence declined almost altogether. It could be feared that the king's forces would be considerable: appeals abroad, at least to his Protestant English subjects, were thought necessary – worryingly inflammatory action in Charles's eyes. Arguments already made in defence of the Covenant were extended into a more public justification of

119

resistance even by arms in obedience to divine will – and for preservation of Scottish liberties. While the king rode north to claim his subjects, the latter seemed ever more identifiable in distinction or separation from his sovereignty. Potentially it was a problem for the Covenanter leadership that Scots might rebel against their prevailing line. However, as long as Charles seemed committed to giving little or nothing in concession, there was a very limited attraction to his person: he was, after all, advancing to invade his northern kingdom with arms. Some continued to seek his favour directly; for others, it might still be plausibly maintained that this distant king was under evil counsel.

The statement about counsel suggested an appeal to Charles to take better ways. In the most general terms the enemy target remained the popish plot which threatened all Protestant nations. As is well known, more specific foundation was not lacking for the plot theme; though the Scottish bishops had little to say on the ways of force, Catholics and English bishops were involved, albeit not in isolation. Personal attacks were levelled; on the positive front church themes continued obviously to be significant, though with a wider range of concerns coming on behind. But whatever the attacks on his counsel, Charles clearly wished to take responsibility for his own decisions. His progress through to the Pacification of Berwick underlined the intensity of his involvement.

Civil war was not a desirable prospect, either for domestic or European well-being. Both king and Covenanters sought to avoid it, paradoxically given their extensive preparations in words and action. Charles came as far as the Scottish border but no further. The Covenanter achievement was, or at least seemed to be, decisive in Scotland, for the king's potential support, unable to provide an effective rival focus, was either quashed or driven out. Charles by his personal presence might have helped, but in the event it was not to be so. Meanwhile his war effort in England – despite his participation – had disappointments as well as success; and in Ireland hopes of the Earl of Antrim were ill-placed. All things considered, an intended drive into Scotland had to be abandoned, or rather postponed. Charles yielded to open talks with the Covenanter leaders he had despised, and by personally attending in debate tried to win his way. For the counsellor of accommodation, like Hamilton or Sir Thomas Hope, this was a forum of hope. Still, however, Charles had little to offer. The Scots would talk, but they could not simply surrender. On these terms of mutual defiance, the crisis of government could only grow more severe.

The Marquis of Hamilton's departure from Scotland at the end of December 1638 was no signal for the Covenanters to relax their guard. Others would still work hopefully to continue his policy of breaking the Covenanter unity which had recently achieved such heights at the Glasgow Assembly. Against this a common directive urged unity throughout the country in support of that achievement. Together with other paper defences of proceedings, a petition was sent on 7 January 1639 to the king. Alexander Henderson and Archibald Johnston were the official signatories on behalf of the late assembly. Charles was asked to accept the conclusions made and to indict a parliament as promised.[1]

An accompanying letter sent to Hamilton contrasted the 'simple truth' with the biased information to be expected from enemies of the church and the state – and, in terms of a gentle threat, Hamilton was advised to stand by the former. Truth was not easily communicated while the king was in England – 'for be the fountain never so pure the streams may and ofttimes are corrupted'. But truth once shown was bound to persuade, since right actions aimed for the glory of God and the honour of the king.[2]

Hamilton presented the petition to the king, but no answer was ever given – something the Covenanters complained about six months later.[3] The supposedly pure fountain had a dirty taste. It is doubtful that Charles believed much honesty underlay this focus on truth as discovered by the Glasgow Assembly. Certainly he did not want to believe it, for the political implications were not only Scottish. What was abjured as contrary to the Word of God implied consequences for all humanity, not just the Scots. More specifically, Arminianism in England had been found to contain all points of popery apart from the Pope himself; and the testimony of an anonymous English cleric had been read in support of presbyterian government.[4] The Covenant vision was potentially very wide. The threat Charles saw ranged further than against his rule of Scotland.

In terms of rhetoric the Covenanters acted decently, as the Earl of Roxburgh noted, but their stand had to be more than verbal.[5] Rumours, often accurate, were coming to Scotland of the king's military preparations. These excused thorough preparations in the shires to muster able-bodied soldiers and appoint commanders; a stop was put on all levies of Scots for service on the Continent.[6] On the king's side, there had been and still would be to some

[1] HMC *Various Collections* (55), vol. V, pp. 234–5; A. Peterkin, *Records of the Kirk of Scotland* (Edinburgh, 1838), pp. 41–2; GD 112/40/2/2/127.
[2] GD 406/1/768.
[3] R. Baillie, *The Letters and Journals*, ed. D. Laing, BC (3 vols., Edinburgh, 1841–2), vol. I, pp. 114–15; GD 406/1/776; BL Add. Ms. 38847, fol. 10v.
[4] Peterkin, *Records*, pp. 156–60; NLS Wod. 8vo. 10, fols. 88, 90, 95v; GD 112/43/1/11. See too M. C. Kitshoff, 'Aspects of Arminianism in Scotland' (unpublished University of St Andrews M.Th. dissertation, 1967).
[5] GD 406/1/1112.
[6] GD 406/1/996, 991, 988; GD 406/M1/49; NLS Ms. 2263, fols. 73–8; *Diary of Sir Archibald Johnston of Wariston, 1632–1639*, ed. G. M. Paul, SHS (Edinburgh, 1911), p. 406; D. Stevenson, *The Scottish Revolution 1637–1644* (Newton Abbot, 1974), pp. 127–30. The

extent attempts to cover work up. Publicly the king gave notice that he would come to York for 1 April; no mention was made of the force that was to accompany him. Fears of what might happen worked to Charles's disadvantage in Scotland – though at the same time Covenanter intelligence dismissed the accuracy of some English brags which forecast a superior royal force to be in the forming.[7]

Brags as well as secrecy illustrated the variety of options present in the royal effort at the outset of 1639. Although the task of raising forces in England was seriously intentioned, the fact that Hamilton kept the most prominent position under the king was indication that support within Scotland would be nurtured as far as possible. Positive news of preparations in the south was partly intended as a means of encouragement for the anti-Covenanter party. Hamilton interpreted the 'decision' to delay filling the border garrisons as a sign of the king's contempt for the Covenanters' military strength or daring; there had actually been no choice.[8] To the Marquis of Huntly, he gave an unreservedly positive picture of what was being done in England – principal cities generous in giving, and all nobles keenly offering service. The facts were otherwise, but Huntly was being warned that if submission was not made, civil war was to be expected.[9] Charles might hope for anything and everything, but the passing of time distanced normality even further.

Civil war was not desirable, but was it even a possibility? Some Scottish areas at least gave the king hopes of support in the early months of the new year, when fighting was in any case a distant prospect. In Aberdeen, the bishop, Adam Bellenden, was desired by Huntly to call a 'sub-synod', which met on 15 January. Resolutions were made to strike against the proceedings in what was called the 'pretended assembly' of Glasgow; on the next day fifteen ministers of the diocese sent a petition to the king asking for help against intimidation.[10] Huntly reported some 'doctors' hitherto reticent being prepared to join Drs Barron and Sibbald in writing for the king's cause. He sent also to the Bishop of Moray to convene his closest clerical friends as in Aberdeen. Many freeholders in Aberdeenshire still supported the king, with highlanders and the old faithful, the Earl of Caithness and the Clan Donald, further in support. Charles sent them letters of encouragement. Huntly was still collecting signatures for the King's Covenant as late as

---

king encouraged French levies, even in April 1639 – *RPCS*, 2nd Series, vol. VII, p. 103; Bod. Clarendon Ms. 16, fol. 69.

[7] Baillie, *Letters*, vol. I, p. 188. Cf. GD 406/1/1005, 992; Johnston, *Diary*, p. 410.
[8] GD 406/1/776, 771; P. H. Donald, 'The king and the Scottish troubles, 1637–1641' (unpublished University of Cambridge Ph.D. dissertation, 1988), p. 197n.
[9] GD 406/1/775. The English effort is briefly discussed below, pp. 133–6.
[10] GD 406/M1/48, 47. Seven more ministers present on the 15th did not sign the petition on the 16th.

February 1639. In early March, he organised a protestation for general subscription by ministers and heritors in his two shires.[11]

If the north-east remained, perhaps predictably, in large part unmoved by
the Glasgow Assembly's conclusions, information retailed to England was
not bad for other areas either. Traquair's reports focused on Angus, Perth-
shire and the Borders, and, as names of nobles and lairds were given, so again
letters from Court, often signed by the king, were distributed to them.
Occasionally such a letter would be addressed, mistakenly or perhaps too
late, to one who professed support of the other side. There was something of a
peaceful struggle. The Earl of Southesk and Lord Ogilvie competed with the
Earl of Montrose; the Earl of Queensberry acted as a bulwark against the
Covenant, as did Sir William Scott of Harden and the Laird of Grandtully. It
was an achievement for the king's side to win the people of Atholl against the
will of their earl, and the people of the junior Earl of Erroll against the
endeavours of Covenanting nobles.[12]

The Covenanters' shire meetings were attended by all gentlemen of the
area, so that loyalist figures had a chance to put their case. Apart from ideological issues, material considerations could potentially play an important
part in weakening the cause of the Covenant. Shire meetings hesitated to erect
councils of war.[13] While the Earl of Southesk thought that the burden of
taxation might work for the king, the Covenanter Earl of Wemyss gave a case
in point. As the king knew himself, administrative burdens in war could be
damaging. While any threat from the south seemed far off, those worked to
Charles's advantage, but it would not continue so for long. Apart from problems raised by his own war effort, he subsequently heard that Wemyss nevertheless offered only his civil obedience, standing out still on 'matters of
religion'.[14]

Charles was given reason to believe that not all of Scotland was against
him. Evidence sent to Court from agents in the north of England supported
the picture of disunity offered from Scotland. Similar lines were emphasised,
the difficulties faced by the Covenanters in mobilising a war effort, the threats
and consequent fears of what would come from England against them.[15]
These assurances were taken seriously in the south. Archbishop Laud did not
hesitate to back the preparation of force despite his worries on how sufficient
finance would be raised. He expressed also his hope for the party in Scotland,
referring more than once to the particular achievement of the Marquis of

[11] GD 406/1/412, 753, 758, 775, 1007.
[12] GD 406/1/1008, 1007, 1005, 986, 751, 780; *HMC Various Collections*, vol. V, p. 234.
[13] GD 406/1/779, 769, 1005; NLS Ms. 81, no. 82; Stevenson, *Scottish Revolution*, pp. 128–9.
[14] GD 406/1/769, 1008; GD 45/14/24; NLS Crawford Ms. 14/7/45.
[15] *CSPD 1638–9*, 409/51, 413/32, 89, 415/11; BL Add. Ms. 15392, fol. 44.

Huntly. Viscount Wentworth took up the theme, although possibly less convinced of its value – not so much from a consideration of the facts as from his ingrained notion that the English were needed to defeat the Scots once and for all.[16]

Charles was determined to assert his wishes despite what the Glasgow Assembly had done. For the cause of episcopacy, he made three replacements for the dioceses made vacant by betrayal – Caithness, Orkney and Dunkeld. Dr Robert Hamilton, who had represented the bishops at Glasgow, was confirmed for Caithness on 30 January; his predecessor, who had taken the Covenant, had since died.[17] Dr Robert Barron and Mr David Mitchell were given their appointments later, in April, although the choice of Mitchell, an Arminian *cause célèbre* at Glasgow, was known by Traquair in early February. Charles did not publicise his choices, but this was hardly a victory for conciliation, given the names chosen.[18] Bishops resisted where they could; the Bishop of Moray, John Guthrie, wrote an apologia for his office when under imminent attack in April.[19] The court of session was to ignore summons of bishops that denied them their office, thus doing nothing that implied acknowledgement of the Glasgow Assembly. Traquair rigidly followed this through in January, and the same principle applied for letters passed under the signet.[20] Favour in the court of session was not confined to bishops. The magistrates of Aberdeen, as also the Earl of Kinnoul, were to be protected from untimely prosecution of cases of debt. At the end of February the king ordered that no Covenanters be allowed any new rights of estates or casualties, or any admittances to new properties: these were forfeited by their disobedience.[21]

Those in opposition had to be seen as wrong. Laud was pleased to discover from a Scottish source a loaded explanation for the assembly's ruling against bishops. One William Wilkie maintained in a letter to Dr Balcanquhal that the nobles had consented out of their jealousy of the bishops' domination of the Lords of the Articles. However much truth lay in that, it clearly reduced

---

[16] *The Works of the Most Reverend Father in God, William Laud, D.D.*, eds. W. Scott and J. Bliss (7 vols., Oxford, 1847–60), vol. VII, pp. 507, 510, 520, 535, 537; PRO SP 81/46, fol. 66; WWM Str. P. LB 7, fol. 164.

[17] See GD 406/1/703, 571; J. Spottiswood, *The History of the Church of Scotland*, BC (3 vols., Edinburgh, 1850), vol. I, p. cxxv.

[18] BL Add. Ms. 23112, fols. 91, 93; GD 406/1/986. For lack of publicity, I assume that Rossingham is a reliable gauge. He reported, erroneously, news of one of the promotions only in September 1639 – BL Add. Ms. 11045, fol. 52v. Dr James Hannay, the infamous Dean of Edinburgh, was named to succeed the deceased Bishop of Dunblane near the end of 1639 – GD 406/M1/92; CSPV 1636–9, p. 594.

[19] NLS Wod. 4to. 83, fols. 53v–64; D. G. Mullan, *Episcopacy in Scotland: The History of an Idea, 1560–1638* (Edinburgh, 1986), p. 193.

[20] GD 406/1/991, 987, 1006, 1005; Johnston, *Diary*, p. 408; NLS Wod. Fo. 63, fol. 10.

[21] BL Add. Ms. 23112, fols. 91–2; GD 406/1/1007.

religious motivation to a sham; Laud quickly repeated the idea to Wentworth.[22] But royal government was in a weak position. This was why the episcopal nominees remained undisclosed; this too was why business slowed to a trickle in the court of session. Effective authority, effective pressure lay with the Covenanters.

Although many Scots may not naturally have been Covenanters, hopes of a royalist party were not answered. In the early days of 1639, it was to some extent an open contest for position. As long as people eschewed full-blown conflict, this would continue. One of those from within the privy council who transferred across to the ranks of defectors was the Earl Marischal.[23] Of the councillors who continued to serve, most wished Charles to adopt a policy of greater concessions. Moderate realism demanded it.

Traquair, frustrated in early January when he was kept from coming to Court to offer his advice, felt again under attack by malicious rivals. At a time when Covenanter military preparations seemed to him daunting, he suggested that the king at best might approve the Acts of the general assembly. But he was conscious of the personal risk of pushing too far, and wrote thus to the Earl of Morton, not to Hamilton. How consent to Glasgow might be with honour he confessed not to know, but reckoned it the only way to preserve meaningful royal authority. It may be that his choice of recipient issued from knowledge that his letters to Hamilton were read out for the king; his advice a little later, in February, returned to the terms pursued before the assembly. He argued that a statement of Charles's position on concessions would be very popular, especially if it included a clear commitment to the 'limitation of bishops'.[24]

This later advice judged the problem to be a shortage of trust in the king's concessions, and it reflected the sense of available support for Charles. Whether it was less promising after Glasgow than before is one important question; as over the earlier period, we should not underestimate the potential of divisions. Traquair would suggest that all possible Scottish noble support for the king be sent home when Charles arrived in York, as was now planned. Was his optimism a chimera? Surely not, although it must be said that the complexity of the situation offered no easy solutions. These people were wishing and praying for normality. In their many and different ways, they could not come together. The Earl of Southesk, like Traquair, asked for

---

[22] Baillie, *Letters*, vol. I, p. 486; Laud, *Works*, vol. VII, p. 518. Cf. Johnston, *Diary*, pp. 403–4; *A Diary of the Public Correspondence of Sir Thomas Hope of Craighall, Bart., 1633–1645*, ed. T. Thomson, BC (Edinburgh, 1843), p. 92; [Charles I], *A Large Declaration*, STC 21906 (1639), pp. 6–15.

[23] GD 406/1/751, 775, 992, 758, 759. For Baillie's view of the whole situation, see Baillie, *Letters*, vol. I, pp. 117–18.

[24] NLS Ms. 81, nos. 83, 96; GD 406/1/1007, 986, 992.

the king to uphold the explicit limitation of bishops; by late March he still felt unable to support the stance of the Covenanters, but tried hard to promote some kind of peaceful settlement of differences, fearing the alternative consequences. If Charles supposed all his leading opponents to be subversive hypocrites, Southesk could not happily fall in; he wished each man freedom to follow his conscience, but without breaking with friends of 'the contrary judgement'.[25] Traquair found Southesk's conduct bravely loyal; Sir John Hay by contrast noted dilatoriness in his response to Covenanter force.[26]

Traquair acted for the king as best he could. When Charles's letter about coming to York was read before the privy council – 'that we may be the more near to that our kingdom for accommodating our affairs there in a fair manner' – the Earl of Argyll tried to get a motion through for composing an advice for the king. Despite the hidden dimension of Charles's progress, Traquair's judgement that an advice would not please Charles gained sufficient support. The Covenanters then tried to present a petition honestly stating that they had no intention of invading England, as was charged; they had support within the council for that, but it was refused on the grounds that it was given in without names attached. It was averted on another occasion by Traquair before finally a specific libel against the Covenanters alleging their plans to invade England forced the issue. On 1 March the privy council decided by a majority to forward the Covenanters' petition to the king; a reply to the king's intimation about York was at last agreed. Charles was advised 'to resolve upon a course without force of arms or showing of your princely power to settle this deplorable-conditioned kingdom'. Traquair did not or could not stop it.[27] A few days before this, the court of session had observed a Covenanter fast, despite plans it should do the contrary. The slight hold of restraint was yielding. Having delayed a little more over the petition, Traquair at last received permission to go up to Court, and took it with him.[28]

The Earl of Argyll kept a regular attendance at the council and Session until early March that was symbolic of his continuing hopes for peace, but the gap was not easily to be bridged. Standing by the Glasgow Assembly, he had pursued his wish for reconciliation by writing personally to Charles and in return was invited to Court. Argyll's response was not immediate, which worried Archibald Johnston, who had known Argyll's past wishes for compromise; it gave Traquair some hope, but in the end Argyll made excuses.[29] He would not admit either, to Charles or to Hamilton, that he had advised with Loudoun

---

[25] GD 406/1/769; *HMC Laing* (72), vol. I, pp. 202–3.
[26] GD 406/1/802, 1001.
[27] *RPCS*, 2nd Series, vol. VII, pp. 106, 113, 115; GD 406/1/1005, 959, 986, 992, 796, 997, 985, 1130.
[28] GD 406/1/997; SRO CS 1/5, fol. 130.
[29] GD 406/1/776, 1007, 1315; Johnston, *Diary*, p. 406; cf. GD 112/40/2/2/125.

and others, nor that during his apparent hesitations he had been active in musters.[30] Nevertheless he honoured as long as possible his past signing of the King's Covenant, albeit with an anti-episcopal interpretation on it. His earlier proposal for a compromise around this had not altogether died.[31] Only in the worsening political circumstances of April 1639 did he at last agree to sign the main Covenant. This, with its new explanation attached to uphold the Acts of Glasgow, had been widely pressed for subscription since February and Argyll could no longer stand out; others before him had been obliged to conform.[32]

A tract probably from the Aberdeen circle argued the case against subscribing the Covenant with its new addition, but the king's cause could make only limited ground.[33] Although Charles was confident in himself, his refusal to offer an unambiguous programme of reform, and the increasing instability of the situation, worked him little advantage. In reply to the council's letter of general advice, he would only insist that such action as was necessary would be taken. His message for Argyll was plainly insulting, a public command to come to Court or else stay confined to his house.[34] It was not helpful either that the Catholics, especially Nithsdale, Ogilvie – and Huntly if he may be called such – and other resolutes like Sir John Hay, Sir Robert Spottiswood or Sir John Scrimgeour the Constable of Dundee, were in the vanguard of his support. Although the king had also academic and clerical defenders of royal authority, on the other hand there were conciliators who in some measure wished him to yield more than he would yet accept; it hardly made the potential royal party homogeneous, let alone convincing. Would the king's personal presence and military back-up have helped? Meanwhile the Covenanters could well exploit the uncertainties of the vacuum. They urged a Protestant and patriotic cause that effectively marshalled strength in the face of the perceived threats.

To date, the movement of protest had required, both for defence and forward momentum, considerable organisation of words and action. This became increasingly necessary as the possibility of a clash of arms drew nearer. At the end of January, the news that the king was coming to York prompted a run of Covenanter publications. A more substantial version of a protestation to answer the December proclamation concerning the assembly dissolution was

---

[30] GD 112/40/2/2/124, 127; GD 406/1/1008; Stevenson, *Scottish Revolution*, p. 128.
[31] Hope, *Diary*, p. 91.
[32] GD 112/39/763; see also GD 406/1/959, 757, 366; Baillie, *Letters*, vol. I, pp. 181–4; GD 112/39/761, 762.
[33] GD 406/M9/76.
[34] *RPCS*, 2nd Series, vol. VII, p. 116; NLS Adv. Ms. 19.1.25, fol. 21; GD 406/1/710; Sir W. Fraser, *The Chiefs of Grant* (3 vols., Edinburgh, 1883), vol. II, p. 67.

at last issued, alongside the separately published *Information* for 'all good Christians' in England. The urgency of wooing sympathies in England picked up again after its lull in the latter part of the previous year.[35] There was also published, on 14 February, an answer to Hamilton's declaration on the meaning of the King's Covenant, and after that the Acts of the general assembly. These printings presumably aimed for a more open publicity than could be achieved by manuscript circulation.[36]

Internal propaganda importantly included justification of resistance to the king, for with Covenanters as eminent as the Earls of Cassilis and Eglinton worried, this was needed as well as stiff organisation to overcome reluctance over the war effort. The king's advance threatened to make divisions in Scotland. Both Archibald Johnston and Robert Baillie set to work, but Alexander Henderson produced the most significant piece.[37] Deliberately it was not published, so that it might be used only in the right hands: it could therefore be read from the pulpit and by 'well affected professors in private conference'.[38] In the event, an answer was made in print some two months later, published in Ireland and dedicated to Wentworth, which attempted to castigate the Scots in the eyes of potential English and Irish friends. Interestingly, the Henderson work, whatever its contemporary success, was reissued at a later date in print – on the eve of the civil war in England.[39]

In the original context the intention was to assure the hearers of the legitimacy of resistance against the anointed king. Henderson began with a short rehearsal of recent events to affirm that no invasion of England was intended; indeed he suggested that invasion, that is aggression, would be unjust. The distinction was made between obedience to God and obedience to the king if the latter contravened the will of God. The king's mistake was to be misled. This was phrased, as in the letter to Hamilton, so as to suggest that the king was badly advised because he was far from Scotland; the ambitious implication was that all Scots were united for the truth. All the people were there-

---

[35]   Baillie, *Letters*, vol. I, pp. 115–16; *Protestation of the Generall Assembly*, Aldis 952 (1639) – revised 8 January; Ms. draft in NLS Wod. Fo. 64, fols. 84–94, 157–8. *Information to All Good Christians . . .*, Aldis 946 (Edinburgh, 1639); Johnston, *Diary*, p. 408; GD 406/1/986; NLS Wod. Fo. 54, fol. 264. The propaganda for the English is discussed in chapter 5 below.
[36]   *Answer to the . . . Marquess of Hammilton*, Aldis 937 (n.p., 1639); *Acts of Assembly. The Principall Acts . . . 1638*, Aldis 936 (n.p., 1639); GD 112/39/753.
[37]   Baillie, *Letters*, vol. I, pp. 53, 189, 489; BL Add. Ms. 63057A, fol. 32; NLS Wod. Fo. 66, fol. 130; Johnston, *Diary*, pp. 408, 410; Stevenson, *Scottish Revolution*, p. 133. For Baillie and his text, see Baillie, *Letters*, vol. I, pp. 81–2, 116; EUL New College Ms X15b 3/1, vol. II, fols. 118v–23. I have not yet discovered Johnston's work – but cf. NLS Wod. Fo. 61, fol. 264 (4 June 1638).
[38]   Henderson's authorship is attested in Baillie's transcript – EUL New College Ms. X15b 3/1, vol. I, fol. 131.
[39]   [J. Corbet], *The Ungirding of the Scottish Armour*, STC 5755a (Dublin, 1639); [A. Henderson], *Some Speciall Arguments . . .*, STC 21909 (Amsterdam, 1642).

fore together to follow God's will if the king stood out of line in the Great Chain of Being.

A concluding section urged that the religious questions at issue were fundamental. This did not mean 'necessary to salvation'; more that the definition of matters fundamental was dictated by the degree of revelation – what was known at one time or in one kirk: 'The kirk of Scotland having from the certain knowledge of the unlawfulness of episcopal government (were it of never so little moment) abjured it divers times, and spewed it out, we must not return to our vomit.' Episcopacy was a principal cause at stake, yet it was within the frame of a 'greater' cause – 'a free national kirk' and 'our civil liberty', which was the defence against being led along the way to Rome.[40]

Rhetoric kept open fairly wide options on the way forward. The tract basically expanded on ideas long since considered over the period of the troubles; it did not apparently lie within the tradition of George Buchanan. The movement of events in consequence of Charles's intransigence would bring on more. A sermon by Henderson in August 1639 laid its emphasis on the importance of the positive union with God, which led him to a conclusion at once more logical and outspoken than in his justification of defensive arms. His prayer was not just for Scots: 'Lord, let thy kingdom come on England, France and all other parts.'[41] Certainly by then, other Scots were echoing such hopes – Charles's nightmare. Johnston of Wariston dreamt in February 1639 of God's Providence possibly reaching further, even perhaps to Charles's death.[42]

Practical work by the Covenanters consisted initially of their highly organised military preparations. The first incident of force, the unexpected seizure of Inverness Castle in February by the Mackenzies, was an indication that there was a contest for influence in the north.[43] It was on 7 March that there entered the period of the Covenanters determinedly taking the whole of Scotland under their effective control.[44] Strongholds were attacked and taken – Edinburgh, Dalkeith, Dumbarton, Stirling – and the fortification of Leith begun; the Marquis of Douglas's castles were captured; the Earl of Nithsdale

---

[40] The paper is also printed in A. Stevenson, *History of the Church of Scotland* (Edinburgh, 1840), pp. 356–60. For similar arguments, see *A Remonstrance of the Nobility . . .* , Aldis 954 (Edinburgh, 1639), pp. 21–6.

[41] NLS Wod. Fo. 27, fols. 36–8; Wod. Fo. 48, fol. 26v. I am grateful to Dr Jenny Wormald for remarks on the tradition.

[42] Johnston, *Diary*, p. 410.

[43] GD 406/1/992, 756; J. Spalding, *The History of the Troubles and Memorable Transactions in Scotland and England from M.DC.XXIV to M.DC.XLV*, BC (2 vols., Edinburgh, 1828), vol. I, pp. 135–6.

[44] EUL New College Ms. X15b 3/1, vol. I, fols. 136–7; GD 406/M1/328/10. For the Covenanter military, see Stevenson, *Scottish Revolution*, pp. 128–31, 137; D. Stevenson, 'The financing of the cause of the Covenants, 1638–51', *SHR*, 51 (1972), 89–123; E. M. Furgol, *A Regimental History of the Covenanting Armies, 1639–1651* (forthcoming).

fled from his and went to the king at York. Expeditions were sent to root out opponents in Kintyre and Mull. A meeting at Perth, attended by Argyll, preceded a northern expedition: Aberdeen was occupied, and the Marquis of Huntly subsequently taken.[45] In short the enclaves of possible resistance were overtaken. The king's party in their fortified strongholds could make only weak resistance; and Charles's institutional machinery was almost completely undermined. One of those who fled was James Gordon, the Keeper of the Signet; he was replaced by a Covenanter nominee.[46] It was not coincidental that March was the month of the king's northern progress. The Covenanters prepared a force to march to the Borders, which it did at the beginning of April.[47]

The other spur to the Covenanters for finally settling their control in Scotland seems to have been a proclamation issued by the king on 27 February 1639, actually intended to demonstrate to his English subjects the 'rightness' of his cause.[48] For the Scots, Charles publicly had been cautious in avoiding direct provocation – hence the non-committal tone of the statement about his coming to York; this was the advice of his Scottish councillors. He considered that the unwritten threat kept his options open and in a good light. However, the likelihood of using force of arms against the outwardly united Scots needed some public justification. The Covenanters in their *Information to All Good Christians* had appealed for English sympathy. All possible efforts were made to detect those who spread the Scottish pamphlet; the proclamation was a printed retort to its arguments. It was something of a stopgap, since a rather lengthier declaration was already in preparation. Even so, ten thousand copies were made for circulation so that it might be read in every parish church.[49] Copies incidentally were sent at least to Huntly and Lord Ogilvie in Scotland, which encouragement they greatly appreciated; in Amsterdam, where publications by the other side had proliferated, it was translated and spread about.[50]

Charles characteristically portrayed the perceived threat in extreme terms. A traitorous faction of Scots had combined for the sake of private ends and for the casting off of monarchical government.[51] He complained of how they had opposed the Covenant he had sponsored, and how they now planned the invasion of England. The assault on monarchy was argued by reference to

<hr />

[45] Stevenson, *Scottish Revolution*, p. 140; BL Add. Ms. 15392, fol. 110; NLS Wod. Fo. 54, fol. 269; GD 406/1/4571; GD 112/39/762; GD 112/40/2/2/97.
[46] GD 406/1/776, 587; SRO CS 1/5, fol. 124.
[47] GD 112/39/389.
[48] Cf. GD 406/1/1001; also Baillie, *Letters*, vol. I, pp. 487–9.
[49] Laud, *Works*, vol. VII, p. 528; J. F. Larkin, *Stuart Royal Proclamations* (Oxford, 1983), vol. II, pp. 662–7. Search efforts are discussed below in chapter 5.
[50] GD 406/1/710, 759, 780; HMC *Montagu of Beaulieu* (54), p. 125.
[51] Cf. PRO SP 16/410/24, 76. The faction allegation by Charles was very typical.

how the Covenanters had assumed the functions of government. Charles did not hesitate to stand by his own former assurances. Episcopacy was to be defended both by statute and by its consonance with monarchical government; the prayer book, claimed to be innovation, was supported as deriving from the wish to have a uniform form of holy worship in all three kingdoms. There was no novelty underlying the rhetoric, only a restatement of deeply entrenched opinions.

Finally, the proclamation answered points raised in the *Information to All Good Christians* that might find sympathy in England – the employment of papists in the army, the advice of prelates for the king's taking of arms and the Scottish claims that they acted only in defence. The king denied the first, not admitting that recusants were attending musters;[52] and explained that he had consulted with bishops, but that they had advised for peace – although in an ambiguous context, it was not made clear how they had done this.[53] On Scottish defence he was categorical that there could be no just defence by arms, alleging that it was the Covenanters alone who contravened laws, which somewhat simplified that issue.[54]

Such a statement could still cause some worries within Scotland, despite all that had passed; the battle by words was not unimportant. Not all Covenanters were necessarily reconciled to resistance. The Earl of Rothes pitched in with a private paper which directly denied any royal pretensions to 'absolute power' in the church. Confuting the arguments of the proclamation, he was concerned to frustrate the ongoing efforts to cause division within Scotland. His view readily admitted the possibility of venturing beyond the enacted law – 'before we lose Christ or part from his clear and undeniable truth'.[55]

Strikingly, and in reflection of the Covenanter self-image, the printed response to the king in contrast gave no evidence of any breach in the unity of the movement. This *Remonstrance*, for vindicating almost the 'whole kingdom' of Scotland from the crimes alleged in the proclamation, was published in English and Dutch. With its final revision by Wariston, it made a detailed response for careful consideration by the English. It was probably the first published piece explicitly to warn the English that the popish plot which had scourged Scotland boded ill for them. The common cause of true religion was urged, to cut against the imputations of treasonable rebellion made on the king's part. Charles's past desire to bring Scotland, like Ireland, into confor-

---

[52] The recusants were apparently unarmed at musters – *CSPD 1638–9*, 409/24; cf. BL Add. Ms. 15392, fol. 64; *HMC Buccleuch and Queensberry* (45), vol. I, p. 281, vol. III, p. 383; C. Hibbard, *Charles I and the Popish Plot* (Chapel Hill, NC, 1983), p. 125.

[53] Laud was not intimately involved with decision-making in January – Laud, *Works*, vol. VII, p. 517; he for one was unsure about the effectiveness of the means of force – *ibid.*, p. 513.

[54] Larkin, *Stuart Royal Proclamations*, vol. II, pp. 662–7.

[55] NLS Crawford Ms. 14/7/45. Endorsed 'E of Rothes April 1639'; holograph of the earl.

mity with England was rejected as unjustifiable – 'our church was no *tabula rasa*'. Episcopacy was 'antichristian', 'prejudicial to civil peace', a 'pernicious enemy to monarchies', unnecessary in parliaments. Prelates who had opened a door to popery put a 'stumbling-block' in the king's way to heaven, a hindrance to the queen's conversion and an offence to all reformed kirks – words of very little restraint.[56]

The king's fear of the Covenanter attack on episcopacy having implications beyond Scotland was well justified, and as ever it was more than an ecclesiastical matter. His official defence denied power to general assemblies to override parliamentary legislation; the English would be expected to agree by comparison of the respective powers of convocation and parliament. Against him, the popish plot theme, trumpeted ever more shrilly, could comprehend fears of an assault on 'liberties' generally, and was a powerful rhetoric that easily linked upset of religion with upset of the state.[57] Religious motives were mixed up with others, and sympathies ran between the nations, as will be seen. Men across two kingdoms groped their way forward with some mutual understanding. The imperative for defence and settlement moved the Covenanters to join their propaganda voice to calls within England for an English parliament.[58]

Charles had no specific answer to make to the *Remonstrance*, but the promised justification of his cause appeared in due course for the English. The *Large Declaration* was written substantially by Walter Balcanquhal, but was published as if by Charles himself around Easter 1639. It gave an extensive historical account of the troubles to date in the best possible light, affirming Charles's commitment to uphold the reformed religion and castigating his opponents as seditious rebels with only a pretence of leading for purer church practice. In the closing section there was a relevant word to the Scots, an insistence that Charles did not wish to challenge Scottish identity – that there was no intention to make Scotland a 'province', or a 'conquered kingdom'. This was supposed to overturn the Covenanters' arguments for a better Anglo-Scottish understanding on account of the alleged threats to the true religion. It was suggested that the king's expedition against the rebels was 'a means to tie [the nations] in a stronger bond of love forever together . . . both

---

[56] *A Remonstrance of the Nobility* . . . , dated 22 March 1639. The Reformed churches may not have been as unanimous as was argued – PRO C 115/N.8/8854; *HMC Montagu*, p. 125; P. Du Moulin, *A Letter of a French Protestant*, STC 7345 (1640); J. K. Cameron, 'The Swiss and the Covenant', in G. W. S. Barrow (ed.), *The Scottish Tradition* (Edinburgh, 1974), pp. 155–63.

[57] [Charles I], *A Large Declaration*, STC 21906 (1639), esp. p. 349; P. Lake, 'Anti-popery: the structure of a prejudice', in R. Cust and A. Hughes (eds.), *Conflict in Early Stuart England* (1989), pp. 72–106.

[58] See below, chapter 5; *Information to All Good Christians*, Aldis 846; *A Remonstrance of the Nobility* . . . , Aldis 954.

of them meeting in this point and centre viz. the defence of our person, and of our royal crown and dignity'. Charles himself was held up as the source of unity.[59] The Union at heart indeed remained purely dynastic; it was an appealing vision – but for the fact that unconditional loyalty to this particular king was showing signs of severe strain.

As king of three kingdoms, Charles might rely on forces outside Scotland to help him somehow to suppress the rebels. If it came to civil war, his strength within Scotland was not necessarily crucial; this of course was the Covenanters' worry. While his Scottish counsellors continued naturally to be concerned for the recovery of domestic support, as a means to long-term security, the king in England supported plans in January 1639 for an army of thirty thousand, with noblemen and others bringing their followings in attendance. News was that the Covenanters had received arms sufficient for eighteen thousand men. With fears circulating of possible Scottish invasion, the English border counties were spared from supplying soldiers for the king's main force; if necessary a second reinforcement army was to be drawn from there.[60]

Charles attended the meetings of the committee of war and endorsed the conclusions, many of which pursued ideas raised in earlier orders. Much of the detail may remain outside our attention. Financial anxiety was one major factor in compelling shifts of tactics. In early February the plan changed to marching a force of six thousand from the southern counties. These were moreover to be pressed men rather than trained bands, for it was understood that counties would be reluctant to release their trained bands for service outside the county limits; but trained bands, five thousand men, were still appointed to accompany the Marquis of Hamilton, who was to go north by sea. Probably this was to be the most crucial line of strike, for these men might offer the most direct support to the hoped for party in Scotland.[61] The third prong of the strategy, envisaged long ago but still advanced with little urgency, involved most prominently the Earl of Antrim. Antrim had made bold claims, not devoid of personal ambition. He could look for support on both sides of the Irish Channel, but his competence, and even more his Catholic religion, came in for criticism by Wentworth. The Irish Catholics

[59] [Charles I], *A Large Declaration*, pp. 423, 429–30. For the composition and chronology, see Donald, 'The king and the Scottish troubles', pp. 215n., 227n.
[60] *CSPD 1638–9*, 409/106, 107, 410/24; GD 406/1/775. For the fullest treatment of the English military, see M. C. Fissel, '*Bellum episcopale*: the bishops' wars and the end of the "Personal Rule" in England 1638–1640' (unpublished University of Berkeley Ph.D. dissertation, 1983).
[61] S. R. Gardiner, *A History of England . . . 1603–1642* (10 vols., 1883–4), vol. VIII, pp. 384–5; Fissel, '*Bellum episcopale*', pp. 363–403; *CSPD 1638–9*, 409/100.

were themselves regarded as potential rebels.[62] Charles would not readily abandon the option, but money factors again may have played a part. Towards the end of March, Wentworth was instructed not to give Antrim supply – although not altogether to discourage him. Instead the Lord Deputy himself was to send ships to the west of Scotland as a show of strength against Argyll, to do damage and plunder if expedient.[63]

The management of finance for the expedition required various proceedings, not least because it was evidently decided not to call a parliament. Parliaments were the usual means of war supply, though notorious alternatives had been explored in the 1620s.[64] Now loans were taken on the security of anticipated Crown revenues, from leading City figures and companies, from judges, and from officers of the army. At the time that the change was made to taking pressed men, the king offered to accept money instead of personal attendance from his nobles.[65] A clerical contribution was looked for, and later a notorious contribution from the Catholics, the idea for which dated back to the previous year. Money also was requested from London, and then generally throughout the country; letters were sent to individual gentlemen in various southern counties asking them for help.[66]

Charles's counsel was probably divided on the parliament question, but it is worth noting that advisers trod warily on the issue, perhaps even avoided raising the subject with Charles. Whatever the king thought, however, the issue was in the air. In the autumn of 1638 there had been general rumours that a parliament might be called; they had similarly arisen earlier in the 1630s when an intervention in the European war seemed most likely. The Florentine Salvetti imagined that 'puritans' in England did what they could to spoil an accommodation in Scotland to force a war, and therefore a parlia-

[62] GD 406/1/1149, 1150; W. Knowler (ed.), *The Earl of Strafforde's Letters and Dispatches* (2 vols., 1739), vol. II, pp. 184, 305–6; *HMC Cowper* (12), vol. II, pp. 162–3; A. Clarke, 'The Earl of Antrim and the first Bishops' War', *Irish Sword*, 6 (1963–4), 108–15.

[63] WWM Str. P. LB 10b, p. 66; LB 11, pp. 218–19; Knowler, *Strafforde Letters*, vol. II, p. 314. Cf. *State Papers Collected by Edward, Earl of Clarendon*, eds. R. Scrope and T. Monkhouse (3 vols., Oxford, 1767–86), vol. II, p. 33.

[64] C. Russell, 'The nature of a parliament in early Stuart England', in H. Tomlinson (ed.), *Before the English Civil War* (1983), p. 148; R. Cust, *The Forced Loan and English Politics 1626–1628* (Oxford, 1987).

[65] Bod. Bankes Ms. 5/45; BL Stowe Ms. 326, fol. 53;0 *HMC Buccleuch and Queensberry*, vol. I, pp. 282, 284; *CSPD 1638–9*, 413/117. See Gardiner, *History of England*, vol. IX, pp. 7, 25–6; T. A. Mason, *Serving God and Mammon: William Juxon 1582–1663* (1985), pp. 125–8. Professor Fissel's work in preparation aims to cover thoroughly the financing of the war.

[66] *CSPD 1638–9*, 410/76; BL Add. Ms. 15391, fol. 345v; C. Hibbard, 'The contribution of 1639: court and country Catholicism', *Recusant History*, 16 (1982), 42–60; PCR, vol. VI, pp. 299, 317; *HMC Cowper*, vol. II, p. 219; *CSPD 1639*, 417/66, 418/45; Gardiner, *History of England*, vol. IX, p. 25.

ment, in England.[67] If a parliament was called to grant supply, it would also be a forum for speaking on English grievances; that this might be counter-productive was certainly a rationale behind the king's resistance to issuing a summons.[68] Ship money was amongst the issues at stake. Whether it was this or, possibly more likely, past memories which prevailed in the king's mind, the outcome had its problems.[69] If Charles's abstinence from ordinary parliamentary means was also in part influenced by the relatively small subsidies thus available, the alternative of contributions seems to have yielded poorly. The clergy may have been the exception, relative to the peers, the City of London, the gentry at large, and indeed the Catholics. The shortage of ready cash was noticed often.[70]

Difficulties were also met in the localities in answering the demands made upon them for soldiers; numbers and quality were low. Making war in England in 1639 was a traumatic and unpleasant experience for most people, whatever the cause of the king. Organisational efficiency both at centre and in locality was open to wide variation.[71] Nevertheless, besides administrative difficulties, positive hostility to the king's course, commented on by Covenanters and foreign ambassadors, or in criticism raised later in parliaments, did not help. The effort may have been particularly testing for those who in some measure might hold sympathies for the Covenanters, although this cannot easily be measured.[72]

Few Englishmen were in a position to mount significant protest to the king's courses. Private grumblings and stratagems of non-participation were dangerous to advertise. Some public attention was however attracted to the responses of the English peers. The Earl of Hertford's reaction was awaited as 'a sign of the times'.[73] Not alone, but probably most prominently, Viscount Saye and Sele and Lord Brooke stood out for their objections; Brooke was reported as refusing to attend unless commanded by a parliament, but both

---

67 *CSPV 1636–9*, pp. 457–8; BL Add. Ms. 27962H, fol. 184; Add. Ms. 15392, fol. 23; *CSPD 1637–8*, 395/29, 397/26; *HMC De L'Isle* (77), vol. VI, p. 156; A. Collins (ed.), *Letters and Memorials of State* (2 vols., 1746), vol. II, pp. 578–9; PRO SP 81/46, fol. 101v; Laud, *Works*, vol. VII, p. 568; E. Cope, *Politics without Parliaments, 1629–1640* (1987), pp. 11–43.
68 Cf. Knowler (ed.), *Strafforde Letters*, vol. II, p. 186; WWM Str. P. LB 10b, p. 9.
69 Cf. WWM Str. P. LB 7, fol. 148. For perceptive comment on the general issues, see Cust, *The Forced Loan, passim*, esp. pp. 316–37.
70 Russell, 'The nature of a parliament', pp. 142–5; Hibbard, 'The contribution of 1639'; Gardiner, *History of England*, vol. IX, pp. 24–5; Fissel, '*Bellum episcopale*', pp. 404–22.
71 Cf. Cope, *Politics without Parliaments*, pp. 165–80; D. Hirst, 'The privy council and the problems of enforcement in the 1620s', *JBS*, 18 (1978), 40–66.
72 More work is needed here. For a good case study, see V. Stater, 'The Lord Lieutenancy on the eve of the civil wars: the impressment of George Plowright', *HJ*, 29 (1986), 771–93.
73 *CSPD 1638–9*, 410/80; Collins, *Letters*, vol. II, p. 593.

relented to make offers of personal attendance.[74] A petition was rumoured to
be prepared for presentation to the king but it did not materialise. By early
March, Laud wrote to Wentworth that 'most nobles and gentry' supported
the king in his campaign; and Charles decided to ignore what opposition had
surfaced, which, with the advice of councillors and judges, he had at first
thought to punish.[75] If trouble lay under the surface, the king would still
pursue his ends – with perhaps an ominously open mind to means.

Charles was also looking abroad for assistance. The Prince of Orange,
solicited for troops in mid-February, could not oblige because of his ongoing
anti-Spanish commitments; but his standing promise to stem the flow of
seditious printed matter from his country was continued.[76] However,
Charles's words of a 'narrow friendship' with Orange would have been difficult to reconcile with the parallel approaches of one Colonel Gage, who
with Secretary Windebank's backing looked to procure troops from Spanish
Flanders – with even Papal finance in the original scheme! These plans went
far, but ended in failure through the reluctance of the Spanish to risk their
own safety, news that was heard in early March.[77]

Mainly on account of the quest for arms and experienced commanders,
the Scottish troubles had by this stage gained a noticeable European dimension. Aiming to minimise the implications of this – except where Charles
could gain positive advantage – Charles's own questing approaches were not
publicised.[78] The King of Denmark, who offered his mediation, was politely
turned down.[79] Alliance with France for the sake of intervention over the
Palatinate cause was still technically under discussion, and the Scottish
troubles cut across this. For Charles, the worsening domestic situation was
forcing his hand – although probably not against his preference – to put aside
thoughts of action in the European war of the day.[80] The French kept apart,
themselves reluctant over commitment to an alliance, although they had a
regular interest in levying troops from Charles's kingdoms for their own
armies. Scots had strong recent connections with France on this front and

---

[74] *CSPD 1638–9*, 412/134, 413/92, 117. There is an analysis of the response in P. Haskell, 'Sir
Francis Windebank and the Personal Rule of Charles I' (unpublished University of
Southampton Ph.D. dissertation, 1978), pp. 427–9.

[75] GD 406/1/985; Laud, *Works*, vol. VII, p. 541; BL Add. Ms. 15392, fol. 60v.

[76] BL Add. Ms. 12093, fol. 15; G. Groen van Prinsterer, *Archives ou correspondance inédite
de la Maison d'Orange-Nassau*, 2nd Series, vol. III (Utrecht, 1859), pp. 144–5; Berks. RO
Trumbull Misc. LXI (Weckherlin's diary, 22 February); PRO SP 84/155, fols. 136, 146.

[77] *State Papers . . . Clarendon*, vol. II, pp. 23–4, 28, 50–1; Bod. Clarendon Ms. 16, fol. 109;
Hibbard, *Charles I and the Popish Plot*, pp. 105–7.

[78] Cf., with regard to the Prince of Orange, *HMC Rutland* (24), vol. I, p. 509.

[79] Laud, *Works*, vol. VII, pp. 530, 559; PRO SP 81/46, fol. 224.

[80] Hibbard, *Charles I and the Popish Plot*, pp. 72–89; cf. PRO SP 81/46, fol. 49; *CSPD
1639–40*, 448/42.

also, for example, over beneficial tariff privileges.[81] Charles could only hope
to counter anything more ominous. Increasingly suspicions were voiced that
France was encouraging the Covenanters.[82]

The urgent task was to assemble armies in strength, and this, despite all the
various problems, the king more or less achieved. Privately Wentworth
analysed the causes of difficulties as before in terms of the lack of 'thorough':
men sought too far their own ends, and in his view Charles lacked decisive
rigour. It was a simple reading, grounded on optimism that English loyalties
could be pushed even by unusual means to curb the Scottish menace;
Wentworth had, however, made the important point that soldiers needed to
be guaranteed their pay. He had little respect for any of the king's commanders. Besides being particularly venomous against Antrim, he scorned the
greed of Hamilton and the Earls of Arundel and Holland. He advised the king
to go no further than York, sceptical that English preparations could be completed before August.[83] Encouragement was mixed with restraining advice,
but Wentworth was distant from the realities of the situation. However,
Charles had his own opinions to carry him. As ever, his attention to counsel
was selective.

What the king wanted shaped the running. Wentworth for himself kept an
interest in the possibility of a parliament, but he would argue to Laud that, no
matter how many people wanted it, it was inadvisable unless Charles was
'vigorously' set that way; if Charles did change, 'it would be a work for
earnest and must be done accordingly; *Quid Romulo ardentius?* would serve
the cause wondrous well'.[84] As yet this was untested hypothesis; the
impression is that Charles avoided even discussion of the parliamentary
possibility.

Wentworth's responsibilities in Ireland and Yorkshire brought him
unambiguously into three-kingdom politics. Never faltering in his hatred of
the Covenanters and wish to defeat their cause, he wrote to the king with
increasing frequency; Laud told him that Charles appreciated this.[85] Pessimistic realism prevailed amongst others of the king's counsel, not least in
Laud himself. There was a sense that the king's efforts to gather support in

[81] See PRO SP 78/107, fols. 107–9; SP 78/108, fol. 1; *State Papers . . . Clarendon*, vol. II, p. 43;
      Collins, *Letters*, vol. II, pp. 596–7; *CSPD 1639*, 420/120, 158. Soldiers and tariffs were also
      central to the Dutch interaction with Scotland – see PRO SP 84/155, fols. 100, 127.
[82] For example, PRO C 115/N.9/8854; PRO SP 81/47, fol. 14v; PRO 31/3/71, fols. 16–17, 19;
      BL Add. Ms. 15392, fols. 74, 76, 122; Knowler, *Strafforde Letters*, vol. II, p. 322; Bod.
      Clarendon Ms. 15, fols. 157–8; *CSPD 1639*, 417/58, 422/28. For the early history of this,
      see below chapter 5.
[83] WWM Str. P. LB 11, pp. 158–60; Knowler, *Strafforde Letters*, vol. II, p. 279.
[84] WWM Str. P. LB 7, fol. 166. For Laud's reply, see Laud, *Works*, vol. VII, p. 542.
[85] Laud, *Works*, vol. VII, p. 536.

England were falling short of what was needed.[86] The Earl of Northumberland was also concerned about a war effort in circumstances of inadequate
preparation. His discussions by letter with Wentworth touched as before on
the parliament question, and also indicated a shared distaste for the dominance of the Marquis of Hamilton. The king appeared far too secretive over
his intentions, which were revealed only as and when necessary – yet
Hamilton had his confidence.[87]

Laud, interestingly, did not readily share the hostility to Hamilton's
employment. At the end of February he pronounced that there were 'good
grounds' for trust since the marquis's return to Court. In a subsequent letter
he coupled Hamilton's achievement with that of the Marquis of Huntly; even
when news of the latter's surrender to the Covenanters was known, Laud's
good faith in Hamilton remained unshaken, despite what Wentworth wrote.
He conceded, however, that many besides Wentworth thought differently.[88]
One factor in the critical view of Hamilton was anti-Scottish prejudice,
heightened in the circumstances of apparent rebellion. Many of the king's
English counsel would encourage little or nothing of a rapprochement with
the Covenanters.

Although Hamilton was not uninvolved with the English military, his first
responsibility was the leadership of Scottish forces; he with Traquair and
Nithsdale had powers to authorise the distribution of arms.[89] In March the
lieutenancies earlier projected came into being, at least the one for Huntly in
the north; Hamilton's eventual own commission was to be Lord General of
the king's forces in Scotland. Within the royal strategy, Hamilton was to take
his English soldiers by sea with a sizeable group of Scottish officers, to link up
if necessary with the royalists in Scotland.[90] How the Scottish situation
would turn out was unknown. Although the king and the Covenanters made
their preparations in all earnest, neither looked to the prospect of war as
inevitable.

With the king having reached York, there was a new proclamation drawn
up which offered pardon to all those in Scotland who would submit on certain terms. Charles's influence was clear in so far as the substance of these was
merely the lesser form of concessions offered at the beginning of the Glasgow
Assembly. The proclamation also made exceptions of a number of named
individuals. These were to submit for trial, or else be liable to be pursued, for

[86] Laud, *Works*, vol. VII, pp. 516–17, 519, 526, 539, 542, 550; BL Add. Ms. 15392, fol. 35.
[87] Knowler, *Strafforde Letters*, vol. II, pp. 175–6, 250; PRO SP 81/46, fol. 186; *The Camden
      Miscellany*, vol. IX (1895), pp. 9–11; *CSPD 1638–9*, 410/80.
[88] Laud, *Works*, vol. VII, pp. 529, 535, 565–6. Cf. *CSPD 1639*, 417/26; BL Add. Ms. 15392,
      fols. 74, 85v, 104, 111; WWM Str. P. LB 18, p. 177; GD 406/1/1204.
[89] *CSPD 1638–9*, 413/113 (undated); GD 406/1/775.
[90] See BL Add. Ms. 5754, fols. 42–50; Donald, 'The king and the Scottish troubles', p. 225n.

monetary rewards, to their deaths. This made in a grimmer fashion than ever the assumption that the disenabling of a few would go towards solving the trouble. The root assumption had a wide currency, but this was a new way of proceeding from it.[91] More generally, in what may have been the core idea for the proclamation, uncooperating landowners stood to forfeit rights over their vassals. The king would try to win loyalty among the people if not among the leaders of society. Eight days were generally allowed for submission.[92]

Sir John Hay, one of many now in exile from Scotland, wrote out the proclamation in York, where it had 'very few alterations', and it was sent to Hamilton for checking on 3 April.[93] Charles thereafter made further changes, most notably extending his policy to promise favours on debts to those who might repent of their past rebellion; another copy was sent to Hamilton.[94] Hamilton made comments on the first copy and advised that publication be as soon as possible and, while not all his suggestions were accepted at Court, indicated a close sense of approval of the text. Scottish news underpinned much of the thinking behind the text – whatever the origins of the idea for executions without trial.[95] The severity of the proclamation may have been an inflamed response to the offensive *Remonstrance*; news of the successes against royal strongholds in Scotland was not then available. That such passionate ruthlessness was injected on the sudden seems to be confirmed by the *Large Declaration*, published around the same time, which assumed the difference between the leaders in Scotland and those who were 'seduced', but stated merely that these leaders would be tried under the law for their crimes.[96]

The possible royal attack covered all three fronts, but initially the design was thoroughly to upset the Covenanter unity, and to pre-empt the invasion of England which was feared. The hope was that Scots who had taken refuge in the English camp would return home to give assistance to the issue of the new proclamation, and Hamilton, had he not been long delayed in getting his troops aboard ship, would have made to join the king at York. The disastrous showing of the king's party in Scotland pushed on more determined thinking.

---

[91] Cf. Knowler, *Strafforde Letters*, vol. II, p. 261; Baillie, *Letters*, vol. I, p. 187; BL Add. Ms. 11044, fols. 82–3.

[92] *CSPD 1639*, 418/50.

[93] G. Burnet, *The Memoires of the Lives and Actions of James and William, Dukes of Hamilton and Castleherald* . . . (1677), pp. 118–19.

[94] SRO Hamilton Red Book ii, 116; Burnet, *Memoires*, p. 120; GD 406/1/588. The text thus became what is printed in *CSPD 1639*, 418/50. The king seems to have thought of the favours idea himself.

[95] S. R. Gardiner (ed.), *The Hamilton Papers*, Camden Society (1880), pp. 70–2; GD 406/1/940.

[96] [Charles I], *Large Declaration*, p. 422; above n. 59. That the proclamation allowed any time at all to submit was an extra suggestion – Burnet, *Memoires*, p. 119.

While the proclamation underwent debate, Hamilton's commission was processed authorising him to use hostility against all who had taken arms in Scotland.[97] The marquis was to sail north therefore, and the king would follow after.

Hamilton and Sir Henry Vane with Charles had to some extent worked out the contingency plans in advance; here both encouraged the king to advance.[98] At this time of new urgency the marquis was keen that the Earl of Antrim's part in the Irish dimension should be encouraged – although he was not to go alone. Wentworth was to draw forces from the north of Ireland to be ready at a day's notice to transport them across to Ayr, Irvine, or the Firth of Clyde.[99] Hamilton's hopes for Antrim were to prove ill-founded. In early May Sir Henry Vane informed him that the prospects were poor – this was before Wentworth and the council finally ruled the same (with pleasure) in Ireland – and encouraged him to coordinate tactics with the Lord Deputy alone, to which Hamilton agreed.[100]

Some decisions were taken as necessity demanded. Fears that the Covenanters were about to march on Berwick resulted in the Earl of Essex, who had just finished a visit, being returned there for defence.[101] Further news of Covenanter successes in the north-east raised a question whether Hamilton should aim for the Firth of Forth or even only for Holy Island so as to meet the king for new counsels. The marquis argued for the former, holding that a loyal party would rise up in Scotland if the 'rebels' invaded, and if not he would follow the agreed course to enter into a war with the enemy – that is, after the eight days allowed beyond the publishing of the proclamation. However, he sounded concerned at the confusion of orders, and appealed to Charles himself to write. The mention of 'war' should not be misread. There was a question of whether the king should attempt anything other than a defensive action and sporadic strikes for advantage. Full battle at the best of times had risks.[102]

Charles was pleased to be directly approached. He affirmed his care to direct, that Hamilton might act 'as it is just, upon my own absolute command'.[103] Reflection, with some Scottish counsel, caused him now to restrain the passion which had informed the proclamation text in the offing. The citing of individuals for summary punishment was to be omitted together

[97] GD 406/1/812, 588; SRO Hamilton Red Book ii, 121; Gardiner, *Hamilton Papers*, pp. 70–2; Burnet, *Memoires*, p. 121.
[98] Cf. also GD 406/1/1188, 1179.
[99] GD 406/1/1190; Knowler, *Strafforde Letters*, vol. II, pp. 318–19; WWM Str. P. LB 10b, pp. 73–5; LB 3, p. 68 (11, 10 April).
[100] WWM Str. P. LB 10b, p. 75; GD 406/1/1197; Clarke, 'Antrim and the first Bishops' War'.
[101] *CSPD 1639*, 417/93; *HMC Rutland*, vol. I, p. 504.
[102] GD 406/1/1190, 1261, 1213; Gardiner, *Hamilton Papers*, pp. 72–3.
[103] Burnet, *Memoires*, p. 122.

with the references to the Glasgow Assembly and the Covenant. It was feared that singling out individuals would only unite further the opposition, which was now apparently all-powerful in Scotland. Charles limited his hopes to getting at least 'civil obedience' – leaving the managing of 'better terms' on church matters for a later date.[104]

What the king was offering in positive terms had not changed at all – and as it was it touched heavily on church matters! A parliament was offered only as before to confirm as much as was promised by Hamilton in the Glasgow Assembly. In effect, therefore, all conclusions of that assembly were denied. The king's word overruled the votes of a general assembly; the parliament would not be free. Charles had no real interest in negotiated accommodation. Instead he fervently hoped that those who would stand out after the revised proclamation would be few. The only change was that he would not stay in his present position in York. With Hamilton commanded to use fire and sword in any necessary pursuit, Charles aimed for the Scottish border. It was agreed that Scottish nobles and others at Court were to return home as a matter of urgency to add their efforts to the enforcement of the proclamation. Writing to Hamilton to leave the north until they had dealt together with the south, Charles closed, 'hoping to have a merry meeting with you in Scotland'.[105]

The king had a reasonable English army: he trusted he would redeem Scotland in person. Charles did not doubt the power of his presence.[106] At York, he had his feudal host around him; as Clarendon later noted, the expedition had much to offer in pomp and show.[107] The largeness of the vision could overlook the practical problems although these loomed large and often. Charles alone was fitted to the vision; his advisers were of necessity on a different level. These men wished to offer advice for the realities of the situation – from Wentworth, in his apparent readiness to countenance any effective policy, to Sir Thomas Hope, who dared still to offer counsel while restraining his sympathies for the other 'side'. Hamilton in his major responsibility of service echoed as far as he could his royal master; but his eyes focused equally on the practicalities of power. Charles, as it were, stayed on his throne.

Faith posited in this personal mission therefore tried to overcome the grim-

---

[104] Burnet, *Memoires*, pp. 122, 123 (latter 20 April, not 10 April as printed – SRO Hamilton Red Book ii, 127); GD 406/1/1212. Charles also wrote briefly to Windebank – *State Papers . . . Clarendon*, vol. II, p. 38.
[105] Burnet, *Memoires*, p. 123; SRO Hamilton Red Book ii, 128 (23 April – imperfect in Burnet, *Memoires*, p. 123).
[106] Cf. WWM Str. P. LB 18, p. 117.
[107] E. Hyde, *The History of the Rebellion and Civil War in England . . .* , ed. W. D. Macray (6 vols., Oxford, 1888), vol. I, pp. 153–4; BL Add. Ms. 15392, fols. 143–4.

ness of the present state of affairs north of the border. Aberdeen had held out only a little better than the rest. The Marquis of Huntly was reported to have subscribed a statement acknowledging the rightfulness of the Glasgow Assembly – a paper that was circulated as a great coup for the Covenanters.[108] In advance of his defeat, Huntly had blamed the poor supply of arms from England for putting his area at risk, for which he had grounds, but had vowed that there would be no 'sparing ourselves'; in the event he apparently surrendered peaceably, at which Charles was definitely not impressed.[109] He was not the only victim of Charles's frustration. Traquair was committed in some disgrace at York for not offering resistance at Dalkeith.[110] The captain who lost Dumbarton Castle had no mean effort to try to excuse himself from blame.[111] Roxburgh came under suspicion when his son Lord Ker gave over the area of his main estates to the Covenanters while he was absent; Windebank already had suspicions concerning the earl. Roxburgh excused himself to the Earl of Stirling, but Lord Ker's subsequent defection to the Covenanters rebounded on the father, who was committed in York.[112] Although Huntly and Traquair were reconciled quickly enough, the foundations for royal recovery were not good.[113]

Those in Scotland who resisted signing the Covenant as long as the king withheld his approval, and some of the ones who fled to York for safety, wished a peaceful solution which required Charles in some measure to yield ground. In late March the Lords of Session had sent the Justice-clerk, Sir John Hamilton of Orbiston, with a letter to the king, making unambiguous the fact that those who upheld the Glasgow Assembly outnumbered those who opposed it; it described the king's 'professed dislike' to be 'worrying' – 'violence and arms are bitter remedies'. Sir James Carmichael followed a fortnight later, apparently for the same purpose, namely to ask the king to hear the advice of the council and Session.[114] The larger backing for the second embassy convened on the mistaken belief that the king was already in Newcastle; nineteen members of council and Session met together in the hope somehow of preventing what seemed like imminent bloodshed and wrong.

---

[108] Hope, Diary, pp. 92–3; Stevenson, Scottish Revolution, pp. 139–40.
[109] GD 406/1/753, 759, 780, 762; SRO Hamilton Red Book ii, 116, 128 (imperfect in Burnet, Memoires, pp. 119, 123).
[110] Cf. CSPD 1639, 417/29; Burnet, Memoires, p. 119; Hope, Diary, p. 93; GD 406/1/587; BL Add. Ms. 15392, fol. 112v.
[111] Gardiner, Hamilton Papers, pp. 68–70; GD 406/1/826. Edinburgh Castle was taken by force rather than by device as at Dumbarton – NLS Wod. Fo. 54, fol. 274.
[112] PRO SP 16/412/80; SP 16/413/89; Donald, 'The king and the Scottish troubles', p. 232n.
[113] For Huntly, a second paper was circulated which had him committed against subscribing the Covenant – CUL Add. Ms. 335, fol. 42; Staffs. RO D661/11/1/5/1; Spalding, History, vol. I, pp. 128–9; BL Add. Ms. 15392, fol. 128.
[114] Peterkin, Records, pp. 211–12; NLS Wod. Fo. 54, fol. 275; Hope, Diary, pp. 88, 90; GD 406/1/818.

Although there were squabbles with the Covenanting leadership, it seems that a measure of shared ideas arose in the heat of events.[115]

Despite the circumstances, the persistence of such counsels is striking when to us the possibility of finding common ground, given the opposite positions, seems to have been remote. The will for a harmonious peace with the king was very strong. Approaches of conciliation were fobbed off in York, however, since Charles would hear only 'propositions worthy of his hearing'.[116] Carmichael was used as a carrier of the new proclamation. The Earl of Southesk brought the news of Huntly's defeat to Charles with a similar appeal for accommodation; he might have stayed at York – had he not feared arrest, being distrusted like Roxburgh. By mid-May he would argue the need to remove the bishops altogether for any hope of settlement.[117] Traquair in his release from imprisonment secured permission to attempt an informal embassy to the Covenanters alongside Lord Dalzell, who was further ennobled around this time. They proposed that Covenanters should come to speak with the king. Charles's coolness indicated how he had no genuine wish to talk. On the other side the circumstances were unpropitious; besides everything else, the original form of the proclamation had been leaked to Scotland, which had given plain evidence of the vindictiveness to be feared.[118]

Given the poor show of resistance against the Covenanters in Scotland, the Scots who circulated around Court at York attracted some animosity.[119] General distrust of Scots was reflected in the special oath required of them, first in Ireland and subsequently in England; the officers who sailed under Hamilton were equally obliged.[120] In the camp, where there were conflicting reports of the Scottish situation, speculation abounded on how far the king himself would go and whether or not there would be war. The royal itinerary was released only in stages.[121]

Within a current of opinion that was reluctant to engage, the Earl of Holland, General of the Horse, spoke to fellow peers of his wishes for a peaceful accommodation – and so distanced himself from the Lord General, the

[115] Hope, *Diary*, pp. 89–92.
[116] NLS Adv. Ms. 33.4.14, fols. 229–30; Hope, *Diary*, pp. 92–3, 95.
[117] WWM Str. P. LB 19, fol. 47; Knowler, *Strafforde Letters*, vol. II, p. 342; CSPD 1639, 421/21; GD 406/1/818, 1197.
[118] NLS Ms. 21183, fol. 110; NLS Ms. 2263, fol. 164; CSPD 1639, 418/72; GD 112/40/2/2/97; GD 112/39/765. For the leak, see NLS Crawford Ms. 14/7/45; cf. CSPD 1639, 417/3.
[119] Cf. HMC Rutland, vol. I, p. 508, but also p. 510; Burnet, *Memoires*, p. 122; GD 406/1/1198; WWM Str. P. LB 19, p. 41.
[120] A. Ford, *The Protestant Reformation in Ireland, 1590–1641* (Frankfurt on Main, 1985), pp. 267–76; PCR, vol. VI, pp. 419, 426, 431, 437; CSPD 1639, 424/12; BL Add. Ms. 11045, fol. 29; GD 18/2386.
[121] For example, CSPD 1639, 417/85, 92, 107, 418/6, 29, 41, 420/106; *Letters and Papers of the Verney Family*, ed. J. Bruce, Camden Society (1853), pp. 209–11; Berks. RO Trumbull Misc. XLIX, no. 40; HMC De L'Isle, vol. VI, pp. 163–4.

Earl of Arundel. Arundel in the past had suspected him of sympathising with the Covenanters.[122] The Earl of Bristol and others opined that the king should not go any further north but instead return to London. The caution shown here was linked later, at the Scottish border, with an appeal for an English parliament. Sir Henry Mildmay, from a different perspective, considered that there existed a large measure of sympathy for the Covenanters, although not all peers felt well represented by Bristol's outspokenness.[123]

An account of the strength of sympathy for the Covenanters is hardly possible, given the many questions at issue, but realism or non-commitment could work against any grand thoughts of aggression. Wentworth could not conceive that Charles's presence was necessary beyond York. His suggestion was that the troubles be contained in Scotland until the next year; while he himself ruled firmly in Ireland, he reckoned that a more coordinated and thorough direction of forces was required for successful action. A good flow of money was a necessary element.[124] Different concerns moved the Countess of Westmorland, who feared for the well-being of the English state in this drive against the Scots; she feared the strain of war might create too serious divisions at home. She had little interest in the Scottish cause *per se*, thinking that a moderate settlement respecting their laws might be managed, with any royal honour lost in the process possible to regain later.[125]

The king had determined the changes in the Scottish proclamation on 20 April, and on the 21st the Earl of Arundel led in bringing to the peers a new oath, for the maintaining of the possible struggle 'to the uttermost of life and fortune'.[126] All those present took the oath – except Saye and Sele and Brooke. Their opposition, which stood out against being committed to invade Scotland or to kill Scots or, in Brooke's words, against the taking of an oath not sanctioned by a parliament, caused a famous stir; as Charles was reported to say – 'I find you averse to all my proceedings.'[127] The two peers

---

[122] *HMC Rutland*, vol. I, pp. 508–9; BL Add. Ms. 15392, fols. 39–40, 330v; Laud, *Works*, vol. VII, p. 523.

[123] GD 406/1/1207; BL Add. Ms. 15392, fol. 170; GD 406/1/1203; Verney, *Letters*, p. 237. Bristol spoke out again at the end of May – *CSPD 1639*, 421/169, 422/62, 78, 423/67; *HMC Rutland*, vol. I, p. 513; Verney, *Letters*, p. 251. Cf. Collins, *Letters*, vol. II, p. 602.

[124] Knowler, *Strafforde Letters*, vol. II, pp. 313–14, 324, 325–7; WWM Str. P. LB 7, fols. 166–7, 179–80; LB 10b, pp. 63–9, 70; LB 11, pp. 218–19; Ford, *Reformation in Ireland*, pp. 267–76.

[125] *CSPD 1639*, 420/70.

[126] The episode has been fully discussed in M. L. Schwarz, 'Viscount Saye and Sele, Lord Brooke and aristocratic protest in the first Bishops' War', *Canadian Journal of History*, 7 (1972), 17–36; Hibbard, *Charles I and the Popish Plot*, pp. 117–20; Cope, *Politics without Parliaments*, pp. 170–2.

[127] *HMC Rutland*, vol. I, pp. 507–9; BL Sloane Ms. 650, fol. 91; *CSPD 1639*, 418/99. On Saye, cf. N. P. Bard, 'The ship money case and William Fiennes, Viscount Saye and Sele', *BIHR*, 1 (1977), 177–84; on Brooke, cf. A. Hughes, *Politics, Society and the Civil War in Warwickshire, 1620–1660* (Cambridge, 1987), pp. 24–5, 120–5.

were imprisoned and interrogated in consequence, but after a few days were sent home. They suffered little more – but, unlike in February, not for want of trying on the king's side.[128] It was another of these practical setbacks; it was not ruinous to Charles, though concessions followed. For the peers who subscribed, there was a modification to save their followings from being engaged outside their personal command. And, whereas the oath was originally intended for administration to the whole army, there is no evidence that this was now attempted.[129]

The peers were esteemed 'martyrs' while under the king's displeasure, and awareness of their stand became widespread. Robert Woodford, the puritan, heard the news quickly of the 'godly and gracious lords' being committed into custody; for Walter Yonge, a Devonshire man already considerably stirred over the Scottish troubles, the incident raised serious constitutional questions.[130] The king's vision was open to question, and from a British perspective. There were perhaps grounds in Sir Thomas Hope's description of the lords as 'intelligencers to the Scots nobles'.[131]

Hamilton's arrival in the Forth on 30 April tied up relatively well with the king's estimated time of arrival in Berwick of mid-May. The proclamation was to be published and eight days given – from its publication throughout the country, not just in Edinburgh – and then the marquis would offer hostilities. A concerted input of intimidation might thus precede the king's own entry to claim the civil obedience of his Scottish subjects.[132]

Although severe fright was taken at the surprise appearance of the ships, there was no collapse of resistance. The Covenanter strength held out. Charles would have to learn that threats from a king outside Scotland at the head of an alien army would, in the main, be counter-productive. It was difficult to get the proclamation received on shore, let alone read in the capital, where it was denounced as the work of evil counsellors. The exiled lords meant to help elsewhere had hesitated to leave Court, fearing for their own safety; the king's estimated time of arrival was delayed. On board ship, the marquis's own men inspired little confidence.[133] Hamilton justifiably felt

[128] *State Papers . . . Clarendon*, vol. II, pp. 38, 41, 45, 56; *CSPD 1639*, 418/114. Cf. also PRO SP 77/29, fol. 192.
[129] *HMC Rutland*, vol. I, p. 508; BL Add. Ms. 15392, fol. 135; GD 406/1/1215.
[130] GD 406/1/1207; *HMC 9 (II)*, p. 498; BL Add. Ms. 35331, fols. 72–3. For Woodford, see J. Fielding, 'Opposition to the Personal Rule of Charles I: the diary of Robert Woodford, 1637–1641', *HJ*, 31 (1988), 769–88; for Yonge, see below, chapter 5.
[131] Hope, *Diary*, pp. 93–4; cf. BL Add. Ms. 15392, fol. 136; Baillie, *Letters*, vol. I, pp. 199–200.
[132] GD 406/1/1203, 1202; Gardiner, *Hamilton Papers*, pp. 76–8.
[133] GD 112/40/2/2/94–5; *Diary of Sir Archibald Johnston, Lord Wariston, 1639*, ed. G. M. Paul, SHS (Edinburgh, 1896), p. 36; Burnet, *Memoires*, pp. 125–6; Stevenson, *Scottish Revolution*, p. 143.

weak, and tried to express this in a confidential letter to Charles. He recommended the acceptance of some form of interim settlement, pointing to the
desperate lack of influence in Scotland and the 'great difficulty and vast
expense' of winning by force, not to mention the poor state of his men. The
counsel had to sound palatable. He referred to a recent Covenanter letter
which offered 'civil obedience' – a term to answer possibly the hopes of the
undelivered proclamation; and he tried to cover himself against any charge of
'falsehood or feebleness'.[134]

The king sent back by return of carrier. He implied that he understood
Hamilton's train of thought, but underlined that civil obedience had to be
understood by the Covenanters' asking for pardon and releasing all that they
unjustly possessed, a demand in effect for surrender, in particular of the royal
castles. Charles had newly received and commissioned Lord Aboyne, who
had a hopeful plan for the north-east, yet he acknowledged his basically weak
position against the Covenanters; nevertheless he trusted 'by the grace of
God' somehow to force obedience – 'the which rather than not do, I shall first
sell myself to my shirt'. Honour was important above all, and Charles could
not doubt but that he would be vindicated.[135] In practical terms, he also sent
around this time a strategy for taking control of the keypoints in Scotland. In
accuracy of information, if nothing else, it was flawed; Hamilton, given
discretion, rejected it.[136]

The marquis was bound to accept the king's words about honour, but he
equally felt obliged to extend his practical arguments. It was to be dreaded,
he wrote, that the problem might become the 'national quarrel' they had
striven for so long to avoid. Many of the Scots at Court seemed to be agents
for the Covenanters; he even raised doubts about the English, referring to
supplications that the Covenanters were now sending through them.
Troubles had to be redressed: he suggested that the English peers concerned
should be made to declare their abhorrence of the Covenant. Any encouragement for the Covenanters should be censored. On the one hand it was to be
admitted that 'compulsion' was needed, by efforts on all three fronts; but
Hamilton mentioned also overtures of peace. The opponents offered civil
obedience humbly – albeit with a 'damnable but', that the king must abolish
bishops, or at least listen to 'just reasons' against them.[137]

In stating the alternatives Hamilton had professed political reasons; his

---

[134] GD 406/1/1201, 1200; Gardiner, *Hamilton Papers*, pp. 78–80; *HMC Hamilton* (21), p.
       106; Hamilton's Diary, M3/1 at Lennoxlove, seen through NRA (S).
[135] SRO Hamilton Red Book ii, 133 (misplaced and incomplete in Burnet, *Memoires*, p. 136);
       BL Sloane Ms. 650, fol. 95; GD 406/1/1199; *HMC De L'Isle*, vol. VI, p. 165.
[136] Burnet, *Memoires*, pp. 107–9.
[137] GD 406/1/1197; Gardiner, *Hamilton Papers*, pp. 80–3. Cf. Verney, *Letters*, p. 231; Bod.
       Tanner Ms. 67, fol. 109; *CSPD 1639*, 420/77.

doubts about the king's grand statements of determination seemed to repeat the June 1638 situation, while his additional correspondence was exchanged with Sir Henry Vane instead of with Laud as in the previous year. Hamilton was possibly even less sure now about the way forward, although the 'damnable but' had an earlier parallel in the explanation of the Covenant. Here again he feared also what the Covenanters might further press on the king, and found his greater comfort in upholding Charles, as a letter to Eleazar Borthwick on 12 May most clearly showed. He detested the situation of subjects being in arms against the king. The main problem was discerning how those ashore in Scotland could be brought to yield.[138] Might trust yet be won? He enclosed proposed terms for treaty for the king, which had originated in discussions with possible middle men, the Earl of Southesk, Lord Innerpeffer, and Borthwick himself.[139]

The terms on paper were a reasonable starting point. The king's wishes were respected in the opening clauses for the Covenanters' laying down of arms, delivery of castles and request of pardon. It was further allowed that words against bishops might be heard at the approaching parliament, likewise other matters from the Glasgow Assembly, to be ratified or denied as was 'just'. Civil obedience was to be offered to the king; the making of fortifications was to be stopped, although those already existing were to remain until the parliament was over. The definition of 'justice' was left open, but the terms were far from approving wholesale the Acts of Glasgow.[140]

Borthwick showed signs of distancing himself from the prevailing direction of the Covenanters. Someone like Robert Baillie may well have been prepared at this stage to accept the simple removal of bishops, as Southesk suggested, without any massive abjuration of the institution.[141] But the odds ran against Hamilton. Given his own position in the Forth, he was not well placed to attract trust; his propositions, made within a background of threat, met threats in return from the Covenanters. Many of them would not willingly abandon the Glasgow achievement. From Charles, he found only superficial approval, for the king judged them to be only a useful time-wasting device while he made his progress towards the Scottish border. Charles certainly wanted 'castles and ornaments of his crown' returned before any meeting of parliament, but his words, when he arrived at the border, dwelt as much on the possibility of hostilities. The marquis came near despair.[142]

[138] GD 406/1/940. See too GD 406/1/1201, 855; Burnet, *Memoires*, pp. 126–7.
[139] GD 406/1/1197; Gardiner, *Hamilton Papers*, pp. 82–3; Hamilton Diary M3/1, 13 May.
[140] The heads, annotated by Charles, are printed in Burnet, *Memoires*, pp. 130–2 (GD 406/M1/54); the draft, with slight differences, is GD 406/M1/79.
[141] *HMC Hamilton*, pp. 106–7; Baillie, *Letters*, vol. I, pp. 177–9; GD 406/1/1197.
[142] GD 406/M1/54; SRO Hamilton Red Book ii, 135; GD 406/1/1189, 836, 1102, 924, 923, 1103, 1100, 925, 922; GD 406/M1/53/1; Burnet, *Memoires*, p. 130; Johnston, *1639 Diary*, p. 48.

The failure of the proclamation only brought Charles to search out strength by other ways. In the camp he had talks with his English nobility of plans for the drive forward. There was a sense that perhaps more might be needed in terms of aggression.[143] Reinforcements were ordered – although not as many as was publicly to be made out by Windebank; in London, Windebank began to research possibilities of a Papal loan. The earlier obstacle of lords not allowing anyone else to command their men was now overcome. Hamilton's delayed commission was hurried on, and an assignment was made to him of £18,000. Sir Donald MacDonald of Sleat, who met with Charles probably around this time, had encouragement to send to the Earl of Antrim, that yet again that expedition might be revived for sending men into the western isles of Scotland.[144] What would actually happen was still open. The king certainly did not give up on the hope of winning loyalty from some of his Scottish subjects. There was a new proclamation on 14 May, published from New-castle, to offer a promise that there would be no hostility if there was civil obedience. Charles wished to show his intention of being shortly 'at our good town of Edinburgh'. He referred settlement to the Scottish parliament he yet hoped to dominate. At the same time, the proclamation contained a threatening ultimatum. The Scots were to be destroyed if they came with their army within ten miles of the border.[145]

The Covenanters did not want war, which was apparent not only in their (novel) obedience to this latest proclamation, but before this in their keenness to work more by petitions than by movement of armies; it was to be different in 1640. They suggested concessions by the king with a conference of 'well-affected men' or some other means to prepare the ground for settling the troubles. It was an appeal for maximum English involvement, failing an English parliament; the most natural participants would be the nobility of both sides. A messenger sent to the Earl of Holland communicated the formula which struck at the heart of the issue – 'we shall be governed in ecclesiastical matters by general assemblies and by parliament in civil matters'. These exchanges were interpreted by the Covenanters as 'treaty', but the king's predictable replies continued the impasse.[146]

Hamilton had referred to English peers possibly sympathising with the Covenanters, alluding to the latter's approaches made from mid-April 1639. At the Earl of Essex's second entrance into Berwick, a letter was sent to him

[143] GD 406/1/1198; cf. WWM Str. P. LB 10b, pp. 87–90, 94–100.
[144] GD 406/1/832, 1189; *State Papers . . . Clarendon*, vol. II, pp. 42–3, 46–8; BL Add. Ms 15392, fols. 159, 162–4; *HMC Rutland*, vol. I, p. 511; Bod. Clarendon Ms. 18, fol. 8; *HMC Hamilton Supp.*, p. 47; PRO C 231/5, p. 243; *HMC Cowper*, vol. II, p. 239; WWM Str. P LB 19, p. 63; LB 3, pp. 74–5; LB 10, fols. 109–11.
[145] Larkin, *Stuart Royal Proclamations*, vol. II, pp. 680–1; GD 406/1/1195; *CSPD 1639* 422/78.
[146] Johnston, *1639 Diary*, pp. 39–43, 46, 48–9.

justifying the Covenanters' cause, and complaining that other Scots had brought about the troubles. It was therefore part of the campaign to neutralise English animosities, and as such was circulated in Scotland; it suggested a peaceful clearing of disputes 'in a way thought fit by both sides'.[147] Essex was important at least on account of his commanding position; whether he gave the Covenanters much encouragement seems unlikely. He forwarded the petition to the king, claiming not to have read it, although he was given a copy.[148] Similar addresses made to the Earl of Holland and others a few weeks later were also designed to get sympathy – and for that reason sending to Arundel or Vane was not considered expedient.[149] Again results were not startling. Holland's replies asked the Covenanters to shun violence and to retire their forces; they were scrutinised at Court, perhaps especially following Hamilton's advice, but Holland served the king well in publicising the new May proclamation.[150]

As the king marched for Berwick, the expectation was that Hamilton would begin any conflict, but, before Charles arrived, Hamilton sent a warning of the likely invasion of England. It was perhaps an exaggerated conclusion from the indications that peace hung on the ratification of the Acts of the Glasgow Assembly, but the situation looked bleak. He suggested sending two of his regiments to the king, who might have greater need since no hope of a significant royalist showing in Scotland remained. 'For ought I can learn, [they] will either make themselves a commonwealth or a conquered kingdom.'[151]

Hamilton's pessimism had foundation, even though some Scottish nobles were at last arriving to do what little they could in the country. The Earl of Tullibardine was one who publicised the new proclamation in his area; Lord Aboyne also came, disappointingly supplied. Hamilton sent him on to the north-east, where the stance on the Glasgow Assembly still met with opposition. He was to arrive there just in time to turn back those forced to retreat by sea from Aberdeen. There alone the king's party could put up a struggle.[152]

In general, the uncertainties of the king's military strategy were felt not only by the marquis. Charles was also concerned enough to warn Hamilton to be ready to come to his aid.[153] The difficulties for the king of finding money and

---

[147] *CSPD 1639*, 418/9 (19 April); NLS Crawford Ms. 14/7/44, 14/3/35; NLS Adv. Ms. 29.2.9, fol. 107.

[148] Baillie, *Letters*, vol. I, p. 204; Verney, *Letters*, pp. 226–7. Cf. GD 112/39/653.

[149] *CSPD 1639*, 420/143, 422/77 – to the Earls of Newcastle, Holland and Pembroke.

[150] Johnston, *1639 Diary*, pp. 36–7, 38–9; GD 406/1/1195. Hamilton saw copies of the letters – GD 406/1/1197, 1087.

[151] Gardiner, *Hamilton Papers*, pp. 83–4; cf. *HMC Hamilton*, pp. 106–7; GD 406/1/837.

[152] Fraser, *Chiefs of Grant*, vol. II, p. 67; Gardiner, *Hamilton Papers*, pp. 89, 90–1; GD 406/1/1194, 334, 1184, 1196, 1192, 837; Stevenson, *Scottish Revolution*, pp. 147–8.

[153] Burnet, *Memoires*, p. 133.

supplies were not insignificant, as no doubt those around him gave warning; but a major clash with a Covenant army on the Scottish border had never been wished. Since Hamilton's troops were mobile Sir Henry Vane on 23 May requested that the two regiments offered be sent to Holy Island.[154]

It was important that Charles could at least defend himself, and Hamilton's assessment offered little more; echoing Wentworth's advice of some weeks past, he opined that a sustained policy of blockade might sufficiently wear down 'this rebellious nation' by Michaelmas, or at the longest within a year.[155] Since that kind of emphasis gave no desirable prospect, he tried after the royal arrival at Berwick, and though the Covenanters' goodwill was fast waning, further to work overtures of peace.

The Covenanters had in fact no intentions of invasion and were pursuing their own line for settlement. Rothes on 29 May appealed to Hamilton himself to go to Berwick to establish the 'possibility of accommodation'; three days later, he was asked to take part in a treaty that might involve also English nobles and the king. Compared with the approaches to the English nobles, these suggestions came relatively late, but Hamilton fobbed off the request for him to go south by saying he would treat where he was, pleading to Rothes that he could not desert his charge, but also encouraging a petition to the king as from 'humble subjects'.[156] On board ship on 1 June, he conceded that a newly indicted general assembly might settle the controverted issues. It was an advance – except that he wished to argue, for the first time as far as is known, that the king had a negative voice there. This the Covenanters would not acknowledge.[157]

Hamilton's attempt to mediate here was probably on his own initiative; in his words about a general assembly he had no specific authorisation in his support. The king had latched present hopes on to the still forthcoming parliament; Hamilton's concession grasped at the possibility of moving away from the clash over authority in parliament that might be expected if it alone were held. He tried to conciliate on the negative voice argument too, by suggesting that all might work out if the assembly operated on 'legal and customary lines'; it was nevertheless a warning against the manipulation of elections.[158]

However, the alternative option was not far off amidst the frustrations and the unknowns, with distrust on both sides. While he kept up talks, Hamilton

---

[154] GD 406/1/1188, 1187, 1186. Cf. Verney, *Letters*, p. 232; Gardiner, *Hamilton Papers*, pp. 75–6.
[155] Gardiner, *Hamilton Papers*, pp. 86–9; GD 406/1/1183, 1192.
[156] GD 406/1/1195, 921, 1105, 926; HMC *Hamilton Supp.*, p. 57; Hamilton Diary M3/1, Johnston, *1639 Diary*, p. 59.
[157] Burnet, *Memoires*, pp. 133–5. For the negative voice question, see above, p. 107.
[158] Burnet, *Memoires*, pp. 133–5; GD 406/1/921, 926, 853.

also vented his passion in letters south, wishing that the Covenanter leaders might be declared traitors if they refused to cooperate.[159] Charles still wanted punishments, so while his slow and unsure progress held back the commencement of attacks, the Covenanters rightly did not take chances.[160] Balmerino saw Hamilton's attitude in the opening days of June as 'harsh'; Robert Baillie, usually generous to Hamilton in seeing him as a bound servant of the king, made an account of these days that turned far more on the danger of the situation and the fears of an armed clash. The closing days of May, when the king came through Berwick, saw frenzied activity among the military command in Scotland.[161]

The proclamation language calling for the submission of the Covenanters was impracticable given the opposing conceptions of what was good to submit upon. On 2 June Charles authorised an offensive. Efforts to publish the recent May proclamation in the Scottish borders as a means of winning support had had disappointing results, with no open defections; the king commanded Hamilton to do what 'mischief' he could. Separately he ordered a ready flow of money as an urgent priority.[162]

This 'war' came to very little. Hamilton, lacking authority to proceed any further with mediatory propositions, transmitted Charles's command to Lord Ogilvie, and the next day himself sailed east with his men as far as Inchgarvie, where there were shots fired at his fleet, and then to the opposite side of the Forth, where at Barnbougle a boat was run aground; the plan was to attack Burntisland. He also heard the latest report from Lord Aboyne, whose latest plea for help reported Covenanter approaches by the Earls of Montrose and Marischal, albeit against a strong current of support in Aberdeenshire and Banffshire.[163]

Meanwhile, the king had received intelligence on 3 June of a Scottish force camped at Kelso, the first breach of the ten-mile limit. About two thousand foot and two hundred horse under the Earl of Holland set out in the middle of the night to inflict an exemplary blow. This force was not small, but the Covenanters managed to repel them, and without a stroke; English eyewitnesses complained the Scots had managed superior numbers. It pointed to a failure in English intelligence, and the Kelso action increased worries about English strength. Holland's retreat may have been sensible enough, but his

[159] GD 406/1/1196, 1192; Gardiner, *Hamilton Papers*, pp. 87–8, 90–1.
[160] Cf. BL Add. Ms. 15392, fols. 174, 277; Bod. Clarendon Ms. 16, fol. 162.
[161] Johnston, *1639 Diary*, p. 59; Baillie, *Letters*, vol. I, pp. 202, 205–6. For the end of May, and Archibald Johnston's prominence, see Johnston, *1639 Diary*, pp. 44–6, 47, 50, 51–2, 57, 59; NLS Wod. Fo. 63, fols. 60ff.; Stevenson, *Scottish Revolution*, p. 150.
[162] *CSPD 1639*, 432/12, 13; Johnston, *1639 Diary*, pp. 43, 46, 49; Bod. Clarendon Ms. 18, fol. 8; *State Papers . . . Clarendon*, vol. II, p. 52.
[163] Hamilton Diary M3/1; PRO SP 84/155, fol. 180; Burnet, *Memoires*, p. 138; Johnston, *1639 Diary*, p. 69; GD 406/1/334; Stevenson, *Scottish Revolution*, pp. 147–8.

earlier keenness to treat with the Scots raised suspicions, even if unfounded.[164]

The Covenanters were not without problems in their own armies, nor was their intelligence faultless. Their strength at Kelso had derived from drawing together a number of companies after warning received of the English advance as Holland's men left their camp. Though the king's attacking role may have boosted their internal unity, they were still not prepared to engage in battle; they feared repeat attacks by the English.[165] Neither side was wholly confident against the other.

Even Charles seems to have been disturbed as the Scots continued in refusal to submit despite his own presence at the head of an army.[166] In this situation Sir Henry Vane wrote to Hamilton on his behalf, to ask him to join the king in person, 'safe, and in a good posture', and to consult on the best way forward.[167] Hamilton, still not directly engaged in conflict, therefore turned to sail south and arrived in Berwick at 2 p.m. on 7 June, whence he went immediately to the king's camp nearby at Birks.[168] By then there had been talks between Covenanters and Scottish courtiers; one Robin Leslie had gone to see the Scottish general, Alexander Leslie. This all ran to one purpose, namely that the Covenanters should petition the king for talks to be opened. They initiated the move, but, by sending Robin Leslie to encourage a supplication, Charles took on what for him was an alternative option. It was in that context that he had considered it important to have his prime counsellor alongside him.[169]

Although the Scottish army was in sight at Duns, and the king did not have the news from the north-east to hand, this was not a surrender by any means. Charles sent away two commissions for the use of aggression on 5 and 11 June, and, as speculation abounded on whether or not there would be peace, the Covenanters were rightly concerned lest he was merely hanging fire.[170] The opening of talks was unpropitious. Charles was falsely persuaded that his condition for treaty – the reading of the April proclamation in the Scottish camp – had been fulfilled; it did not happen. But the Covenanters

---

[164] Cf. *CSPD 1639*, 423/12; *HMC Rutland*, vol. I, p. 513; Verney, *Letters*, pp. 243–4; *CSPD 1639*, 423/27, 29. For fuller accounts, see Gardiner, *History of England*, vol. IX, pp. 27–31; Fissel, '*Bellum episcopale*', pp. 76–95.

[165] Baillie, *Letters*, vol. I, p. 200; Johnston, *1639 Diary*, pp. 42, 49, 57, 59, 62–3, 65; Burnet, *Memoires*, pp. 139–40.

[166] Cf. GD 406/1/1066; but also *HMC 4*, p. 295. As Professor Russell has noted to me, Charles took seriously the Earl of Bristol's approaches at this time – *CSPD 1639*, 423/67.

[167] Burnet, *Memoires*, p. 139 (4 June). Cf. GD 406/1/1195; *CSPD 1639*, 423/46.

[168] NLS Wod. Fo. 66, fol. 64; Hamilton Diary M3/1.

[169] Johnston, *1639 Diary*, p. 63; Stevenson, *Scottish Revolution*, pp. 150–1.

[170] Stevenson, *Scottish Revolution*, pp. 151–2; also PRO SP 84/155, fol. 182v; BL Add. Ms. 15392, fols. 181–2.

wanted to talk; their justification for the deception was that the limitations of the proclamation, neither sanctioned in the ordinary way by the Scottish privy council nor valid to pronounce as it did on traitors, made it unacceptable; their argument still stood that it had originated from bad counsel. Was the king alone deceived? The Covenanters went to pains to have their position explained at least to the English peers.[171]

Charles's rather blind hope of the condition deserves attention. Still the royal majesty, the royal terms of settlement, the royal will were to hold sway: this the reading of the proclamation was to symbolise. If he was ever told, he overlooked the deception in which Sir Edmund Verney, his standard-bearer, had acquiesced; he hoped in any case to win some interim settlement. He was convinced that he should participate in the talks himself. At his appearance on the first day of treaty, he explained to the surprised Covenanters who attended that he wished to hear clearly since it had been said that he had closed his ears to the allegedly just complaints of his subjects.[172] By this stage, however, much was expected of him – and his new readiness for accommodation was again strictly limited. True communication between the two sides was to prove once more elusive.

The Covenanters sent initially a delegation of four to the talks at Birks. The Earl of Rothes and Lord Loudoun gave an element of continuity with respect to the long duration of the troubles, and were accompanied by the Earl of Dunfermline and Sir William Douglas of Cavers, the sheriff of Teviotdale. Only one of these four, Dunfermline, had not been blacklisted in the original form of the April proclamation; he had in fact let Hamilton know of his uneasiness concerning the radical nature of the Glasgow conclusions.[173] Two further speakers who attended to even numbers were more resolutely committed – the ex-Moderator, Alexander Henderson, and the ever-diligent Archibald Johnston of Wariston; Johnston was clearly important at all stages in drawing up the far-reaching statement of desires and supporting arguments.

The Covenanters had requested that they talk with 'a few worthy Englishmen, well-affected to the true religion and to our common peace'. Charles conceded to appoint negotiators, six initially, his military commanders with some other privy councillors. He had no scruples about adding to this group subsequently, but in his own attendance he personally dominated the meetings, showing himself coherent and persistent in argument. In intention there was little room for compromise. Notably, however, on what became the

[171] Johnston, *1639 Diary*, pp. 66–8; Stevenson, *Scottish Revolution*, pp. 151–2. Con in London knew that the king's desire had not been obeyed – BL Add. Ms. 15392, fol. 180.
[172] Johnston, *1639 Diary*, p. 71.   [173] *CSPD 1639*, 418/50; GD 406/1/366.

crucial day of the talks, the second meeting on Thursday 13 June, he had
alongside him the Marquis of Hamilton.[174]

Four days of discussions led to an agreement sealed on 18 June. Charles
talked in the only way he knew, stating his readiness to accept submission to
his judgement. As the Covenanters had been so insistent on the bad counsel
around him, he would now hear in person both 'sides' of the case; but his
prejudice against the Covenanters was more than apparent. They were ready
to talk about the justifiability of their case, but final determinations were
reserved for the parliament that they still expected. Charles was grudging
about hearing them out, but a debate of the issues did ensue; however, he
insisted that all substantial points be committed to writing. Though discussion was not to lead to final settlement in advance of the parliament, he
would try by the force of his personal presence to secure the best possible
terms.

Rothes and Loudoun argued for the importance of the law and customs of
Scotland, the practice of the established church and, above all, for the need to
uphold God's honour. This covered the desires put to the king and the validity
of the Glasgow Assembly in particular. Following instructions written at
Duns, they were asking for ratification of the Glasgow Acts at a parliament
in Edinburgh on 23 July, and this was of primary importance. They further
asked the king to declare that all ecclesiastical matters would be treated in
general assemblies and all civil matters in parliaments (with other inferior
judicatories); and also for a Pacification, under which were required specific
points of disbandment and the return of excommunicates, incendiaries and
informers to Scotland.[175] It seems clear that the Scottish negotiators put the
final shape on what was written down as 'Desires' for the king; memoranda
composed by Johnston of Wariston could be helpful – including notably a
request for parliaments every two or three years which was included – but
some of the originally suggested 'means' for Pacification were apparently
smoothed over, namely the desire for a reparation of losses and also for the
recalling of hostile proclamations and copies of Charles's *Large Declaration*.
Johnston's suggestion to secure good public appointments by the king
nominating with consent either of parliament or the council or Session in
interludes was not presently adopted.[176]

---

[174] For this and the account that follows, detailed reference is eschewed. The principal sources
are Johnston, *1639 Diary*, pp. 64–95 (Johnston's official record?); accounts in PRO SP
16/423/92, 104, 119, SP 16/424/13, 26, 64; and the less well-known account by Sir Edward
Walker, in BL Add. Ms. 38847, fols. 3–5, 10–13, 15–16 and Lansdowne Ms. 255,
fols. 333–4.
[175] *CSPD 1639*, 423/80. For the enemies of the Covenant, see Johnston's Memos nos. 2, 5, 6 (in
1639 Diary, pp. 72–4).
[176] For drafts towards the final text, see NLS Wod. Fo. 63, fols. 80–1; Johnston, *1639 Diary*,
pp. 70–1.

Charles asked how the interpretation of what was right in Scotland could be determined. Who would judge on the laws over which king and Covenanters had such disagreements? Rothes insisted that the written records were self-explanatory, but it was hardly as simple. Early on Charles directed the writing of a brief general statement by Loudoun, possibly dictating it, that the Scottish desires were 'only the enjoying of our religion and liberties according to the . . . laws'; as long as that was observed together with the offering of 'civil and temporal' obedience to the king, Charles would be satisfied.[177] With this the Covenanters were sent away to procure powers to conclude an interim agreement, and the king assured them that he would then commit himself in writing. At the next meeting he confirmed his approval of this general statement; on the issues at stake, he believed that it might adequately serve his purpose. For themselves, the Covenanters feared that matters could not be closed at that.

Reasons as requested for the lengthier main 'Desires' were drawn up by Argyll, Gibson of Durie, Sir Thomas Nicholson and Wariston. It was to be made clear that the total abolition of bishops in Scotland was required. With Wariston and Henderson joining the contingent who carried these back for the second session of talks, there was once more full debate on authority, in particular that of the king over the church in Scotland; Hamilton spoke in Charles's support. Charles was refusing to acknowledge the Glasgow Assembly Acts which were made against his wishes, standing still by the concessions he had offered at the time. The episcopal issue was naturally raised; Rothes, Loudoun and Henderson all spoke up, but the king would offer only the censure of individual offenders.

On the subject of the king's authority in general assemblies, Charles pressed for a full set of queries to be answered in writing. Verbal debate was allowing very little: it was on this day that Charles elicited the famous retort from Rothes that if he were king and committed David's fault, the kirk might excommunicate him. Heading Charles's list of queries were the king's powers of indiction and dissolution, and the negative voice question which Hamilton recently had opened up; also questioned was the status of the king's assessors and the qualifications of electors of assembly commissioners. Blunt argument also about the relative and independent force of acts of general assemblies as against those of parliaments prompted another royal request for a statement. The answers, presently spoken or as later written, were not complimentary to the king. Parliaments would by their ratification give civil force to general assembly legislation which otherwise might be enforced only by church censures, but the assembly's role in formulating the legislation was taken to be both primary and exclusive. The king had a right to indict assemblies

---

[177] *CSPD 1639*, 423/80.I.

above any other, it was conceded, but this could not absolutely hinder the kirk under necessity from convening assemblies under God's direct blessing. On the question of dissolving and the negative voice, Charles was plainly denied. The views blatantly contradicted those held by the king – but final resolutions on principles were reserved to the general assembly. As Charles delayed his answer to the main 'Desires', this pointed a possible way forward.[178]

The king probably received two noteworthy advice-papers, which have survived, at about this stage. The 'Remonstrance to his Majest anent the demands' began by suggesting that ratification of the Glasgow Assembly conclusions was inadvisable given that the members had proceeded against the king's will to make conclusions affecting the consciences and religion of his subjects. Far more preferable, for the king's honour, and to give satisfaction, was the calling of a new assembly. The author proceeded to discuss Charles's three main queries put to the Covenanters on 13 June. In so far as assemblies dealt with 'doctrine and manners' and the 'discussing appeals from presbyteries and synods', that is, regular and necessary business, the king should look to maintain his authority as God's lieutenant: the advice therefore was to have yearly assemblies, with the king designating time and place. The important point was to secure subjects on points presently touching their consciences and to provide a good assembly system for handling judicial matters. Things might be freer with regard to future making of canons and constitutions of kirk government; the author reckoned in that case that people would yield the king's sole right to indict, with some power for dissolving and a negative voice. The suggestion was that the king did not have to surrender authority felt proper to him.

The 'Remonstrance' was also accommodating on the matter in dispute of the force of acts of the general assembly before they were ratified in parliament. As far as this affected parliamentary statutes in force, the author trusted that the king making concessions for his subjects in matters of conscience presently controverted would remove tensions; in his opinion there was some existing 'contrary' parliamentary legislation – nothing was named but the references were obvious enough. For future acts, the author maintained optimistically that these would follow general assembly acts passed under the king's approval, so there would be no problem! As a concluding point, the author reflected that Charles might be satisfied on the Covenant question if one were to be subscribed that was approved by the king in a general assembly, for the 'purity' of God's truth but consonant with civil

---

[178] See BL Add. Ms. 38847, fols. 12v–13; GD 406/M1/56/2; NLS Wod. Fo. 66, fol. 63. Cf. Johnston, *1639 Diary*, pp. 80–2; *Reasons for a Generall Assemblie*, Aldis 931 (n.p., 1638).

obedience. The most probable author of this worthy effort of mediation was Sir Thomas Hope of Craighall.[179]

In the second advice-paper a line restricted on the other side of the argument justified both the indicting and dissolving of assemblies on the grounds that past practice reinforced declared royal prerogative: for a general assembly to be independent of the Crown was considered a dangerous assertion that, if nothing else, ran contrary to the supremacy legislation of 1606. Membership was discussed in terms that excluded the recent employment of ruling elders. The precedents used went far back and included the parliamentary statutes of 1597 and 1612 concerning the place of bishops. The conclusions of Glasgow had to be dismissed simply because they were declared null by the king. Not a very original piece for the king's cause, it would have little impressed the Covenanters.[180]

Charles found room to take on board the ways of compromise – typically, as ever, in a half-hearted fashion, and so yet again coming some way short of the moderate suggestions from the other side. He seemed now to attempt to procure a Pacification in earnest, having hitherto kept his alternative option of force well open. He presented terms in the form of a declaration, submitting them to his councillors, Scottish and English, on 14 June and then to the Covenanters at the third session of talks on the next day. Awareness of the serious financial burdens of his army could have played a part, as important if not more so was the king's apparent weakness within Scotland – although news was about to arrive of Montrose's discomfiture at Aberdeen.[181] For whatever reason, counsel for a peaceable accommodation – such as Sir Thomas Hope had offered – had won through to Charles, though no doubt with some modification of thought injected by its hearer.[182]

The statement made it unambiguous that Charles would not approve the conclusions of the Glasgow Assembly, following his various earlier proclamations on the subject and other 'weighty considerations'. In positive terms almost the same concessions as before were being offered, including the regular discipline of all persons 'of what quantities, titles or degrees soever', according to their faults, by both general assemblies and parliaments.[183] It

---

[179] GD 406/M1/45. The handwriting is that of Hope's secretary. For Hope's attendance on Charles, see GD 406/M1/90; *HMC Rutland*, vol. I, p. 514; Hope, *Diary*, p. 98.

[180] GD 406/M1/46; another copy in NLS Crawford Ms. 14/3/45. For similar arguments in 1638, see GD 406/1/676; NLS Wod. Fo. 66, fol. 75.

[181] BL Lansdowne Ms. 255, fol. 333; Berks. RO Trumbull Misc. LXI (Diary, 14 June); *CSPD 1639*, 423/119.

[182] I note that a heavily amended draft of the declaration survives in Hamilton's hand, dated 13 June – GD 406/M1/55; but cf. *HMC Rutland*, vol. I, p. 514.

[183] That Johnston's record referred specifically to the accountability of 'bishops' may be a distortion of chronology – Johnston, *1639 Diary*, p. 83; cf. PRO SP 16/424/13; GD 406/M1/55.

was not new either that assemblies were to be held 'so oft as the affairs of the kirk and kingdom shall require'; but in allowing the presently requested general desire for matters civil and ecclesiastical to be handled in their respective judicatories, the king indicated a shift. He announced his intention to attend personally not just a parliament but a new general assembly, to be held in Edinburgh.

Like the Covenanters, the king in his statement proceeded further to address the present state of action. Disbanding was to take place, but only in return for precise moves by the Covenanters, including the dissolving of 'pretended tables and conventicles'. They were expected to renounce all the means of their internal strength. Would or could the Covenanters trust so far? Moreover, their desire for punishment of traitors and incendiaries was countered by a promise for an Act of Pardon and Oblivion to be passed. Finally, the king's righteousness was upheld: it was written that calamities which might follow through disobedience would be occasioned only by those who followed such ways.[184] It was a thinly disguised threat; whether Charles could seriously support it was another matter.[185] The problem was that, as with the general assembly idea, much hope was placed on uncertain ground.

Archibald Johnston's record of the Scottish reaction to this statement focused objections mainly on what was basically a prelimitation on the future assembly and parliament with regard to bishops. That Charles adhered to specific proclamations, to any oath for ministers, and to mere mention of bishops after the December 1638 conclusions was taken to be offensive. The king, however, was assuming there could be a contest over this. He was insistent that his statement be read out in the Scottish camp, and sent someone to hear this happen; he sounded optimistic for settlement. Also, he had desired a public reading of his approval of the Loudoun paper and his own queries; perhaps he was still ignorant of what had happened before the talks began. The thought was that if those who talked with the king were amongst the most factious of the Covenanters, the rest might, when they heard of the king's generosity, and respecting his title and his army, cooperate to overrule them. Political manœuvring ran alongside conscience: 'if you keep my benignity from my people, you must expect to answer before God'.[186]

Charles would act the king, indeed by the conditions to be observed before he disarmed, the king in renewed strength amongst his Scottish subjects. A paper, scripted around this, dealt with what might follow the disbandment of the Covenanting forces – the restoration of royal castles and garrisons, the return of arms and loyal subjects' houses and losses, and the demolition of the

[184] *CSPD 1639*, 423/107.
[185] Cf. BL Add. Ms. 38847, fol. 15v; *State Papers . . . Clarendon*, vol. II, p. 53.
[186] BL Lansdowne Ms. 255, fol. 333.

Covenanters' fortifications. The first two of these were included within the king's ambitious statement of 15 June; the castles, for their practical worth and the matter of honour, were the most important.[187] Two other proposals never became public. It was thought to re-establish bishops and exiled ministers in their various churches, complete with payment of stipend dues. The theme was close to Charles's heart, yet far from realisable; the late inclusion of 'bishops' on the manuscript suggests a measure of hesitancy even in its writing. In the event, not even troubled ministers had much hope of resettlement.[188]

The second proposal – which has rings of Hamilton's influence – was that some of the 'most discreet' noble Covenanters and the 'most moderate ministers' might meet with some royal councillors, and bishops possibly, in order to confer and prepare matters for the new general assembly. As a whole, the counsel embraced the king's wishes, but it included a slight change of emphasis. Charles was advised to consider how far with honour he might condescend to the petitioners' desires, so that the burden of having matters concluded might be laid on his servants. The king might still direct, but perhaps preferably at a respectable distance.[189] Was the suggestion a tactical concession to some words from the Covenanters? Or an anticipation of what might happen at the assembly to the detriment of the king's honour? The negative voice question looked unpromising. With the form of the coming settlement remaining uncertain, Hamilton shared in the king's longing for peace but was careful to ponder cautiously the political options. He was over-heard to express hopes of the ministerial element in the new assembly as opposed to the elders; he seems to have believed that the opposition to the Five Articles and episcopacy had got far out of hand. This kind of talk under-pinned Charles's hopes – yet surely it was a slender basis for effecting a massive reversal.[190]

This last paper contained no ambiguity as to the standing of bishops. In verbal debate Charles was at first crisp and unyielding when he was asked for the abolition of episcopacy; but the issue was not left in black and white. Tactically he pressed for other matters to be discussed. When pushed, he conceded that a 'free assembly lawfully called' might theoretically re-enact the conclusions of Glasgow; we may be sure that he hoped it would not happen. 'Free' and 'lawfully' were important words. On 17 June, he almost played to

---

187 Hamilton was to recover the castles in person – *CSPD 1639*, 423/117; BL Add. Ms. 38847, fol. 16v.

188 Cf. Charles's interlineations on 'The several breaches of the Articles of Pacification' – Traqr. Mss. Bundle 27. For ministers, see also GD 406/M1/72/1–2; PRO E 351/1748; NLS Wod. Fo. 63, fols. 121–203.

189 GD 406/M1/81 (*c.* 15 June, perhaps earlier; as written out, it gave food for thought).

190 *CSPD 1639*, 423/117; Johnston, *1639 Diary*, pp. 87–8; Collins, *Letters*, vol. II, p. 603; BL Add. Ms. 38847, fol. 11. See also above, p. 150.

the Covenanters' complaints in avoiding any pronouncement on episcopacy, giving his reason as not wishing to prelimit his vote, and still suggesting that he would abide by the decision of a general assembly – 'agreeable to the laws of kirk and state', the crucial qualifying clause.[191]

If this has been drawn correctly, it suggests that Charles, like his Scots counsellors before him, was engaging with the task of breaking up peacefully the engendered unity of the Covenanters. However, his perspective remained narrow and domineering. He understood clearly enough how an opposing line of argument was upheld but, refusing to believe that it was either right or generally popular, sought to recover the initiative – through the craved for national assemblies. At root his views diverged far from those of his Scottish subjects – he continued to approve the service-book, which had started off the whole chain of events – so that, although owing to the resistance shown his immediate targets had been redefined, his negotiation, not surprisingly, was a tension-ridden process. However, the other side of the picture was the unattractiveness of a 'national war' option. As it stood, Charles had too little to hope from in Scotland; in England the poor cash flow was discouraging. The first orders for English disbandments preceded the signing of the Pacification documents. The king's choice was limited.[192]

Charles's declaration was closely debated. He made a few concessions of phrasing, without removing all ambiguities; but it was indicative of the rift that the Covenanters offered a whole alternative form. That they had an agenda apart from matters of the church was affirmed in their hope for parliaments triennially or as often as state affairs demanded.[193] Scottish frustration had gone far. Wariston stood out for his willingness to engage in quite sharp debate with the king, but Charles kept to his terms. He refused to give any firm promise of yearly assemblies, and the matter in the end was referred to the coming general assembly. On the other hand his offer of a pardon, which as all along implied that wrong had been done on the Covenanters' side alone, was omitted to leave simply a proposed Act of Oblivion. The final clause of the declaration, that made threats against future disobedience, was retained despite objections. Seven articles covered the details of disbandments and restoration of normality.[194]

The documents were signed on 18 June. The important questions were still open. Charles could hope that by his personal presence the forthcoming

[191] BL Add. Ms. 38847, fols. 15v–16; cf. Johnston, *1639 Diary*, pp. 87, 95.
[192] *State Papers . . . Clarendon*, vol. II, pp. 54–6; Bod. Clarendon Ms. 17, fol. 24; *HMC 3*, p. 40; GD 406/1/308, 1177; *HMC Rutland*, vol. I, p. 518; Bod. Firth Ms. c. 4, p. 360.
[193] Johnston, *1639 Diary*, pp. 84–7, 75; NLS Wod. Fo. 63, fol. 83. GD 406/M1/56/2 is Hamilton's copy of part of this.
[194] PRO SP 16/424/1 or SRO Hamilton Red Book ii, 147; Stevenson, *Scottish Revolution*, p. 155; Donald, 'The king and the Scottish troubles', p. 264.

Edinburgh Assembly would endorse his adopted line of moderate concessions, which he believed to be, unlike the demands made by the Covenanters, consonant with the laws of Scotland. The king did not doubt that the problem of suppressing what he saw as extreme demands still lay in the future. But he was hopeful in so far as he trusted in his own mission.[195] Symbolically he refused to visit the Covenanter army.[196] The Pacification of Berwick, as it became known, was to be far more than a truce.

The incomplete resolution of the troubles was manifest, however. Promptly issued, the Covenanters' 'Information against all mistaking of his Majesty's declaration' was a protestation that set the party line to affirm the validity of Glasgow.[197] After that came 'Some heads of his Majesty's treaty', which set out points alleged to have been agreed verbally with Charles. These points can be verified in the surviving accounts of the talks, except that the Covenanters made the royal concessions of phrasing sound as if they were the only possible logical course, and they omitted altogether the proviso so important to Charles, that proceedings on matters referred to the general assembly had to be faithful to the 'established laws and constitutions' as he read them.[198]

These latest pieces of Covenanter propaganda were mainly distributed in Scotland, where there seems to have been some popular pressure for their composition.[199] 'Some heads', however, was also sent to English lords as a 'modest information against mistaking', a gentle phrase which hid the depth of the rift now clearly visible between the Covenanters and the king. The cultivation of potential English sympathisers by Wariston and his colleagues took on ever greater significance. The noble figures amongst them had been independently briefed at the outset of the talks. Wariston privately considered the welfare of English 'favourers to Christ's cause'; another of his memoranda sought to clear errors of understanding about the Scottish Reformation, by showing it to have been *contradicente magistratu*. From that topical issue – and although it was always proudly Scottish, demanding the exclusion of English bishops and statesmen from handling affairs outside England – he proposed that English people should be allowed to enjoy conformity with the Scots in 'judgement or practice anent religion either in doctrine or discipline'.[200]

[195] HMC 5, p. 638; Knowler, *Strafforde Letters*, vol. II, p. 362.
[196] Johnston, *1639 Diary*, p. 92; CSPD *1639*, 424/26. Charles did, however, receive Argyll – GD 112/40/2/2/80.
[197] Johnston, *1639 Diary*, pp. 88–90, 92, 96.
[198] Johnston, *1639 Diary*, pp. 93–5. For another piece, the 'Army's declaration', see for example PRO SP 16/424/113.
[199] Johnston, *1639 Diary*, p. 95; Stevenson, *Scottish Revolution*, pp. 157–8.
[200] Johnston, *1639 Diary*, pp. 92–3, 63–5, 68, 73–4.

How far the contents of Wariston's memoranda were communicated remains unclear. Robert Baillie's sense was that English sympathisers did not show themselves readily enough – 'there was nought among them but a deep either sleep or silence'.[201] He was disappointed, but the circumstances did not favour such a showing. Whether or not his hopes had foundation, the general feeling in the English camp probably looked rather for peaceful settlement than a compounded rebellion.[202] How far this stretched to sympathy with the Scots can only be guessed at; at the same time the king was complimented for his moderate conduct during the treaty, and some writers, like Sir John Borough, were persuaded by Charles's arguments as opposed to those of the Covenanters, or else showed a predisposition against the Covenanters' insolence.[203]

However, conduct of the talks in the English camp and the exchange of visits, mainly in their aftermath, gave open opportunity for contact and so the possible growth of mutual understanding.[204] The Earl of Pembroke, Charles's Lord Chamberlain, attracted Scottish favour. He stood in for the Earl of Holland on at least one day in the treaty; these two were leading recipients of copies of 'Some heads'.[205] Later there was a correspondence made public between Rothes and Pembroke in which the former alleged that the Lord Chamberlain had been more friendly in June 1639 than he now appeared. Pembroke denied it, for Charles remained harsh towards any shows of contact with the Covenanters.[206] Before this, Pembroke with others had to answer before the English privy council for his copy of the Scottish paper, which was taken to be most offensive.[207]

Ideally the king wished to keep the arena of troubles well confined to Scotland, and persecution, with its limitations of method and effectiveness, could not fully secure this. That he had led an English army to the Scottish border was costly enough in terms of money and energy. That Charles then committed himself to representative assemblies to provide solutions to troubles would be noted by those who felt aggrieved at their lack in his other kingdoms. For the Scottish situation, Charles had little choice, unless, as Wentworth had suggested, he postponed a more aggressive campaign to another year. The king went through the other options first.

---

[201] Baillie, *Letters*, vol. I, p. 219.
[202] Cf. Donald, 'The king and the Scottish troubles', p. 267n.
[203] Verney, *Letters*, p. 252; *HMC Various*, vol. II, p. 254; PRO SP 16/423/104; *CSPD 1639*, 424/50, 425/46; Collins, *Letters*, vol. II, p. 604.
[204] *CSPD 1639*, 424/28; NLS Wod. 4to. 25, fol. 154; *HMC Rutland*, vol. I, p. 515.
[205] BL Add. Ms. 38847, fol. 15; *CSPD 1639*, 423/119; Berks. RO Trumbull Misc. LXI (Weckherlin's diary, 13 June); Johnston, *1639 Diary*, pp. 88, 92–3; BL Add. Ms. 35331, fols. 73v, 74; Add. Ms. 15392, fol. 193; *CSPV 1636–9*, p. 558.
[206] BL Add. Ms. 4106, fols. 187–9; GD 406/1/8351, 955; *CSPD 1639–40*, 447/52; NLS Crawford Ms. 14/7/23. Cf. *Information from the Estaits*, Aldis 967 (n.p., 1640), pp. 6–7.
[207] *CSPD 1639*, 425/86, 427/14.

The weakness of the king's government in Scotland had been freely exposed, but Charles hoped that this might once again come under control. The air of expectancy was short-lived. For a time there were noises that the Scottish general, Alexander Leslie, and his army might go off to the Palatinate.[208] On another pole of assumptions Bellièvre, the French ambassador, applied his best efforts to counter the likely ill effects for his country of an Anglo-Scottish alliance.[209] Charles's limited optimism, envisaging a situation to be healed by his own presence, was expressed to Wentworth in Ireland in three letters in the closing days of June; the Lord Deputy dutifully wrote replies which acknowledged that a lasting peace was the thing looked for. But a more guarded letter from Charles of 30 June prompted an answering warning that all three kingdoms needed to be secured – the suggestion being that, if necessary, force had to be used to procure obedience in Scotland.[210]

Charles perhaps did not need to be told, but his final decision to go not to Edinburgh but to London showed a realisation that his own presence at the assemblies would not achieve the desired end. Ominously, he wrote to Wentworth on 23 July to invite him to come over to England. His hope that Wentworth might be available for some time was explained by the comment, 'the Scots Covenant begins to spread too far'. It was probably a reference to the Scottish situation, though the king had his worries about sympathies elsewhere. In short, the Scottish interpretation of the Covenant was reckoned to be both prevalent and unacceptable; therefore Charles wilfully determined to attempt an external conquest by force. A few days later he emphasised to Wentworth that there was no hurry for his arrival; winter would be early enough.[211] A second campaign came to be on the horizon.

The stages towards this may be rehearsed. After the Pacification, Charles had been left by his nobles and troops as he waited to go to Edinburgh for the assemblies. The original intention to return south for a month before the general assembly on 6 August was the first casualty of the peacemaking plan. Hamilton had gone north, where he was permitted to retake Edinburgh Castle and to install Lord Ettrick as commander, but was reviled in the streets by a mob unhappy with the Pacification as it stood. They must have felt an element of anticlimax after a draining military effort; Hamilton's advice to Charles was not to leave the north in the present circumstances.[212] In reply

---

[208] PRO SP 81/47, fols. 130–1; Collins, *Letters*, vol. II, p. 602. Cf. *CSPD 1639*, 421/34.
[209] PRO 31/3/71, fols. 85, 95, 99, 105. The fear, since late May 1639, was of Charles aligning with Spain.
[210] WWM Str. P. LB 19, p. 68; LB 3, pp. 75–6, 80; Knowler, *Strafforde Letters*, vol. II, pp. 362, 372; *HMC 5*, p. 638.
[211] Knowler, *Strafforde Letters*, vol. II, pp. 372–3, 374.
[212] GD 406/1/1175 (23 June); *CSPD 1639*, 424/42, 77.

Charles left it open. English advice urged the king not to risk insult in going into Scotland, but he certainly contemplated going immediately; uncertainties multiplied as to his plans.[213]

Other royal castles were surrendered and most of the Covenanter army disbanded. Charles, disbanding his main army but maintaining the two border garrisons, allowed captured Scottish ships and goods to be returned; he even approved a limited warrant to allow 'conventicles' to be held for the purpose of settling in Scotland some internal relief of common burdens, which gave an excuse to the Covenanters to continue meeting together. Hostilities were to be stopped in the north-east.[214] However, since Charles had reserved some ships and the garrisons, the regiment of Colonel Monro remained undisbanded around Edinburgh and the Covenanters submitted a strong protest concerning Berwick and Carlisle. In the west of Scotland Argyll kept his doors figuratively locked by continuing the building of boats. There was no prompt release of detained loyalists. Huntly, who was freed, came to stay with the king at Berwick, but the Covenanters complained that 'broken men', supposedly under Gordon control, were ravaging the countryside. Steadily the bitter words increased in number, on both sides.[215] On 1 July, the Earl of Traquair read the summons for the general assembly: it included bishops, and there was a protestation. Traquair and others were assaulted by the crowds the next day.[216]

The protestation was a reminder that Charles's intention not to renounce episcopacy was running against well-organised, determined opponents. Nothing was done to establish who had been responsible for the riot, although the former provost of Edinburgh, Sir Alexander Clark, went to the king to excuse it as an uncontrolled action by women and boys – a familiarly ominous tale. Lord Loudoun also went to see Charles, most probably to explain the protestation. Traquair, warning of this, begged Hamilton to persuade the king not to commit himself one way or the other until he could come to give advice.[217]

How could the king attend a general assembly in these circumstances?

213 GD 406/1/1174; *State Papers . . . Clarendon*, vol. II, p. 57; BL Add. Ms. 15392, fols. 197, 205; *CSPD 1639*, 425/44; Bod. Clarendon Ms. 17, fol. 19; Berks. RO Trumbull Misc. LXI (Diary, 29 June).
214 WWM Str. P. LB 3, p. 80; *CSPD 1639*, 424/59; HMC *Cowper*, vol. II, pp. 237–9, 241–2; PCR, vol. VI, pp. 450, 453, vol. VII, pp. 529, 535; BL Add. Ms. 23112, fol. 110; Inveraray Castle, Argyll Mss., Bundle 11; GD 406/M1/57; NLS Wod. Fo. 64, fol. 2.
215 Gardiner, *Hamilton Papers*, p. 93; *CSPD 1639*, 424/59, 96; GD 112/40/2/2/92, 85, 78; GD 112/39/774; D. Stevenson, *Alasdair MacColla and the Highland Problem in the Seventeenth Century* (Edinburgh, 1980), pp. 69–70; GD 406/1/1165, 1164, 1098; Traqr. Ms. 4/116; BL Add. Ms. 23112, fol. 96.
216 *CSPD 1639*, 425/1, 22; GD 112/40/2/2/33; RPCS, 2nd Series, vol. VII, pp. 122–3. Cf. Johnston, *1639 Diary*, p. 88; Baillie, *Letters*, vol. I, p. 220.
217 GD 406/1/969; Hope, *Diary*, p. 100.

Hamilton had further disturbing words to offer on 5 July. It seemed that, if the assembly was held, episcopacy would be found to be abjured by the Covenant and contrary to the constitutions of the church of Scotland; and a parliament would ratify that, probably whether the king allowed it or not. Hamilton raised the possibility that the king's negative voice in the parliament might be put at risk. Should he therefore attend the assembly? The alternative of discharging the assembly altogether would be worse, for a meeting would take place anyway, with support of the generality of the kingdom, and so all civil authority would be lost. Then Charles would certainly have to consider anew 'the kingly way', in other words force, which introduced a need for money, and possibly an English parliament, with its outcome vulnerable to 'hazard and their discretions'; there were bleak prospects also in leaving the Covenanters untouched for another year. The weight of the advice therefore was for concession, by a veritable lessening of royal power in ecclesiastical affairs, but doing as much as possible to maintain civil authority. Hamilton turned his words to win the king.[218]

Another advice-paper, when it still looked as if the king would go north, came from the Bishop of Raphoe, who was in attendance. He spoke much in line with Wentworth's thoughts, although it is not clear that the Deputy had sent him. More directly than Hamilton he advised against the journey, arguing that compromise by a king in person was neither fitting nor safe, and concluding that Charles should wait for his opportunity to stand 'in full posture to give the dead stroke to rebellion'; in the meantime he might try to win some of the nobility by offering posts or money. There was a consciousness of the king's English worries; at this time action was in the offing concerning recipients of the Scottish propaganda, and the bishop dared to hope for better English loyalty when Scotland was well settled.[219]

On the same day as this, 8 July, Hamilton proposed reasons to excuse himself from acting as Commissioner for the forthcoming assemblies if the king did not go, which seems to cast important light on the turn of events. He apparently could assume that Charles had more or less decided not to go north in person; and moreover that a settlement more concessionary than before was to be offered in Scotland, namely the 'so odious' allowing of the abolition of episcopacy. Hamilton's argument was that it could only be detrimental for the present royal service if he served again the leading role within Scotland, and bad for himself. The settlement would be hated by all who loved the king, and not easily accepted at Hamilton's hands by those on the other side.[220]

---

[218] Burnet, *Memoires*, pp. 144–5 (GD 406/M1/60 – holograph).
[219] Traqr. Ms. 12/32. Cf. Knowler, *Strafforde Letters*, vol. II, p. 423.
[220] Burnet, *Memoires*, pp. 146–8.

What happened in these few days? In the earlier advice, Hamilton still apparently left room for a concessionary church settlement to be worked in Scotland; he hardly painted attractively the alternative of force, nor the one in which Charles himself went to Edinburgh. Charles then decided not to go – and to allow even the abolition of episcopacy in Scotland – but Hamilton's wish not to be employed was reflection that Charles was by no means sincerely giving ground. Charles did take on board the idea of not simply abandoning Scotland for the year, but whether Hamilton was pleased at this minimal concern seems doubtful. A Commissioner was needed: Hamilton had no chance of bowing out of affairs, but it was surely to his relief that Traquair was subsequently entrusted in his place – with a near-impossible brief.[221] Hamilton saved himself but at the cost of endorsing an awful turn of policy.

Again on this same day, through Lord Loudoun, who had newly come with Traquair from Scotland, the king summoned certain named Covenanters to Berwick 'for receiving our pleasure in some particulars which cannot be so well expressed in writing'.[222] One thing intended was to discuss the offensive propaganda paper 'Some heads'; more than that, Charles was seemingly wanting to clear his own mind about not going north. In Scotland, however, warnings were raised that he might detain those who went to him, and in the two sets of meetings which took place the attendance was correspondingly poor.[223] The contest of wills was clear to those who attended, as Charles complained at length of the alleged breaches of the Pacification, and the Covenanters raised their own grievances; they tried to give the king satisfaction on his.[224] The clash achieved very little, except that the king satisfied his questionings. He tried to establish what they intended to have in place of bishops and what would be the ecclesiastical power allowed to him; Hamilton was secretly instructed to use any means whatsoever to discover this.[225] Deception was the name of the new game; Charles believed that he was forced to it.

Hamilton was the most closely trusted counsellor in these moves by Charles. Traquair, who in Edinburgh had oversight of the Covenanter disbandment and the good manning of the royal castles, at first was as ignorant as any other of the king's decision to change plans.[226] While the Covenanters

---

221 For Traquair's position, cf. Traqr. Mss. Bundle 28[i] – words collected against the marquis.
222 *CSPD 1639*, 425/33; SRO RH 1/7/8.
223 GD 406/1/905; NLS Wod. Fo. 63, fol. 95; GD 112/402/2/2/69. The king was attended by Scottish and some English councillors – Berks. RO Trumbull Misc. LXI (Diary, 17, 18, 25 July); *CSPD 1639*, 426/21, 23; Stevenson, *Scottish Revolution*, pp. 158–60.
224 *CSPD 1639*, 426/21, 22, 50; NLS Wod. Fo. 54, fols. 315–19; Traqr. Mss. Bundle 27 – especially 'The several breaches of the Articles of Pacification'.
225 GD 406/1/809 (partially in Burnet, *Memoires*, p. 148). Hamilton had discussion with both Lindsay and Rothes – GD 406/1/8351; GD 112/40/2/2/69; HMC 6, p. 457.
226 Cf. Gardiner, *Hamilton Papers*, pp. 94–5.

were not very cooperative, either in handing over seized royal arms or in coming to see the king, he used energies in looking for chances to build support. Interestingly, he interpreted the long disputes that took place in Edinburgh over the king's summons of individuals to Berwick as signifying some division amongst the Covenanters. Leading in their hostility to Charles were Argyll and Balmerino; but it seems that the Earls of Montrose and Lothian were almost restrained from obeying the summons.[227] Traquair could not report that he had gained positive help from anyone, but his efforts were noted: a letter from Hamilton subsequently remarked that the king did not doubt of Montrose's carriage 'in all civil points'. It was only to be said that the earl would do well if he would come to understanding with the king on matters ecclesiastical.[228]

The church business was the primary sticking-point as far as Charles was concerned. The news that Charles would go south was made public after the second visit of the Covenanters; the letter to invite Wentworth over was already sent. Instructions for Traquair to serve as Commissioner were also drawn up in private around 27 July. They aimed to maximise support for Charles, as far as possible on his own terms. Episcopacy might be abolished if the assembly so decided; but it was emphasised repeatedly that this was not to be through any positive will of the king nor through any acknowledged arguments against it, only 'in satisfaction to the people, for settling the present disorders and such other reasons of state'. It might be abjured as contrary to the kirk's 'constitution' if this was the only way to avoid immediate trouble; but its abjuration as a point of popery or as contrary to the Word of God or the Protestant religion could not be countenanced, for this would necessarily have implications elsewhere. The hopes of some Covenanters, if not of others, in this direction had to be denied.[229]

The same idea of calculated concession informed much of the text. The next year's assembly was to be arranged, at Aberdeen or else Glasgow, in order to avoid the demand made for yearly assemblies. Permission was given to lay elders to be assembly commissioners, but not voters on 'fundamental points of religion' nor approved electors; grounds for declaring the assembly proceedings null in the future were to be left open.[230] Even so, on some points Charles would make no surrender. There was to be absolutely no debate con-

---

[227] Gardiner, *Hamilton Papers*, pp. 92–3, 94–5, 97–8; GD 406/1/1095; NLS Wod. Fo. 63, fols. 95–6.

[228] Traqr. Ms. 7/10a (partly in *HMC 9 (II)*, pp. 260–1, but wrongly attributed to Lennox; c. 6 August 1639).

[229] The original survives as two separate documents – GD 406/M1/75, M1/61 (Burnet, *Memoires*, pp. 149–51). For a working paper drawn up by Hamilton, and annotated by Charles, see GD 406/M9/88/4.

[230] Cf. *HMC 9 (II)*, p. 260.

cerning royal power in assemblies: if this threatened, prorogation was preferable. Charles knew well what he might expect, and commanded silence on the
matter. Other subjects here were unrealistic. The assembly was not to meddle
in civil matters without permission; all reference to the Glasgow Assembly
was likewise to be avoided; the Covenant was to be signed, but not including
the abjuration of episcopacy. There were unambiguous instructions that
ministers deposed unjustly by the Covenanters should be restored, and those
who had given cause for offence should be tried anew in this assembly by
committee; an additional instruction asked Traquair to get the sentence of
excommunication on bishops removed. The Instructions said nothing concerning the parliament, other than providing for the anticipated new conditions of electing Lords of the Articles. Purely civil business was not at this
stage Charles's concern.[231]

The king hoped that no burdens for the late war might be laid on non-
Covenanters. Letters were sent to loyalists, to confirm them in their obedience and cooperation; Traquair was given some unaddressed to carry with
him for others not certainly known.[232] The bishops were not to appear at the
assembly, not even to protest, with which they cooperated; but Charles had
Archbishop Spottiswood assured of future efforts on their behalf. A protestation was to be made, reserving the king's right to be heard for redress since
he was not to be personally present. Thus future action – royal intentions not
divulged – was left free.[233]

Hamilton's words in support of the two-edged plan rang somewhat
hollowly. His letter to Lord Lindsay, his brother-in-law, which he read to the
king, intimated that Traquair's instructions would satisfy, 'if you be not
devils'. Privately afterwards he expressed more agony that he was caught
between two stools.[234] Hamilton wished that the king might truly reign, but
the difficulty of the situation was telling.[235] Traquair had a brief that was
more unambiguously time-wasting than any to date. To the Bishop of Ross,
Hamilton claimed that his conscience was offended by what was happening
over episcopacy – but with what degree of sincerity we can only guess. Was
not his problem as much that Charles was leading not for a settlement as good
as could be managed, but for a second war?[236] Hamilton was in any event less
than happy.

[231] Burnet, *Memoires*, pp. 149–51; GD 406/1/1030.
[232] M. Napier (ed.), *Memorials of Montrose and his Times*, MC (2 vols., Edinburgh, 1848–51),
        vol. I, p. 250; Traqr. Ms. 12/34; GD 406/1/8329; Traqr. Mss. Bundle 28[iii].
[233] GD 406/1/1030 (Burnet, *Memoires*, pp. 153–4) – draft by Hamilton with amendments by
        Laud; another draft is PRO SP 16/427/23. For the bishops' response, see *HMC 9 (II)*,
        pp. 257, 254.
[234] GD 406/1/937, 928.
[235] See Traqr. Ms. 7/10a; GD 406/1/933 (16 August, answering GD 406/1/1119); GD
        406/1/870.
[236] GD 406/1/944.

Charles had led a large expedition to intimidate and if necessary crush the troublemakers of Scotland. The military effort was large, although not as large as ideally the king might have wanted; it had its difficulties, perhaps considerable ones, of supply and administration. Yet it marched north, flanked by a naval force on the east and preparations in Ireland, only to be sent home again without any final result for its labours. Although very few people knew it, Charles within a month of that interim conclusion had resolved to perform again with military forces. In 1639 the king had looked for a surrender, or at most a struggle of minor proportions. At extreme moments he had believed that the removal of a few factious individuals might solve much of the troubles; at his most openminded he had dared to place faith in representative assemblies – albeit ones to be attended and very carefully managed by himself.

Whether by a degree of fighting or by presiding at assemblies, Charles had every intention of dominating his people. However, the option of fighting was severely put in challenge first by the king's weakness in Scotland. Although his arming in the early stages threatened to succeed in frightening the people of Scotland into divisions, this did not happen. As he drew near to the Scottish border, the Covenanters themselves gathered an impressive defence force and indicated to him that they would receive him only without his armies. Charles originally was hoping to have gained mastery through the anticipated parliament, and spurned talks of any other kind, but interim talks were forced upon him by the impasse reached on the Scottish border. Then it seemed that a new general assembly might be the best way to proceed – though again on sharply curtailed lines. Willingness to negotiate only just showed its head: Charles showed an ability to share in the double-talk long since practised by his Scottish counsellors, but there was no real mistaking his intentions. In the end he would not accept the chance to go into Scotland because his own terms, episcopacy with royal honour, were not met.

The royal expectations were a fundamental weakness. Ought a king at the head of an army have been able to compel obedience? More was needed, but a belief in the royal mission, a hope for what ought to have happened, sustained Charles to some extent apart from consideration of reality. Reality, however, bore constantly in on him, whether in the form of the shortages of cash in England, the inadequacies of the Earl of Antrim, or the failures of his heterogeneous support in Scotland. His counsellors provided him with varying arguments. Charles did consult – and was not altogether blind to what was needed – but, arguably, he made things more difficult for himself as time passed by. The cost of settlement mounted.

Yet, on the other hand, the king had great interests at stake which are not to be denied. In the British context, politically and ecclesiastically, uniformity

of church government had been important for his father James; the Covenanters in their turn agreed utterly that it was desirable, even if cast differently. At a practical level it was a vital counter to troubles, however these
were construed; it was tied up with the unity of the church under Christ; but
almost as importantly it touched to a critical extent on concepts of
sovereignty. There was no question of Charles giving way lightly on such an
important issue, and his problem was that the Scottish party against his
purposes kept an equally determined front.

In Scotland church questions continued to be at the fore. The prospect of a
parliament there demanded from the leadership some careful thought on far-
reaching constitutional issues in the light both of the problems confirmed and
the progress made. The abolition of episcopacy had multiple ramifications.
As for more purely civil matters, opinion on the desirability of regular parliaments has already been mentioned; much more on government generally
would appear in due course, with reference to history both of the recent and
more distant past. The national interest had been defended against predomi-
nantly English armies, but leading was a very presbyterian vision – the idea
that church matters should be completely determined within the forum of the
general assembly in which the king was but a principal member with no
special sovereign rights.

All together, a stiff and demanding challenge for any king – so would more
careful listening to counsel have helped Charles? For the counsellors, to keep
royal favour and yet be realistic in counsel was a hazardous exercise.
Traquair and Roxburgh were vulnerable to attack despite their continuing
efforts to find a middle way. Hamilton, although undoubtedly angry over
Covenanter excesses, was chained probably as much by observed royal con-
straints; in his winding ways he seems only just to have kept above water. The
removal of episcopacy had to be expressed as a 'damnable' option. The
suggestion he moved towards on the eve of the Pacification – to think in terms
of a new general assembly – was to some extent a last-ditch hope. Success as
Charles wanted it was near-impossible, with the election system so soundly
overtaken by the Covenanters and with the king's lack of influence within any
assembly meeting. But what was to be done? Within Charles's narrow programme, there was little alternative but to hope – vainly? – for an effective,
external fighting force, such as Wentworth dreamed of and to which the king
came round. Genuine moderate compromise meanwhile – flawed in many
ways, given the polarities at hand – was never fully tried. Charles had fixed
limits. But he found himself obliged to forget them, to delay yet longer, to
wait for conquest; he thought it better than to bow to negotiation with people
he could only label as rebels.

The involvement of his other kingdoms brought the king help and problems together. Non-Scottish counsellors had mixed feelings about their rela-

tive exclusion from the primary decision-making. If their own major responsibility was elsewhere, a few like the Earl of Northumberland were unhappy that they were kept so much in the dark as to the king's intentions. There were hesitations over the king's strategies – and undoubtedly some feeling that Charles should have proceeded by more regular means, namely a parliament. People generally in the king's other kingdoms could not now fail to be aware of the Scottish troubles. Many of them bore some direct cost, and not always lightly or with good will. It seems likely that many of the problems in the second war effort of 1640 would be due simply to the burden being so soon repeated.

On the Scottish side, concern arising from the general problems of regnal union was naturally heightened by the circumstances of events. Though creative proposals took time to emerge formally, the military atmosphere of 1639 had compelled defensive moves, including appeals, written and verbal, to sympathisers in England and Ireland. Appeals abroad, in spite of all the suspicions entertained on the king's side, were rather more limited in nature. Arms and commanders certainly had been sought; but requests for direct encouragement were held back. Two letters were in fact prepared, one to the Estates of Holland and one, later notorious, to the King of France, but neither was sent. There was a fear of antagonising the more immediately important English support should the correspondence become known, with some hesitation also as to the advantages of an alliance.[237] It is commentary on what was still – just – a defensive movement in Scotland. For Charles, closure of all possible channels of support was attempted, but the cause of the Covenant had its outgoing effects. The Scots hoped for English sympathy, because Charles naturally derived his greatest aggressive strength there – and also because there were grounds to believe that sympathy could be forthcoming. And it is to the history of this British dimension that we should now turn.

---

[237] Stevenson, *Scottish Revolution*, pp. 137–8.

5

A British problem
July 1637–July 1639

A necessary assumption in Charles's mind when he resolved to venture a second military expedition against the Covenanters was that an efficient and effective fighting force could be raised from his other kingdoms. Administratively and financially this would prove to be a challenge too great to be met, but within that there were political troubles. The processes set in motion gave rise to major crises in both England and Ireland. The explanation of much that happened is to be sought where most commentaries have looked, namely in the relevant domestic arenas. What is attempted here is rather an examination of particular aspects of the background to the British dimensions of those troubled years.

The Scottish troubles developed out of problems involved in the rule by one king over three kingdoms. In particular they focused on ecclesiastical policy, but the resentment at allegedly anglicising corruptions could be shared by many who felt unhappy about Scotland's relations with England. The contrasts were often drawn in black and white; the Covenant cause was the patriotic one for Scots. At the same time, their feeling for the Reformed communion and their knowledge that there were some in England and Ireland of similar mind naturally brought Scots complainers to consider the extent to which their own plight was a common one, with a common enemy in popery. Finally, as the king threatened force of arms against what was reckoned to be a stance on truth, it became expedient as well as desirable to cultivate sympathies outside Scotland.

The king and his counsel were bound to oppose mutual contacts which involved Scots seen to be rebels; Charles's notion of bringing his kingdoms into closer conformity of church and government was strictly to be guided from above. His administration tried to crack down on informants and sympathisers. A presupposition shared to some extent was of an inherent subversive tendency among puritans. In many respects the discoveries of the administration, undoubtedly patchy, revealed that there was no serious concerted plot against the king's well-being; yet the fears of this intensified and, though much went unrevealed, not altogether without reason. Up to July

1639, Charles hoped to achieve a Scottish solution to the Scottish troubles, even with his joined forces in support; the problems, however, were not so easily confined.

On the one hand, as has been seen, the king could not successfully negotiate a means of accommodating the Scottish protest. His reluctant concessions and accompanying threats only stirred the Covenanters – as they became – to enter upon ever new heights of daring. By law they vigorously defended their position of the early months of protest; subsequently by arms they met the more aggressive threats of the king. They sent abroad for supplies and support. Charles tried to frustrate their chains of contact and encouragement at home and abroad, but without much success.

On the other hand, there were some – perhaps not very many, but significant enough figures – who themselves found encouragement from the course of the Scottish troubles. The Scots had dared to stand up to the king, and at a distance and with their cause and organisation had won considerable ground. Might not this bode well in turn for the settlement of troubles in England and even Ireland? None would have been able to predict how events would turn out – and next to nothing can be said here about many of the complex themes agitating centre and locality. What follows is not to argue a necessary shape for 1640 and beyond. It is, however, to sketch out the context for what in high political terms were mutual cross-border contacts of some importance. The Scottish affair showed Charles's absolutist rule to be vulnerable: it was part of the background to the various and many troubles of the new decade.

The riot in St Giles's Cathedral, Edinburgh, and its sequel was news sufficient to excite some early comment in England on the Scottish troubles, an interest which in the event was to become sustained. Lord Newburgh was writing at the end of August 1637 of the riot that had women throwing stools – 'most men stand at gaze to see how it will be prosecuted'.[1] George Garrard had the same story – and more – in October. In his second letter on the subject William Hawkins, correspondent with the Earl of Leicester, reported nobles leaving the church and people triumphing in supposedly a second refusal of the book offered to be read; rumour overtook the facts. All the writers assumed that what was involved was an attempt to impose the English Book of Common Prayer – 'the discipline of the Church of England', 'our English church service', 'our common prayer book'.[2] Given the principle of the king's church policy, they were not far wrong.

[1] *HMC* 4, p. 293.
[2] *HMC* 4, p. 293; W. Knowler (ed.), *The Earl of Strafforde's Letters and Dispatches* (2 vols., 1739), vol. II, p. 117; *HMC De L'Isle* (77), vol. VI, p. 127.

How the news came is unclear, but doubtless the Court was an important source. There were enough comings and goings by Scots to provide plenty of news, not to mention private letters. The time-lag involved in reporting varied; Hawkins's next report, of the October riot, was remarkably early.[3] One surviving example of a letter between two Scots was written by the Supplicant Earl of Lothian to his father, the courtier Earl of Ancrum. Lothian justified his own peaceful opposition to 'these things pressing on us . . . so much against forms and order and laws'.[4] Other correspondents with Lothian were the Earl of Bedford and his son Lord Russell, and Dr Isaac Dorislaus, an academic maintained by Lord Brooke, was active in this connection.[5] These names at least later would assume importance in the Anglo-Scottish connection. Clearly, direct news channels between Scots and English should not be ruled out. While the Supplicants were proud of their Scottish religious heritage, they were probably prepared from an early stage after July 1637 – and not only about the recent 'innovations' – to share their cause with the English 'godly'.

A distinctively Scottish church identity had been a cause for worry at the time of the Union. That hurdle passed, it was the seat of the monarchy being in England which continued the threat of change. Someone like Archbishop Spottiswood could argue that anglicising influence was not necessarily bad, but not all agreed, and especially after the latter years of James's reign.[6] Robert Baillie is a good example of one who in the 1630s kept close tabs on what he saw as disturbing theological trends south of the border.[7] Apart from noting publications, such people would perhaps have had friendly contacts, probably most often fellow Scots living in the south. In the post-Union years, the flow of Scots southwards was always greater than the complementary traffic, but there are noteworthy examples of the latter trend. Sir William Brereton on his journey in 1635 into Scotland noted many smouldering Scottish grievances over church matters.[8]

[3] *HMC De L'Isle*, vol. VI, p. 130. For general comment on the spreading of news, see R. Cust, 'News and politics in seventeenth-century England', *P and P*, 112 (1986), 60–90.

[4] D. Laing (ed.), *Correspondence of Sir Robert Kerr, First Earl of Ancrum, and his Son, William, Third Earl of Lothian* (2 vols., Edinburgh, 1875), vol. I, pp. 93–8.

[5] Laing, *Ancrum Correspondence*, vol. I, p. 93. For Dorislaus, see *DNB*; Warwicks. RO CR 1886/CUP4/21A. I am grateful to Dr Ann Hughes for the last reference.

[6] Above, chapter 1; D. Lyndesay, *A True Narration of . . . the Proceedings in the General Assembly of the Church of Scotland . . .*, STC 15657 (1621), pp. 21–46.

[7] R. Baillie, *The Letters and Journals*, ed. D. Laing, BC (3 vols., Edinburgh, 1841–2), vol. I, pp. 1–2, 28, 30, 113–14, 116–17; EUL New College Ms. X15b 3/1, vol. I, fols. 32–4 and vol. II, fols. 66–7. For those who disturbed Baillie, see N. R. N. Tyacke, *Anti-Calvinists* (Oxford, 1987).

[8] Sir W. Brereton, *Travels in Holland, the United Provinces, England, Scotland and Ireland M.DC.XXXIV–M.DC.XXXV*, Chetham Society (1844), pp. 99–121. Cf. C. Lowther, *Our Journall into Scotland, Anno Domini 1629 . . .* (Edinburgh, 1894); Bod. Rawlinson Ms. D49, fols. 1–6.

The more radical tradition in England and Scotland was an area of common ground. Pamphlet literature, much of it published in the Low Countries, kept alive a critique of the English prayer book and other church practices in which Scot and English could share. *The Trial of the English Liturgie*, first published in 1637, was reissued in 1638. It, like an attack on Archbishop Laud's speech against the notorious English nonconformists, William Prynne, John Bastwick and Henry Burton, published in 1638, showed a remarkable facility in linking together Scottish and English political and ecclesiastical themes. Laud was readily singled out in this context.[9] The famous *Dispute against the English-Popish Ceremonies* by George Gillespie, published in 1637, was addressed to everyone in the Reformed churches of Scotland, England and Ireland.[10] The fractious reaction in Scotland to the new liturgy no doubt lay in the background to pamphlets like these, but this was not explicitly the subject addressed. The tradition went back to David Calderwood, who in his writings around the Perth Articles controversy had often attacked English practices; some of his works indeed were reissued in the mid-1630s, when he was still active.[11] In 1628, Peter Smart, the ousted prebendary of Durham, had used the press in Edinburgh as well as in London to publicise his grievances against ceremonies.[12] Further back, the sense that the English Reformation was neither as full nor as perfect as that of Scotland had got ingrained in this strand of what might be called puritan thinking. Probably the English could not so well identify with this, but the argument that their church had not sufficiently separated itself from Rome and so-called popery was both powerful and emotive. Apocalyptic thought linked Rome with the antichrist. Even where the papacy exercised no positive influence, the cry of popery was an immediate means of branding the enemy.[13]

The printed output from the Low Countries attracted critical attention, but, as has been suggested in earlier chapters, the existence of nonconformist dissent did not necessarily pose a major problem for a royal government. It made difficulties, but the eruption of a major crisis required a concatenation of circumstances. In this respect Charles's English government in 1637 had

---

[9] *The Trial of the English Liturgie*, STC 16452 (n.p., 1637, reprinted 1638); *Divine and Politike Observations* . . . , STC 15309 (n.p., 1638).
[10] [G. Gillespie], *A Dispute against the English-Popish Ceremonies* . . . , Aldis 885.5 (n.p., 1637); Baillie, *Letters*, vol. I, p. 90.
[11] [D. Calderwood], *The Altar of Damascus* . . . , STC 4352 (n.p., 1621); *A Re-examination of the Five Articles* . . . , STC 4363.5 (n.p., 1636); *Quaeres Concerning the State of the Church of Scotland*, STC 4362 (n.p., 1638).
[12] J. G. Hoffman, 'The Arminian and the iconoclast: the dispute between John Cosin and Peter Smart', *Historical Magazine of the Protestant Episcopal Church*, 48 (1979), 279–301.
[13] See A. H. Williamson, *Scottish National Consciousness in the Age of James VI* (Edinburgh, 1979), esp. pp. 143–5; P. Collinson, *The Birthpangs of Protestant England* (1988), esp. pp. 8–27; P. Lake, 'Anti-popery: the structure of a prejudice', in R. Cust and A. Hughes (eds.), *Conflict in Early Stuart England* (1989), pp. 72–106.

difficulties rather than crisis. For the most part, folk in England cared little for
the Scots – and perhaps knew even less about them. That Charles should have
extended the use of the prayer book, albeit in a locally modified form, to Scotland, might generally have commanded approval from those who happened
to hear of it. It was not necessarily an issue for the English.[14]

At the same time the survival in English archives of some copies of papers
composed by the Supplicants is noteworthy. 'Reasons why the service-book
cannot be received' is commonly found, as a separate item or together with
the privy council letter to the king of 25 August 1637, an important tract in
the Scottish organisation of the movement, although, as it was printed in
1638, some of the manuscript copies may have been made then.[15] The dispersion does not always tell us about sympathies. Viscount Conway was
interested to get a copy, having heard of one in the Earl of Ancrum's hands.[16]
Information could be channelled from Court consciously or otherwise.

Newsletter accounts of day-to-day happenings circulated from the very
beginning, within an operation crowned in 1637 by the Earl of Rothes's full
'Relation' of events from 23 July to 21 December, may have found their way
south also. Some of these were written primarily to provide information for
encouragement and coordination within Scotland; their wider circulation
was not, it would seem, centrally organised. However, Rothes's work, which
was carefully vetted by other prominent figures, was written specifically for
Court. The Earl of Traquair was supposed to take it when he went in January
1638; as a compromise, given his delicate mission, it was carried by the
accompanying Justice-clerk, Sir John Hamilton of Orbiston. At that time the
Scottish troubles raised passions, but did not seem insurmountable: the con-
sistency of the king's hard line was yet to appear. The intention of sending to
Court was to clear the Supplicants from hostile reports.[17]

At the English end, amongst the most interesting survivals are the copies
known of the petition of 18 October 1637. Sometimes an example could be

---

[14] PRO SP 16/387/79; *RPCS*, 2nd Series, vol. VI, pp. 536–7; E. Cope, *Politics without
Parliaments, 1629–1640* (1987), pp. 44–93; E. Hyde, *The History of the Rebellion and Civil
War in England Begun in the Year 1641*, ed. W. D. Macray (6 vols., Oxford, 1888), vol. I,
pp. 145–6. For attachment to the prayer book, see J. S. Morrill (ed.), *Reactions to the English
Civil War 1642–1649* (1982), pp. 89–114.

[15] *Reasons . . . Service-Booke . . . Ought to Bee Refused*, Aldis 932 (n.p., 1638). Manuscript
copies have various titles – for some examples see CUL Ms. Mm. 4.24; GD 124/10/373; NLS
Dep. 175 Box 81/1; Beds. RO J. 1409; BL Add. Ms. 28011, fol. 39; BL Loan 29/172, fols.
157–8.

[16] Knowler, *Strafforde Letters*, vol. II, p. 129.

[17] For examples, see BL Sloane Ms. 650, fols. 25–32, 33–7; Sloane Ms. 1467, fols. 41–4;
GD 406/M1/38; NLS Wod. Fo. 29, fols. 23–5; Baillie, *Letters*, vol. I, pp. 25–7; John Leslie,
Earl of Rothes, *A Relation of Proceedings Concerning the Affairs of the Kirk of Scotland*, ed.
D. Laing, BC (Edinburgh, 1830), esp. pp. 45, 52, 53; *Diary of Sir Archibald Johnston of
Wariston, 1632–1639*, ed. G. M. Paul, SHS (Edinburgh, 1911), pp. 288, 295–7, 304.

included within a narrative text, such as one which, after quoting the petition, expounded the differences between the Scottish and English episcopates, demonstrating how the former had usurped their function as laid out in the 1600s.[18] However, Walter Yonge, in Colyton in Devon, transcribing the petition into his diary probably in November, and Sir Roland St John made copies with identical distortions of the original. The petition was thus addressed to the privy council of England; where bishops were blamed, they were described as bishops who had been entrusted with the government and affairs of the English church – in other words, they who had innovated with the 'seeds of superstition, idolatry and false doctrine'. Then, at the end of both the copies, was written a note that it had been presented to the king on 26 October and had been answered almost immediately, to the effect that the Scots gained a reprieve from being obliged to accept the controversial liturgy for three years. This final gloss was not at all accurate, but it suggested that the Scottish troubles would be quieted in consequence of the strong opposition among the people. Yet the arguments within the petition would not have emphasised so much any Scottish point that English bishops had interfered in affairs, for in the original the intention was to attack the *Scottish* bishops; rather, altered as it was, it served as an unmitigated indictment of English bishops. The English reader would be led to reflect on the bad church leadership of England as much as to sympathise with those troubled in Scotland.[19]

In confirmation that this copying was more or less contemporary was the mention of the service-book being suspended from being pressed for three years. This was repeated, after a fashion, in various letters out of London in November and December 1637; foreign correspondents too took on board the false rumour, a sign of how interest was being stirred.[20] Yonge and St John continued to collect Scottish papers as best they could, and Yonge in his diary made cross-reference in the margin to his later-obtained copy of the 'Reasons why the service-book . . . '. Nothing is known of the source of the copies, other than that Yonge made his from one in Sir John Pole's hands; Pole in time also provided a copy of the December petition that he had received from Mr How the minister.[21]

---

[18] BL Sloane Ms. 650, fol. 10v.
[19] BL Add. Ms. 35331, fols. 67–8; Beds. RO J. 1347. For the uncorrupted version (above, p. 52), see D. H. Fleming, *Scotland's Supplication and Complaint . . . 18th October 1637* (Edinburgh, 1927).
[20] Knowler, *Strafforde Letters*, vol. II, p. 129; CSPV 1636–9, p. 350; BL Add. Ms. 27962H, fol. 78. Cf. F. J. Levy, 'How information spread among the gentry, 1550–1640', *JBS*, 21 (1982), 26–7, 33.
[21] BL Add. Ms. 35331, fols. 68, 69v. Pole's son later sat alongside Yonge in the Long Parliament – M. F. Keeler, *The Long Parliament* (Philadelphia, 1954), 'William Pole'. For St John, see Beds. RO J. 1347, 1355, 1409, for example.

Walter Yonge, a zealous puritan, would also note in his diaries the aspects that he disliked in English church policy under Laud.[22] His interest in Scotland was not exactly new, for in 1633 he commented on the tax legislation alongside articles propounded for the church in Scotland; that the latter included an act giving the king 'power to alter, add or make and ordain any ceremonies' points to an obvious hostility somewhere along the line, interpreting the significance of the legislation. Again with the radical strain in 1637, Yonge noted that liturgy, ceremonies, episcopal government 'after the English manner' caused Scottish opposition.[23]

It cannot be supposed that Yonge was an isolated example of one who reflected on these things, though the survival of such a revealing source is not common.[24] His receptiveness and interest were not dulled in 1638. A letter of 20 July told him of what Hamilton had offered in Scotland against what the Covenanters had further demanded. The latter was supposed to include 'the perpetual abrogation of the authority and names of bishops'; Hamilton's correspondence of this period did not dwell so much on fears for the institution of episcopacy, but there was open preaching on the subject.[25] In England as well as in Scotland there would be an audience for the propaganda put forward by the Covenanters. They set out that their liturgy was little short of being a Missal. Popery was a common enemy.[26]

Here, in written controversy as opposed to straightforward information, the prominent Scots might claim the support of those – the 'best and ablest' – they alleged were restless under the English Book of Common Prayer; here they might voice hopes that there could be a common drive for purity of religion, perhaps even by extending the Covenant, with its Negative Confession at the heart.[27] When the appeal first came to be made more widely, there was less emphasis on the incompleteness of the English Reformation and more on the possibility that the Scottish liturgy was devised within a scheme to bring all three kingdoms nearer to Rome.[28] National prejudice and fears remained despite, indeed partly because of the incompleteness of, the

[22] 'Religion laboured to be suppressed' – BL Add. Ms. 35331, fol. 53.
[23] BL Add. Ms. 35331, fols. 52v, 67v. Cf. above, p. 30; PRO C 115/M.31/8155, 8156, 8158 – I owe these references to Ms Sabrina Alcorn.
[24] For English presbyterianism, cf. P. Lake, 'Anti-popery: the structure of a prejudice', in R. Cust and A. Hughes (eds.); *Conflict in Early Stuart England* (1989), pp. 95, 97.
[25] BL Add. Ms. 35331, fol. 71r; GD 406/1/556; Baillie, *Letters*, vol. I, p. 86.
[26] Cf. also J. Fielding, 'Opposition to the Personal Rule of Charles I: the diary of Robert Woodford, 1637–1641', *HJ*, 31 (1988), 769–88.
[27] EUL Laing Ms. I, 293; *Reasons . . . Service-Booke . . . Ought to Bee Refused*; EUL New College Ms. X15b 3/1, vol. II, fols. 44–66, 67–93; NLS Wod. 4to. 26, fols. 7–20, 22–9, 30–43; Baillie, *Letters*, vol. I, pp. 53, 69, 90; Rothes, *Relation*, pp. 10, 40, 78, 122, 144.
[28] *A Short Relation of the State of the Kirk of Scotland . . .*, Aldis 934.5 (n.p., 1638), sig. C3. Cf. Johnston, *Diary*, pp. 310–11; Baillie, *Letters*, vol. I, p. 90. For the wider English picture, see P. Lake, 'Calvinism and the English church, 1570–1635', *P and P*, 114 (1987), 32–76.

union of the kingdoms under one crown. In time of danger, the Covenanters hoped for support as wide as possible; while there was no fudging of their Reformed stance, there was an understandable wish not to offend their English neighbours.

In England Charles trusted principally to loyalty to the Crown, but cross-kingdom tensions were potentially to his advantage when the troubles came near war; the Protestant cause in its widest application was something that cut against him from the Covenanters' side. It seems significant that in the first stirrings of Covenanter panic about war, in summer 1638, that a rumour circulated that the Scots would send and pay for a massive army to help the Palatinate cause. It was, apparently, an offer conditional on the settling of the Scottish troubles. There is no certain evidence that such an offer was genuinely made, but it was timely, building in both England and Scotland on consciences wishing to combat Catholic forces in Europe.[29] Charles, not least in his preoccupation with the Scottish troubles, was not offering action. The rumour would have emphasised the relative undesirability of an Anglo-Scottish war. Some of the king's leading servants, the Earls of Northumberland and Essex among them, chafed at the European inaction. In the aftermath of the Pacification of Berwick, the Scots made (or repeated) the same offer.[30]

The foreign correspondents in London entertained few doubts that there were direct links across the border; they rarely cited details, however. As in the radical tradition, they singled out Archbishop Laud from the beginning as the central figure of policy. Most of them were Catholics, and seeing Laud generally more hostile to 'puritans' than Catholics, they made assumptions before they had proof that English and Scottish puritans would encourage each other. That assumption could mix dangerously with fact should not be forgotten when using these reports: the Venetian ambassador was obsessed with the threat of Spain, and from the first maintained mistakenly that the Spaniards had a hand in the Scottish troubles; the Supplicants would hardly have welcomed that.[31]

George Con, the Papal nuncio, was by far the most prominent of the 'foreign' Catholics, since he shared the regular confidence of the king. Well placed to hear the news from Scotland, he at first thought it not worth reporting, and so reflected the general sense in government that the trouble was regrettable but not serious. News brought with Lennox in September 1637

---

[29] BL Add. Ms. 35331, fol. 71r; PRO C 115/N.8/8821.
[30] C. Hibbard, *Charles I and the Popish Plot* (Chapel Hill, NC, 1983), pp. 72–89; *CSPD 1639–40*, 448/42 (20 March 1639); PRO SP 81/45, fol. 265; SP 81/46, fol. 49; SP 81/47, fols. 130–1.
[31] BL Add. Ms. 27962H, fols. 66v, 75–6; *CSPV 1636–9*, pp. 259–60, 273, 316; *CSPD 1637*, 369/41; BL Add. Ms. 15391, fol. 74r.

evidently changed this general attitude, and soon thereafter Con was com-
menting that the puritans in England celebrated the valour of the Scots which
was superior to their own. It seems likely that there was some basis of fact for
this, but how far it was a significant phenomenon even in London is not
known.[32]

Scots had a tradition of hearing from informers in England, but traffic the
other way, news and other material from Scotland for English audiences, was
probably for most people a new experience – and its circulation, especially
among potential sympathisers, was discouraged. Positive interest in the
Covenanter cause was bound to be concealed as far as possible; to some
extent, unless minds were open, knowledge of what was happening would
spread only gradually.

In mid-December 1637, Laud took note of the case of John Bartlett, a
stationer, who confessed to having sold schismatical books, Bastwick's
Litany, Burton's *Appeal*, and more. He had also received the 'Scottish news'
and caused several copies to be made. His material included letters to the
Scottish privy council – 'tending to sedition and disparagement of His
Majesty's service and government'. He revealed only that it was a Scotsman
who had brought the news, of which the original copy was in a Scottish hand;
the same hand had copied out some of the English material. Bartlett was committed to the Fleet until he revealed more information: one Secretary for each
of the kingdoms, Sir Francis Windebank and the Earl of Stirling, were to
examine him. Thus a case first brought by Sir John Lambe for the court of
high commission was heard instead before the privy council with the king
present. Stirling, who did not sign the warrant for the committal to the Fleet,
was obviously specially brought in by Charles. Laud interpreted the case as
signifying the link between Scots and English that he had feared.[33]

Con believed that these fears inspired a heightened drive by Laud against
Catholics at the end of 1637. While Laud was indeed writing of feeling persecuted by puritans and Catholics – 'very like corn between two millstones',
Con read that the archbishop was keener than ever to clear his name, and his
church policy, from aspersions that it was popish.[34] On 3 November, he
wrote of Laud being frightened of the ever-worsening Scottish troubles and of
a pasquinade that had him in correspondence with Con himself. The latter
was the theme which the apostate priest Thomas Abernethie would take up

---

[32] BL Add. Ms. 15390, fols. 400v, 436r, 457; G. Albion, *Charles I and the Court of Rome*
(1935), pp. 222–6. There was rumour in April 1638 of action by the apprentices in London
– Baillie, *Letters*, vol. I, p. 65.
[33] *The Works of the Most Reverend Father in God, William Laud, D.D.*, eds. W. Scott and
J. Bliss (7 vols., Oxford, 1847–60), vol. VII, p. 402; *CSPD 1637–8*, 374/13; *PCR*, vol. II,
p. 463; BL Add. Ms. 15391, fol. 181.
[34] Laud, *Works*, vol. VII, p. 380.

with a vengeance in 1638, but it was quite untrue.[35] Laud went to the king for help, and in this counselled Charles to introduce stricter measures against Catholics, as being the only way to quieten the tumults of Scotland. The king was sympathetic to Laud but not unfriendly to Con either, who in his letters to Rome suggested that Charles would have liked to quieten the puritans of Scotland without prejudice to the Catholics. Nevertheless, a proclamation against Catholics was eventually issued on 20 December. Only after the privy council had passed a secret order for the issuing of this did Con hear of it and attempt – not wholly without success – to moderate the terms. Charles's justification to Con was that he had the advice of the whole council – that he had to maintain good government over his kingdoms. Con's response that it was not even 'half-good' to quieten puritans by issuing edicts against Catholics was rejected.[36]

Laud and Charles had more than one kingdom in mind at this time, but Con's account made some distortion. Laud was hardly alone a schemer against Catholics, and it was unfair to portray him as such. He had the king's support, particularly in opposing proselytising, which Con was actively encouraging in the Court. In generalisation Laud and Wentworth would liken the Covenanters and the Catholics in respect of their civil disobedience.[37] If Con would have denied that aspersion, he nevertheless kept links with foreign powers which were not beyond reproach. In September 1637, Richelieu's almoner, one Thomas Chambers or Chalmers, came to London to represent the cardinal's interest in the Scots – that is, first in recruiting Scottish mercenaries for French service, a tradition of many years' standing, and secondly to build up Scottish support for the French Crown in its troubles. Richelieu's idea here was to provide an enormous gift to build up and maintain a strong Catholic clergy in Scotland.[38] Con was very uneasy about putting to Charles even the request for Scottish regiments; although England and France were in treaty for an alliance, relations were cool between the two kingdoms as France delayed to join in full commitment. And there was no question of Con telling Charles of this real 'popish plot' for blatant Catholic mission.[39]

Con's report of harsh measures against Catholics in England because of the

---

[35] BL Add. Ms. 15390, fols. 469–70; T. Abernethie, *Abjuration of Poperie*, Aldis 897 (n.p., 1638); Hibbard, *Charles I and the Popish Plot*, pp. 113–14.

[36] BL Add. Ms. 15390, fols. 470–1, 481, 498–501; PRO 31/9/124, fols. 215–16; PRO 31/3/70, fol. 65; Bod. Clarendon Ms. 5, fol. 155; Albion, *Charles I and the Court of Rome*, p. 465; Hibbard, *Charles I and the Popish Plot*, pp. 61–2.

[37] Albion, *Charles I and the Court of Rome*, pp. 212–13; Hibbard, *Charles I and the Popish Plot*, pp. 51–6; Laud, *Works*, vol. VII, pp. 390, 454; WWM Str. P. LB 7, fol. 106v. See, likewise, [J. Corbet], *The Epistle Congratulatorie of Lysimachus Nicanor*, STC 5751 (n.p., 1640).

[38] BL Add Ms. 15390, fols. 415–16.

[39] BL Add. Ms. 15390, fols. 417, 434–5; Hibbard, *Charles I and the Popish Plot*, pp. 74–6.

Scottish crisis in fact had only a tinge of truth. The English proclamation was not in itself meant to appease the puritans of Scotland, rather it was directed to the recent spate of Court conversions; English fears of Catholicism gave reasons in plenty for it, and the English council which backed it had no formal responsibility in Scottish affairs. Con meanwhile missed news of the contemporary proclamation for Scotland. Laud for himself had still fairly specific reflections on the ills of the Scottish situation to offer to the king; fears of major conspiracies, however, would grow in time.[40]

Thomas Chambers was a Scots Jesuit who certainly visited Con again in March 1639 and also Scotland, on account of which there arose suspicions that he brought French encouragement for the troubles.[41] The deterioration of Charles's relations with France from the spring of 1638 started off multiple speculation that the French might try to exploit the Scottish situation. It had actually been discussed in the highest French circles from the early date of November 1637; probably the contribution of Chambers's own mission in bringing the matter to attention should not be discounted. In the summer of 1638 the Earl of Leicester in Paris was quick to fasten suspicion on Chambers, and not without reason. The French were bound to be interested in the course of Charles's domestic troubles; it is incidentally at least suspicious that the transcripts of Bellièvre's dispatches contain no references to Scotland before December 1638.[42] Rumours widened that the Spanish too were ready to exploit Charles's weakness.[43] How far anything went though was a perplexing question for Charles and his support; given the very high Catholic profile of Chambers's work in particular, it seems hard to believe that much significantly worked against the king. Although the questions and suspicions multiplied in 1639, the French threat remained potential rather than actual.

What arose out of the history of Franco-Scottish relations was only one aspect of the European dimensions of the king's troubles. Leicester's suspicion that French ships might operate to supply arms to the Scots out of the Low Countries brings us to another.[44] As has been suggested in the previous chapter, until the latter part of 1639 the Covenanters were probably innocent of charges of calling in foreign powers; but they did seek arms and

---

[40] Albion, *Charles I and the Court of Rome*, pp. 221–9, 415–16; Laud, *Works*, vol. VII, p. 402.
[41] BL Add. Ms. 11044, fol. 85v; PRO 31/3/71, fol. 36; PRO SP 16/439/66; *Mémoires de Richelieu*, vol. X (Paris, 1823), pp. 463–4; D. Stevenson, *The Scottish Revolution 1637–1644* (Newton Abbot, 1974), pp. 184, 187.
[42] BL Add. Ms. 15391, fol. 181; Add. Ms. 26962H, fols. 130, 108; Add. Ms. 11044, fol. 95; M. V. Hay, *The Blairs Papers, 1603–1660* (1929), pp. 126–8, 250–3; PRO SP 78/106, fols. 11–13, 34, 74–5, 166.
[43] Bod. Clarendon Ms. 14, fols. 142, 90; PRO SP 77/28, fol. 361; SP 94/40, fols. 189–90; SP 81/45, fol. 198.
[44] PRO SP 78/106, fol. 166; A. Collins (ed.), *Letters and Memorials of State* (2 vols., 1746), vol. II, p. 572.

men abroad. To counter this, Charles used both his English and Scottish agents abroad. In the Low Countries Sir William Boswell was chiefly employed, with local government cooperation. While shipping was obliged to go unauthorised, no blockade on the Maas could be agreed upon; and the Covenanters could draw on good local support, although a proposal for the Covenant to be taken in Campvere, the Scottish staple, failed. They complained at any stoppage.[45] In Sweden, Sir Thomas Roe at the end of July 1638 was told to investigate supplies of arms and money being given after Field-Marshal Alexander Leslie returned there. Roe duly reported that Leslie departed for Scotland on 22 August 1638, having taken his discharge from Swedish service. A few months later, further military supplies bought in Sweden came under investigation. Charles was not without support: the King of Denmark agreed to have them landed.[46]

Propaganda would be the other matter with international consequences, but, before that, mere information with a Scottish perspective was suspect, as Bartlett's case showed. The alternative, of information given so to speak officially from the king, was remarkably sparse before the serious military efforts of 1639 – and was rare enough during these! Court-linked interest in the troubles was not surprising. Besides the sizeable Scots contingent that was resident, the Marquis of Hamilton's mission in 1638 was closely followed by his enemies as well as his friends.[47] The commentary of the time increasingly remarked on the widespread discussion of the situation in Scotland.[48] However, George Con, for all his frequent conversations with the king, was remarkably vague on the details of what was going on. He heard of the 4 July proclamation after the event, and early in October admitted his own ignorance of exact details. The reports of the Venetians, Zonca and Giustinian, could be even more speculative, although they made great efforts to keep well-informed, both keen to reflect on the seriousness of trouble for the king in all three of his kingdoms.[49] Charles and Laud did not reveal publicly what

[45] Berks. RO Trumbull Misc. LXI (Diary, 10 August 1638); *CSPD 1637–8*, 397/44; *HMC Cowper* (23), vol. II, p. 191; PRO SP 84/154, fol. 129; NLS Wod. Fo. 66, fol. 113; Rothes, *Relation*, pp. 155–6.
[46] Bod. Clarendon Ms. 14, fol. 116; PRO SP 81/44, fols. 224, 262v; SP 81/45, fols. 8, 83v, 101v, 290; SP 81/46, fols. 93, 121, 130; Baillie, *Letters*, vol. I, p. 110; Sir W. Fraser, *The Melvilles Earls of Melville and the Leslies Earls of Leven* (3 vols., Edinburgh, 1890), vol. I, pp. 391–2; S. R. Gardiner (ed.), *The Hamilton Papers*, Camden Society (1880), p. 17; Stevenson, *Scottish Revolution*, p. 130.
[47] GD 406/1/1156; BL Add. Ms. 27692H, fols. 141–2, 226; *CSPD 1637–8*, 393/71; Collins, *Letters*, vol. II, p. 579; *HMC Egmont* (63), vol. I, p. 108; *HMC De L'Isle*, vol. VI, p. 159.
[48] Cf. WWM Str. P. LB 18, p. 57; PRO C 115/N.8/8817.
[49] BL Add. Ms. 15391, fols. 202–3, 288; *CSPV 1636–9*, pp. 418, 423, 427, 436, 439, 442, 479. Cf. BL Add. Ms. 27962H, fols. 152, 158, 162; *CSPD 1637–8*, 393/71; PRO 31/3/70, fols. 110, 116. Hibbard, *Charles I and the Popish Plot*, pp. 93–101 gives a slightly one-sided account of Con.

was sent to them from Scotland. At the time of the debates at Court in September 1638, it was reported that the king tried to hide the news of the Scottish obstinacy in England by spreading false news; Wentworth was advising Laud at the same time to do just that – 'Paint not that lion full as fierce as he is.'[50]

It was not therefore straightforward to procure information on the troubles as long as Hamilton served his personal mission. The Earl of Arundel was sent for in mid-November 1638 at first only to be told by the king that matters were getting worse, nothing more; the decision that he should command the king's army came subsequently. This was the dimension of secrecy that so frustrated Northumberland in 1639.[51] Sir James Douglas in Berwick assumed, or perhaps was given, the post of informer to Secretary Windebank of what was happening in Scotland. He sent on papers to show what the Covenanters were doing, and served as a rare independent source of Scottish news. Roger Widdrington, the postmaster, also sent occasional reports and by 1639 was thought suitable to organise a spy network to operate inside Scotland. Both men were probably Catholics. Hamilton himself recommended a Catholic servant when the proclamation of April 1639 was being prepared for publication.[52] Perhaps trustworthiness was thereby assured – but it hardly countered well the allegations of popery from the other side.

The concern in government was that the rebellious Scots would encourage, or be encouraged by, contacts from outside. Even before the Bartlett case came to light, Windebank followed up a disclosure apparently by James Maxwell, one of the Scottish Grooms of the Bedchamber, and heard Robert Innes tell of his highly topical conversations with Scotsmen in London.[53] In Ireland Wentworth expressed his concern in November 1637 about the great interest taken there in the Scottish troubles. The immigrant Scots population, not to mention their often radical pastors, would continue to be a cause for concern, although some certainly took the chance to return to their home of origin.[54] In the same November Traquair, in Edinburgh, had questioned Rothes on what he knew of a 'ticket' supposedly sent to the Supplicants from puritans in England. The further discovery in England of the Supplicant paper that urged solidarity in complaints against the Scottish bishops seemed only to confirm the existence of a mutual traffic.[55]

---

[50] *CSPV 1636–9*, pp. 468, 449; WWM Str. P. LB 7, fol. 131.
[51] BL Add. Ms. 15391, fols. 311v, 313–14.
[52] *CSPD 1637–8*, 386/34, 397/45; *CSPD 1638–9*, 413/89, 91; GD 406/1/940.
[53] *CSPD 1637–8*, 363/77.
[54] WWM Str. P. LB 7, fols. 85, 95; GD 406/1/652; D. Stevenson, *Scottish Covenanters and Irish Confederates* (Belfast, 1981), pp. 12–21.
[55] Rothes, *Relation*, p. 31 – I do not know what a 'ticket' is; above p. 57.

The king's councillors were concerned lest a united front be forged against them. To some extent the efforts of Windebank and others to restrain the wider effects of the troubles in Scotland reflected on themselves as well as on those who came under investigation. Wentworth corresponded with Laud about a puritan plot, the counterpart to the popish plot; Laud suspected that John Williams, the Bishop of Lincoln, who was in the Tower, operated with contacts in England and Scotland and that there was a plan by subversives to have an English parliament summoned in order to uproot the work of recent years. Wentworth offered reassurance based on inherent optimism; he doubted that Bishop Williams would be up to much, and minimised the size of any English opposition group – 'Lord Saye and the rest of that fraternity', as he described them elsewhere, made noise but were not truly powerful. What was the truth of it? It remained unclear.[56]

Wentworth had no difficulty in Ireland in directing stern measures against the Scots, who he seems generally to have despised. Various matters nevertheless called for attention, such as the widespread dispersion of propaganda, at first handwritten, later printed; some were forward to take the Covenant or to speak out in its favour. Given the number of Scots in Ulster, he hoped to increase the strength of his Irish army to ensure against uprisings inspired from the Scottish mainland. He also tried to keep a special watch on the Irish ports for incoming material, and talked with Dr Henry Leslie, the Bishop of Down, who in due course delivered a confutation of the Covenant at his diocesan visitation on 26 September 1638; this was published the next year in London.[57] For Laud, the news that rumours passed in English dioceses of the Scottish liturgy being popish was no comfort.[58] With detection methods of variable efficiency, fears were built on evidence hardly plentiful but sufficient to keep the king's men on the alert. To a large extent their expectation was that the trouble would come from predictable types of people.[59]

It is not possible to gauge the proportion of cases extant of those which were discovered, but it is likely that there has survived a reasonable cross-section. Many of these were of only minor importance; informers might for instance report cases of seditious words. Not surprisingly these were more frequent in the time of approaching war in 1639, but there were examples in

[56] Laud, *Works*, vol. VII, pp. 454, 468, 471, 501–2, 505, 511, 513, 517, 539; WWM Str. P. LB 7, fols. 62–3, 83–5, 122–3, 131–2, 148; LB 10, fols. 232–3. Cf. Baillie, *Letters*, vol. I, p. 111; D. Hirst, *Authority and Conflict: England 1603–1658* (1986), pp. 164–9, 178–9; Lake, 'Anti-popery', pp. 84–7.
[57] WWM Str. P. LB 7, fols. 85, 95–6, 113–14, 132v; H. Leslie, *A Full Confutation of the Covenant*, STC 15497 (1639); Knowler, *Strafforde Letters*, vol. II, p. 226; Stevenson, *Scottish Covenanters and Irish Confederates*, pp. 14–21.
[58] Laud, *Works*, vol. V, p. 353.
[59] For example, GD 406/1/327, 374, 423. On conflict beliefs, cf. introduction to Cust and Hughes, *Conflict in Early Stuart England*.

1638, such as one John Alured who, living on the English border with Scotland, was charged with having welcomed the prospect of a Scottish invasion. This would lead to an English parliament, he believed; he described the Scots as 'our own nation and our own blood'. A Henry Spier of Reading felt that the Scots would soon be good subjects – and not because of change on their part.[60] Such cases would usually be followed up and disciplined; it seems possible that they largely reflect a religious current answering Covenanter hopes.[61]

The Covenanters had a sense of their likely target audience; equally Scots outside Scotland became particularly vulnerable to government attentions. This was hardly without reason. The minister who served for a time in exile amongst Ulster Scots, John Livingstone, distributed copies of the Covenant in London after its first signing; Eleazar Borthwick was another who clearly served the Covenant cause while he was there. In 1639 Laud would note that support was rallied in London amongst common soldiers.[62] Attempts were made from an early date to intercept correspondence, and it is notable how for many extant cases the Scottish connection is obvious. Thomas Livingstone, a tailor in the Strand, lost a whole series of letters, mainly from Lord Almond his cousin. Was Windebank marking certain other people – like the zealous 'J.P.' who wrote to the notorious puritan minister of Berwick, John Jemmatt?[63] How the system worked is unclear, but in August 1638 Windebank introduced the interception of letters at the Scottish border, to discover some 'ill-affected of our own', he explained to Hamilton. A fortnight later, Hamilton received predictable complaints from the Covenanters. The period of war would only increase the pressure and discrimination against Scots outside their home country – most notably by the imposition of oaths.[64]

Threat of war caused the Covenanters to produce explicit propaganda for outside readership, which gave a more ominous challenge to the king and his administration. The first pamphlet of this nature, the *Short Relation of the State of the Kirk of Scotland . . .* , was published in July 1638 to take issue with Hamilton's threatening words about English force. It appealed against

---

[60] *CSPD 1637–8*, 395/29, 83, 397/40; *CSPD 1640*, 463/77, 97.
[61] Cf. E. Cope, *Politics without Parliaments 1629–1640* (1987), pp. 175–8. The main sources are State Papers, Domestic and Bod. Bankes Mss. I am grateful to Professor Russell for discussions around this point.
[62] Cf. *CSPD 1637–8*, 393/52, 395/14; Laud, *Works*, vol. VII, p. 542; W. K. Tweedie (ed.), *Select Biographies* (2 vols., Edinburgh, 1845–7), vol. I, pp. 159–60; Stevenson, *Scottish Revolution*, pp. 57, 83–4.
[63] *CSPD 1637–8*, 393/38, 45, 397/58; PRO SP 16/400/50, 401/1. Livingstone's house was searched – *CSPD 1638–9*, 413/72.
[64] PRO SP 16/397/34; GD 406/M9/109/10. Merchants' letters were often opened – GD 18/2386 and State Papers, Domestic, especially for February 1639. For oaths, see *PCR*, vol. VI, pp. 419, 426, 431, 437; *CSPD 1639*, 424/12; BL Add. Ms. 11045, fols. 29, 39.

the justice of the king's so acting, but far more against the possibility of the English joining in. The mutual interest of the two kingdoms was upheld, not without some generous glosses, for instance in the allusion to peaceful commercial relations. However, it was the predominant emphasis of the tract to justify the movement of protest; Johnston of Wariston was its chief author. The narrative told of the course of the reformation in Scotland and its corruptions since the time of James. The Scottish bishops were principal targets, but the model of much that had gone wrong was English: aspersions were cast upon the admittedly lawfully established English liturgy, and even upon the English bishops, who might join in incensing the king to war. The popish plot might come in turn to threaten the people of England. The mutual interest might be more than the defence of the truth in Scotland.[65]

There was no printed reply to this work. The only counter-publications in London in 1638 were editions of the Aberdeen doctors' writings; not until the new year did documents in support of the other side run more freely from the English press. By the end of July 1638, the emphasis of Hamilton's commission had shifted to a greater concentration on accommodation in Scotland: it was hoped somehow to silence the opposition rather than engage with it.[66] In 1639, with war more positively again on the agenda, the king would explain his position to the English – though even then speed was not apparently of the essence. The Covenanters pre-empted him with their *Information to All Good Christians within the Kingdome of England*, published on 4 February 1639. Here the popish plot led the argument which was designed to counter prevailing rumours in England that the Covenanters intended invasion; again Wariston was involved. The themes of mutuality were upheld as before, but the plot to be exposed was that which threatened to take Scotland and England on the way to Rome. English churchmen had offended greatly. Now in the wake of the Glasgow Assembly, the Covenanters defended their own stance which had cast out bishops as contrary to their reformation and confession of faith.[67]

That Charles attempted to have this second statement answered in a proclamation was an indication of the mounting concern that the Covenanters could reach a popular audience outside Scotland. Ten thousand copies

---

[65] Above, pp. 85–6; *Short Relation of the State of the Kirk of Scotland* . . . ; Johnston, *Diary*, pp. 361, 367. For contemporary comparisons, see Rothes, *Relation, passim*; NLS Wod. Fo. 64, fols. 217–19 (Johnston, *Diary*, p. 359(?)).

[66] J. D. Ogilvie, 'The Aberdeen doctors and the National Covenant', *Papers of the Edinburgh Bibliographical Society*, 11 (1912–20), 73–86; *The Declinator and Protestation of the Archbishops* . . . , STC 22058 (1639 – 23 January); *His Majesties Proclamation in Scotland*, STC 22001 (1639); above, chapter 3.

[67] Above, pp. 127–8, 130; *An Information to All Good Christians* . . . , Aldis 946 (Edinburgh, 1639); Johnston, *Diary*, p. 408; Baillie, *Letters*, vol. I, p. 189. For the first draft, see NLS Wod. Fo. 63, fols. 24–6.

of the proclamation were printed.[68] But the problem had wide ramifications. Both the *Short Relation* and the *Information* were translated and printed under cover in the Low Countries. It was the beginning of a trend in respect of Covenanter publications, but it was well rooted in the tradition there of radical printing, notably of English libels.[69] A Scot named 'Hage', probably the William Haig of 1633, was printing the proceedings of the 1633 parliament. So much was done that a senior minister in Amsterdam, John le Maire, took it upon himself to campaign on Laud's behalf against any printing of books which in his view tended to attack 'British government or Anglican hierarchy'.[70] The Covenanters' answer to the king's English proclamation of February 1639, the *Remonstrance*, would certainly have fallen in here: it contained unmistakably a general attack on episcopacy. Prelates of England and Scotland, by opening the door to popery, could, moreover, be putting a 'stumbling-block' in the king's way to heaven, a hindrance to the queen's conversion and an offence to all reformed kirks. These were not the only reasons for the Scots' defensive arms, but they were words that showed little restraint. In some quarters the struggle became known as the bishops' war.[71]

These were not small operators who were under investigation. A Scotsman, Thomas Crawford, commissioned ten thousand copies in English and three thousand in Flemish of one offensive work; John le Maire could congratulate himself on having foiled the plans for translations into French, but he believed that the English copies would be shipped into Scotland. By February 1639 titles included works on the limits of political obedience, including a reprint of Buchanan's *De Iure Regni Apud Scotos*.[72] Sir William Boswell acted for Charles by communicating publicly with the Estates in the Low Countries to have the publishers of libels punished. As over arms, the Covenanters did not monopolise sympathies. One item translated for Charles was the proclamation of 22 September 1638 – perhaps an interesting reflection of Dutch sympathies for that relatively concessionary document.[73]

If anything, foreign versions of the various libels intensified personal hostilities against Archbishop Laud. His Scottish opponents would share

---

[68] J. F. Larkin, *Stuart Royal Proclamations*, vol. II (Oxford, 1983), pp. 662–7.

[69] *Cort Verhael van de Misdaden . . . die de Schotse Bisschoppen . . .*, Aldis 941 (Amsterdam, 1639); *Informatie aen alle goede Christenen . . .*, STC 21905b.5 (Amsterdam, 1639); PRO SP 16/387/79; K. L. Sprunger, *Dutch Puritanism* (Leiden, 1982), pp. 70–6; S. Foster, *Notes from the Caroline Underground* (Hamden, CT, 1978), pp. 58–62.

[70] PRO SP 16/387/79; cf. Laud, *Works*, vol. VII, p. 426; PRO SP 84/154, fols. 44, 312; Sprunger, *Dutch Puritanism*, pp. 306–18.

[71] *A Remonstrance of the Nobility . . .*, Aldis 954 (Edinburgh, 22 March 1639), esp. pp. 20–2; *Remonstrantie vande edelen . . .*, STC 21908.5 (Amsterdam, 1639); Cust and Hughes, *Conflict*, p. 213.

[72] PRO SP 84/155, fols. 6, 31–2, 79; Laud, *Works*, vol. VII, p. 544.

[73] PRO SP 84/154, fols. 113, 146, 150–1, 248.

in this, but such a specific attack was restrained in the writings completed for English consumption – at least until the Covenanters needed to answer specific points of controversy in the March 1639 *Remonstrance*; mention of Laud's name had actually been struck out after the draft stage of the February *Information*. Manuscript separates in circulation before this were less hesitant, presumably since any who received these would have been more specially targeted.[74]

Whatever Charles did, the flow of information and deliberate appeals for support, both printed and manuscript, could not easily be stopped. Attempts to cure the symptoms of the problem in any case were but partial expedients. At the same time many of his subjects outside Scotland criticised the 'rebellion' in the north, and by 1639 fewer and fewer could claim ignorance of it; the king's war preparations if nothing else saw to that. The circulation of literature did arouse hostile comment. George Butler's attitude to the 'devilish books' being vented out of Scotland by self-styled merchants, whom he described as 'bare, roguish pedlars' fell in here. This was not just inbred hostility; Butler had read a recent Covenanter protestation.[75] Rumours did not die that the Covenanters might be aggressive towards England; they built on natural fears, like the suggestions that the Scots would come in search of rich pickings.[76]

Thomas Dugard, a schoolmaster in Lord Brooke's circle, was a more likely one who was sympathetic to Scots appeals; a book about the Scottish Covenant – probably the *Short Relation* – got to him at the end of October 1638, and some more literature came later.[77] Henry Oxinden made extensive notes on the *Short Relation*, including a curse on any who did not wish for peace – provided that the gospel of peace was safe![78] The Earl of Northumberland also read the *Short Relation*, although when is not known. He noted the charges made that the bishops had been imposed on Scotland as a political move and had done only wrong there. He put alongside this notes on the king's *Large Declaration* of 1639. These emphasised the Scottish reluctance to be under the church of England, and the basic similarity of the Scottish liturgy to the service-book of England (with the argument drawn on that for the king), but also drew attention to the Scottish supplication to be allowed to live under their own laws. Northumberland had plenty of

---

[74] PRO SP 84/155, fol. 6; *Remonstrance* . . . , pp. 17–18; NLS Wod. Fo. 63, fols. 24–6. For examples of manuscript papers in circulation around this time, see *CSPD 1638–9*, 398/18, 415/1; BL Loan 29/172, fols. 195–8.
[75] WWM Str. P. LB 18, p. 142.
[76] Cf. Knowler, *Strafforde Letters*, vol. II, p. 268; WWM Str. P. LB 10, fol. 192r.
[77] BL Add. Ms. 23146, fols. 80v, 82v; A. Hughes, 'Thomas Dugard and his circle in the 1630s – a "Parliamentary-Puritan" connexion?', *HJ*, 29 (1986), 771–93.
[78] BL Add. Ms. 28011, fol. 39.

prejudice against the Scots, but it was apparently important to him to consider the rival contentions.[79]

The Covenanters had made progress at home in special circumstances and with considerable central organisation. What happened elsewhere was for the most part beyond their control: it was a tricky business to assess responsiveness to the Covenant, let alone the political implications of that. The story here too is one of partial insight. As they applied their best efforts to wooing support, comment on English affairs attempted to take stock of the state of military preparations and the troubles which might hinder them. In the early summer of 1638, Baillie heard a report not only of how Scottish bishops at Court fomented war, but also that the English council had refused to be interested: 'English councillors . . . are said to have spoken of the injustice of such a course, and the danger which it was like to bring to the state of England as things went, their deep malcontents lying for many years but overplastered, without any solid cure.' The story rather exaggerated on truth, but it was attractive news to a minister who found encouragement in the reported contemporary troubles of England.[80]

Sometimes the news recounted could be bad, such as for the Earl of Home in late July 1638, who expected the worst since the nobility of England had reputedly undertaken to serve the king, to the latter's delight. More positively, a newsletter giving information of the English military preparations would urge its recipients to seek the prayers of the godly in the south; another, likewise in autumn 1638, suggested that the Earls of Holland and Pembroke opposed the use of force. Each of these strands needs careful judgement now to assess their significance; they were no easier then to interpret accurately. For the most part, however, the picture was one of encouragement, as the king's councillors feared, and that was perhaps the important thing.[81] English military news was important too; interestingly Walter Yonge got prompt information on this himself, at least once from Sir Walter Earle.[82] Belief in a unity of truth drew life from encouragement through words and events. Solidarity with the reformed communion was important.[83]

---

[79] Alnwick Mss., BL Microfilm 285, fol. 286. The archive shows that Northumberland owned copies of other Scottish papers. Walter Yonge also studied the *Large Declaration* – BL Add. Ms. 35331, fol. 73.

[80] Baillie, *Letters*, vol. I, pp. 71–3; also pp. 95, 117; cf. NLS Wod. 4to. 25, fol. 14v; Wod. Fo. 66, fol. 111; GD 112/39/548.

[81] GD 112/40/2/1/5; Baillie, *Letters*, vol. I, pp. 73, 90, 111–12, 117; Sir W. Fraser, *The Annandale Family Book* (2 vols., Edinburgh, 1894), vol. II, p. 296; NLS Dep. 175/324 (early September 1638); NLS Ms. 2263, fols. 71–2; GD 112/40/2/2/119; NLS Wod. 4to. 106, fols. 195, 199; *CSPD 1638–9*, 415/11.

[82] BL Add. Ms. 35331, fol. 71v.

[83] Cf. J. K. Cameron, 'The Swiss and the Covenant', in G. W. S. Barrow (ed.), *The Scottish Tradition* (Edinburgh, 1974), pp. 155–63; NLS Wod. 4to. 24, fols. 67–8; BL Sloane Ms. 654, fols. 196–223.

For the English administration, it was not always advisable to proceed to the prosecution of likely friends of the Covenanters, though a concerted effort was made to discover them. House searches carried out after the publication in February 1639 of the *Information to All Good Christians* revealed around forty recipients; included in the caches were some copies of the Acts of the Glasgow Assembly and some of the related protestations by the Covenanters.[84] A list compiled by Charles Calthorpe, 'intelligencer', named mostly ordinary folk, but one of the letters from Scotland 'fell flat' on Lord Brooke. Hamilton and Laud considered together whether he should be arrested, but decided that nothing was to be done for the time being, probably so as to avoid public confirmation of the Covenanters' approaches gaining sympathy. There was greater strictness at the time of the oath for the peers.[85]

Fears of the puritan menace, like those of the popish plot, encouraged a block labelling of the enemy – a polarisation of the political world that was run through by religion. It is not surprising that, as Caroline Hibbard has argued, the period of crisis in the British context saw an intensification of fears expressed concerning popery – fears with many contemporary grounds for evidence.[86] The underlying reality of the supposed puritan menace was equally tantalising to some of the governors of the day. As far as we are concerned here, they came at least near to discovering some of the cross-kingdom contacts.

On 3 July 1638 Wentworth wrote to Laud to report that the tenants of Londonderry had sent their agent, Sir John Clotworthy, to supplicate the king for them, concerning the issue of the plantation of their area, but there had been a detour: 'the puppy is so much for the common cause of the brethren that he is gone to Edinburgh to see what becomes of the kirk'. That Clotworthy had been more interested to pursue the Covenanters than his appointed mission was for Wentworth an Irish problem; Ulster was filled with such people. Laud and the king took Wentworth's point about being wary of Clotworthy on his supposed primary task; but what of 'Mr Johnson's [*sic*] alchemies'?[87] Clotworthy had gone to Edinburgh, and had had talks with Archibald Johnston on 11 June before travelling south to conduct his other business.[88]

---

[84] *CSPD 1638–9*, 413/6, 51, 72, 73, 77, 109, 120; 412/90; *HMC Cowper*, vol. II, p. 217; *PCR* vol. V, p. 130.

[85] PRO SP 16/413/120–1. Some of the individuals were investigated further – *CSPD 1638–9* 414/54, 86, 128 – yet Sir John Meldrum was imprisoned at York for suggesting that some English peers were Covenanters at heart – *CSPD 1639*, 417/110. For the oath, see above pp. 144–5.

[86] Hibbard, *Charles I and the Popish Plot*; see too R. Clifton, 'Fear of popery', in C. Russel (ed.), *The Origins of the English Civil War* (1973), pp. 144–67.

[87] WWM Str. P. LB 7, fols. 113–14; Laud, *Works*, vol. VII, p. 464; T. W. Moody, F. X. Martin and F. J. Byrne, *A New History of Ireland*, vol. III (Oxford, 1978), pp. 265–6.

[88] Johnston, *Diary*, p. 351; *CSPI 1633–47*, pp. 194–5; Bod. Bankes Ms. 6/6.

The Londonderry business showed clearly Wentworth's many prejudices against the Scots. Clotworthy, however, was an Englishman; in 1640 he would be selected -for the Long Parliament in two seats, one under the patronage of the Earl of Warwick; he was related to John Pym by marriage; in 1635 he had received John Winthrop's son to discuss emigration to Massachusetts. In short, he was of a group of active malcontents – and through his Irish land interests, not to mention religious sympathies, particularly well connected with Scots.[89]

When Clotworthy reached London, he kept a correspondence with his friends in Scotland which both satisfied their concern as to how affairs were carried at Court and went further. At first Clotworthy sent correspondence through Mr Thomas Livingstone – one of Windebank's targets – who apparently was acting as a channel for such post; the letters were directed to Mr John Fleming, a merchant in Edinburgh. In these earlier letters, mainly bearing news, Clotworthy used cipher heavily. He told on 21 June how the king and Laud ('56', '66') alone handled the Scottish business, both answering the dispatches that came from Hamilton in Edinburgh. He wrote that they planned to arm 20,000 men and that Wentworth ('81') had promised to bring out of Ireland 15,000 in support – at that time, as far as we know, no more than rumour. Hamilton ('201'), in one possible interpretation of the cipher, was not keen to support this unless it was without risk; he was promising nothing at this 'hard pinch', but meanwhile the king could not sleep for want of him. On English sympathy, Clotworthy related that the 'protestants' and the 'precisians' heartily desired that the Scots should accept no settlement unless within a parliament – and that they should find pardon with other like conditions of peace for friends. There should be no agreement with Hamilton just for the name of three or four: 'all will be disappointed and all your so happy work be disappointed. Wherefore clear the root and branch.'[90] The next surviving letter, of 26 June, is more obscure, appearing to deal with mercantile affairs, but making little grammatical sense; it made clear mention, however, of the Earl of Antrim's intentions to go across to Ireland, which in the prevailing atmosphere had ominous overtones.[91]

'Root and branch' acquired a specific meaning in the politics of the Long Parliament, touching the abolition of episcopacy. Was it as directed in this 1638 context? It seems hard to conclude otherwise, given the Scottish situation of the day. In the *Short Relation* written by Johnston, concluding harsh

---

[89] Keeler, *Long Parliament*, 'Sir John Clotworthy'; *Winthrop Papers*, Massachusetts Historical Society, vol. III (Boston, 1943), p. 193.

[90] PRO SP 16/393/31 and /33. Holograph, unsigned. A John Fleming was a Covenanter in Edinburgh – M. Wood (ed.), *Extracts from the Records of the Burgh of Edinburgh 1626 to 1641* (Edinburgh, 1936), pp. 106, 161.

[91] NLS Wod. Fo. 66, fols. 92–3. Holograph, unsigned.

words against the English episcopate drew on a plea to the English if necessary to help to 'root out these Canaanites, who are pricks in their sides'.[92] The apparent distinction between Protestants and precisians may also be recognised here. The differences of approach in propaganda tailored to fit the receiver have already been noticed; here was the kind of assessment that would encourage the type of propaganda written in the event in July 1638 and February 1639, words for the Protestant church of England at large, although not without an unmistakable injection of radical godly thought. Ambitions for reformation, in Scotland and in England, could reach up high. One of the costs for Charles of the Scottish troubles being prolonged was the increase of confidence in the expression of these, in heart and mind if not in concrete political action.

Windebank's agency seized on the first of Clotworthy's letters described above. Its anonymity may have preserved its author from investigation; another letter from him, of 11 July 1638, shows he was aware of the danger of letters being intercepted. Sending by a trusted messenger, Clotworthy wrote free of code on this occasion. He warned his 'worthy friends', his addressees, to warn Mr (Eleazar) Borthwick of the risks of using the mail. The future plan would be for letters sent to Clotworthy to be sent still to Thomas Livingstone, but superscribed only with the symbol *Π*. It would be a regular correspondence, but he specially requested to be sent six of the 'printed letters which are cried about the streets', with the same number of Covenants and any other items lately circulated.[93]

Clotworthy could now tell that the king had talked about Scotland with councillors other than Laud. He updated the news of the Earl of Antrim, who was correctly reported to have been recommended by the Marquis of Hamilton to the king for leading an expedition of MacDonnells from Ireland to land in Scotland. He wrote again of Wentworth making military overtures to the king to bring 16,000 men from Ireland, but here exercised critical judgement on the rumour, doubting that this was possible with Ireland itself not quiet. The Earl of Arundel apparently had a commission to go into the northern parts, and there were to be raised 20,000 men; flat-bottomed boats were already prepared, twelve or twenty of them. All possible information was being gathered, and accuracy was reasonably good. Clotworthy could believe that the king would do everything he could for a strike of force; Charles was said not to doubt that this would be welcomed, but Clotworthy believed that it was more likely that the king's hopes would be frustrated. He

[92] *Short Relation*, sig. C3v.
[93] June 1638 publications – *Reasons . . . Service-Booke . . . Ought to Bee Refused*, Aldis 932; *Reasons for a Generall Assemblie*, Aldis 931; *Reasons against the Rendering of our Confession*, Aldis 930 – cf. Laud, *Works*, vol. VII, p. 542.

expressed doubt that the king could raise even two hundred men! Some preparations were so public, he argued, that it made him think that the intention was more to intimidate.

In suggesting that the king might not be able to do as he wished, Clotworthy captured the hopes of Baillie and the fears of Laud; and he offered evidence to his Scottish readers. They would not believe, he wrote, how heartily their cause was taken by 'nobility, gentry and commonalty'. Some of the nobles had attempted to form a group for jointly petitioning the king to cure their grievances, but only two had been prepared to go so far; the names were not written, but Lords Brooke and Saye seem most probable – 'you may guess who they are'. Was this the first planning of the petition rumoured to be ready in February 1639, or even pointing towards the famous petition of the peers in 1640? Clotworthy in due course would help in distributing early copies of that latter important document.[94] The two prominent lords would not stay much longer in England, but Clotworthy could tell, on the unanimous consent of many leading persons, that they hoped to find their 'America in Scotland'; all 'designs foreign' were stopped until it could be seen what were the results in Scotland of resistance to the king. And 'if a liberty can be had with you', he continued, very many would want to come to Scotland, men of great wealth, who were prodigious spenders – 'I could number 40 or 50 of them'.

Writing in these terms was presumably not meaningless for his Scots readers. Clotworthy emphasised that such men hoped that any final agreement would include a dropping of all barriers between the kingdoms with complete freedom of movement, as was proper for 'subjects of the same government and members of the same body'. The malcontent in England saw a way of wooing the Covenanters in economic terms – a fascinating reflection on the dimension that otherwise remained largely unaddressed by the Covenanters until later, in 1639 and beyond. The Covenanters might stand for the general liberties of Scotland against the seen abuses of government, but they stood vitally too for religion. Clotworthy gave assurance that no challenge would be made to their 'gospel'.[95]

Saye, Brooke, the Earl of Warwick, and one Henry Darley in March 1638 are known to have declared their intention of travelling to Providence Island as soon as possible; they never went.[96] Given Clotworthy's connections, his account is plausible, his contacts with significant nobles and gentry almost certainly genuine. Whatever the accuracy of the figures he gave, his letter

---

[94] GD 406/1/985; Lancs. RO DdHu/46/21. The peers' petition is discussed below in chapter 7.
[95] NLS Wod. Fo. 66, fols. 109–10. Holograph, unsigned. Printed in D. Dalrymple, *Memorials and Letters Relating to the History of Britain in the Reign of Charles the First* (Glasgow, 1766), pp. 39–45, as anonymous.
[96] J. T. Cliffe, *The Puritan Gentry* (1984), pp. 204–5.

revealed the character of notable discontent in England, constrained while lacking means of redress without a parliament and prepared, before the Scottish troubles, to consider emigration as the only escape. The Covenanters' audacity to stand against the king was indeed celebrated.

Clotworthy's writing would imply that religious sympathies were central to the feeling of common ground with the Scots. As with Scots individuals, it is risky to generalise on the basis of limited evidence, but Clotworthy's position was clear; he was active in opposing allegedly popish ritual in Ireland in 1635.[97] For his Covenanter correspondents, he enclosed a New Testament that included 'such abominable pictures that horrible impiety stares through them'. The same thing was later to be described in Charles's name as a 'very slender ground' for complaint; but it clearly upset a number of people. For some at least, there was a spiritual gulf.[98]

The politics of the situation in mid-1638 seemed open, in the eyes of the king's Scottish counsellors, to moderate compromise. Clotworthy opposed this because of its risks. He singled out the Earl of Cassilis and Lords Loudoun and Lindsay who amongst others had found the king's offers through Hamilton fair; Clotworthy's fear was that the marquis merely hoped to make division.[99] He specifically warned against trusting Lord Reay, who had apparently signed the Covenant as a tactical measure in order to become an infiltrator.[100] Scottish internal news was being thoroughly digested by one Englishman at least. At the same time, he admitted that English 'wellwishers' were concerned lest the bishops' allegations came true and the Covenanters struck against government and established sovereignty – beyond any 'quarrel of conscience'. For instance, it was difficult to know whether the Scots should do anything against the king's preparations; and yet necessary defence was advisable. The border towns should be secured, even at risk of being accounted an open act of rebellion. Some possible support might be upset, he warned, but he offered too his prayers and the prayers of many – 'I think multitudes' – that the 'holy cause and profession' would not suffer; it was after all amazing that the Scots had preserved themselves hitherto against all criticism.[101]

---

[97] A. Ford, *The Protestant Reformation in Ireland, 1590–1641* (Frankfurt on Main, 1985), p. 273.

[98] [Charles I], *A Large Declaration*, STC 21906 (1639), pp. 112–13; *HMC 9 (II)*, p. 497; G. D. S. Henderson, 'Bible illustration in the age of Laud', *Transactions of the Cambridge Bibliographical Society*, 8/2 (1982), 173–216; E. S. Cope and W. H. Coates (eds.), *Proceedings of the Short Parliament of 1640*, Camden Society (1977), p. 238; Collinson, *Birthpangs of Protestant England*, pp. 115–21.

[99] Cf. above, chapter 3. Cassilis was a patron of George Gillespie but was hesitant about approving resistance by force – Tweedie, *Select Biographies*, vol. I, p. 330; Baillie, *Letters*, vol. I, pp. 53, 189.

[100] Cf. Rothes, *Relation*, p. 104; Johnston, *Diary*, p. 347.

[101] NLS Wod. Fo. 66, fols. 109–10.

The points are important to rehearse for confirming the picture already presented of the uncertainties and flux within the course of the Scottish troubles. Charles was threatening in his words and actions, feeble though the latter were in the event. At the other end it was not the wish to bypass the royal sovereignty endowed by God, but there was undoubtedly a godly opposition which desired to shape the king's direction. Obedience first to God, for Clotworthy and Johnston an immediate and pressing vision, for others perhaps something tending towards an excuse, led to action Charles could only castigate as intolerable. For many, perhaps most, people the middle ground might have been more or less attractive, yet there were forces which encouraged a distancing from this.

Was the problem Charles's incapacity for realism? There was also a positive quest on the other side. 'Mind Christ and his gospel': in the last letter available, of 28 July 1638, Clotworthy repeated the theme of guarding against division. Obedience such as he suggested threatened an extreme, but Clotworthy here was still more confident that the king could not seriously intend war. The Marquis of Hamilton would try to minimise the terms, but would then have to close on whatever could be agreed; the advantage might lie with the Covenanters. Clotworthy gave amongst his reasons the difficulties of the collection of ship money: 'the king will rather comply with you than lose the sweet morsels of what is to be had from England'.[102] Charles's attitude in fact made the advice in both cases very mistaken.

The mention of ship money, undoubtedly a considerable grievance amongst various people in England in the summer of 1638, was indication that domestic concerns remained important in these cross-kingdom contacts. The political cause was not alone one of religion. That Englishmen could contemplate exile in Scotland was to be described as the Covenanters' 'negative help' to them. However much discontent people had – and frustrations felt over the ship money court cases or over Charles's long-term resistance to calling a parliament were only aspects of this – the Scottish situation brought sparks of fire to highlight attention directly focused on Charles's central government. The crisis was to have momentous consequences.[103]

In 1638 and 1639, the possibility of a parliament in England, raised as the king contemplated the use of force against the Scots, came to nothing. But Englishmen and Scots might share common feeling in supporting each other's

---

[102] NLS Wod. Fo. 66, fol. 111 – a contemporary copy, but the content is strongly suggestive of Clotworthy; phrases of other letters are echoed.
[103] NLS Wod. Fo. 66, fol. 111. Cf. A. Hughes, *Politics, Society and Civil War in Warwickshire, 1620–1660* (Cambridge, 1987), pp. 105–11; Cope, *Politics without Parliaments*, pp. 106–22; P. Lake, 'The collection of ship money in Cheshire during the sixteen-thirties: a case study of relations between central and local government', *Northern History*, 17 (1981), 44–71; B. Whitelocke, *Memorials of English Affairs* (1682), p. 27.

calls for representative assemblies; indeed the 'puritan' cause could grow in strength through its attraction to parliaments. The misapprehension of ordinary Englishmen that the Covenanters wanted a settlement simply through a parliament indicates well English assumptions; at the same time it shows how distance and mutual ignorance or misunderstanding could, alongside disparate domestic priorities, raise difficulties for the formation of Anglo-Scottish thinking. At least for a time Clotworthy shared in the error – likewise Wentworth and many others.[104]

Scots were not immune from the obverse mistake. The February 1639 *Information* was the first of a number of documents to appeal openly for the holding of an English parliament. In Scottish terms this was so that the justice of the Covenanter case might openly be heard – though matters could scarcely rest at that. In the draft of the statement, however, probably by Sir Alexander Gibson of Durie, the appeal was for a general assembly and parliament in England – in other words, for a Scottish-type solution in England; it was corrected in the revision stage.[105] Furthermore, it was important to the Covenanters that the possible hearing of their case in England did not imply any subordination, as had often been aired by the English around 1603, of 'a church and kingdom as free, ancient and independent as any other in the world'. Closer union in terms of visions for commerce and the church was beginning to emerge as an issue from these Scottish troubles, but, if the Scots had their way, the union could be nothing less than federal and between equal partners.[106]

The king, however, called no English parliament. Political advances over this were still distant in 1638 when Clotworthy kept his links so closely with the Covenanters. Wentworth from Ireland still assumed that the king might command ready loyalty from his English people, particularly if soldiers were well paid. He emphasised the need for firm and decisive action, whether with a parliament or without. Wentworth's apparent overestimation of the capacity of royal government to overcome serious hindrances both administrative and ideological would ill serve the king, who placed his hopes here after the failure of the Pacification of Berwick.[107]

In so far as the Union of the Crowns involved the third kingdom of Ireland, Covenanter awareness of Wentworth's activity against them became increasingly hostile. He had had a run of critical correspondence with Lord Lorne in the latter part of 1638 which became fairly well known; in 1639 especially,

---

[104] PRO SP 16/393/31; Knowler, *Strafforde Letters*, vol. II, p. 191; PRO SP 78/106, fol. 74v.
[105] NLS Wod. Fo. 63, fols. 24–6.
[106] *Information*, pp. 10–11; D. Stevenson, 'The early Covenanters and the federal union of Britain', in R. Mason (ed.), *Scotland and England, 1286–1815* (Edinburgh, 1987), pp. 163–81.
[107] For example, WWM Str. P. LB 10b, pp. 23–4.

his persecution of Scots and other Covenant sympathisers in Ireland won him enemies.[108] If anything, the Catholics in Ireland fared even worse in Covenanter eyes, in part of course out of the abortive Antrim expedition, but at root in the light of the battle against popery. The Covenanters' official line would be to hope for the reformation in Ireland to follow exactly the lines of England.

In each of the kingdoms, most of those actively concerned in the high political situation would have home issues to the forefront of their thinking, and understandably so. Only a small number of individuals became involved in daring cross-kingdom contacts. If there were suppressed troubles in England, responsiveness to wider British issues was even slower to show. The course of the Scottish troubles nevertheless awakened a greater interest and involvement which sometimes made a public mark. An English preacher like Jeremiah Burroughs might defend the Scottish Covenant cause; another, a Dr Mosely, would attempt an independent mission of reconciliation to the Covenanters as the king drove north with his army; both attracted critical attention from the king's men.[109] In Scotland, visions for the reformation in England would be expressed – regardless of what most English folk would have thought of them – and at times optimism ran high. The Earl of Rothes was as aware as someone like Alexander Henderson that the episcopal hierarchies were potentially up for challenge.[110] In the prelude and aftermath of the Pacification, contacts were made, thoughts formulated – in short a great deal that ran at least to some extent counter to Charles's dictatorial approach to the Scottish situation.

The king commanded considerable service, but criticism ran within the king's camp as well as praise. While one Secretary, Windebank, was open to various expedients involving Catholics, the other, the aged Sir John Coke, with his assistant Weckherlin, showed distaste for the same. Sir Edmund Verney made a daring decision to put aside thoughts of hostility when he misled the king on the matter of the opening condition of the talks at Berwick.[111] Whether out of expediency or principle, the king's servants questioned their

---

108 Knowler, *Strafforde Letters*, vol. II, pp. 187, 209–10, 220–1, 225, 232, 246–8, 291–2; EUL New College Ms. X15b 3/1, vol. I, fols. 134–6; Moody, Martin and Byrne, *New History of Ireland*, p. 268.
109 W. Hunt, *The Puritan Movement* (1983), p. 278; *CSPD 1639*, 420/173, 421/60, 176, 422/77; HMC *Cowper*, vol. II, pp. 225–6; Baillie, *Letters*, vol. I, p. 204.
110 Gardiner, *Hamilton Papers*, pp. 98–100; NLS Wod. Fo. 48, fol. 26v; *Diary of Sir Archibald Johnston, Lord Wariston, 1639*, ed. G. M. Paul, SHS (Edinburgh, 1896), p. 79. Cf. also NLS Wod. Fo. 54, p. 310.
111 Hibbard, *Charles I and the Popish Plot*, pp. 53–4, 104–8, 121; M. B. Young, *Servility and Service. The Life and Work of Sir John Coke* (1986); Berks. RO Trumbull Misc. XLIX, nos. 41, 44; Misc. LXI (Diary 11 June, 25 July 1639); PRO SP 81/47, fol. 126; *Letters and Papers of the Verney Family*, ed. J. Bruce, Camden Society (1853), pp. 246–9.

master. Hamilton evidently felt no need to conceal from the king the point that many Englishmen did feel ambivalent about Charles's approach to the problems.[112]

Charles appeared only partly to hear – only partly to attend to the significance of the warnings of caution. Accommodation on a middle ground might have satisfied very many if it could have been achieved, but on his 'side' Charles – no doubt also with many in obedience to him – declined properly to enter in. He was susceptible to the views described above of the puritan conspiracy. The troubles were British because their king was; Charles continued to *wish* for suppression of the undesired implications of this. The decision for a second war effort invested hope in a 'national' war, English against Scots; he conceded it was not likely that the strong, outwardly united Covenant front could be broken from within. Charles wanted the three kingdoms only upon his terms. The ambivalent attitudes, the uncertainties, the troubles could not simply vanish however. In defence but also with their own forward visions, the Covenanters kept as far as they could upon the British stage.

Puritanism and popery were labels used by opposing parties who sought to label with prejudice. For that reason, as terms they lacked accuracy. They failed to distinguish, for example, those who might be described as ideological opponents of aspects of the regime from those who purveyed and received criticism in a relatively passive manner; they failed to distinguish the aims of Archbishop Laud and George Con. They conveyed well the pervasive relevance of Christian religion in the politics of the day; they less successfully penetrated to the political motive forces. Laud with Charles may have been interested in recovering a catholic heritage for the church which ran to some extent against reformed emphases, but he was not intending a simple rapprochement with Rome. The Covenant leadership may have had offended church sensibilities to the fore, but this did not preclude it from careful politics and due attention to questions of expediency. Non-ecclesiastical politics became subsumed under both labels. Popish and puritan were flexible notions.

Opposition was a problematic phenomenon, when political thought exalted the idea of king and subjects living in harmonious order under the one ruler of the universe. In the period after 1637 it was a phenomenon clearly affecting not just one of Charles I's kingdoms. The king had tended towards an order of unity between the kingdoms; in crisis he naturally wished to keep the problems isolated, but could not. For his own vindication he was advised

[112] G. Burnet, *The Memoires of the Lives and Actions of James and William, Dukes of Hamilton and Castleherald . . .* (1677), pp. 147–8; Johnston, *1639 Diary*, pp. 87–8.

to use forces from his other kingdoms at least to weaken the impression of unity given from within Scotland. This obliged the involvement of each of the societies; the Covenanters equally were, for their self-defence, moved to counter allegations voiced against them. They denied that they were plotting invasion; more fundamentally they challenged whether the English should come in arms against them. They justified their cause and presented their history, and they appealed to ideals of union between the kingdoms as well as between king and subjects.

The king's men tried to suppress their mere information, not to mention their explicitly directed appeals, but this was a battle not won. Government could not extend to an effective clampdown; in England and even in Ireland, despite Wentworth's best efforts, information got through, sympathies were expressed, hopes for domestic reform were raised. In the Low Countries and increasingly within Scotland itself the printing press was used. Whether or not the more radical statements of godly reformation found willing ears, consciousness of the Scottish troubles was spread widely; for the king it spread to the sphere of his foreign relations as well as to his subjects at home. A few particular contacts across kingdom boundaries involved figures aspiring to roles in national as well as local politics. There were visions for church and for state – matters less and less the monopoly of the king and his counsel. The king's men naturally had concern or sometimes fears. What faced them was united by thin or even invisible threads, despite what they sometimes appeared to think; they themselves also had troubles and mutual tensions. Charles trusted to his royal will. Many in 1639 seemed well to appreciate the weakness of this for uniting king and subjects. This was the main point; it was one of its consequences that some were beginning to grope their way forward to explore remedies for its weakness in the union of the kingdoms.

6

Parliaments and war
August 1639–September 1640

Although the king had given precise instructions to the Earl of Traquair for the new general assembly, with a parliament to follow, his own decision to return to the south signalled a departure from the allowances he had hitherto made to Scottish politics. Superficially he was yielding yet more ground to the Covenanters, and a full programme of reform would result from it; but he harboured thoughts of suppression and revenge. Such thoughts had never truly been absent from Charles's mind, but through the efforts of Hamilton and cautious English advisers he had gone far, as he thought, in being responsive to the Scottish situation. Now the negative dimension was more overwhelming. He would attend to Traquair's dispatches more to ensure that his few caveats were not overstepped than to look for signs of a loyal group in Scotland.

Charles, however, was not one altogether to close his options. Though Wentworth had received his summons to lend his support at the king's side, the projected campaign was for the new year. Particular care for the border garrisons and the preparation of the war effort would await the ending of the Scottish assemblies – in case any advantage could be won. Until then the Covenanters were to be allowed thoroughly to disgrace themselves, if for no other reason than for the sake of the king's esteem and the benefit of his support. Direct military threats would therefore be held off, as indeed was expedient also for reasons of cost.

The Earl of Traquair tried hard to act more positively on the king's behalf, not to mention his own, and it involved him as ever in a measure of double-talk. He had to be wary of Charles's disfavour if he went too far with the Covenanters, yet he had to exceed the king's own sense of propriety if he was to gain ground at all. The Marquis of Hamilton, out of the centre of affairs, was to some extent relieved of the near-impossibility of that task, although he continued as Charles's principal secretary in the business. The rivalries, even enmities, around him at Court and beyond continued as he sought at least to look for signs of breakthrough in the impasse of the troubles; he was suspected of doing more. Since he had frustrations over this both with king and Covenanters, his own position kept apparently relatively open. Given his standing and wealth, he was unlikely to desert Charles; but Wentworth's rise to influence and the prospect of a second war strained his 'conscience' as much as anything to date.

The king's stand brought him to call parliaments in Ireland and England, for supply and support in preparations for a new war. He was persuaded that this might be a serviceable way forward, despite the risks. Wentworth injected his characteristic counsel on the need to attend to the effectiveness of the policy. However, the English parliament sorely failed to answer expectations and was dissolved precipitately; alternative means had to be used to prosecute the military preparations. Significant delays and difficulties marked the ensuing months, but more crucially the Covenanters pre-empted Charles by invading England in August 1640. They further demanded settlement of their troubles within parliaments in both England and Scotland – an intervention alongside English petitions which was intended to give Charles little choice.

Within Scotland, Charles found the assumption that he held controlling sovereignty severely challenged, and now in the parliament as well as in the general assembly. Was the same to happen elsewhere? The British dimension of the Scottish troubles took on heightened importance. Most publicly it had brought an end to the so-called 'Personal Rule' in England; Charles nevertheless had no intention of handing over the reins. It was not in him to abandon hope, but a heavy critique directed at his counsel was being mounted, not least through the links across the kingdom boundaries. Some Englishmen took great interest in the various Scottish assemblies of 1639 and 1640. Information and propaganda continued to flow southwards, and news northwards. At the time of the Short Parliament there were underhand contacts designed to further the common cause. The fears and the attentions of Charles and his counsel were justifiably raised: it can be shown that the process of secret exchanges was there in the background to the Scottish invasion. Still Scottish and English interests would have divergences, and leaders would be at pains to maintain or create unities of purpose, but from Charles's perspective the threat seemed major indeed. The atmosphere was conducive neither to trust nor to an easy resumption of harmonious government.

Traquair, acting as the King's Commissioner, was conscious of Charles's future intentions, but tried nevertheless in Hamilton's spirit to work for a settlement that might win a significant backing in Scotland, both for the sake of peace and his own glory. Other Scottish privy councillors, such as the Earls of Roxburgh and Winton, complained that they were uninformed.[1] Personal

---

[1] GD 112/40/2/2/55.

rivalries of this nature were perhaps the least of Traquair's problems, though he had a similar obstacle with individuals on the Covenanter side. Argyll and Rothes keenly guarded their prominence in the strong grouping which pressed forward with a formidable programme of demands.[2] The immediate contentiousness of the Edinburgh General Assembly also stirred the king to keep a direct correspondence with Traquair. Charles insisted that concessions were to stand as in his instructions, and that any contrary proceedings were to be protested against and not ratified in parliament.[3]

Hamilton performed the role of Laud and Vane before him, supplementing the king's dispatches but fully aware of Charles's preferred line; drafts of the king's letters survive in his hand. Whether he could be anything more than an amanuensis is unclear. He specifically reminded Traquair of the care to be taken with ratifying the Covenant, so that the interpretation of the text could be compatible with the king's future intentions. Episcopacy was not to be abjured irrevocably. There was also an insistence that the band approved in the King's Covenant – or, more precisely, the band subscribed by James VI – should pass. The king still wished to constrain the Scots as far as possible. Leeway given in the Scottish situation could too readily have reverberations elsewhere. The Covenanters were not even to assume that the parliament would immediately be held: Charles threatened to prorogue it to the spring if necessary. In British terms a king obliged to a parliament was a wholly objectionable precedent.[4]

First in the general assembly Traquair tried to fulfil his commission.[5] Presenting a version of the grievances felt in the Scottish church together with the approved proposed solutions, he maintained in several speeches the need to respect the king's different views, not least because he was king in England. There was to be no question of like concessions south of the border; the recent public exchanges by Rothes on the subject of episcopacy in England demanded a clear line on that.[6] It was hopefully a line to be accepted by the generality of Scots. In attempting to woo them, Traquair may have disclosed a partial version of his instructions.[7] The Act of 17 August 1639 pronounced on all the grievances to the satisfaction of the Covenanters. Episcopacy with the rest was abolished, being described only as 'according to the constitutions

[2] Cf. GD 112/40/2/2/55, 54, 51; PRO 31/3/71, fol. 108.
[3] G. Burnet, *The Memoires of the Lives and Actions of James and William, Dukes of Hamilton and Castleherald* . . . (1677), pp. 156–7.
[4] GD 406/1/1032, 585; Traqr. Ms. 8/6, 7/10A.
[5] The sources used for the assembly are A. Peterkin, *Records of the Kirk of Scotland* (Edinburgh, 1838), pp. 204–9, 237–72 and NLS Wod. Fo. 63, fols. 235–51. Detailed reference will be eschewed here.
[6] S. R. Gardiner, *The Hamilton Papers*, Camden Society (1880), pp. 98–100.
[7] NLS Wod. Fo. 63, fols. 231–2.

... unlawful in this kirk'. Traquair added his consent.[8] The question of the Covenant was not yet involved.

The Act was a statement designed to accommodate all views, and Charles could grudgingly allow it, although he found the narrative section which had singled out the causes of the troubles 'damnable'. He would not, for instance, have wished to describe canons or service-book as containing heads of popery and superstition. Traquair did his best to persuade Charles not to interrupt the process if at all possible, either in the present assembly or in the approaching parliament, since, if demands ran too far, the king would always retain his right to deny or question conclusions through appropriate declarations by his Commissioner. It seemed to Traquair, the Scot, that Charles could only benefit by the conciliatory course which fulfilled standing promises. Though only some members of the assembly pushed aggressively for far-reaching change, it was likely that few would stand out from the pack if the king on his side broke the agreement sealed at Berwick.[9]

With respect to his instructions, Traquair managed to avoid dispute of the royal power in assemblies, but had trouble in plenty besides, notably over the question of yearly meetings which the king still hoped to deny; also over the condemnation of the *Large Declaration* issued earlier in the year in Charles's name, the handling of deposed ministers, for whom Charles had had high hopes, and the administration of ex-episcopal patronage.[10] On the vexed question of the membership of assemblies, the Covenanters had failed to win Charles over at Berwick, but it was no deterrent to action. Before the assembly a memorandum was circulated to encourage the re-election of those who had been commissioners at Glasgow.[11] Charles, little moved, wrote that he allowed a free assembly and parliament, but this did not by any means guarantee that he would 'ratify all their fancies or anything derogatory to royal authority'.[12] But what would he approve? There were plainly opposing ideas of freedom: to hold the middle ground required something little short of acrobatics.

Traquair's behaviour with the Covenant pushed ambiguous courses to their limits. The assembly wanted the text to stand as revised after Glasgow. Traquair signed it with the assembly on its last day of meeting, 30 August,

[8] Stevenson, *The Scottish Revolution 1637–1644* (Newton Abbot, 1974), pp. 163–4. For the draft Act, and the copy sent to Court, see NLS Wod. Fo. 63, fols. 117–18; GD 406/M1/69.
[9] GD 406/1/900; Burnet, *Memoires*, pp. 156–7; Traqr. Mss. Bundle 28[iii] – letters of 10 Aug. to marquis, 24 Aug. to king and to marquis, 30 Aug. to king.
[10] Besides assembly records, see Traquair's letters, especially of 21 Aug. to marquis, 26 Aug. to marquis and to king, of 1 Sept. to king – Traqr. Mss. Bundle 28[iii], Traqr. Ms. 12/35; also GD 406/M1/39, M1/70. For the Instructions (Burnet, *Memoires*, pp. 149–51), see above chapter 4.
[11] NLS Wod. Fo. 63, fol. 84.
[12] Traqr. Ms. 4/117 (29 Aug., incomplete in *HMC 9 (II)*, p. 249).

and afterwards in response to a petition permitted a privy council order to back national subscription. Only on the band could Traquair make some progress with a modifying statement that announced signatories would be bound to join together as commanded by royal authority as well as for the more unlimited defence of the king in preservation of religion, liberties and laws. The act of council made no conditions regarding the interpretation of the Covenant, and was used as justification for a nationwide campaign thereafter to compel subscription.[13] However, what Traquair had meant when he signed was the point of controversy. The manœuvring in which he involved himself stretched understanding at Court then, and provoked the Covenanters to bitter attacks later.

Apparently he signed first as Commissioner, making reference to the Covenant's meaning as found in 1580, 1581 and 1590, but also unconditionally as a private individual.[14] He further made a closing declaration which restated his approval of the Act of 17 August, and protested firmly against the king being committed further, such as to the retrospective approval of Glasgow or necessarily to reform in church patronage or the civil places of churchmen.[15] This naturally moved his opponents to argue the interpretation of the 1581 Confession which in their minds underlay the reforms, though it had not been explicitly stated; they refused to allow the declaration to be entered in the official assembly record. Consequently, when Traquair again subscribed the Covenant, in the two ways, on 6 September in the Articles, he had his declaration entered instead in the book of the privy council, dated as 30 August; Huntly and others tried to subscribe the Covenant on 11 September with the proviso that they complied with this declaration.[16]

Charles noted the ambiguity of the act of council; Traquair defended it by observing the advantage of not losing the face of authority despite the challenge against the original instructions to him.[17] The king allowed it, but the earl's device forced the differences with the Covenanting leadership into the open. Whether or not Traquair had adequately covered himself by protestations during the assembly, his critics argued now that he threatened

---

[13] *RPCS*, 2nd Series, vol. VII, pp. 131–2; Traqr. Ms. 14/10; draft in NLS Wod. Fo. 63, fols. 252–3; *CSPD 1639*, 428/36. Whether the Covenanters had held off pressing for nationwide subscription before this time was contested – *CSPD 1639*, 427/104.

[14] NLS Wod. Fo. 63, fol. 233; cf. Traqr. Ms. 8/6; [Charles I], *A Large Declaration*, STC 21906 (1639), pp. 66–8.

[15] *RPCS*, 2nd Series, vol. VII, pp. 132–3.

[16] 'Anent Acts of 17 and 30 August' – Traqr. Mss. Bundle x; *APS*, vol. V, pp. 593, 599; GD 112/39/786; Traqr. Ms. 12/35 – letters of 1 Sept. to king, 4 Sept. to marquis, 15 Sept. to king; NLS Wod. Fo. 64, fols. 4v, 227; Traqr. Ms. 4/121; Traqr. Mss. Trial VI, VII. The various disputes make the issue still very confusing!

[17] Traqr. Ms. 14/17.

to destroy its achievement. He had never in fact been free to do otherwise, and the Covenanters ably exploited this. As the Earl of Lauderdale said, there was no dealing with anyone at the assembly since whatever was urged there was described as articles of faith. The loss of trust in the king had reversed the previous order of whose religion should prevail in the kingdom.[18]

As a means of settlement, parliaments and general assemblies together had captured most people's hopes in the early days of the troubles; by 1639 they were understood to be themselves part of the settlement. A programme of constitutional reform was contemplated. The line-up of social forces was already familiar from the course of the troubles; nobles, now in particular Argyll and Rothes, would be prominent, but not without significant showings from the other groups in Scottish society. The organisation of the Covenant movement, with the Tables at the centre and various committees in the peripheries, had indeed encouraged this. For parliaments, the abolition of episcopacy opened up possibilities. There was a desire to escape from the domination of parliaments by the Lords of the Articles, a move for more to be achieved in plenary sessions – as happened in England, for example. As a replacement for the bishops, an estate might be formed by the lairds in their own right, instead of their being counted alongside commissioners for burghs; thus there would be still three estates to elect representatives on to the Articles. The church would not need representatives since all conclusive legislation would first proceed through assemblies. In sum the parliament would be far less within royal control than before.[19]

Representatives for both shires and burghs were also keen to formulate numerous proposals for the resumption of ordinary government to be considered by the parliament now due to meet, a reflection on how reformation excitement had extended to matters civil as well as ecclesiastical. Five principal demands sent up to Court from the gentry on 30 August 1639 were but a foretaste of numerous items raised in separate documents. Recent policies for the king's cause were within the background to the first two, which concerned the issue of relief of debts and the selection and jurisdiction of sheriffs. Then appeals were made for consent by nobles or gentry to be necessary for appointments or dismissals from the court of session, and for annual conventions for the gentry such as the burghs already enjoyed, so that there might be a forum for presenting grievances to the privy council. There was clear innovation here on both counts; the appointments proposal, again perhaps recently born, entrenched most directly on the prerogative. The last

---

[18] GD 406/1/1022; cf. NLS Wod. Fo. 63, fol. 204; *Diary of Sir Archibald Johnston, Lord Wariston, 1639*, ed. G. M. Paul, SHS (Edinburgh, 1896), p. 79.

[19] Traqr. Mss. 28[iii] (21, 30 Aug.); Traqr. Ms. 12/35 (4, 15 Sept.); Stevenson, *Scottish Revolution*, pp. 166–9.

matter touched on was the work of the Lords of the Articles.[20] Charles had given little advance thought to legislation to be proposed from below. On the constitutional question, however, Traquair's instructions had anticipated the problem arising from the lack of bishops. Before he had heard any news of the parliament itself, Charles utterly rejected the alternative overtures. As a token, he offered verbal assurance against the defrauding of creditors.[21]

In the first instance the parliament had been requested as the necessary means of sealing church legislation, and Traquair was keen to move Charles to allow the maximum concessions, at least for the present, and particularly by ratifying in parliament the principal legislation of the assembly. The purely civil programme was something different, and it seemed to Traquair that 'many of the better sort' might be happy to be guided.[22] It was in this context that the discussion applied of the probable civil obedience of the Earl of Montrose; Traquair's assessment with respect to him was confirmed by the Earl of Airth and Menteith, recently reappointed a privy councillor, who tried independently to keep the king informed of proceedings. Despite Charles's stance on the church, Traquair would try hard to persuade people of the advantages of resting content with a simple resolution in that area – where the troubles overtly had had their origin.[23]

Traquair's hopes were not without foundation. Now, with this parliament – such as had been awaited from the outset of the troubles – the language of conciliation could open new breaches in the Covenanting movement. Certainly, as in the history of the troubles, breaches involved more than the ideology through which the king and Covenanter leaders expressed their differences. For Montrose, rivalry with Argyll may have played its part, with dislike of pressing the king too far through both kingdoms; Traquair's own relationship with Argyll was strained.[24] Weariness of drawn-out courses may have influenced others, perhaps also fear that the troubles could be getting out of control. The splits came despite intensive organisation of arguments for a united line, but the far-reaching demands now made pressed the likelihood of peace ever further away. Cooperation with discontented Englishmen

---

[20] GD 406/M1/68. Cf. above, p. 21; A. Collins (ed.), *Letters and Memorials of State* (2 vols., 1746), vol. II, pp. 613–14; NLS Wod. Fo. 64, fols. 78–81 (n.b. Rothes's marginalia); also *Information from the Estaits . . . of Scotland*, Aldis 967 (n.p., 1640), pp. 17–20; *A True Representation of the Proceedings of . . . Scotland*, Aldis 981 (n.p., 1640), second part.

[21] NLS Wod. Fo. 64, fol. 3 (Hamilton draft, GD 406/1/585).

[22] Traqr. Ms. 12/35 (4 Sept.). Among his efforts to win support, see Traqr. Ms. 14/16.

[23] Traqr. Ms. 7/10A; M. Napier (ed.), *Memorials of Montrose and his Times*, MC, vol. I (Edinburgh, 1848), p. 258; BL Add. Ms. 11045, fol. 45v; Add. Ms. 23112, fol. 94; GD 49/513–14.

[24] Cf. E. C. Cowan, *Montrose. For Covenant and King* (1977); D. Stevenson, *Alasdair MacColla and the Highland Problem in the Seventeenth Century* (Edinburgh, 1980). For Traquair's strained relationship with Argyll, see Traqr. Ms. 12/35 (27 Sept.); Traqr. Mss. Trial VI, VII.

might also have been counter-productive; encouragement to conclusions in the general assembly was no doubt appreciated, but how many were happy about the massive questions involved in any possible operation to influence events within England?[25] However, the breaches could serve the king only if he allowed it; the parliament had to fulfil its purpose of ratifying at least church reform as far as it had now gone.

If Charles still pressed hard on unaccommodating courses, unity amongst the Covenanters was more likely. The king had no desire for this parliament, fenced (formally opened) on 31 August, to last long. He would allow ratification of assembly Acts – but without any coercive sanction, a poor half-way compromise which marked his distaste for the presbyterian proceedings. It remained the case that all matters which exceeded the original instructions should be resisted by means of the negative voice. It gave Traquair very little room for movement, even though the king apparently wished to protect himself against public challenge on his future intentions. Where he expressed his feelings of principle to Traquair, they were not for public advertisement.[26]

For replacement of the bishops in this present parliament, Charles had no intention of effecting anything permanent; his concession that laymen might be used was to be unique. Bishops had latterly dominated the process of electing the Lords of the Articles; but Traquair had permission to choose the noble members himself – if that was advisable – which he did despite great protestations on the other side that this likewise should not count as a binding precedent.[27] For the bishops' estate now made vacant, Traquair adopted hopes early on of using abbots and priors, equally royal nominees, which was legally justifiable by statutes in force, although none presently held such titles; he probably meant them to be laymen.[28]

Sir Thomas Hope, the King's Advocate, was helpful here in giving advice. His attitude towards having the lairds counted as the third estate was cool, probably on account of concern lest it overshadow and discredit the more worthy aim of having the Acts of the general assembly ratified. For him the Act of 17 August had been climactic, the 'unspeakable joy of all them that fears the Lord and waits for his salvation'.[29] While protestations were being made in plenty against the procedure of choosing the Articles, introduction of the general assembly Acts was withheld by the hard-core, who argued that what was not done now was lost for ever. Sir Thomas Hope most often made

[25] Cf. Traqr. Mss. 28[iii] (10 Aug.); Traqr. Ms. 8/6.
[26] Traqr. Ms. 8/7, 4/121; NLS Wod. Fo. 64, fols. 2–3, 22.
[27] Burnet, Memoires, pp. 149–51; GD 406/1/900; HMC 9 (II), p. 249; NLS Wod. Fo. 64, fol. 22; APS, vol. V, pp. 252–4; GD 112/39/786; Stevenson, Scottish Revolution, pp. 170–1.
[28] Traqr. Mss. 28[iii] (21, 26 Aug.).
[29] A Diary of the Public Correspondence of Sir Thomas Hope of Craighall, Bart., 1633–1645, ed. T. Thomson, BC (Edinburgh, 1843), pp. 104, 106–7, 92.

the counter-protestations for the king – much to the displeasure of the Earl of Rothes and others.[30] Charles, perhaps on account of the nature of Hope's religion, was hardly enthusiastic about this abbots and priors proposal. A true clerical third estate was not in Sir Thomas Hope's mind.[31]

The business of the parliament was focused, as in the past, in the meeting of the Articles. On the one hand the priority of ratifying the principal assembly Acts dominated – including an Act Rescissory to repeal all contradictory legislation, most notably anything in favour of episcopacy; on the other was the process of legislating on the constitution of parliaments. The Articles easily approved the Acts of 17 and 30 August; Traquair was obliged by his instructions to register declarations which reserved to the king a future right to question.[32] The Act Rescissory caused bigger trouble for him, despite help from Sir Thomas Hope, who tried in his own way to keep it conducive to the king's service. The text positively upheld the presbyterian 'Golden Act' of 1592 and annulled legislation in favour of episcopacy and the Perth Articles; Charles would not welcome it and yet Johnston and Hope of Craighall were in agreement. Reasons of principle and three-kingdom politics together kept the king more desirous of a rupture than of ratification of such unacceptable legislation. Therefore, although the Act was passed in Articles on 24 September, Traquair obediently made a declaration reserving Charles's future right of challenge.[33]

At the same time a draft of an Act of Constitution had been submitted – followed by a draft composed by the Advocate.[34] The original expressed that the nobility, barons and burghs as the three estates had full and undoubted power, and that the present meeting was a precedent for the future; and went on to repeat the repeal of the Jacobean statutes which established bishops as the third estate.[35] Sir Thomas Hope's draft was apparently sparse by comparison. It acknowledged that this was a full and good parliament, but made reference to the right of abbots and priors to sit as the third estate. This was passed in the Articles, also on 24 September – but it was left to the king to consider and signify his pleasure to the next parliament.[36]

---

[30] *APS*, vol. V, pp. 252–4; Hope, *Diary*, pp. 104, 107, 112.
[31] NLS Wod. Fo. 64, fols. 2, 22.
[32] *APS*, vol. V, pp. 593, 598.
[33] NLS Wod. Fo. 64, fols. 47, 22, 123; *APS*, vol. V, pp. 594, 599, 601; Traqr. Mss. Bundle 27 – 'Acts of the noblemen . . .'.
[34] 7, 12 Sept. – *APS*, vol. V, pp. 594, 598.
[35] EUL New College Ms. X15b 3/1, vol. I, fol. 218.
[36] *APS*, vol. V, pp. 599, 601. I have not found a copy of the text. See *Hope's Major Practicks*, *1608– 1633*, ed. J. A. Clyde, Stair Society (Edinburgh, 1937), pp. 12, 14, 28; Hope, *Diary*, p. 107; Traqr. Ms. 12/35 (15 Sept.); GD 112/40/2/2/34, 32. The arguments penned at least partly by Johnston of Wariston are our fullest indirect source – 'Our prejudices from the reference of the act of constitution' – NLS Wod. Fo. 64, fols. 25–6; 'Anent the act of constitution drawn by the Advocate and passed in the Articles' and 'Anent the act of constitution given in by us and in the Articles referred to the king' – Traqr. Mss. Bundle x.

Argyll and Rothes 'and many others' supported the more radical measure.[37] Wariston, in his characteristic role, amended and probably composed the works of propaganda written to persuade a general agreement on this programme. In papers dated 15 and 20 September, he emphasised the need to remove all claims of bishops to sit in parliaments, and tried to confute as the main objection the argument that this diminished the king's power. Subsequently he responded pointedly to the Advocate's ideas for abbots and priors. The rhetoric of the duty owed to God was as prominent as ever. Traquair gathered copies of these papers as best he could; some at least got to Court.[38]

These two principal bills were made to link with one another in a tactical move by Johnston of Wariston and his fellows. They proposed that the Act Rescissory should include within it a denial of all parliamentary rights to abbots and priors. Sir Thomas Hope received a rebuff, but the general issue of the third estate was seriously divisive. Traquair for his part forwarded yet another idea to the king, given to him not from Sir Thomas Hope but from some nobles and others who had met with him and some of the privy council. This was for the fourteen ex-bishops' places to be taken by six earls' sons in their majority, five lairds and three burgesses. It was a compromise not so generous to the lairds as the proposal for honouring them as a full estate. Traquair could claim the support of some noblemen on the Articles – but not enough to outnumber others joined with gentry and burghs against him. The king, however, rejected any permanent proposal for substitutes for the bishops.[39]

The more extreme lines of reform were insistently pressed. The implications of Traquair's saving declarations were exploited; it was seen as worrying that he yet again had avoided being fully committed to the achievements of the general assembly, and unacceptable that there was a loophole for the king to allow prelates to sit in future parliaments. Writing was accompanied by action, but not just on the commonly agreed church issues. Lord Loudoun and others not technically members of the Articles protested on 26 September and produced the alternative Act of Constitution to go through the Articles. They rejected both the Act referred and the action of reference, and looked for support from the prospective meeting of the parliament in full session. At least one relatively uncontentious matter could be said

---

[37] Traqr. Ms. 12/35 (4, 15 Sept.).
[38] NLS Wod. Fo. 64, fols. 5–6, 9–10, 13–14, 15, 19–20, 25–6; EUL Ms. X15b 3/1, vol. I, fols. 217–19; Traqr. Mss. Bundle x; GD 406/M1/87, M9/93/41, 45; PRO SP 16/432/51.
[39] APS, vol. V, p. 599; Traqr. Ms. 12/35 (19 Sept.); GD 112/40/2/2/34, 31; NLS Wod. Fo. 64, fol. 22.

to be at issue. Traquair's manœuvre had in effect left this present parliament without valid status.[40]

Traquair would suffer at Court for allowing the action of Loudoun and his group but, as he then said, he had been powerless to stop it.[41] The argument as to the validity of the parliament was reasonable and Traquair, unless authorised, could only engage in verbal assurances as reply; the agenda behind the Loudoun manœuvre was the original form of the Act of Constitution, however, which was not Traquair's first line of concern. As a concession, it was proposed on the Covenanters' side that the clause applying to future parliament meetings be dropped. The issue of triennial meetings was not even explicitly in question at this point; the point offered indicated a hesitancy about encroaching on the king's parliamentary power – the crisis would have moved on by 1640. For the present the hard-liners had little joy, for there were others whose support Traquair cultivated. Nevertheless the irony was that, if the king's ecclesiastical stance was taken unmodified, Sir Thomas Hope and his sort had little about which to be satisfied. Logically Traquair ought to have appealed to the king to allow true grounds on which to rebuild trust between him and his subjects. Because of Charles's rigid stand, he could only try to phrase arguments for the advantage of *interim* peaceable conclusions.[42]

Always the king limited the achievement of conciliation by the counsellor. If the counsellor was to give advice at all, caution had to be observed; if he was to keep his position, he had to have his work approved. Traquair asked for the king's comment on his declarations, and Charles noted a mistake: the earl had allowed the word 'unlawful'. This went further than 'abolished within this kirk', since what was absolutely unlawful in one church could not be lawful in another professing the same religion, whether episcopacy or the civil powers and places of kirkmen. The word comprehended God's law; it was not authorised within the earl's instructions, and most certainly not for any parliamentary Act.[43] Charles was thus far correct; Traquair dutifully explained how he had used this compromise in order to satisfy religious discontent yet without agreeing to abjuration on account of the Word of God – an action in the interests of peace, not intended to disturb the church of England 'nor his Majesty's own judgement'.[44]

[40] *APS*, vol. V, pp. 602–3; Traqr. Mss. 28[iii] (6 Oct.). The papers of arguments in circulation (n. 38) again are a vital source.

[41] Traqr. Ms. 14/17.

[42] Traqr. Mss. Bundle 27 – 'Acts of the noblemen . . . '; Bundle x – 'Anent the act of constitution'; Traqr. Ms. 12/35 (15, 19, 27 Sept.).

[43] Traqr. Ms. 12/35 (27 Sept.); NLS Wod. Fo. 64, fol. 22; Burnet, *Memoires*, pp. 158–9. The marked copy of the declaration is in Traqr. Mss. 28[iii].

[44] Traqr. Mss. 28[iii] (6 Oct.). Traquair had mentioned the word 'unlawful' to cover himself on 10 August, but it had not been picked up – letter in Traqr. Mss. 28[iii]. Cf. *HMC De L'Isle* (77) vol. VI, p. 199; BL Add. Ms. 11045, fol. 68.

Traquair went as far as he dared. Despite the king's lack of commitment to the Scottish assemblies, ground had been made, and might yet be made, for the sake of peace. Trying his best to moderate Charles's inevitable displeasure at his letter, Traquair also took the step on 6 October of sending Lord Dalzell in person to convey the still optimistic message that division might be managed – by a means not to be set down on paper. He disputed Charles's willingness for a rupture: if people could be satisfied with the Acts of the assembly and allowing of the Covenant, it was quite probable that in civil matters the king could get his own way.[45]

Sir Thomas Hope must have regretted the Commissioner's conditional approval of the assembly Acts, yet on many other matters he served Traquair and the king well. He believed that the king's role in the constitutional questions was fundamental.[46] It is an open question how many might have followed him out of the present mainstream Covenant politics given the chance; but it was here that Traquair was concentrating his attention. As Dalziel was sent off, the future organisation of the Lords of the Articles was the prominent issue and there was a question of referring this in its entirety to the king. Traquair tried his strength and found a result in the Articles very like his assessment of mid-September when the same subject was under debate: Roxburgh, Huntly, Marischal, Montrose, Lauderdale and Southesk voted for referral to the king, together with three officers of state, the Advocate, the Justice-clerk, Sir John Hamilton of Orbiston, and the Treasurer-depute, Sir James Carmichael, but of the rest only the Lairds of Cavers (the Sheriff of Teviotdale) and Lag and the commissioner for Aberdeen joined. All the rest, a majority, although only of two, voted for referral to the parliament in full session – as with the legislation for the constitution of parliaments.[47]

Traquair's effort was defeated narrowly by the hard-liners around him. As usual, a paper had been written to try to keep them together.[48] His attempt the day before this vote to raise the pressure by privately intimating the riding of the parliament (here: a formal procession at its end) could not be sustained; he consented to postpone the end, and was obliged to make this public. In the event the riding was to be postponed eight times. Traquair's fear was that the parliament might sit on regardless of his order; members were as concerned that they should have an opportunity to vote on legislation before any conclusion.[49] Far-reaching propositions continued to be made. The lairds'

---

[45] Traqr. Mss. 28[iii] (6, 8 Oct.). Dalzell was already the Earl of Carnwath.
[46] *APS*, vol. V, pp. 593, 594, 598, 599, 601, 602, 607; *Hope's Major Practicks*, esp. p. 1; Hope, *Diary*, p. 115.
[47] GD 112/39/789; Stevenson, *Scottish Revolution*, pp. 174–5.
[48] NLS Wod. Fo. 64, fols. 15, 19.
[49] Traqr. Ms. 14/12; Traqr. Mss. 28[iii]; GD 112/39/791; Sir J. Balfour, *Historical Works* (4 vols., Edinburgh, 1824–5), vol. II, pp. 351–2; EUL New College Ms. X15b 3/1 vol. I, fols. 217–19.

demand for each to have a single vote instead of one per county addressed a constitutional issue; more directly challenging to the king's authority was the demand for parliamentary control of appointments to the commands of castles, or the one for the conduct of privy councillors and sessioners to be censurable by parliaments. Neither here in Scotland nor subsequently in England could Charles entertain such presumptions. Later, in his defence, Traquair said that most of the major bills originated in the Articles, where for the nobles sat most notably Argyll, Rothes and Lindsay; a contemporary account was that bills principally, although not entirely, of narrower import were presented daily from the gentry and burghs.[50] The truth is that these lower social groups were as capable as the nobles of forwarding major items, as can be seen from the extremely long list of 'Instructions' from the gentry to the Lords of the Articles available by 6 October; there was likewise one from the burghs.[51]

State as well as church was the object of reformation. Was it a reflection on problem-filled years under Charles I, or perhaps on a longer period in the context of the Union and 'British' government? To what extent did it pick up on the deep forces of social and economic change in Scotland aside from 1603 and its consequences? There are no simple answers here, and much careful research remains to be done.[52] Social distinctions carried through, yet individuals like Argyll and Rothes had the interests of many parties to consider. Charles's offence which had brought the political opportunity and occasion was only a part, albeit a vital one, of the whole picture.

The king's intransigence had given presbyterianism the advantage in Scotland and, if at heart many Scots were not represented by that radical line, some of the multitude of civil proposals were also divisive. Two notable points in Wariston's programme at Berwick did not even see the light in the 1639 parliament: triennial parliaments, as has been noticed, and the demand for parliamentary consent to major appointments. Disagreements and divisions were doubtless repeated in the country at large, but at the same time there were signs that active dissent was to become a punishable offence. Persecution began at the centre, with the more extreme Act of Constitution

---

[50] Traqr. Ms. 14/17; GD 112/40/2/2/28; GD 406/M9/88/4. The draft Act for the Articles provided that all bills in future should be presented to parliament in full session – NLS Wod. Fo. 64, fol. 48. For England, see A. Fletcher, *The Outbreak of the English Civil War* (1981), pp. 55–9, 136–46.

[51] *APS*, vol. V, p. 614; Traqr. Mss. 28[iii] (6, 13, 19 Oct.); GD 406/M1/76; L. B. Taylor (ed.), *Aberdeen Council Letters*, vol. II (1950), pp. 145–8; Traqr. Ms. 14/19; BL Add. Ms. 11045, fol. 65.

[52] Cf. W. Makey, *The Church of the Covenant* (Edinburgh, 1979); A. I. Macinnes, 'The origin and organization of the Covenanting movement during the reign of Charles I, 1625–1641; with a particular reference to the west of Scotland' (unpublished University of Glasgow Ph.D. dissertation, 1988).

striking against not just the bishops but against all those absent from their summons; the 'well-affected' had been positively encouraged to attend. Traquair rose to the defence over this, hoping to serve his ends, not to mention those of the king.[53]

Another major piece of legislation over which Traquair struggled was an Act of Pacification which was supposed to enact the king's concession at Berwick for an Oblivion. There were two parts fo this, a narrative section describing the late troubles and a legal provision for securing all subjects, whether offenders of the king or of the 'laws and liberties' of the kingdom. The earlier version of the narrative tended to be less than complimentary to the king – and Wariston was associated with its making; there was also a very clear indication of the deep opposition to any suggestion that past Covenanter conduct required a royal pardon, such as had been not only in Charles's mind at the Pacification but throughout in the thinking of Sir Thomas Hope. Agreement on a compromise form was eventually reached. Related and as troublesome was the matter of relief for aggrieved parties.[54]

Traquair might fight a very major civil programme but the king's agreement to the more generally espoused religious settlement was his other obstacle. As long as Charles refused to move on this, the earl's course had to remain ambiguous. A possible escape from giving over all advantage was to prorogue the parliament rather than attempt to end it altogether. This would avoid the potential disaster to be caused by the king breaking with church issues in the air. In Scotland it could be argued to be giving the king time to consider the civil issues raised – and direct petitioning of him might be encouraged, which would draw out time. Traquair's hope was for the possible settlement of peace; but Charles would in any case be agreeable given the schedule for his military design.[55]

The hard-liners, all along suspicious even to the point of aggression of the king's future intentions, hoped to secure a final settlement on their own terms within this present parliament. From early on in its sitting, they had considered directing approaches to Charles to try to oblige him to state his position unambiguously. Their opposition to a premature end to the parliament was readily reformulated as opposition to the idea of a prorogation; they argued that prorogation needed the consent of the Estates, and devoted

---

[53] Johnston, *1639 Diary*, pp. 73–4; NLS Wod. Fo. 54, fols. 328–9 (a list of absents); Wod. Fo. 63, fol. 99; Wod. Fo. 64, fols. 37–9; EUL New College Ms X15b 3/1 vol. I, fol. 217v; Traqr. Mss. 28[iii] (6 Oct.); BL Add. Ms. 11045, fols. 55, 59. The Act against leasingmakers was to be revived – *APS*, vol. V, pp. 604, 607.

[54] *APS*, vol. V, pp. 607, 609, 611, 613, 615; GD 112/40/2/2/31; GD 16/40/5; *CSPD 1639–40*, 432/52. Five drafts of the Act of Pacification survive – NLS Wod. Fo. 64, fols. 27, 29–30, 31, 58, 60.

[55] Traqr. Mss. 28[iii] (6, 8 Oct.).

considerable energy to persuading the Estates that it was not to be desired unless various conditions were first fulfilled.[56]

Charles took what he wanted from Traquair's advice. It is worth noting incidentally that, while Traquair was assured of the king's trust, Charles at least received information from other sources. The Earl of Airth's report in mid-September sounded critical that Traquair discussed all affairs in private with an 'officer of state' who was among those the king had wanted watched. Traquair had indeed been directed, and on his own advice prior to the parliament, that Sir Thomas Hope should be used as little as possible.[57] Given Hope's service, that was a small problem, but Airth interestingly asked the king's directions on the matter of signing the Covenant and giving advice to Traquair; Charles did not encourage the former nor, however, the latter – 'For I suspect the issue will not be so fair but that he [Traquair] will be glad to lay the burden on other men's shoulders.'[58] The king had no expectation of a good outcome from Traquair's labours. Another aspiring counsellor, the Earl of Nithsdale, came close to meeting Charles's true spirit. As the Edinburgh General Assembly drew to a close, Nithsdale explained how, as he had feared at Berwick, prospects were growing ever bleaker. He criticised the king's agents, who would make 'a molehill into a mountain'. The criticism necessarily hit Hamilton as much as Traquair; Nithsdale made his addresses firstly to Secretary Windebank in his effort to insinuate himself once more into the king's close counsel. To judge by results, he was not immediately successful; perhaps Hamilton blocked the message en route.[59]

Charles's response to Dalzell's information was delayed while he took consultation on 'kingly ways'. Admittedly at this time, English domestic concerns must have taken some attention, but Wentworth had arrived, and with Hamilton and Laud also the Scottish situation was discussed. About 20 October, a new committee for Scotland was formed, with a corresponding increase of involvement for people like the Earl of Northumberland. More specific orders and arrangements began to be made, for instance concerning the border garrisons.[60] Charles was prepared to concede the prorogation idea, but his interpretation of it was quite plain.

Two letters were addressed to Traquair on 19 October. One was a version

---

[56] Traqr. Ms. 12/35 (15 Sept.); GD 406/M9/67/4; BL Add. Ms. 11045, fols. 58v, 60; GD 406/M1/87; R. S. Rait, *The Parliaments of Scotland* (Glasgow, 1924), p. 339.

[57] Traqr. Ms. 8/8, 7/10A.

[58] GD 406/M1/39; GD 406/1/1070; Napier, *Memorials of Montrose*, vol. I, pp. 251–4. Airth's contact at Court, James Livingstone, was also a correspondent with Hope! – Hope, *Diary*, p. 106.

[59] *CSPD 1639*, 427/100.

[60] Cf. Traqr. Ms. 12/28; S. R. Gardiner, *History of England . . . 1603–1642* (10 vols., 1883–4), vol. IX, pp. 56–69; Collins, *Letters*, vol. II, pp. 613–15; *CSPD 1639–40*, 431/53. Cf. lack of news in BL Add. Ms. 11045, fol. 70.

designed for public consumption, and it stated that matters in debate required 'greater conference' with the Commissioner and some other privy councillors; therefore the parliament should be prorogued to a time thought 'satisfactory to the subjects'. No possible supporters were to be lost.[61] The second version of the same letter, drawn up by Hamilton with Charles's holograph corrections, was rather less polite. It was evident, wrote the king, that the subjects aimed not for religion but at the 'whole frame' of Scottish government and for the 'total overthrow' of royal authority. Dissolution was the only proper course, but a prorogation might be conceded, to 2 June of the next year – and the enemies' reasons for their proceedings would be heard. Traquair was to attend Court with all the relevant papers and having consulted with the council and others on how to settle the business; and the Covenanters might send representatives to Court, whom Traquair would name once the parliament was prorogued.[62] The tactics appeared careful to retain and increase all possible support and to that extent had taken on board Scottish advice; Lord Dalzell also wrote, encouraging Traquair to work on those whose support he had by great labour won – the names of the Earls Marischal and Montrose were mentioned – and yet the king offered no substantial concession. Only a part of Traquair's message had penetrated.[63]

The prorogation therefore was Traquair's last battle with the parliament in 1639. With the hard-liners he opposed their arguments for the need for consent to the action, believing it to be only the thin edge of the wedge, tending towards a precedent whereby parliaments could only be interrupted or broken up with their own consent. With Charles he had a hard struggle to gain some kind of acknowledgement for the validity of the present parliament, as an expedient to draw support, if nothing else. In passion of argument to Court, he staked his personal continuance as Commissioner on the point. Similarly with the unsettled church business, he tried to persuade that ratification of assembly business was the only means to a sure division. The Pacification of Berwick had to be seen to be honoured; there was a risk otherwise, he wrote, of 'universal opposition' in England to any forthcoming war.[64]

As events built to a head, Traquair with the privy council sent the Earl of Kinnoull to negotiate with Charles concerning the prorogation; the Covenanters themselves tried without success to obtain a warrant for the Earl of

[61] NLS Wod. Fo. 64, fol. 32; GD 112/40/2/2/18.
[62] Traqr. Ms. 12/30, 9/1, 12/28 (19 Oct.).
[63] NLS Wod. Fo. 64, fol. 152; Traqr. Ms. 11/43; GD 406/1/1092; see too R. Baillie, *The Letters and Journals*, ed. D. Laing, BC (3 vols., Edinburgh, 1841–2), vol. I, p. 224.
[64] Traqr. Mss. 28[iii] (27, 31 Oct.); *APS*, vol. V, p. 616; Hope, *Diary*, p. 109; GD 112/40/2/2/18; GD 406/M1/87; GD 406/1/1118; NLS Wod. Fo. 63, fol. 99; Balfour, *Historical Works*, vol. II, pp. 351–2.

Dunfermline and Lord Loudoun to go on an immediate embassy south.[65] They travelled then without it, but Charles was utterly dismissive towards them; he was little better about yielding ground on his ideas about the status of the sitting parliament, more concerned that Edinburgh Castle should be well secured for defence, which was done by General Ruthven, now Lord Ettrick.[66] Finally the parliament was prorogued, on 14 November 1639, without the consent of the Estates, but not without trouble and a remonstrance to the king. The latter was used to justify a continuing central organisation for the Covenanters, for, while the king's answer was awaited, a Committee of Estates was appointed to remain in Edinburgh to represent the parliament. For practical reasons, not everyone could stay put, as was originally intended; but it was a clear enough statement of political defiance.[67]

Traquair would not have underestimated his contribution for strengthening the royal cause in Scotland, but Charles was going on with his war almost regardless of it. Only on his own terms did he, at the same time, receive any who came to him. One of these was the Earl of Seaforth, whose name was linked with an anti-Covenanter plot; he was given warrant to come up to Court on 19 September.[68] More significantly Montrose and a number of others received a prompt invitation at the ending of the parliament; Sir Thomas Hope was included as evidently back within favour.[69] Montrose for one had suggested such a summons on 1 November, when in a letter to Charles he declared his distaste at the course of proceedings in Scotland, counting himself amongst those 'most faithfully disposed' to the royal service. There was no doubt some subtlety here, with perhaps advice from a privy councillor like Roxburgh to him to write the letter; but it was an approach that fell flat. Charles responded but Montrose excused himself,

[65] Traqr. Mss. 28[iii] (1, 5 Nov.); *RPCS*, 2nd Series, vol. VII, p. 139; EUL New College Ms. X15b 3/1 vol. I, fols. 213–14. Patrick Maule of Panmure also went south at this time – Hope, *Diary*, p. 110.
[66] Traqr. Ms. 12/26, 12/29 (cf. incomplete copy in NLS Wod. Fo. 64, fol. 44); D. Dalrymple, *Memorials and Letters Relating to the History of Britain in the Reign of Charles the First* (Glasgow, 1766), pp. 76–7; Baillie, *Letters*, vol. II, pp. 449–50; GD 406/1/1092, 929; Traqr. Ms. 9/11.
[67] *APS*, vol. V, pp. 255–8; *RPCS*, 2nd Series, vol. VII, pp. 141–2; GD 112/40/2/2/53; PRO SP 16/475/97; Stevenson, *Scottish Revolution*, pp. 176–8; NLS Wod. Fo. 64, fol. 125. For the remonstrance sent south, see PRO SP 16/436/4; GD 406/1/1125; Balfour, *Historical Works*, vol. II, pp. 367–9.
[68] Traqr. Ms. 12/34, 12/28; *HMC 9 (II)*, p. 254 (Traqr. Ms. 14/14, 15 – which show little in addition apart from the important point that Sir James Lamont went to work while the parliament sat; Sir W. Fraser, *Memorials of the Earls of Haddington* (2 vols., Edinburgh, 1889), vol. II, p. 182.
[69] GD 220/3/85; Fraser, *Haddington*, vol. II, pp. 177, 179; Lord Lindsay, *Lives of the Lindsays*, vol. II (1849), p. 35; NLS Crawford Ms. 14/7/23; Sir W. Fraser, *The Red Book of Menteith* (2 vols., Edinburgh, 1880), vol. II, p. 61; BL Add. Ms. 11045, fol. 83; Hope, *Diary*, p. 113.

declining to leave the Covenanter fold – where, it might be noted, he was kept very welcome, if nothing else in the interests of continuing the face of internal unity.[70] Sir Thomas Hope did not move either – and quickly became once more the object of the king's wrath.[71]

The king only felt the need to have the relevant parties answer before him. Both Traquair and the Covenanter delegates to whom Charles now made the gesture of inviting south had to defend their conduct.[72] While the king attempted to assert his own line in all the various exchanges, Traquair's efforts of conciliation were in effect brushed aside. He was obliged to make a report of his commission before the full English privy council, which the Covenanters made out as the significant background to the determination made for a second war effort. A sense of national identity, but much more than that, was offended in this unprecedented account given of the proceedings of representative assemblies: it could be argued that laws, liberties and independence were at once trodden down. Since Traquair did not speak sympathetically, his reputation in Scotland all but collapsed.[73] It is notable that Hamilton, who had also given a report, escaped heavy censure; he had done well to retreat from the limelight. Traquair did keep the king's favour, though, through all the charges made against him – a comment that through his ambiguous manoeuvrings he had managed, just, to act the royal servant; against the Covenanters, Charles would intend to preserve him.

While probably the loss of a significant division in the Covenanting movement was the cost once again of Charles's intransigence, English interest outside the Court was another dimension to the king's Scottish troubles in late 1639. One of the great concerns in Charles's mind had been about the British dimension of over-large concessions on episcopacy in Scotland; he might justifiably have worried about more than that, given the many aspects of the Scottish affair that later seemed to be imitated, or at least repeated, in England from 1640. English newswriters, in particular Rossingham, regularly provided the latest items or rumours of interest to their readership, which supplemented direct channels from Scotland.[74] One report which

---

[70] GD 406/1/878; GD 220/3/85; Gardiner, *Hamilton Papers*, p. 103; Dalrymple, *Memorials*, p. 52; GD 3/5/229. Cf. *Information from the Estaits . . .* , Aldis 967 (n.p., 1640), p. 20.
[71] GD 406/1/1286 (Jan. 1640).
[72] GD 112/40/2/2/1; CSPD 1639–40, 436/32; Traqr. Ms. 14/17; Collins, *Letters*, vol. II, p. 620; Dalrymple, *Memorials*, pp. 76–7; NLS Wod. Fo. 64, fol. 43.
[73] *Information from the Estaits . . .* , pp. 9–10; Traqr. Mss. Bundle 28[iii]; Trial VI; *His Maiesties Declaration . . .* , STC 22006 (1640), p. 39. Traquair's name was also besmirched over the Lamont plot – NLS Acc. 7360; Fraser, *Haddington*, vol. III, p. 179; cf. Traqr. Mss. 28[iii] (24 Aug.); GD 406/1/8351.
[74] See BL Add. Ms. 11045; there were also Diurnal Occurrents of the Edinburgh General Assembly – PRO SP 16/427/44, 46; BL Loan 29/172, fols. 195–8; HLRO Braye Ms. 2, fols. 46–9, 50–61. Cf. for expression of interest CUL Add. Ms. 335, fol. 33v; HMC 4, p. 294.

mentioned the presence of a son of Viscount Saye and Sele, probably Nathaniel Fiennes, amongst the large number of Englishmen attending the general assembly and parliament would perhaps have been of particular concern to the king and his counsel. Traquair wrote of the son's presence in connection with 'English intelligence' – people who assured the Covenanters of their support as well as pressing for a parliament to be called in England, encouraging the drive for far-ranging ecclesiastical reform in Scotland.[75]

Scots reciprocated the interest, particularly after mid-November 1639, as the aggressive intentions of the king began to strike home. Loudoun and Dunfermline apparently distributed papers whilst they were in England, and made contact where they could; Rothes wrote to the Earl of Pembroke.[76] A new batch of printed propaganda would dwell on the evils brought about by papists and prelates in the other kingdoms. The Covenanters sought out both suppliers of news and fellow-sufferers in a quest for a common defence, a task given a particular focus once the king decided for his own ends to call an English parliament.[77] A non-parochial awareness had been manifest in some of the clearest thinking on royal authority during the sitting of the parliament; this alone could have excited interest elsewhere, though it was a sensitive subject. With this spread alongside the explicitly religious theme, the Scottish struggle would have found a cross-section of sympathisers.[78]

Samuel Rutherford almost certainly visited Warwick Castle to stay with Lord Brooke and to preach there, going first at the end of December 1639 and again three months later. Warwick Castle stood at the centre of a haven for 'puritan' preachers. While with the likelihood of a second Scottish war English nonconformist thought would generally express fears of a judgement of God, much could take off from that. Bad direction in the civil government and the church could be criticised; there were hopes for the approaching English parliament. As might be expected given the climate of suspicions and sensitivities in high government circles, the sources are relatively silent over the Scottish troubles.[79] And, though Laud and so-called Canterburian

[75] BL Add. Ms. 11045, fol. 52; Gardiner, *Hamilton Papers*, p. 263; E. Hyde, *The History of the Rebellion and Civil War in England Begun in the Year 1641*, ed. W. D. Macray (6 vols., Oxford, 1888), vol. I, p. 69; Traqr. Mss. 28[iii] (10 Aug.); Traqr. Ms. 8/6.
[76] BL Add. Ms. 4106, fols. 187–9; *CSPD 1639–40*, 432/49, 447/52; GD 406/1/883, 955, 1806, 8351; NLS Crawford Ms. 14/7/23; PRO 31/3/71, fols. 139–40.
[77] Fraser, *Haddington*, vol. II, pp. 176–7, 184; GD 406/1/1256; NLS Adv. Ms. 33.4.14, fols. 290–3; NLS Crawford Ms. 14/3/50; *CSPD 1639–40*, 447/92; EUL New College Ms X15b 3/1 vol. I, fols. 240–1; GD 112/40/2/2/15.
[78] NLS Wod. Fo. 64, fol. 14; Traqr. Mss. Bundle x – 'The resolution of particular men'. For English thought, cf. J. P. Sommerville, *Politics and Ideology in England 1603–1640* (1986).
[79] BL Add. Ms. 23146, fols. 87, 88v; Warwicks. RO CR 1886/CUP4/21A – 'gifts' (I am grateful to Dr Ann Hughes for her help here); A. Hughes, 'Thomas Dugard and his circle in the 1630s – a "Parliamentary-Puritan" connexion?', *HJ*, 29 (1986), 771–93; BL Harl. Ms. 379,

churchmanship and theology, often lumped together with the Catholics, had their opponents, criticism in the English context was not confined there. Above all, English expectations of their parliament turned first to English grievances, but insular feelings were under challenge. While leaders who embraced a British vision may have been few, the fact was that this might be the only way forward for both English and Scots. The king's troubles were spread across his kingdoms.

Charles was persuaded to summon parliaments in Ireland and England, since advice apparently coalesced that this was the best means of supply for war, at least in the first instance. Subsidies might be slow and small but they might serve as security for loans; that they constituted the 'ordinary way' was another point made, and an important one as a means of confuting the many rumours of English sympathy for the Scots which Wentworth for one believed to be more noise than substance. Though it was put to the king that the people should grant him supply, if that failed to happen, 'extraordinary' ways were to be upheld, a point hardly uncontroversial given past experience under Charles. Both Laud, who shifted from his customary antipathy, and Hamilton lent their voices to counteract the king's own contrary leanings, but Wentworth was probably the principal moving force, whose confidence that both parliaments could be managed drew heavily on his Irish experience. Though he was right to expect a good example from Ireland, this was not necessarily to be enough, but hopes for money were not focused entirely on parliament in any case; negotiations began in December 1639 for a loan from Catholic Spain, though with simultaneous discussions about a marriage alliance with the House of Orange.[80]

All councillors seemed agreed that the 'insolences' of the Covenanters had to be curbed, but Northumberland, for example, had strong feelings against the incendiaries who led for war. Most accurately this would have included Wentworth, who in December 1639 described the potential war as 'most just, necessary and honourable', but the existing correspondence between these two continued much as before. Northumberland remained hostile to what the Scots were doing but saw trouble to be as much within government as out-

fols. 60–1; Harl. Ms. 383, fols. 170v, 172; Berks. RO Trumbull Misc. XLIX, no. 37; BL Add. Ms. 35331, fol. 74v; *Winthrop Papers*, Massachusetts Historical Society, vol. IV (Boston, 1944), pp. 205, 207, 214, 218, 220, 221, 237–8, 243–4; *HMC Buccleuch* (45), vol. III, p. 382.
[80] Gardiner, *History of England*, vol. IX, pp. 75–7, 89–91; T. W. Moody, F. X. Martin and F. J. Byrne, *A New History of Ireland*, vol. III (Oxford, 1978), pp. 271–4; J. H. Elliott, 'The year of the three ambassadors', in H. Lloyd-Jones, V. Pearl and B. Worden (eds.), *History and Imagination* (Oxford, 1978), 165–81.

side it.[81] Although he was one of the most closely involved English councillors with regard to the Scottish problem, his sense of not carrying influence is good commentary on the very limited extent to which Charles shared the issues; membership of the committee re-formed in October 1639, even generalship of Charles's northern land forces such as Northumberland was given, seemed to count little. While in foreign policy his concern for the Palatinate cause could not accommodate the contemporary pro-Spanish trend, his disillusionment with Charles's leadership, and Hamilton's influence, only mounted through this period, especially when the poverty of means for the assumed war became apparent.[82]

The Spanish connection was important beyond the Court. Baillie believed that it helped to encourage unity amongst the Covenanters against the king; Spain and Catholics, no matter how financially or politically attractive as allies for Charles, offered yet more substance to fearers of the popish plot, Scottish and English.[83] France, in both foreign and domestic terms, was less attractive to Charles, not least because the Prince Elector was imprisoned there in November 1639; Secretary Windebank was once more alert for news that France was fomenting the Scottish troubles. The French in turn were highly sensitive to the turn of events in England, and it was not without significance that Lord Loudoun spoke with the ambassador Bellièvre whilst he was on his abortive mission in London.[84]

The military plans at the outset were for a larger army than before, 35,000 foot including 8,000 from Ireland, which financially seemed bound to outrun any possible parliamentary grant.[85] Strategically the priority was to secure the garrisons both in Scotland and in Berwick and elsewhere in the north, and it was for the latter particularly that Charles with some success appealed first to his lords of council, later to his Household servants, for a very substantial loan.[86] A council of war was constituted at the end of December 1639. Hamilton more than the king attended the meetings of this council, with an

[81] See Collins, *Letters*, vol. II, pp. 604–59; T. D. Whitaker (ed.), *The Life and Original Correspondence of Sir George Radcliffe* (1810), p. 191. Northumberland's attitudes are well documented, but he would not have been alone – cf. Kent AO U269/C267/6–7; BL Add. Ms. 24023, fol. 17.

[82] Collins, *Letters*, vol. II, esp. pp. 614, 617.

[83] Baillie, *Letters*, vol. I, p. 224; cf. GD 112/40/2/2/28, 20; GD 112/40/2/3/39; PRO SP 81/48, fol. 28.

[84] PRO SP 78/108, fols. 189v, 201v; SP 78/109, fols. 85–6; *CSPD 1639–40*, 439/66; *HMC De L'Isle*, vol. VI, p. 208; PRO 31/3/71, fols. 139–40, 154, and 31/3/72, fol. 16; Gardiner, *History of England*, vol. IX, pp. 91–2.

[85] *CSPD 1639–40*, 432/86; Professor Mark Fissel's study in preparation will deal thoroughly with this dimension.

[86] *CSPD 1639–40*, 432/53, 435/37, 441/29; PRO SP 78/108, fol. 209; Collins, *Letters*, vol. II, p. 629. The extensive correspondence involving Lord Ettrick and Sir Michael Ernley is mostly printed in *CSPD 1639–40* and W. D. Macray (ed.), *Ruthven Correspondence*, Roxburghe Club (1868).

appointment this time to command artillery.[87] Scots loyalists no longer constituted the leading part of the attack, although the few who resided at home were to make what stand they could.

Hamilton had done well by resigning as Commissioner, since he had had good words from both Traquair and the Covenanters at the Edinburgh General Assembly, and he still slept in the king's Bedchamber.[88] His proximity to Charles still brought him approaches from the Covenanters in the new year, for he was urged by Lord Lindsay at the end of January 1640 to work for peace and oppose any war. In one letter he sent back at the beginning of March, admittedly approved by Charles, he affirmed his past efforts for a peaceable solution, but for the most part upheld what was now being done. He was as capable of encouraging Henrietta Maria and the Catholic effort on the king's behalf.[89] To Lindsay he conceded that the way of force was undesirable, but pointed out that it was hardly desirable for Charles either – and he simply offered that Charles guaranteed 'the true Protestant religion and the laws of the kingdom'. On the question of possible foreign support for the Covenanters, he denied the implication that this could make them insuperable – a 'few factious spirits' corresponding from England could make little difference; Wentworth could not have put it better. Lindsay replied quickly, insisting not only that Charles was going the wrong way but that Covenanter strength with help from others was indeed considerable.[90] The Covenanters began their preparations, of arms and money, in great earnest – though not without their own problems of local cooperation.[91]

Nithsdale's efforts to procure the king's favour bore meagre fruit, perhaps because they were referred to Hamilton. Trying to catch the tide by writing in praise of the Lord Deputy Wentworth, he maintained that the English were better subjects than the Scots, and that the king's leading men in Scotland were 'puritan'. He denigrated those who held out hopes of a king's party. He spoke some truth, since he himself faced severe challenges locally; and

[87] PRO SP 16/441/29–30, 442/143; C 231/5, p. 366; Alnwick Mss. vol. XV, fol. 66 (BL Microfilm M286).

[88] GD 406/M1/70; Peterkin, *Records*, p. 252; *CSPD 1639–40*, 430/54.

[89] GD 406/1/1837 (n.d.).

[90] GD 406/1/1109, 1268; Burnet, *Memoires*, pp. 163–5; GD 406/1/8351. See too *HMC Hamilton Supplementary* (21), pp. 59–60.

[91] *CSPD 1639–40*, 442/134, 447/52; GD 406/1/1268, 1236; *The Journal of Thomas Cunningham of Campvere, 1640–1654*, ed. E. J. Courthope, SHS (Edinburgh, 1928). The band made for common relief on 18 January 1640 was probably genuinely meant, for the matter had not been settled in the parliament – cf. D. Stevenson, *Scottish Revolution*, p. 178; D. Stevenson, 'The financing of the cause of the covenants, 1638–1651', *SHR*, 51 (1972), 89–123. For objections to it, see NLS Wod. Fo. 64, fol. 62; GD 406/M9/89.

Traquair, back in Scotland to keep intelligence, lasted only until the end of January 1640. The Covenanters were in strength.[92]

The distance between Court and Edinburgh, or rather between the king and his subjects, was very obvious in the exchanges between Hamilton and Lindsay. Lindsay wished to plead his allegiance to the king, who though he had right and descent lost his people's obedience by his course in religion. Lindsay would suggest that his loyalty would endure better than that of some others, but he did not spare criticism of Traquair, against whom he had sometimes voted in the parliament; he glossed over the contentious issues of that meeting. Religion obviously mattered to him, as he called on Hamilton to seek what was right in God's eyes, but the crisis was as much of politics as of ideology. Civil war was in prospect for a second time.[93] However, gestures of force by the Covenanters were restrained in the weeks of waiting for the English parliament. Though their rhetoric tended to exaggerate their strength as much as the king's servants played it down, their wish for external support in this new year was considerably more sustained than before, partly (mainly?) in fear at what the king might achieve, but helped too by signs of encouragement.

Four self-styled commissioners from Scotland arrived at Court on 12 February, Loudoun and Dunfermline again together with the Sheriff of Teviotdale and Mr Robert Barclay, the provost of Irvine. As they came they almost certainly distributed copies of a new *Information from the Estaits of . . . Scotland*.[94] This was addressed to the 'kingdom' of England, not just the 'well-affected', as had been the case in the 1639 propaganda. It attacked heavily the few bad patriots and churchmen of Scotland who urged a second war without just cause – acting like the 'whore of Babel' – and offered a general defence of present demands as justifiable under the law. At the same time was included the usual important proviso that the English judicatory should not however judge the Scottish laws or parliament. There was one particular audience which was to take note. The members of the English parliament summoned to supply this intended war were called upon not to be misled, given the incendiaries and their own relative ignorance concerning the Scottish situation; those who had done evil were to be exposed before them, for the good of the church and state in both kingdoms. The English were

[92] GD 406/1/883 (13 December 1639); *State Papers Collected by Edward, Earl of Clarendon*, eds. R. Scrope and T. Monkhouse (3 vols., Oxford, 1767–86), vol. II, p. 82; *CSPD 1639–40*, 436/41, 442/134; Fraser, *Haddington*, vol. II, p. 177; PRO SP 16/449/51. Traquair's return to Court, however, was at royal command – NLS Ms. 81, no. 77.

[93] GD 406/1/8351.

[94] *CSPD 1639–40*, 446/48, 448/23; *CSPD 1640*, 450/41; *His Maiesties Declaration*, p. 2.

asked to join in petitioning the king for a resolution of this particular history of grievances.[95]

This tied up well with the instructions to the commissioners, for they were to demonstrate to Charles in person the justice of the essential demand to have the Scottish parliament ratify the conclusions of the general assembly, which included the abjuration of episcopacy and the abolition of civil places for kirkmen. Church-linked reforms were not to be compromised, and the steering of unity was conscious. Traquair, who had returned again from Scotland also to attend, was singled out for heavy criticism, while it was argued that the resolutions of the past sitting of parliament should command more credence and respect than the narration of a single individual. Charles was quick to defend his Commissioner, not least because the implication otherwise was that he was obliged to accept all legislation that could be argued to be legitimate in Scots law and custom, whether or not he wished it. The Covenanters used the fact of the king's absence from the parliament to argue that there could be no further substantial deliberations; his meeting with commissioners after the event was meant only for clarification and explanation.

Charles made them wait to see him, and when he granted an audience did so with Traquair and apparently the whole Scottish committee present, though he for his part dominated the speaking; Hamilton, Laud and Traquair gave him some support.[96] The commissioners, or 'petitioners' as the king would have them called, defended the opposition to the prorogation of the parliament and their own authorisation which Charles challenged, but most of all dwelt on justifying the various conclusions and articles raised when parliament had been in session. They led the talks, on 3 March when Lord Loudoun made a major speech, and indeed on the 9th when Archbishop Laud challenged the justice of these principles. The case for the Acts of Rescission and Constitution notably began from the Acts of the assembly, the point at which most Scots could agree. The underlying principles were stressed, the 'regnum constituendum' but 'ecclesia restituenda' that was Scotland, with independent judicatories of church and state as acknowledged at the time of the Pacification. The differences with England were urged, the total independence of the laws and church of their country and the unique standing of the general assembly where was represented all the Protestant population of the

---

[95] *Information from the Estaits of ... Scotland*, Aldis 967 (n.p., 1640) – Amsterdam edition STC 21916.5. A manuscript answer to this is in NLS Ms. 3044, no. 120.

[96] PRO 31/3/72, fols. 43, 52–3. The main talks may be reconstructed from Windebank's notes (PRO SP 16/447/18, 19, 58, 96, 448/12); J. Rushworth, *Historical Collections* (8 vols., London, 1659–1701), vol. III, pp. 998–1014; and *A True Representation*, Aldis 981 (n.p., 1640). Detailed reference will be eschewed here. The Scottish petition of 24 February is misplaced in *CSPD 1638–9*, 413/80.

country; Laud's various contrary objections were answered. Here Charles had little to say. He spoke up only to restrain the Covenanters' presumption on the English scene, attempting to quash their hopes for the English parliament or the support of the Earl of Pembroke.[97]

When pressed by Traquair, the Covenanters admitted that they did not stand to every one of the articles under discussion, since these strictly speaking were still to be considered by the Estates in full parliament and by the king. Some of their arguments, such as that for the lairds each to have a single vote, were logically rather than legally founded. One single and notable point of restraint exercised by the Articles they boasted upon was that parliaments every two or three years had not been demanded, describing it as a thing desirable but nevertheless one that might encroach upon the king's prerogative to his displeasure. The aim was to show the pervading force of religion and conscience as the prime mover in Scotland, and as such the point had propaganda value for divided hearts at home as well as for the English audience for whom it was stressed in the *True Representation* published after the talks. Within three months, however, such professed moderation would be laid aside.

Charles neither believed that he needed to learn principles nor did he consider his prerogative uninfringed, as was implied. Strikingly, he chose in his words to the English privy council on 11 March to focus on two issues nearly all Covenanters might have thought long ago closed. He maintained that the Covenant in any form other than that authorised through Hamilton in September 1638 was unacceptable, and particularly the band which did not exclude the king from being combined against; Traquair's conduct was alleged in support, apparently without mention of its complicated history. The Earl of Arundel spoke up to pronounce against the neglect 'unprecedented in the Christian world' by the Covenanters of the interests of their ruler. Secondly, but more fundamentally, Charles claimed his 'right' to summon and dissolve assemblies and to have a negative voice. At Berwick he had considered rival cases in writing, but now it was said to be a thing to be enjoyed 'as in all powers of Christendom'. The king overlooked again the details of Scottish law, a confession perhaps that his legal case on these points was weak, but equally evidence that he claimed an innate right. Whether or not he had ever thought otherwise, he was now determined to remove all ambiguity, to present his essential objections to the whole Covenanting movement.[98] He did not speak only to the English council; the same argument was published in *His Maiesties Declaration*, where with respect to the parlia-

---

[97] On parliament and the Earl of Pembroke, see PRO SP 16/447/19.
[98] *PCR*, vol. VIII, pp. 358–60; PRO SP 16/447/87.

ment a contrastingly detailed case was filled out with Traquair's help.[99] The king wished to ban the presbyterian case even from being discussed. However, they were to refute him in *A True Representation*, where in 1639 the king's *Large Declaration* had gone unanswered in print.[100] The struggle was becoming ever more serious. Could battle by arms yet be staved off through battle by words?

The public nature of the debate caused the two cases to be shaped carefully. By consequence of the concession of abrogation made in the Edinburgh Assembly, Charles's case for bishops stressed their place as the third estate in the parliament more than their spiritual roles, 'wherein the civil power of kings is so much concerned'.[101] Nevertheless Laud, with Charles's explicit backing, had for some time been encouraging Bishop Hall of Exeter to publish a defence of *iure divino* episcopacy. Episcopacy was to be compared with lay presbytery, with the contrasts for obvious reasons drawn especially sharply. *Episcopacy by Divine Right Asserted* when finished was directed to English and Scottish readers.[102]

Accepting an invitation during debate to raise points of objection on particular Acts of parliament, Charles concentrated on the visible attacks on the prerogative – matters such as the prorogation of parliaments, the defining of the Articles, the authorisation of coinage, the matter of customs duties, appointments to royal castles and the judicial functions of the exchequer. The major constitutional matters arising from the general assembly acts were virtually ignored, for the reason that radical civil proposals had so thoroughly corrupted their handling – an argument that struck hard at what had caused the divisions in Scotland.[103]

When the Covenanters pressed for a quick end, Charles raised objections on twenty-five more of the subjects treated in the Articles.[104] Though the month of March 1640 Charles was obviously playing for time, and mean-

---

[99] *His Maiesties Declaration*; PRO SP 16/449/50; Traqr. Mss. Bundle 27 – charges v. Traquair. Secretary Windebank and Robert Reade were also heavily involved; early sections may have been written as early as September 1639 – PRO SP 16/422/128, 449/49; *CSPD 1639–40*, 447/87; *CSPD 1640*, 450/61.

[100] *A True Representation*: Ms. draft in NLS Wod. Fo. 64, fols. 169–72, 173–4, 179, 228–231. The second part, covering the London talks, was published separately as *The Proceedings of the Commissioners*, STC 21927.

[101] *His Maiesties Declaration*, pp. 20–1.

[102] J. Hall, *Episcopacy by Divine Right Asserted*, STC 12661 (registered 10 Feb. 1640); *CSPD 1639*, 429/40; *CSPD 1639–40*, 430/50, 431/2, 65, 432/38, 63, 436/45; cf. *A True Representation*, pp. 80–1. See too, also by Hall, *Certain Irrefragable Propositions*, STC 12646b; *CSPD 1639–40*, 433/55 (calendared too late?).

[103] PRO SP 16/448/12.

[104] The king endorsed the paper of objections – Traqr. Mss. Bundle 27; he marked also *CSPD 1639–40*, 447/71 [must post-date 15 March, not 10 March as calendared].

while had authorised Lord Ettrick in Edinburgh Castle to use force.[105] Responses to the explanations offered by the Covenanters were cursory, and the process of reporting matters to the privy council met with delays.[106] Attentions were shifting when on 24 March letters of summons were issued for seven Scots to answer a serious charge – a veiled reference to a letter addressed to the French king which subsequently was made public at the Short Parliament; it seems likely that Traquair had brought this with him when he last came from Scotland.[107] Separately, though in expectation of refusals, Argyll and Balmerino were also strictly summoned.[108] Thus Charles prepared to meet his English parliament, with formal orders now going out for mobilisation and letters to the loyal Marquis of Douglas and to Nithsdale to warn that by 13 April, the day of the parliament opening, peace with the 'Covenanting rebels' would be at an end.[109] Two days before the parliament assembled, Charles had Lord Loudoun arrested as one of the signatories of the French letter, along with the three other Scottish commissioners in London. Of the remaining signatories in Scotland none had answered their summons, but the king's action was dramatic enough. By publicising their contacts with France in the main opening speeches he looked to animate the parliament by exposing Covenanter treason; those he cast as his opponents were to be seen in their worst light. The address on the French letter was interpreted to be such written only from subjects to their own king.[110]

Charles was more than ready to find evidence of treason, but there was probably more than a tactical move involved here. While the letters to Louis XIII and the Earl of Leicester in France were carefully timed to avoid too early publicity, Windebank's assumed tone in these, together with the secret investigations to pin down the carrier, a Mr Colville, marked an uncertainty on the French position.[111] Reports were received of Franco-Scottish connections which were no doubt as unwelcome as they had been throughout the period of the troubles.[112] The interrogation of Lord Loudoun on 14 April

---

[105] *CSPD 1639–40*, 446/30, 448/27.
[106] *CSPD 1639–40*, 449/29: this paper appears to be the king instructing Windebank, not Windebank the committee.
[107] PRO SP 16/449/51 (fols. 125, 129 with Traquair additions); *CSPD 1639–40*, 449/53; GD 406/1/1305/1; Traqr. Mss. Trial XI; Stevenson, *Scottish Revolution*, pp. 179–81.
[108] *CSPD 1639–40*, 449/55, 56; PRO SP 16/449/57 shows Charles's holograph points on the wording. The king attempted to strike against Argyll's local power base – GD 406/1/1305/2–3, 1271, 1272; NLS Acc. 7360.
[109] *CSPD 1639–40*, 447/41, 448/44, 71, 74 etc.; *PCR*, vol. IX, pp. 392–400; Sir W. Fraser, *The Book of Caerlaverock* (2 vols., Edinburgh, 1873), vol. II, p. 15; Macray, *Ruthven Correspondence*, p. 61; *CSPD 1640*, 450/38.
[110] E. S. Cope and W. H. Coates (eds.), *Proceedings of the Short Parliament of 1640*, Camden Society (1977), pp. 53–4, 95–6, 115–22, 293–4.
[111] *CSPD 1640*, 450/60–1, 452/4, 455/83, 456/6; Collins, *Letters*, vol. II, pp. 645–8, 653.
[112] *CSPD 1640*, 451/118; PRO SP 16/451/27 (the Calendar is misleading).

and was thorough and his answers were felt to be less than satisfactory.[113] Although there was no mention of the letter in the king's second speech to the parliament, it was subsequently still referred to by his Lord Keeper.[114] It was symptomatic of other problems in this English arena that the tactical use of the letter fell flat.

Considerable efforts had gone towards securing the attendance of cooperative members in the parliament – with limited success – for they were to be asked only to supply money. Charles justified the war but would not be questioned on it. *His Maiesties Declaration* was published which set out at length the Scottish story to date; but in the opening speeches on 13 April that story was only alluded to, while the news that there had been a generous grant in the Irish parliament was mentioned as an encouragement to supply. Grievances in England, it was said, would be dealt with in due course – after the alleged danger of Scottish aggression was past. The view meanwhile presented was a rosy one of the years without parliaments.[115]

The rallying of discontent across the national borders would have predisposed the king to be alert to trouble now as he had experienced in plenty in the English parliaments of the 1620s. Then, as recently in the Scottish situation, he had tended to blame small numbers of disaffected individuals for disturbing the harmony that was the ideal between king and subjects.[116] Counsel for this parliament had offered that the country would support him in this exigency. Prejudices and impatience showed in his dissolution of the parliament after only three weeks, it having failed in its declared purpose. The Commons did not unite to obey him on the matter of supply – and Charles blamed a small factious number.

This was not a simple victory for the Covenanters, but did they have reason to celebrate? Charles's impatience, together with varying motives which had impelled English members to their delays, counted probably more than the later argument of Covenanter propaganda, namely that the parliament had been persuaded that the king lacked a just cause of war, especially a war between two closely linked kingdoms.[117] However, there had been a wide and

---

[113] *CSPD 1640*, 450/85–6; Cope and Coates, *Proceedings*, pp. 58, 134.

[114] Cope and Coates, *Proceedings*, pp. 164–7, 176; *LJ*, vol. IV, pp. 62–3.

[115] J. K. Gruenfelder, *Influence in Early Stuart Elections 1604–1640* (Columbia, OH, 1981), ch. 5. The declaration was available by 16 April at latest – *CSPD 1640*, 451/40; cf. GD 112/40/2/3/30. For Ireland, see PCR, vol. X, pp. 421–3; Moody, Martin and Byrne, *New History of Ireland*, vol. III, pp. 270–4.

[116] Cf. R. Cust, *The Forced Loan and English Politics 1626–1628* (Oxford, 1987), esp. pp. 16–23, 87–90, 324–37. Again I am grateful to Dr Cust for sharing his unpublished work with me.

[117] *A True Representation*, p. 98 (second part).

sustained appeal in print and otherwise to the English to consider carefully the matters at issue; and Charles had been very aware of it.

The potential for hostility and misunderstanding should probably not be underestimated. Early on the Covenanters took pains to try to clear themselves of undesirable aspersions; the French letter exposed by the king had in fact never been sent. But their slate was not clean – though they never admitted this except to their closest confidants – and they feared rousing English indignation. To answer the confusion in England touching the date of the letter, a vital part of their defence, they insisted that it had been drafted in time of extreme stress in 1639 before the Pacification; that it was not treasonable but in any case was covered by an Oblivion.[118]

In private they maintained correspondence and contacts wherever possible. Amongst the best evidence of this is a memorandum of 30 April from Edinburgh which discussed the strategy of response to Loudoun's continuing detention. Any important papers, it recommended, should be given to 'friends' for safekeeping. As the king's intention was perceived to be to limit information available for those in the parliament, the author urged the 'friends' to move the members to demand either the release of Loudoun or a public hearing – which was Loudoun's own aim. This was far preferable to anything done from Scotland since the potential of published statements was said to be already exhausted. If members justly refused to meddle while the situation was so delicate, the author continued, the other Scottish commissioners might at least be able to give favourable information to offset the plotting of the enemy who otherwise kept the majority in tow. English friends should tell their fellows that there was no aggression being shown by the Covenanters in Scotland.[119]

A letter of the same date directed to a 'particular friend in the par[liament]' contained very similar arguments. It exhorted English action, using fairly strong terms over the responsibility owed to God and to the welfare of both the kingdoms; the Scots waited 'in a lingering suspense' to see how the English acted by themselves on their behalf. Ireland, wrote the author, was to be no example as the king wanted it, for it was a conquered nation, an unattractive model for either Scotland or England. As an afterthought the author insisted that, should anything be revealed of present Scottish contacts with France, Holland and Denmark, it should be shown that these ongoing links were conceived 'in fair terms for intercession with our prince' – unable

---

[118] Cf. PRO 31/3/72, fol. 111; *Remonstrance Concerning the Present Troubles*, STC 21927.5 (n.p., 1640), dated 16 April; NLS Ms. 3368, fol. 16; Cope and Coates, *Proceedings*, pp. 58, 76–7 (Lords' debates); *CSPD 1640*, 450/89; Stevenson, *Scottish Revolution*, pp. 184, 187. The Act of Pacification with Oblivion of course still lacked the king's assent.

[119] NLS Wod. Fo. 64, fol. 163. Loudoun himself petitioned for release or a trial – *CSPD 1640*, 450/87; Burnet, *Memoires*, p. 169 (GD 406/M1/298 – misplaced in Burnet).

to bear any false interpretation as had been attempted with the other. There were names for the recipients of this letter or their receivers, a Mr Darling and a Sir John Hopton at Parliament Main Lodge.[120]

For Wariston, who wrote these, and his fellow leaders, there were immediate practical priorities in the appeals made in both papers for good information of armed movements on the part of the king, but there was also the sense of divine mission against a common enemy. In the memorandum mention was made of a paper that some parliament members should have to make use of, for informing a case against the bishops of England. This was almost certainly Robert Baillie's *Ladensium ΑΥΤΟΚΑΤΑΚΡΙΣΙΣ or the Canterburians' Self-Conviction*, which Baillie sent for approval to Wariston and others in late March. It consisted of a lengthy indictment of Laud and fellow English divines for promoting the present war effort and all the recent troubles of Scotland, and further accused them of 'gross Arminianism, plain popery and setting up barbarous tyranny, which is the common quarrel of all the reformed kirks with the Kirk of England'. Popery, cast as the joining with Rome, her authority, her idolatry, her heresies, ran towards tyranny in the church and the state.[121] Could this be a leading issue of the parliament? The English had more time to bring it to the fore in the so-called Long Parliament later in the year.[122]

Equally damning against Laud and his supposed faction but also against Wentworth, now the Earl of Strafford, the Scottish *Remonstrance* published at the opening of the parliament went rather beyond the critique of Scottish stirrers of troubles which marked the earlier *Information from the Estaits*. Here were exposed the great plotters against the welfare of both kingdoms, not simply in the recent history of the Scottish troubles described but also touching heavily in England on the controversies of the 1620s, and the rule since without parliaments; the popish agents of Rome and Spain were said to have acted in collaboration. However, the present great need was to secure the religion and liberties of Scotland; about such matters the English parliament ought to be concerned, as it had been in the English context in the past – for 'since in regard of the situation of this whole isle, and the union under one head, we are all, as it were, one house; if it fall, we shall all be buried in the ruins'.[123]

---

[120] NLS Wod. Fo. 64, fols. 165–6. For possible channels of communication, cf. *CSPD 1640*, 450/79; GD 112/39/797.

[121] Aldis 971.5; Baillie, *Letters*, vol. I, p. 243. Printed in April; but cf. BL Sloane Ms. 1467, fol. 113v.

[122] Cf. J. S. Morrill, 'The attack on the Church of England in the Long Parliament, 1640–1642', in D. Beales and G. Best (eds.), *History, Society and the Churches* (Cambridge, 1985), 105–24.

[123] *Remonstrance Concerning the Present Troubles* (Dutch editions, STC 21927.7, 21928). Quote from p. 15, Bryson edition. Cf. GD 112/40/2/3/34; BL Add. Ms. 28011, fols. 54–5.

Charles had caused offence to claims for liberties to the point that in the history now of both nations strong pleas for definition had been advanced, but it was still his counsel who received the brunt of the attack. In Scotland the cry of religion and liberties had implied a strong appeal to law through representative assemblies as a defence of what was right, but here in the *Remonstrance* the emphasis was on the Union that was at stake. What ought to have been a blessing with mutual benefits was being turned under evil influence to a war between the kingdoms. In complaining to the English the Scots demanded more serious attention be paid to the Union, for the evils which struck their own kingdom could easily spread further; the offence of Strafford was that he was seen to be using the Irish and English parliaments for utterly wrong purposes. All of these points would be subsequently developed. It might be noted that the address was to the English parliament alone, the Covenanters crying out for the punishment of Laud and Strafford and others who had created danger not just for the kingdoms but for the king himself; and that they hoped that the parliament might hear a 'true', uncorrupted representation of the Scottish grievances, for these, it was argued, were of the most serious nature, far outstripping what might be the expected agenda of the English now in 1640. It was in the northern kingdom that the rule of law was most severely under threat: might not the English devote their attentions there?[124]

In respect of these high expectations, the Short Parliament perhaps did not give much satisfaction, and, to return to the documentation of underhand contacts, it might be suggested that the passion and sense of urgency there arose in some measure from disappointment in the highest circles at what had happened to date; it may be that the revelation of Covenanter secrets indicated an attempt to gain confidence of men in another kingdom. High hopes for the rhetoric of union were perhaps temporarily dampened, since the draft heads for the memorandum omitted any idea that the English parliament, if it overlooked Loudoun's suffering, could bring on irreconcilable rupture between the kingdoms; the finished product aimed more singlemindedly at encouraging public, well-informed debate of the issues in the Covenanter cause. This was precisely what Charles wished to avoid.[125]

The parliament did not give satisfaction to the king, most obviously in failing to meet his appeal for immediate help against the Scots. There was a strong inclination in the Commons to consider domestic grievances before

---

[124] *Remonstrance Concerning the Present Troubles.*
[125] Above, p. 229; NLS Wod. Fo. 65, fol. 178; 64, fol. 163. Wariston holograph. The endorsement is 'Memorandum for our Scots commissioners', but the paper does not seem to be written to them directly. All four are described in the third person; they were all under restraint until late April – *CSPD 1640*, 451/66, 452/103. The recipient is addressed as 'your lo.'; he is connected with 'the factorie' and a messenger, Mark Home.

supply.[126] That this was to be the order seemed likely from the beginning of the session, and a resolution was passed accordingly on 23 April. John Pym's lengthy speech on the 17th aroused a good deal of interest – even a very sympathetic diarist commented on the stark nakedness of his words – by listing grievances under three heads, and this was used as a model for proceeding after the voting of the resolution. Religion and property were the issues alongside privileges of parliament; there was much debate on the troubles of the 1629 dissolution, and demands were put forward for annual meetings to deal with grievances seen to have arisen since then. Such matters had figured in some of the elections, and they were evident in the few county petitions received which, in one account, 'stunned the royalists more than anything, to see county join together against the new and illegal courses; of which petitions some beforehand said that they were the Scottish Covenant wanting only hands'.[127]

These reported divisions were by no means clear-cut. Various office-holders were prominent in often reminding the Commons of the king's sense of priorities or bringing Charles's messages. Pressed by Charles that there would be a time fitter than the present to deal more fully with grievances, their words might have run counter to those of other members and, though there was no united party structure, nevertheless there existed a degree of opposition that stood out against the king's wishes.[128] In the Lords Charles's prospects were brighter, with a considerable majority supporting him when he made his momentous appeal to them on 24 April not to uphold the Commons' resolution on priorities. For Archbishop Laud, presumably acting for the king, the names of the dissentients were worth noting here, for offence was taken; for the Scot Archibald Campbell, the opposing lords were giving a vote in favour of the Scots.[129]

The message of the 'country' that there was first a need for reform in

[126] Cf. *CSPD 1640*, 450/103, 451/66. I am most grateful to Judith Maltby for sharing her work on the Short Parliament with me prior to publication. For secondary accounts of the parliament, see E. S. Cope, 'Compromise in early Stuart parliaments: the case of the Short Parliament of 1640', *Albion*, 9 (1977), 135–45; G. E. Aylmer, *Rebellion or Revolution?* (Oxford, 1986), pp. 11–14. The Earl Russell will deal far more fully with the parliament in his forthcoming work. I am grateful to him for discussions on it.

[127] Cope and Coates, *Proceedings*, pp. 234 (BL Harl. Ms. 4931), 148–57, 299–300; cf. *CSPD 1640*, 451/66.

[128] Besides Cope and Coates, *Proceedings*, see J. D. Maltby (ed), *The Short Parliament (1640) Diary of Sir Thomas Aston*, Camden Society (1988). For general comment on the structure of politics, see especially, C. S. R. Russell, *Parliaments and English Politics 1621–1629* (Oxford, 1982).

[129] PRO SP 16/451/39; Cope and Coates, *Proceedings*, pp. 79n., 229; E. S. Cope, 'The Earl of Bedford's notes of the Short Parliament of 1640', *BIHR*, 53 (1980), 257; GD 112/40/2/3/34. The irregularity of the king going thus to the Lords and their subsequent votes caused much debate in both Houses thereafter.

England did not necessarily preclude a wish to satisfy the king in his purposes, but it created a situation which Charles found very troublesome. Those who spoke of removing thorns in the foot before marching on, or of winning the hearts of Englishmen as well as their money were appealing possibly for no more than practical remedies; sensitivity to various grievances undoubtedly bore on many members. Some rhetoric possibly sounded more ominous, such as Sir Francis Seymour's mention of the need to clear the sun of mist and the fountain of muddy waters, a repeat of themes recently expressed by Covenanters. Lord Digby and Edward Kirton pushed the argument that English problems should be remedied first before the Scottish disease – rebellion – took over in the south.[130]

As Charles saw it his delineation of priorities was challenged, which he resented if he did not take it as an attack; in the questions that arose, he was reluctant to lose time or honour in talking. Ship money, which with military charges was a prominent issue from the beginning of the session, attracted most of the reporting from this Short Parliament, for it was objected that the country could not give parliamentary subsidies if it was to be liable to these unpopular, expensive and dubiously legal levies. From his second appearance in the parliament Charles tried to explain. On 21 April he told the House by the Lord Keeper that ship money was levied on account of extraordinary necessity; on the 24th he suggested that some alternative means might be found to replace it if that was desired. This option of an alternative was repeated by Windebank on 2 May, although any question of the illegality of either levy was not conceded.[131] Another option mooted earlier came through with the king's agreement only on 4 May, when twelve subsidies were requested and the dropping of ship money offered in return. An earlier resolution for the king's agents to justify his case for the levy was laid aside so that the Commons might waste no more time – but this did nothing to calm uncertainties as to what could recur in the future.[132]

To some extent Charles enlarged his problem through manufacturing the degree of urgency involved on his side; they had a point who objected that he might have called the parliament sooner.[133] Supply was needed, and moneys had been engaged already, as the king said, but the threat from the Scots was not so very pressing – deliberately so, as far as the Covenanters were concerned, although they appointed their commanders while the parliament still

---

[130] Cope and Coates, *Proceedings*, pp. 77–8, 191, 207, 222–3; Maltby, *Aston Diary*, pp. 36–44, 124–5.

[131] PRO SP 16/450/88; *LJ*, pp. 62–3; Cope and Coates, *Proceedings*, pp. 70, 264–6; Maltby, *Aston Diary*, pp. 124–5.

[132] Maltby, *Aston Diary*, pp. 128–44; *CSPD 1640*, 450/94, 452/20, 33. Cf. for April PRO SP 16/451/29.

[133] Cope and Coates, *Proceedings*, pp. 178, 240–1; Maltby, *Aston Diary*, pp. 67–8.

sat.[134] The king's evidence of Scottish provocation was paltry, the reports given of the Scottish troops on the border exaggerated.[135] In 1639 the king's fears of Scottish invasion had been sincere; this was not so much the case now, and he was himself undoubtedly an aggressor.

In the end, in a characteristic sweep doubting that there were as many grievances 'as the public voice doth make them', the king singled out a small group of troublesome members of the Lower House as causing the dissolution.[136] Whether such a group did or could have control seems doubtful – though there was wide concern that English people should have some satisfaction from this parliament – but it is important finally to note that some perhaps had stood out for a hard line. A few had dwelt much, for instance, on privileges of parliament or on religious heads of grievances; they had even defied the king's wishes by talking directly of the Scotland business.

In the Lords, Viscount Saye and Sele had spoken up to the point of asking that the Scottish troubles be left out of immediate consideration – on which he was firmly answered by Strafford, Laud and Lords Maynard and Cottington. When in the Commons on 23 April the example of the 1621 parliament was alleged to encourage support for the king's war supply, John Pym disagreed with the precedent, saying that King James had declared the business to the House and asked their advice concerning the Palatinate, which was then the concern, whereas in the present case the king had been pleased neither to inform nor to ask counsel. Since at other times a number of speakers would affirm that no one opposed the granting of supply altogether, and Pym himself guarded his comments with acknowledgement of the king's prerogative powers on determining peace or war, it must be appreciated that what one could acceptably say was limited.[137] Sir Robert Cooke's contribution, which fastened the origins of the war on the clergy, was exceptional in its outspokenness, but arose out of a wish that the war might be debated.[138] Pym rather asked that the king explain the causes of the war, on the grounds that the country should know what it was paying for; a few did follow him,

---

[134] For example, the 21 April speech – *LJ*, vol. IV, pp. 62–3; *CSPD 1640*, 450/89, 98, 103, 451/11, 46–7; GD 112/40/2/3/30; Sir W. Fraser, *The Melvilles Earls of Melville and the Leslies Earls of Leven* (3 vols., Edinburgh, 1890), vol. III, pp. 164–7. The Covenanter military effort will be fully treated in E. M. Furgol, *A Regimental History of the Covenanting Armies 1639–1651* (forthcoming).

[135] Cope and Coates, *Proceedings*, p. 176; *CSPD 1640*, 450/64, 113, 114, 451/23.

[136] *LJ*, vol. IV, p. 81; Cust, *The Forced Loan*, pp. 331–7. The closing speech, with minor holograph corrections by Charles, survives in GD 406/1/1805.

[137] See Cope and Coates, *Proceedings*, pp. 74–9, 173, 192, 239; NLS Adv. Ms. 33.1.1, vol. XIII, no. 7.

[138] Cope and Coates, *Proceedings*, pp. 195–6; Maltby, *Aston Diary*, p. 131; Hyde, *History of the Rebellion*, vol. I, p. 179. Cooke's connections with people opposed to the war are well documented – PRO SP 16/448/79. I am grateful to Professor Russell for this reference.

but others opposed.[139] How far members could bear such discussion is questionable; but the listing of those for and against from diary evidence has obvious shortcomings. Concern for the recovery of order might join with more ambitious lines of opposition; the middle stance in debate could be lost in reporting, as for example by the puritan outside the parliament who wrote that the 'honest men' had stoutly resisted giving money for war against the Scots because they wanted peace.[140]

Charles was not prepared to tolerate a long parliament, but the raising of the Scottish dimension may have pushed him the more urgently to dissolve. Money questions, tied up with the rights and wrongs of ship money, animated the Commons on 4 May when the king's new offer was made; the mood seemingly was positive for granting the king subsidies, but not without resolutions on the issues involved in the ship money to be dropped. Merely on this question of delay the king's representatives warned of the possibility of dissolution, as had been Charles's position from at least 23 April, if not the start of the parliament.[141] The dissolution on 5 May seemed to proceed for this reason, with opinion in the king's council divided; but almost immediately the property of prominent members in both Houses was searched for papers, and reporting of the fact connected it with the Scots or the Scottish war.[142] On 9 and 10 May Secretary Windebank interrogated two of the Scottish commissioners, Cavers and Barclay, on contacts with members of the parliament – directly following the information provided in an anonymous, undated paper, which told that it had been planned to produce before the Lower House on 5 May a book entitled 'The Scottish declaration to the English' as a means by which to draw the House to investigate the causes of the war.[143] Had knowledge of this paper prompted the English house searches, and possibly brought forward by a few hours the act of dissolution? It has been observed that the prevention of the Speaker from taking his chair showed extreme urgency on the king's part.[144] The king was certainly

---

[139] See Cope and Coates, *Proceedings*, pp. 190–7, 207–10, 228; Maltby, *Aston Diary*, pp. 122–44.

[140] *Winthrop Papers*, p. 243. Again we look forward to the Earl Russell's account.

[141] Cf. *HMC De L'Isle*, vol. VI, pp. 252, 254, 263; *CSPD 1640*, 451/54, 452/33; Cope and Coates, *Proceedings*, p. 173; Maltby, *Aston Diary*, pp. 39, 41; PRO SP 16/450/113.

[142] PRO SP 16/452/37; GD 112/40/2/3/34; Gardiner, *History of England*, vol. IX, p. 117; *CSPD 1640*, 453/24; BL Sloane Ms. 1467, fols. 104–5. Papers found are listed in Bod. Tanner Ms. 88*, fols. 115–17.

[143] *CSPD 1640*, 452/115, 102, 104. No book of that title is known. The delay in interrogations may be explicable by the Scots at that time being somewhere at liberty, possibly in hiding. Windebank's letter to Conway on 7 May gave little away – *CSPD 1640*, 452/69.

[144] PRO SP 16/452/46; Gardiner, *History of England*, vol. IX, p. 117. Intercepted papers of Scotsmen become common at this period, perhaps because of special alertness – *CSPD 1640*, 452/26, 28, 44–7.

offended by the Commons' procrastination; he would equally have been very
keen to frustrate any possibility of their discrediting his cause.[145]

The interrogations revealed little of substance for the king; 'Mr Darling'
and 'Sir John Hopton', as far as we know, remained undiscovered.[146] It is
interesting, though, that the anonymous information touched closely on the
desires of the Committee of Estates as expressed in the memorandum by
Wariston. The Earl of Dunfermline, whose name there had been linked with
the possibility of defection to the king, was untouched by Secretary Windebank; later in May he would be trusted on a royal commission to Scotland.[147]
The councillors of the king were not far off the track. At the same time, it must
be asked what might have happened had the parliament not been so suddenly
ended. Perhaps it is doubtful that members would all readily have responded
to the information to be offered – though Scots eagerly noted that their news
was discussed in London after its dissolution. *A True Representation*, the
very substantial justification of the recent history of the Covenanters which
attempted to answer the king's printed declaration, was published presumably as soon as possible.[148]

For the immediate task in hand Charles would look to alternative means of
supply. Debate in the close committee for Scottish affairs raised questions
affecting strategy and approaches. Northumberland's contribution was
rather spiritless, as he had little hope either of straightforward supply or willingness to fight – he was one who had opposed the council advice for dissolution – but Strafford, drawing on arguments raised in advance of the Short
Parliament, urged the offensive. He emphasised the king's ability to exploit
all possible means since the parliamentary failed him, an argument that elsewhere would be hotly opposed. Strafford's words in this debate would be
later used against him, including his alleged remarks that the Irish army could
be used to compel English cooperation as well as Scottish obedience. Whether
or not he contemplated such a thing, it was not meant here; the Irish army of
eight thousand would be aimed at the west of Scotland.[149] There were complementary tactics for a naval assault on the east coast, for which Hamilton
was consulted, and some Scots were again involved. The main army was to
thrust northwards, with apparently no change in its size despite the outcome

---

[145] *CSPD 1640*, 452/33, 69; also *State Papers . . . Clarendon*, vol. II, pp. 83–4.
[146] *CSPD 1640*, 452/102, 104.
[147] Cf. BL Add. Ms. 11045, fol. 74v; *CSPD 1640*, 451/66; NLS Wod. Fo. 64, fol. 163.
[148] GD 112/40/2/3/34; NLS Wod. Fo. 64, fol. 163.
[149] HMC 3, p. 3; *CSPD 1640*, 452/31, 457/98; HMC *De L'Isle*, vol. VI, p. 262; Gardiner, *History of England*, vol. IX, pp. 119–25; Bod. Carte Ms. 1, fols. 181–9, 194. If the Vane record is authentic, the silence of Hamilton in so crucial a debate is striking.

of the parliament. Defence would be assured, but more than that was intended.[150]

It seems to have been harder than in 1639 to find the required cash and soldiers; while the parliament was still sitting, original rendezvous dates were postponed from 20 May to 10 June.[151] War revived and exacerbated troubles born of localism or administrative inefficiency, especially since this was the second campaign in as many years, but there was widespread unhappiness in the aftermath of such a parliament. Opposition to non-parliamentary ways of finance had a strong recent history. A meeting of convocation at the end of the parliament gave those sensitive to current church policy yet more cause for antagonism. An oath for clergy explicitly to uphold episcopal government and a resoundingly clear statement on the king's absolute authority were both topical in the light of the Scottish troubles and potentially provocative. Political troubles were building in England which would explode centrally when Charles came to call another parliament later in the year; discontent contributed to his interim difficulties in many parts of the country. A campaign of the thoroughness Strafford had envisaged was not managed, and uncertainties with further postponements marked the preparations.[152] The Earl of Northumberland, one among many, had little joy.[153]

Less than three weeks after the end of the Short Parliament, the king sent to prorogue the Scottish parliament imminently due to reconvene. Such a respite was probably the only option open to him; it seems that he tried to back the order with a show of force – even at the time that new postponements of English army movements were instructed. Rumour suggested that Charles was looking for a peaceful solution, wishful thinking perhaps, but hardly probable.[154] Rather than Hamilton or Traquair, it was the Earl of Dunfermline who was persuaded to carry the warrant for prorogation which the King's Advocate and the Justice-clerk, Hamilton of Orbiston, received on 1 June. Sir Thomas Hope was still heavily suspected by Charles, but ironically

---

[150] Alnwick Mss., BL Microfilm 285, fol. 199 (Hamilton holograph); *HMC De L'Isle*, vol. VI, p. 318. This was the policy as before – Collins, *Letters*, vol. II, p. 652; *CSPD 1640*, 452/33.

[151] *CSPD 1640*, 452/16–17. Again Professor Fissel's work will address the history of the whole operation.

[152] J. S. Morrill, *The Revolt of the Provinces* (1976), pp. 16–31; E. S. Cope, *Politics without Parliaments, 1629–1640* (1987), pp. 185–95; C. Hibbard, *Charles I and the Popish Plot* (Chapel Hill, NC, 1983), pp. 147–62; T. A. Mason, *Serving God and Mammon: William Juxon, 1582–1663* (1985), pp. 128–33.

[153] *CSPD 1640*, 451/33, 458/60, 459/97, 460/55, 461/16, 463/70; PRO SP 16/457/7; Collins, *Letters*, vol. II, pp. 653–7; *HMC De L'Isle*, vol. VI, pp. 270, 285, 300; BL Add. Ms. 28103, fol. 34v.

[154] GD 406/1/1305/3–4, 1222; *CSPD 1640*, 451/33, 454/1, 44–5, 47–9, 61–8, 70, 82, 455/3, 456/6, 457/7; BL Sloane Ms. 1467, fol. 114; *CSPV 1640–2*, p. 52; *HMC Rutland* (24), vol. I, p. 520; Gardiner, *History of England*, vol. IX, pp. 154–5n.

the king was keeping to the usual form in addressing the warrant to him.[155] The two officers of state judged the warrant to be sufficient but on the next day two of the lords named in the commission would not agree. Lords Napier and Elphinstone objected on a technicality – they were not without backing – and the parliament proceeded to meet. Frustration with Charles's single-mindedness had compelled severer courses.[156]

Covenanter leaders meeting together on 1 June had discussed whether the parliament should meet against the king's will; there had been talk of a more serious alternative – apparently the question of whether deposition of a king was possible.[157] Passions were high, and with fears circulating of the ruin of the kingdom, the parliament sat and considered legislation which was finally voted on 11 June. A huge number of Acts was passed, in the name of the 'estates of parliament presently convened by his Majesty's special authority' – a suitable façade of legitimacy.[158] Earls present numbered half of those present in 1639 and the number of lesser nobles had dropped slightly, which possibly represented a fall in the active ranks of the Covenanters. There was little restraint as the parliament both ratified the outstanding general assembly Acts and enacted many of the parliamentary bills not voted in 1639. It was unequivocal now that the lairds were to be a separate estate, and in parliaments which were to be held every three years; the pursuit of anyone who backed courses destructive of liberties in kirk or kingdom was sanctioned. In this new turn of events, the king's civil authority was blatantly undermined and limited.[159]

The declaration or remonstrance made at the end of the parliament asked the king merely to attach his name to the measures already passed. This was followed by a list of demands for a well-grounded peace safe from 'evil counsels'.[160] The statement would last as the basis of the treaty begun later in the year. Accompanying was a letter to Hamilton's brother who was now the king's Scottish Secretary, the Earl of Lanark, which justified the Acts passed

---

[155] PRO 31/3/72, fol. 170; BL Harl. Ms. 383, fol. 168. Dunfermline may nearly have been tempted to keep with the king – GD 406/1/1273; A. B. Grosart, *Lismore Papers* (10 vols., 1886–8), vol. IV, p. 147. Stevenson, *Scottish Revolution*, p. 192, seems over-harsh on Charles's decision to send to Sir Thomas Hope; in any case, there was provision for Sir Lewis Stewart to be used if necessary.

[156] GD 406/1/1301, 1223, 1273, 1224; GD 406/M9/111/2; Sir W. Fraser, *The Elphinstone Family Book* (2 vols., Edinburgh, 1897), vol. II, pp. 161–2; GD 112/40/2/3/39; *CSPD 1640*, 457/36. The commission used was that of 20 August 1639.

[157] M. Napier, *Montrose and the Covenanters* (2 vols., Edinburgh, 1838), vol. I, p. 362 (from NLS Wod. Fo. 67, fol. 35); Stevenson, *Scottish Revolution*, pp. 190–2. Cf. PRO SP 16/447/19.

[158] The usual form was 'Our sovereign lord with consent of the Estates' – Traqr. Mss. Bundle 27, 'The acts of the noblemen etc.'.

[159] *APS*, vol. V, pp. 251, 258–300; Stevenson, *Scottish Revolution*, pp. 193–6.

[160] *APS*, vol. V, pp. 299–300; *CSPD 1640*, 456/72, 457/96.

as upholding religion and liberties – necessary to remedy extremities far worse than any threatened by violence on land or sea, it was argued; but it made also a direct threat. If the king passed over this remonstrance sent from the parliament, the Scots were to prepare and provide for their 'own deliverance and safety'.[161]

The Covenanters went on to bring Scotland to a military readiness for an invasion of England. A central core group had met before as well as after the parliament to coordinate finance and mustering both of soldiers and enthusiasm; an Act authorised the title now of Committee of Estates. Complementary to the propaganda directed southwards, which had left open possibilities of action *in extremis*, were pieces written for internal consumption, to justify the opposition and, in consequence, the invasion.[162] As in 1639, there were obvious centres of potential resistance to be overcome – in the south-west, particularly the Earl of Nithsdale; elsewhere, Dumbarton and Edinburgh Castles, the Ogilvies in the central Highlands and the Gordons and their followers in the north-east. Local power struggles played their part, but the efforts by Monro in the north-east and Argyll against the Ogilvies and others quashed the determination of these islands of support for the king.[163] Resistance was stoutly maintained, however, in the fortresses south of the Highlands, where hope of the king introducing some aid still continued.[164]

The king was kept informed both by these various individuals in Scotland and by regular intelligence from Viscount Conway and Sir Michael Ernley on the borders. However, though it was an encouragement on the English side to see the constant resistance being made there and the apparent difficulties for the Covenanters of bringing together troops for attack, the king's Scottish supporters had reason to bemoan the lack of material support they received. It was part of the king's larger problem in the south of making only gradual headway in the preparation of his assault.[165]

Meanwhile in and around Court many, including the Marquis of Huntly, were in exile and unwilling to return to Scotland as Charles might have wished. Roxburgh told Charles that with estates forfeited there was little

---

[161] Burnet, *Memoires*, pp. 167–8.
[162] D. Stevenson, *The Government of Scotland under the Covenanters*, SHS (Edinburgh, 1982), pp. xxi–xxvii; *Remonstrance Concerning the Present Troubles*; NLS Adv. Ms. 33.4.14, fols. 290–3.
[163] Stevenson, *Scottish Revolution*, pp. 197–9; also GD 406/1/1143; GD 112/40/2/3/40; PRO 31/3/72, fols. 187–8; *CSPD 1640*, 458/58; GD 112/43/1/7/41.
[164] Besides Macray, *Ruthven Correspondence*, for example GD 406/1/1240–2; Bod. Rawlinson Ms. A1, pp. 9–12; Carte Ms. 1, fols. 194, 307, 333v–5; *CSPD 1640*, 454/51, 457/15, 458/58, 460/10, 18, 467/5, 135; NLS Ms. 2618, fols. 10–15.
[165] E.g. *CSPD 1640*, 454/34, 76, 98, 455/3, 456/64, 457/45, 101, 458/60, 62; PRO SP 16/457/7, 60; Gardiner, *History of England*, vol. IX, pp. 157–64; M. C. Fissel, '*Bellum episcopale*: the bishops' wars and the end of the "Personal Rule" in England 1638–1640' (unpublished University of Berkeley Ph.D. dissertation, 1983), pp. 300–62.

point – perhaps a realism not far removed from that of the Earl of Northumberland.[166] The king's absence from Scotland doubtless contributed to the shows of loyalty being limited to the few prepared, for whatever reason, to count the cost there, but Charles had apparently lost interest after the débâcle of summer 1639 for making a personal appeal by going north himself. It was a reflection on his narrow expectations, which together with the enforced delays of action, did nothing to gain him advantage within the Covenanting movement. Moderating counsel still tried somehow to break through. According to Rossingham, two versions of an oath for the Scots were considered at this time. The first had a very full acknowledgement of the king's royal supremacy and a heavy denunciation of the Covenant; the second, later version was notably less harsh in its terms, making only vague reference to the king's royal power and authority – surely an advised concession, but still leaving a gulf to be crossed.[167]

Lanark's immediate reply to the remonstrance from the Scottish parliament asked for time for Charles to consider, but a royal response followed quickly. This was defiant, saying that the subjects had gone much too far by their so-called Acts of parliament, and telling them to show a 'clear respect' to the royal power. The king would stand by what he had promised at Berwick, a statement that was determined to yield no propaganda advantage to the other side; by implication the king still promised to conclude the parliament as agreed.[168] It was considered expedient to encourage English loyalties, but also somehow to defuse the now explicit Scottish threat, and in this context Lord Loudoun was specially released from the Tower to carry the reply north.

Charles had had no intention of releasing his prisoner, but in this period of impending war, the Marquis of Hamilton seems to have carried the main work of diplomacy.[169] In terms of principle, the leading issue was the challenge to royal authority within parliaments, and of the instructions to Loudoun the primary one was that he should try to persuade the Covenanters to petition the king for the appointment of a royal Commissioner who might settle religion and laws according to the articles of the 1639 Pacification in an utterly new parliament. The other heads made topical provision to have the worries about Scottish invasion averted through dispersing of troops; also to ensure the personal safety of Lord Ettrick; and for the upholding of the king's authority with respect to the question of the bishops' estate in parliaments.[170]

[166] GD 112/40/2/3/34; GD 406/1/1242.
[167] *CSPD 1640*, 457/36, 104.
[168] GD 406/1/1297, 10800, 1298; cf. Stevenson, *Scottish Revolution*, p. 193.
[169] Cf. GD 406/1/1305/7; PRO 31/3/72, fols. 175, 180.
[170] Burnet, *Memoires*, p. 170.

A companion paper explored the various reasons and motives for such an approach, as they might be argued in Scotland. The Covenanters would save money by dismissing soldiers, but would still have the option of quickly reconvening forces if necessary; Ettrick was personally under threat following an Act in the parliament, and generous treatment would be a testimony of mercy not just for him but for others in danger of capture, thus hopefully dampening tensions; the king's 'power' was highly concerned in the abolition of the ecclesiastical estate in parliament, so that if bishops and clergy were not to be allowed to continue, the loss to that 'power' had still somehow to be compensated. The duty and allegiance of subjects to acknowledge the king's sovereignty which resided especially in parliament was the main point on the foremost issue. None would deny that royal consent was both necessary and desirable in matters of the state – thus, even over the church, subjects had preferred a new general assembly in 1639 to insistence on the controversial Glasgow Assembly. The oath of the Covenant obliged subjects not to diminish the king's greatness and authority, but on the contrary to defend him and his sacred power. It was not fitting therefore that legislation in a parliament without royal consent should then be passed on to the king to be ratified. The best way forward would be by means of a new meeting of the Estates.[171]

The king was well honoured by this language, but how much by accepting he wished another parliament must be questionable; in his Secretary's letter he would only leave options open.[172] In 1639 he had been persuaded to yield on matters within a general assembly only by his optimism that the situation might soon be reversed; to postpone the issue yet again was on his part a hollow manoeuvre. The proposals certainly came from below, with Loudoun himself writing out the papers. What for Charles were disposable terms for accommodation did nothing to affect his continuing preparation of arms. He wished to have it all his way, and Loudoun, for his benefit, further promised that he would not discuss the instructions with anyone in England unless with royal permission. The point was raised not least since latterly Loudoun had been under relaxed conditions of restraint, meeting apparently all kinds of people besides Scottish courtiers – 'English nobles and others'. The general rumour still picked up that Loudoun's journey offered the possibility of peace, but as long as this reflected to Charles's advantage it would have pleased him well enough. The Earl of Northumberland, unaware of the

---

[171] GD 406/M9/119/15 (Loudoun holograph, undated). Copy in NLS Wod. Fo. 63, fol. 46. Cf. Stevenson, *Scottish Revolution*, p. 194.
[172] GD 406/1/10800, 1298.

details, rightly doubted that the king was much interested in changing his mind.[173]

If Charles had given his consent presumably for little more than tactical gain, what of Hamilton, who had been instrumental in procuring Loudoun's release, and Loudoun himself? It seems probable that Hamilton's frustration with the king's attitude had reached far; perhaps too that he was wishing to cover himself against harm from within Scotland. For 1639 there may be evidence that he had wished simply a final settlement to be allowed through the Scottish parliament, probably something such as Traquair had worked for.[174] Here in 1640 a record of thoughts communicated between himself and Loudoun suggests that the two nobles worked earnestly on a strategy to find something like a mutual agreement. Loudoun committed himself to the combination of 'religion, laws and liberties' and the king's honour in a 'happy peace' – even with probable pain and expense on his part. He and the marquis bound themselves to 'trust, fidelity and secrecy' in what each would attempt to this same end. Thus Hamilton would do what he could with Charles, including, in happy circumstances, intercession on Loudoun's behalf for the king's recognition. The tone of realism was not absent, for Loudoun noted the need to resolve on action in the case of war – 'to condescend what course we shall take for keeping of correspondence'. Hamilton at least was willing to listen.[175]

Self-interest and public matters were overlapping, and revolving naturally around the personal monarchy. The marquis was open to a common basis of operation with Loudoun to complement his own continuing efforts to advise the king whose benefits he so richly enjoyed. Loudoun, ultimately hopeful of an earldom in a restored peace, did engage and, though he gave warning of the likely extreme courses pending should matters not be resolved, he agreed that a parliament in which the king had not been represented was inadequate – that royal authority was a vital sanction for legislation. Given his record in 1639, his civil vision was relatively radical amongst Scots, though firm conclusions are difficult here. In that earlier context, he had stood up against an ambitious, constrained and in many ways unsatisfactory lead given by Traquair on behalf of the distant king. If he had outwardly disagreed with Sir Thomas Hope then, he now appeared to be nearer an approach with which Hope could have concurred. Our hypothesis is awkward; regrettably there are many unknowns.

---

[173] *CSPD 1640*, 457/96, 458/60; GD 112/40/2/3/39, 41. Loudoun was given easier conditions when Dunfermline was sent north in late May 1640. The original of the instructions is GD 406/1/949.

[174] Traqr. Mss. Bundle 28[i] – 'Words spoken'. Cf. Baillie, *Letters*, vol. I, p. 220.

[175] Burnet, *Memoires*, p. 171; see too GD 406/1/1220. The Burnet/Oldmixon story about Hamilton saving Loudoun's head may refer to a rumour in December 1640 – BL Loan 29/172, fol. 356.

In a wider context this venture gives good insight into the politics of inter-action between Court and outside. It is a commonplace that courtiers did not necessarily serve the king's own preferred courses. Though Hamilton was away from Scotland, there were expectations that he, like any other Scottish figure but particularly in regard of his closeness to Charles, would still work for a solution to the Scottish troubles. It is also worth noting that the Coven-anters' public front of accusing the king's men of various kinds of crimes and especially bad counsel did not stop them at the same time wishing still to exploit the position of some of these individuals in Court, whether for the sake of information or, as here, for particular ends like the release of Lord Loudoun. Private hopes could easily be included within the larger pro-cesses.[176] The courtiers did not have it at all easy; other, English enemies of Hamilton, whether for public or private reasons, would later accuse him of betraying the king by this incident of collusion![177]

Hamilton risked a pact with Loudoun for the time being, but the general circumstances of mutual distrust perhaps not surprisingly meant that the Covenanters' response to the king was courteous but defiant. There was still reason to worry at what was happening with royal armies; intransigence was not confined either to Charles, despite Loudoun's arguments for what theoretically ought to have been agreeable. Sir Thomas Hope was among the many who, given the outcome, ended up constrained to uphold the legislation of the 1640 parliament.[178] Subsequently there was another petition which stressed that the Acts of the parliament had to be accepted by Charles. For Hamilton and Loudoun, what understanding there had been managed in London was progressively worn down because of the distance. The black and white perspective of the king or of the public rhetoric of the Covenanters created two sides, neither of which was truly a unity.[179]

The critical tendency of people who wished less generous freedom to the movement of events within Scotland was captured elsewhere around the charismatic Earl of Montrose, who on the 'side' against the king nevertheless forged the Cumbernauld band, with some eighteen or nineteen other nobles in July 1640. This was an agreement which pledged support to the original ideals of the Covenant 'in defence of religion, king and country' – a striking coincidence with the words of Loudoun in his earlier talks; the Band's language and later defences suggested that a minority was regarded as having

---

[176] *APS*, vol. V, pp. 286–7, 189–90. For other contemporary links between Scots and Court, see NLS Wod. Fo. 63, fol. 178; PRO 31/3/72, fol. 112; NLS Ms. 3134, no. 7; Fraser, *Haddington*, vol. II, pp. 179–84.
[177] *CSPD 1640*, 459/61; PRO SP 16/466/34; Staffs. RO D661/11/1/5 no. 4.
[178] Cf. GD 112/40/2/3/45; Burnet, *Memoires*, pp. 172–3; GD 406/1/1217.
[179] NLS Adv. Ms. 33.4.6, fol. 3 (17 July). For later Loudoun–Hamilton letters, one of which was circulated, see GD 406/1/1218; *CSPD 1640*, 464/48; GD 406/1/1219, 1278, 1216.

stepped beyond these ideals. Words of principle passed over personal animosities which existed, since talk of the possible need for a temporary 'dictator', together with the unpleasant personality clash over the expedition against Atholl and the Ogilvies, lay in a background which included poor relations between Montrose and most obviously, the Earl of Argyll. Loudoun could not be numbered here – he was if nothing else a Campbell; but there were more than half of the earls who had attended the 1640 parliament, a collection of prominent Covenanters, even if within the history of the Scottish troubles a high proportion had had what must be called a variable history of commitment.[180]

Rumour had reached a Scot in London shortly after the ending of the 1640 parliament on 11 June that there was a likely plan by the Covenanters to invade England, to pre-empt the aggressive strike by the king and its undesirable bloodshed, and to attempt in as peaceful manner as possible to oblige the king to yield to demands.[181] The argument of justification had to be extreme necessity. The impasse was as much in the king's mind as in the suffering felt directly under his blockade of Scotland, but it was the more visible pressure which furnished an excuse at least for propaganda purposes, with the final decision to march not being taken until 3 August, the crossing of the Tweed following on the 20th of the same month.[182] The king was preparing a military attack, though his progress towards that was uneven; however, for the Covenanters to cross on to English soil carried risks far beyond any arising from correspondence with foreign powers. However reluctant English people were to undergo the cost and effort of this war, the invasion of their home soil would be bound to stir up enmity. To persuade the English that the cause was reasonable, the printed output of the Covenanters took a key role in the operation; integral too were the private contacts which were nurtured as far as possible. There was substantial advance planning.

By late June troops were beginning to be gathered for the king at Selby in Yorkshire. The royal war effort was problem-filled but by no means hopeless. Shortage of money rather than of men was probably the main reason for delay, at least in England; in Ireland there was also a lack of ships. Troop movements in Scotland caused the king and his establishment to ponder whether the Scots would dare to invade now that events had reached such a high pitch; opinion seems to have fluctuated. The Covenanters' bragging

---

[180] Napier, *Memorials of Montrose*, vol. I, pp. 254–5; Stevenson, *Scottish Revolution*, pp. 197–9, 206–7; Napier, *Montrose and the Covenanters*, vol. I, pp. 376–7; cf. Baillie, *Letters*, vol. I, p. 247.

[181] BL Harl. Ms. 383, fol. 174. Sir John Seton was the individual.

[182] Johnston, *1639 Diary*, p. 97; NLS Adv. Ms. 33.4.6, fols. 1–2; GD 112/40/2/3/2; Baillie, *Letters*, vol. I, pp. 256–9; Stevenson, *Scottish Revolution*, pp. 208–9.

about English friends was regularly discussed in dispatches to and from the north. Strafford believed that Scottish invasion was bound to meet severe English resistance. Windebank thought 'companions in iniquity' more than anything else to be behind the real troubles of raising soldiers and coat and conduct money; only at a particularly low point did he feel like acknowledging the possibility of support for the Scots in England. But questions concerning this became more and more searching.[183]

Worries became sharply focused when the Scottish soldiers drew up on the banks of the Tweed and their printed propaganda began to circulate as the preparative act for their crossing. Here in early August news of contacts across the border was taken very seriously.[184] In the period of invasion a Scot detained for distributing tracts and maintaining contacts with Englishmen in the north, the Laird of Lochtour, was ordered to be clapped in prison and examined by fair means or foul on what exactly was going on. Involved here was Sir Henry Vane, who felt corrected on his previous assumption that national hostility was greater in the north than in the south.[185] It is worth noting that there had been cross-border contacts even in 1639. However, the area needed careful treatment by the Scots; they found friends, as Vane realised, but they equally received criticism, which the burdens of occupation in time would multiply.[186]

The king's men tried hard to dig into the question of subversive contacts, but made only limited ground in what nevertheless was an important high-level dimension of the invasion process. When Lord Loudoun returned to Scotland at the end of June 1640, he almost certainly brought with him reports of English friendship.[187] Although not all of the source material can be authenticated, it seems possible to construct a narrative of that Anglo-Scottish dimension in the crucial period around the time of invasion.

A letter in the other direction said, plausibly, to have been written by Johnston of Wariston had come to Loudoun only a short time before his

---

[183] The reports are frequent in *CSPD 1640*, but see especially 457/25, 459/41, 460/14, 64 (Windebank quote), 461/16, 59, 463/62; GD 406/1/1231; *State Papers . . . Clarendon*, vol. II, p. 89; *The Works of the Most Reverend Father in God, William Laud, D.D.*, ed. W. Scott and J. Bliss (7 vols., Oxford, 1847–60), vol. VII, pp. 606–9; Collins, *Letters*, vol. II, p. 659.

[184] *CSPD 1640*, 461/57, 463/2, 11, 31, 39, 54, 81. Sir John Conyers sent an early copy of the *Intentions of the Army of . . . Scotland*, Aldis 970 (n.p., 1640) to Sir Henry Vane about 9 August; Windebank received one from Conway – *CSPD 1640*, 463/91.

[185] *CSPD 1640*, 464/41, 77–8, 95, 465/27, 38; GD 406/1/1691. Cf. Thomas Triplett – *CSPD 1640*, 458/19. Lochtour was the brother of William Carr, who was already an object of suspicion – *CSPD 1640*, 461/57, 463/2, 11, 71; for his eventual release, see NLS Adv. Ms. 33.4.6, fol. 33.

[186] GD 406/1/1008; *CSPD 1640–1*, 466/76, 89; PRO SP 16/467/142; NLS Adv. Ms. 33.4.6, fols. 2–6; Adv. Ms. 33.4.7, fol. 4.

[187] GD 112/40/2/3/45.

sudden release. Wariston was asking for assurance of English concurrence at the time of invasion and he requested particularly the signatures of 'some eminent person or persons' on a solemn engagement. The common enemy was the papist and prelate, the common aim the well settling of the churches and kingdoms: might there then be a possibility of a common league or band? The Covenanters would prepare a declaration to justify themselves to the English, on grounds which had already been advised by the 'friends', but otherwise all would be done in secrecy until after the Scots were in England.[188]

The codename used here, Nathaniel Black, was one which lasted the years of secret plotting on the Covenanter side; Loudoun another time would be known as Nathaniel White. Separately, the Earl of Rothes in his correspondence hinted that events were coming to a head. Again, rumour picked up by the French ambassador fastened on ideas that the Scots would demand a final settlement within a new English parliament, which was certainly the eventuality and, given the past, most likely an important foundation of cross-kingdom talks.[189] The alleged cause of tendencies to popery was not neglected either. Before the end of July, when the Scottish army was already drawing together in the Borders, Wariston was involved in settling the 'quickest passages in hand of our agreement and mutual concurrence'. Although the immediate priority was the coordination of approaches to the king, he expressed concern that the friends still needed to be persuaded from 'their doubts and scruples anent the kirk government'.[190] Covenant talk was in the air. Possibly it was Wariston who also around the same time, in a pamphlet entitled 'Grounds of God's aim and call to this voyage as the means to the end', developed arguments for the abolition of episcopacy in all three kingdoms.[191]

Early in July, if the copy source is to be believed, one Englishman at least had given a positive reply to Wariston's letter. He told that the friends were prepared to unite themselves into a considerable body and to draw up a remonstrance for the king as soon as the invasion took place, this to bear reference to the grievances of both Scots and English; he agreed with the idea of a covenant. The Scottish army was the 'sole and principal means' of achieving satisfaction of desires. Practically it was envisaged that the army should

---

[188] Like Gardiner, I am accepting the authenticity of this letter transcribed in J. Oldmixon, *The History of England during the Reigns of the Royal House of Stuart* (1730), pp. 141–2. See Gardiner, *History of England*, vol. IX, p. 179.

[189] NLS Wod. Fo. 66, fols. 201, 203; NLS Ms. 81, no. 13; PRO 31/3/72, fol. 214.

[190] NLS Wod. Fo. 64, fol. 203 (pre-28 July; Wariston holograph marks are on this paper). Cf. Baillie, *Letters*, vol. I, p. 275. Wariston was later rewarded under Oliver Cromwell for his 'special hand in the brotherly assistance given to England in 1640' (and 1643) – NLS Wod. Fo. 68, fol. 18.

[191] EUL New College Ms. X15b 3/1 vol. I, fols. 245–8.

come to London, where nobles and the City would give their support. On the way everything should be paid for – including what was taken from papist and prelate; fighting was to be avoided if possible. A good reputation might thus be won with those who were not ill-affected. Information was given on the state of the English defences. As significantly, the Covenanters were told that money was being collected for them, and there was a promise of some English troops, particularly among the horse, giving their direct support. The specific points of reform were not touched upon; but, as was the case with Wariston, the author considered the invasion in terms of 'deliverance' – 'of the poor and fettered gospel in both kingdoms, and a just judgement on the authors of these desperate counsels'.[192]

An account ascribed to Viscount Mandeville, later second Earl of Manchester, associated a supposedly forged letter of encouragement signed by himself and six other peers to the 'falseness and impudence' of Lord Savile. A text provided later by the historian Oldmixon was artificially squared with this, but deserves attention for its likely authentic substance. The authors entered upon less full assurances here, keen to encourage but cautious about publicly showing this; the Covenant idea of forces and money being supplied to the invading Scots amounted to treason under English law. Nevertheless Scottish 'deliverance' was to be hoped for.[193] The Manchester memoir set out to deny that treason had ever been committed by himself with the others; written retrospectively, and when Savile's reputation was thoroughly sullied, we should not readily place our trust here, as will be seen. Were the seven peers – Bedford, Essex, Warwick, Saye and Sele, Brooke, Savile and Mandeville – truly engaged in cross-kingdom contacts? It is certainly possible.[194]

However great English responsiveness, the Scots gave the real moving-force by their action. In dialogue that took place, Wariston's mention of disagreements over church government raised one aspect of differences between English and Scottish godliness and political vision which would dog future good relations. This was particularly relevant in the Scots' pursuit of the idea of a mutual covenant. With agreement not essential given the immediate priorities, the time for this had to be postponed. The Covenanters did not

---

[192] Oldmixon, *History*, pp. 143–4, where the letter is ascribed to Lord Savile. The text is at least a little corrupted.

[193] Oldmixon, *History*, pp. 142–3. The ascription of authorship seems to have been taken from the Manchester memoir.

[194] BL Add. Ms. 15567, fols. 7–8; below, p. 252. See Stevenson, *Scottish Revolution*, pp. 188, 358, and further on Walter Frost, BL Add. Ms. 4460, fol. 74v; Warwicks. RO CR 1886/CUP4/21A – travelling charges and gifts in Lord Brooke's accounts. My conclusions differ slightly from those in Gardiner, *History of England*, vol. IX, pp. 179–81. The letter must have a late date given that the peers apparently allude to Scottish propaganda on the eve of the invasion – i.e. in early August 1640.

wish to stand still. Careful planning to allay wider English hostilities, in particular resentment at possible burdens an invading army might bring, informed the more public stance of the Covenanters. In propaganda specially produced and widely distributed, the aim avowed was the presentation of long-standing grievances to the king and thereby a resolution of the troubles. They claimed that their invasion was defensive, impelled by the strains of approaching war, but were confident to announce that they were under God's special blessing and therefore deserved the support of those in England who loved the truth. The English were 'reminded' of the Short Parliament's unwillingness to finance a war against the Scots since members' speeches, complaints and grievances had shown that England's cause was the same; the support of London was called as witness. Together with purely Scottish ends, they called as before for the trial and punishment of the English authors of the troubles in their own parliament – and thus 'against papists the extirpation of popery; against prelates the reformation of the kirk, against atheists the flourishing of the gospel, against traitors and firebrands a perfect and durable union and love between the two kingdoms'. In such general terms they hoped to maximise the appeal of their case, a rhetoric not repeated in the address to Charles at this time.[195] Subsequent statements would be both more specific and more demanding.

The communication sent to the Covenanters after their entry into England by one who signed 'N.F.' gives important confirming evidence of the state of underground contacts. The author, quite probably Nathaniel Fiennes, wrote after the invasion had taken place to tell the Covenanters of the petition addressed by twelve English peers to the king; his father Saye and Sele was among those who signed.[196] The petition had been sent on 28 August to ask Charles for redress of particular grievances and especially for an end to the war, for which the signatories hoped that the king might summon a parliament, both to remedy the troubles and punish the causers of them. Was this not the 'remonstrance' anticipated in the earlier Anglo-Scottish correspondence?[197]

---

[195] *Intentions of the Army of . . . Scotland*, Aldis 970 (n.p., 1640; also in Latin and Dutch, Aldis 965; STC 21921, 21919.5); *Information from the Scottish Nation, to all . . . English*, Aldis 968 [1640]; GD 406/1/1293. See S. A. Burrell, 'The apocalyptic vision of the early Covenanters', *SHR*, 43 (1964), 1–24; *CSPD 1640*, 465/12, 86; BL Harl. Ms. 383, fol. 182; Johnston, *1639 Diary*, p. 97.

[196] Cf. *Vindiciae Veritatis*, Wing F884 (1654), p. 29. I am grateful to Dr John Adamson for drawing my attention to this pamphlet, for which see J. S. A. Adamson, 'The *Vindiciae Veritatis* and the political creed of Viscount Saye and Sele', *Historical Research*, 60 (1987), 45–63. For the communication here described, see P. H. Donald, 'New light on the Anglo-Scottish contacts of 1640', *Historical Research*, 62 (1989), 221–9.

[197] *CSPD 1640*, 465/16. The original signatories numbered twelve – the Earls of Bedford, Hertford, Exeter, Essex, Rutland, Warwick, Bolingbroke and Mulgrave, Viscounts Saye and Sele and Mandeville, Lords Edward Howard and Brooke. Copies of the petition exhibiting

The letter informed the Scots that, in the event of an unsatisfactory answer, the lords were resolved to stay together in one body and thus to work for a solution. The City of London and 'all the gentry' would second this petition with one of their own. Most significant, though, was the provision for action appropriate for the 'peers of England to do in regard of their great interest [in religion, liberty and laws] for the safety of both king and kingdom and their own neighbour nation and church of Scotland'. If necessary, forces might appear to be called the 'armies of the commonwealth', and there was detail of what might be hoped for; there were nine colonels in Charles's army who with all their regiments would join in the cause. The mood was optimistic, noting that gentry everywhere would willingly join with them.[198]

To balance this the condition of the king's army was described. It was said to be fortunate that the Scots had not entered England as early as planned, for the king was still poorly supplied and the stated Scottish aim of petitioning and non-aggression would therefore be the more convincing. The author asked whether the Scots would march south from Newcastle to press a quick victory, in conjunction with help from the peers and others. The king would not willingly capitulate, and it was necessary to coordinate tactics. It was offered that the peers intended to ask Charles to appoint a treaty in order to prevent spilling of blood. This was preferable in so far as it would look better if the Scots acted unaided and that by their pacific carriage they win the affection of the English nation; the king would be portrayed in this way not as an underdog who might attract support but as a figure appealed to by two popular groups. One other practical cause of disturbance was anticipated: the Scots were advised to give assurance to London that the coal trade would continue – an important point if the City and commons were not to be alienated.[199]

The strategy of invasion was a sensitive business. National antipathies might be aroused; invasion might be construed to be against the person of the king instead of in order to ask him for settlement. Both sides had hopes that the Scots would not meet with serious resistance. The purpose was to ensure peaceful settlement in particular by the sacrifice of enemy counsellors; the king was not personally threatened – but his authority and administration were, and particularly those who had led cooperatively in government of

---

other names (which are numerous) are less straightforwardly handled; some peers certainly signed later – *CSPD 1640–1*, 467/88. I am grateful to Professor Russell for discussions around this.

[198] On the peers' interest, cf. C. S. R. Russell, 'The first army plot of 1641', *TRHS*, 5th Series, 37 (1987), 105–6. On the gentry cf. PRO SP 16/446/75; EUL Ms. Dc. 4.16, fol. 4v.

[199] EUL New College Ms. X15b 3/1 vol. I, fol. 262; another copy in NLS Adv. Ms. 33.1.1, vol. XIII, no. 28; Donald, 'New light on the Anglo-Scottish contacts'. Sir Henry Vane was likewise unclear on the geographical target of the Scottish army – *CSPD 1640–1*, 466/2, 17, 30, 76.

church and state. The peers petitioned the king at a crucial moment; at least some of them seemed prepared even for direct confrontation by arms should Charles still determine to fight the Scots.

The peers claimed a backing far beyond their own group, probably exaggeratedly optimistic, and Scots were not likely to contradict this. Networks of course involved non-noble figures, including people who would be prominent in the House of Commons like John Pym and John Hampden; Sir John Clotworthy, who distributed copies of the petition, would defend the petition in the subsequent English Long Parliament.[200] Since indeed the call was above all for a parliament, and positive siding with the Scots was not admitted, the appeal of the petition cast widely, although it did not lack criticism at the time.[201]

The Covenanters knew of support from groups in London in August and September, and they followed the advice to give assurances to the Mayor there. The Londoners' petition, advertised to the Scots in advance, was sent to Charles despite the best efforts of privy councillors and the Lord Mayor. It echoed the demands of the peers' petition, indirectly criticising the war and asking for a parliament to be summoned.[202] The apprentices too, their own self-description, made a public stand on the Covenanters' behalf, for when the proclamations were issued denouncing the invaders as rebels, they publicly declared them 'good and loyal subjects', at the same time condemning Laud, Strafford and all other incendiaries. Apprentices had rioted after the end of the Short Parliament, when Laud had been a principal target. In early September 1640, a different paper called on 'gentlemen and apprentices and all other brave spirits that do resolve to do anything for religion'. It brought the examples of soldiers who had cast down altars and other perceived symbols of idolatry across the country in recent months, and exhorted the group to forward the cause of reformation – a secret oath was mentioned, so that if anyone individually suffered all should suffer, or else all should be relieved.[203] This was a 'covenant' in England, and Windebank came to hear

---

[200] *State Papers . . . Clarendon*, vol. II, pp. 94–5; *The Camden Miscellany*, vol. VIII (1893), p. 2; Lancs. RO DdHu/46/21; BL Add. Ms. 4460, fol. 74v; *D'Ewes (N)*, pp. 41–2, 365, 538; *CJ*, vol. II, p. 30; HLRO Main Papers, 25 November, 12 December 1640, 9 March 1641; *LJ*, vol. IV, pp. 98, 188, 189; BL Harl. Ms. 6424, fol. 52r.

[201] Cf. *State Papers . . . Clarendon*, vol. II, pp. 110–12; PRO SP 16/466/75, 91–2; Staffs. RO D 661/11/1/5; Collins, *Letters*, vol. II, pp. 659–60.

[202] *CSPD 1640–1*, 467/75, 9, 135; BL Add. Ms. 24984, fol. 7; V. Pearl, *London and the Outbreak of the Puritan Revolution* (1964), pp. 99–102.

[203] NLS Adv. Ms. 33.1.1, vol. XIII, no. 12 (27 August); Baillie, *Letters*, vol. I, p. 261; Gardiner, *History of England*, vol. IX, pp. 132–4; EUL New College Ms. X15b 3/1 vol. I, fol. 260. Note also Baillie, *Letters*, vol. I, p. 65.

of it.[204] At a higher level, Johnston of Wariston would still be pressing towards a covenant for both nations.[205]

Significant efforts therefore had gone into cementing links across kingdom boundaries, though such designed unity, incomplete in its as yet only roughly formulated goals, was only one aspect of Charles's troubles. His military standing was never finally tested, but the Scots' invasion was an affront he did not take lightly. In the early days of August, Viscount Conway in the north was the first to receive warning that invasion and a drive towards Newcastle were imminent. He sent for reinforcements from Yorkshire.[206] Charles was immediate in his response; the news that the Earl of Northumberland, his general, had suffered a tertian ague at exactly this time prompted him to suggest that he should go himself to the defence of Newcastle – and beyond, as was possible. He put this to a full meeting of the privy council on the Sunday, 16 August. It was a stroke of decisiveness, of gritted-teeth response, which seemingly took the council by surprise, for he answered passionately the objections raised in plenty, notably by Hamilton and Strafford.[207]

Strafford had also had ill-health, but having readjusted from initial indignation at what he had seen as scaremongering on Conway's part, he was appointed Lieutenant-General to follow the king, whose 'life and courage' he openly admired. Hamilton, equally forward to serve, travelled with Charles in his coach.[208] Thus the three-prong offensive was dropped in favour of a defensive thrust. Charles hoped that his presence would encourage his people to give of their energies, especially since his Lord General being ill might have discouraged them. At the same time he was determined to show the Scots that the arguments of their propaganda were false. If there was a party in support of the Scots, as they wished – and as was at least loosely the case – no opportunities were to be given to it. He left London on the day that the Covenanters crossed into England.[209]

Charles went as far as Northallerton in Yorkshire, where on 29 August he tried to rouse the local men. However, the next day was when the Covenanters, having had to fight at Newburn, took Newcastle in a major strategic gain – and without a struggle. As Viscount Conway retreated, the king moved back to York. The English military preparations had achieved little. As for the efforts to establish what collaboration ran across the border, an initial northern focus gave way to investigation of the possibly more national

---

[204] *State Papers ... Clarendon*, vol. II, p. 113; *HMC Various Collections* (55), vol. II, pp. 258–9; PRO SP 16/467/75.
[205] NLS Wod. Fo. 64, fols. 190, 203; cf. Wod. Fo. 66, fol. 223v.
[206] *CSPD 1640*, 463/50, 451/33.
[207] PRO SP 16/463/91; *CSPD 1640*, 463/99, 464/2, 8.
[208] *CSPD 1640*, 464/3, 27; BL Harl. Ms. 383, fol. 184.
[209] Cf. Gardiner, *History of England*, vol. IX, pp. 182–91.

dimension. Two of the signatories of the peers' petition had to answer before the privy council sitting in London. Coincidences could not be missed; a petition from the Covenanters, dated 2 September, reached the king hours before the peers' petition, asking in general terms for relief of the pressing grievances and for the settling of a firm and durable peace with the advice of the 'estates' of the kingdom of England convened in a parliament.[210] Had Englishmen invited in the Scots? The king had questions, but no certain answers.[211]

The full nature of the contacts which passed secretly between discontented parties remained largely undisclosed. The Scots had sent a copy of their petition to their English friends; they received back a letter signed apparently by nearly thirty English peers, which offered approval and an update of news from their end. This reported that the shock in the king's camp at the English petition gave hope that a short time would suffice to see a capitulation of some kind. They told that the king's army was weak; that the nine 'commonwealth' regiments were still assured. What they could not send was money or victuals, so they echoed the Scots' own intentions in asking that for this interim period they should try to subsist without oppressing the local people. A treaty was to be hoped for as a result of the Scottish petition. The letter closed with an affirmation that the English would be as careful of the Scottish interest as of their own.[212]

A sense of shared purposes, at least after the event of invasion if not before, knew its negative targets better than its positive ones, but everything awaited conclusion with the king in parliament. The polarisation put Hamilton, because of his position if not his inclination, on the other side. He remained closely associated with the king and a line that feared and often detested 'popular' stirrings. Besides the Covenanter denunciation of Scottish individuals who were to be called to trial, the English encouragers of the Covenanters in the quest for settlement reminded them to ensure that not only 'interested' English privy councillors be excluded from participating in the expected treaty talks, but also Scottish courtiers such as Lennox or Hamilton. At this time the marquis had to find his protection with the king.[213]

---

[210] Staffs. RO D 661/11/1/5; NLS Dep. 175/Box 80 unfol.; *State Papers . . . Clarendon*, vol. II, pp. 110–12; PRO SP 16/466/75; *CSPD 1640–1*, 465/38, 466/36 (original GD 406/1/1290), 467/5, 9, 61; NLS Adv. Ms. 33.4.7, fol. 5; Crawford Ms. 14/3/80.

[211] Cf. *State Papers . . . Clarendon*, vol. II, p. 120; *CSPD 1640–1*, 468/23; PRO SP 16/468/137 (second letter); BL Add. Ms. 11045, fols. 122, 125.

[212] EUL New College Ms. X15b 3/1 vol. I, fols. 262–3; Donald, 'New light on the Anglo-Scottish contacts'. The copy notes only some of the signatories – the Earls of Bedford, Hertford, Bolingbroke, Exeter and Mulgrave, Viscounts Saye and Sele and Mandeville, Lords Howard and Brooke.

[213] EUL New College Ms. X15b 3/1 vol. I, fol. 263; GD 406/1/1278, 1219, 1216, 1284; BL Add. Ms. 35838, fol. 164.

Charles, determined and aggressive towards the Covenanters, had no intention of capitulating to any treaty save on his own terms, but shortage of money and fears of defeat at the hands of the Scots obliged a measure of restraint. The king's servants looked to his army and possible means of reinforcing it from the south, but they also considered how to unite a strong English force with the king to stand up against the Scots – questions political as well as military. For army prospects, Strafford could advise only a defensive; small sums of money channelled north somehow kept his men in order, and in the south Windebank and the council hesitated to do more than send out orders for military readiness. The drawing together of troops was deliberately held back when money was so short and tempers so uncertain.[214]

Sir Henry Vane on 29 August, without mention of the king's agreement, suggested that the councillors in London consider how to advise the king, a loaded request in the circumstances. Vane, who had replaced Sir John Coke as Secretary of State, inclined more readily to a peaceable end to the problem than his colleague, who retained longer the feeling of the king, that a solution by means of force was best; and Windebank in reply asked for direction.[215] Very quickly, however, on the 30th, from the news that Newcastle had been taken without resistance, Charles himself recommended the London group to consider 'other counsels', that is, besides the immediate practical organisation of the army.[216]

It was following directly from this that debate on 2 September in the privy council in London produced advice for the summoning of a great council of the peers. 'Other counsels' might have been for a parliament, but few in London supported this as opposed to a great council; the rest divided between favouring both or just the Council. At first it was supposed that the Council would be held in London, as a quick means to help the king by widening the base of counsel behind him in his dealings with the Scots. The country's present disunity was seen as a weakness to be overcome. But Secretary Windebank admitted in his writing to the king the advantages of a full parliament, which by dealing with grievances might be the best means for giving the king forces and money, the practical requirements for waging war. Charles was not wholly dismissive, but the subject had to be raised cautiously, even without knowledge of the direct demands of the peers' petition and Scots propaganda.[217] A great council was similarly up for debate

---

[214] See for example *CSPD 1640–1*, 466/2, 107, 467/28; GD 406/1/1231; *State Papers . . . Clarendon*, vol. II, pp. 89–91, 94–9; Whitaker, *Radcliffe Correspondence*, pp. 203–4.

[215] *CSPD 1640*, 465/38, 56; see too PRO SP 16/466/76, 84, 467/19, 20, 60, 76, 142, 468/116; Bod. Clarendon Ms. 19, fols. 39–40. Vane and Windebank were perhaps not always completely frank to each other.

[216] *CSPD 1640*, 465/50. Cf. *CSPD 1640–1*, 467/60; Bod. Clarendon Ms. 19, fols. 111–12.

[217] PRO SP 16/466/11, 12; *State Papers . . . Clarendon*, vol. II, pp. 94–5. See too C. S. R. Russell, 'Why did Charles I call the Long Parliament?', *History*, 69 (1984), 375–83.

around the king in York. As an institution it had been in abeyance for over a
century, but Charles presumably hoped that it would be less troublesome
than a parliament, for he asked to hear from Windebank which people had
preferred the latter. He resolved to summon his nobility to a Council to be
held at York on 24 September.[218]

However clear the king's wishes, hopes did not die for a parliament, and in
the light of the peers' petition there was concern that many might refuse to
attend the Council. Following another letter from Vane, the council in
London debated again the question of a parliament. As earlier in the month,
although now more unanimously, there was a strong argument for Charles
summoning a parliament by his own volition rather than visibly under
pressure, and so keeping his honour.[219] The beginning of a stream of county
petitions as well as one from ministers and others concerning the notorious
oath passed in Convocation earlier in the year made inroads against wishes
for English unity, but the army in any case was in no state at that point to face
the enemy.[220] Although Charles rejected the advice of some to be harsh
towards the carriers of the petitions, since they had strong backing, he came
round just shortly before the Council met to agree that the best time for
summoning a parliament was not to be lost.[221]

Charles continued to believe that the English should merely follow his lead
with respect to the affairs of the Scots, and it was in line with this that he still
kept separate the responsibilities for Scottish affairs. Sir Henry Vane learnt of
the first main Scottish petition after Charles had answered it, and received no
more promptly details of subsequent Covenanter statements. Whether or not
Vane was correct in his understanding that Strafford was consulted for
Charles's answer to the first petition, Charles's endorsement was on a copy
written out by Hamilton, and Lanark made the copy which Vane sent on to
the privy council in London.[222] Charles also sent for Traquair, fulfilling a
promise that no treaty would be made without him.[223] Furthermore he
avoided giving answer to the Covenanters, referring them to the Council to be
held at York – and meanwhile was quite happy for chances to be taken to
make life uncomfortable for them; though there was a risk of displeasing

---

[218] *CSPD 1640–1*, 466/54; *State Papers . . . Clarendon*, vol. II, pp. 113–15.

[219] *CSPD 1640–1*, 467/5, 60, 75.

[220] Cf. Cope, *Politics without Parliaments*, pp. 194–5, 198; P. H. Donald, 'The king and the
Scottish troubles, 1637–1641' (unpublished University of Cambridge Ph.D. dissertation,
1988), p. 364n.; *CSPD 1640–1*, 467/28, 60.

[221] The decision seems to have been made around 22 September – cf. *CSPD 1640–1*, 467/101;
PRO SP 16/466/42, p. 37, 467/119, 135; *State Papers . . . Clarendon*, vol. II, pp. 118, 120;
D'Ewes (N), p. 393.

[222] *CSPD 1640–1*, 466/54, 76, 467/5. Vane made no mention of the first Scottish petition in his
letter of 5 September. PRO SP 16/466/76; GD 406/1/8328.

[223] Traqr. Ms. 11/48 (12 September)

Londoners through disrupting coal supplies to the south, he authorised a complete blockade of Newcastle.[224]

Covenanters and peers had asked for settlement within an English parliament; as for these peers, the Covenanters' first response to the news of the great council was cold. They were direct in their insistence that this would not avert the need for an English parliament, and laid down for the king basis for an agreement under eight 'heads'.[225] Publicly they rejoiced in their easy progress to date, and thanked Providence, but decided, contrary to their original thoughts, to set up a long-term base in the north-east – in agreement with the suggestions of the 'N.F.' paper.[226]

To march no further might have averted the likelihood of battle, but occupation of one area was not without problems, including desertions in the ranks and arguments higher up.[227] They had hindrance as well as help from locals, for not all necessarily viewed them as the 'redeemers' they cast themselves to be. Raised expectations and excited vision had to cope with the relative disappointment of finding positive support so limited in the English people they met.[228] The army had to be fed and paid; collaborators were appointed to find supplies for them, and the Scots leaders met with officeholders and gentry in Northumberland, County Durham and Newcastle to fix a regular loan contribution towards the upkeep of their army. Such diplomacy hoped to reduce the inevitable tensions which would arise; the land of Catholics and churchmen, however, seems to have been more cavalierly exploited. Feeling at last assured that Charles was not strong enough for present aggression, the Covenanters prepared for as long a stay as was necessary for their desired ends.[229]

The year between the king's journey south from Berwick and his return north to York can have given little cause for joy to Charles. Scottish troubles had forced a retreat where grand visions of the sway of majesty had to bow to a nation of rebels. If that had not sufficiently fired the king's wrath, the revel-

---

[224] GD 406/1/8328 – Hamilton may have acted as more than a scribe, for he wrote originally of a working towards 'reconciliation' in this reply to the Covenanters of 5 September, which the king amended to 'happy conclusion'! For incidents, and the blockade, see *CSPD 1640–1*, 467/28, 75–6, 119, 470/4, 69, 74; *State Papers . . . Clarendon*, vol. II, pp. 116, 118.

[225] GD 406/1/1295 (copy in *CSPD 1640–1*, 466/82); GD 406/1/1291 (*CSPD 1640–1*, 467/59); NLS Adv. Ms. 33.4.6, fols. 9–10 (cf. *CSPD 1640–1*, 468/39).

[226] Cf. letters from Newcastle of 2 and 8 September in NLS Crawford Ms. 14/3/80; also see GD 112/40/2/3/2; Balfour, *Historical Works*, vol. II, pp. 388–9.

[227] NLS Crawford Ms. 14/3/80; NLS Adv. Ms. 33.4.6, fols. 5–6; EUL Ms. Dc. 4.16, fol. 4; NLS Wod. Fo. 31, fols. 27–9; GD 112/40/2/3/7; Napier, *Memorials of Montrose*, p. 220.

[228] Cf. NLS Adv. Ms. 33.4.6, fols. 5–6; Baillie, *Letters*, vol. I, pp. 257–8, 262.

[229] *CSPD 1640–1*, 467/28, 59; p. 61; 467/76; NLS Adv. Ms. 33.4.6, fols. 3–6; Grosart, *Lismore Papers*, vol. IV, p. 135; P. Yorke, *Miscellaneous State Papers, from 1501 to 1726* (2 vols., 1778), vol. II, pp. 215–16.

ation of demands civil as well as ecclesiastical in the Edinburgh parliament had then to be stomached, as well as a continuation of that parliament which dared to sit and pass legislation in the summer of 1640 in the absence of any royal representative. The final blow had been the invasion of a Covenanter army, with which Charles's own passionate response was powerless to deal. The king had driven north only to be nearer news of English losses; he was offered expressions of discontent from his English subjects that bore all too many familiar tones. A popular menace evidently had to be faced in both kingdoms.

His Scottish advisers shared in the suffering, though in different terms. Counsel to the king to yield more positively on the leading religious questions seemed to offer grounds of hope which were frustrated first at Court and then by the hostile unanimity of the Covenanters. Traquair tried to make friends and allies, but ended up a public target of scorn and ire. He carried much of the cost of Charles's singlemindedness; however much the Covenanters knew the king himself to be the fount of the problems, they continued to keep their attack within a traditional framework, though much of their practice was all but revolutionary. At the same time they had gone beyond simply peaceful means; in contrast to 1639, the possibility of a pitched battle against royalist forces was seriously in the reckoning in 1640. Hamilton would also be their target, bound to be accused for his failure to press a Covenant settlement for which he probably had little taste. However, while these Scots near the king were vulnerable, Covenanter ambitions would be turning ever more to institutionally guaranteed forms of settlement, as a means of ensuring the king was 'well' counselled – though for some individuals there would be a tension here. Competitive ambition might yet be the king's way into divisions for his advantage.

Charles's rigidity of stance, which almost wished to deny that the troubles were real, had support even if Strafford, who backed him positively in his aggression, was unable with others to overcome in time the many practical problems of waging this intended war. For Charles the major issue remained his authority in the Scottish church, but though this took in the whole question of sovereignty, as the story of the National Covenant had shown, his isolation in the Scottish scene is very striking. His English councillors might support him, and not least Archbishop Laud, alongside Strafford a principal target of the Covenanters; but in Scotland not even the Aberdeen doctors made much of the king's preference as they defended themselves in 1640.[230] There was a structural problem, but it was one which Charles by his approach exacerbated. Did distance in miles count as much as distance in ideology? Scottish politics demanded an engagement which he was plainly unable to

---

[230] At the 1640 general assembly – Baillie, *Letters*, vol. I, p. 248; AUL Ms. 635, pp. 381–97.

offer, save by the tools of bloodshed and oppression. The events of the next few years would confirm that a general attitude was involved on his part, but his three-kingdom responsibility undoubtedly aggravated the situation. Despite the high terms which the struggle had reached, civil war in 1640 would have had few Scots on the king's side.

For the Scots, who invaded first, matters of kirk and state went together; parliamentary legislation was supposed to reinforce enactments of general assemblies so as to add coercive force and to cover all civil implications, but there were distinct areas of action. The narrative here has hardly touched on the many purely civil items before the Scottish parliament of 1639–40 – items of trade and the economy, of local jurisdiction and law and order as well as of central government, royal appointments, parliamentary procedure, privy council accountability. Many of the wide range of matters considered belonged only tangentially to this particular crisis, yet they had become firmly part and parcel of it.

The Covenanters Charles opposed were far from united, but his threatening aspect near forced them to be. Traquair's assessment of divisions was well founded even though Johnston of Wariston and his co-workers did all they could to argue their increasingly multi-faceted cause. Those who did not opt out altogether naturally continued to look for settlement of religion and liberties, as had been the banner of the troubles at their origin, but for a long time Charles was not capable of listening to their words. Certainly it remains true that to have separated off a moderate settlement from the highest demands being made would not have been without difficulties, but this was hoped for by many – and denied to all. Covenanter leaders nevertheless were vital for continuing impressively to mould the operation of resistance; finance and men were managed through a complex organisation, not without problems but sufficient to create an army of invasion well supported centrally by the Committee of Estates. The next stage was to engage earnestly with the British dimension of settling peace.

The Scottish invasion was inspired by both apocalyptic vision and fears for national security, but it was an integral aspect of the preparation that English friendship should be wooed, so as to make likely a reasonable outcome. Certain parties in England may have been highly amenable to this, though whether the enthusiasm of many for the Scottish cause against existing patterns of government allowed for invasion of English soil may be doubted. Private contacts contributed, but the public appeal was as important. Reform for Scots, English and Irish demanded change in the king's counsel, and it happened that this could be conjointly channelled primarily against Laud and Strafford, though many others within the current establishment were also vulnerable; that reform was to be by means of representative assemblies was another clear point of linkage. How significant was all of this? Evidently supporters of the English peers' petition consciously took a concern in Covenanter progress after the invasion, and they hoped to carry the country with them. There was no united cause between the kingdoms – but it seems likely that in the circumstances hostility was to some extent dampened. If nothing else, many English folk were to appreciate the parliament that after a month was summoned in consequence of the disgrace of invasion; in Ireland an opportunity to attack Strafford drew nearer.

Although sources make it difficult to assess pro-Scottish feeling as a contributory factor to Charles's military shortcomings, it is not probable that this was his main problem in England. If it played a part, it was alongside administrative ineffectiveness, antipathy to the cost and effort of war, shortage of supply, popular English disaffection. It was part of the king's weakness, however, that, having himself hoped to invade, he could not even risk a defensive battle against his Scots opponents, in spite of having two other kingdoms. He had hoped to skate over the debates and issues of the Short Parliament which he had summoned with such reluctance. In hope of recovering his position, he was persuaded to encourage more consultation through a great council and a parliament. But the Scots hoped to hold him down to conclusions to be ratified in all the kingdoms. With such a crisis over his authority, his problems would range very widely; where the Scots had begun, the English, and Irish, would seek to follow.

7

Projected settlements
September 1640–November 1641

That Charles consented to summon a second English parliament in 1640 was the outcome of the Scottish invasion, although in intention the king was not acceding to the demands of the Covenanters, the English peers and many others of his English subjects. The summons did not necessarily signal the end of the force option as a means of defeating the Scots, but it quickly turned that way. Militarily Charles had to admit to weakness while the armies stayed on foot and money shortages became a crucial factor in the story; this as the background to a political struggle that embraced more than one kingdom pushed him to learn, albeit inadequately, the possibilities of compromise and negotiation that could get the Covenanters back to Scotland in peace. The king wished each of the kingdoms to be separately under his rule; his prag-matic concessions were not generously given. The peace for Scotland would be fragile and short-lived.

Three phases followed one another in this last period to be considered here. The forum of talks between Scots and English representatives at Ripon saw the king abandoning his immediate hopes of making progress by means of his army, forcing concentration instead on the negotiation of terms for supply of the occupying army while treaty was taken as far as possible towards con-clusion. The financial burden, which fell initially on the northern counties where money was borrowed and food and necessities supplied, was referred to the king's English parliament, which sat from 3 November 1640. It con-strained Charles's freedom, but, along with the Covenanters' demand for reparations for losses sustained over the whole of the struggle, gave general cause for tensions, not least since the king's army also had to be supplied. Those unhappy about the disgrace of the Scots invasion had a concrete sub-ject of grievance which weighed heavily on England as a whole.

Talks directly over the Scottish troubles were moved south to London for the meeting of the parliament. Charles had to accept that most of the proceed-ings would be reported not just to himself but to that body. It was confir-mation that the demand for punishment of his counsellors had concomitant positive implications, namely that he should in future be obliged to rule

259

having regard to the conclusions of regular representative assemblies. That the Covenanters envisaged a British settlement, to solve what in many respects seemed to them to have been born of the three-kingdom situation, laid wide open a further set of issues. Charles had no wish to lose authority in two more kingdoms to the extent that the Scots had forced his hand. Therefore, as on account of the financial question, he sought to have the opposing army returned to Scotland with all possible haste. Some dared to resist this, though on the whole English people were sensitive to the imposition of things primarily amenable to the Scottish interest.

As the months drew on, the patience both of negotiators and armies dropped, which moved both king and subjects to conclude and return the business to Scotland. Charles decided to go north himself to attend the Scottish parliament. Initially his own underhand negotiations made him feel hopeful of the possibility of a conclusion with some salvaged honour. In the event he carried through the visit with a more reduced brief, which if nothing else had to prepare the way for recovering the advantage in England. He would have yielded far, yet his negotiating position was weakened by the ramifications of the plots in which he simultaneously engaged. Even at this intended conclusion, he could neither trust nor be trusted.

The few who with energy and daring led in pressing for the realisation of major reform in government, whether Scots or English, were often hard pressed to persuade their fellow nationals; cooperation across the kingdom boundaries was strained, hardly surprising in this novel situation of union politics from below. It may be that most Scots wanted to return home to be ruled by a king more sympathetic to their many and various interests, and that most English folk wished likewise – ideals of unity to which Charles's monarchy was central. There were clear hesitations over encroaching on the king's prerogative though solutions were wished to afflictions of the past. Tensions arose around the attacks made on his counsellors and the possible ways forward to guard against repeat troubles. Even if the words which were used spared Charles attack, the references made to reform linked to the direction of his counsel struck home. The question addressed was how far he could be left to rule alone.

Through this prolonged crisis over central authority, Charles was very seriously challenged, and this he did not take easily. Stability seemed all too unlikely as he came near the end of the Scottish parliament. Ambitious groups of people lined up against him in each of the three kingdoms. His will to control seemed never to be dented by the limitations which events and direct counsel urged upon him. A rising by Catholics in Ireland in the event pitched him into hard straits. On his mainland, he had threatened as well as wooed, plotted while others had plotted against his counsellors, sought to divide as well as unite. In short, the manœuvring he had manifested during the course of the Scottish troubles to date, and in this and previous meetings with his English parliaments, was repeated in a chain that contributed eventually in bringing about a major struggle by arms.

Charles met the great council at York and declared his intention to summon a parliament. He gave terms for both meetings by stating his desire to be rightly understood by his English people and urging a timely remedy to the current evils; he wanted help to proceed to the 'chastisement of these insolences and securing of my good subjects'. The immediate practicalities were moderately couched – a way of answering the petition of the 'rebels' and continuing to support his own army – for Charles intended to steer the Council as far as he could. He was inclined neither to be responsive nor generous towards the Covenanters; his interim conciliation was offered because he lacked a present alternative. Therefore his moderate sounding offers to leave the Council to debate without him were on the understanding that it might follow a brief; Traquair should explain at the very beginning the king's cause against the Covenanters, whereby it was hoped that the dishonour of opening dialogue with rebel invaders might be avoided. Given that the war was justly grounded, means for the king's army were the priority.[1]

General reactions to this opening were quite favourable, as in the circumstances many did feel that the king was to be supported, but this did not mean that his guidelines were not to be questioned.[2] The silence that first followed Charles's speech was broken by the Earl of Bristol, who was to emerge as a leading spokesman of the next month, probably self-appointed; he neither shared the sympathies of some for the Covenanters nor would he be the yes-man of the king. He had dared to suggest long ago, while accompanying Charles to the Scottish border in 1639, that open debate of issues might help all round, and now again he asked whether it was not necessary to suspend judgement until the Scots were heard. Observing that the approaching parliament would be critical of improvident action, he emphasised that in relative strategic weakness Charles had to be prepared to talk, and especially since the Scots alleged that their coming into England was in order to be rightly understood where ill-wishers had misrepresented them. A strong realism had an element with it of criticism for the king's courses to date; Bristol might still obey the king, but he implied that there was room for reformulation of policy – a counsel reminiscent of Hamilton or Traquair. Theoretically the possibility of the peers helping Charles to force the Scots to reason remained, should the

---

[1] Sir J. Balfour, *Historical Works* (4 vols., Edinburgh, 1824–5), vol. II, p. 405; A. B. Grosart, *Lismore Papers* (10 vols., 1886–8), vol. IV, pp. 124–6.

[2] BL Add. Ms. 11045, fol. 118v; PRO SP 16/468/23; *CSPD 1640–1*, 468/24; Grosart, *Lismore Papers*, vol. IV, pp. 136–7; Bod. Tanner Ms. 65, fol. 129.

latter refuse to yield to that – but with the definition of what was 'reasonable' left open, Bristol successfully proposed there should be a treaty.[3] On these grounds English negotiators were to be peers who the Covenanters might accept. Charles allowed sixteen to be named as commissioners, including seven signatories of the peers' petition; he offered to stand by what settlement they could reach, but at the same time retained the catch-clause of what might be done in case of 'unreasonableness' on the other side.[4] Bristol meanwhile argued for selling provisions to the Scots in return for the release of English soldiers detained after Newburn, so leaving aside the question of honour in preference to a politics that might build foundations of trust; he also opposed administering the oath of supremacy to Covenanters whose 'religion' prevented them from taking it. The disagreement with Charles's thinking was evident, as acceptance of the oath with related releases of prisoners on the king's side continued to be a sticking-point.[5]

None of this meant that war was dropped from the agenda. The primary business of the great council remained the finding of a means of maintaining the king's army; Sir John Borough's semi-official record began only with this. At least defence against further invasion obviously depended on it and the peers did not disappoint, in the end offering conjointly their security for a loan of £200,000 to be sought from the City of London. They were evidently cautious to avoid any encroachment on what might be regarded as the sphere of parliamentary business.[6]

Charles, more simply, was joyful at this outcome. He could now forget fears of the Scots being in an overweening position, and he made a special effort to conciliate the Londoners. The pattern of small popular gestures indicated the direction of his thoughts.[7] Though Lord Savile and Viscount

---

[3] Grosart, *Lismore Papers*, vol. IV, pp. 124–5, 130. For Bristol, cf. *CSPD 1639*, 421/169, 422/62, 78, 423/67; *State Papers Collected by Edward, Earl of Clarendon*, eds. R. Scrope and T. Monkhouse (3 vols., Oxford, 1767), vol. II, p. 115.

[4] Grosart, *Lismore Papers*, vol. IV, p. 130. The names were apparently suggested to Charles, not by him – NLS Adv. Ms. 33.4.6, fol. 10; P. Yorke, *Miscellaneous State Papers, from 1501 to 1726* (2 vols., 1778), vol. II, pp. 219–20, 225; *CSPD 1640–1*, 468/23; Beds. RO J 1375 – letter of the Earl of Bolingbroke.

[5] Grosart, *Lismore Papers*, vol. IV, pp. 126–9. Cf. NLS Adv. Ms. 33.4.6, fols. 10, 33; R. Baillie, *The Letters and Journals*, ed. D. Laing, BC (3 vols., Edinburgh, 1841–2), vol. I, p. 261.

[6] Yorke, *State Papers*, vol. II, pp. 209–17; *CSPD 1640–1*, 468/23, 83; Grosart, *Lismore Papers*, vol. IV, pp. 132–3. Sir John Borough did not arrive late in York – *CSPD 466/54,15*. I usually refer to his notes as printed in Yorke, *State Papers*, vol. II.

[7] Grosart, *Lismore Papers*, vol. IV, pp. 134–5 (another important copy of this letter, with variations obviously geared to winning approval for the king, survives in Corp. of London RO Hist. Papers I, no. 14, 113A; I am grateful to Mr James Robertson for providing me with a transcript); *State Papers . . . Clarendon*, vol. II, pp. 121, 123; *CSPD 1640–1*, 468/61, 81, 115; C. S. R. Russell, 'Why did Charles I call the Long Parliament?', *History*, 69 (1984), 378–9.

Mandeville cast slurs on the adoption of an aggressive war policy without means – a matter of tactical phrasing with which Bristol could join – Charles with the Earl of Strafford replied by alleging the failure of the country to oblige as expected: they offered the country a further chance to show its loyalty and service. The king made much of accounts of Scottish plunder and violence in all of the northern counties, news that was to be spread in the south, for he looked forward with more optimism to the future.[8]

The defining of stiff instructions for the lords commissioners occupied the next few days and Charles, stern against those who implied that there was room for debate, made it clear that the 1639 Pacification was to be his basis for treaty. The peers, he said, were to advise 'just', 'honourable', 'safe' things, but their judgement of the Scottish business was to be directed.[9] Traquair's relation and copies of relevant papers would be at their disposal and, seemingly at the peers' request, Scottish 'assistants' for specialist advice to accompany them to Ripon; Traquair, Lanark and Morton were named, all of whom were present in the great council. Charles may not have been too keen to concede that issues were open to debate, but nevertheless he sent for the lawyer Sir Lewis Stewart.[10] Reluctantly he was drawn to respond to the more realistic objections around him that the Scots would press for more than was written in the Pacification. The rule remained hard and fast: anything beyond it should be referred to him, and should there be any differences of interpretation he, and his English peers, were to give judgement.

The king observed that, as it stood, the Pacification altered laws and constitutions in Scotland; but it was to these that anything further wished by the Scots should be referred, and he asked the Council whether it would thus bind them. Bristol replied by noting that the Scots were too strong to be compelled to anything. Charles denied this, asserting that, if the country was united, compulsion – 'just and right' – might indeed be threatened.[11] It was hardly mentioned that the Pacification, like the concept of reasonableness, had left many things open, yet Charles maintained that, should the Covenanters not keep faith on its terms, he would consider himself absolved from observing it – hopefully with the peers' support.

The Covenanters in one of their demands asked for reparation of losses, which though it struck sharply against the king himself could be portrayed as

---

[8] Grosart, *Lismore Papers*, vol. IV, pp. 131–2, 135; Yorke, *State Papers*, vol. II, pp. 212, 208–9, 211, 216; NLS Adv. Ms. 33.4.6, fols. 17, 19–21, 27–8, 32–3; *The Demands and Behaviour of the Rebels of Scotland*, STC 21915 (1640); *A Briefe Relation of the Scots Hostile Entrance*, STC 22007.5 (1640).

[9] Cf. *CSPD 1640–1*, 468/39.

[10] *State Papers . . . Clarendon*, vol. II, pp. 217–19; J. Nalson, *An Impartial Collection of the Great Affairs of State* (2 vols., 1682–3), vol. I, pp. 451–2; *CSPD 1640–1*, 468/23, 39; GD 112/40/2/3/13; NLS Adv. Ms. 33.4.6, fols. 17, 19.

[11] Yorke, *State Papers*, vol. II, pp. 217–23.

an insult to the English nation. By insisting that he would be acquitted, the king showed his readiness still to go to war. He sounded confident, then on 26 September, and again the next day. Strafford backed him, doubting that the Covenanter army was better than the English, although hesitating to advise fighting at that time. A cessation of arms was to be moved, but the Scots were to be challenged on the justice of their demands and their conduct in invasion. They were brave words, but, with the overtures to London as yet only in the making, they remained to be put to the test.[12]

There had been obvious tensions in these exchanges, but instructions were settled so that treaty might go ahead.[13] Although some peers were content to follow Charles, in debate or just silently, he did well in exploiting the wounded honour argument; a fairly substantial debate over the question of a safe-conduct for the Scots commissioners ended to his advantage.[14] It did not seem that he would move to win a Scottish party, but perhaps there continued to be possibilities of that, even if not in the present emergency. The Earl of Montrose was committed briefly in the Scottish camp for private correspondence, possibly with Patrick Maule of Panmure, around the opening of the great council.[15]

From York, the lords commissioners went to Ripon on 2 October, where the Covenanters came likewise with strict instructions. The Scots were wary of what might happen given the lack of progress so far; it was already a month since they had taken Newcastle. The general tenor of their instructions had been already presented to the king in correspondence, but the more precise demand now was to ask for maintenance of their army during the course of any treaty that might develop. This would overcome the existing need to exact contributions locally, with all the accompanying problems, and they pitched their demands high. For those who would come to talk with them, the Covenanters expected the opportunity to provide full information of what had allegedly gone wrong through the evil offices of both Scots and Englishmen, particularly 'their [the English] prelates who have been too busy in our affairs for [a] way to erect popery'. It was anticipated that at least some of the English lords would need convincing.[16]

The Covenanters took exception to Traquair's employment; he and a few

---

[12] Yorke, *State Papers*, vol. II, pp. 234–40. Yorke omitted two vital folio sides of debate; therefore see also BL Harl. Ms. 456, fols. 12v–13.

[13] *CSPD 1640–1*, 468/83, 87; Bod. Clarendon Ms. 19, fol. 54; Grosart, *Lismore Papers*, vol. IV, pp. 137–9; HMC *Rutland* (24), vol. I, pp. 523–4; Nalson, *An Impartial Collection*, vol. I, pp. 448–9.

[14] Yorke, *State Papers*, vol. II, pp. 228–34; *CSPD 1640–1*, 468/83.

[15] E. C. Cowan, *Montrose. For Covenant and King* (1977), p. 109; GD 112/40/2/3/14; BL Add. Ms. 11045, fol. 125. Sir James Mercer carried this letter, therefore on 23 September, not the 8th, as Cowan has it – NLS Adv. Ms. 33.4.6, fols. 8, 9v.

[16] Baillie, *Letters*, vol. I, p. 263; Balfour, *Historical Works*, vol. II, pp. 408–11.

others were pursued foremost of the seventy or so named on a list newly published of Scottish 'incendiaries' to be heard before the coming Scottish parliament for their conduct.[17] This caused Bristol some offence at the Covenanters' presumption, but he was quickly mollified. Loudoun on the other side suggested a middle course, which was ultimately adopted – after the king was asked – namely of having the Scottish assistants absent but able to be consulted. Traquair agreed, prepared, like Hamilton who was also on the list, to answer all charges made against him; Sir Henry Vane came in to attend the talks. The Covenanters also put their request for maintenance; Bristol proposed the rule of the Pacification on his side, faithful to the letter of the royal instructions, but attention was diverted to the request for a cessation of arms.[18] As spokesman he was not uncompromising. His use of the word 'invasion' caused offence at first, but in quick defence he excused perjuring the Scots; he may even have admitted that the English were the first invaders, in the literal sense of the word, since they had sent ships to blockade the Scottish coast.[19]

Once the king's permission on the assistants question was obtained, the extent of the Scottish request for supply was announced to be £40,000 sterling per month. The demand apparently shocked the English, who suggested what had been talked over at York – either the disbanding of the Scottish army or its supply by some Scottish means.[20] The Scottish commissioners, cautious but prepared to talk, conceded that the sum for maintenance was open to negotiation. They allowed as a compromise that their demand in writing should be phrased conditionally; thus maintenance was requested in terms of a *sine qua non* of treaty and cessation. They agreed, at least privately, that there were some advantages in Bristol's suggestion for the treaty being removed to York so as to be near the king, although this was in the event resisted. They offered, and had tentatively accepted by Bristol on the other side, copies of a new piece of propaganda, *The Lawfulness of our Expedition into England Manifested*. Hopeful of being well represented at York, they

[17] *CSPD 1640–1*, 467/114; the names of those summoned are in NLS Adv. Ms. 33.1.1, vol. XIII, no. 20. I count 69 – cf. *HMC De L'Isle* (77), vol. VI, p. 337; BL Add. Ms. 11045, fol. 129. Proceedings against Traquair had opened after the June 1640 parliament – Traquair Mss. Bundle 26[i].

[18] J. Bruce (ed.), *Notes on the Treaty Carried on at Ripon between King Charles I and the Covenanters of Scotland, A.D. 1640, Taken by Sir John Borough*, Camden Society (1869) (hereafter *Ripon*), pp. 5–16, 19–20; NLS Adv. Ms. 33.4.6, fols. 18–19, 21; Yorke, *State Papers*, vol. II, p. 235; *CSPD 1640–1*, 470/3.

[19] Bruce, *Ripon*, p. 24; NLS Adv. Ms. 33.4.6, fols. 44–5. It was the rule to have statements of consequence in writing, all of which were copied in the official Scottish letter-book (NLS Adv. Ms. 33.4.6) and I shall reference them from there.

[20] Bruce, *Ripon*, pp. 21–3. Cf. debate of 29 September at York.

deliberately avoided raising their more contentious demand for general reparation of losses.[21]

The demand for maintenance prompted Charles in York to open debate on whether he might instead win by force; he would have had the matter of reparations well to the fore. His appeal to the lords for support assumed that none would advise the high dishonour of giving money if it was possible forcibly to repel the Scots. He sounded more confident than before in propounding a strategy of entrenching the English forces and thus wearing out the Scots over time, while preventing their further advance; Strafford had advised as much – though it was hardly an ideal option.[22]

Charles had not yet yielded anything substantial to the Covenanters. Their requests alongside the matter of the assistants were only partially met, as he offered limited postways strictly for those on treaty business and denied freedom of seaways for the present.[23] To his great council he was correct in maintaining that the Covenanters' position would not be eased by the extension of time. However, the other side of the argument was put powerfully by Bristol and others of the lords commissioners. They noted the danger of irritating the Covenanters. On the one hand it seemed risky to place reliance on a good supply for the king's army; Bristol stressed rather more that the Scots might not only overcome a blockade but cause devastation to the occupied counties and their neighbours. Put thus the question was whether to offer maintenance, maybe reluctantly, in order to work for an accommodation, or to abandon parts of England to the Scottish army. The picture was not greatly distorted. If it was possibly counter-productive to the Covenanters to be violent within England, the circumstances of poverty, blockade and desertions may have perforce pushed them to that in time; as it was they intended to spread their forces as far as the Tees for ease of supply.[24]

To give maintenance was seen as a negative act on Charles's part, and on the other hand as something positive. The debate lasted a few days while the king tried to have the Covenanters come to York following Bristol's suggestion; a hard line on the Scottish side defeated that idea.[25] A middle way was found on 12 and 13 October. Bristol suggested that the Scots find as much as possible for themselves so that the English contribution could be small.[26] The

[21] Bruce, *Ripon*, pp. 23–4, 72–7; NLS Adv. Ms. 33.4.6, fols. 17, 23, 25–6. I take it that Bristol was one who advocated the move to York – cf. Grosart, *Lismore Papers*, vol. IV, p. 129; Yorke, *State Papers*, vol. II, p. 249, for his earlier proposal of the same.

[22] Cf. Yorke, *State Papers*, vol. II, pp. 210–11; *CSPD 1640–1*, 469/42; Grosart, *Lismore Papers*, vol. IV, pp. 146–8.

[23] Bruce, *Ripon*, p. 28; Nalson, *An Impartial Collection*, p. 453; NLs Adv. Ms. 33.4.6, fols. 27, 30–2.

[24] NLS Adv. Ms. 33.4.6, fols. 16, 38, 45–6.

[25] NLS Adv. Ms. 33.4.6, fols. 29–30; cf. *CSPD 1640–1*, 469/63.

[26] This hearkened back to the consensus of 29 September.

means proposed of the least dishonour was that the northern counties might 'voluntarily' supply the money, thus saving any direct contribution by the king.

Charles was concerned that the plundering of the northern counties should be prevented, and to this extent Bristol's words won him; perhaps he was also looking to the future. That the London response, generous initially in principle, was still being worked out caused uncertainties in York. The king certainly could not consider aggressive war at present; winter, but probably more importantly the parliament, was approaching.[27] He insisted that, if the proposed means of supply were adopted, every effort should be made to finish the rest of the business; the treaty on their main demands should not be delayed. While Lord Savile reminded him that the Scots expected the parliament's name to be on any conclusion, the king's reason for haste was probably not caused by a wish to avoid that entirely – his parliament would be involved, but if possible in the closing stages.[28] Scottish involvement in English politics was as unacceptable as it was threatening, and it was equally desirable to minimise participation the other way. Immediate action of some sort was therefore necessary, whether covering against the Scots potentially laying waste to the north of England or else quickly proceeding with the treaty.[29]

The Earl of Strafford maintained extreme hostility towards the Scots. When Charles had begun to listen to Bristol's arguments, which included optimism for a final settlement, Strafford put the counter-case. There was dishonour in a king buying a cessation unless it was absolutely necessary, which he doubted since the Scots had previously claimed they would pay their own way; moreover it was questionable whether the English in the north would be secured by any maintenance. He argued for having the English united in confronting the Scottish pretensions. Critical as before of the recent war effort, he poured scorn on the peers' willingness now to settle a means of supplying a rebel army.[30] Such words prolonged the debate, but Charles tended the other way. There was considerable voiced support for his concern for honour; he was assured that the Scots would cooperate on this middle way. Strafford interestingly shifted his ground when he saw this line prevailing, and argued that only the northern counties should be the suppliers for the

---

[27] Yorke, *State Papers*, vol. II, pp. 281–4; *CSPD 1640–1*, 469/50, 61, 85. It was Scottish wishful thinking that Bristol persuaded Charles of the justness of the Covenanter cause – cf. NLS Crawford Ms. 14/3/70; NLS Wod. 4to. 25, fol. 50.

[28] *CSPD 1640–1*, 469/92. Cf. the Lord Keeper's speech – Yorke, *State Papers*, vol. II, pp. 263–4.

[29] For other perspectives, see BL Loan 29/172, fol. 306; A. Collins (ed.), *Letters and Memorials of State*, vol. II (1746), pp. 661–2.

[30] Yorke, *State Papers*, vol. II, pp. 264–6, 247; NLS Crawford Ms. 14/3/70 (but see n. 27 above).

Scots, not their neighbours if at all possible. Vane and Lord Keeper Finch encouraged the proceeding with the maintenance and treaty; the king repeated insistently his desire for advance of the whole treaty. For speed's sake, the lords' wish for more ample discretion in their negotiations was granted – though flexibility was still clearly limited on the substance of the main Scottish articles.[31]

In Ripon the English lords collectively tried to steer the course of the talks on the maintenance. At first they would not name a sum as the other side wanted, Bristol repeatedly pressing on the Covenanters their own argument that they were in a friends' country and therefore did well not to cause too great offence. Never compromising his obvious concern for the well-being of the occupied northern counties, he continued to ask for the reduction in size of the Scottish army, which his hearers would hear nothing of. He insisted even more strongly that they should not increase their forces, as was in the offing.[32] At the same time, however, he was increasingly prepared to warn the Scots of their enemies on the English side. Rather as he had warned the king and peers of Scottish aggressiveness, he advised the Scots not to provoke by aggressive action. The York balance was fragile.

The Covenanters reduced their desired sum to £30,000 a month; Bristol wanted to push them to less.[33] The feeling that it was important that the Covenanters should not act alone any further made the peers themselves deal with northern locals on how to provide the money. Pushed at last by the Covenanters to name a sum, they fastened on £850 a day – the exact amount which was already being lifted as a contribution from the occupied counties.[34] The locals agreed to be bound to pay for one month and the lords assured themselves that somehow money for the other month would be found. A confident front was presented meanwhile to the Covenanters, who were given extra conditions such as ending the exploitation of papists and high church folk and the uncontrolled seizure of coal customs and forage. Problems arose over the Covenanters' insistence on having a security properly settled for the provision of maintenance, a dispute which lasted some days, but a large part of this was that certain means could not quickly be found.[35]

After the offer of £850 a day was reported in York, there was a repeat of

---

[31] The preceding has been derived from the debates of 6–13 October – Yorke, *State Papers*, vol. II, 241–79. For new directions to the lords commissioners, see PRO SP 16/469/90; *HMC Salisbury* (9), vol. XXII, p. 324.

[32] Cf. NLS Crawford Ms. 14/3/80; *HMC Laing* (72), vol. I, p. 205; GD 112/39/820, 821; *CSPD 1640–1*, 469/74; Baillie, *Letters*, vol. I, p. 260.

[33] He named £20,000. Cf. 12 October – Yorke, *State Papers*, vol. II, p. 259.

[34] I.e. £25,500 a month. See Savile on 6 October – Yorke, *State Papers*, vol. II, p. 246.

[35] Bruce, *Ripon*, pp. 28–45. For varying English responses, see *CSPD 1640–1*, 470/3; Bod. Carte Ms. 103, fol. 196.

former arguments with the Earl of Strafford. He dwelt particularly on the talk of need to involve Cumberland and Westmorland in the maintenance, and so urged the possibility of armed resistance to the Scots. With continuing problems over the supply of the king's army, he would not readily accept that the Covenanters should be put in the advantageous position.[36] Bristol, not without casting slurs on the recent English military organisation, addressed the peers to encourage them to honour their agreement to support the maintenance, and he found Charles still behind him. With time drawing on, the king would not embrace thoughts of military strike – provided that the treaty could be advanced.[37]

Therefore the Scottish commissioners were persuaded to enter on preliminary talks over their main demands before the terms of either maintenance or cessation were fully concluded – despite their own instructions and while arguments continued on the security question. The English peers' claims of their earnestness in dealing were believed. The Scottish commissioners' reports to Newcastle reflected a recognition that the treaty stood or fell on their own readiness to negotiate. It was taken now that the immediate risk of fighting was past, and the Earl of Argyll accordingly journeyed south from Edinburgh, leaving his main body of troops behind.[38]

In Ripon on 21 October the Covenanters' letter of 8 September sent to the king's Scottish Secretary was formally read out. This made mention of eight heads of demands, led by one for publishing the Acts of the 1640 parliament. Others touched the manning of Edinburgh Castle and other fortresses; the disrespect for the Covenant by imprisonment of its signatories and refusers of royal oaths; the proclamations made against the Covenanters, which were to be recalled. The restoration of ships and goods taken was sought, and the general reparation of all losses and wrongs sustained. Included too was the just censure of all incendiaries, and an open-ended final article asking for the removal of the English border garrisons and of restraints on passages between the nations and, in a catch-all reminiscent of 1638, for all other particulars which might settle a firm peace.[39]

Hoping to publicise the demand for general reparations to his advantage, Charles delayed permission for the formal removal of the treaty to London while he asked for details. Bristol passed on the request, but the peers would not have the king so jeopardise their talks; their successful reply to Charles's

---

[36] Yorke, *State Papers*, vol. II, p. 287; also see HLRO Braye Ms. 2, fols. 77–8 (paraphrased in *HMC Braye* (10), p. 137), which account mistakenly puts all the debate on Sunday 18 October.

[37] Yorke, *State Papers*, vol. II, pp. 279–90.

[38] NLS Adv. Ms. 33.4.6, fols. 41v, 46; GD 112/39/820, 821; GD 112/40/2/3/109, 111, 144; Baillie, *Letters*, vol. I, p. 263.

[39] Bruce, *Ripon*, pp. 56–8; NLS Adv. Ms. 33.4.6, fols. 40–1; *CSPD 1640–1*, 466/82.

letter, which came after the Scots had proceeded to air their main demands, insisted that everything possible was being done, and that this kind of delay was highly undesirable – '[we] would be very critical of the advisers of that'. The Covenanters exerted pressure to get the conditions of the occupation settled.[40]

In Ripon, Lord Loudoun presented the other two basic documents of the Covenanter cause, the first petition of 2 September and the preamble to the 1640 Acts of parliament. He proceeded at length to show the origins of the Scottish troubles as innovation in religion and law dating back to James's reign, offering to explain each of the recent Acts for the lords commissioners. In the context of the whole the king's wished-for emphasis was premature. The English lords, however, seemed disinclined to accept the Acts as offered. Bristol thought that some might be ratified, in the king's own way, and that the Covenanters should welcome such a ratification by authority since their parliament had sat without Charles being represented; he seemed less than interested in the tale of a grand cause. The idea of selection and ratification was not one which would recommend itself to the Covenanters, whose line was to maintain all the Acts already as law, merely lacking a usual means of publication. Moreover, Bristol's suggestion that the validity even of the parliament might be questioned was sternly refuted.[41]

As none of these points passed in writing, no detailed report was made to Newcastle, where the priority was still to settle the practical details on the table. The tensions already manifest over the maintenance and its security were slightly paralleled in the debate of the articles of the cessation. The Covenanters would have liked the settled maintenance not to be limited to two months' duration, but the peers advised against pressing this. They hoped that the treaty might be finished by then; but in any case it was not possible to press the local gentry for an indefinite period of supply, nor was it advisable to take such a request presently to York where, the peers declared, 'the most part did murmur and complain that the two months was too long a time'. If the necessity arose for an extension, a separate arrangement would have to be made.[42] As concession to circumstances and Covenanter insistence, the participation of Cumberland and Westmorland was embodied formally in the articles for the maintenance, and committees were appointed of gentlemen and lords who would have responsibilities for overseeing the operation.[43]

---

[40] *CSPD 1640–1*, 470/30; Bruce, *Ripon*, pp. 81–2, 60, 63–4; NLS Adv. Ms. 33.4.6, fols. 46–7.
[41] Bruce, *Ripon*, pp. 59–63.
[42] NLS Adv. Ms. 33.4.6, fols. 45–6; Bruce, *Ripon*, pp. 36–8. Cf. Paget and Bristol at York – Yorke, *State Papers*, vol. II, pp. 276, 259.
[43] Articles 13 and 14 of maintenance agreement, which was entitled 'for easing of the counties ... and for settling the competency' – NLS Adv. Ms. 33.4.6, fols. 47–8, 56–8.

The Committee of Estates at Newcastle made only a few brief demands for the actual cessation, excising a number of the articles provisionally agreed at Ripon, but little was gained by the twelve heads concluded. The request to have no English garrisons north of the Tees was not granted, and is interesting for showing the peers' care for the king's honour which in this case exceeded what Charles himself might have insisted upon.[44] A united front was erected against Scottish demands over the matter of the customs and the payment of the maintenance. The Covenanters were not on any account to be allowed to distrain customs or money if there was local defaulting; as requested there was a clause allowing distraining of goods from individuals, but the other was, in the peers' words, 'odious' in itself and advantageous to the Covenanters' 'enemies'.[45] The mutual desire to have understanding, variously motivated as it was, won through. Differences were open, but in the end they were never destructive; the Bristol–Strafford duel had threatened more. Both sides had an eye on final settlement; they might reasonably have anticipated results from further talks.

The king hesitated to sign the papers concerning the maintenance and cessation, which for him were only the unpleasant groundwork of the main business with the Scots. Strikingly, however, Bristol far outdid Charles in speaking negatively of the treaty as one 'of the greatest disadvantage that hath [been] signed since the conquest'. Viscount Mandeville, whom we suppose to have been sympathetic to the Covenanters, pointed to what had been gained against their preference. Whatever personally was felt, publicly the Covenanters would be little praised for their occupation of the north of England: the English at large were uneasy over it. The justificatory paper which the lords commissioners drew up on their own account emphasised the conditions of necessity which had guided their work. However, in so doing, they underlined another dominant factor – and the Earl of Strafford took offence, which was as surely meant as it was overtly denied. Many of the peers at least agreed with the Covenanters that there had been bad agents in action.[46]

The pronouncement by Hamilton that he was satisfied with the peers' work preceded Charles's eventual decision to sign the agreement; perhaps the words of one so closely alongside him made a difference, but there was little option. Hamilton had kept something of a low profile during the treaty; although his few recorded remarks tended to support the finding of a settle-

---

[44] Bruce, *Ripon*, pp. 57–8; NLS Adv. Ms. 33.4.6, fols. 81v–2, 90, 93; Yorke, *State Papers*, vol. II, pp. 297–8.

[45] Article 8 of maintenance, article 5 of cessation – NLS Adv. Ms. 33.4.6, fols. 45–6. Article 7 of the cessation was to some extent ambiguous on how the Scots might find agreed sums; part of the maintenance was to be paid in kind – cf. NLS Adv. Ms. 33.4.6, fol. 50.

[46] Yorke, *State Papers*, vol. II, pp. 290–7; cf. BL Harl. Ms. 457, fols. 117–19; T. D. Whitaker, *The Life and Original Correspondence of Sir George Radcliffe* (1810), pp. 214–18.

ment by a measure of concessions, he also had to defend himself against a slur by Bristol on his past military conduct.[47] Concern, moreover, at his own vulnerability in the light of his being confirmed as an incendiary in the Covenanters' list prompted him at the close of the treaty to entrust his brother Lanark to speak on his behalf with Lord Loudoun. Loudoun was asked to clear the marquis's name before the Covenanters, to show that he was no 'unnatural countryman' full of malice. Loudoun was a natural addressee especially in the light of their recent contacts; and he was furthermore to be encouraged to facilitate the treaty, as might be expected of him. Could the king too be brought to yield with good grace? The English context did not make it easy. Lanark's meetings with Loudoun aroused suspicions in Sir Henry Vane and Bristol that Charles was attempting underhand dealing.[48] All around him Charles seemed to face uneasiness and distrust.

However, the king's quest for a united people behind him had not been utterly disappointed by the great council at York. Though there was criticism of military courses taken to date, the proceedings hinted that the Covenanters might not be able to count on substantial positive support from the English. Charles at least went to the parliament still looking to chase the Scottish 'rebels' from English soil.[49] The rumour that prominent English figures had supported the invasion and the certain coincidence of the petitions would remain still in his mind, but he preferred to focus his attention on loyalty that he as a king might expect. Treaty had been opened, which he did not find ideal – and especially since in the event so little progress had been made at Ripon on the substance of the Scottish demands; in London, with the parliament sitting, he would hope still to restrict severely the demands being made by the Scots.

Charles would tend always to view in terms of black and white but little was as simple; the English aspect which was darkest, the perspectives of those whom the Covenanters thought of as friends, had rarely surfaced in the York and Ripon talks. Settlement of the conditions of the occupation had been the obvious priority. On this there was a need for further provision as long as the treaty continued, and this would be a burden that would count in many other people's minds against the Scots. However, although it could certainly be expected that Charles would not prolong the parliament any more than necessary, his financial problems meant that the Scots occupation of the northern counties was a guarantee for its continuance. It would be a point

---

[47] Yorke, *State Papers*, vol. II, pp. 216–17, 225, 235, 238–9, 252, 284, 296; BL Harl. Ms. 456, fol. 13; *HMC Braye* (10), p. 137; GD 406/1/1437; Grosart, *Lismore Papers*, vol. IV, pp. 144–8. For Charles, cf. *HMC 4*, p. 621.

[48] GD 406/1/876, 1257/2; Bruce, *Ripon*, p. 59. Cf. Traqr. Mss. – 'Traquair papers no. 49'.

[49] Russell, 'Why did Charles I call the Long Parliament?', pp. 380–1.

underpinning friendly English approaches to the Covenanters, though it did no harm to keep a low profile on it. A few had spoken their turn at York, with care. The first important thing was that, by a combination of causes, armed conflict was now unlikely. Where the opportunities of days to come would move remained to be discovered.

Realism and hopes for change outside the circle which had positively cultivated friendship with the Scots would be critical of Charles's rasher statements. That the Covenanters had come so far in their criticism of bad counsels was impressive, since in England and Ireland too there were obvious matters which required consideration. Disappointment after the dissolution of the Short Parliament meant, if anything, a greater expectancy in the country at large for what reforms might be achieved in the winter of 1640–1, much of which is outside the scope of the account to be offered here. People varied in their attitudes towards the Scots from outright hostility and fear to if not friendship, tempered concern that at the least normality should be restored by a measure of concessions from the king. All together it conveyed a familiar point, that Charles could not have the obedience he wished – the parliament was not to be manipulated as he directed.[50]

However, parliaments did not usually last very long, and, though the Scottish trouble held Charles to this one, the passing of time would come to his advantage. Financially, keeping both Scottish and royal armies on foot was an enormous expense which it was highly desirable to end. Secondly, the British vision adopted by the Covenanters had direct ramifications on the English domestic scene, an important extra element through which a legacy of English national differences and prejudice towards the Scots was provoked. Amongst the Covenanters too, though they pressed British topics so as to settle Scotland's position better within the Union of the Crowns, there was a strong desire, for their own many domestic reasons, not to extend this abnormal period in England longer than could be helped. As with regard to the Short Parliament, they wished Scottish business to have top priority.[51]

Over the Scottish proposals, if it is asked how far a common vision got through the underhand contacts, it is difficult to see how closely the English side was coordinated – perhaps not very much, and the bonds were certainly casual in contrast with the organised unity of the Covenanters. The Scottish programme was well defined, above all in those eight articles sent to the king shortly after the invasion and more recently brought up for wider consideration at Ripon. On the first seven of these, which addressed the existing issues

[50] What follows is by no means a full account of the English parliament in the period under discussion. I have benefited from A. Fletcher, *The Outbreak of the English Civil War* (1981); the Earl Russell's comprehensive study is keenly awaited.

[51] *Remonstrance Concerning the Present Troubles* . . . , STC 21927.5 (n.p., 1640); PRO SP 16/471/22 – cf. NLS Wod. Fo. 64, fol. 190.

of the conflict, the Covenanters would make their case well known, hopeful that there would be no serious arguments, save possibly on points of detail, as will be seen; the less precise eighth article opened up the wider vision which, picking up from the Scottish achievement, pointed further, British ways forward.

British heads, in the instructions at the opening of the parliament to the Covenanter commissioners to be 'urged as expedients, as you shall find opportunity', included the idea of having parliaments in both kingdoms every two or three years, amongst other things to preside over the implementation of the treaty and to censure evil counsellors. The processes of declaring war and peace were also to be focused within parliaments. *Conservatores pacis*, keepers of the peace, were to be appointed in each kingdom to work in the interim periods. The Scots were going to make demands concerning those who might attend Court, and about the future marriage of the Prince of Wales. It might thus be hoped to counter the popish influence which had so threatened religion and liberties; and, as discussed privately at Ripon, there was the notion of a common 'confession of faith' for both kingdoms – in other words the Covenant.

The effect would be to confine the freedom of movement of the king and his counsel in England as well as in Scotland. The evidence for this British vision is Scottish; in what appears to be a draft by Archibald Johnston of Wariston were other points omitted in the instructions such as an idea for annual church assemblies in England as in Scotland. On the church the abjuration of episcopacy already made in Scotland was to stand, and specific Scottish perspectives covered a number of the 'expedients' in the instructions; more points would yet be formulated for the making of a 'settled peace'. Therefore, was the main work of coordinating efforts between Scots and English still to come? It seems most likely. In both kingdoms there were of course many topics on which there was no overlap; the instructions had to allow for the possibility that Scottish business might proceed *pari passu* with English.[52]

Zeal or vision did not get a free hand; the practical difficulties of getting money to the armies, divisions in England and differences amongst the Covenanters themselves prevented that. If everyone agreed in wishing peace and unity, the terms on which that might be settled were diverse; but people could not foresee any fixed outcome. For the Covenanter commissioners, the instructions were private, and it was a part of strategy that demands and

---

[52] PRO SP 16/471/22; NLS Wod. Fo. 64, fol. 190; Wod. Fo. 66, fol. 223v. For various hopes amongst the Scots, see NLS Wod. Fo. 67, fol. 3; D. Laing (ed.), *Correspondence of Sir Robert Kerr, First Earl of Ancrum, and his Son William, Third Earl of Lothian* (2 vols., Edinburgh, 1875), vol. I, p. 105.

requests would be made at times of the greatest advantage.[53] There was going to be a struggle; reports from the commissioners in London to the Committee at Newcastle would frequently make mention of the 'well-affected'. It is worth remembering that this could be simply in contradistinction to 'enemies', a polar opposite, as well as more positively designating the friendship of some English people. Nevertheless there was an optimism and excitement in the air from all quarters, as great expectations converged.[54]

After the opening speeches in parliament on the Scottish problem, a few days lapsed before the Scottish commissioners arrived in London to continue the talks begun at Ripon. The Earl of Bristol, prominent as before, reported to the Lords and then in a conference to both Houses what had passed from the beginning of the great council. He emphasised the necessity of treaty on account of English military weakness, and concluded by showing the reasons for offering supply to both armies. The Scots were shown to be still a potentially dangerous aggressor.[55] Bristol declined to comment on events prior to the invasion, but the Lords, almost certainly against the king's desire, appointed a select committee to investigate the whole Scottish business which had led to the Council of York. The implication was that the case against the Covenanters by which the recent war had been justified was open. The Covenanters welcomed at least the idea; they would have wished it still to be clear, however, that neither they nor their laws were to be judged in an English parliament.[56]

Charles allowed the re-appointment of the lords commissioners for the treaty, but showed his keenness to have such talks quickly dispatched by appearing in person on the first day of the meeting in London. He tried to suggest that there should be no problem in this, but Bristol and Holland agreed with the Covenanters that it would not be helpful. That Charles raised the significant point of Traquair's exclusion suggests that his own presence was to re-affirm the settlement of the issues as he saw them. The Covenanters' firm refusal to entertain the king's presence led Bristol to suggest to Charles

---

[53] How the paper of Scottish instructions came to be in State Papers remains a mystery, although Montrose is an obvious suspect – cf. GD 112/40/2/3/113; M. Napier (ed.), *Montrose and the Covenanters* (2 vols., Edinburgh, 1838), vol. I, pp. 374–7; NLS Wod. Fo. 65, fol. 154v; NLS Adv. Ms. 33.4.6, fol. 98.

[54] Cf. NLS Adv. Ms. 33.4.6, fol. 55v; Baillie, *Letters*, vol. I, p. 283; BL Loan 29/172, fols. 363–7; Fletcher, *Outbreak*, pp. 1–3; J. S. Morrill, 'The religious context of the English civil war', *TRHS*, 5th Series, 34 (1984), 155–78.

[55] *LJ*, vol. IV, p. 90; Nalson, *An Impartial Collection*, vol. I, p. 524; *HMC Montagu* (54), vol. III, p. 387. One Robert Benson attempted unsuccessfully to blacken the peers' efforts of September and October – *LJ*, vol. IV, pp. 90, 98; HLRO Main Papers, 25? November; *HMC Montagu*, vol. III, p. 394.

[56] *LJ*, vol. IV, pp. 90–1; HLRO Braye Ms. 95, fol. 176; Baillie, *Letters*, vol. I, p. 274; *HMC Montagu*, vol. III, p. 391. Cf. *D'Ewes (N)*, p. 20. The committee apparently never reported its conclusions.

that he might instead regularly view all treaty papers with his 'Scottish counsel'.

The king withdrew to consult with lawyers on his position, but although receiving a favourable judgement he did not reappear. Bristol may have been the moderating force; certainly he did not allow the Scots any binding statement that the king could not attend, but told them that the Commons with the Lords had now approved the peers' commission, thus stifling the unprecedented Scottish request to have that commission issued as from the king and parliament. The Scots had asked for the parliament's opinion on Charles's attendance, believing that most members would oppose its legitimacy. Clearly it avoided an awkward situation for Charles to hold back silently. Bristol pressed on by asking for the delivery of the first article, for ratification of the 1640 Acts of parliament; the concern from the Covenanters for the maintenance of their army could be answered at this stage by news of an order in the Commons already made on the subject.[57]

Bristol had no obvious wish for extra delays; the process of negotiation was to some extent bound to be prolonged since parliament was sitting. The practice of the treaty became daily afternoon talks between the commissioners, frequent consultation with the king – including interviews sometimes involving the Covenanters – and reference at least at the end of each Scottish article to both Houses of parliament. Following the practice at Ripon and as a counter to any misconstruction such as had followed the Berwick agreement, all written exchanges were available to both king and parliament besides the Committee of Estates split between Edinburgh and Newcastle. It was unavoidably a slow way of action, prone to delays.[58]

Charles continued to play a very active role, both individually and jointly with his parliament, despite his exclusion from the formal treaty debates. He was notably involved in controversy surrounding the first and fourth articles of the eight, namely the one asking for royal approval and publication of the 1640 Acts, and the one concerning the treatment of incendiaries. In their correspondence north the Covenanters alleged as ever that the king was led astray by ill-minded Scottish counsellors still around him, whereas the king's disagreements with them had little that was novel. Traquair was alongside Sir Robert Spottiswood and Sir John Hay in tendering advice; he later maintained that he had advised Charles in November to 'ratify' the Acts,

---

[57] BL Harl. Ms. 457, fols. 3–9; Stowe Ms. 187, fols. 2–3; NLS Adv. Ms. 33.4.6, fol. 59; *LJ*, vol. IV, p. 91; *CJ*, vol. II, p. 33; *D'Ewes (N)*, pp. 49–50. The Stowe manuscript is the Scottish record kept in London until June 1641. Most of the written exchanges are preserved here, so although some have been printed in various works (esp. Rushworth, Nalson and *HMC Salisbury*, vol. XXII), I shall cite them from the manuscript.

[58] D. Stevenson, *The Scottish Revolution 1637–1644* (Newton Abbot, 1974), p. 215.

especially those relating to the 1639 general assembly and Covenant.[59] However, with the official Covenanter line going beyond that, as had already been shown to the Earl of Bristol at Ripon, the king for his own part directly challenged the legitimacy of the 1640 parliament and its legislation. He offered to consent to all the other articles save this one, for remedy of which he suggested another parliament, which the Covenanters, both in common sense and on principle, had to reject. Personally, he singled out a number of Acts for particular criticism; it is highly unlikely that he was at all satisfied by the answers made to him.[60]

The status of the 1640 parliament session concerned not only Englishmen like Bristol but also apparently folk within the Covenanter camp. Wariston was one of its most confident defenders. He drew parallels between this parliament and that of 1560, the maker in other words of momentous conclusions by the Scottish people against the will of the monarch – which, incidentally, in the sixteenth century had had English help; moreover it was to be distinguished from the Glasgow General Assembly which, though it sat on after Hamilton's departure, had its enactments replaced by those of Edinburgh in 1639. Presumably the special emergency of 1640 gave the parliament its justification and an achievement of legislation that could not lightly be abandoned. It was proposed that even if the Acts were to be re-read in a subsequent parliament session, they were still to be published unchanged with the original dates kept. If the king wished to add his name to the further prorogation of the parliament, that might also be allowed, though it was a concession, not being thought necessary – as Traquair had been told in 1639. But for the Covenanters there was to be no question of nullifying the 1640 session, and ideally the issue was not to be discussed, raising as it did explicit questions over royal power and, conversely, what subjects might do in the extreme necessity for the preservation of religion and liberties. Abstract questions were not the business of this moment to which religious and political troubles had brought them: they would only confuse the issues, especially since it had been subtle manoeuvre and not clear-cut 'revolution' at the beginning of the 1640 session. Nevertheless queries on the instructions stated one of the assumed principles, namely that the king was obliged *de pacto* to assent to what the parliament decided – an unambiguous denial of the negative voice.[61]

[59] NLS Adv. Ms. 33.4.6, fol. 66; Napier, *Montrose and the Covenanters*, vol. I, p. 350; Baillie, *Letters*, vol. I, p. 276; BL Stowe Ms. 187, fol. 10; NLS Crawford Ms. 15/2/2; Traqr. Mss. Bundle 26[i] – interrogatories for the Earl of Morton *et al.*

[60] BL Stowe Ms. 187, fols. 7–12; Harl. Ms. 457, fols. 13–14; NLS Adv. Ms. 33.4.6, fol. 60v; Wod. Fo. 63, fol. 90. For an analysis of the legislation made for Charles, see Traqr. Mss. Bundle 27.

[61] PRO SP 16/471/22; cf. Bruce, *Ripon*, pp. 70–1.

By 3 December 1640, one month into the parliament, the publishing of the Acts as they stood was finally conceded; it was agreed to lay aside and forget some of the written exchanges over the article. It was a mammoth concession, over which there would be further dispute although with little gain for the king in the autumn of 1641 at the Scottish parliament; Charles dropped even the specific reservations he had made. It must be asked why the king so quickly moved from his position held since Berwick, and in the process conceding all at once not just the ecclesiastical but also a very substantial civil programme. Both Wariston and Baillie implied that pressure from the English lords commissioners brought Charles to full concession in the end.[62] However that impression arose, it seems likely that the important point for Charles was that the concession was taken as signalling the imminent end of the treaty and occupation. The Covenanters had been asked whether all their demands were contained in their September statement.[63] Although much was still to be disclosed, they had been agreeable to continuing the prorogation of the Scottish parliament in November no further than a new date in January 1641.[64] The Earl of Argyll, hoping to gain personal and public advantage by his presence at the conclusion of treaty, received encouragement from the Earl of Rothes later in December, who was getting an invitation for him from the English lords commissioners; Hamilton's goodwill was also avouched – a continuation of his own effort to recover influential Scottish favour.[65]

An early ending did not necessarily bode ill though the agenda was large, not least on religion; Scots, and probably many English members, could easily be over-optimistic about reaching their goals. Moreover, for the English the expense of the treaty as long as it lasted was a matter in itself; the cessation of arms agreement which included the maintenance was each time renewed only for one-month periods. For the Scots it was plain inconvenience made worse by poor supply lines that was felt, particularly by the army in the north.[66] What was Charles's concern – to minimise the damage in an English parliament safe against dissolution as long as the Scots army could threaten? Crisp denunciation of a popish plot in the opening days had led to the

---

[62] Baillie, *Letters*, vol. I, pp. 276–7; Napier, *Montrose and the Covenanters*, vol. I, pp. 349–51; BL Harl. Ms. 457, fols. 12–21; Stowe Ms. 187, fols. 6–14; NLS Adv. Ms. 33.4.6, fols. 60–1, 65–6.

[63] On 23 November. Possibly the copy of secret instructions had not reached the king.

[64] NLS Adv. Ms. 33.4.6, fols. 56, 84; GD 112/40/2/3/113. Cf. Baillie, *Letters*, vol. I, pp. 276, 283; *D'Ewes (N)*, pp. 105–6.

[65] Argyll and Bute District Archives, Argyll Mss. TD 40/8. It was later alleged that Rothes wished to know whether Argyll wanted to be Lord Chancellor – Napier, *Montrose and the Covenanters*, vol. II, p. 59; *APS*, vol. V, p. 639.

[66] *CJ*, vol. II, pp. 44, 62; *D'Ewes (N)*, pp. 52–3, 105–6, 214–15; NLS Adv. Ms. 33.4.6, fols. 50, 56, 63–4, 80; GD 112/40/2/3/123.

impeachment of the Earl of Strafford, who had been his key figure in recent military strategy.[67]

The difficulties on the other hand of quick proceeding, however, were to work against Charles's purposes. The second and the third articles of the Scottish settlement passed rapidly, though again it was certainly novel that the king conceded points over the manning of castles and the administration of oaths. However, Charles could not yield so easily over the fourth article, asking for the punishment of incendiaries; as a result the Scottish parliament had again to be prorogued.[68]

The attack upon the incendiaries touched upon many who had served the king faithfully, and moreover held implications not only for Scots. Besides the constant pressure of hostility directed particularly against Traquair, Charles was also here concerned for the fates of Strafford and Laud. On the Scottish side, singled out especially with Traquair were Sir John Hay, Sir Robert Spottiswood and Dr Walter Balcanquhal besides, as a group, the 'prelates'. The civilians were at least to be debarred from all future officeholding.[69] Charles gave the English negotiators no discretion to admit that there were any incendiaries in his attendance and insisted that he would give 'all just protection to his servants'; Bristol, under instructions, moved to have the article transposed to the end of the treaty. No ground was given, which drew the king to concede that he would not prohibit, or better hinder, parliamentary trial of suspected persons – which merely brought him in line with one of the statutes of 1640. The Covenanters now named all those excepted, and extended their demand to ask for cooperation in sending those cited to Scotland for trial, expressing their hopes that none of these people might return to credit with the king.[70]

Eventually, on 30 December, Charles accepted a minimum by pledging that he would employ no person who was judged incapable by Act of parliament without the parliament's consent. He reserved still Traquair's case for challenge only in his own presence, since he had given the earl his orders while he acted as Commissioner: the charge as it stood dwelt principally on Traquair's conduct in 1639–40. Traquair could be included in the more general settlement only if he was charged with doing anything unlawful.[71] It was no satis-

---

[67] Fletcher, *Outbreak*, pp. 3–4.

[68] BL Harl. Ms. 457, fols. 22–4; Stowe Ms. 187, fols. 14–15; NLS Adv. Ms. 33.4.6, fols. 66, 76, 80–1, 84, 98.

[69] Napier, *Montrose and the Covenanters*, vol. I, p. 350; NLS Adv. Ms. 33.4.6, fols. 74–5, 83, 94–5.

[70] Cf. Napier, *Montrose and the Covenanters*, vol. I, p. 350; Sir W. Fraser, *The Sutherland Book* (2 vols., Edinburgh, 1894), vol. II, p. 170; NLS Wod. Fo. 65, fol. 188; GD 406/M1/128. Sources for the list of incendiaries are cited above, n. 17.

[71] BL Harl. Ms. 457, fols. 23–45; Stowe Ms. 187, fols. 15–16, 25–6; NLS Adv. Ms. 33.4.6, fols. 76, 83, 96–7; Baillie, *Letters*, vol. I, pp. 279, 285. For Traquair's charge at this date, see NLS Wod. Fo. 64, fols. 135–42.

factory resolution for the Covenanters, who continued to see Traquair serving the king against their better interests while he, like many of the others cited to appear before the Scottish parliament, remained untroubled in the protection of the king's Court.[72] For Charles, however, it was a vital point in saving something of his honour vested in one he had chosen to be responsible to him alone.

As might have been anticipated from the year's printed propaganda, the Covenanters had also extensive charges to make against Archbishop Laud and the Earl of Strafford. Charges against Laud began with a heavy indictment of his part in composing the service-book and promoting the wars of 1639–40, and importantly it was made to figure in a prosecution moved, as with Strafford, from the House of Commons. The coincidence of timing appears to have been deliberate, possibly less neat than it might have been, for while the Scottish charge was signed and given to the English peers on 14 December when the 1640 Canons, and then Laud's name on the 15th, were under attack in the Commons, the contents of the charge were not published until the 17th, when Bristol had it read to a conference of both Houses.[73] From the report of this conference, John Pym led the House to accuse the archbishop of treason; Laud in quitting the House of Lords wanted to collect papers for his defence against the Scottish charge, which was all that was known at this stage, and this was indeed done.[74]

The Scottish charge had undergone alteration (and so delay) before being made public, for the king, and the lords commissioners after him, managed the omission of an introduction and conclusion which cast heavy aspersions in general terms on English bishops, in particular on the ill effects of episcopacy on Scotland owing to the English influence. The Covenanters would try again to raise this central question; therefore the influence of the king caused it to be dropped for only a short time, and the charge was curiously left

[72] A revised roll was issued on 9 February 1641, but later demands concerning these people named only the most prominent, leaving the rest unspecified – GD 406/1/1515; GD 406/M9/118/1; NLS Wod. Fo. 73, fol. 103; *A Diary of the Public Correspondence of Sir Thomas Hope of Craighall, Bart., 1633–1645*, ed. T. Thomson, BC (Edinburgh, 1843), p. 121; BL Sloane Ms. 1467, fols. 102v–3; *RPCS*, 2nd Series, vol. VII, 510–12. See too Traqr. Mss. Bundle 27 or NLS Adv. Ms. 33.1.1, vol. XIII, no. 59 (summons against Traquair + 19). Besides the main list, at least 131 more people were listed in a paper of 10 March 1641 – GD 406/M9/86/5.

[73] *CJ*, vol. II, pp. 51, 54; *LJ*, vol. IV, p. 111; *D'Ewes (N)*, pp. 162–3, 169–70; CUL Ms. Kk. 6.36, fols. 120–3; *Note Book of Sir John Northcote*, ed. A. H. A. Hamilton (1877), pp. 72–3, 78–81; Baillie, *Letters*, vol. I, pp. 280, 275; NLS Wod. 4to. 25, fol. 118.

[74] *LJ*, vol. IV, p. 111; *HMC Montagu*, vol. III, pp. 399–400; *The Works of the Most Reverend Father in God, William Laud, D.D.*, eds. W. Scott and J. Bliss (7 vols., Oxford, 1847–60), vol. III, p. 377. The Scots were asked to prove their charges early in January 1641 – *CJ*, vol. II, p. 62; BL Harl. Ms. 457, fol. 51v; also *D'Ewes (N)*, p. 325; Baillie, *Letters*, vol. I, pp. 474–5; *HMC House of Lords (17)*, vol. XI, pp. 432–3.

with pieces of paper pasted over the offending paragraphs as if to signify the reluctance behind their omission.[75]

The Covenanters were never on their own in England, but nor was their programme easily effected. They had received warning of the king's first coming to the treaty; and before this had met with some of their friends at Lord Savile's house to air the idea of having some members of the Commons on the English side of negotiators. Their friends' answer was revealing, generous despite the lack of precedent, but pointing out the risk of opening a door for other peers to be included on the commission 'who might do more harm than those [i.e. the Commons members] could do good'.[76] On the abolition of episcopacy question the Covenanters assisted with the organisation of the massive London 'root and branch' petition, presented on 11 December – after which their original paper against Laud followed. Anti-episcopal support appeared to be found more readily outside the parliament since, inside, consideration of what was a divisive issue was postponed – although at the end of December, private Anglo-Scottish discussions made for close consideration of the religious question.[77] The Covenanters also kept contacts with ministers preparing their famous remonstrance, which was presented to the House in January 1641.[78]

Whoever the Covenanters' friends were over the English church issue – the 'godly' in Baillie's eyes – it is clear that Scots threw themselves in. Popery and episcopacy had received strong batterings in the Scottish context, which at least went towards encouraging an imitation of their reforming zeal; there was at the same time plenty of domestic incentive and enthusiasm – even if not necessarily for the British presbyterianism the Covenanters had as their positive vision. In the divisions which arose Scots joined in opposing the moves and counter-petitions which favoured the bishops.[79] Charles would not have approved.

[75] BL Harl. Ms. 457, fols. 29, 31; HLRO Braye Ms. 2, fols. 92–5 (and v. Strafford, fols. 96–7). See too NLS Wod. Fo. 64, fols. 191–3, 195; Baillie, *Letters*, vol. I, pp. 278, 280.

[76] NLS Adv. Ms. 33.4.6, fol. 59. The Englishmen present were not named.

[77] Baillie, *Letters*, vol. I, pp. 273–4, 275, 280, 285–7; Napier, *Montrose and the Covenanters*, vol. I, p. 349; NLS Wod. 4to. 25, fols. 117v–18; *CSPV 1640–1*, p. 97; Fletcher, *Outbreak*, pp. 91–2. Two diarists wrote as if an earlier London petition also struck against bishops – CUL Ms. Kk. 6.38, fol. 22 (Palmer); Bodleian Film 39, p. 8 (Peyton); cf. NLS Crawford Ms. 14/3/75. Lord Maitland journeyed south on 29 December with further instructions on matters of the eighth article, and so probably including points concerning unity and uniformity between the churches; Maitland served again on this issue later – NLS Adv. Ms. 33.4.6, fol. 96; Wod. Fo. 67, fol. 20; Baillie, *Letters*, vol. I, pp. 473–4; *RPCS*, 2nd Series, vol. VII, p. 316. I am grateful to Professor Russell for discussions on this.

[78] Baillie, *Letters*, vol. I, pp. 282, 286, 291–2. Cf. BL Add. Ms. 24863, fol. 48.

[79] Baillie, *Letters*, vol. I, pp. 291, 296, 303; PRO SP 16/473/45. For the English dimension, see for example Fletcher, *Outbreak*, pp. 91–124; J. S. Morrill, 'The attack on the church of England in the Long Parliament, 1640–1642', in D. Beales and G. Best (eds.), *History, Society and the Churches* (Cambridge, 1985), pp. 105–24.

The supply of money both to the Covenanters and the king's forces took up time in the Commons from an early stage. Members agreed more easily to make a grant than on how to pay it and as in April 1640 there were questions on the supply–grievances balance. The final manner of supply was not resolved upon until almost a month after the debate opened, when on 10 December a grant of two subsidies was decided. The requirements of the two armies virtually forced another grant of two subsidies less than two weeks later. The Scots in London read optimistically what happened; the king meanwhile was faced by far-reaching demands.[80] One was that the parliament should directly handle the collection of the money; calls for legislation against superstition and idolatry, and for annual, or later triennial, parliaments came in around the money bills.[81] Further delays in approving these bills affected too the flow of credit, and around this arose yet more attention to English grievances. The two armies were paid up to early or mid-December, but then received nothing until March 1641.[82]

That the armies and consequently their area of occupation suffered in this political process was not necessarily taken with equanimity. Members from the north were noticeably urgent for final settlement, as too those who spoke for disbanding the Scots with little care for the settlement of their treaty. On the other hand John Pym, surely with Scottish approval, stood out against credit procrastinations, and the Covenanters were vocal in their own complaints.[83] Divisions of opinion over the threatening aspect of the Covenanters seemed to surface when it was proposed to disband the Irish army before the two armies in England. The proponents had financial considerations little in mind, it being far more a matter of disarming papists who they supposed to proliferate in the Irish force; their opponents valued the security against the Covenanters whose potential they feared.[84]

Treaty negotiations in January 1641 continued in the familiar vein of some

---

[80] *CJ*, vol. II, pp. 48–9, 57; *D'Ewes (N)*, pp. 33–5, 110–11, 134–6, 170, 183–5; NLS Adv. Ms. 33.4.6, fol. 60.

[81] *CJ*, vol. II, p. 28; *D'Ewes (N)*, pp. 33–5, 204, 327; BL Add. Ms. 56103, 13 November (unfol.); Bod. Rawlinson Ms. C956, fols. 38v–45v (partly printed in *D'Ewes (N)*, pp. 534–6); CUL Ms. Kk. 6.38, fols. 44–5; Fletcher, *Outbreak*, pp. 39–40.

[82] The subsidies bill was ready for royal assent only on 16 February, and then not without mistakes – *CJ*, vol. II, p. 105; *D'Ewes (N)*, p. 491. For a study of credit, see W. P. Harper, 'Public borrowing 1640–1660. With special reference to government borrowing in the City of London between 1640 and 1650' (unpublished University of London M.Sc. dissertation, 1927).

[83] For example, *D'Ewes (N)*, pp. 74, 203–4, 265–6, 277, 333, 335, 345, 351, 356–7, 367, 371, 380–4, 390–2; NLS Adv. Ms. 29.2.9, fol. 151.

[84] Fletcher, *Outbreak*, pp. 18–19; *D'Ewes (N)*, pp. 204–5, 213, 229–30, 357, 486–7; M. Jansson (ed.), *Two Diaries of the Long Parliament* (Gloucester, 1984), pp. 16, 19; *HMC Cowper* (23), vol. II, p. 274; BL Harl. Ms. 6424, fols. 23v–4v; HLRO Lords' Minute Book (5/E/7/1/7), 19 February.

hard argument alongside a mutual readiness for dialogue. To the fifth article asking for the restoration with damages of all ships and goods taken during the troubles, the English lords represented the king's line that this was acceptable only if done reciprocally, with damages paid on both sides.[85] The Scots changed their approach, not without advice from their friends, and pressed for ships in detention to be returned to them, the question of damages being transferred to the all-inclusive sixth article. A sum of money was asked specifically for setting ships out to sea, which the English beat down to £4,000. The speed of this conclusion recommended itself to both sides, and Scots and English commissioners reported it to Newcastle and the two Houses respectively.[86]

The Covenanters benefited from advance collaboration with English friends over the next, potentially difficult article which asked for general reparations.[87] Long before the Covenanters had officially presented it, Bristol in mid-December for the king had raised the matter before both Houses as an opposite device to encourage speed in ending the treaty.[88] He did not succeed, and was compromised when, following the eventual reading of the massive schedule of general Scottish expenses, he asked whether the sum total – over £500,000 sterling – was demanded of the English. If the king still hoped, as at York, that the Scottish paper in itself would be enough to incense an anti-Scottish reaction, Bristol's question by contrast was conciliatory, picking up from the Scottish wording the notion of 'friendly assistance';[89] but the Scottish reply, phrased to elicit a definite statement of English support for their cause in any grant made in response, went further than the earl wanted. They would have borne their own charges had they been able, they argued, but needing at least some help they hoped it might be done by 'the justice and kindness of the kingdom of England'.

Justice had been the theme of a letter from the Newcastle Committee which the lords commissioners had heard read: it acknowledged that the English parliament had not moved the war, but said that England had benefited from Scottish ships and goods taken and used; that English 'churchmen' had been the worst incendiaries of all; and that Scottish suffering over three and a half years deserved its reward – 'Justice craves we should not return beggars or

[85] BL Harl. Ms. 457, fols. 51, 54; NLS Adv. Ms. 33.4.6, fol. 114.
[86] BL Harl. Ms. 457, fols. 45–50; Stowe Ms. 187, fols. 26v–7v; NLS Adv. Ms. 33.4.6, fols. 97–8, 104. Ships were not immediately released – NLS Adv. Ms. 33.4.6, fol. 132.
[87] Baillie, *Letters*, vol. I, pp. 285, 289–90; NLS Adv. Ms. 33.4.6, fols. 77, 98. A proposed format for the paper, endorsed by Wariston, survives in NLS Wod. Fo. 66, fol. 117.
[88] *LJ*, vol. IV, pp. 111–12; *D'Ewes (N)*, p. 165; CUL Ms. Kk. 6.38, fol. 121; Northcote, *Note Book*, p. 78; NLS Adv. Ms. 33.4.6, fols. 83–4.
[89] BL Harl. Ms. 457, fol. 50v; Baillie, *Letters*, vol. I, p. 289.

bankrupts.'[90] Justice went near acknowledgement that the Covenanters had been right in their cause and actions, which was the tenor of the long introductory narrative to the main demand. Bristol, presumably under pressure from Charles, tried in vain to have his question and the Scottish answer removed from the written record.[91]

The same earl's speeches to the two Houses who met in conference to hear matters reported were faithful to the record, and not ungenerous to the Covenanters; the expediency of granting something of the demand was that it indicated a readiness in the Scottish guests to depart. What might be given could be regarded as a 'viaticum' of kindness, though it was certainly an enormous request and regrettable for the time that it would take to be answered.[92] In a fuller speech on the matter of general reparations, he argued that, though this appeared sad and dishonourable to the nation, the dishonour more properly fell on those 'ill instruments' who had given 'improvident counsels'. His continuing harshness implied against Strafford cannot have endeared him to the king, but his appeal was focused more importantly by a rhetoric to uphold future unity, a unity which might draw in all three kingdoms under Charles. This unity, with the ideal of love and concord among the people under God, unlike Charles's hope at York, would involve concessions on religion and liberties not only to the Scots, as had already happened, but to the English as well. The Scottish army may have startled in the past, may have offended the honour of the king and English people; Bristol dwelt now on the vision of one king and one island and so one nation.[93]

Unity was appealing, but this picture was only one optimistic possibility which left many matters untouched, as the background for example of debates in the Commons and Lords showed; there was animated dispute concerning the reasonableness of the Scottish demand. Despite his vision Bristol still served the line of wishing the early end of the Scottish occupation and, though attendances of English peers at the treaty were low, he pressed the Covenanters to allow interim proceedings on the other remaining articles while the parliament prepared an answer on the reparations matter; the king encouraged it. The Scots resisted, stressing that it was expected of them to finish individual articles before further proceeding, but they were by no

[90] NLS Adv. Ms. 33.4.6, fol. 83–4, 95; BL Harl. Ms. 457, fol. 48 – the part explicitly about justice was not summarised in Borough's notes.
[91] BL Harl. Ms. 457, fol. 50; Stowe Ms. 187, fols. 27–32; Baillie, *Letters*, vol. I, p. 289; NLS Adv. Ms. 33.4.6, fol. 104v. By contrast, the Covenanters had been happy to shun publicity after the dispute over the 1640 legislation – BL Harl. Ms. 457, fol. 18.
[92] Bod. Dep. c. 165, fol. 11 (12 January 1641). Cf. Baillie, *Letters*, vol. I, p. 290.
[93] *D'Ewes (N)*, p. 247; Bod. Dep. c. 165, fols. 12–13. Cf. Jansson, *Two Diaries*, pp. 26, 28 (22 March).

means adamant on the question, for they were not all prepared for an indefinite stay.[94] As the time for another month's renewal of the cessation in early February drew near, Bristol almost singlehandedly continued his efforts by suggesting, twice, the appointment of select committees within the English parliament to handle a quick ending to the treaty; in the Commons some suggested that this should be the last month for the payment of maintenance.[95] However, the Lower House had resolved by majority that it was fit to give friendly assistance and relief though without specifying for the present the sum involved or the manner of raising it. The Covenanters' insistence on knowing the precise sum involved consequently meant some further delay before all was settled.[96]

The king so far had had to endure the parliament's comprehensive assault on many of the policies of recent years, but as divisions seemed possible he delivered a speech on 23 January to state his own terms for unity. Supply for the armies and the longer-term expense of the navy were obvious heads; he hinted that the triennial act then in passage might be acceptable if some things were changed, but regarding bishops, while allowing room for reformation, he categorically blocked any question of their complete removal.[97] The ministers' remonstrance for precisely that extreme course was presented on the same day. Robert Baillie, among the Scots, had support for the words on parliaments, but felt that resentment at the role of bishops in parliament would in consequence of the king's words join with the 'root and branch' campaign. The Covenanters continued to inject their efforts. Alexander Henderson's work on the case against limited episcopacy was ready for publication, and further encouragement was probably given to the London campaign.[98]

With the prosecution of Strafford also coming to full readiness, this was the time that Charles explored possibilities of gaining English ground with the help amongst others of the Earl of Bedford and John Pym – a projected settlement which also conceivably was to draw such people away from reliance on the Scottish presence. There were rumours of bridge appointments to the

---

[94] BL Harl. Ms. 457, fols. 52–4; Stowe Ms. 187, fol. 32; NLS Adv. Ms. 33.4.6, fols. 114, 116; Baillie, *Letters*, vol. I, p. 289; *D'Ewes (N)*, pp. 292–4.

[95] BL Harl Ms. 6424, fol. 16; *D'Ewes (N)*, pp. 333–4.

[96] *D'Ewes (N)*, pp. 272–5, 268–9 (22 January 1641). The debate lasted unusually long, until 2 p.m. Cf. Baillie, *Letters*, vol. I, p. 290. There were no treaty meetings between 26 January and 5 February – BL Harl. Ms. 457, fol. 60.

[97] *CJ*, vol. II, p. 72; *LJ*, vol. IV, p. 172; *D'Ewes (N)*, pp. 263–5, 277, 280, 331, 354; BL Harl. Ms. 379, fol. 79; *HMC Montagu*, vol. III, p. 411; BL Harl. Ms. 6424, fol. 12.

[98] Baillie, *Letters*, vol. I, pp. 291–2, 295, 302–3; [A. Henderson], *The Unlawfullnes and Danger of Limited Prelacie*, Wing H1444; NLS Wod. 4to. 25, fols. 141–2; J. D. Ogilvie, 'Church union in 1641', *RSCHS*, 1 (1926), 143–60.

privy council.[99] Additionally, and presumably with the king's blessing, Traquair tried to bribe the Covenanters into a speedy withdrawal, even before the Commons named the sum to be awarded as friendly assistance.[100] Nothing immediately could be achieved. The Commons came round to offer £300,000 as a 'brotherly assistance' – albeit with quite a contest of exchanges.[101] Generally this prompted some optimism about an approaching end, though the opening of debates on the contents of the ministers' remonstrance and the 'root and branch' petition were timely reminder of what was left to do on possibly a British front. The Scots put their charges against Laud and Strafford into print, together with the papers exchanged over the sixth article; and, to catch the moment, the paragraph which attacked English bishops and episcopacy, struck out in December under royal pressure as an unacceptable opening, was included at the end of the document against Laud.[102]

After agreement on the seventh article, for restoring publicly the Covenanters' reputation in England,[103] the eighth and last article was opened, at least in part, with a far-reaching demand both for the removal of the border garrisons and the slighting (razing) of their fortifications. It was argued that, with the hoped-for lasting peace, there would be no need to maintain even the potential of such fortifications, an idea that James VI and I had espoused as symbolic of Anglo-Scottish understanding. This first of the British heads for 'securing a settled peace' caused reflection on the whole period since 1603.[104] Although the full schedule for the eighth article seems then to have been deliberately withheld in order to oblige English friends, no long delay of the end was anticipated, or wanted, by the Scots.[105] Argyll was summoned to join the

[99] C. Roberts, 'The Earl of Bedford and the coming of the English revolution', *Journal of Modern History*, 49 (1977), 600–16. I am grateful, however, to Professor Russell for his help and for letting me see an unpublished paper on this subject.

[100] Baillie, *Letters*, vol. I, p. 290; NLS Wod. Fo. 64, fol. 143; Traqr. Mss. Trial XI – depositions of Cavers and Wauchton.

[101] *CJ*, vol. II, p. 78; *D'Ewes (N)*, pp. 320–1; BL Harl. Ms. 457, fol. 60; Stowe Ms. 187, fol. 33v; NLS Adv. Ms. 33.4.6, fols. 118–19, 122; NLS Wod. 4to. 25, fols. 145v–6; J. G. Fyfe, *Scottish Diaries and Memoirs, 1550–1746* (Stirling, 1928), p. 124.

[102] Fletcher, *Outbreak*, pp. 91–9; Baillie, *Letters*, vol. I, pp. 290–1, 297, 300; *The Charge of the Scottish Commissioners against Canterburie and the Lieutenant of Ireland*, Wing C4201J (1641).

[103] BL Harl. Ms. 457, fols. 62–4; Stowe Ms. 187, fol. 34. The written exchange has not survived – cf. *APS*, vol. V, pp. 339–40. To some extent this demand for recalling hostile proclamations touched upon a *fait accompli* – GD 406/1/1313.

[104] BL Harl. Ms. 457, fols. 65–6; Stowe Ms. 187, fol. 34; NLS Adv. Ms. 33.4.6, fols. 118–19, 123. See too NLS Adv. Ms. 33.1.1, vol. XIII, no. 72 (1 March); D. Laing (ed.), *Correspondence of Sir Robert Kerr, First Earl of Ancrum . . .* (2 vols., Edinburgh, 1875), vol. I, p. 115; NLS Wod. Fo. 73, fol. 89v.

[105] Baillie, *Letters*, vol. I, pp. 297, 301; *CSPV 1640–2*, p. 127.

negotiators in London, invited by the English lords as Rothes earlier had suggested; the Marquis of Hamilton invited Lord Lindsay, his brother-in-law, to share in the honours, and Lord Almond was also to come.[106]

As preparative for further demands, the Covenanters asked Charles to consider a more regular residence in Scotland. The request, tactical to some extent since compensatory motions were intended to cover his necessary absence, hit a serious point in stating the wishes for royal justice and Court life with its accompanying benefits. The king should not abandon his English responsibilities – as some Englishmen feared – but Scotland should enjoy still his personal presence. It was asked that the prince should have some of his upbringing in the north.[107]

Against this smooth progress, royal conciliation which extended to making some of those rumoured appointments gave the Covenanters some alarm – made worse by rumours that they, doing well themselves, were no longer concerned for the English cause against episcopacy and the fate of the English incendiaries; the flow of loan money seemed to be at stake. On 24 February a paper was composed on the Covenanter side to refute the rumours; delivered first to the English lords commissioners, it was also printed – according to Johnston of Wariston – because of groundless anxiety in some of his colleagues that some Scots were being attracted by royal preferments. A crisis blew up by the king taking extreme offence at the Covenanters' so direct words about English politics.[108]

The king's stake in the truth of the rumours suggests that Johnston's suspicion that Traquair had been active in kindling jealousies may have been justified; Charles was in effect testing his English strength.[109] Debates over

---

[106] NLS Adv. Ms. 33.4.6, fol. 96; *HMC 4*, p. 624; BL Harl. Ms. 457, fols. 68, 70, 72v; NLS Adv. Ms. 33.4.6, fol. 139r; Baillie, *Letters*, vol. I, p. 306; Laing (ed.), *Ancrum Correspondence*, vol. I, p. 111. Lord Almond's sponsor is unknown. Some of those cited as incendiaries petitioned in early February to be allowed to go home, presumably to cut their losses – NLS Adv. Ms. 33.4.6, fols. 119, 122v.

[107] BL Harl. Ms. 457, fol. 67; Stowe Ms. 187, fols. 35, 37; NLS Adv. Ms. 33.4.6, fol. 123; Baillie, *Letters*, vol. I, p. 301; NLS Wod. Fo. 67, fol. 19.

[108] BL Stowe Ms. 187, fols. 38–9; *From the Commissioners of Scotland, 24th February 1641* (*sic* – English spelling though) BL Thomason 669.f.3; NLS Wod. Fo. 66, fols. 207–8. The reading of Johnston's letter is a little obscure (not to mention the handwriting!). Johnston named Dunfermline, the Sheriff of Teviotdale, John Smith (?) and the Clerk (Adam Blair) as the likely actors, and himself with Rothes and Loudoun as those feared to be heading for royal promotion. See too NLS Adv. Ms. 33.4.6, fols. 129–30, 133; GD 112/43/1/4/4; Laing, *Ancrum Correspondence*, vol. I, p. 110; Baillie, *Letters*, vol. I, pp. 303–6. Baillie was reasonably happy that the king was given the printed paper; Bristol, a less 'good friend' to the Covenanters than the Earl of Holland, had handed the manuscript copy to Charles – BL Harl. Ms. 457, fol. 71. Mr Thomas Henderson, who was linked with the printing, was used subsequently by the Scottish commissioners – NLS Wod. Fo. 73, fol. 97.

[109] NLS Wod. Fo. 66, fol. 207. For the Newcastle response, see NLS Adv. Ms. 33.4.6, fols. 117, 132, 135. Cf. PRO SP 16/471/22; GD 3/5/242. I owe the suggestion about the king's stake to Professor Russell; I am grateful for discussions with him on this.

reparations for the Covenanters had shown clear splits, as Charles had always expected; and though over Strafford the Scottish presence might still have been seen to be helpful, the Covenanter ecclesiastical vision was found offensive by many.[110] The 24 February paper, which touched on both issues, exposed again the division of attitudes within the parliament; its message allowed the serious financial worries in the Commons to be linked clearly for the first time with complaints against the Scottish presence being lengthened to give support to the anti-episcopal lobby. Edward Hyde told the House of his success in finding individuals who would have lent the much-needed cash for the armies but for this provocative Scottish paper. The Commons was plunged into hectic and to some extent rival money debates on 27 February, and some equally divisive exchanges directly over the Covenanters. The Scottish paper was not, however, in the end condemned; John Hampden and William Strode, and so almost certainly John Pym, were if anything open in its support.[111]

The king's reactions were quite clear as, in Johnston's words, he ran 'stark mad' at the paper.[112] The words against Strafford came at a time of tense exchanges in the Commons over the preparations for the trial, but the odds on the king stopping anything much at this stage were small; Sir John Culpepper, a defender of episcopacy whom Hyde had supported on 27 February, expressed as strongly as any other the urgent need to prosecute the business.[113] On the other hand Charles could more popularly vent his anger on the visible impudency of the Covenanters expressing themselves on the sensitive church question; that the paper had been printed gave him extra grounds. Although the Covenanters as yet were saying little that was new, the king seized his opportunity. He fully intended to recall the paper from circulation by a proclamation of his own, a threat which hung over the Covenanters for some days and which obliged them to present to the peers a mollifying explanation of the earlier paper – which they had to allow to be printed. This acknowledged that the English should decide their own church settlement; and Charles awaited from them their fuller statement on the whole question.[114]

Charles had blamed the Covenanters for causing divisions in England –

---

[110] See NLS Adv. Ms. 33.4.6, fols. 130, 133, 135v–6, 138, 139v, 150.

[111] *D'Ewes (N)*, pp. 417–18; BL Add. Ms. 14828, fols. 7v–9; NLS Wod. 4to. 25, fols. 151–2; Jansson, *Two Diaries*, pp. 12–13.

[112] NLS Wod. Fo. 66, fol. 207.

[113] *D'Ewes (N)*, pp. 371, 381–4, 417. The delays were imputed to the lords newly made privy councillors working with Hamilton – Baillie, *Letters*, vol. I, pp. 305, 310–11; NLS Wod. 4to. 25, fols. 148v–9; NLS Wod. Fo. 67, fol. 23; *HMC De L'Isle*, vol. VI, p. 384; Staffs. RO D (W) 1778/Ii/14.

[114] NLS Adv. Ms. 33.4.6, fols. 129–30, 135–6; BL Harl. Ms. 457, fols. 71–2; Baillie, *Letters*, vol. I, pp. 306–7; *CSPD 1640–1*, 478/1; SRO PA 13/1, p. 1; NLS Wod. Fo. 66, fols. 207–8.

which was at best a half-truth.[115] These days of crisis were serious. For the Covenanters they dashed the hope of ending the treaty very soon – Argyll's coming was delayed once again – and for the king they apparently marked a turning-point in the parliament. He was disappointed with the Bedford-Pym 'group', but found elsewhere that he did not have to be isolated. All he could do to secure the early departure of the Scots and so his honour would be done, with hopefully the saving of Strafford and some form of episcopacy. It was to be a struggle, but he would not be bound. He would engage dangerously with plotting that was beginning amongst the English army in the north.[116]

Court and parliamentary politics were linked, and the Marquis of Hamilton's position gives an interesting perspective on this. Being on the Scottish list of incendiaries until a revision in February 1641, and vulnerable to attack in the English scene as a monopolist, Hamilton more clearly than ever was attempting to balance his defence between the king and the Covenanters.[117] Courting the latter with their English friends, he had still tried to promote a path of accommodation with royal blessing – for example by securing the solicitor-generalship for Oliver St John, one of the earliest 'bridge appointments', and encouraging Charles's consent to the English triennial act; along with that it was not coincidence that he contemplated marrying the Earl of Bedford's daughter and giving his own daughter to be wedded to Argyll's son.[118] However, around 3 March charges were raised against him in the English parliament, including a substantial indictment of his commission in Scotland; the Earls of Strafford, Arundel and Berkshire were said to have concerted the move. Information against him had been furnished by the Earl of Montrose, another rising figure of hope for Charles, as will be seen. Most unusually for this parliament Hamilton escaped – thanks not to the king but to his links formed with the Covenanters and their English friends – though it was not the end of attacks. Certainly later in the year, but no doubt also at this time, Viscount Saye and Sele and John Pym were amongst his supporters. The competition around the king gave Hamilton's double-game serious risks; while he remained where he was most

---

[115] NLS Adv. Ms. 33.4.6, fol. 129.

[116] NLS Adv. Ms. 33.4.6, fols. 129–30; C. Russell, 'The first army plot of 1641', *TRHS*, 5th Series, 37 (1987), 85–106.

[117] NLS Adv. Ms. 33.1.1, vol. XIII, no. 20; Wod. Fo. 67, fol. 35v; Adv. Ms. 33.4.6, fols. 123–4; Baillie, *Letters*, vol. I, p. 277; *HMC Cowper*, vol. II, p. 268; PRO 31/3/72, fol. 339; E. Hyde, *The History of the Rebellion and Civil War in England Begun in the Year 1641*, ed. W. D. Macray (6 vols., Oxford, 1888), vol. I, p. 253; Argyll and Bute District Archives, Argyll Mss. TD 40/8.

[118] Sir W. Fraser, *Memorials of the Montgomeries Earls of Eglinton* (2 vols., Edinburgh, 1859), vol. I, p. 243; *HMC De L'Isle*, vol. VI, p. 386; NLS Wod. Fo. 65, fol. 192; GD 406/1/1657, 1459; GD 112/40/2/3/139; *HMC Hamilton Supplementary* (21), p. 53.

comfortable, at Court, he doubtless wished fervently for a return to some kind of normality.[119]

Although the Covenanters realised that many disliked their printed message, they still looked for the support of some friends – but these made known their resistance to the Scots in any sense dictating an ecclesiastical settlement for England, which at least was highly impolitic, given the spectrum of English opinion. The Scots offered their fullest statement on 10 March, to request unity in religion and uniformity in church government for the sake of 'nearer union' and truth, but acknowledged again that the separate kingdom of England should determine its own destiny. Politics were a necessary part of advancing God's kingdom; every endeavour was to be used in the negative struggle against the adversary – even force of arms should the latter turn aggressive – but ways forward into truth would be left in the hands of Providence. Whatever the ideal, it was true that, beyond the realm of prayer, Scottish resources were not inexhaustible. The English could only be encouraged to see where their 'best' interests lay.[120]

The Covenanter ideology was assured and predictable, offered in timely coincidence with a vote in the Commons for the exclusion of bishops from parliament, which restored some optimism dented by the sobering reflections in the wake of the February troubles.[121] However, the refusal of the king and Bristol to allow this paper of arguments to be made public was heeded – and the circulation of the document restrained even in Scotland; the friends advised it. While Bristol represented a defence that the 'established laws' in question were in any case under current debate, the Scots friends confirmed an anticipated argument for the Covenanters that their helping presence for Strafford's trial would be better without reviving divisive motions around the subject of religion.[122]

Caution by the Scottish negotiators, an attention to 'law and reason' and an appeal to the Newcastle Committee to allow them discretion, marked the further progress of heads under the eighth article.[123] The aim was the best

[119] NLS Wod. Fo. 65, fols. 192–3; Wod. Fo. 67, fol. 20v; Baillie, *Letters*, vol. I, 309–11; *HMC De L'Isle*, vol. VI, p. 289; *D'Ewes (N)*, p. 430; GD 3/5/244. For the later attacks, see NLS Wod. Fo. 66, fol. 177 (15 April); BL Harl. Ms. 6424, fol. 55v; *CSPD 1641–3*, 482/23, 486/15; Hyde, *History*, vol. I, pp. 258–9, 280; GD 406/1/1507; below, p. 313.

[120] Baillie, *Letters*, vol. I, pp. 291, 303, 305–8, 312; NLS Wod. Fo. 67, fol. 23; Adv. Ms. 33.4.6, fols. 130, 133, 135–7, 139, 147–8; BL Stowe Ms. 187, fols. 41–8; Cf. PRO 31/3/72, fols. 476–7; BL Harl. Ms. 457, fol. 31. P. Collinson, *The Birthpangs of Protestant England* (1988), pp. 134–5, has wise remarks to make in this regard.

[121] NLS Wod. Fo. 67, fols. 23, 30; NLS Wod. 4to. 25, fols. 152–3; Baillie, *Letters*, vol. I, pp. 307–9; BL Harl. Ms. 6424, fols. 44–6. There were encouraging divisions also in the Lords.

[122] NLS Adv. Ms. 33.4.6, fols. 138, 150; BL Harl. Ms. 457, fols. 75, 76v–8; Stowe Ms. 187, fols. 41–8; EUL Ms. Dc. 4.16, fol. 88v; Baillie, *Letters*, vol. I, pp. 313–14.

[123] See NLS Adv. Ms. 33.4.6, fols. 138–9, 146–7.

possible Scottish settlement in restricted bargaining circumstances; an index of all demands was submitted also on 10 March, with provision that extra points might still be added. These together with ongoing shortages of money weakened and in time killed the hope that the Scottish parliament presently due to reconvene in April might then be held. Fears grew that Charles might attempt a counter-strike; Johnston, with a sense deeper than most of both vision and politics, anticipated more positively the need for yet another pro-rogation for Scotland.[124]

Because of the various distractions, agreement on the first part of the eighth article had come in the parliament a month after its first being submitted. All strongholds on both sides of the border were to be returned to their state before the troubles began, after the armies had been disbanded – an evasive answer to the request that the fortifications should be both abandoned and slighted.[125] From the king through to the Commons, there was pressure on the Covenanters to release the remainder of their demands; they for their part wished no great delays, conscious of the suffering in the north, and beyond the general index, at the end of March, came two extensive papers on British themes, one offering proposals under the broad head of making a lasting peace, the other detailing a programme for arrangements relevant to trade and commerce. They had held back a little for Strafford's trial, but as this sub-sequently drew on, Charles with the Earl of Bristol encouraged every effort to advance settlement of the issues – to which, in the main, they had a good response.[126]

The mounting difficulty of the situation forced differences among the Covenanters to come near the surface. In the exchanges over the secret instructions to their commissioners in November 1640, there had been fullest dispute over a demand concerning the appointment of the king's council within the list of 'expedients' for a solid peace, where it was asked that council and Session be 'reduced' to the practice of the years before 1603; a parliamentary say in appointments was meant. A query on this implied that some felt that this entrenched too far on the king's prerogative, besides being a demand not previously made.[127] In March 1641, at least three members of the

[124] BL Harl. Ms. 457, fols. 74, 77; Stowe Ms. 187, fols. 39–40, 48v–9; NLS Adv. Ms. 33.4.6, fols. 119, 122, 133–5, 137–8, 150v; NLS Wod. Fo. 67, fol. 23 (Johnston on 9 March).
[125] Even in June 1641 the Covenanters could get only part of what they asked. *LJ*, vol. IV, pp. 174, 175; *CJ*, vol. II, pp. 97, 98, 175; *D'Ewes (N)*, pp. 434, 444–5, 451, 454; *APS*, vol. V, p. 340; NLS Adv. Ms. 33.4.6, fols. 133, 136v; Wod. Fo. 73, fol. 92; BL Harl. Ms. 457, fols. 79, 93; Stowe Ms. 187, fols. 39, 60–1.
[126] BL Stowe Ms. 187, fols. 50–6; NLS Wod. Fo. 73, fol. 76v; Wod. Fo. 67, fols. 17, 28. There were no treaty meetings between 19 March and 8 April. For the trial, see Fletcher, *Outbreak*, pp. 7–15; J. H. Timmis III, *Thine is the Kingdom* (Alabama, 1974).
[127] PRO SP 16/471/22; cf. NLS Wod. Fo. 64, fol. 203; Napier, *Montrose and the Covenanters*, vol. I, pp. 376–7.

Scottish delegation in London were uncomfortable about it, according to
Wariston, who had long espoused it. He maintained that he stood firm along
with Rothes and Loudoun – that is, in his view firm for the 'country'; others,
he suggested, worried for their own advantage with the king.[128] The Committee of Estates directed that the demand should be pressed as far as possible
although not to the point of making a breach.[129]

This was a subject that was to go before the king only, and not to the
English parliament – it being consciously argued that it stemmed from the
fact of the king's habitual absence from Scotland – and therefore was a
demand for unique Scottish circumstances. The arguments of law and
precedent, which were available not least through Wariston's efforts, were to
be left aside on this particularly sensitive area.[130] The commissioners in
London reported that the king would not go further than to allow parliamentary advice as opposed to consent on appointments to council, Session and
the principal offices; they gave no indication that they would press hard
against this, nor against Charles's wish to free the advocate Sir Lewis Stewart
from his citation since February as a likely incendiary.[131] They advised
against the idea of now legislating for yearly conventions for noblemen and
lairds to match those of the burghs, the reason being that Charles would
oppose the continuation of anything resembling the Tables; he had quickly
indicated his related displeasure at the idea of *conservatores pacis*, committees to safeguard the peace between triennial parliaments. This was
caution on pressing the king too far, and an indication of a yearning simply
to return to normality. Some of the Scots at least wanted to avoid more long
delays. Any intimation of division, however, was still avoided.[132]

Division was a feared beast not least on account of worries about the Earl
of Montrose. A leading figure by his own choice, it could not be doubted that
there were others behind him. Due to Lord Boyd's confession in late 1640,
discovery of the Cumbernauld band had lately caused shock-waves to run
through the Covenanting movement, and it was a reflection on a somewhat
precarious unity that the Committee in Edinburgh and Newcastle was neither
sure of the extent of support for the signatories at Cumbernauld nor

---

[128] NLS Wod. Fo. 67, fol. 20; cf. *Diary of Sir Archibald Johnston, Lord Wariston, 1639*, ed.
G. M. Paul, SHS (Edinburgh, 1896), pp. 73–4. Johnston named the Sheriff of Teviotdale, the
Clerk Adam Blair and William Drummond of Riccarton.

[129] BL Stowe Ms. 187, fols. 48v–9; NLS Adv. Ms. 33.4.6, fol. 135.

[130] Cf. GD 406/M9/93/44; NLS Wod. Fo. 64, fols. 96–7, 99–100; EUL New College Ms. X15b
3/1, vol. I, fols. 326–30 or Buckminster Park, Tollemache Ms. 4106; Johnston, *1639 Diary*,
pp. 15–16.

[131] Cf. NLS Adv. Ms. 33.4.6, fols. 147–8, 123v–4, 139; NLS Wod. Fo. 73, fol. 83; also below,
pp. 295–6.

[132] NLS Adv. Ms. 33.4.6, fols. 135, 147–8; NLS Wod. Fo. 67, fols. 23, 32; EUL Ms. Dc. 4.16,
fol. 89; Stevenson, *Scottish Revolution*, pp. 219–20.

altogether united in condemning Montrose. The Banders had declared that they meant nothing against the Covenant or the public good, and that they would eschew causes of offence, but they upheld consistently 'indirect practising' as the reason for their combination. In short, bound to keep the language of the 'cause', they were opposing the ascendancy of a clique around Argyll. Montrose certainly lost the trust of many of his non-associated colleagues, but he escaped major prosecution. As to the truth of what he had stood against, there was no investigation but rather an unsuccessful effort to draw all elements of the Covenanters together.[133]

From the time of the 1639 Pacification Montrose had had thoughts of direct approaches to the king, caused probably by a mixture of his local jealousies with a vision that did not strongly identify with the increasing demands being made of Charles. He avowed that the Cumbernauld band was signed because of talk of a possible dictatorship in Scotland, linked with Argyll and designed to overcome the present king's inadequacies, which had led on to proposals for cantoning Scotland to the hands of private persons; he claimed for himself that he upheld the true spirit of the Covenant. None of this would have been of great comfort to Charles, and probably Montrose knew it, since he denied that he ever sent him a copy of the Band.[134] His statements of criticism over the instructions to the Scots commissioners on the eighth article rather stood to gain support from moderates within the Covenanter party – and so possibly also those who sought moderately to advise Charles.[135]

In the period of the treaty at London, attention came to be around Sir Archibald Stewart of Blackhall, Sir George Stirling of Keir, Lord Napier and Montrose. Although the whole story may not be clear, it seems that Blackhall and Keir met together shortly after Lord Boyd's funeral; their talks then as subsequently expressed concern at the continued lengthening of the quest for settlement – and their feeling that all might be solved by the king holding a parliament in person.[136] Montrose and Napier were found to be sympathetic, and proposals were made for disbanding the Scottish army and for postponing all appointments until the king was in Scotland. Therefore regret which had lasted since Charles's failure to come in July 1639 seemed to be more directed against the consequences of royal absence than, as Wariston and

---

[133] NLS Adv. Ms. 33.4.6, fols. 102v–3, 115–16, 119; Laing, *Ancrum Correspondence*, vol. I, p. 126; Baillie, *Letters*, vol. II, pp. 468–9; GD 406/M9/93/7–8 (28 January); J. Murray, 7th Duke of Atholl, *Chronicles of the Atholl and Tullibardine Families*, vol. I (Edinburgh, 1908), p. 110; Stevenson, *Scottish Revolution*, pp. 223–7.

[134] Napier, *Montrose and the Covenanters*, vol. I, pp. 373–4, 377, 380–3, 386–90, vol. II, pp. 50–1, 59.

[135] GD 220/3/57; Napier, *Montrose and the Covenanters*, vol. I, pp. 376–7, vol. II, pp. 42–3.

[136] Evidence by Blackhall – NLS Wod. Fo. 65, fols. 68–9; Napier, *Montrose and the Covenanters*, vol. I, pp. 461–3. The depositions dated from some time after the event.

colleagues steered it, against Traquair. The Montrose group in effect was presenting a rival claim for leadership in a settled Scotland. They intended contact with the Duke of Lennox; Lieutenant-Colonel Walter Stewart, acting for them, linked assuredly with Traquair about 3 March. The dating might confirm our notion of rival settlements, since it ties up with the summons of Argyll to attend in London.[137] Blackhall would not assume responsibility for the ideas, but he did not deny his support for them.[138]

Traquair listened to ideas for settlement within the future Scottish parliament, ideas which upheld a concept of 'religion and liberties';[139] he heard words which spoke of the Earl of Argyll's treason – and now, if not already before, he commissioned in return a search for friends in Scotland who would see him defended from the Covenanter charges prepared against him. He employed the same Lieutenant-Colonel Stewart, and enjoyed the support of Lennox, his patron.[140] Wariston, who heard of the Traquair contact with the Montrose group almost immediately, connected it at first with Traquair's personal cause; the larger truth dawned in time.[141] Traquair embraced with relish the chance to mount a case against both Argyll and his ally Rothes, which from Traquair's perspective offered increased chances as a means of escaping censure himself.[142] He told Charles about his Stewart meeting and was briefed, in general terms at least, for subsequent return visits.[143]

Whatever Charles felt about the Cumbernauld band, the effect of the coincidence of the approach from Scotland and his increased disenchantment with the Scottish commissioners in London and their partisan English support should not be underestimated. Talk of disbanding the Scottish army could mix with anti-Scottish feeling amongst English army officers which was the background to what has become known as the first army plot. Montrose's original notion of disbanding the Scottish army probably did not differ from the point included in the main treaty which asked for the disbandment of both armies as the desirable means of return to settled civil government.[144] How-

---

[137] Napier, *Montrose and the Covenanters*, vol. I, pp. 453–4; Traqr. Mss. Trial VIII, 15th argument.

[138] Napier, *Montrose and the Covenanters*, vol. I, pp. 420–2, 424–30, 442–3, 449–50, 453–4, 466; NLS Wod. Fo. 65, fols. 68, 71; D. Stevenson, 'The "Letter on Sovereign Power" and the influence of Jean Bodin on political thought in Scotland', *SHR*, 61 (1982), 25–43.

[139] NLS Wod. Fo. 65, fol. 72; Traqr. Mss. Bundle 28[iii] – letter from Traquair to Stewart, 9 March.

[140] Traqr. Mss. Bundle 26[iii], [ii]; Napier, *Montrose and the Covenanters*, vol. I, p. 446; Lennox corresponded with Montrose on Traquair's behalf – NLS Wod. Fo. 65, fols. 43, 45, 70v.

[141] Napier, *Montrose and the Covenanters*, vol. I, pp. 363–4; see too EUL Ms. Dc. 4.16, fol. 89.

[142] NLS Wod. Fo. 65, fols. 43–4; Napier, *Montrose and the Covenanters*, vol. I, pp. 360–1; Traqr. Mss. Bundle 28[i].

[143] Traqr. Ms. 37/10, 16.

[144] Cf. NLS Wod. Fo. 65, fol. 70v; GD 220/3/57; M. Napier, *Memorials of Montrose and his Times*, MC (2 vols., Edinburgh, 1848–51), vol. I, pp. 285–7.

ever, Professor Russell's argument is very plausible that Charles exploited another possibility by attempting to have the Scots disbanded or at least neutralised so that English soldiers might be free to intimidate untrammelled the parliament in Westminster, hopefully on his behalf. The Covenanters subsequently alleged as much when evidence of Montrose's plotting came to light.[145]

Charles's involvement in plotting was part of his hard efforts to save Strafford's life. The army plots (for they were plural) showed once again the king's readiness to engage in all and every means possible to achieve his ends. Apparently deliberate leaks of information served to complement the 'planning' of the use of force, a tactic already tried through the Scottish experience. But the outcome was little better than before. Impulsive action only brought more trouble. It worked counter to Strafford's own last-ditch appeals that he might be allowed to retire quietly away from politics; and severely dismayed even the king's supporters in the Commons. Conciliation and threats together were a bad pair, but Charles never learnt the lesson.[146]

For Scotland also, where the parliament was prorogued to near the end of May, Charles contemplated ideas both threatening and hopefully conciliatory. He insisted that the Scottish army had to be disbanded before he would send any royal Commissioner to the parliament, so exerting pressure for a later date than the Covenanters suggested. He suspected now for the Scottish end of things that he could actually gain by the drawing-out of time. By 20 April at the latest, he had decided that he would attend the parliament in person in the light of more news of his potential support there, for Lieutenant-Colonel Stewart had returned to London earlier that month.[147]

At the same time, with some of the Scots commissioners itching to have things ended, he tried to woo people more generally. Money was offered to enable a quick end to the treaty should the English parliament be too slow about it, and there was talk of a major tactical concession on the question over official appointments. The request had been that the various leading government appointments should be made with appropriate consent, with Lords of Session furthermore guaranteed their places *ad vitam vel culpam*.[148] Charles's initial response had been only to concede that misconduct might be censurable in parliament, and to give general assurance that he would

---

[145] Russell, 'The first army plot'. Montrose's talk of leading troops to fight for the Prince Elector may have been genuine, but the presence of Commissary Wilmot, an English army plotter, at the interview with Charles is intriguing! – Traqr. Ms. 14/20 (re week 18–25 April). Cf. Baillie, *Letters*, vol. I, p. 357.

[146] For this context, see Russell, 'The first army plot'.

[147] EUL Ms. Dc. 4.16, fol. 89; Napier, *Montrose and the Covenanters*, vol. I, p. 367; Traqr. Ms. 37/10; NLS Wod. Fo. 73, fol. 92; Baillie, *Letters*, vol. I, p. 350.

[148] Cf. M. Lee, Jr, *The Road to Revolution: Scotland under Charles I, 1625–1637* (Urbana and Chicago, 1985), pp. 22–3; above, pp. 21–2.

appoint able and qualified individuals to the various positions; the Covenanter commissioners not surprisingly had found this insufficient but had
themselves offered a compromise formula, which Charles now apparently
indicated he would accept. Parliaments, council and Session might suggest
names for appointments or at least offer comment on any that he proposed;
judges would have their places *quamdiu se bene gesserint*. The king followed
through on these verbal exchanges in writing on 9 June. By then, however, the
possibilities of mutual understanding were again sullied.[149]

The various rumours and manœuvres in April were disquieting through the
uncertainties they engendered, but particularly to those who conceived of
themselves as the objects under attack. Johnston of Wariston kept himself
well informed by his English contacts and, suspecting that Montrose was
aggressive, was on the alert.[150] Furthermore, besides the general threat (as he
took it) contained in the intimation of the king's journey, Wariston faced
threats against his own person and Argyll and Rothes, for Charles tried to
blackmail them into surrender on the Scottish incendiaries question; the
names of Saye and Sele and Pym came into the talks. Evidence collected by
Traquair was to be used to bring charges if they persisted in their
standpoint.[151]

Wariston was confident, no doubt justifiably, that he might face any
charges with impunity before a trial in Scotland, but in London the incendiaries issue nearly caused a split with some of his 'comrades'.[152] The problem
had been raised anew through a request for Acts of Oblivion in all three kingdoms which excepted criminals and those cited to answer to the Scottish
parliament: Charles refused the exceptions despite what he had already conceded about the trial of incendiaries under the fourth article of the treaty, and
some of the Scots commissioners seemed ready to quit a rigid approach.
Although Wariston was surely right in seeing Traquair's interest and therefore his counsel employed here, that earl was not alone under challenge, and
principles were involved on both sides.[153] Where originally pursuit had been
argued necessary for confessions that might serve the honour of king and
kingdom, now in passion Wariston called for blood, because of Traquair's
ongoing conduct. Charles continued to deny that loyalty to himself could be
punishable, but the Covenanters in the end respected the orders of parliament

[149] NLS Wod. 4to. 25, fol. 160v; BL Harl. Ms. 457, fols. 80, 85v, 87, 99; Stowe Ms. 187,
fols. 48–9, 59, 61, 67v; *APS*, vol. V, pp. 340–1; Napier, *Montrose and the Covenanters*,
vol. I, pp. 366–7; Russell, 'The first army plot', pp. 102–3.
[150] NLS Wod. Fo. 67, fols. 28, 23, 25v, 35v; Wod. Fo. 66, fol. 177. Cf. Bod. Dep. c. 165,
fols. 55–9. The Commons responded to rumours by restraining troop movements – *CJ*,
vol. II, p. 116; BL Harl. Ms. 162, fol. 399; Harl. Ms. 163, fols. 9–10.
[151] NLS Wod. Fo. 67, fols. 35, 37, 21; Traqr. Mss. Bundle 28[i].
[152] Rothes's word – NLS Wod. Fo. 66, fol. 183.
[153] BL Harl. Ms. 457, fol. 93; Stowe Ms. 187, fols. 58–9, 62; NLS Wod. Fo. 73, fols. 85, 93.

and Committee of Estates which bound them to a common course. Charles's attempt at conciliation could not yet break this barrier. Those like the Earl of Dunfermline who were drawn into talks with the king were assailed by Wariston with arguments strongly asserting a bound commitment to the full prosecution of incendiaries.[154]

Wariston's suspicions that the idea both for recrimination and for the king's journey had stemmed from Scotland, in particular from Montrose, were soon enough confirmed. The prospect of Charles travelling north was by no means appealing; Wariston hoped, presumably with his English friends, that it could never happen because of the many problems still to be remedied in England, yet the plotting raised threats to personal survival. In his correspondence Wariston referred also to a threat to attack Englishmen who could be incriminated for their contacts with the Covenanters. Little materialised in the event until the attack intended against the five members in January 1642, but the possibility had a long history; in October 1641, before the Scottish incendiaries were processed, Charles allowed a counter-attack in Scotland in what was known as 'the Incident', in which context the threats against Englishmen were renewed.[155] Charles was surely misguided to tread on such a path. The question in April 1641 was how to restrain him. Lord Balmerino and Adam Hepburn of Humbie received the confidential communications direct in Edinburgh; with Montrose as yet inside the Committee of Estates, the news was to be told only to General Leslie, the Earls of Cassilis and Lothian and Lord Lindsay. Wariston did not name his Court source, but it seems highly probable that it was the Marquis of Hamilton. Whatever Hamilton thought of the British vision against Charles, in these days of plots he could not trust his interest only to the king.[156]

The bulk of the eighth-article agenda made its sporadic progress through the months of April and May 1641. The lords commissioners were quick to send their first responses, on many of the commercial heads, adopting the Scottish timesaving suggestion of referring matters to a committee; some of these heads, as remedies for the 'defaults' of the post-Union period, looked to extend advantages for Scottish trade *vis-à-vis* the other kingdoms, which was to stretch English tolerance to its limits. In the other 'peace' group fell together the highly contentious issues of Oblivion and religious uniformity; also war, where extensive mutual cooperation between the nations was requested along with other relevant matters, and the *conservatores pacis*;

---

[154] NLS Wod. Fo. 67, fols. 35, 37, 21.
[155] Below, pp. 312–14 – GD 406/M1/117.
[156] NLS Wod. Fo. 67, fols. 35, 37–8. The Earl of Lothian was approached independently by Traquair for help! – Traqr. Mss. Trial VIII (15th argument).

proposals for disbanding included a demand for first breaking up the Irish army. An explicatory paper for briefing the parliament about the various aspects of the programme was prepared by the Scots on 12 April.[157]

Some of these matters were inspired by the present crisis, but, as some had a more general reference to the multiple-kingdom state of affairs, it is worth noting how the Covenanters expressed their consciousness of Ireland, which had not been explicit before. They aired specific hopes over matters such as free trade and equal standards of coinage, punishment of incendiaries, and certainly ratification of the treaty. They could assume that Ireland might generally be taken under the name of England – which was hardly fair to their situation, and symptomatic of the kind of imperialism to which Irish Catholics in particular were opposed; by contrast Charles was paying good attention to his potential Irish support, a quest, however, that later he might have regretted as a contributory factor to the outbreak of the rebellion there.[158]

The whole agenda had to go to the parliament, except that the lords faithfully represented the king's wish that the innovatory notion of *conservatores pacis* be dropped altogether; the Covenanters could not agree to that, though some, as has been seen, had hesitations. At some point, probably in the first half of April, a paper in Lord Loudoun's hand explored the possibility of a compromise alternative for the *conservatores*.[159] There was an attempt to negotiate around the particularly Scottish topics in the eighth article, where the king's first answers had conceded little. Might the king attend more regularly in his northern kingdom? It had also been asked that the Prince of Wales might have some part of his education in Scotland, and that Scots might be guaranteed places in his as in the king and the queen's household. On each of these Charles predictably resisted being tied down, and was adamant on his own discretion as to the employment of papists around Court, over which he was also being challenged in the English parliament at this time. As over appointments, the king chose to open up more in April, but at most to modify turns of phrase; Court life was a very special province. His conclusion on the question of copper coinage ran more amply to the strategy of wooing

---

[157] BL Harl. Ms. 457, fols. 81–4; Stowe Ms. 187, fols. 50–9; NLS Adv. Ms. 33.4.6, fol. 134; Wod. Fo. 73, fols. 76v, 84–5.
[158] BL Stowe Ms. 187, fols. 52, 55v, 56–7; SRO PA 7/2/78B; A. Clarke, 'The genesis of the Ulster rising of 1641', in P. Roebuck (ed.), *Plantation to Partition* (Belfast, 1981), pp. 29–45; C. S. R. Russell, 'The British background to the Irish rebellion of 1641', *Historical Research*, 61 (1988), 166–82. English views of Ireland and the Irish were also confused – I owe this point to Professor Michael Perceval-Maxwell.
[159] NLS Wod. Fo. 65, fol. 35; NLS Wod. Fo. 73, fol. 85.

support; points of grievance he accepted might be remedied with the help of the coming parliament.[160]

Over the troubled incendiaries question, however, Charles continued to resist and he found cooperation anew from his Advocate, Sir Thomas Hope of Craighall. Having helped Traquair in some measure in 1639, and yet also having believed God's blessing to be on the Scottish invasion in 1640, Hope was prepared to appease Charles in the face of the mainstream drive against the incendiaries; since the parliamentary legislation was now accepted, royal favour seemed once more desirable. He was trusted with the several prorogations of parliament, and in January, April and May 1641 tried to avoid implication in protestations which were read to exclude the possibility of Traquair returning as royal Commissioner.[161] He himself protested when the Covenanters put his name on the Signet summons of the incendiaries, insisting on the need for the king's express warrant; Charles gave explicit warrant to the contrary in order to frustrate the summons. An alternative summons took the names of four other leading advocates, but Hope was under considerable pressure to comply, particularly at the prorogation in May. His was an unhappy position; he withdrew rather than be obliged to make a protestation for his stand.[162]

This latest prorogation was to delay the parliament until mid-July, and Charles's mounting hopes for good returns at his attendance led him down paths which revealed how little changed were his presuppositions. His letter to prorogue caused some ado because it was seen to imply a reassertion of the claim to be able to prorogue the parliament without consent; there was unease when the machinery of the privy council was stirred into action to manage the details of the royal visit. Worse, the Earl of Winton, a Catholic, was the king's chosen recipient of the letter summoning the council to its first meeting.[163] The moderate tendency amongst the Covenanter commissioners continued under the burden of the long occupation, however, with some in late May commending the king's decision to make the journey north, and generous to the queen for her enabling role. William Drummond of Riccarton

---

160 BL Harl. Ms. 457, fols. 71v, 76, 80, 85v, 87, 99; Stowe Ms. 187, fols. 35–8, 53, 59–61, 67–8; NLS Wod. Fo. 73, fol. 84v. The Covenanters did not readily abandon the request for Scots to attend at Court – cf. Buckminster Park, Tollemache Mss. 4109, 4110. I am grateful to both Professor Russell and Dr John Adamson for drawing my attention to the Tollemache family archive.

161 Hope, *Diary*, pp. 119–20, 124–5; GD 406/1/1514, 1521; *APS*, vol. V, pp. 302–3, 304, 305–7, 620, 621, 623.

162 GD 406/1/1513, 1514, 1322, 1515, 1516, 1517, 1519, 1334, 1520, 1521, 1522, 1345, 1525, 1346, 1524, 1349, 1351, 1350, 1357, GD 406/M9/93/9; cf. GD 406/1/10830; Hope, *Diary*, pp. 122, 124, 126–9, 131, 137; *APS*, vol. V, pp. 307, 621–3.

163 *APS*, vol. V, p. 306; GD 406/1/1344, 1347, 1345, 1362. The council was summoned to meet on the same day as the parliament had been due.

wrote to Sir George Stirling of Keir and, in a letter which dealt with the current questions over the incendiaries, mentioned his disbelief that Keir could possibly be involved with a Montrose faction as was rumoured. Drummond's characterisation of some who sought their own private ends followed on the words of the king and not on the thoughts of Wariston.[164]

Feeling amongst the Scots that the occupation should not be unduly extended was shared in the parliament, but not necessarily with much regard to the treaty. In early April the House of Commons divided on whether to allow another cessation of arms for a mere fortnight, which those in support only narrowly carried; the Lords subsequently were persuasive that a month was needed because of the length of the eighth article.[165] Fortnightly cessations began in May, however, with expressions of impatience for the end increasingly common, it seems.[166] Shortly afterwards afternoon sittings were revived, although they failed to attract good attendances; more significantly a standing committee of Lords and Commons (26 + 52) was appointed to meet in effect almost daily to speed the process. As Gervase Holles among others discovered, outright hostility to the Scots was still never countenanced, but through it all Charles might have seen some encouragement for his own drive to recover control.[167]

Money paid to the armies in March had brought the period covered to mid-January; not until late May was there more. As the cessation of arms was repeatedly extended, projected capital accumulation almost immediately fell short of needs; an Act for two subsidies to bring the total to six passed after debate had already opened on another means of supply, a bill to raise £400,000, the equivalent of about eight subsidies, by equal rating on the counties.[168] The search for immediate cash went on separately. The money question played its part in slowing progress. Consideration of ways to disband both armies begun on 13 March, following Covenanter appeals, produced a scheme around 21 May which assumed that the Scottish army might return north before payment of any part of the brotherly assistance. The Scots gave a regretful refusal; their financial needs were too great, and their treaty

---

[164] NLS Wod. Fo. 66, fol. 178; Wod. Fo. 73, fols. 97, 99, 104; Laing, *Ancrum Correspondence*, vol. I, p. 120; Baillie, *Letters*, vol. I, p. 354. But cf. Baillie, *Letters*, vol. I, pp. 383–4, 388; Balfour, *Historical Works*, vol. III, pp. 27–30, 75.

[165] *CJ*, vol. II, p. 118; *LJ*, vol. IV, p. 212; BL Harl. Ms. 164, fols. 161, 163v; Harl. Ms. 162, fols. 391, 399; Harl. Ms. 163, fols. 9–10; Harl. Ms. 1601, fols. 54–5; Bod. Tanner Ms. 66, fol. 50. See Fletcher, *Outbreak*, pp. 21, 23–4.

[166] *CJ*, vol. II, p. 140; BL Harl. Ms. 164, fol. 202; Harl. Ms. 163, fols. 213, 234, 287.

[167] For Holles, see *CJ*, vol. II, p. 152; BL Harl. Ms. 163, fols. 206–7; Harl. Ms. 164, fol. 188; Harl. Ms. 477, fol. 10. Cf. Harl. Ms. 163, fols. 178, 190, 310; Harl. Ms. 477, fol. 74; Harl. Ms. 478, fol. 57. Holles holograph copy of speech – BL Lansdowne Ms. 207 (f), fols. 37–8.

[168] *CJ*, vol. II, pp. 92, 142, 145, 149, 158, 161; BL Harl. Ms. 163, fols. 170, 174–5, 196–7, 228–9; Harl. Ms. 164, fol. 188v; Harl. Ms. 477, fol. 93v.

unfinished in any case. However, they accepted a following offer of £80,000 of the assistance now with the rest to be paid later as a necessary surrender to save time. It allowed concrete thinking to begin on the details of disbanding, but the onus of finding the money remained.[169]

The substance of the eighth article was put before both Houses on 14 April, and the Lords managed resolutions – long before the Commons, who were more fully occupied on the financial questions. The proceedings against Strafford also made time limited, but some argued for hastening that process for the sake of other affairs including the treaty.[170] The Lords' votes on the treaty more or less upheld the proceedings of the peers who had negotiated with the Scots. They hesitated to encroach on the prerogative in matters of war and joined in trying to allay the Covenanter demands against incendiaries and for uniformity of religion.[171]

The king's troubles in early May – the débâcle of the first revelations of the army plots coinciding with the end of Strafford – were the last hindrance to the Commons' debates. It was a crisis met most notably by the famous Protestation and the Act against the dissolution of parliament without its own consent; there were calls for the publication of the Remonstrance then in preparation, and for control over the appointment of royal councillors. The king's scheming was very directly confronted. To link such actions with Scottish precedents may not be altogether conclusive, though the links between prominent figures were real. The Protestation fell short of being a Covenant such as Scots wished, as it was argued to be neutral on the existing church government and ceremonies of England; but it was explicitly against popery, and stated the link on this between the three kingdoms which had been drawn on also during Strafford's trial. The Scots would consciously imitate the same oath at the eventual opening of the Scottish parliament.[172] A positive urge for progress within the parliament marked the subsequent days towards the end of the treaty, for it could be expected that Charles on his journey to Scotland would call the parliament's end. The majority probably would have been content at that prospect; some feared more acutely for the future, perhaps those who prepared most actively for the trial of Archbishop

---

[169] The proposal here assumed payment of the Scots only up to the end of May, when the present cessation ended. *CJ*, vol. II, pp. 104, 153; *LJ*, vol. IV, p. 268; BL Harl. Ms. 457, fols. 88, 90–2, 95v; Stowe Ms. 187, fols. 63–7; NLS Wod. Fo. 73, fol. 96v.

[170] See *LJ*, vol. IV, pp. 231–2.

[171] *LJ*, vol. IV, pp. 222, 224, 268.

[172] Fletcher, *Outbreak*, pp. 15–17; Russell, 'The first army plot', pp. 103–6. For the Scottish imitation, see NLS Wod. Fo. 66, fol. 223; Baillie, *Letters*, vol. I, pp. 351–2, 384; *APS*, vol. V, p. 332.

Laud or who keenly debated for the abolition of episcopacy in England, but English civil war if a possibility was not imminent.[173]

Discussions on the treaty produced some divisions in the Commons. The House agreed to shelve the question of religious uniformity in English hands, as allowed for in the Scottish desire, but the lobby most critical of episcopacy narrowly led the House to extend a vote of thanks to the Scots for their concern.[174] On other matters, hesitations over the Scottish vision seem to have cut across the whole spectrum of opinion. Guarding their privilege as ever, the Commons would take direction from the responses of the lords commissioners; in general it was after these had been given that the House added any remarks of substance and there were few such remarks on the distinctively English responses on the heads of trade.[175] The Commons also agreed that it went too far to have the consent of both parliaments necessary for the levying of war, only allowing, with sufficient caveats, some conditions to be placed on any future levying of war between the kingdoms.[176]

The Commons also had little to add on the proposed Oblivion, but for the English parliament Scottish incendiaries were not technically in the reckoning here. However, they appeared in the eleventh item of the trade heads, where it was asked that incendiaries, and any guilty of offences in the Middle Shires, might be remitted to the home country for treatment. With the king's antipathy well known, the relevance of this was not missed, although it apparently became tied up with a debate on the normal propriety of handing over refugees to persecution in their own country. The majority narrowly won the vote for a compromise resolution that 'persons' committing an offence might be sent home to be censured as incendiaries.[177]

The Covenanters picked up on the incendiaries issue at the end of this whole process, first by specific comment to the lords commissioners; Charles would give little ground, but with the Covenanters then appealing to the parliament, he insisted that his reasons be heard.[178] Five days after this, how-

---

[173] Cf. Fletcher, *Outbreak*, pp. 99–108; P. Crawford, *Denzil Holles, 1598–1680* (1979), pp. 48–52; Russell, 'The first army plot', pp. 105–6.

[174] *CJ*, vol. II, p. 148; BL Harl. Ms. 163, fols. 184, 188, 191–3, 215; Harl. Ms. 379, fol. 85; Harl. Ms. 477, fols. 74v–5; Sloane Ms. 3317, fol. 22; Harl. Ms. 457, fols. 93, 97, 99; Stowe Ms. 189, fol. 3; PRO 31/3/72, fol. 565.

[175] *CJ*, vol. II, pp. 154–5; BL Harl. Ms. 163, fols. 215–16, 311v; Harl. Ms. 477, fols. 91, 93v, 129; Sloane Ms. 1467, fol. 76. The final workings on the trade heads were not concluded by the relevant committees until 7 July 1642 – SRO PA 13/2, fol. 97.

[176] *CJ*, vol. II, pp. 150, 152, 156; *LJ*, vol. IV, p. 222; BL Harl. Ms. 163, fols. 202–3, 204–6, 208–9, 234v–5, 311; Harl. Ms. 477, fols. 80, 82, 83, 128v–9. For a memo by Loudoun in consideration of these decisions, see NLS Wod. Fo. 65, fol. 76 (16 June).

[177] *CJ*, vol. II, pp. 150, 154–5; BL Harl. Ms. 163, fols. 194, 216, 223, 229v; Harl. Ms. 477, fols. 76v, 96, 129; Bod. Film 39, p. 132.

[178] *CJ*, vol. II, p. 175; *LJ*, vol. IV, pp. 274–5; BL Harl. Ms. 163, fols. 310–11, 333v; Harl. Ms. 478, fol. 57v; Bod. Rawlinson Ms. D1099 (fol. 62); NLS Wod. Fo. 73, fols. 96–7, 102–3; BL Stowe Ms. 187, fols. 61–2, 68–9; Harl. Ms. 457, fols. 93–100; NLS Wod. Fo. 65, fol. 76;

ever, on 19 June and amidst divisions the Commons approved the exclusions to the Scottish Act of Oblivion. The House divided yet again on the eleventh 'commerce' head for the sending home of civil offenders, since the Covenanters substituted an explicit clause to specify that incendiaries should be thus remanded. The earlier compromise was uprooted, and the Lords backed the change.[179]

Charles's position had limited appeal. The problem of incendiaries was all too plausible in days when the army plotting was still topical – the army plotters were exceptions on the English side of the Oblivion – and new unsettling news was coming in from Scotland. From Edinburgh in early June the Committee of Estates had sent to the king to remove from Court all those cited, phrasing it almost as a condition of his coming to make peace in Scotland.[180] Montrose was among the signatories, but he was soon thereafter challenged for his recent underhand contacts with Traquair. Investigation of people who had defamed Argyll in 1640 had led to the interception of Lieutenant-Colonel Walter Stewart, amongst whose baggage was a royal holograph letter to Montrose and a set of cryptic instructions which Stewart fastened on the earl and his fellows.[181] There was no question as before of quietly ignoring this evidence of secret links with the Court: Johnston of Wariston was asked to hurry up to Edinburgh though the treaty in London was still unfinished. It became a concern that Montrose's supposed design to have had the Scottish army disbanded was linked with the English army plot; but the great fear was that the vital unity of the Covenanters was in peril. Sir Thomas Hope was pressed to cooperate in the prosecutions.[182]

The English lords commissioners first heard the news on 14 June as relevant to the Covenanter cause against the incendiaries; but English friends of the Covenanter commissioners delayed publicising it for almost a week. Enough of the bare outlines of the Stewart story were known to allow a scare to be fashioned on the scale of early May.[183] Again the safety of the kingdom

HMC *Salisbury*, vol. XXII, p. 354; Beds. RO J.1382. For the king's reasons, see Traqr. Ms. 14/40; BL Harl. Ms. 457, fols. 100–2. The undated paper from Scottish bishops to the parliament may date from this time – HMC *House of Lords*, vol. XI, p. 243.
[179] *CJ*, vol. II, p. 180; *LJ*, vol. IV, p. 281; BL Harl. Ms. 478, fols. 92–3; BL Harl. Ms. 163, fols. 333v–4v. For the final version, see *APS*, vol. V, pp. 343–4.
[180] SRO PA 12/1, fol. 2 (5 June); NLS Wod. Fo. 73, fols. 101–2 (7 June).
[181] Napier, *Montrose and the Covenanters*, vol. I, pp. 374–7, 472–4; Napier, *Memorials of Montrose*, vol. I, pp. 272–3; GD 406/1/1345, 1358; GD 406/M9/61/126; SRO PA 7/2/63; NLS Wod. Fo. 64, fols. 39, 77.
[182] NLS Wod. Fo. 73, fols. 101, 104v, 106; SRO PA 12/1, fol. 2; Laing, *Ancrum Correspondence*, vol. I, pp. 126–7; GD 406/1/1531, 1532.
[183] Napier, *Montrose and the Covenanters*, vol. I, pp. 535–6; BL Harl. Ms. 457, fols. 101, 104v; Stowe Ms. 187, fol. 69; Harl. Ms. 163, fols. 339v–40, 342; Harl. Ms. 478, fol. 100; Harl. Ms. 5047, fol. 32; HMC *Portland* (29), vol. I, p. 24. Sir Arthur Heselrig mentioned to the Commons meeting with the Covenanters only 'last Saturday', i.e. 19 June, but the first meeting was on the 15th.

was seen to be at stake; the committee of seven which had handled the army plots withdrew, and made proposals to counter the popish plot which John Pym delivered, the so-called Ten Propositions. It was stated firmly that the king should not go into Scotland until both armies were dissolved and the affairs of the kingdom generally settled – a highly pitched English target cutting against Charles's wishes – but one with which Wariston notably could sympathise.[184]

Members of this English parliament were meeting threats with a determination no less serious. The king tightened his dedication to solving the Scottish problem as a means of freeing himself. Traquair's sudden departure from Court after the news of Stewart's capture was no doubt calculated to minimise the English ramifications of the affair as well as to gain Scottish advantage. At the same time, Charles wrote his own letter to Argyll to assure him of his good intentions, despite almost certainly knowing of the self-incriminating words uttered by the earl. Given Argyll's past, it was a wise move, whatever Wariston might have thought, and Traquair quite possibly encouraged the king; it is certain that he now supported Charles's resolution to use amongst others Hamilton in his Scottish affairs.[185] Even the Earl of Rothes was drawn towards the Court – though he asked for the opinion of Wariston and other nobles and was unrepentant against Traquair.[186] Charles would still hope for a settlement not wholly disastrous in Scotland, by whatever means, but with the incendiaries controversy still open, peace was not yet guaranteed. The king was feared, and over these days of public scares people held back from giving him full trust. Politics swung against Charles, and the most obvious indication of this was that now his agreed concession on the demand concerning appointments was taken to be inadequate, and the matter had to be referred for final conclusion within the Scottish parliament.[187]

Charles was further conciliatory in his instructions to the Earl of Wemyss, chosen Commissioner for the general assembly in late July. Alexander Henderson, once again the Moderator, was appointed as Royal Chaplain for the forthcoming visit. Charles would astound the English when he went north

---

[184] *CJ*, vol. II, pp. 183–4; BL Harl. Ms. 478, fols. 107–8; Fletcher, *Outbreak*, ch. 2, esp. pp. 42–4, 55–9, 64–8; NLS Wod. Fo. 67, fols. 37v–8.

[185] Napier, *Memorials of Montrose*, vol. I, pp. 282–3 (12 June); Traqr. Ms. 12/37. Balcanquhal also left Court, but not Sir John Hay – *CSPD 1641–3*, 481/61; BL Harl. Ms. 457, fol. 109.

[186] *CSPD 1641–3*, 481/42, 483/96; D. Dalrymple, *Memorials and Letters Relating to the History of Britain in the Reign of Charles the First* (Glasgow, 1766), pp. 136–7. For other commissioners and the king, see GD 406/M9/93/36; GD 406/1/1461; Baillie, *Letters*, vol. I, p. 380; Balfour, *Historical Works*, vol. III, p. 25.

[187] *APS*, vol. V, pp. 310, 340–1; BL Stowe Ms. 187, fol. 67.

by his willingness to accept Scottish churchmanship.[188] His hope expressed presently for the 'much altered' government of the church of Scotland nevertheless needed some interpretation at the Scottish end – 'that by their actions and whole carriage they give real proof that the government of the church by assemblies and presbyteries may consist with monarchy and royal authority'. Was he leaving a loophole for the future? The assembly welcomed the generous tone of concessions but in its closing address aptly replied by noting that duty to 'supreme authority' included honour due to the king 'by all laws divine and human'. Whatever Charles's hopes for authority, members of the assembly would still wish to consider ways of achieving uniformity with the English.[189]

Traquair continued to advise the king on Scottish affairs after leaving Court, particularly on the proposed Act of Oblivion and his own case in relation to that. After the Act was passed in both Houses, he drafted for Charles a declaration to be subjoined to it which admitted the reciprocal exceptions as specified – with reference to Traquair's willingness to be lawfully tried over the conduct of his Treasurership, an aspect of his career as yet only a minor part of the charges.[190] This was complemented by submissions to the Scottish parliament in which Traquair offered to retire permanently from Court and demit all public office if necessary; he denied incensing trouble by his talks with Lieutenant-Colonel Stewart.[191] Charles readily accepted them for use, adding his own words that all others cited to the parliament should be let off unless a great crime was involved. Still no scope was allowed for the trial of Traquair's conduct as Commissioner in 1639–40. The king was consistent on this point, giving Traquair full assurance of his protection – an interesting comment on Charles's outlook given that the 'protection' of Strafford had so recently failed.[192]

Charles's cautious assent to the Act of Oblivion did not reveal everything. Traquair raised subtly in his submission over Stewart the subject of words and information against both Argyll and the Marquis of Hamilton; the king

[188] Napier, *Montrose and the Covenanters*, vol. I, p. 368; Baillie, *Letters*, vol. I, pp. 359–61, 363, 385–6; *CSPD 1641–3*, 483/68, 82, 484/1; G. F. Warner (ed.), *The Nicholas Papers*, vol. I (1641–52), Camden Society (1886), pp. 23–4. Wemyss was apparently second choice to the Earl of Southesk.

[189] GD 406/M9/110/3; GD 406/1/10789, 1393, 1394, 1399, 1404; A. Peterkin, *Records of the Kirk of Scotland* (Edinburgh, 1838), pp. 292–3, 296–7; Baillie, *Letters*, vol. I, pp. 360, 364–5. See too Stevenson, *Scottish Revolution*, pp. 232–3; W. Makey, *The Church of the Covenant, 1637–1651* (Edinburgh, 1979), pp. 63–4, 66–7.

[190] Traqr. Mss. 12/37, 37/15, 37/17, Bundle 28[iii].

[191] *APS*, vol. V, p. 624; Traqr. Mss. Bundle v, Bundle 26[iii]; PRO SP 16/481/50. Traquair's note of the submissions for the benefit of the English parliament survive in GD 406/M1/192/3. For the small concern with his Treasurership, see Baillie, *Letters*, vol. I, p. 384; NLS Wod. Fo. 64, fols. 135, 150–1, 128. The final 'dittay' is Traqr. Mss. Trial VI.

[192] *APS*, vol. V, pp. 309–11, 628–9; *HMC 9 (II)*, p. 243; GD 406/1/1369.

might yet have cards to play. The threats of mutual recriminations known by Wariston in April remained potentially useful; to borrow a metaphor, Charles might again wield the stick as well as the carrot.[193] Traquair meanwhile was in no hurry to cross the border, and preparations went ahead confidently for the royal visit.[194]

The Committee of Estates was uncompromising that incendiaries should come north, and the Scottish parliament on its first day of sitting, 15 July 1641, rejected Traquair's submissions, accepting instead a very substantial charge drawn up against the earl; on the next day the complete roll of those cited was read. The parliament sat without the king to prepare business; in line with the changes of 1640, there was a President, and no Lords of the Articles. As was now highly customary, Wariston helped to marshal unity by a memorandum.[195] On the treaty the members confirmed that the appointments question was to undergo further discussion once the king arrived, and among other points repeated the demand for men of reformed religion to attend the prince, which the king had answered only by vague assurances; there was a similar English request in the Ten Propositions. The propriety of consultation for war continued to be pressed, to be agreed in some form by a committee to be appointed in addition to the *conservatores* whose appointment was still requested.[196] The Covenanters did not expect challenges here, and very little time was allowed for the treaty to be concluded in England before the king's journey north; Lord Loudoun brought the amendments to Westminster on 5 August, where despite the tight circumstances there was little difficulty.[197]

Traquair worked hard in clarifying for Charles the details of his likely defence, and further wrote an address to explain his position to the parliament of England so as to counter the Covenanter appeals against him.[198] Whether this reached that parliament is uncertain; Traquair's hoped for allies, surprisingly, were Viscount Mandeville and his father the Earl of Manchester, but many including the Earl of Bristol refused to back down on

---

[193] *APS*, vol. V, p. 624; Traqr. Mss. Bundle 26[ii]; cf. Traqr. Ms. 12/40. For the metaphor, cf. Russell, 'The first army plot'.
[194] Hope, *Diary*, p. 145; GD 406/M9/121/1 (end June 1641?).
[195] GD 406/1/1381, 1378, 1380, 1382, 1386; *APS*, vol. V, pp. 311–14, 625–7; NLS Wod. Fo. 64, fols. 50–1, 153; Stevenson, *Scottish Revolution*, pp. 193, 229–32. Charles had a copy of Traquair's charges sent secretly to him – Traqr. Ms. 37/10.
[196] *APS*, vol. V, pp. 316–17, 343–4, 630, 649–50, 681; SRO PA 7/2/78B; Fletcher, *Outbreak*, p. 57. The other committee was appointed on both sides; only on the Scottish side is there a record of *conservatores* names – NLS Wod. Fo. 65, fol. 254; *APS*, vol. V, 404–5.
[197] BL Harl. Ms. 457, fols. 111–12; *LJ*, vol. IV, pp. 343–5; *CJ*, vol. II, p. 242; BL Harl. Ms. 164, fols. 3v–4.
[198] Traqr. Mss. 37/16, 37/10, 12/39; Bundle 27; NLS Wod. Fo. 73, fol. 107.

the Oblivion question – and, despite Traquair's efforts, English peers cooperated with the Covenanters by hearing witnesses in his case. The Scottish point was agreed that bad counsel should be tried.[199]

Charles did what he could to stave off challenges in Westminster while Commons and Lords worked through the practicalities of a poll tax, the last and one of the more efficient financial expedients, but his efforts to appear open-handed bore success as mixed as his motivation. Early in July his proposal to marshal active support for the Protestant cause in Europe delighted the Earl of Bristol, who was taken yet further into royal favour; it also produced a favourable reaction in Scotland. On the other hand Charles was vulnerable to outcry over his permission given to Irish officers to join the French and Spanish Catholic armies![200] Diverse interests were pulling on him; the prospect of his journey to Scotland likewise was still variously regarded. Charles would have limited the brief of the parliament during his absence, but he faced objections in the Commons which were unresolved at his departure. He was pressed to stay longer, but with sufficient money available for the Covenanters' army, there was no question of it.[201] And while the Scottish army straightforwardly withdrew, there were scares of trouble from within the king's army, and even of the king using the Scottish or Irish armies to his own advantage. The Earl of Holland, named originally to accompany the king into Scotland as his new Lord General, in the end did not go.[202] The gulf of distrust between Charles and some in and outside his parliament was considerable, and the issue of counsel was coming as much to the fore here as in Scotland.[203]

Concern for the future lay behind the move of sending delegates from both Houses to attend Charles while he was in Scotland. In so far as they might have been commissioned under the Great Seal, that is, with royal authorisation, they were meant to be acceptable, but the king, seeing the scheme to presume upon the role of the privy council, brusquely rejected it.[204] But Charles was not supposed to have a choice: those concerned, Lord Howard

---

[199] Traqr. Mss. Bundle 27, letter from Traquair to Countess of Home, 8 December 1641; BL Harl. Ms. 457, fols. 109, 112; *APS*, vol. V, pp. 319–20; *HMC House of Lords*, vol. XI, pp. 284–6; HLRO Main Papers, 16 August 1641; Traqr. Mss. Bundle v (Lord Wharton); *LJ*, vol. IV, pp. 365, 359.

[200] Cf. *CSPD 1641–3*, 482/27, 483/34, 36; *CSPI 1633–47*, pp. 330, 338; *APS*, vol. V, pp. 645, 647; SRO PA 7/2/74; CC Nicholas Box – letters of Northumberland and Bristol, 13, 28 and 31 August. The Scots in their turn were offered the same proposal for the Palatinate – *APS*, vol. V, pp. 699, 701; Balfour, *Historical Works*, vol. III, pp. 144, 146; GD 406/1/1458.

[201] Cf. Baillie, *Letters*, vol. I, p. 388.

[202] For the king's entourage, see GD 406/M9/121/1.

[203] See especially Fletcher, *Outbreak*, pp. 47–81.

[204] W. Bray (ed.), *The Diary of John Evelyn*, vol. IV (1852), p. 59; cf. Warner, *Nicholas Papers*, p. 9; Guildford, Bray Ms. 85/5/2 (5, 8). I am grateful to Dr John Adamson for drawing my attention to this last collection of Nicholas papers.

of Escrick, Sir Philip Stapleton, Sir William Armyn, Nathaniel Fiennes and John Hampden, were already on their way, and the further authorisation in the form of a parliamentary ordinance given to them *before* Charles's answer was heard betrayed this. Nor did the ordinance precisely repeat what had been asked of the king, most notably the phrase that the commissioners should 'certify both Houses of parliament such accidents and occurrences, as may concern the good of this kingdom'.[205]

The Scottish troubles had forced out into wide recognition the significance of the British nature of Charles's monarchy; those who were forward in the English parliament were necessarily British in their concerns in August 1641 as Charles journeyed north. Hamilton, who went with the king into Scotland, became a regular recipient of correspondence from Saye and Sele, who was prominent in the Lords like Pym in the Commons.[206] Hamilton was advised to trust the Lords' commissioner, Howard of Escrick, and, among the Commons' group, especially John Hampden. The further message was simple, that the marquis who had won an interest in England in the hearts of the 'best-affected and most potent in this kingdom' should not endanger that for anything in Scotland. Saye's confidence in his own party asserted itself against anything that might be engineered by the king, or, as he put it, 'honest men will live and die together in that which shall be for the king's *best* service and the union of both kingdoms' (my emphasis). A group which found common cause with the Covenanters and their achievement stood firm at this juncture to oppose to their limit all tendencies to the contrary.[207]

The Covenanters' army, having returned into Scotland, did not completely disband for their own reasons of security. The English army was being more slowly broken up, principally on account of the shortage of money, but the Covenanters were particularly nervous of the border garrisons, which had never been surrendered by the king during the time of the Scottish surrounding occupation; there were also memories that complete disbandment had been espoused by the Montrose group.[208] The English parliament's commissioners in Edinburgh advised their London colleagues to hasten the

---

[205] *CJ*, vol. II, pp. 249, 253, 256, 258–9, 262–3, 264, 265–6; *LJ*, vol. IV, pp. 361, 362, 366, 368, 370, 372–3; Fletcher, *Outbreak*, p. 76.

[206] Cf. Warner, *Nicholas Papers*, p. 3; Guildford, Bray Ms. 52/2/19 (22). Viscount Mandeville joined with Saye, though it may be noted that Hamilton received addresses from all kinds of people, including still Scottish bishops – GD 406/1/1495, 1408, 1407, 1412, 1410, 1509, 1422, 1430; *CSPD 1641–3*, 482/50.

[207] GD 406/1/1409, 1411, 1505. Cf. GD 406/1/1506, 1417, 1427; Bray, *Evelyn*, p. 76. Hamilton and Argyll were friendly to the English commissioners – Bod. Carte Ms. 103, fol. 67; I am grateful to Professor Russell for this reference.

[208] SRO PA 7/2/74; *APS*, vol. V, pp. 346–7; Yale, Escrick Mss., correspondence from 1 September, esp. Corr. 2/10; CC Nicholas Box – letter of Thomas Webb, 19 August. I am grateful to Professor Russell for drawing my attention to these Nicholas letters.

removal of the border garrisons, representing the Covenanters' complaint that some Scottish troops had to be kept on foot because of them. John Pym, chairing the Commons' recess committee and regarded certainly by the commissioners as their leading supporter, obliged by drafting the orders himself, on 14 September.[209] Although the Scottish army could no longer serve to guarantee the southern parliament's life, the partisan incentive for close cross-kingdom cooperation was not removed – and on this matter was justified, given Charles's later attention to the garrisons in the period around the time of the Incident.[210]

Basically Charles hoped to dissolve the English parliament after settling affairs in Scotland, and he was encouraged to look forward to the chance of resuming ordinary rule – whatever that might mean for the future. Edward Nicholas, corresponding in the greatest secrecy with Charles and the Duke of Lennox[211] from the start of the royal journey north, criticised the intentions of those who promoted the parliamentary commission to attend the king in Scotland. He commented on unnamed figures in close attendance on the king who had been accustomed to keep such people informed: Secretary Vane was the intended target here, but Hamilton may not have been beyond aspersions. Nicholas reflected optimism for the future in England, once the king had contained the Covenanters at home in peace and quietness. It was a simplification (with a large measure of truth) that Charles would have been delighted to read – the party which had so much depended on the Scottish army would be 'out of countenance and esteem'; the 'good people of England' would be ready to respect their king so much that he would have to moderate his 'happiness and power' as he had previously borne restraint and opposition.[212]

At the Scottish parliament against the preference of those seen as his opponents in England and Scotland, Charles therefore believed that he might achieve more than a settlement of the northern troubles which had preoccupied him for four years. He would be ready to promise that he would go to Ireland in the new year.[213] As the English prominents knew, a settlement in Edinburgh would have ramifications beyond Scotland. Because a three-kingdom recovery was at stake, Charles's patience was as limited as ever, but it was important to be secure in the north. However, fears of what the pro-

---

[209] Yale, Escrick Mss. Corr. 3/17, 19, 22; APS, vol. V, pp. 663, 355, 364, 347, 671, 680–1; *CSPD 1641–3*, 484/29–31, 39, 43; Houghton Library Mss., Sotheby's Catalogue, 16 March 1964. I am grateful to Professor Russell for the last reference.

[210] PRO SP 16/485/22.1; *D'Ewes (C)*, p. 11; Bray, *Evelyn*, pp. 87, 94. Charles tried to hold back the emptying of the Berwick garrison.

[211] After 9 August 1641 Lennox was also Duke of Richmond, in the English peerage.

[212] Guildford, Bray Ms. 52/2/19 (2, 8); Bray, *Evelyn*, pp. 68–9; cf. *ibid.*, pp. 71–6; GD 406/1/1397; GD 406/M9/93/3; Fletcher, *Outbreak*, pp. 45, 47–8.

[213] T. Carte, *A Collection of Original Letters and Papers Concerning the Affairs of England from the Year 1641 to 1660* (1739), pp. 8–9.

jected settlement might bring kept the English situation highly volatile; and in Scotland the making of that settlement was run through with considerable tensions.

Charles made some conciliatory gestures. His novel turns of courtesy towards presbyterian churchmen have already been mentioned; an equally radical turnaround was his nomination of Lord Balmerino to act as president of this parliament. The Earl of Roxburgh dared to express optimistic hopes that peace would now reign in place of conflict. As everyone now was to swear to uphold the Covenant, the character of that peace would be to some degree different from that of the years prior to 1637, but the lingering worry had to be that factious spirits – or 'bad counsel' – would again upset it. Moreover, the king who was presently charming towards his Scottish subjects would not remain with them for long. There is no reason to suppose that Charles's basic outlook had changed, as anyone alert to the signs could have told. The king for one managed to avoid signing the Covenant – a reflection on the gap which remained between him and his Scottish subjects, a gap even more readily sustainable once he was in his other kingdoms where the Covenant was not the law of the land.[214]

Shadows therefore loomed over this parliamentary meeting from the very outset. The final enactment of the treaty within the Scottish parliament should have been a straightforward matter. Charles, however, made a last-ditch attempt to ratify the Acts of the 1640 parliament, contrary to his earlier concession, made under duress, simply to authorise their publication in the name of king and estates of parliament, still dated 11 June 1640. He lost the point – and his name was required as little more than a rubber-stamp; he nevertheless mounted a more sustained struggle in respect of the Acts passed in the present sitting before his arrival.[215]

In English terms a quick end was desirable, but could Charles work consistently for that in the Scottish circumstances? Problems crowded in. With Montrose disabled, the king could happily try to skirt any extended controversy over appointments. A degree of concession was in order, provided that there could be cover against English claims for the same concession. The Scots' tactful stress within the treaty on the importance of his normal distance from Scotland as the motive for the demand suited Charles, but difficulties surfaced in demands now made in the parliament which in effect opened new discussions. The moderate compromise of April 1641 was shelved as the question of appointing judges *ad vitam vel culpam* returned, such as had been in the original March demand. Charles decided to allow this; Hamilton and

[214] *APS*, vol. V, p. 333; CC Nicholas Box – letters of Roxburgh and Thomas Webb, 18 and 19 August.
[215] *APS*, vol. V, pp. 311, 333–45, 644–6, 648, 650, 654, 354, 356, 669, 364, 679–80, 699; Baillie, *Letters*, vol. I, pp. 388–9; Buckminster Park, Tollemache Ms. 4110.

Argyll were prominent in all of the talks, and under their guidance the nobility as an estate fell in with his wishes. However, the other two estates pushed further; most significantly it was asked for appointments made between parliamentary meetings, that is with consent of council or Session as appropriate, to be subject to the next parliament's approval, thus another constitutional restraint on the king, and more immediately undermining the tenure of those already in office. Charles, grossly offended, withdrew his concession.[216]

It was perhaps over-optimistic to believe in the security of keeping the concession within Scotland, which after all had already been mooted in the House of Commons, but this demand was a very direct insult to Charles.[217] Eventually, after almost a fortnight, he was persuaded to allow legislation which modified the wording he had earlier preferred. The forces against him were strong. His attempt to have explicit emphasis in a postscript on the key point for English observers, namely the peculiarly Scottish character of the concession, was not approved for publication, and omitted from the record altogether was his firm determination to retain any in office for whom there were no grounds for displacement. The king's discretionary powers of appointment were wholly taken away, and suddenly he had no officers of state. Though some of these in time were reappointed, the further damage was that Charles's return to England was delayed.[218]

Valuable days were given over to argument with Argyll on possible candidates for the major offices. It appears that Argyll was offered the most lucrative post of Lord Treasurer but he refused, at least for the time being, also resisting Charles's intention to have the Earl of Morton as Lord Chancellor, the position of supreme dignity albeit lesser financial worth. Morton had been too much around Court in recent years.[219] In the end Charles took names to the parliament, with Lord Loudoun cast as Treasurer, and together with a list of officers a roll of the proposed privy council. Morton's candidacy was opposed, Argyll himself speaking up but certainly not alone, for besides questions over his suitability and calls for a smaller

[216] *APS*, vol. V, pp. 354–5, 663, 653–7; SRO PA 7/2/87, 92; GD 406/M9/93/46; Warner, *Nicholas Papers*, pp. 39–42, 47; Bray, *Evelyn*, pp. 61–2; CC Nicholas Box – letter of Thomas Webb, 19 August.

[217] Cf. Bray, *Evelyn*, pp. 76, 80; Warner, *Nicholas Papers*, p. 52. However, in the subsequent English controversy, Charles appealed to the Scots for support – Fletcher, *Outbreak*, pp. 143–5; GD 406/1/1750, 1766.

[218] *APS*, vol. V, pp. 354–5, 663, 387–8; Guildford, Bray Ms. 52/2/19 (13); Bray Ms. 85/5/2 (6); Bray, *Evelyn*, pp. 67, 70–1; Bod. Carte Ms. 103, fol. 84. Again the king wanted to be presented positively in England on this – Bray, *Evelyn*, p. 68; *CSPD 1641–3*, 485/49.

[219] Guildford, Bray Ms. 85/5/2 (6); Warner, *Nicholas Papers*, pp. 48–51. Cf. Stevenson, *Scottish Revolution*, pp. 236–7. It seems likely that Morton was offered his position long in advance – NLS Adv. Ms. 33.1.1, vol. XIII, no. 73.

council size, the wider issue of the king nominating still did not command agreement. That Morton stood down after an initial struggle hardly eased matters, for another week lapsed before the Estates were asked to consider Loudoun as the king's new candidate for Chancellor.[220] Charles would not yield any new rules about nomination. The compromise was for a vote on Loudoun's fitness to be Chancellor which would not determine the future process of nominations, but this was reached by the king in effect giving an ultimatum to his Estates. The public nomination, immediately following, of Lord Almond to be Treasurer only re-opened the debate. Charles's response was to speak of adjourning the parliament so that all attention might be directed to 'finding' the desired consent.[221]

Although lack of agreement over royal appointments was probably the sorest point under discussion in the opening weeks of October 1641, it was not the only rub, and yet people hoped that the end was near. Charles was not alone in wishing to return south, for both English commissioners and Scots were inclined to expect an early ending of the king's troubles in his northern kingdom. The crisis around what became quickly known as the 'Incident' rudely intervened here.[222] It was rude intervention for those who had wished moderation or compromise in place of singlemindedness or force; it came ironically as the king was being engaged in controversial bargaining by those against whom it was designed. In short, though the Incident could be justly attributed to factious behaviour or 'bad counsel', Charles was tempted. The Incident was a vengeful strike primarily against Hamilton and Argyll. Over the vexed question of incendiaries, Argyll was attempting – but certainly not with unanimous popular support – to have the majority of processes stopped. This was to be in return, most notably, for guarantees against the future employment of the individuals still to be prosecuted, a condition certainly not in line with Charles's own preference; whether it pushed him over the edge remains uncertain, but clearly it was not ideal.[223] Perhaps the dominance retained by Argyll and Hamilton through these days seemed too much to serve themselves so that the king, frustrated in the feeling that he was being

---

[220] *APS*, vol. V, p. 667; Warner, *Nicholas Papers*, pp. 50–1; Bray, *Evelyn*, pp. 78–80; Guildford, Bray Ms. 52/2/19 (16).

[221] Balfour, *Historical Works*, vol. III, pp. 70–89; *APS*, vol. V, pp. 356–7, 366–7, 665–7, 672, 675–7; NLS Wod. Fo. 64, fols. 114, 116; Warner, *Nicholas Papers*, pp. 51–2; Buckminster Park, Tollemache Ms. 3751; Carte, *Letters*, pp. 1–5. The choice of Almond for the Treasurership was known as early as 27 September, i.e. before public debate on Loudoun – Warner, *Nicholas Papers*, p. 51.

[222] Cf. Yale, Escrick Mss. Corr. 2/14, 3/17, 21–3, Docs. 3/20; *APS*, vol. V, pp. 681–2; CC Nicholas Box – letters of Roxburgh and Endymion Porter, 13 and 19 October.

[223] Cf. Baillie, *Letters*, vol. I, p. 393; GD 406/1/121; NLS Wod. Fo. 64, fols. 49, 147–8, 155; Buckminster Park, Tollemache Mss. 4109, 4110; working papers in Yale, Escrick Mss. Docs. 1/3; *The Truth of the Proceedings in Scotland*, BL Thomason E.173(29), pp. 4–7.

dictated to, lost patience. Whatever the case, he apparently sanctioned a desperate, but all too characteristic, change of tactics.

Hamilton had been conscious of his fragile position in the king's favour since the emergence of the 1641 plottings around Montrose. The king might have dared to hope once more for a party which would allow him a settlement less straitening in its terms. Hamilton's support of the Covenanters alongside Argyll after his arrival in Scotland lost him not only the king and Lennox, but provoked feelings of discontent on quite a wide front. Possibly the revival of words alleging Hamilton's claim to the Scottish crown was significant; perhaps more fundamentally jealousies such as Montrose had tried to harness were stirred by the fact of Hamilton and Argyll's ascendancy.[224] Competition came into the open. Hamilton's English friends by contrast were dismayed to learn that the marquis was supposedly thinking of remaining in Scotland.[225]

The Incident bears comparison with the English army plots since the intrigues were most likely suggested from outside though to a king with willing ears. A difference was that material for accusations had built up over many months in 1641, and the king aimed now more for punishment than for threat.[226] The affair owed much to its immediate circumstances. After a public insult given to Hamilton by Lord Ker, followings came out on to the streets behind the marquis despite a more than generous exoneration and humiliation of Ker in a full session of parliament.[227] After this – as the deposition and defence accounts would allow us to reconstruct – William Murray of the Bedchamber, using letters from Montrose who was detained in the Castle, and meeting with some nobles and army officers at the Earl of Airth's house, stirred up hostilities, particularly against Hamilton. Some of the troops still in arms were potentially available. One design was concocted whereby the Catholic Earl of Crawford apparently hoped to have Hamilton and Argyll murdered; in a more moderate way, Lord Almond looked for a public trial as the best means of felling them, but played his part in organising men to resist any defence by them using force.[228]

Approaches within this plotting to one Captain William Stewart leaked the plot in advance. Hamilton at first hesitated to act, possibly unwilling to believe this was actually being attempted; but when he got confirmation on

[224] Carte, *Letters*, pp. 1–9, but esp. p. 8. For other observers speaking of 'Argyll's party' – Yale, Escrick Mss. Corr. 1/4, 2/10; cf. *ibid.*, 3/23; Baillie, *Letters*, vol. I, pp. 393–4; CC Nicholas Box – letter of Endymion Porter, 19 October.

[225] GD 406/1/1510, 1432.

[226] Cf. Russell, 'The first army plot'. I have enjoyed discussions with Professor Russell on this.

[227] *APS*, vol. V, pp. 675, 366, 369; Carte, *Letters*, pp. 7–8; GD 406/1/1544, 1554; Balfour, *Historical Works*, vol. III, pp. 82–6; Yale, Escrick Mss. Corr. 3/23; BL Sloane Ms. 1467, fol. 151v; Baillie, *Letters*, vol. I, p. 391.

[228] The deposition accounts are printed in full in *HMC 3*, pp. 163–70 (House of Lords' Mss.), as they were sent to England for consideration there. See too GD 406/M1/112.

the morning of 12 October, he kept well away from the king's quarters. Hearing that Charles would come accompanied even by soldiers to the parliament in the afternoon, he left Edinburgh, Argyll and Lanark going with him. That Hamilton later claimed that this was the best way of avoiding armed clashes between followings left the point unspoken that Charles had intended to mount a public attack.[229]

The argument for Charles's implication begins with his knowledge of the plotters and their strategies. William Murray was well known to be close; Lord Ker had been Charles's trusted messenger in September.[230] Revealing too was Charles's prompt insistence that there should be a public trial in parliament of those who had fled, for they had hurt his honour; he hinted more than once that he had incriminating evidence against the marquis. It seemed to suit well enough that the legal approach supplanted the possible clash by arms, but Charles would have known of both. As individuals the plotters were nearly all active in wooing the king's favour; he ever was a king who directed, and a confident strike was to advantage him in England as well as in Scotland.[231] Was the Hamilton-Argyll threat too closely aligned to what was feared around 'King Pym' in England?[232] Charles may well have had it in mind, however the plotters formulated their plans; given the Anglo-Scottish connections, there were to be British consequences again.

Though Charles may have inspired, there remains doubt how far he actually initiated. Traquair's letter to him from Berwick on 27 September was explicitly critical of Hamilton, for the first time in his extant correspondence, reminding him of the evidence Traquair had gathered to be available for use against the marquis. But Traquair was thinking of it as a means to oblige Hamilton's cooperation; that he criticised Montrose on 3 October for assuming, as he heard, something of a personal mission to damage the marquis is of interest. Probably it reflected Traquair's sense of politics; he would still have hoped to benefit from the king allowing sway to the then dominant Hamilton-Argyll group.[233] The Incident was perhaps aptly named, a relatively sudden piece of action which an enraged king saw fit to countenance.

---

[229] GD 406/M1/121; GD 406/1/1438, 1575, 1573, 1572; S. R. Gardiner, *History of England ... 1603–1642* (10 vols., 1884), vol. X, pp. 23–7. A son of Huntly, Lord Gordon, went out of Edinburgh with the others. Lanark's closeness to his brother Hamilton seems to be the explanation of why he went too.

[230] Cf. Bray, *Evelyn*, pp. 64, 70. Murray's son acted as a carrier for Charles on 5 October; Murray himself was promoted in the aftermath – *ibid.*, p. 78; *CSPD 1641–3*, 485/72.

[231] Cf. Warner, *Evelyn*, pp. 78, 80, 81–2, 85; Guildford, Bray Mss. 52/2/19 (16, 21), 85/5/2 (10).

[232] Bray, *Evelyn*, pp. 79–80; Guildford, Bray Ms. 52/2/19 (16); CC Nicholas Box – letter of Roxburgh, 13 October.

[233] Traqr. Mss. 12/40; Bundle 27, letter from Traquair to Southesk, 3 October; Bundle 26[ii]; Bundle 28[i]. Cf. Traqr. Mss. 'Traquair Papers', no. 49. Traquair was surely jealous of Hamilton – cf. GD 406/1/1754, 1755.

Pressing for a public trial, at which he showed no keenness to have the refugee lords present, Charles was answered by their friends in parliament who argued for a trial in camera. There was argument for over a week on this, with the king speaking often on his own behalf. He certainly received support – but simply not enough (Hamilton's sense of Scottish politics was better). The successful switching of the focus of supposed guilt on to the plotters by the other group frustrated Charles's plan altogether. To add to the bitterness, renewed aspersions were cast on incendiaries who were said still to attend on the king. For a time there was a proclaimed risk of public disorder, news which ironically was exploited in England to the king's disadvantage.[234]

Hamilton and the others kept closely in touch with their friends, meeting with Lords Loudoun and Lindsay for instance. As significantly, the marquis used William Murray as a channel for regaining the king's favour. This might at first seem contradictory, but makes sense since Hamilton's wish still was not to lose the king, despite what had been attempted against him. Uncertain while the nature of any trial was under debate and hearing news of forces raised to press an attack against him and his fellows, Hamilton apparently took the safest policy of stressing that the Incident was a matter of public significance – in line with the efforts of supporters within the parliament; in other words trying to deflect the king's wish for personal recrimination.[235] A jealous individual, like the plotter Earl of Crawford, therefore was to be sacrificed, but Hamilton and Argyll were to return to the public scene where they could promote an accommodation between king and subjects. Despite what Charles thought of this, the time lost and strength of the opposition led to his allowing the trial of the Incident by private committee.[236] Hamilton, Argyll and Lanark returned in the end with their honours guaranteed by the parliament, the product of various papers composed by themselves.[237] The conclusion of the Scottish settlement then ensued.

The effects of the Incident outside Scotland ran beyond the prominent figures who had worried exceedingly at Hamilton being under attack; in continuation of their correspondence they sent assurances of friendship and trust

---

[234] Balfour, *Historical Works*, vol. III, pp. 94–118; *APS*, vol. V, pp. 374–5; Warner, *Nicholas Papers*, pp. 56, 57; Yale, Escrick Mss. Corr. 3/24, 25; GD 406/M1/117, M1/113; NLS Wod. Fo. 65, fols. 31–3; Fletcher, *Outbreak*, pp. 132–3.

[235] GD 406/M1/121 is an excellent summary of the events, borne out by surviving correspondence – GD 406/M1/109/1–2, M1/116; GD 406/1/1568, 1544, 1439, 1554, 1567, 1064, 1569, 1438, 1575, 1573, 1572. See too memos by Lanark, GD 406/M1/107 (to Lindsay, 18 October?); GD 406/M1/106 (to Will Murray, 23 October?).

[236] GD 406/1/1493, 1545, 1440, 1550, 1542 (two copies in *CSPD 1641–3*, 485/13, 17); GD 406/M1/115, M1/105; *APS*, vol. V, pp. 374–5, 685–6; Balfour, *Historical Works*, vol. III, pp. 128, 130; Yale, Escrick Mss. Docs. 3/24–6. For the processes intended against Crawford and others, see GD 406/M1/114. For Charles, cf. Bray, *Evelyn*, p. 121.

[237] GD 406/1/1564, 1449, 1556, 1548, 1562; GD 406/M1/119; *APS*, vol. V, p. 378; HMC 4, p. 258.

once news got through.[238] English parliamentary politics generally were further destabilised. Edward Nicholas bemoaned his lack of knowledge which made him unable to fend off questions, and a motion passed the Commons to affirm that the parliament offered the fullest support against any who challenged the peace between the kingdoms. The Incident was interpreted as an aspect of a general popish plot; it lost the king advantage.[239] If Charles had hoped to get his English troublemakers frightened, it became more urgent than ever for him to return to master the situation.

Besides this, and before the return of the noblemen into Edinburgh, the news of trouble in Ireland gave further reason for the king's early return south. This Catholic rising grew out of a situation where the recent British concessions by Charles on the one hand had raised hopes, while on the other hand fear of a concerted anti-Catholic action from England with the Covenanters in alliance probably helped to push forward any advance planning.[240] The Covenanters – particularly those on the west coast of Scotland who kept close links with *émigré* compatriots across the Irish Channel – offered troops quickly to quell the rising. Charles encouraged this, although it was novel where Ireland had been an English concern. By thus identifying with the Scots he hoped to strengthen his position, but the unpredictable burgeoning of the Irish troubles into something big instead reduced his freedom of movement, and his own good faith came under suspicion.[241] The English parliament gained another cause for its continued sitting which had momentous consequences; the Covenanters readily grasped a new opportunity to instruct commissioners for London, appointed to conclude on matters left over from the treaty, to negotiate also on details of collaborative action in Ireland – and so further to promote Anglo-Scottish union.[242]

In the prior, rapidly concluded Scottish settlement, the means of royal government were profoundly altered. Ground was at last yielded over appointments; amongst the mass of legislation at the conclusion of the parliament were the nominations 'with the advice and approval of the Estates' of principal officers of state, privy councillors and Lords of Session. The Treasurership went into commission, Traquair still under prosecution and

---

[238] GD 406/1/1506, 1427, 1442/1, 1443, 1451; Warwicks. RO CR 2017/C1/103; Guildford, Bray Ms. 85/5/2 (17, 25); *CSPV 1640–2*, pp. 231–2; Hyde, *History*, vol. I, pp. 415–18.

[239] Bray, *Evelyn*, pp. 85, 91–3, 97; Guildford, Bray Ms. 85/5/2 (19, 24, 25, 26), Ms. 52/2/19 (37); *CJ*, vol. II, pp. 290, 292; *LJ*, vol. IV, pp. 400–1; *D'Ewes (C)*, pp. 26–7; *CSPD 1641–3*, 484/68; Fletcher, *Outbreak*, ch. 4, esp. pp. 130–3.

[240] Clarke, 'The genesis of the Ulster rising'; Russell, 'The British background to the Irish rebellion'.

[241] Stevenson, *Scottish Revolution*, p. 243; *APS*, vol. V, pp. 688, 378; Balfour, *Historical Works*, vol. III, pp. 119–20, 128–9, 134, 141–4, 147, 153; Bray, *Evelyn*, pp. 97, 101.

[242] Fletcher, *Outbreak*, pp. 143–4; D. Stevenson, *Scottish Covenanters and Irish Confederates* (Belfast, 1981), pp. 39–99.

wrangling over names finally closed; the king did better with the replacement for Sir John Hay as Clerk-register, for the ambitions of the pugnacious Johnston of Wariston were apparently overcome in Charles's naming of the younger Gibson of Durie.[243] The revised roll of the council, however, showed some changes so as to accommodate hard-line Covenanters who had been omitted in Charles's original list, and a host of elevations and promotions included Argyll, General Leslie and even Wariston amongst the beneficiaries.[244] Nor did the establishment stop there, for commissions for finishing business related to the recent struggles, not least the controversial *conservatores pacis*, were approved. Over the incendiaries the compromise solution aired in the days before the Incident returned, with the king able only to quibble on wordings. The prosecution of the majority of incendiaries was dropped while the Estates reserved proceedings against the five principals long since singled out together with Montrose and his three fellow plotters, Napier, Keir and Blackhall, whose examinations were already advanced. The degree of compromise was suggestive of Argyll being again in the ascendant; Charles gave in struggling but to some extent relieved in so far as punishment of any crimes proved was to be left to his discretion.[245] The picture was not absolutely black but it was surely with feelings of defeat and discontent that Charles looked for future goodwill from his Scottish subjects. Had he by so great a surrender in Scotland found a route towards calm waters? Given the multiple-kingdom dimension so clearly in the immediate background, the prospect for his boat was still a rocky course.

Charles had been forced by the inadequacy of his military response to Covenanter aggression to widen his appeal to the English people, first by a great council of the peers and then by a parliament. That the king should consult his people was a principle that the Covenanters could share, and they looked keenly for an English response in their favour. Already their actions in Scotland spoke eloquently of the same principle; in treaty with the king and his representatives they would seek its formal acknowledgement. A king whom they claimed had been badly counselled was to be steered towards better ways

---

[243] Buckminster Park, Tollemache Ms. 4110; Baillie, *Letters*, vol. I, p. 396. Durie was a compromise; Sir John Hay had originally demitted in favour of Sir John Hamilton of Orbiston – NLS Adv. Ms. 33.1.1, vol. XIII, no. 71; *Questions Exhibited . . . Concerning the E. of Montrose*, BL Thomason E.172(3) (1641). For Wariston's long ambition for the post, see D. Mathew, *Scotland under Charles I* (1955), p. 66.

[244] *APS*, vol. V, pp. 387–9, 391–420; Balfour, *Historical Works*, vol. III, p. 164; Buckminster Park, Tollemache Ms. 3751; Stevenson, *Scottish Revolution*, pp. 239–40. For a list of knights dubbed, see NLS Adv. Ms. 33.2.7, fols. 126–8.

[245] *APS*, vol. V, pp. 705–6; Buckminster Park, Tollemache Mss. 4105, 4110; *Questions Exhibited . . . Concerning the E. of Montrose*. Bishop John Maxwell had been added to the original four.

– in his Court, in his Scottish administration, in his parliament. The projected settlement was to serve the best interests of Scottish religion and liberties: Charles was within the vision, and so were the English and Irish.

Three-kingdom troubles raised hopes of a three-kingdom solution, but the powerful unity of the Covenanters which achieved so much for Scotland could not bring settlement of what in their eyes admittedly were less urgent troubles in the two other kingdoms; to an extent the Scots added to troubles elsewhere, both directly and indirectly. No attempt has been made to cover those other distinct histories, except to explore how the king like the Covenanters made his moves across a wide and demanding stage; much more may yet be said. That Charles and his counsel were under attack from various directions is vital explanation for why he yielded so utterly where he had so long struggled. After all his consuming attentions over Scotland from the early part of 1638, his surrender at the end of 1640 came very quickly – and though it was by no means a final solution at that time to agree to the Scottish legislation, it was a pointer to how the king's troubles had taken a new turn.

Charles's approach to Scottish religion and liberties had been overthrown, and his officers were attacked; in the last ditch he tried desperately to save them, for it was a strike against monarchy shared in his other kingdoms. Against Charles were arguments that servants of the Crown were accountable to the high courts of parliament as well as to himself; it is clear from his sustained protection of Traquair and the rest how he wished to deny the principle, or at least restrict its effects. A king never did command fully the actions of his servants, but some actions were more expressly under royal direction than others. Traquair was designated by the other side as a victim for all that had recently, and perhaps longer ago, gone wrong in Scotland; Charles could not bear the prospect of his own policy being thus cast open to denunciation. It was his privilege, he believed, to direct and not to be directed; to hold trial and not to be tried; to pardon and not to be punished. Formally this was so, but the nature of the persecution of his servants rebounded heavily upon him.

The scope of the Covenanter programme was considerable, an ambitious vision that looked as freely to the long term as to the short. However, it would be unwise to press the idea of revolution too far for what has been covered here.[246] Much remained unsettled in the British vision at the end of 1641. Rather, commissions were appointed to deal with the difficult subjects of trade and defence; presbyterianism was far from being positively established outside Scotland; a British arrangement of the king's journeyings or the establishment of the Court had no secure guarantees. The concern positively to

---

[246] Stevenson, *Scottish Revolution*, pp. 315–26, attempts to argue that 'revolution' should be used for this whole period.

direct the lines of the king's counsel had made ground. Scottish holders of major offices were to be appointed with clear reference to the king's parliaments as much as to the king himself, and these parliaments were to meet triennially. It remains significant, however, that there was no inevitable course with these most radical changes. Although proposals for reform regularly exceeded the foundations of precedents eagerly searched out, the recurring desire to negotiate with Charles is as apparent as the daring and organisation within the process. Where Charles, in weakness or through tactics, could talk with his subjects, English or Scottish, there were possibilities of his gaining ground. At the same time, crises of religion and liberties produced leaders profoundly set at distance; and, for Scotland, the part of the ever enthusiastic Archibald Johnston of Wariston will still repay full study. He would resist with all his gifts the possibilities of scheming, deviation and even vindictiveness that flourished around the Lord's anointed.

Charles survived as king while the societies over which he ruled struggled like him to cope with the crises at the centre and their ramifications. His counsel ranged from the cooperative words of Strafford through the varying attempts at diplomacy of Hamilton or Traquair to the more direct challenges both verbal and written which sought to affect his direction by felling those to whom he had given his confidence. The remarkable way in which he went from plot to submission, defiance to words of wooing, reflects well on how major a battle his leading critics fought to have ill counsels turned to good: the king in short was his own master. Each 'side' had ideas about its enemies. Where there were the most passionate fears of sedition and popularity alongside fears of popery, the problem was to find a consensus by which most people could go forward. This was not at all easy: unity wished for was far from unity gained, and it was not the latter which was settled through the Scottish parliament in November 1641. The fragility of the settlement lay not in its Scottish context alone but in its British one. Charles was still potentially in conflict with numbers of his subjects. With one dramatic plot newly sorted in Edinburgh while another stood ready to be exposed in Ireland, the story of the king's troubles was not at an end.

8

'An uncounselled king

The title requires justification: it cannot be doubted that Charles I was intentionally a counselled king, and that his subjects likewise expected this. When it suited him, as it did in January 1626 over the Revocation or later in the preface to the Scottish liturgy, Charles boasted that he had taken counsel. Institutionally he appointed privy councils in each of his three kingdoms whose duty it was among other things to give him advice. In the privacy of his Court any who could gain access, whether member of the Household like the Marquis of Hamilton or visitor like the Earl of Nithsdale, had opportunities to speak out. After 1603 Scots with a distant king might argue very easily that policies ill pleasing them were the result of bad counsel given to a monarch who sadly was removed from the realities of the situation. If the king could do no wrong, then his servants, whether they had counselled him or not, were vulnerable to criticisms and attack. This reaction was not necessarily misplaced. Competition for the ear of the king was keen; rivalries and jealousies, popularly taken to be the stuff of life at Court, were often real; anglocentric policies could be supposed to have come from English advice. Can it be said that Charles was uncounselled – or only that he was wrongly counselled in the eyes of particular critics?

Just as in modern parlance an ill-advised action does not necessarily proceed from the steerings of a third party, there could be some ambiguity in attacks on the king's counsellors. In the Scottish troubles the Supplicants or Covenanters had reason to complain of poor counsel which touched upon both king and those who sought to go alongside him in his courses. If the king was misled, in either sense, subjects might hope for an improvement by his direction. The counsellors blamed may only have been acting as servants, but contemporaries could not readily make the distinction – nor was it desirable that they should.

Direct criticism of the king was not acceptable. For Charles the doctrine that the king could do no wrong was to be keenly defended – but beyond the limits, spoken or otherwise, that some contemporaries would have wished. It was easier for his supporters – preachers, politicians and writers – to join him over the broad doctrine than to face the many practical questions too readily glossed over. James VI and I wrote treatises on the subject of kingship but was equally adept in the political sphere; Charles was both less eloquent on paper and much less ready to compromise in practice.

Charles did turn to and was evidently influenced by counsel, though he could keep a deliberate privacy to the process. Often advice-papers were submitted, that he might with more freedom contemplate his options; and much of the insight into counsel recorded in this book has been derived from such papers, written in or around the king's presence. Charles was also able to engage in debate, less famously than his father but with considerable persistence, as our accounts of councils at Berwick or York or in Court have most clearly shown. His part in privy council business has been less central to this story, however, which is not without relevance. His earliest meetings with the full English council on the Scottish business were brief, admitting of little debate. The major decisions over the Scottish troubles, though they had enormous implications for English government, were taken in far smaller circles, and often apparently in one-to-one exchanges with Hamilton. Fears of the popish plot meanwhile found substance to some extent on account of the Catholics around the king. As for the Scottish privy council, we have presented an account of a meeting from 1626; the barrier of geographical distance in the later period of the troubles was felt acutely by councillors. Nevertheless, the king's commanding role in government constantly brought him into contact with would-be advisers. For the period covered in the main part of this book, very many meetings and discussions have undoubtedly escaped the record. People expected the king to be counselled – many tried to be the givers of counsel themselves. It is an important point that those who met with Charles knew and usually accepted that his decisions were to be final, but there was no supposition that counsel was useless. In his humanity the king was by no means to be beyond correction or beyond being steered – whatever the theory.

Thus criticism levelled at counsellors was ambiguous. It could be attacking the individuals in question, for personal or political reasons – certainly much of the advice given to Charles was contentious – but it could also be a message that the king was to desist from 'ill-advised' paths. In public exchanges the king was specially immune from direct criticism; but the indirect was not necessarily to pass him by. Charles, however, was particularly sensitive over this. It even appears that he was sensitive over counsel offered to him personally. Opposition to declared purposes could be castigated as disobedience. In 1626 he had determined on courses over which he did not wish to be questioned. From 1637 there was the manner of church government with specific policies challenged by the Scottish protest; the king could not accept that he might materially have to yield. The care required by his bishops, by

Traquair and Hamilton – to take the documented examples – to put their cases to Charles over the period of crisis was considerable. His readiness to threaten required the lay counsellors particularly to play a double-game – to attempt to bridge a gap which the king by his unwillingness to listen to popular pressures helped to widen. Those in direct contact with Charles tried to push him to move; their successes were determined by his reluctant concessions, not to the protesters, but to political expediency. How best could the troublemakers be overcome? The factiousness was apparently always on the other side, as if the king thought he was always right.

The king was being counselled, but in Charles's mind there was no question that it was his receptiveness and decisions which counted. As he wrote to Hamilton during the 1639 campaign, it was utterly correct that the king's 'absolute command' should be sought for action.[1] This was what kings were meant to give. Charles's consciousness of the divine right of kings was uncompromising, even regardless of law or precedent. Natural and divine law the king heeded; by these rightness was attached to his office. The approach appeared at the beginning of his reign as clearly as when he proceeded to dictate for the Scottish church without regard to the national or general assembly.

If there ever was a Scottish crisis of counsel caused by a narrowing of distant channels into Court, this was only part of the problem in respect of the Covenant troubles. Plainly there were people of the greatest possible influence with the king who did not simply fall in with his courses. The English close committee for Scottish affairs had opinions divided; Traquair and Hamilton showed a willingness at least to listen and engage with the movement of protest, though they were not of themselves in a position to be part of it. Charles, however, could not well listen or engage. Though practically there were all kinds of limitations on absolutism, and not least the extent to which he was steered, whether he acknowledged it or not, by the exigencies of events and the counsel which responded to these, he tried to maintain a principled stance – and not surprisingly found himself toppled. He turned to counsel as it suited him but showed a staggering unwillingness to listen to moderate judgement. We could imagine how Hamilton might well have enunciated a critique of the courses of this ill-advised king; Wentworth, in his secret correspondence to Laud, indicated his own prejudices on a different tack.

A king then in some measure uncounselled, or unable to be counselled? No one, not even Charles, would admit it, but it was in any case only one important aspect of the troubles. Archibald Johnston's thought that the Lord might

[1] G. Burnet, *The Memoires of the Lives and Actions of James and William, Dukes of Hamilton and Castleherald . . .* (1677), p. 122.

find it good to remove Charles brings us to another. Ideas of rightness were held strongly within the core of the Covenanting movement where there was a very different stance on religion relative to that of Charles – and where there was as striking a contrast in the attention paid to practical politics. God was seen to bless a resistance to the prayer book which became powerfully organised. To maintain sovereignty in this context was a worrying task.

Charles's stance on his royal authority fuelled him to see resistance to particular policies as disobedience or worse towards his person. Pretence of religion more than puritanism was to him intolerable, and popularity, in the sense of playing to the people's worst instincts, the enemy of good order and respect for hierarchy. He was more than ready to single out individual factious spirits for animating society against him. The accuracy of the analysis, however, was never put to the test, just as on the opposite side where the broad cause of anti-popery with its more precise focus in the evil counsellors and their influence never quite managed to secure the king outside their orbit. Suspicions of conspiracy therefore remained and were perpetuated.

Conspiracy possibilities, with their range going beyond the particular individuals to the phenomena of popery or factious disobedience, were met most positively with something like constitutional stances. The king in a supremely discretionary role resisted being tied down but found his weakness in the practicalities of politics. Charles might consciously have striven to rule without parliaments in England but that did not in the event mean an end to parliaments; in Scotland he was persuaded – with only partial success on Hamilton's part – to use the general assembly, which he had avoided from the outset of the reign by upholding the counsel of the bishops as a representative body. Popular feeling, however, called out for annual parliaments and annual assemblies as had been supported in the nations' past history; later, as a means to remedy bad counsel, the king was asked to make appointments with the advice of parliaments. Disinclination to innovate was pushed to its limits in crisis, as was evidenced in the 1640 parliament in Scotland, both by its legislation as a whole and perhaps, most notably, its triennial Act – which so clearly lacked Scottish precedent. Attempts at constitutional redefinition went still further in the peace heads of the 1641 treaty.

The king and his counsel faced major challenges. While many tried so hard to bridge the divide which opened up with the Scottish troubles, the greatest – or most rash – daring ran in the face of the unity all claimed equally to desire. The divide encouraged polarisation and worked against middling ways, but for much of the time there were personal interactions. For the Covenanters, Traquair or Hamilton were as frustrating as they were helpful, and at severe times were positively to be attacked for their part in the 'plot' on the popery side. They were not without responsibility, just as opposite them were Rothes and Argyll and many others – especially Wariston – who helped to drive the troubles to their greater heights. Accusations went that people were serving their own interests; no doubt, to a greater or lesser extent, but they could also less selfishly be serving their king or the very many people in Scotland who were moved by fears of popery.

To the shape of the crisis Charles himself nevertheless contributed significantly. For him the protest started as an aberration; it quickly descended into treason, primarily in his mind, but even persuaded otherwise he could not truly listen – let alone open policies to the conclusions of a general assembly. His sense of mission and firmness of purpose led him into conflict with a people who progressively were further alienated. James's *Basilicon Doron* had emphasised far more the parliamentary sphere, and it was by parliamentary laws that Charles took his stance when challenged, though these were to some extent only a secondary part of his thinking. The steering of requests for an assembly into presbyterian lines only stiffened his resolution in no way to be committed to it. Presbyterian thought placed the determination of matters ecclesiastical within the general assembly alone, leaving the king no negative voice and obliging the king in parliament to ratify legislation. That was an extreme line, but Charles's inability to see the need for politic concession was arguably critical for the outcome. The conflict in origins was not bound to see the victory of presbyterianism, but this proved to be the cost. Charles preferred to rest his hopes in threat and ultimately in force, half-heartedly and inadequately yielding ground while the practical side of organising this went forward. He was not a keen warrior and the shortage of means in 1638 was perhaps not crucial; in 1639 show was preferred before battle. However, the latter year's preparations were on an enormous scale in the hope that there would be no question of the majority on the other side capitulating. Finding that even his personal presence had poor prospects of securing an amenable assembly and parliament, he then turned more decisively to the option of fighting.

Trust in the direction of the church by king and bishops was plainly insufficient in Scotland in 1637 at the introduction of a highly controversial liturgy. For folk who had resisted the Perth Articles and episcopal presumptions in the church there was an acute cause of provocation to which others from all society sooner or later found themselves ready to join. Anti-popery in Scotland was readily although not exclusively tied up with patriotic sentiment; Scots would welcome outside encouragement. Religion gave a uniting thrust – and was thus more than a mere cloak – to protest which came to cover far more than simply matters of the church. Directed by a very determined core, the people overcame inhibitions to resist, and by 1639 even by arms. Presbyterianism was made to appear the only possible answer to what was offered. In short the National Covenant, ambiguous at its first signing, answered a need, and though the history of the early Covenanting movement was not the history of the whole Scottish nation, it affected most if not all of the Scots people profoundly; the movement focused around a clear stance of opposition to policies for church government, very much concerted by organisation within and in resistance to what threatened to come from without. The obsessive concern for unity never overcame tendencies to division but with Charles as he was, the breaking of that unity was considerably delayed.

The central government of Scotland depended on an administration physically distant from the king, a natural source of misunderstandings and failures of communication. But as delay and unrealistic hopes characterised the whole course of Charles's response, it may be concluded that for counsel the distance between Edinburgh and London was not crucial, though it allowed the patriotic movement to exploit the weaknesses of the king's case as well as his lack of means of coercion. The many and complex manœuvrings, above all of Traquair and Hamilton, to turn him were in vain. They continued their efforts generally with a reasonable assessment of the possibilities but the enforced double-game, fraught with risks, became increasingly impossible.

By the time of the Edinburgh Assembly in August 1639 the struggle for presbyterianism had been won in Scotland; but Charles's determination by his three-kingdom strength to win his point extended the crisis further. Chances of Scottish support were squandered for the sake of having things his own way – a perilously short-term perspective which was defeated even in its initial stages because of shortage of resources for the armed forces in England and Ireland. From Scotland a civil as well as a church programme would be forced upon the king who was unwilling to talk. For a time Charles's tunnel vision blinded him to the serious discontent manifest in his principal kingdom during 1640, which rebounded to disadvantage if not through the Short Parliament then through its successor at the end of the same year. Then a military and financial predicament and major English assaults on a variety of fronts, not least the ecclesiastical, pushed Charles to yield ungracefully to the Covenanters. His subsequent responses to the length of the invasion and the possibilities of advantage, Scottish and English, only enlarged gaps of distrust. English folk in resistance to Charles's 'only way' grew determined; the cost of settlement with the Covenanters became near as high as could have been imagined. Irish troubles joined in.

It was neither normal nor desirable that king and subjects should be so deeply sundered. As Covenanters would not blame themselves or Charles, Traquair bore the brunt for the 1639 assembly and parliament and their consequences. Awareness of English sympathy with the religious dimension of the struggle stimulated more and more daring contacts, as also approaches to foreign powers, whilst the king set about preparing armies for a second time. On the liberties dimension English and Scottish common interests would diverge in detail, the first year of the Long Parliament confirming the problems of joint action. However, the invasion of 1640 had above all the target of solving the Scottish crisis of government; its British dimension, with important concerns for security and long-term vision, had to be shelved, consequently leaving uncertainties for the future. After 1641 likelihood of a new civil war would stir fears and ambitions within Scotland, and the king and those in parliament who opposed his proceedings would each look to gather northern support; as the crisis progressed Hamilton and Argyll would split once more.

The multiple-kingdom context cannot be ignored in any account of the troubles, for there were inherent instabilities. Although a uniform church policy was appropriate to kingdoms under a single monarch, for Charles I it proved to be a very costly pursuit. Other causes of offence given in the peripheral kingdoms came in afterwards as religion united determined segments of the Scottish population. Religion was a divisive area in this reformation period. However, while there were splits also in England and Ireland, in Scotland the unity achieved was considerable, even though the Scottish tradition which won the advantage was itself one-sided.

If through the various political turns it did not come to a civil war in Scotland, it was not for Charles's want of trying. Again the three-kingdom dimension was relevant, for Charles could threaten easily by reckoning on his English strength, and though it was less easy in practice two military campaigns were organised, which in turn were important for cementing Scottish unity. One of the weaknesses of Charles's isolated stand around principle was to intensify the Court–country split that was commonly perceived. In many respects the links between Court and Scotland were not so severely disjoined as that perspective suggested – although there were problems, whether distinctively Scottish or not – but the Covenanter stand, most obviously in facing a king in England advancing with armies, more successfully drew in the Scottish people than appeals for people to show their personal loyalty to their sovereign. Meanwhile English and Irish administrations were to some extent forced into foreign courses without wide consultation; more specific dislike of those courses was expressed in action and word. Although the three-kingdom arrangement finally prompted Charles's surrender in Scotland, the complex interaction of discontent across the kingdoms had helped to widen the boundaries of his troubles, which together with his bitter and erratic responses opened a decade of extreme instability.

Charles ruled therefore at a difficult time and in difficult circumstances. Without a truly British council body, Scottish and Irish alienation was likely and even more so as policies were pursued from the centre which were likely to cause notable discontent. The Scottish reaction to the liturgy exceeded expectations, and from the king's point of view was most disastrously handled, though such a crisis bore no easy solution. The emphasis here has been on the interplay around Edinburgh and in Court of the king and those who sought to counsel him and therefore the importance of the short-term – the immediate high-political considerations – alongside more far-seeing visions in shaping the Scottish troubles. It has been asked how issues of importance going back into James's reign attained such significance in national politics in the period after July 1637; and how Charles so patently failed to engage not merely with extreme presbyterianism but with this general Scottish protest except by ineffectual declarations and insufficient military aggression. However much in advance views could be opposed and political thought seriously diverge, and conflict both local and central build up, the shape of the major troubles ensuing upon the liturgical policy had a particular history which this account has, albeit incompletely, attempted to address. With consequences for Charles and so his other kingdoms, the Scottish troubles were a major testing-ground which a king with counsel, yet often despite it, failed well to handle.

BIBLIOGRAPHY OF MANUSCRIPT AND PRINTED PRIMARY SOURCES

MANUSCRIPT SOURCES

Aberdeen: University Library
  Ms. 635 – diary of John Forbes of Corse
Argyll and Bute: *see* Inveraray
Bedford: Bedfordshire Record Office
  J. 1347–1409 – St John of Bletsoe Mss.
Berks.: *see* Reading
Buckminster: Buckminster Park Estate Office
  Tollemache Family Archive Mss.
Cambridge: University Library
  Kk. 6.38 – journal of Geoffrey Palmer
  Ee. 5.23; Gg. 4.13; Mm. 4.24; Add. Ms. 335 – miscellaneous
  Microfilm 771 – calendar of Bridgewater and Ellesmere Mss.
Edinburgh: National Library of Scotland
  Mss. 79–84 – Morton correspondence
  2263 – customs accounts and other papers
  2618, 3044, 3368 – miscellaneous
  2687–8 – English parliament
  2933, 3134, 3368 – letters and papers
  3012 – Bishop of Galloway
  3139 – Cunninghame of Robertland
  3145 – royal letters, etc.
  7032, 7109, 20774–5 – Yester papers
  9303, 9931 – miscellaneous
  15950 – Samuel Rutherford's letters
  Ch. 16396 – Fleming of Wigtown
  Ms. 17498 – Fletcher of Saltoun
  21174, 21183 – Marischal papers
  Acc. 7360 – Argyll correspondence
  Advocates' Mss. 1.2.2 – miscellaneous letters
  7.1.19, 19.1.25 – miscellaneous letters
  15.2.17 – papers relevant to the 1633 visit
  17.1.5 – Exchequer
  22.2.15 – royal writs
  29.2.8, 29.2.9 – Balcarres papers
  31.3.10 – signet commissions

31.6.1 – Exchequer
32.4.8 – contemporary history
33.1.1, vols. XI, XIII; 33.1.3, 33.1.4, 33.2.7, 33.2.23, 33.7.7 – Balfour of Denmilne
33.2.1 – Glasgow Assembly
33.2.13 – papers relating to the principality
33.4.6, 33.4.7 – registers of the Committee of Estates
33.4.8 – army in Ireland
33.4.14 – copies
33.7.26 – Denmilne correspondence
34.3.12 – re history of Aberdeen
34.5.15 – King's Covenant
35.1.10 – accounts of Sir John Clerk
Crawford Mss. – muniments of the Rt Hon. the Earl of Crawford and Balcarres
Deposit 175, boxes 80, 81, 87 – Gordon Cumming of Altyre and Gordonstoun
Wodrow Folio Series 16 – kirk session register, SE parish of Edinburgh
25, 27, 29, 31, 42, 43 – church and state papers
48 – sermons
54 – miscellaneous papers
61–8 – church and state papers, letters
73 – Committee of Estates papers
Wodrow Octavo Series 10 – Glasgow Assembly
11 – miscellaneous
Wodrow Quarto Series 9 – contemporary history
20, 24, 25 – letters and papers
26 – miscellaneous
29, 106 – church and state papers
72 – Glasgow Assembly
75 – papers on various ministers
76 – David Calderwood papers
83 – life of the Bishop of Moray
[Edinburgh]: Scottish Record Office
CS 1 – court of session, books of sederunt
E 4 – Exchequer act book
E 5 – Exchequer minute book
E 17 – Royal letters and warrants
E 26 – Treasury accounts
GD 1/164 – Sir Thomas Hope of Craighall
GD 3 – Earls of Eglinton
GD 16 – Earls of Airlie
GD 22 – Cunninghame Grahame of Ardoch
GD 26 – Earls of Leven and Melville
GD 37 – Airth papers
GD 40 – Marquesses of Lothian
GD 45 – Earls and Marquess of Dalhousie
GD 49 – Barclay Allerdice muniments
GD 112 – Marquesses and Earls of Breadalbane
GD 124 – Earls of Mar and Kellie
GD 150 – Earls of Morton
GD 156 – Lord Elphinstone

GD 157 – Lord Polwarth
GD 220 – Dukes of Montrose
GD 250 – Sempills of Craigievar
GD 406 – Dukes of Hamilton (including Red Books)
PA 7 – Scottish parliament
PA 11, 12 – Committee of Estates
PA 13 – papers of the Scots commissioners in England
PA 14 – Scottish parliament
PA 15/1 – 1639 accounts
PC 11 – registers of the Scottish privy council
PS 1 – privy seal registers
PS 6 – privy seal minute books
RH 1, 9 – miscellaneous copies and transcripts
SP 13 – state papers, miscellaneous
[Edinburgh]: University Library
  Dc. 4.16 – register of the Committee of Estates, 1640–1
  Laing Mss.
  University Library, New College
  X15b 3/1, 3 vols. – original Mss. of Baillie's letters
Floors Castle, Roxburghshire
  Mss. of His Grace the Duke of Roxburghe (seen through NRA (S))
Glasgow: Strathclyde Regional Archives
  T-PM 113 – Stirling-Maxwell of Pollok muniments
Guildford: Guildford Muniment Room
  Bray Mss. 52, 85 – Nicholas's papers
Inveraray: Sheriff Courthouse
  Archives of the Argyll and Bute District Council
  TD 40 Argyll Mss. – photocopies
Inveraray Castle, Argyll
  Mss. of His Grace the Duke of Argyll
Kent: *see* Maidstone
Lancs.: *see* Preston
Lennoxlove, East Lothian
  Mss. of His Grace the Duke of Hamilton (seen through NRA (S))
London: British Library
  Add. Mss. 4106, 4460 – Birch's transcripts
  5754 – papers relating to Scotland, etc.
  6521 – diurnal occurrents, English parliament
  11044 – Viscount Scudamore
  11045 – Rossingham's newsletters
  11056 – miscellaneous
  12093 – royal autographs
  14828, 56103 – diary of Framlingham Gawdy
  15389–92 – Roman transcripts
  15567 – Manchester's memoires
  15914 – Sydney letters
  15970 – Howard letters
  18738, 19398, 19402, 21406, 21506 – original letters
  23112 – Earl of Stirling's register
  23113 – Earl of Lauderdale

23146 – diary of Rev. Thomas Dugard
23242 – royal letters
24023, 28103 – original letters
24863 – miscellaneous political papers
24984 – papers relating to 1640 invasion
27962H–I – Florentine transcripts
28011 – political papers, Oxinden
28082 – military papers
32093 – state papers
33259 – Burnet's *Memoires*, Ms.
34216 – state papers, transcripts
34486 – deciphered passages in D'Ewes's journals
34600 – Spelman's letters
35097 – Scudamore's letter-book
35331 – diary of Walter Yonge
35838 – Hardwicke papers
36779 – Borough's notes of Ripon
36913–14 – Aston papers
37343 – Bulstrode Whitelocke's annals
38847 – Sir Edward Walker's notes of Berwick
63057A–B – Burnet's *History of his Own Time*, Ms.
Egerton Mss. 2597 – Earl of Carlisle's correspondence
3371 – Leeds papers
Harleian Mss. 162–4 – D'Ewes's journals
286, 374, 379, 382–3, 386 – D'Ewes's correspondence
456–7 – Borough's notes of York and London
476–8, 541 – John Moore's journals
1601 – English parliament journal
4612, 4707 – Scottish papers
4931 – state papers
5047 – English parliament journal
6424 – bishop's parliament journal
7000, 7001 – original letters
Lansdowne Mss. 207 (f) – Gervase Holles's papers
255 – Walker's notes of Berwick
Sloane Mss. 29 – paper on the Irish people
650 – Scottish papers
654 – John Dury's correspondence
1467, 3317 – miscellaneous political papers
1519 – original letters
Stowe Mss. 184 – miscellaneous
187 – treaty in London papers
189 – original papers
322, 325, 326 – financial, customs papers
Microfilms M285, 286, 390 – Alnwick Mss. (Northumberland)
M485/29 – Hatfield Mss. (Salisbury)
M636 – Claydon House Mss. (Verney)
Loan 29/119, 172, 173, 202 – Harley papers
[London]: House of Lords Record Office
Braye Mss. 2, 95

Main papers 1640–1
Minute book of Lords' proceedings, Jan.–Mar. 1641
[London]: Public Record Office (Chancery Lane, unless otherwise stated)
    C 115/M.31, M.35, M.37, N.8, N.9 – various correspondence
    C 231/5 – Crown Office docquet book
    E 351/1748 – an account of the Marquis of Hamilton
    E 403/2567–8, 2984 – privy seals and warrants
    LC 3/1, LC 5/133–136A – Lord Chamberlain's papers
    LS 13/30, 169 – Lord Steward's papers
    PRO 31/3/68–72 – French transcripts
    PRO 31/9/18, 124 – Roman transcripts
    SP 16/343–485; SP 20/7 – state papers, domestic series
    SP 75/15 – state papers, Denmark
    SP 77/28–30 – state papers, Flanders
    SP 78/105–10 – state papers, France
    SP 80/10 – state papers, Germany (Empire)
    SP 81/44–50 – state papers, Germany (states)
    SP 84/153–6 – state papers, Holland
    SP 85/7 – state papers, Rome, Italian states
    SP 94/40–1 – state papers, Spain
    T 56/12–13 (at Kew) – privy seals
Maidstone: Kent County Archives Office
    U269/C267–86 – Sackville Mss.
    U269/F3/1; U1475/A99, C82–161, Z1/8–9, Z47; U1500/C2/40–5 – De L'Isle
    Mss.
    U350 – Dering Mss.
    U565/F45; U601/O13 – Darnley Mss.
Northampton: Northamptonshire Record Office
    Isham letters 225–60
    SJ 85–94 – St John Mss.
Oxford: Bodleian Library
    Add. Mss. c. 69, c. 286 – correspondence
    Bankes Mss. 5, 6, 8, 9, 10, 14, 15, 18, 37, 38, 42, 58, 59, 62, 64, 65 – miscellaneous
    papers of Attorney-general Sir John Bankes
    Carte Mss. 1–4, 63, 65, 80, 103 – Irish and English political papers
    Clarendon Mss. 5, 14–21, 23 – state papers
    Dep. c. 165, 172 – Nalson deposit, state papers
    Firth Ms. c. 4 – Essex lieutenancy book
    Ms. Film 39 – diary of Sir Thomas Peyton
    Rawlinson Mss. Letters 52
      A1 – Thurloe papers
      C956, D932, D1099 – Sir John Holland's journal
      D11, D49 – papers relating to Scotland
    Tanner Mss. 63–7, 66*, 88*, 144*, 177, 239 – mainly correspondence
[Oxford]: Christ Church College
    Nicholas Box
Preston: Lancashire Record Office
    DdHu/46/21 – letter from John Pym to William Jessop
Reading: Berkshire Record Office
    Trumbull Misc. Mss. XLIX, LXI – Weckherlin papers

Sheffield: Central Library
  Wentworth Woodhouse muniments, Strafford papers
  Letter-books 3, 5, 7, 10, 11, 17–21, 34
Stafford: Staffordshire Record Office
  D 661/11/1/5 – Dyott Mss.
  D (W) 1778/Ii – Dartmouth Mss.
Traquair House, Peebleshire
  Mss. of Mr Peter Maxwell Stuart, relevant to 1st Earl of Traquair
Warwick: Warwickshire Record Office
  CR 1886/CUP4/21A – Accounts of Major John Halford
  CR 2017/C1 – Feilding of Newnham Paddox Mss.
Yale University, New Haven, Connecticut: Beinecke Library
  Howard of Escrick Mss.

PRINTED PRIMARY SOURCES – CONTEMPORARY PAMPHLETS

Abernethie, T. *Abjuration of Poperie*, Aldis 897, n.p., 1638
Acts of Assembly. The Principall Acts . . . 1638 . . ., Aldis 936, n.p., 1639
Andrewes, L. *A Sermon Preached before His Maiestie at Whitehall, on Easter Day Last, 1618*, STC 623, 1618
Answer to the . . . Marquess of Hammilton, Aldis 937, n.p., 1639
An Answere to M. J. Forbes of Corse, Aldis 898.5, n.p., 1638
Arguments Given in . . . Perswading Conformity of Church Government . . ., BL Thomason E. 157(2), 1641
[Baillie, R.] *Ladensium ΑΥΤΟΚΑΤΑΚΡΙΣΙΣ or the Canterburians' Self-Conviction*, Aldis 971.5, n.p., 1640
  A Parallel or Briefe Comparison of the Liturgie with the Masse-Book, the Breviarie, the Ceremoniall and other Romish rituals, Wing B 465, 1641
  The Unlawfullnes and Danger of Limited Episcopacie, Wing B 470, 1641
The Beast is Wounded, STC 22031.5, Amsterdam, 1638
A Briefe Relation of the Scots Hostile Entrance, STC 22007.5, 1640
Buckeridge, J. *A Sermon Preached before His Maiestie at Whitehall March 22 1617 . . . to which is added a discourse concerning kneeling at the Communion*, STC 4005, 1618
[Calderwood, D.] *The Altar of Damascus*, STC 4352, n.p., 1621
  The Pastor and the Prelate . . ., STC 4359, n.p., 1628
  Quaeres Concerning the State of the Church of Scotland, STC 4361.5 and 4362, n.p., 1621 and 1638
  A Re-examination of the Five Articles Enacted at Perth, Anno 1618, STC 4363.5, n.p., 1636
Certain Instructions Given by the L. Montrose . . . with a True Report of the Committee for This New Treason . . ., BL Thomason E. 160(26), 1641
Certaine Reasons Tending to Prove the Unlawfulness and Inexpediency of All Diocesan Episcopacy, Aldis 994, 1641
The Charge of the Scottish Commissioners against Canterburie and the Lieutenant of Ireland, Wing C 4201J, 1641
[Charles I] *A Large Declaration*, STC 21906, 1639
Confession of Faith, BL Thomason 669.f.4, 1641
The Confession of John Browne, a Jesuit, Wing B 5118, 1641

[Corbet, J.] *The Epistle Congratulatorie of Lysimachus Nicanor*, STC 5751, n.p., 1640

The Ungirding of the Scottish Armour, STC 5755a, Dublin, 1639

A Declaration of the Proceedings of the Parliament of Scotland, BL Thomason E. 172(15), 1641

The Declinator and Protestation of the Archbishops . . . , STC 22058, 1639

The Demands and Behaviour of the Rebels of Scotland, STC 21915, 1640

A Description of the Forme and Manner of Public Thanksgiving, BL Thomason E. 171(16), [1641]

A Discourse Concerning Puritans, BL Thomason E. 204(3), 1641

A Discourse Shewing . . . *the Three Kingdomes* . . . , BL Thomason E. 160 (27), 1641

The Discoverie of a Late and Bloody Conspiracie at Edinburgh, BL Thomason E. 173(13), 1641

The Diurnal Occurrences, Wing E 1526, 1641

Divine and Politike Observations . . . , STC 15309, n.p., 1638

Downing, C. *A Discoursive Conjecture* . . . , BL Thomason E. 206(10), 1641

A Sermon Preached . . . *1st September 1640*, BL Thomason E. 157(4), 1641

The Duke of Lennox his Speech . . . *October 28th 1641*, BL Thomason E. 199(20), 1641

Du Moulin, Pierre, the younger *A Letter of a French Protestant*, STC 7345, 1640

The Earle of Crawford his Speech . . . *October 25th 1641*, BL Thomason E. 199(19), 1641

The First and Large Petition of the Citie of London . . . , BL Thomason E. 156(20), 1641

Forbes, J. *A Peaceable Warning*, Aldis 910, Aberdeen, 1638

A Forme of Thanksgiving . . . *to Be Used throughout the Diocese of Lincoln* . . . , BL Thomason E. 171(12), [1641]

From the Commissioners of Scotland, 24th February 1641, BL Thomason 669.f.3, 1641

From Scotland Two Coppies of Letters . . . , BL Thomason E. 171(9), 1641

General Demands Concerning the Late Covenant, with Vindication, 'It Will no Doubt Seem Strange', Aldis 912, 1639

[Gillespie, G.] *A Dispute against the English-Popish Ceremonies* . . . , Aldis 885.5, n.p., 1637

A Greate Discoverie of a Plot in Scotland, BL Thomason E. 173(12), 1641

The Grievances Given in by the Ministers before the Parliament Holden in June 1633, Aldis 856.5, n.p., 1635

Hall, J. *Certain Irrefragable Propositions*, STC 12646b, 1639

Episcopacy by Divine Right Asserted, STC 12661, 1640

Harris M. *Brittaine's Hallelujah*, STC 12807, [Hamburg], 1639

[Henderson, A.] *Some Speciall Arguments Which Warranted the Scotch Subjects Lawfully to Take up Arms*, STC 21909, Amsterdam, 1642

The Unlawfullnes and Danger of Limited Prelacie, Wing H1444, 1641

His Maiesties Declaration . . . , STC 22006, 1640

His Majesties Proclamation in Scotland, STC 22001, 1639

An Honorable Speech Made in the Parliament of Scotland by the Earl of Argile, BL Thomason E. 199(17), 1641

Information from the Estaits . . . *of Scotland*, Aldis 967, n.p., 1640

Information from the Scottish Nation, to All . . . *English*, Aldis 968, [1640]

An Information to All Good Christians . . . , Aldis 946, Edinburgh, 1639

The Intentions of the Army of . . . *Scotland* . . . , Aldis 970, n.p., 1640

King Charles his Resolution Concerning the Governement of the Church of England, BL Thomason E. 174(5), 1641
The Lawfulness of our Expedition into England Manifested, Aldis 972, 1640
Leslie, H. *A Full Confutation of the Covenant*, STC 15497, 1639
The Lord Hume his Speech, BL Thomason E. 199(9), 1641
The Lord Loudoun his Learned and Wise Speech . . . Sept. 9th 1641, BL Thomason E. 199(13), 1641
Lyndesay, D. *A True Narration of All the Passages of the Proceedings in the General Assembly of the Church of Scotland . . .*, STC 15657, 1621
The Marquis Hamilton's Speech . . . November 6th 1641, BL Thomason E. 199(22), 1641
Morton, T. *A Defence of the Innocencie of the Three Ceremonies of the Church of England . . .*, STC 18179, 1618
  A Sermon Preached before the King . . ., STC 18196, copy in CUL 8.28.15, Newcastle, 1639
The Nationall Assembly of Scotland, Wing C 4231BB, 1641
News from Scotland, STC 22013, Amsterdam, 1638
A Noble Speech Spoken by the Lord Cambel of Lorne, BL Thomason E. 199(15), 1641
Peace Again in Sion, BL Thomason E.171(7), 1641
Peacham, H. *The Duty of All True Subjects*, STC 19505, 1639
The Proceedings of the Commissioners, STC 21927, 1640
Protestation of the Generall Assembly, Aldis 952, n.p., 1639
Questions Exhibited . . . Concerning the E. of Montrose, BL Thomason E. 172(3), 1641
Reasons against the Rendering of our Confession, Aldis 930, n.p., 1638
Reasons for a Generall Assemblie, Aldis 931, n.p., 1638
Reasons . . . Service-Booke . . . Ought to Bee Refused, Aldis 932, n.p., 1638
A Relation of the King's Entertainment into Scotland . . ., BL Thomason E. 166(5, 6), 1641
Remonstrance Concerning the Present Troubles . . . April 16th . . ., STC 21927.5, n.p., 1640
A Remonstrance of the Nobility . . ., Aldis 954, Edinburgh, 1639
A Second Speech Made by the Lord Loudoun, BL Thomason E. 199(15), 1641
A Short Relation of the State of the Kirk of Scotland . . ., Aldis 934.5, n.p., 1638
Smart, P. *The Vanitie and Downefall of Superstitious Popish Ceremonies*, Aldis 690, STC 22640, n.p., 1628
The Trial of the English Liturgie, STC 16452, n.p., 1637
A True Representation of the Proceedings of . . . Scotland, Aldis 981, n.p., 1640
The Truth of the Proceedings in Scotland Containing the Discovery of the Late Conspiracie, BL Thomason E. 173(29), 1641
Tweeds Tears of Joy, Aldis 957.5, 1639
Ussher, J. *The Reduction of Episcopacie*, Wing U 216, 1656
Valentine, H. *God Save the King. A Sermon . . .*, STC 24575, 1639
Vindiciae Veritatis, Wing F 884, 1654
Whereas Some Have Given Out . . ., Aldis 917, Edinburgh, 1638

PRINTED PRIMARY SOURCES – OTHER

The Acts of the Parliaments of Scotland, 12 vols., eds. T. Thomson and C. Innes, Edinburgh, 1814–75

Acts of the Privy Council of England (1629–30), 1960

Akrigg, G. P. V. (ed.) *Letters of King James VI and I*, 1984

Aston, J. 'The journal of John Aston', in *Six North Country Diaries*, Surtees Society, 1910

Baillie, R. *The Letters and Journals*, ed. D. Laing, 3 vols., BC, Edinburgh, 1841–2

Balfour, Sir J. *Historical Works*, 4 vols., Edinburgh, 1824–5

Baxter, C. *Selections from the Minutes of the Synod of Fife M.DC.XI–M.DC.LXXXVII*, Abbotsford Club, Edinburgh, 1837

Botfield, B. (ed.) *Original Letters Relating to the Ecclesiastical Affairs of Scotland*, 2 vols., Edinburgh, 1851

Bray, W. (ed.) *Diary of John Evelyn*, vol. IV, 1852

Brereton, Sir W. *Travels in Holland, the United Provinces, England, Scotland and Ireland M.DC.XXXIV–M.DC.XXXV*, Chetham Society, 1844

Bruce, J. (ed.) *Notes on the Treaty Carried on at Ripon between King Charles I and the Covenanters of Scotland, A.D. 1640, Taken by Sir John Borough*, Camden Society, 1869

Bund, J. M. W. (ed.) *Diary of Henry Townshend of Elmley Lovett, 1640–1643*, vol. I, Worcestershire History Society, 1920

Burnet, G. *The History of My Own Time*, 6 vols., Edinburgh, 1753

   The Memoires of the Lives and Actions of James and William, Dukes of Hamilton and Castleherald . . ., 1677

Calendar of Clarendon State Papers Preserved in the Bodleian Library, vol. I, eds. O. Ogle and W. H. Bliss, Oxford, 1872

Calendar of State Papers, Domestic Series, eds. J. Bruce, M. A. E. Green and W. D. Hamilton, 1858–97

Calendar of State Papers Relating to Ireland, ed. R. P. Mahaffy, 1901

Calendar of State Papers . . . Venice, ed. A. P. Hinds, 1922–5

The Camden Miscellany, vols. VIII, IX, XII, 1893, 1895, 1910

Cameron, J. K. (ed.) *The First Book of Discipline*, Edinburgh, 1972

Carte, T. *A Collection of Original Letters and Papers Concerning the Affairs of England from the year 1641 to 1660*, 1739

   An History of the Life of James, Duke of Ormond, 3 vols., 1736

The Ceremonies, Form of Prayer and Services Used . . ., 1685

Coates, W. H., *The Journal of Sir Simonds D'Ewes from the First Recess of the Long Parliament to the Withdrawal of King Charles from London*, Yale, 1942

Coates, W. H., A. S. Young and V. F. Snow (eds.) *The Private Journals of the Long Parliament. 3 January to 5 March 1642*, Yale, 1982

Cobbett's Complete Collection of State Trials, 34 vols., 1809–28, vol. III, 1809

Collins, A. (ed.) *Letters and Memorials of State*, 2 vols., 1746

Colvin, H. M., O. R. Ransome, and J. Summerson *The History of the King's Works*, vol. III (part 1), 1975

Cope, E. S. 'The Earl of Bedford's notes of the Short Parliament of 1640', *BIHR*, 53 (1980), 255–8

Cope, E. S., and W. H. Coates (eds.) *Proceedings of the Short Parliament of 1640*, Camden Society, 1977

Craigie J. (ed.) *The Basilicon Doron of King James VI*, STS 3rd Series, 2 vols., Edinburgh, 1944–50

Craigie, J., and A. Law (eds.) *Minor Prose Works of King James VI and I*, STS, Edinburgh, 1982

Crawfurd, G. *The Lives and Characters of the Officers of the Crown and of the State in Scotland*, vol. I, Edinburgh, 1726

Dalrymple, D. *Memorials and Letters Relating to the History of Britain in the Reign of Charles the First*, Glasgow, 1766

Diary of John Rous, ed. M. A. E. Green, Camden Society, 1856

A Diary of the Public Correspondence of Sir Thomas Hope of Craighall, Bart., 1633–1645, ed. T. Thomson, BC, Edinburgh, 1843

Diary of Sir Archibald Johnston, Lord Wariston, 1639, ed. G. M. Paul, SHS, Edinburgh, 1896

Diary of Sir Archibald Johnston of Wariston, 1632–1639, ed. G. M. Paul, SHS, Edinburgh, 1911

Dickinson, W. C., and Donaldson, G. (eds.) *A Source Book of Scottish History*, vol. III, 1961

Donaldson, G. *The Making of The Scottish Prayer Book of 1637*, Edinburgh, 1954
  'A Scottish liturgy of the reign of James VI', in *Miscellany of the Scottish History Society*, vol. X, Edinburgh, 1965

Ferguson, J. (ed.) *Papers Illustrating the History of the Scots Brigade in the Service of the United Netherlands, 1572–1782*, SHS, Edinburgh, 1899

Fleming, D. H. *Scotland's Supplication and Complaint against the Book of Common Prayer . . . the Book of Canons, and the Prelates, 18th October 1637*, Edinburgh, 1927

Forbes-Leith, W. *Memoirs of Scottish Catholics during the XVIIth and XVIIIth Centuries*, 2 vols., 1909

Fraser, Sir W. *The Annandale Family Book*, 2 vols., Edinburgh, 1894
  The Book of Caerlaverock, 2 vols., Edinburgh, 1873
  The Chiefs of Grant, 3 vols., Edinburgh, 1883
  The Douglas Book, 4 vols., Edinburgh, 1885
  The Elphinstone Family Book of the Lords Elphinstone, Balmerino and Coupar, 2 vols., Edinburgh, 1897
  History of the Carnegies Earls of Southesk and their Kindred, 2 vols., Edinburgh, 1867
  The Melvilles Earls of Melville and the Leslies Earls of Leven, 3 vols., Edinburgh, 1890
  Memoirs of the Maxwells of Pollok, 2 vols., Edinburgh, 1863
  Memorials of the Earls of Haddington, 2 vols., Edinburgh, 1889
  Memorials of the Montgomeries Earls of Eglinton, 2 vols., Edinburgh, 1859
  The Red Book of Grandtully, 2 vols., Edinburgh, 1868
  The Red Book of Menteith, 2 vols., Edinburgh, 1880
  The Scotts of Buccleuch, Edinburgh, 1878
  The Sutherland Book, 2 vols., Edinburgh, 1894
  Wemyss of Wemyss, Edinburgh, 1888

Fyfe, J. G. (ed.) *Scottish Diaries and Memoirs, 1550–1746*, Stirling, 1927

Galloway, B. R., and B. P. Levack (eds.) *The Jacobean Union*, SHS, Edinburgh, 1985

Gardiner, S. R. (ed.) *The Constitutional Documents of the Puritan Revolution, 1625–1660*, Oxford, 1906

The Hamilton Papers, Camden Society, 1880

Gordon, J. *History of Scots Affairs, from M.DC.XXXVII to M.DC.XLI*, 3 vols., Spalding Club, Aberdeen, 1841

Gordon, Sir R., of Gordonstoun, and G. Gordon, of Sallach *A Genealogical History of the Earldom of Sutherland*, Edinburgh, 1813

Groen van Prinsterer, G. *Archives ou correspondance inédite de la Maison d'Orange-Nassau*, 2nd Series, vol. III, 1625–42, Utrecht, 1859

Grosart, A. B. (ed.) *Lismore Papers*, 10 vols., 1886–8

Hacket, J. *Scrinia Reserata*, 1693

Haller, W. *Tracts on Liberty, 1638–1647*, New York, 1934

Hamilton, A. H. A. (ed.) *Note Book of Sir John Northcote*, 1877

Hamilton, G. *A History of the House of Hamilton*, Edinburgh, 1933

Henderson, J. M. 'An "advertisement" about the service book, 1637', *SHR*, 23 (1925–6), 199–204

Heylyn, P. *Aerius Redivivus*, Oxford, 1670
   Cyprianus Anglicus, 1668
   A Full Relation of Two Journeys . . . , 1656

Historical Manuscripts Commission (*HMC*):
   HMC 1–9, appendices
   Salisbury, parts XXII, XXIV (9)
   Eglinton, Braye, Gawdy, Westmorland, Abergavenny (10, 11, 13, 15)
   Skrine (16)
   House of Lords, vol. XI new series (17)
   Hamilton, Hamilton Supplementary (21)
   Cowper, 3 vols. (23)
   Rutland, vol. I (24)
   Atholl and Home (26)
   Portland, vols. I, III (29)
   Kenyon of Peel (35)
   Ormonde, vols. I–II old series, vol. I new (36)
   Buccleuch and Queensberry, vols. I, III (45)
   Montagu of Beaulieu (54)
   Various Collections, vols. II, V, VIII (55)
   Bath, vol. V (58)
   Mar and Kellie, Mar and Kellie Supplementary (60)
   Egmont, vol. I, part 1 (63)
   Denbigh (68)
   Laing, vol. I (72)
   De L'Isle and Dudley, vol. VI (77)
   R. R. Hastings, vols. I, IV (78)

Hope – see *Diary*

Hope's Major Practicks, 1608–1633, ed. J. A. Clyde, Stair Society, Edinburgh, 1937

Hutton, W. M. 'Two letters of Archbishop Laud', *EHR*, 45 (1930), 107–8

Hyde, E. *The History of the Rebellion and Civil War in England Begun in the Year 1641*, ed. W. D. Macray, 6 vols., Oxford, 1888

Imrie, J., and J. G. Dunbar (eds.) *Accounts of the Masters of Works*, vol. II (1616–49), Edinburgh, 1982

Jansson, M. (ed.) *Two Diaries of the Long Parliament*, Gloucester, 1984

Jeffs, R. (ed.) *Fast Sermons to Parliament*, vol. I (November 1640–November 1641), 1970

Johnston – see *Diary*

Journal of the House of Commons, vol. II

Journal of the House of Lords, vols. IV–V

The Journal of Thomas Cunningham of Campvere, 1640–1654, ed. E. J. Courthope, SHS, Edinburgh, 1928

Kenyon, J. P. *The Stuart Constitution*, 2nd edn, Cambridge, 1986

Kerr, J. *The Covenants and the Covenanters*, Edinburgh, 1895

Kirk, J. (ed.) *The Second Book of Discipline*, Edinburgh, 1980

Knowler, W. (ed.) *The Earl of Strafforde's Letters and Dispatches*, 2 vols., 1739

Laud – see *Works*

Laing, D. (ed.) *Correspondence of Sir Robert Kerr, First Earl of Ancrum, and his Son, William, Third Earl of Lothian*, 2 vols., Edinburgh, 1875

Larkin, J. F. *Stuart Royal Proclamations*, vol. II, Oxford, 1983

Larkin, J. F., and P. L. Hughes *Stuart Royal Proclamations*, vol. I, Oxford, 1973

Leslie, J., Earl of Rothes – see Rothes

L'Estrange, H. *The Reign of King Charles*, 1656

Letters and Papers of the Verney Family, ed. J. Bruce, Camden Society, 1853

Lindsay, Lord *Lives of the Lindsays*, 1849

Lowther, C. *Our Journall into Scotland, Anno Domini 1629, 5th of November from Lowther*, Edinburgh, 1894

McNeill, C. (ed.) *The Tanner Letters*, Dublin, 1943

MacPhail, J. R. N., *Papers from the Collection of Sir William Fraser*, SHS, Edinburgh, 1924

Macray, W. D. (ed.) *Ruthven Correspondence*, Roxburghe Club, 1868

Maitland Club Miscellany, vol. II, Edinburgh, 1840

Marwick, J. D. *Extracts from the Records of the Burgh of Glasgow, 1573–1642, 1630–62*, Glasgow, 1876, 1881

May, T. *The History of the Parliament of England*, 1647

Mémoires de Richelieu, vol. X, *Collection des mémoirs relatifs à l'histoire de France*, vol. XXX, Paris, 1823

Memoirs of Archibald, First Lord Napier, Written by Himself, Edinburgh, 1793

The Memoirs of Henry Guthry, Late Bishop of Dunkeld, Glasgow, 1747

Memoirs of his Own Life and Times by Sir James Turner, ed. T. Thomson, BC, Edinburgh, 1829

Miscellany of the Maitland Club, vol. I part 2, Edinburgh, 1834

Murray, J., 7th Duke of Atholl, *Chronicles of the Atholl and Tullibardine Families*, vol. I, Edinburgh, 1908

Nalson, J. *An Impartial Collection of the Great Affairs of State*, 2 vols., 1682–3

Napier, M. (ed.) *Memorials of Montrose and his Times*, 2 vols., MC, Edinburgh, 1848–51

Montrose and the Covenanters, 2 vols., Edinburgh, 1838

Northcote – see Hamilton, A. H. A.

Notes of Proceedings in the Long Parliament, temp. Charles I, by Sir Ralph Verney, Knight, ed. J. Bruce, Camden Society, 1845

Notestein, W. (ed.) *The Journal of Sir Simonds D'Ewes from the Beginning of the Long Parliament to the Opening of the Trial of the Earl of Strafford*, Yale, 1923

Oldmixon, J. *The History of England during the Reigns of the Royal House of Stuart*, 1730

Oppenheim, M. (ed.) *The Naval Tracts of Sir William Momnson*, vol. III, Navy Records Society, vol. XLIII, 1913

Peterkin, A., *Records of the Kirk of Scotland*, Edinburgh, 1838

Privy Council Registers in Facsimile, 12 vols., 1967–8

The Records of Elgin, 1234–1800, eds. W. Cramond and S. Ree, 2 vols., New Spalding Club, Aberdeen, 1903–8

The Register of the Privy Council of Scotland, 1st and 2nd Series, Edinburgh, 1877–1908

Reliquiae Baxterianae, 1696

Rogers, C. (ed.) *The Earl of Stirling's Register of Royal Letters Relative to the Affairs of Scotland*, 2 vols., Edinburgh, 1885

Historical Notices of St Anthony's Monastery, Leith, Grampian Club, 1877

Rothes, J. Leslie, Earl of *A Relation of Proceedings Concerning the Affairs of the Kirk of Scotland*, ed. D. Laing, BC, Edinburgh, 1830

Row, J. *The Historie of the Estate of the Kirk of Scotland*, 2 vols., MC, Edinburgh, 1842

Rushworth, J. *Historical Collections*, 8 vols., 1659–1701
   The Tryal of Thomas Earl of Strafford, 1700

Rutherford, S. *Letters*, ed. A. A. Bonar, Edinburgh, 1984

Saint-Léger, A. de, and L. Lemaire (eds.) *Correspondance authentique de Godefroi Comte d'Estrades de 1637 à 1660*, Paris, 1924

Sanderson, W. *A Compleat History of the Life and Raigne of King Charles from his Cradle to his Grave*, 1658

Scot of Scotstarvet, Sir J. 'A trew relation of the principall affaires concerning the state', *SHR*, 11 (1914), 164–91; 14 (1917), 60–7

Scot, W. *An Apologeticall Narration of the State and Government of the Kirk of Scotland Since the Reformation*, WS, Edinburgh, 1846

Scottish History Society Miscellany, vol. I, Edinburgh, 1893

Selwyn, E. G. (ed.) *The First Book of the Irenicum [1629] of John Forbes of Corse*, Cambridge, 1923

Snow, V. F., and A. S. Young *The Private Journals of the Long Parliament, 7 March to 1 June 1642*, 1987

Spalding, J. *The History of the Troubles and Memorable Transactions in Scotland and England from M.DC.XXIV to M.DC.XLV*, 2 vols., BC, Edinburgh, 1828

Spottiswood, J. *The History of the Church of Scotland*, 3 vols., BC, Edinburgh, 1850

Sprott, G. W. *Scottish Liturgies of the Reign of James VI*, Edinburgh, 1871

State Papers Collected by Edward, Earl of Clarendon, eds. R. Scrope and T. Monkhouse, 3 vols., Oxford, 1767–86

Trevelyan, W. C. and C. E. (eds.) *Trevelyan Papers*, part 3, Camden Society, 1872

Tweedie, W. K. (ed.) *Select Biographies*, 2 vols., Edinburgh, 1845–7

Warner, G. F. (ed.) *The Nicholas Papers*, vol. I (1641–52), Camden Society, 1886

Warwick, Sir P. *Memoires of the Reigne of King Charles I*, 1701

Whitaker, T. D. (ed.) *The Life and Original Correspondence of Sir George Radcliffe*, 1810

Whitelocke, B. *Memorials of English Affairs*, 1682

Winthrop Papers, vols. III–IV, Massachusetts Historical Society, Boston, 1943–4

Wishart, G. *Memoirs of the Marquis of Montrose*, Edinburgh, 1819

Wolfe, D. M. (ed.) *Complete Prose Works of John Milton*, vol. I (1624–42), 1953

Wood, M. (ed.) *Extracts from the Records of the Burgh of Edinburgh 1626 to 1641*, Edinburgh, 1936

The Works of King Charles the Martyr, 1662

The Works of the Most Reverend Father in God, William Laud, D.D., eds. W. Scott and J. Bliss, 7 vols., Oxford, 1847–60

Yorke, P. *Miscellaneous State Papers, from 1501 to 1726*, 2 vols., 1778

INDEX

341

Cambridge Studies in Early Modern British History

Also published as a paperback